D0076862

# Police & Society

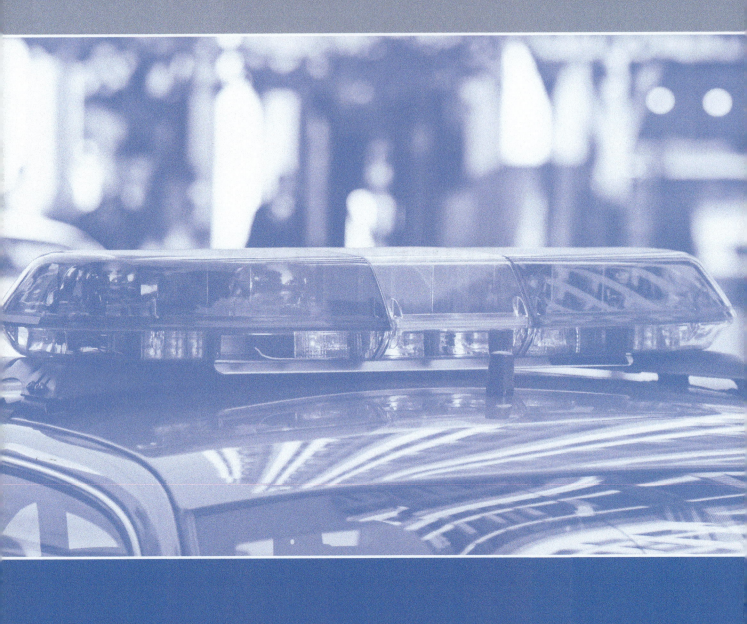

# Police & Society

### Ninth Edition

Kenneth Novak

Gary Cordner

Brad Smith

OXFORD

UNIVERSITY PRESS

# OXFORD
### UNIVERSITY PRESS

Oxford University Press is a department of the University of Oxford.
It furthers the University's objective of excellence in research, scholarship,
and education by publishing worldwide. Oxford is a registered trade mark
of Oxford University Press in the UK and in certain other countries.

Published in the United States of America by Oxford University Press
198 Madison Avenue, New York, NY 10016, United States of America.

© 2022, 2020, 2017, 2015, 2012, 2009 by Oxford University Press
© 2004, 1999, 1996 by Roxbury Publishing Company

For titles covered by Section 112 of the US Higher Education Opportunity
Act, please visit www.oup.com/us/he for the latest information about
pricing and alternate formats.

All rights reserved. No part of this publication may be reproduced,
stored in a retrieval system, or transmitted, in any form or by any means,
without the prior permission in writing of Oxford University Press,
or as expressly permitted by law, by license, or under terms agreed with
the appropriate reprographics rights organization. Inquiries concerning
reproduction outside the scope of the above should be sent to the Rights
Department, Oxford University Press, at the address above.

You must not circulate this work in any other form
and you must impose this same condition on any acquirer.

Library of Congress Control Number: 2022945096

CIP data is on file at the Library of Congress
ISBN 978-0-19-761741-0

9 8 7 6 5 4 3 2 1
Printed by Marquis, Canada

Dedicated to Roy Roberg

Scholar, educator, friend

# BRIEF CONTENTS

# CONTENTS

# PREFACE

*P*olice *& Society* offers a comprehensive introduction to policing in the United States. The text is both descriptive and analytical, covering the process of policing, police behavior, organization, operations, and historical perspectives. Contemporary issues and future prospects are also addressed. Throughout the text, an emphasis is placed on describing the relationship between the police and the public and how this relationship has changed through the years. To adequately explain the complex nature of police operations in a democracy, we have integrated the most important theoretical foundations, research findings, and contemporary practices in a comprehensible yet analytical manner.

*Police & Society* is unique for several reasons. Because of the substantial increase of published research in the field and consistent with previous editions of this text, we have attempted to include in the ninth edition only the most valid and reliable research currently available, leading to the "best policies and practices" in policing. We emphasize in-depth discussions of critical police issues rather than attempting to cover—in a relatively brief manner—every conceivable topic or piece of research in the field. We believe this approach contributes more substantially to the intellectual and practical development of the field of policing.

This edition of *Police & Society* was revised during a unique period of American policing. In 2020, several factors coincided that directly and indirectly impacted the nature of policing. The world confronted a global pandemic, which significantly affected social interaction and global economies. As many Americans were isolating themselves during the early weeks of the COVID-19 pandemic, we watched disturbing videos involving the killing of George Floyd during an encounter with the Minneapolis Police. Images spread quickly through social and news media, leading to public protests in many cities in the United States and worldwide. While many demonstrations were nonviolent and peaceful, others involved police and public conflicts. By summer, many cities began to report increases in violent crime. These events (and others) stimulated conversations about the role of the police in a democratic society, with discussions about defunding or even abolishing the police becoming commonplace. Building trust and legitimacy in policing, highlighted in the President's Task Force on Twenty-First Century Policing (https://cops.usdoj.gov/pdf/taskforce/taskforce_finalreport.pdf), dominated conversations.

The pandemic, George Floyd's murder, and rising crime rates forced the authors to reassess many topics in a new, and perhaps more urgent, light throughout this textbook. It encouraged renewed discussion of what it means to police in a democracy (Chapter 1) and raised numerous issues relating to officer legal liability (Chapter 2), officer behavior (Chapter 9), the use of force (Chapter 10), and officer accountability (Chapter 11). As many called for increasing diversity and inclusion in policing (Chapter 12), police departments experienced challenges recruiting and retaining officers during the Great Resignation (Chapter 6).

Pundits wondered what policing strategies effectively address increasing crime rates (Chapters 4 and 7) without adversely impacting police legitimacy (chapter 8). As public trust in the police waned, the number of officers killed in the line of duty hit a 20-year high, and officers (like many essential and front-line service workers) died from complications related to COVID-19 (Chapter 13).

Several types of features are included to provide the most realistic and up-to-date view of the police. "Inside Policing" boxes provide a brief description of real-world police issues and operations or biographical sketches that highlight the contributions of influential police leaders. We have also incorporated contemporary discussions from *Modern Policing* (https://gcordner.wordpress.com/), a blog managed by one of the authors (Gary Cordner). Here, students are directed to additional articles, reports, op-eds, editorials, and news stories directly related to topics within the chapter. "Voices from the Field" boxes highlight nationally recognized experts who provide their insights on contemporary police practices and problems in a thought-provoking format. We have also selectively added links to podcasts on policing; these inclusions give the students an additional medium to consume discussions about policing in society and stimulate critical thinking about issues in policing that complement the text of the chapters. Many of these colorful podcasts were produced by Jerry Ratcliffe and are featured at *Reducing Crime* (https://www.reducingcrime.com/).

The ninth edition features an expanded glossary of key terms, and each chapter begins with a listing of key terms. Ancillaries to enhance instruction include a **Companion Website** and a revised and expanded **Ancillary Resource Center for Instructors**.

This is the first edition of *Police & Society* in which our colleague Roy Roberg did not participate. Roy Roberg and Jack Kuykendall wrote the first edition in 1996. They sought to write a college textbook that focused on contemporary issues in policing and emphasized integrating the best scientific research to guide students in a critical examination of policing. While society and policing have changed considerably over the years, their framework and early contributions remain embedded in the ninth edition. Roy brought each of us into this project over the years, and together, we labored to stay true to the original vision of *Police & Society*. We appreciate Roy's invitation to collaborate on this project and continue to value his perspective, admire his passion, and recognize his unyielding dedication to his students and the profession.

We thank the many police officers, police executives, professors, and students with whom we have interacted over the years. Their experiences and insights have given us the basis for many of our ideas and for conceptualizing critical issues in policing. We hope this book increases the understanding and appreciation of policing in society and encourages thought-provoking dialogue among students and the police.

# ACKNOWLEDGMENTS

We continue to enjoy an outstanding working relationship with Oxford University Press and thank those who contributed significantly to the production of this edition, including Steve Helba, our editor, and his assistant, Sonya Venugopal. We also thank those who reviewed the book for their thoughtfulness and insight, including John Krimmel, The College of New Jersey; Joseph Schafer, Saint Louis University; Mengyan Dai, Old Dominion University; Nicole Doctor, Ivy Tech Community College; Richard Dewey, Indian River State College; Xioachen Hu, Fayetteville State University; and Frank Jones, New England

College. We appreciate the assistance of the Kansas City (MO) Police Department Media Unit, especially Sergeant Jacob Becchina, and the Baltimore Police Department for providing us with images and artwork that appear throughout this edition.

We especially thank all of the contributors to the "Voices from the Field" features throughout the text. These individuals are experts in policing and academe and have served in policy-making positions within police departments throughout the United States. Their contributions to our discussion on the police are significant, and they have provided a perspective on policing that cannot be found in any other forum.

# ABOUT THE AUTHORS

**Kenneth Novak** received his PhD in criminal justice from the University of Cincinnati and is currently a professor in the Department of Criminal Justice and Criminology at the University of Missouri–Kansas City. He has published scientific research articles on various topics in policing, including officer decision making, citizens' attitudes toward the police, racially biased policing, and program evaluation. He has conducted research with several criminal justice agencies, including the Kansas City (MO) Police Department; the Jackson County Prosecutor's Office; the Bureau of Alcohol, Tobacco, Firearms, and Explosives; and the US Attorney for the Western District of Missouri. Follow Ken on Twitter at @KenNovak_1.

**Gary Cordner** is Academic Director in the Education and Training Section, Baltimore Police Department. He taught for 21 years at Eastern Kentucky University, also serving as director of the Kentucky Regional Community Policing Institute and dean of the College of Justice and Safety. He received his doctorate from Michigan State University and served as a police officer and police chief in Maryland. Cordner has coauthored textbooks on police administration and criminal justice planning and coedited several anthologies on policing. He edited the *American Journal of Police* from 1987 to 1992 and *Police Quarterly* from 1997 to 2002. Cordner is a past president of the Academy of Criminal Justice Sciences and founder and former chair of that organization's Police Section. He completed a nine-year term on the Commission on Accreditation for Law Enforcement Agencies and served as Chief Research Advisor to the National Institute of Justice's Law Enforcement Advancing Data and Science (LEADS) Scholars Program. Follow Gary on Twitter at @gcordner and his blog at https://gcordner.wordpress.com.

**Brad Smith** received his PhD in criminal justice from the University of Cincinnati. He is currently professor and chair in the Department of Criminology and Criminal Justice at Wayne State University in Detroit. His research focuses on policing, and he has conducted research in various areas, including police discretionary behavior, citizens' attitudes toward the police, police stress, the use of deadly force, and police brutality. He is also a coauthor of *Race and Police Brutality: Roots of an Urban Dilemma* (2008, State University of New York Press).

**Part I**

# Policing Foundations

# Police in a Democracy

## CHAPTER OUTLINE

## KEY TERMS

- case law
- civil laws
- consolidated agencies
- contract law enforcement
- counterterrorism
- criminal justice system
- criminal laws
- discretion
- federalism
- homeland security
- jurisdiction
- private police
- proactive
- procedural laws
- public police
- public safety agencies
- reactive
- regional police
- rule of law
- separation of powers
- special jurisdiction police
- substantive laws
- task forces
- tribal police

THE POLICE HAVE POWER and authority, and as we have been reminded over the past several years, the actions they take are frequently controversial. The functions that police perform are critical to the safety of people and communities, but those very functions sometimes collide with our rights and freedoms, even including life and death.

No single event better epitomizes this reality than the police killing of George Floyd by Officer Derek Chauvin in Minneapolis in May 2020. Floyd, a Black man, was suspected of passing a counterfeit $20 bill. During his arrest, while Floyd was handcuffed and lying face down in the street, Chauvin knelt on Floyd's neck for over nine minutes, causing him to stop breathing and die. A year later, in a rare instance of a police officer being found criminally responsible for using excessive or deadly force, Chauvin was convicted of second-degree murder and sentenced to 22.5 years in prison (Olson, Xiong, and Walsh 2021).

In the aftermath of George Floyd's murder, many protests took place around the United States, and in fact around the world, often under the banner of Black Lives Matter. Some protests were peaceful, others violent. Some police departments demonstrated their empathy with protesters and successfully avoided violence, property destruction, and mass arrests (Cassie 2020). Others were not as successful or fortunate. Police in Portland, Oregon, faced perhaps the most challenging situation, with over 100 consecutive days of protests and riots. Officers grew weary and frustrated, in part due to bickering between city, state, and federal leaders over which tactics they could use to respond to organized protest violence (Levinson 2021). Meanwhile, protesters in Seattle took over a police station (Silva and Moschella 2020) and in Minneapolis set fire to one. Overall, riots in Minneapolis caused an estimated $500 million in property damage, one of the highest totals in American history (Penrod and Sinner 2020).

Protesters and activists demanded more police accountability and transparency, and many supported "defunding" the police. A few cities, including Austin, Seattle, and Los Angeles, quickly slashed police budgets (Levin 2021). After some reflection, many others began "reimagining" policing, identifying social problems like substance abuse and mental health crisis that had fallen to the police over the last 50 years but, perhaps, could be handled better and more safely by other specialists. This reimagining approach sounds less radical than defunding, but realistically, most cities will need to shift some funding from the police to other agencies to make it work.

What has been the effect of all this turmoil on American views of the police? Nationally, overall confidence in the police dipped to 48 percent in 2020, the first time it had fallen below 50 percent since polling began and well below the high of 64 percent in 2014. However, the figure rebounded to 51 percent in 2021 (Jones 2021). Compared to other US institutions in 2021, police ranked third highest, behind only small business and the military. Out of 16 institutions, the police were the only one that had an increase in public confidence from 2020 to 2021 (Brenan 2021).

While confidence in police improved in 2021, support for defunding waned. In 2020, almost as many people said they wanted less spending on police (26 percent) as wanted more spending (31 percent). A year later, though, 47 percent wanted more spending, versus only 15 percent who wanted less (Parker and Hurst 2021).

The whiplash of crises following George Floyd's murder and the rebounding support for police illustrate what a crucial and yet controversial role the police play in modern society. And as dramatic as these recent events and developments have been, they are not unprecedented. American police have been in crisis before, whether the issue has been corruption, civil disorder, excessive force, or discrimination.

It is equally important to recognize that the murder of George Floyd and its aftermath have not been the whole story of American policing in recent years. For example:

- Murders and shootings increased dramatically in the United States in both 2020 and 2021. The increase from 2019 to 2020 was 30 percent (Gramlich 2021), possibly the biggest one-year increase ever, while at least 12 cities hit all-time highs for murder in 2021, including Philadelphia, Indianapolis, Columbus, and Louisville (Hutchinson 2021).

- The riot/insurrection at the US Capitol on January 6, 2021, highlighted the severity of threats posed by political extremism, both to democracy and specifically to the police.

- In 2021, there were 34 school shootings, resulting in 14 deaths and 54 injuries (Education Week 2022).

- Although both domestic and international terrorism remain significant threats, no mass terrorist attacks occurred in the United States in 2021, for the first time since 2001 (Byman 2021).

- The COVID-19 pandemic has presented many challenges for police since early 2020, including enforcement of often unpopular public health orders.

- In 2021, 138 officers died in the line of duty from nonmedical causes (mainly gunfire and car crashes), a 28 percent increase over the average of the last three years. A much larger number, 362, died from medical causes, mainly COVID-19, in 2021 (Officer Down Memorial Page 2022).

- An estimated 200-plus officers commit suicide each year. The number is hard to measure accurately due to underreporting (Spence and Drake 2021).

- Recruiting new officers and retaining current ones have become even bigger challenges than usual (Westervelt 2021).

To begin to understand these kinds of situations and controversies, we must start with some basic questions: Why do the police exist? What do they do? What are their problems? How has policing changed over the years? The central theme of this book is an attempt to answer these and related questions about police in the United States.

One note about semantics: Throughout this book, the terms *police* and *law enforcement* are used interchangeably. With either term, the intent is to refer to all those who provide police services, whether they work for a police department, sheriff's office, state police, or federal agency.

This book contains a lot of information. To help you digest it, the book is organized into four sections: *Policing Foundations, Police Administration, Police Behavior,* and *Contemporary Issues.* Each chapter within these sections contains special features called "Voices from the Field" and "Inside Policing." These features provide brief descriptions of real-world police issues, excerpts from research studies, and highlight the contributions of important historical and contemporary figures in law enforcement.

## Policing a Free Society

The police play a double-edged role in a free society. On the one hand, they protect our freedom—not only our rights to own property, to travel safely from place to place, and to remain free from assault, but also such fundamental rights as freedom of speech, freedom of assembly, and freedom to change the government through elections. However, the police also have the power to limit our freedom through surveillance, questioning, search, and arrest. It is particularly important to understand this anomalous situation when thinking about policing in the United States because "the police . . . are invested with a great deal of authority under a system of government in which authority is reluctantly granted and, when granted, sharply curtailed" (Goldstein 1977, 1).

In our democratic system, government is based on consensus of the people, but policing often comes into play when agreement breaks down. In our system, government is expected to serve the people, but police often give out "services" that people do not want—orders, tickets, arrests. In our system, people are largely free to do as they please, but police can force them to stop. In our system, everyone is considered equal, but police have more power than the rest of us. It has been said that "democracy is always hard on the police" (Berkeley 1969, 1). It might also be said that police can be hard on democracy.

These factors indicate why the opposite of a democratic state is often called a police state. Democracy represents consensus, freedom, participation, and equality; the police represent regulation, restriction, and the imposition of government authority on an individual. That is why the police in a democracy are often confronted with hostility, opposition, and criticism no matter how effectively or fairly they operate.

### Police and Government

The word *police* is derived from the Greek words *politeuein*, which means to be a citizen or to engage in political activity, and *polis*, which means a city or state. This derivation emphasizes that policing is every citizen's responsibility, although in the modern world, this responsibility is often delegated to certain officials who do it on a full-time basis. Also, the derivation emphasizes that policing is political—not in the sense of Republicans versus Democrats, or liberals versus conservatives, but in the sense that policing entails carrying out decisions made by the people and their representatives, decisions that benefit some members of society but not others.

Today, we tend to say the same thing in a slightly different way—police enforce the law and carry out the policies of the government. Governments are vested with *police power* to regulate matters of health, welfare, safety, and morality, because a society requires structure and order if it is to be effective in meeting the needs of its members. One important expression of police power in a society is a police, or law enforcement, organization.

The activities and behavior of the police are determined in part by the type of government of which they are a part. In more totalitarian governments, power is exercised by only one person (e.g., a dictator), a small number of individuals, or one political party. The established laws and policies that control all aspects of life in a totalitarian state are intended to maintain the interests of those in power; the social order is preserved at the expense of individual freedom. More democratic governments, by contrast, are based on the principle of "participation of the governed." The members of a democratic society either directly participate in deciding the laws or elect representatives to make such decisions for them.

The United States has a republican form of government known as **federalism**. Some powers are exercised by the national government, but many others are decentralized to state and local units of government, both to allow more people to participate in the political system and to limit the power of those individuals elected to national political office. Significantly, one of the governmental functions that is largely delegated to state and local governments is policing.

Another important organizational feature of the US government is **separation of powers**, which results in three branches of government: executive, judicial, and legislative. This separation exists to provide a system of "checks and balances" so that one branch of government will not become too powerful. In the United States, the combination of federalism and separation of powers results in a governmental system that is highly fragmented, with widely dispersed power and authority. This system is sometimes criticized for being inefficient and incapable of governing effectively, but that is exactly what its designers intended—they wanted a limited form of government (including police) that would not interfere with peoples' freedoms any more than absolutely necessary.

Law enforcement is a responsibility of the executive branch of government in our system. Checks and balances help to constrain policing in two fundamental ways. First, the police do not make the laws they enforce—the legislature does that, along with appropriating the money that police agencies need to operate. Second, the police do not decide what happens to people who violate the law and are arrested—the judicial branch does that, along with interpreting and reinterpreting the meaning of laws in our changing society.

Government and laws are created through a political process or system. Voters, special interest groups (e.g., the National Rifle Association, the American Medical Association, and the American Civil Liberties Union), political parties, and elected officials are active participants in the political process. Theories of political decision making in a democracy take both pluralistic and elitist perspectives. The pluralistic perspective argues that debates, bargains, and compromises determine the allocation of resources and the enactment of laws and policies. Furthermore, although there are many different interests and groups in a society, with some more influential than others, no one group dominates. In contrast, the elitist or class perspective argues that only a limited number of persons (e.g., the rich or special interest groups) have any real influence in the political process. The playing field is not level, so politics results in preferential treatment for the most influential individuals and discrimination against those with little or no influence or power.

These two contrasting perspectives are important for understanding the police. From the pluralist perspective, police can be seen as a benign institution that helps implement laws and policies that result from an honest and fair political contest. From the elitist perspective, police are usually characterized as the "iron fist" that helps protect the powerful and repress the rest of society. Policing is a more noble enterprise within the pluralist framework than within the elitist framework. From either perspective, however, the police wield power and thus deserve careful attention.

### Police and Rule of Law

Democracies are concerned about the rights and freedoms to be given to individuals and about the limits to be placed on the government's use of police power. This concern is usually addressed by creating a constitution. Constitutions may be written or unwritten, but they serve the same basic purpose—to establish the nature and character of government by identifying the basic principles underlying that government. The Constitution of the United States identifies the functions of government and specifies in its first 10 amendments (the Bill of Rights) the most important rights of individuals relative to the government.

The United States has a constitutional democracy in which the exercise of power is based on the **rule of law**. Ideally, laws created through a democratic process are more reasonable and more likely to be accepted by citizens than laws created by only a few influential persons. And although democratic government does not always work in this fashion, ours has evolved so that the rule of law in practice has gradually become less tyrannical and more representative of the concerns of all citizens. One of the reasons why the rule of law is considered necessary is that proponents of democracy assume individuals in power will be inclined to abuse their power unless they are controlled by a constitution, democratically developed laws, and the "checks and balances" built into the structure or organization of government.

Police accountability to the rule of law is an important tradition in democratic societies. According to Reith (1938, 188), the basis for democratic policing "is to be found in rational and humane laws." The significance of the rule of law to democracy and the police is further described in a Royal Commission Report on the British police:

> Liberty does not depend, and never has depended, upon any particular form of police organization. It depends upon the supremacy of . . . the rule of law. The proper criterion [to determine if a police state exists] is whether the police are answerable to the law and ultimately, to a democratically elected [government]. In the countries to which the term police state is applied . . . police power is controlled by a [totalitarian] government [that] acknowledges no accountability to democratically elected (representatives), and the citizens cannot rely on the [law] to protect them. (Royal Commission on the Police 1962, 45)

There are a number of ways to categorize laws; for example, laws may be civil or criminal and substantive or procedural (legal issues are discussed further in Chapter 3). **Civil laws** are concerned with relationships between individuals (e.g., contracts, business transactions, or family relations); **criminal laws** pertain to behaviors that the government prohibits in the interest of protecting society and the individuals within it. Those behaviors that pose a threat to public safety and order (e.g., disorderly conduct, drunk driving, theft, rape, or murder) are considered crimes. The prosecution of a crime is brought in the name of the people as represented by government officials (e.g., a prosecuting attorney). Although police must be familiar with both civil and criminal law, their primary concern is with criminal law.

In the realm of criminal law, **substantive laws** are those that identify behavior, either required or prohibited, and the punishments for failure to observe these laws. For example, driving under the influence of alcohol is prohibited, and such behavior may be punished by a fine or imprisonment or both, along with suspension of the privilege to drive a motor vehicle. **Procedural laws** govern how the police are authorized to go about enforcing substantive laws. Procedural laws specify the level of evidence required to justify an arrest, for example, and whether the police can arrest based on their own authority or must first obtain a warrant.

Important frames of reference for procedural criminal laws are the Bill of Rights (the first 10 amendments of the US Constitution; see Table 1.1) and **case law** (the written rulings of state and federal appellate courts), which more specifically define when and how each procedure is to be used. When enforcing substantive laws, officers are supposed to follow procedural laws, which restrict the power of government and reduce the possibility

**TABLE 1.1   Selected Amendments to the US Constitution**

**Fourth Amendment**

The right of the people to be secure in their persons, houses, papers, and effects, against unreasonable searches and seizures, shall not be violated, and no warrants shall be issued but upon probable cause, supported by oath or affirmation, and particularly describing the place to be searched and the persons or things to be seized.

**Fifth Amendment**

No person shall be held to answer for a capital, or otherwise infamous crime, unless on a presentment or indictment of a grand jury, except in cases arising in the land or naval forces, or in the militia, when in actual service in time of war or public danger; nor shall any person be subject for the same offense to be twice put in jeopardy of life or limb; nor shall be compelled in any criminal case to be a witness against himself, nor be deprived of life, liberty, or property, without due process of law; nor shall private property be taken for public use without just compensation.

**Sixth Amendment**

In all criminal prosecutions, the accused shall enjoy the right to a speedy and public trial, by an impartial jury of the State and district wherein the crime shall have been committed, which district shall have been previously ascertained by law, and to be informed of the nature and cause of the accusation; to be confronted with the witnesses against him; to have compulsory process for obtaining witnesses in his favor, and to have the assistance of counsel for his defense.

**Eighth Amendment**

Excessive bail shall not be required, nor excessive fines imposed, nor cruel and unusual punishments inflicted.

that police will abuse the power they have been given. The law not only provides a framework for police activity and behavior but also is intended to ensure that the police have good reason (e.g., "reasonable suspicion" or "probable cause") to intrude into the lives of citizens. Procedural laws also balance what would otherwise be an unequal relationship between government and the individual, because the government usually has more resources, and often more public support, than a person suspected of committing a crime.

Even when the police have legal authority, however, they do not always enforce the law because of limited resources, public expectations, organizational priorities, and officer preferences. Rather, both the organization and the officer exercise **discretion**; that is, they make a choice concerning what laws will be enforced and how that enforcement will take place. A number of factors influence police discretion; they are discussed in Chapters 9 and 10.

## Police, Terrorism, and Homeland Security

Our commitment to freedom, democracy, and the rule of law has been challenged in the post-9/11 era. The events of September 11, 2001, at the World Trade Center, the Pentagon, and in western Pennsylvania, now more than 20 years in the past, suddenly created new top priorities for American law enforcement—**counterterrorism** and **homeland security**. To achieve these new priorities, the US national government considered and/or adopted a range of responses, including the USA Patriot Act, that impinged on traditional American views about privacy, freedom of movement, and the rights of people accused of crimes. Who was asked to carry out many of these controversial new responses? The police, of course.

The post-9/11 threat posed by international terrorism has been challenging for police in several respects. For example, terrorists operate with a different type of motivation than traditional criminals and often are willing to die to further their causes. Terrorists may employ tools (chemical, biological, or radiological) or explosive weapons of mass destruction that local and state police are ill equipped to resist. When local and state police engage in counterterrorism activities, they often work with national-level agencies that they have not traditionally had much interaction with, such as the Central Intelligence Agency (CIA) and the National Security Agency (NSA). Protecting the homeland engages the police with the military in a way that has historically been discouraged in America (the military has generally been restricted in its role within the borders of the United States). Overall, the counterterrorism and homeland security missions tend to thrust federal agencies into the forefront, which is awkward because local and state police have historically had the primary responsibility for law enforcement and crime control in the United States.

The riot/insurrection at the US Capitol in January 2021 highlighted a different but related threat—domestic terrorism. Current national estimates indicate this is a growing and evolving threat with two main components: "racially or ethnically motivated violent extremists, and militia violent extremists" (Garland 2021). The federal government has recently developed a National Strategy for Countering Domestic Terrorism (White House 2021). Since domestic terrorism originates within the country, local and state police have an even bigger role to play, along with the Federal Bureau of Investigation (FBI), than has usually been the case with international terrorism.

We will have more to say about the specific challenges of counterterrorism policing in Chapter 15. In the big picture, these challenges go to the core issues of democracy and law—how best to ensure safety and order while protecting individual freedoms. Institutions such as Congress, the president, and the courts are responsible for making and reviewing laws and programs designed to support safety with freedom. But there is no more crucial institution than the police when it comes to constructing the reality of safety and freedom on the streets and in our communities. In "Voices from the Field," former Philadelphia police commissioner Charles Ramsey provides his perspective on balancing policing and freedom in the post-9/11 era.

## Police Reform

Even before the murder of George Floyd in 2020, there were significant demands for police reform. Since 1997, numerous police agencies have entered into consent decrees following investigations by the US Department of Justice that found a "pattern and practice" of constitutional violations, often primarily affecting African American citizens (Powell, Meitl, and Worrall 2017). Following the death of Michael Brown in Ferguson, Missouri, in 2014, greater attention began to be paid to deaths in police custody, with the realization that they number over 1,000 per year (Civil Rights Division 2015). The President's Task Force on Twenty-First Century Policing (2015) issued 64 recommendations related to trust, legitimacy, and community policing. The Police Executive Research Forum (2016) published a set of 30 guiding principles designed to emphasize de-escalation of critical incidents and stricter standards on police use of lethal force. In general, public and political attention has become more and more focused on police use of force, misconduct, accountability, and transparency.

Many jurisdictions today are trying to reimagine policing by considering whether to tighten policies on use of force, hire and train differently, implement stronger civilian oversight, become more community-oriented, shift some responsibilities away from police to social service providers, and so on. These and other approaches to police reform are discussed in various chapters throughout the rest of this text.

## Police Systems

At a fundamental level, there are three basic types of police in the United States: citizens, private police, and public police. This book is primarily about public police officers.

It is not uncommon for people in a democracy to participate in the policing process. As citizens, we may make arrests when a felony is committed in our presence (in some states,

---

# VOICES FROM THE FIELD

## Charles H. Ramsey

*Police Commissioner (Ret.), Philadelphia, Pennsylvania; formerly Chief of Police, Metropolitan Police Department in Washington, DC*

When I was chief of the Metropolitan Police Department in Washington, DC, I partnered with the United States Holocaust Memorial Museum and the Anti-Defamation League to build an experiential training program called "Law Enforcement and Society: Lessons from the Holocaust."

With the Holocaust as the historical backdrop, police officers are asked to examine their role in a democratic and pluralistic society. The program gains access to some of the most critical issues facing police officers and law enforcement agencies today—issues such as racial profiling, biased policing, equal treatment under the law, and perhaps most importantly, the role of police officers in upholding the rights of all citizens.

What followed from the state-sanctioned policies in Nazi Germany 70 years ago was nothing short of the denial of the most basic of human rights and individual freedoms. And almost from the beginning, local police were intimately involved in this process. Whether it was providing intelligence information to invading army troops or harassing people who violated Nazi taboos, arresting political opponents or being the foot soldiers in the mobile killing squads, local police soon became integrated into the Nazi reign of repression and brutality. The Holocaust, however, did not just happen overnight. It occurred along a continuum that started with the use of inappropriate language separating people along the lines of religion and nationality and ended with the absolute denial of a person's constitutional rights.

The Law Enforcement and Society program is a critical part of teaching law enforcement officers our core values of democracy—fairness, equality, and compassion. In that moment where a police officer encounters a victim of crime, or is arresting an offender, or is answering a request for directions, or is on routine patrol, she has a choice about how to treat the person standing before her. Does she treat him with dignity and respect? Or does she see him simply as the "other," based on a label such as race, gender, sexual orientation, religion, class, ability, nationality, or ethnicity?

The lesson in the Law Enforcement and Society training is straightforward, but powerful: When police officers violate their oath and their code of ethics, there are consequences—devastating consequences. We cannot close our eyes and divorce ourselves from our own sense of morality. We cannot think of ourselves, as we are so often portrayed, as the "thin blue line" between right and wrong or good and evil. I believe that is an inadequate metaphor and that true "community policing" does not define police officers as a line—thin, blue, or otherwise. We are not now—nor should we ever be—something that divides and separates our communities.

Rather, I like to think of the police as a thread—a thread that is woven throughout the communities we serve and that holds together the very fabric of democracy and freedom in our communities. If the police begin to unravel, then our very democracy begins to unravel as well. That image, much more so than the thin blue line concept, captures the true role of the police in protecting and preserving a free society.

citizens may also arrest for breaches of the peace). When we report a crime and cooperate in the subsequent investigation, we are participating in the policing process. Another type of citizen involvement is related to the legal doctrine of *posse comitatus*, in which individuals can be required to assist police officers. This conjures up the image of the sheriff's or marshal's posse in Western movies, but it also includes the possibility that any of us, if requested, would be required to aid a police officer.

Vigilantism is another example of citizen participation in law enforcement. Historically, vigilantes were community members (e.g., civic, business, or religious leaders) or mobs who took the law into their own hands. These groups developed as the result of a public perception that the existing law enforcement system was inadequate and corrupt, or that it did not serve the interests of the vigilantes (Walker 1977, 30–31). Although it was more common in the nineteenth century, this type of citizen involvement in law enforcement still occurs.

As mentioned, there are also both public and private police. **Public police** are employed, trained, and paid by a government agency; their purpose is to serve the general interest of all citizens. **Private police** are those police employed and paid to serve the specific purposes, within the law, of an individual or organization. A municipal police officer is a public police officer; a guard at a bank or department store is a private police officer. One way in which these lines can be blurred is that public police may sometimes also serve in a private capacity when they are off duty and hired to provide security, such as at a nightclub or shopping center.

Public police agencies fit into the governmental structure in different ways. On the one hand, most police chiefs report to an elected official (the mayor) or appointed official (the city manager) within the executive branch of government, although a few report directly to a city council or quasi-independent police commission. Sheriffs, on the other hand, are elected by the voters and generally report only to them. An important caveat to the independence of sheriffs, however, is that they usually must apply to a county council for a portion of their annual budget. Thus, although sheriffs are directly elected officials, they are typically dependent on other elected officials for the resources they need to operate. This is another example of checks and balances.

Public police organizations are part of the **criminal justice system**, which includes the courts and correctional institutions. The police function as the "gatekeepers" of the criminal justice system, because they determine who will be cited or arrested. The judicial branch and its representatives, including prosecutors, defense attorneys, and judges, process the accused to determine guilt or innocence and to sentence those who are convicted. The correctional part of the system (e.g., probation, treatment programs, jails, prisons, or parole) supervises, rehabilitates, and/or punishes convicted criminals.

Around the world, police systems vary greatly. One feature that varies is the extent to which police systems are unitary or fragmented. Some countries have one police institution for the entire nation; these are unitary systems. Many other countries have more than one police institution but still only a few, such as a national police plus a gendarmerie for rural areas, or a preventive police, an investigative police, and a border police. At the other end of the spectrum are countries that have many separate police institutions, often dispersed among national, state, and local levels of government. Mexico, India, Brazil, Germany, Canada, and England have relatively fragmented police systems.

A second important feature of police systems in different countries is their connection to the military. The modern trend has been toward a clear separation of the police and the military, partly in the spirit of checks and balances on government authority but mainly because the use of military power against a country's own citizens is considered repressive except in the gravest emergencies. In some countries, however, the police and the military are still indistinguishable, or the police are subservient to the military.

It is crucially important to understand that the police system in the United States is distinctive with regard to both of these comparative features. Police in the United States are clearly separate from, and independent of, the military. Even at the federal (national) level, where most military resources and assets are situated, the military is in the Department of Defense, whereas law enforcement agencies are mainly in the Department of Justice and the Department of Homeland Security. And as described in the following section, when it comes to unitary versus fragmented policing systems, ours is the most fragmented in the world by far.

## The US Police System

The most distinctive feature of American policing is that it is fragmented and local. The United States has almost 18,000 public police agencies (Reaves 2011), far more than in any other country. Almost 90 percent (15,273 agencies) are general-purpose local agencies (e.g., city, town, township, village, borough, parish, or county) (Brooks 2019b), whereas the rest are federal, state, or special-purpose law enforcement agencies.

The organization of the US police tends to follow the geographic and political structure of the US government. Each of the levels of government—federal, state, county (or parish in Louisiana), and municipal—has police powers and may have its own police forces. The federal and state levels of government tend to have multiple police forces that specialize in specific types of law enforcement. County and municipal (collectively called local) governments each tend to have just one police force that provides a wide range of police services.

Law enforcement organizations differ in part by their legal **jurisdiction**, including the criminal matters over which they have authority. For example, the jurisdiction of the Internal Revenue Service (IRS) Criminal Investigation Division is limited to violations of federal tax laws. The FBI is the most generalist law enforcement agency of the federal government; it is charged with the investigation of all federal laws not assigned to some other agency (e.g., not assigned to the Secret Service, the Postal Service, or the IRS). By contrast, local police, within the legally incorporated limits of their city or county, enforce all state and local laws that are applicable. Their jurisdiction is defined mostly by geography, whereas federal agency jurisdictions are nationwide but limited to specific federal statutes.

The federal government has more than 60 agencies with law enforcement and investigative powers, over half of which are Offices of Inspectors General (Brooks 2019a). (See Table 1.2 for a list of the 10 largest federal law enforcement agencies.) State governments, in addition to having a state police or highway patrol department (e.g., the Alaska Department of Public Safety, the New York State Police, or the California Highway Patrol), often have other agencies with police powers to address such matters as revenue collection, parks and recreation, and alcoholic beverage control. At the county level, the most common type of law enforcement agency is the sheriff's office, but some counties also have investigators who work for prosecuting attorneys and public defenders. In addition, some counties have police departments (e.g., Nassau County, New York, and Fairfax County, Virginia). When there is a county police department, the sheriff's department is usually responsible for operating the county jail and for assisting the courts, but it does not engage in extensive policing activities. Finally, municipal governments typically have their own police force

**TABLE 1.2** Ten Largest Federal Agencies with the Authority to Carry Firearms and Make Arrests

| AGENCY | FULL-TIME OFFICERS |
|---|---|
| US Customs and Border Protection | 43,724 |
| Federal Bureau of Prisons | 19,093 |
| Federal Bureau of Investigation | 13,799 |
| US Immigration and Customs Enforcement | 12,400 |
| US Secret Service | 4,729 |
| Drug Enforcement Administration | 4,181 |
| Department of Veterans Affairs Police | 3,839 |
| US Marshals Service | 3,788 |
| Bureau of Alcohol, Tobacco, Firearms, and Explosives | 2,675 |
| US Postal Inspection Service | 1,891 |

*Source*: C. Brooks, *Federal Law Enforcement Officers, 2016—Statistical Tables.* (Washington, DC: Bureau of Justice Statistics. 2019). https://bjs.ojp.gov/content/pub/pdf/fleo16st.pdf.

(e.g., the Los Angeles Police Department [LAPD], the Rapid City Police Department in South Dakota, and the LaGrange Police Department in Georgia). County sheriffs and local police are generally involved in patrolling, responding to calls for service, and conducting investigations; however, sheriffs' departments also invest substantial resources in managing jails and providing court services.

Table 1.3 presents information on local police departments by size of the organization. Small agencies are most common. Almost half of all local US police departments have fewer than 10 full-time sworn officers. Nearly 75 percent have fewer than 25 officers, and

**TABLE 1.3** Local Police Departments by Size of Agency

| NUMBER OF FULL-TIME SWORN PERSONNEL | NUMBER OF AGENCIES | PERCENTAGE OF AGENCIES |
|---|---|---|
| All sizes | 12,261 | 100.0 |
| 1,000 or more | 45 | 0.4 |
| 500–999 | 53 | 0.4 |
| 250–499 | 101 | 0.8 |
| 100–249 | 425 | 3.5 |
| 50–99 | 845 | 6.9 |
| 25–49 | 1,587 | 12.9 |
| 10–24 | 3,358 | 27.4 |
| 1–9 | 5,847 | 47.7 |

*Source*: S. Hyland and E. Davis, *Local Police Departments, 2016: Personnel.* (Washington, DC: Bureau of Justice Statistics, 2019). https://bjs.ojp.gov/content/pub/pdf/lpd16p.pdf.

95 percent have fewer than 100 officers (Hyland and Davis 2019). This feature of American law enforcement is important to keep in mind. Although most of us picture the FBI, the New York Police Department (NYPD), or the LAPD when we think of American police organizations, Mayberry RFD is more typical.

The most common type of law enforcement agency is the local police force (e.g., city, town, township, village, or borough). There were 12,261 local police departments in the year 2016 (Hyland and Davis 2019), the latest date for reliable figures. The next most common are the 3,012 county sheriff's departments (Brooks 2019b). Other types of local law enforcement agencies, such as tribal police departments, county police departments, and multijurisdictional regional agencies, account for about 2 percent of the total. There are also more than 600 local constable and marshal offices, many filled by election, though their authority is frequently limited (Reaves 2011).

Although the typical police department in the United States is small, there are some large law enforcement agencies in the country. Thirteen federal law enforcement agencies have 1,000 or more sworn personnel (Brooks 2019a). Each state has a state police or highway patrol agency, all with at least 100 sworn personnel and an average size of more than 1,000. In addition, there are 40 city and county police agencies with 1,000 or more sworn police personnel, plus 11 sheriff's offices (Brooks 2019b; Hyland and Davis 2019). The largest municipal police department is in New York City, with 36,008 full-time sworn personnel. The largest sheriff's department is in Los Angeles County, with 9,351 sworn personnel. (See Tables 1.4 and 1.5 for the 10 largest local police departments and sheriff's offices in the country.)

Agencies are one important aspect of the structure of policing in America; another is the distribution of personnel. Consistent with what has been described earlier, most police officers work at the local level. As of 2016, there were about 468,000 full-time sworn officers in local police departments (Hyland and Davis 2019) and another 173,000 in sheriff's offices (Brooks 2019b). These are followed by 132,000 in federal law enforcement agencies

**TABLE 1.4  Ten Largest Local Police Departments by Number of Full-Time Sworn Personnel**

| AGENCY | FULL-TIME SWORN PERSONNEL |
|---|---|
| New York (NY) Police | 36,008 |
| Chicago (IL) Police | 11,965 |
| Los Angeles (CA) Police | 9,870 |
| Philadelphia (PA) Police | 6,031 |
| Houston (TX) Police | 5,203 |
| Washington (DC) Metropolitan Police | 3,712 |
| Dallas (TX) Police | 3,408 |
| Miami–Dade County (FL) Police | 2,723 |
| Phoenix (AZ) Police | 2,689 |
| Las Vegas (NV) Metropolitan Police | 2,566 |

*Source*: S. Hyland and E. Davis, *Local Police Departments, 2016: Personnel.* (Washington, DC: Bureau of Justice Statistics, 2019). https://bjs.ojp.gov/content/pub/pdf/lpd16p.pdf.

**TABLE 1.5** Ten Largest Sheriff's Offices by Number of Full-Time Sworn Personnel

| AGENCY | FULL-TIME SWORN PERSONNEL |
|---|---|
| Los Angeles County Sheriff's Department (CA) | 9,351 |
| Harris County Sheriff's Office (TX) | 2,207 |
| Riverside County Sheriff's Office (CA) | 2,048 |
| Orange County Sheriff's Department (CA) | 1,744 |
| Jacksonville Sheriff's Office (FL) | 1,577 |
| Palm Beach County Sheriff's Office (FL) | 1,539 |
| Orange County Sheriff's Office (FL) | 1,432 |
| Broward County Sheriff's Office (FL) | 1,425 |
| San Diego County Sheriff's Office (CA) | 1,322 |
| Sacramento County Sheriff's Office (CA) | 1,246 |

*Source*: C. Brooks, *Sheriffs' Offices, 2016: Personnel*. (Washington, DC: Bureau of Justice Statistics, 2019). https://bjs.ojp.gov/content/pub/pdf/so16p.pdf.

(Brooks 2019a) and about 60,000 each in state police (Hyland 2018) and special jurisdiction agencies (Reaves 2011). Thus, about 72 percent of the almost 900,000 sworn law enforcement officers in the United States work for local police departments and sheriff's offices.

The pattern of police agencies and police employment varies substantially across the United States (Cordner 2011). In general, western states have fewer law enforcement agencies and fewer police officers in proportion to their population than midwestern or eastern states. Hawaii and California have the fewest police agencies per population, and South Dakota and North Dakota have the most. Washington and Vermont have the fewest police officers per population, while Louisiana and New York have the most. Rural states tend to rely more on state police than urbanized states do—the most "state police–dependent" states are Delaware, Vermont, West Virginia, and Alaska. Sheriffs' departments play a big role in law enforcement in some states and a negligible role in others. The states in which sheriffs' departments represent the biggest portion of police employment are Louisiana, Wyoming, Florida, and Idaho. At the other end of the spectrum, the least "sheriff-dependent" states (not counting Alaska and Hawaii, which have no counties and therefore no sheriffs' departments at all) are Delaware, Connecticut, New Hampshire, Pennsylvania, and Rhode Island.

## Other Types of Law Enforcement Agencies

In addition to the basic structure of policing described earlier, there are several other forms of public policing, including tribal police, public safety agencies, consolidated agencies, regional police, special jurisdiction police, contract law enforcement, and task forces.

**Tribal police** are law enforcement agencies created and operated by Native Americans. Their jurisdiction is usually, but not always, limited to reservation land. These types of police agencies are separate from the police agencies operated by the Bureau of Indian Affairs, which is a federal agency.

**Public safety agencies** represent the integration of police and firefighting services (and possibly other services like disaster preparedness, hazardous waste disposal, and emergency medical services). This integration can be limited to administrative matters, or it may include the joint performance of both firefighting and police duties. When the duties or work are integrated, employees are trained to perform both police and firefighting activities.

**Consolidated agencies** represent the integration of two or more police departments. This integration can be either by function or by organization. Functional, or partial, integration involves combining the same activity, perhaps communications or training. For example, two or more police departments may decide to share the same communication system or develop a common training academy. Organizational integration involves two or more departments becoming one. This usually occurs between a county and a city department, as in Clark County–Las Vegas, Nevada, or Duval County–Jacksonville, Florida, but it could also involve two or more cities.

Historically, it has been common for communities to consider the consolidation of police departments, particularly in urban areas. Supporters of consolidation argue that a larger police force can provide better service at lower cost. This argument is not always accurate, but it does tend to generate support for consolidation. Opponents of consolidation argue that if the community maintains control of its own police force, it will be more responsive to the needs of that community. Citizens often want to maintain direct control over the use of police power in their community. Although consolidation of functions like Special Weapons and Tactics (SWAT) and communications is relatively common, the complete consolidation of two or more police departments is rare.

**Regional police** can result from full-fledged consolidation, but the term generally refers to a situation in which two or more local governments decide to jointly operate a police agency across their jurisdictions. The regional police agency is often overseen by a board or commission with representation from all participating jurisdictions, and funding is provided by each on a proportional basis. Pennsylvania is distinctive in having several of these types of agencies, such as the York Area Regional Police Department, which serves three townships and six boroughs.

**Special jurisdiction police** usually have the same police powers as the officers employed in other police departments, but they tend to have jurisdiction only in a tightly specified area. Colleges, universities, and public school systems often have their own campus police forces, for example. Also common are transportation/transit police, natural resources police, and specialized criminal investigation agencies such as the Tennessee Bureau of Investigation.

**Contract law enforcement**, or contract policing, involves a contractual arrangement between two units of government in which one agrees to provide law enforcement services for the other. For example, a county sheriff's department might enter into a contract with a municipality to provide a given level of police service for a certain amount of money. The municipality might not wish to pay to establish its own police department, or it might believe it would receive better services from the larger organization. Although it is possible to have a contractual relationship between any two governmental units, the most common relationship is between a county and a city. Contract law enforcement is common in many urban areas.

**Task forces** are a form of functional consolidation but tend to be temporary (i.e., from a few weeks to years) rather than permanent. Some task forces, however, have lasted more than 20 years. Two or more departments may decide to create a task force to respond to crimes such as auto theft, drugs and related problems, or violent crime. Cooperative arrangements can exist at the local level (e.g., several municipal police departments and the county sheriff) or between local and state, or local and federal, law enforcement agencies (e.g., a drug, gun, or gang violence task force). A task force may also include representatives from other criminal justice agencies (e.g., probation and parole) or other governmental and community organizations (e.g., social services). What is unique about this arrangement is that it involves the joint efforts of two or more police departments directed toward common problems.

## Similarities and Differences

Local police, when compared with state and federal law enforcement, have the most employees, cost the most money, deal with most reported crime, respond to the majority of other police-related problems that occur (e.g., traffic accidents, domestic disputes, and barking dogs), and tend to have a closer relationship with citizens. State police, naturally, are spread farther apart, tend not to be as closely connected to local communities, and often have a primary focus on traffic safety. Federal law enforcement agencies, with a few exceptions (e.g., the US Park Police), are mainly investigative and are least connected to local communities.

There are substantial differences within each of these categories, however. Some local agencies are large and have many personnel who perform specialized duties (investigation, traffic, juvenile, etc.), whereas others are small, with no specialization. State law enforcement agencies also vary, especially between state police and highway patrol and depending on whether the state has a separate Bureau of Investigation or whether that function is incorporated within the state police. Even federal agencies that might seem similar have significant differences. For example, the FBI has traditionally emphasized reactive (i.e., after the fact) investigation (although that has shifted to some degree since 9/11), whereas the Drug Enforcement Agency has long emphasized proactive and instigative methods of investigation (Wilson 1978). A significant amount of Secret Service work involves executive protection rather than investigation.

Local jurisdictions vary greatly among urban, suburban, and rural areas, from New York City to rustic West Virginia, remote Alaska, or the Mississippi Delta. Although urban crime rates tend to be higher than rural crime rates, crime associated with urban areas is often exported to rural areas; for example, urban drug trafficking is a driving force behind the spread of drug use and the development of gangs in rural areas. Some of the crimes that tend to be associated with rural areas include growing marijuana and manufacturing methamphetamine; theft of crops, timber, and animals; and poaching. Some crimes in rural areas are more easily solved (i.e., an arrest is made), because homicide, rape, and assault are more likely to occur among acquaintances than in urban areas. Also, rural witnesses may be better able to personally identify observed suspects. By contrast, a crime witness in an urban area is more likely to be describing a total stranger.

Sims (1996, 45) described other differences that exist between urban and rural police:

> Urban police tend not to live where they work, while rural officers do . . . [R]ural law enforcement is personalistic and nonbureaucratic, in contrast to the formality, impersonality and bureaucratization of urban police. Rural law enforcement involves . . . more face-to-face interaction and communication. [It also] . . . includes a greater . . . percentage of police-acquaintance contacts and . . . [fewer] police–stranger contacts.

In addition, rural law enforcement officers, more than their urban counterparts, often work with lower budgets, fewer staff, less equipment, and a smaller number of written

---

**INSIDE POLICING 1.1**  **The Only Cop in Town**

The United States has 2,000 or so single-officer police departments, in many of which the officer is only part-time. This photo-essay highlights "the only cop in town" in three such agencies located in Delaware, Kansas, and Alaska, along with brief audio clips. One common theme for the chiefs is that they know their residents and the residents know them, which has its pros and cons. One comments, "You know everybody, and you know how they are. You're seeing them at their worst, but you know how they are at their best too."

   **Discussion Question:** Sometimes we say that police should treat everybody the same. But we also say that police should use discretion in order to treat us as people, not just pieces of work. Which way do you lean, and why?

SOURCE: *Modern Policing* blog, October 24, 2018, gcordner.wordpress.com/2018/10/24/the-only-cop-in-town/.

---

policies. They typically work alone and must wait longer for back-up assistance. But they also appear to be more efficient than urban police and more respected by the public. The context in which rural police work takes place also affects their activities (see Inside Policing 1.1). Rural citizens may be more likely to rely on informal social controls (i.e., take care of the problem themselves) than to report a "private" matter to the police. In addition, rural residents may be more likely to mistrust government and therefore may be more reluctant to share information (Weisheit, Falcone, and Wells 1994; McDonald, Wood, and Pflug 1996).

## Police Role and Purpose

Egon Bittner (1970, 46) famously described the core of the police role as "the distribution of nonnegotiably coercive force employed in accordance with the dictates of an intuitive grasp of situational exigencies." The police are who we call when something really bad is happening right now, and we give them the authority to deal with it—forcefully, if necessary. Moreover, police have discretion in deciding what to do and how to do it. None of this authority or discretion is unlimited, but the reality is that society needs a mechanism for handling trouble, including trouble that must be dealt with immediately. That mechanism is the police.

   The police are the major representatives of the legal system in their transactions with citizens. The police "adapt the universal standards of the law to the requirements of the citizen and the public . . . through their right to exercise discretion." They are also the "major emergency arm of the community in times of personal and public crisis." In carrying out their mandate, the police "possess a virtual monopoly on the legitimate use of force" (Reiss 1971, 1–2).

   Although using force may be at the core of the police role, the police also provide a variety of more mundane governmental and social services. In doing their job, the police have intimate contact with a wide variety of citizens in a wide variety of situations:

> Police officers deal with people when they are both most threatening and most vulnerable, when they are angry, when they are frightened, when they are desperate, when they are drunk, when they are violent, or when they are ashamed. Every police action can affect in some way someone's dignity, or self-respect, or sense of privacy, or constitutional rights. (President's Commission 1967, 91–92)

The police role refers to the part that police are expected to play in a democratic society. When expectations from different sources are compatible, there is minimal difficulty in deciding what the police should do and how they should do it. When expectations differ, however, conflict can arise over the police role. There are several major sources of expectations concerning what the police should do and how they should do it, including the law, the police organization, the community, and the individual (Roberg, Kuykendall, and Novak 2002):

1. **Legal expectations.** Laws provide the basic framework in which the police are supposed to function. Although the police do not always follow the law, legal expectations have a substantial influence on what they do and how they behave. Police do not enforce all laws all the time, however; rather, they exercise discretion in deciding what laws to enforce and how to enforce them. These discretionary decisions may not always be compatible with what either the formal organization or the community expects.

2. **Organizational expectations.** The formal and informal aspects of a police department produce organizational expectations. Formal expectations are derived from leaders, supervisors, training programs, and the goals, objectives, policies, procedures, and regulations of the police department. Informal expectations are derived from officers' peers, the work group, and the police culture (Crank 1998; Paoline 2001). Officers are strongly influenced by their work experiences and the way in which they adjust to the emotional, psychological, intellectual, and physical demands of police work. They must attempt to do their job in a manner that is acceptable to both the police department and their peers while trying to stay safe and not provoke citizen complaints.

3. **Community expectations.** Societal trends and problems, in general and in each community, create an environment of community expectations. Individual citizens and subgroups—women and men, youth, rich and poor, traditionalists and cosmopolitans, members of minority groups, or immigrants—all have their own opinions about police and their own priorities and preferences. In some communities, there can be a reasonable degree of consensus about the role that the police should play, but in many communities, there are divergent expectations. To add an additional complication, these expectations often change over time in response to specific events, evolving conditions, or shifts in the composition of the community.

4. **Individual expectations.** Police employees' individual expectations refer to their personal perspectives concerning the degree to which their needs are met by the organization and their working environment. All employees expect to be treated fairly and adequately rewarded. They also have their own beliefs about police work and how the police role should be carried out. Those beliefs may be affected by peers and the police culture, but they can also be individualistic—police officers can have "pet peeves" just like anybody else (Linn 2008).

## Law Enforcement or Politics?

What is the most effective way to integrate the role of police into a democratic society? At the extremes, there are two alternatives: one that is rule-oriented and one that is responsive and individualized. The former is a legalistic (i.e., bureaucratic, quasi-military, or professional) approach and assumes that justice is a product of consistent application of laws and departmental policies and procedures. Ideally, these laws, policies, and procedures are rationally developed and free of any bias that would be inconsistent with the fundamental principles of the society.

The responsive and individualized alternative is a more personal or political approach, and there are two different variations of this view of the police role. One is that laws and the police primarily serve the interest of the most influential persons in a community. Such individuals are considered above the law, whereas others are treated more harshly. This view leads to politics of preference and discrimination. The second view focuses on responsiveness and individualization. Its advocates argue that strict enforcement of the rules does not take into account the uniqueness of the problems and needs of individuals and groups in the community. The police response should be lawful but otherwise a function of the situational context and community values as they relate to community problems.

This debate between the legalistic and the personal/political approach emphasizes a long-standing tension in democratic societies—the rule of law versus community expectations. At the one extreme is the uncaring bureaucrat who never deviates from the rules and does not seek opinions about which rules are important or when and how they should be applied. At the other extreme is the tyranny of the majority. However much we subscribe to the rule of law, those who provide government service are often called on to tailor that service to the needs of a particular community. But how can they do this without providing preferential treatment for some (e.g., individuals, groups, or neighborhoods) while discriminating against others? The answer to this question remains elusive, and it varies concerning how, or even whether, it can be done.

The legalistic approach and the personal/political approach to the role of the police identify three possible types of police-community relationships. The *political model* refers to a police–community relationship that is plagued by problems of preferential treatment, discrimination, and corruption. The *legalistic or reform/professional model* is based on the assumption that political influence has a corrupting influence on policing; therefore, the police–community relationship must be more structured or bureaucratic. The *community policing model* is based on the desirability of the police being responsive to individuals and groups while at the same time not engaging in preferential treatment or discrimination.

### Crime-Fighting or Social Service?

The debate about whether the police should only fight crime or should also provide social services influences the priority given to police activities, the type of personnel selected, the way that officers are trained, and the styles that officers adopt. Officers who consider themselves crime-fighters believe that crime is a function of a rational choice made by criminals and that the primary purpose of police is to patrol and conduct investigations to deter crime and apprehend offenders. Officers who consider themselves social service providers believe that crime results from a variety of causes and that other police activities, such as crime prevention education and community building, may also reduce the crime rate. The social service orientation tends to result in more police–community involvement and a less aggressive and authoritarian approach to policing.

There are, of course, no "pure" crime-fighters or social service providers; however, the belief that police are, or should be, one or the other influences how the police role in a community will be constructed. Often, the role expectations vary by source. Some communities, neighborhoods, or groups may expect police to be crime-fighters, whereas others may want a social service orientation. On the police side, officers frequently prefer to think of themselves as crime-fighters, although it is also common for them to say that they joined the police to help people.

### Proactive or Reactive?

**Proactive** police work emphasizes police-initiated activities by the individual officer and the department. **Reactive** police work occurs more in the form of responses to incidents when assistance is specifically requested by citizens. Giving a traffic ticket or other citation or conducting a field interrogation of someone acting suspiciously is proactive. Developing a solution to a crime or other problem that is designed to keep it from occurring is also proactive. For example, undercover decoy programs are proactive, as are "stakeouts" (following suspected career criminals) and picking up truants (who may be committing burglaries when absent from school). Responding to specific incidents based on citizen requests and following up on those incidents are reactive responses.

Proactive responses can be problematic, because they make the police more intrusive in the community—that is, police are more likely to initiate contacts or tactics without being asked, and some proactive efforts are potentially dangerous (e.g., stakeout and decoy programs). Being proactive can be associated with good management, but it may also be intrusive and risky. In recent years, several police departments, including those of Philadelphia and New York, were criticized for excessive use of "stop and frisk" (American Civil Liberties Union of Pennsylvania 2016; New York Civil Liberties Union 2016). A particular concern is that when police proactively stop people they think are acting suspiciously, conscious or unconscious bias may influence who they decide to stop, resulting in racial profiling or other forms of discrimination.

Which is more compatible with democracy—a police force that is primarily reactive or one that is more proactive? Passive, reactive policing interferes with our freedom the least, but it likely also protects us the least. In trying to strike the right balance, it may be important to distinguish the degree to which proactive police work is in response to community expectations (but see Inside Policing 1.2) versus the expectations of the police department or individual police officers. What is clear, however, is that the more proactive and intrusive the police are, the greater the risk to police officers, citizens, and democracy.

---

### INSIDE POLICING 1.2  Not a Police Matter

Police have been called recently to deal with a Black guy wearing socks at a private pool (in Memphis), an 11-year-old Black kid on his first day delivering newspapers (in Cincinnati), a 12-year-old Black kid mowing a lawn who accidentally crossed into a neighbor's yard (outside Cleveland), and a 9-year-old Black girl selling water outside her apartment building (in San Francisco). This article discusses what police should do, including having call takers ask more specific questions and routing such calls through supervisors before assigning them to patrol officers.

**Discussion Question:** These seem to be cases in which the caller (the complainant) thinks something is suspicious, mainly due to the person's race. What should the police do when they get calls like this? What happens if they ignore the call? What happens if they respond and check it out?

SOURCE: *Modern Policing* blog, July 16, 2018, https://gcordner.wordpress.com/2018/07/16/not-a-police-matter/.

### Police Activities and Workload

As these debates about the role of the police suggest, police officers perform a variety of different tasks and activities. Since the 1960s, many studies have attempted to summarize the nature of police work by categorizing different measures of reactive and proactive police work, such as calls to the police, calls dispatched, time consumed, and encounters with citizens. By the 1980s, it had become widely accepted that actual police work, as contrasted with its depiction in the media, was a rich and varied blend of several types of activities, including crime control (e.g., taking crime reports, investigating crimes, and inquiring into suspicious circumstances), law enforcement (e.g., making arrests and issuing traffic citations), order maintenance (e.g., handling disputes and keeping the peace), and service (e.g., finding lost children and helping disabled motorists). The actual mix of these different types of activity varies among different jurisdictions, such as between a city and an affluent suburb, and among different patrol beats within a jurisdiction.

The most comprehensive study of patrol work was the Police Services Study (Whitaker 1982). This study examined patrol work in 60 different neighborhoods, with observers accompanying patrol officers on all shifts in 24 police departments (including 21 municipal and 3 county sheriffs' departments). The observers collected information on each encounter between a police officer and a citizen, detailing nearly 6,000 encounters in all. The fact that this study included so many different police departments and police-initiated as well as citizen-initiated activity makes it persuasive. In a sophisticated reanalysis of the Police Services Study, Mastrofski (1983) examined the most frequent incidents encountered by patrol officers and found the following breakdown:

- 29.1% Crime-related incidents
- 24.1% Traffic regulation and enforcement
- 22.7% Nuisances, disputes, and dependent persons
- 24.1% Services and other miscellaneous incidents

The takeaway from this breakdown is simply that police work is not "just" crime fighting or "just" social services. It is a rich mix of reactive and proactive work, some clearly crime-related and some not, with a fair amount in the ambiguous categories of nuisances, disputes, and miscellaneous incidents.

The Police Services Study also examined the specific actions that police officers took during their 6,000 encounters with the public. The percentages indicate the proportion of all encounters in which police officers took each kind of action. (These numbers add up to more than 100 percent, because officers often took more than one type of action in an encounter.)

- 57% Interviewed a witness or person requesting service
- 40% Interrogated a suspect
- 29% Conducted a search or inspection
- 28% Lectured or threatened (other than threat of force)
- 27% Gave information
- 23% Gave reassurance
- 14% Used force or threat of force
- 11% Gave assistance

- 9% Gave a ticket
- 8% Used persuasion
- 5% Made an arrest
- 2% Gave medical help

The police invoked the law relatively rarely, making arrests in only 5 percent of the encounters and issuing tickets in fewer than 1 of 10 encounters. Officers used force or the threat of force in 14 percent of the encounters (with force actually used in only 5 percent, most of which amounted simply to handcuffing or taking a suspect by the arm). The use of force or its threat was about equally likely in situations involving crime, disorder, and traffic encounters, but was rare in service situations.

Perhaps the most interesting characteristic of police work revealed by these percentages is the importance of interpersonal communication. Five of the six most common actions taken by officers consisted entirely of talking and listening: interviewing, interrogating, lecturing or threatening, giving information, and giving reassurance. Police officers primarily use communication to determine what is happening in any given situation, and it is primarily through communication that an amicable solution is reached. Enforcing the law and using force often come into play only after communication tactics and informal solutions prove unsuccessful. Of course, serious law violations do sometimes require immediate enforcement, and very dangerous suspects may warrant immediate use of force.

The traffic function of policing accounts for a sizable portion of all police–citizen encounters and significantly affects how the public views the police. According to a study based on a large sample of US residents, 53 million Americans aged 16 or older had a police contact in 2015, with vehicle stops accounting for 47 percent (Davis, Whyde, and Langton 2018). Of those involved in vehicle stops, 91 percent said the stop was legitimate, and 90 percent or more said the police behaved properly and respectfully unless there was a search or arrest, in which case 67 percent said the police behavior was proper and respectful.

Police officers typically have a great deal of discretion in making traffic stops and issuing citations, and the level of traffic enforcement varies greatly among individual officers and between different departments. Some departments have no formal policies regarding traffic enforcement, although there are often informal policies and expectations. For example, specialized traffic units may have policies requiring officers to generate at least one citation per hour, whereas regular patrol officers may be expected to write one or two citations per shift. Such policies or expectations can lead to unequal traffic enforcement, with officers scrambling at the end of shifts or at the end of the month to "keep their numbers up" or "meet their quotas." We will have more to say about police behavior and police use of force in Chapters 9 and 10.

## Police Goals and Strategies

In this section, we have discussed several different ways of thinking about the role of the police in a free society and also some information about what police officers actually do. To complete the discussion, we will consider what police officers and entire police agencies are supposed to accomplish (their purpose or goals). We will also briefly touch on the strategies that police agencies use to try to accomplish their goals.

A particularly useful listing of police goals is provided in Table 1.6. Moore and Braga (2003) present these goals as the "bottom line" of policing. This framework illustrates that the police bottom line (i.e., the measuring stick that we should use to determine how well a police agency or individual officer is performing) is actually multidimensional. This is

**TABLE 1.6  Dimensions of Police Performance**

| |
|---|
| Reduce crime and victimization |
| Call offenders to account |
| Reduce fear and enhance personal security |
| Ensure civility in public spaces (ordered liberty) |
| Quality services/customer satisfaction |
| Use force and authority fairly, efficiently, and effectively |
| Use financial resources fairly, efficiently, and effectively |

Source: M. H. Moore and A. Braga, *The "Bottom Line" of Policing: What Citizens Should Value (and Measure) in Police Performance* (Washington, DC: Police Executive Research Forum, 2003), 18.

another way of saying that we expect the police to accomplish several different things, more or less simultaneously. This helps explain why policing is complex and also why different members of the community might have different opinions about how well their police are performing—opinions regarding which goals are most or least important vary from person to person as well as over time.

Individual officers who give the highest priority to the goal of calling offenders to account tend to perceive the police role as mainly law enforcement, in contrast to officers who put more priority on maintaining order (ensuring civility in public places) or reassuring the public (reducing fear). An emphasis on reducing crime reflects the crime-fighter role, whereas the social service role tends to focus somewhat more on satisfying the public by providing quality services. A proactive approach to policing might promise more success in reducing crime or holding offenders accountable, but at the risk of inefficient or unfair use of police power and authority. The interplay among these different dimensions of police performance helps explain the different ways that police officers (and the public) perceive the police role.

At the police agency level, we can see the same thing. Some police departments put their highest priority on reducing crime, perhaps because their jurisdiction has a high crime rate or because the police chief adheres to the crime-fighter role. Other police departments seem to focus more on maintaining order or providing services, perhaps because crime rates are lower in their jurisdictions or in response to different community and political expectations (Wilson 1968). Certain agencies, especially federal and some special jurisdiction agencies, clearly put their greatest emphasis on calling offenders to account. In these agencies, investigation is the dominant activity, and success is measured almost entirely in terms of cases solved.

Efficient use of financial resources has always been perceived as a high priority for taxpayers, but it has come to the forefront in recent years. Tax limitation measures adopted over the past 30 to 40 years have significantly reduced public funds in many states and local jurisdictions. In addition, the economic downturn starting in 2008 caused many police agencies to cut back on services and even lay off sworn personnel. After one or two decades during which police agencies seemed to have favored status with taxpayers, city managers, and mayors at budget time, finances tightened, and police chiefs often had to find places to cut their budgets (see Inside Policing 1.3). The more recent COVID-19 pandemic further decimated budgets in many municipalities and counties.

---

**INSIDE POLICING 1.3** | **Local Policing in Pennsylvania**

Pennsylvania has over 2,500 municipalities and no unincorporated areas. Nearly half the municipalities have their own police departments, while the rest rely on state police, since Pennsylvania sheriffs lack general police powers. This article describes the policing situation in Allegheny County, which has Pittsburgh Bureau of Police and 108 other police departments. Most of these departments are small, and many depend heavily on part-time officers. The result is wide variation in staffing, workload, and pay, with the neediest communities often least able to afford reliable, consistent police service.

**Discussion Question:** The cost of policing has gone up substantially over the last few decades, at a rate faster than the increase in tax revenues. This has been good for police salaries, but local governments are finding it harder to afford their current level of policing. What would you suggest to solve this dilemma?

SOURCE: *Modern Policing* blog, December 19, 2018, gcordner.wordpress.com/2018/12/19/local-policing-in-pennsylvania/.

---

Additionally, the public tends to put a high priority on the "using force and authority fairly" and "quality services" dimensions. If a community believes that its police officers do not treat people fairly or if citizens have unpleasant contacts with officers, public trust and confidence are easily compromised. This seems to be true even if, at the same time, the police department can demonstrate success in achieving other goals, such as reducing crime and holding offenders to account. This characteristic of police performance is now sometimes referred to as procedural justice (Sunshine and Tyler 2003); the lesson is that process can be as important as outcome in judging the effectiveness of the police and maintaining the legitimacy of the police institution, a point to which we will return in Chapter 8.

Another implication of procedural justice and police legitimacy is that *how* the police try to accomplish their goals can be as important as whether they accomplish them, which brings strategies and tactics into the discussion. *Strategies* refers to the broad approaches that police agencies take in trying to accomplish their multiple goals, whereas *tactics* refers to narrower and more specific programs and activities. Community policing is an example of a strategy, whereas foot patrol is a tactic.

Major police strategies can be differentiated in two ways: (1) according to the specific methods that they employ, as noted previously, and (2) according to how much priority they place on the various goals of policing. In Chapters 2, 4, and 8, we discuss several police strategies, including the reform/professional model, community policing, problem-oriented policing, intelligence-led policing, and predictive policing. In a nutshell, professional policing emphasizes reducing crime and holding offenders to account, relying mainly on police presence and strict enforcement of the law. Community policing tends to put more emphasis on the goals of customer satisfaction and fear reduction than the other strategies, and it relies more on personalized policing, community education, and community engagement. Problem-oriented policing emphasizes reducing the harm that is caused by crime and other types of problems, mainly by taking an analytical and preventive approach to identify tailor-made solutions to specific problems. Intelligence-led policing and predictive policing are the newest strategies, focusing mainly on crime reduction aided by high-tech approaches to prediction, prevention, and suppression.

## Looking Ahead

The aim of this chapter has been to lay a brief foundation for your study of police and society. The next three chapters continue in that same vein. Chapter 2 presents the history of police to help you understand when and why modern police departments developed and how they have evolved, as well as what societies did before they had police departments as we know them today. Chapter 3 provides the legal framework of policing, including concepts from constitutional, criminal, and civil law that define the parameters or "guardrails" within which police are allowed to use their power and authority. Chapter 4 focuses on police strategies, especially community policing and problem-oriented policing, which came to prominence in the 1990s and continue to be popular today.

Part II of the book shifts to the organizational or administrative perspective on policing. This approach is important, because police officers are members of police *organizations* and society looks to police *organizations* to make their communities safe and free. Chapter 5 discusses police administration and management, including how police agencies are structured, how police officers are managed and led, and the challenge of achieving organizational change. Chapter 6 targets three specific police administrative processes related to acquiring and developing the right kinds of people to do police work—recruitment, selection, and training. Chapter 7 focuses on the main operational tactics and programs that police use in the field, such as patrol and investigations, while Chapter 8 focuses on contemporary innovations and alternatives aimed at more effectively accomplishing the multidimensional bottom line of policing.

Part III concentrates on police behavior—in other words, what police officers do, why they do it, and how best to control it. Chapter 9 discusses a variety of types of police behavior and misbehavior, along with theories that aim to explain the behavior. Chapter 10 focuses specifically on the core of the police role, exercising force and coercion. Chapter 11 then presents information on the many internal and external methods that are used to try to hold both individual police officers and police agencies accountable for their behavior, including their use of power and authority. It has been said that power corrupts, and that absolute power corrupts absolutely. Police definitely have power, so many mechanisms must be in place to control that power and hold police accountable when power is misused.

Part IV discusses a variety of important contemporary issues affecting police and society. Chapter 12 reviews the experience of women and minorities in policing and explains why it is so important for police agencies to reflect the diversity of their communities. Chapter 13 examines the effects of stress on police officers and considers the highly important topic of police officer safety, including the surprising fact that fewer police die from felonious assault than from suicide, job-related illness, and accidents. Chapter 14 assesses the role of higher education in policing; the necessity of college for police officers is an issue that has been vigorously debated since the 1960s. Chapter 15 then discusses a number of different current and emerging issues in society and within policing, including the impact of modern technologies such as body-worn cameras and the still-evolving police role in homeland security and counterterrorism.

As previously noted, this is a lot of information. Each chapter is full of many important details, but as you digest them, try to keep the big picture in mind as well—policing foundations, police administration, police behavior, and contemporary issues. You might want to use that framework, along with the chapter titles, as a kind of outline or mental filing system to help you keep so much information organized in a coherent and understandable format.

## Summary

The type of police a society has is determined by the society's history, culture, and form of government—totalitarian or democratic. In free and democratic societies, police fill an anomalous and conflicted function. The rule of law is one of the most important means for dealing with this conflict. Laws represent rules that citizens are required to follow, of course, but also rules that the police are supposed to follow in their interactions with citizens. In today's world, terrorism has introduced another new challenge for the relationship among democracy, law, and the police, and most recently, demands to reimagine and reform policing have become stronger.

Police are defined as those nonmilitary individuals or organizations that are given the general right by government to enforce the law and maintain order, and their primary purpose is to respond to problems of individual and group conflict that involve illegal behavior. The police role and what is considered appropriate or inappropriate police behavior are influenced by legal, organizational, and community expectations as well as the personal values and beliefs of individual police officers. When all the expectations arising from these different quarters align, policing can operate from consensus in a smooth manner. In a democratic society, however, expectations often clash, creating conflict over the police role and the specific actions that police take in their approach to crime, disorder, and other issues.

Another challenge faced in policing is a multidimensional bottom line. Society expects police to accomplish several different ends, including reducing crime as well as providing quality services, making public places orderly, and reassuring people that they are safe. In addition, police are expected to treat people fairly and equitably and to accomplish their multifaceted bottom line without expending more tax dollars than absolutely necessary. Several different police strategies currently compete for popular and professional acceptance as the most effective way to deliver policing in the twenty-first century.

## Critical Thinking Questions

1. How is policing different in a free and democratic society as opposed to a totalitarian society?

2. It has been said that "democracy is always hard on the police." Why do you think this is the case?

3. Why is the rule of law important for policing in a democracy?

4. Discuss the ramifications of the multidimensional police bottom line. If you were a mayor, how would you use this bottom line to determine how good your town's police department was and what it should do to improve?

5. The police system in the United States is very fragmented. Do you think this is a positive or a negative feature? Why?

## References

American Civil Liberties Union of Pennsylvania. 2016. "*Bailey et al. v. City of Philadelphia et al.*" Philadelphia: Authors. https://www.aclupa.org/our-work/legal/legaldocket/baileyetalvcityofphiladelp/.

Berkeley, G. E. 1969. *The Democratic Policeman*. Boston: Beacon Press.

Bittner, E. 1970. *The Functions of Police in Modern Society*. Washington, DC: US Government Printing Office.

Brenan, M. 2021. "Americans' Confidence in Major US Institutions Dips." *Gallup*, July 14. https://news.gallup.com/poll/352316/americans-confidence-major-institutions-dips.aspx.

Brooks, C. 2019a. *Federal Law Enforcement Officers, 2016 – Statistical Tables*. Washington, DC: Bureau of Justice Statistics. https://bjs.ojp.gov/content/pub/pdf/fleo16st.pdf.

Brooks, C. 2019b. *Sheriffs' Offices, 2016: Personnel*. Washington, DC. Bureau of Justice Statistics. https://bjs.ojp.gov/content/pub/pdf/so16p.pdf.

Byman, D. 2021. "2021 Saw Plenty of Violence—But No Mass Terrorist Attacks in the US." *Brookings*, December 29. https://www.brookings.edu/opinions/2021-saw-plenty-of-violence-but-no-mass-terrorist-attacks-in-the-u-s/.

Cassie, R. 2020. "Why Baltimore's Protests Are So Peaceful." *Bloomberg CityLab*, June 4. https://www.bloomberg.com/news/articles/2020-06-04/why-baltimore-s-george-floyd-protest-is-different.

Civil Rights Division. 2015. *Investigation of the Ferguson Police Department*. Washington, DC: US Department of Justice. https://www.justice.gov/sites/default/files/opa/press-releases/attachments/2015/03/04/ferguson_police_department_report.pdf.

Cordner, G. 2011. "The Architecture of US Policing: Variations Among the 50 States." *Police Practice & Research: An International Journal* 12(2): 107–119.

Crank, J. P. 1998. *Understanding Police Culture*. Cincinnati, OH: Anderson.

Davis, E., Whyde, A., and Langton, L. 2018. *Contacts Between Police and the Public, 2015*. Washington, DC: Bureau of Justice Statistics. https://www.bjs.gov/content/pub/pdf/cpp15.pdf.

Education Week. 2022. "School Shootings in 2021: How Many and Where." *Education Week*, January 5. https://www.edweek.org/leadership/school-shootings-this-year-how-many-and-where/2021/03.

Garland, M. 2021, June 15. "Attorney General Merrick B. Garland Remarks: Domestic Terrorism Policy Address." Washington, DC: US Department of Justice. https://www.justice.gov/opa/speech/attorney-general-merrick-b-garland-remarks-domestic-terrorism-policy-address.

Goldstein, H. 1977. *Policing a Free Society*. Cambridge, MA: Ballinger.

Gramlich, J. 2021. "What We Know About the Increase in US Murders in 2020." *Pew Research Center*, October 27. https://www.pewresearch.org/fact-tank/2021/10/27/what-we-know-about-the-increase-in-u-s-murders-in-2020/.

Hutchinson, B. 2021. "'It's Just Crazy': 12 Major Cities Hit All-Time Homicide Records." *ABC News*, December 8. https://abcnews.go.com/US/12-major-us-cities-top-annual-homicide-records/story?id=81466453.

Hyland, S. 2018. *Full-Time Employees in Law Enforcement Agencies, 1997–2016*. Washington, DC: Bureau of Justice Statistics.

Hyland, S., and Davis, E. 2019. *Local Police Departments, 2016: Personnel*. Washington, DC: Bureau of Justice Statistics. https://bjs.ojp.gov/content/pub/pdf/lpd16p.pdf.

Jones, J. 2021. "In US, Black Confidence in Police Recovers from 2020 Low." *Gallup*, July 14. https://news.gallup.com/poll/352304/black-confidence-police-recovers-2020-low.aspx.

Levin, S. 2021. "These US Cities Defunded Police: 'We're Transferring Money to the Community.'" *The Guardian*, March 7. https://www.theguardian.com/us-news/2021/mar/07/us-cities-defund-police-transferring-money-community.

Levinson, J. 2021. "Discord over Leadership, Morale, and Discipline Besets a Portland Police Bureau in Transition." *Oregon Public Broadcasting*, June 25. https://www.opb.org/article/2021/06/25/leadership-morale-discipline-issues-beset-portland-police-bureau/.

Linn, E. 2008. *Arrest Decisions: What Works for the Officer?* New York: Lang.

Mastrofski, S. 1983. "The Police and Noncrime Services." In G. Whitaker and C. Phillips (eds.), *Evaluating the Performance of Crime and Criminal Justice Agencies*, pp. 33–61. Thousand Oaks, CA: Sage.

McDonald, T. D., Wood, R. A., and Pflug, M. A. (eds.). 1996. *Rural Criminal Justice*. Salem, WI: Sheffield.

Moore, M. H., and Braga, A. 2003. *The "Bottom Line" of Policing: What Citizens Should Value (and Measure) in Police Performance*. Washington, DC: Police Executive Research Forum.

New York Civil Liberties Union. 2016. "Stop-and-Frisk Practices." New York: Authors. https://www.nyclu.org/issues/racial-justice/stop-and-frisk-practices/.

Officer Down Memorial Page. 2022. https://www.odmp.org/.

Olson, R., Xiong, C., and Walsh, P. 2021. "Chauvin Sentenced to 22½ Years for the Murder of George Floyd." *Star Tribune*, June 26. https://www.startribune.com/chauvin-sentenced-to-221-2-years-for-the-murder-of-george-floyd/600071867/.

Paoline, E. A. 2001. *Rethinking Police Culture: Officers' Occupational Attitudes*. El Paso, TX: LFB Scholarly.

Parker, K., and Hurst, K. 2021. "Growing Share of Americans Say They Want More Spending on Police in Their Area." *Pew Research Center*, October 26. https://www.pewresearch.org/fact-tank/2021/10/26/growing-share-of-americans-say-they-want-more-spending-on-police-in-their-area/.

Penrod, J., and Sinner, C. 2020. "Buildings Damaged in Minneapolis, St. Paul After Riots." *Star Tribune*, July 13. https://www.startribune.com/a-deeper-look-at-areas-most-damaged-by-rioting-looting-in-minneapolis-st-paul/569930671/.

Police Executive Research Forum. 2016. *Guiding Principles on Use of Force*. Washington, DC: Author. https://www.policeforum.org/assets/30%20guiding%20principles.pdf.

Powell, Z., Meitl, M., and Worrall, J. 2017. "Police Consent Decrees and Section 1983 Civil Rights Litigation." *Criminology & Public Policy* 16(2): 575–605.

President's Commission on Law Enforcement and Administration of Justice. 1967. *The Challenge of Crime in a Free Society*. Washington, DC: US Government Printing Office.

President's Task Force on Twenty-First Century Policing. 2015. *Final Report*. Washington, DC: Office of Community Oriented Policing Services. https://cops.usdoj.gov/RIC/Publications/cops-p341-pub.pdf.

Reaves, B. A. 2011. *Census of State and Local Law Enforcement Agencies, 2008*. Washington, DC: Bureau of Justice Statistics. https://bjs.ojp.gov/sites/g/files/xyckuh236/files/media/document/csllea08sol.pdf.

Reiss, A. J., Jr. 1971. *The Police and the Public*. New Haven, CT: Yale University Press.

Reith, C. 1938. *The Police Idea*. London: Oxford University Press.

Roberg, R. R., Kuykendall, J., and Novak, K. 2002. *Police Management*, 3rd ed. Los Angeles: Roxbury.

Royal Commission on the Police. 1962. *Report*. London: Her Majesty's Stationery Store.

Silva, D., and Moschella, M. 2020. "Seattle Protesters Set Up 'Autonomous Zone' After Seattle Police Evacuate Precinct." *NBC News*, June 11. https://www.nbcnews.com/news/us-news/seattle-protesters-set-autonomous-zone-after-police-evacuate-precinct-n1230151.

Sims, V. H. 1996. "The Structural Components of Rural Law Enforcement: Roles and Organizations." In T. D. McDonald, R. A. Wood, and M. A. Pflug (eds.), *Rural Criminal Justice*, pp. 41–54. Salem, WI: Sheffield.

Spence, D., and Drake, J. 2021. *Law Enforcement Officer Suicide: 2020 Report to Congress*. Washington, DC: Office of Community Oriented Policing Services. https://cops.usdoj.gov/RIC/Publications/cops-p429-pub.pdf.

Sunshine, J., and Tyler, T. R. 2003. "The Role of Procedural Justice and Legitimacy in Shaping Public Support for Policing." *Law & Society Review* 37: 513–548.

Walker, S. 1977. *History of Police Reform*. Lexington, MA: Lexington Books.

Weisheit, R. A., Falcone, D. N., and Wells, L. E. 1994. *Rural Crime and Rural Policing*. Washington, DC: US Department of Justice, Office of Justice Programs, National Institute of Justice.

Westervelt, E. 2021. "Cops Say Low Morale and Department Scrutiny Are Driving Them Away from the Job." *National Public Radio*, June 24. https://www.npr.org/2021/06/24/1009578809/cops-say-low-morale-and-department-scrutiny-are-driving-them-away-from-the-job.

Whitaker, G. P. 1982. "What Is Patrol Work?" *Police Studies* 4: 13–22.

White House. 2021. National Strategy for Countering Domestic Terrorism. Washington, DC: National Security Council. https://www.whitehouse.gov/wp-content/uploads/2021/06/National-Strategy-for-Countering-Domestic-Terrorism.pdf.

Wilson, J. Q. 1968. *Varieties of Police Behavior: The Management of Law and Order in Eight Communities*. Cambridge, MA: Harvard University Press.

Wilson, J. Q. 1978. *The Investigators: Managing FBI and Narcotics Agents*. New York: Basic Books.

## CHAPTER 2

# Police History

## CHAPTER OUTLINE

## CHAPTER OUTLINE   (continued)

### KEY TERMS

- class-control theory
- constable
- constable–nightwatch system
- crime-control theory
- disorder-control theory
- frankpledge system
- highway patrol
- kin policing
- marshals
- nightwatch
- patronage system
- political model
- *posse comitatus*
- professionalization
- reform/professional model
- sheriff
- state police
- thief catcher
- urban-dispersion theory
- vigilante

"Those that fail to learn from history are doomed to repeat it."

—Winston Churchill

IT IS IMPORTANT TO understand the history of policing for several reasons. Possessing an understanding of and appreciation for this history allows one to identify enduring aspects of the police. It also allows evaluating prior police reform efforts and provides a basis for anticipating future policing developments (Walker and Katz 2011). Yet despite extensive research into policing since the 1960s, no definitive answers exist as to what the police role should be or what particular activities are consistently more effective in reducing crime while maintaining widespread community support, particularly among the poor and minority members of society. Is it even possible for the police to reduce crime without providing preferential treatment for some while discriminating against others?

This question identifies the fundamental police problem in a democracy. The modern approach to responding to this problem is community policing, discussed in Chapter 4. Before community policing, other approaches were used to make police compatible with democracy. These approaches, called models of policing, are briefly discussed in this chapter.

## Foundations of Policing

The history of policing begins with a consideration of kin policing, Greek and Roman policing, and the development of policing in Europe, particularly in England, because of that country's influence on the formation of modern police departments in the United States.

### Early Policing

One of the earliest methods of policing is known as **kin policing**, in which the family, clan, or tribe enforced informal and customary rules, or norms, of conduct. Often, the response to a deviation from group norms was brutal (e.g., a hand cut off for stealing or a brand on the forehead for being a criminal). In effect, each member of the group had at least some authority to enforce the informal rules (Berg 1992).

The kin policing of clans and tribes began to change during the rise of the Greek city-states and Rome. Until about 594 BCE in Greece and the third century BCE in Rome, public order was the responsibility of appointed magistrates, who were unpaid, private individuals. The first paid public police officer was the *praefectus urbi*, a position created in Rome about 27 BCE. By 6 CE, Rome had a large public police force that patrolled the streets night and day. After the fall of the Roman Empire, anarchy tended to prevail on the European continent until the twelfth and thirteenth centuries, when kings began to assume the responsibility for legal administration.

Their approach included strengthening the **nightwatch**, a group of citizens who patrolled at night looking for fires and other problems, and appointing individuals to conduct investigations, make arrests, and collect taxes. In some countries, such as France, mounted military patrols were also employed.

In the twelfth century in England, a **sheriff** was appointed by the king to levy fines and ensure that the **frankpledge system** worked. This system for keeping order had existed for centuries and was based on an organization of tithings (10 families) and hundreds (10 tithings). Eventually, these hundreds became known as parishes, and several hundred became known as a shire. A shire was similar to a contemporary county.

In this system, men over the age of 15 formed a ***posse comitatus***, a group called out to pursue fleeing felons. In 1285, the Statute of Winchester mandated that every hundred citizens appoint two constables to assist the sheriff. Like the sheriff, the **constable** inquired into offenses (conducted investigations), served summonses and warrants, took charge of prisoners, and supervised the nightwatch. By the thirteenth century, law was administered by magistrates, who were appointed by the king, and by sheriffs and constables. In the late 1200s, the office of justice of the peace was established in England. The county sheriff was responsible for policing a county, and sheriffs were assisted by the justice of the peace, who in turn was assisted by constables.

This arrangement was the foundation for a system of law enforcement that was to stay in place until the 1800s. However, much of the work of these individuals, except the sheriffs, was voluntary and not popular, so the practice of paying for substitutes became commonplace. In many instances, the same person was paid year after year to do the work of those who were appointed to the position but did not wish to serve. Often, the substitutes were inadequately paid, elderly, poorly educated, and inefficient. These deficiencies did not help the image or effectiveness of policing in the eyes of the community.

At the end of the 1700s, families by the thousands began to move to newly established factory towns to find work. Patterns of lives were disrupted, and unprecedented social disorder resulted. Existing systems of law enforcement, primarily the justice of the peace and the constable, were inadequate to respond to the problems associated with these changes. In the **constable–nightwatch system** of policing, the constables, who were appointed by the local justices, patrolled their parishes during the day. The constables had limited power, however, and when they tried to obtain citizen assistance by raising the "hue and cry" to capture a fleeing criminal, they were more likely to be ridiculed than helped. At night, men of the watch were charged with patrolling deserted streets and maintaining street lamps, but these individuals were more likely to be found sleeping or in a pub than performing their duties.

In London, criminals had little to fear from this law enforcement system, and they moved freely about the city streets. Victims of crime, if they were well-to-do, were protected by their servants and retainers (who formed a bodyguard or type of private police). Poorer citizens had no such protection. When property crimes were committed, the usual procedure was for the victim to employ a **thief catcher**. This person, usually an experienced constable familiar with the criminal underworld, would attempt, for a fee, to secure the return of all or part of the stolen property. Often, the thief catcher would supplement his fee by keeping part of the stolen property for himself. Thief catchers were not interested in apprehending and prosecuting criminals, but in getting paid and returning all or part of the stolen property.

## Policing in Nineteenth-Century England

It is important to focus on the early policing models of nineteenth-century London, because this system became a model for policing in England and, to some degree, the United States (President's Commission 1967). Henry Fielding, the magistrate for Middlesex and Westminster, was among the first to believe that police action could prevent crime. From 1754 to 1780, he assisted in the organization of the Bow Street station and is credited with developing the first police investigators. The Bow Street station was organized into three groups that performed specific crime-control functions. Men engaged in foot patrol in the inner areas of the city. Additionally, men on horseback allowed patrols up to 15 miles away from the Bow Street station. Finally, a group of men responded to crime scenes to engage in investigations. These plain-clothed men became known as the Bow Street Runners or Thief Takers, and as such, they represented the first detective unit (Germann, Day, and Gallati 1978).

In 1822, Sir Robert Peel, the British home secretary, criticized the poor quality of police in London. In 1829, he was able to pass the Act for Improving the Police in and Near the Metropolis, also known as the Metropolitan Police Act. This measure resulted in the creation of the first organized British metropolitan police force and the modern- day police (Germann et al. 1978).

Initially, Charles Rowan and Richard Mayne were appointed to develop the force. They adopted a military structure and sought to employ the most competent personnel possible. However, there was considerable resistance to this new type of police among the British populace. They feared the abuse of governmental authority, the kind of secret police that existed in countries such as France, and limitations on individual freedom. Historically, Britain, like other countries, had many problems in this regard. Eventually, the police became accepted, largely because Rowan and Mayne were selective about who they employed and how officers were to behave. By the 1850s, every borough and county in England was required to develop its own police force. Inside Policing 2.1 provides brief descriptions of the contributions of Peel, Rowan, and Mayne to the development of the British police.

One of the most important principles of the Peelian approach was to emphasize the preventive aspects of law enforcement. This attitude resulted in police officers being distributed throughout the city to prevent crimes or to be close by when crimes occurred so that officers could make arrests and help victims. This idea became an important part of

## INSIDE POLICING 2.1 Founders of the British Police

### Sir Robert Peel

In 1822, Robert Peel was appointed home secretary, the person responsible for internal security in England. One of his most important objectives was to establish an effective police force to respond to riots and crime problems. It took him seven years—until 1829—to be successful. Because the idea for a new approach to policing was so controversial, Peel initially asked that the new police be established only in metropolitan London. He intended, however, that a similar type of police organization would eventually be established for all of Great Britain. Peel was a strong advocate of the concept of a civilian (rather than a military) police force that did not carry guns and that was put out in the community to patrol to prevent crime. The new police became known as Bobbies, after the founder of the department.

### Colonel Charles Rowan

Charles Rowan was one of the first commissioners of the new police in London. He served in that capacity until 1850, when he retired. Rowan had a military background that prepared him for such service. Early in the nineteenth century, he served under the major general Sir John Moore, whose approach to dealing with his soldiers likely had a strong influence on how Rowan thought the police should relate to the public. Moore believed that military officers should show respect for soldiers and treat them firmly and justly. Rowan wanted the same type of relationship to exist between police officers and citizens. Both he and Mayne encouraged officers to listen to citizen complaints and be tolerant of citizens' verbal abuse.

### Richard Mayne

Richard Mayne, an Irish barrister, served as a police commissioner until 1868. His extended service enabled the London police to develop a force that was well respected by citizens. Together with Rowan, he organized the force into numerous divisions that varied in size depending on the amount of crime in a division's area. Each division had a superintendent in charge, with inspectors, sergeants, and constables, in descending order of rank. Constables wore a blue uniform and were armed with a short baton and a rattle (for raising an alarm). The uniform was designed so that it would not be similar to military dress. Mayne and Rowan were both concerned that military-style police would have more difficulty being accepted by the public.

SOURCES: Adapted from H. A. Johnson, *History of Criminal Justice* (Cincinnati, OH: Anderson, 1988), 173–175; D. R. Johnson, *American Law Enforcement: A History* (St. Louis: Forum Press, 1981), 20–21.

the development of police in the United States. Other principles were also implemented to guide the development of the new police force. The Peelian principles include the following:

1. The police must be stable, efficient, and organized along military lines.
2. The police must be under government control.
3. The absence of crime will best prove the efficiency of police.
4. The distribution of crime news is essential.
5. The deployment of police strength both by time and area is essential.

6. No quality is more indispensable to a policeman than a perfect command of temper; a quiet, determined manner has more effect than violent action.

7. Good appearance commands respect.

8. The securing and training of proper persons is at the root of efficiency.

9. Public security demands that every police officer be given a number.

10. Police headquarters should be centrally located and easily accessible to the people.

11. Policemen should be hired on a probationary basis.

12. Police records are necessary to the correct distribution of police strength. (Germann et al. 60–61)

Peel may not have created the list attributed to him; rather, these principles may be a summary of the practices developed by Peel, Rowan, and Mayne. Lentz and Chaires (2007) noted that early presentations of the Peelian principles varied, and there is no historical evidence that Peel actually wrote them. They may instead be a product of authors of twentieth-century policing textbooks who sought ways to succinctly describe the values of early English policing practices. Early policing scholars and a subsequent generation of policing textbooks likely interpreted retrospectively emerging police policy, custom, and practice to create a list of principles, conveniently attributing them to Sir Robert Peel.

This understanding is important to promote historical integrity and emphasize that policing should be examined within its social and historical frameworks. A full examination here would be beyond the scope of the current text's goals; however, we recognize (as Lentz and Chaires 2007 noted) that these principles represent an important way to demonstrate that policing was becoming rational. A look toward these principles has also been used to lend credibility and support for modern police innovations or reform. For example, the "absence of crime" emphasizes the importance of crime prevention (and not merely responding to criminal events); the "rational deployment of police strength" reinforces the importance of crime analysis; "proper training" indicates the need for professionalism and education (as championed by twentieth-century reformers); and "accessibility to the public" reinforces principles underscored in community-oriented policing. Bringing Peel back to modern strategies can romanticize the past while having intuitive and political appeal and can offer historical street credibility to would-be reformers. These principles, regardless of origin, have shaped policing in Western democratic societies, and it is not our intent to minimize either this fact or the influence of Peel himself. Rather, we note that the root of the Peelian principles remains unclear.

The remainder of this chapter is divided into three sections: the development of modern policing at (1) the local (county and municipal) level, (2) the state level, and (3) the federal level of government. The historical discussion of modern policing in this chapter ends in the 1960s, but Chapter 4 discusses the development of community policing and other emerging policing strategies since the 1970s.

## The Emergence of Modern Policing in the United States

In the 1600s and 1700s, the English colonists in America brought with them the system of policing that existed in England. This system included the offices of justice of the peace, sheriff, constable, and nightwatch. Over time, the basic responsibility for law enforcement gradually shifted from volunteer citizens to paid specialists. This process of role specialization was the result of a growing and increasingly complex society attempting to master the physical environment and cope with human problems. One consequence of these economic, social, and technological changes was an increasing public concern about deviant and disruptive behavior.

Initially, in some larger U.S. cities, the constable–nightwatch system of policing evolved as a response to the problems of maintaining order and enforcing the law. The system included a limited number of constables who had civil and criminal responsibilities and a patrolling nightwatch staffed with persons who were required to serve as a community obligation. As in England, this obligation was unpopular, and paid substitutes, who were often incompetent, were used until the nightwatch became a full-time, paid occupation.

## The First City Police Forces

Between the 1830s and the 1850s, a growing number of cities decided that the constable–nightwatch system of law enforcement was inadequate. As a result, paid day-time police forces were created. Eventually, the daytime force joined with the nightwatch to create integrated day–night, modern-type police departments. In 1833, an ordinance was passed in Philadelphia that created a 24-person day force and a 120-person night-watch, all of whom were to be paid. In 1838, Boston created a daytime force to supplement the nightwatch, and soon other cities followed. This arrangement provided the foundation for the emergence of modern policing: a force of officers in one department available 24 hours a day to respond, often through patrolling, to crime and disorder problems (Lane 1967; Miller 1977; D. R. Johnson 1981).

Four theories have been suggested to explain the development of police departments. The **disorder-control theory** explains development in terms of the need to suppress mob violence. For example, Boston had three major riots in the years preceding the establishment of its police department (Lane 1967). Mob violence also occurred in other cities during the 1830s and 1840s. The **crime-control theory** suggests that increases in criminal activity resulted in a perceived need for a new type of police. Threats to social order, such as highway robbers and violent pickpockets, created a climate of fear. Concern about daring thieves and property offenses was also widespread in cities during this time (D. R. Johnson 1981). The **class-control theory** regards the development of the police as a result of class-based economic exploitation. Its advocates note that urban and industrial growth coincided with the development of the new police. During this period, many persons of different social and ethnic backgrounds competed for opportunities to improve their economic status. The resulting disruption prompted the middle and upper classes, usually white Anglo-Saxon Protestants, to develop a means to control the people involved, usually poor immigrants, sometimes not Anglo and often not Protestant. This theory holds that modern police forces were merely tools created by the industrial elite to suppress exploited laborers who were being used as fuel for the engine of capitalism (Cooper 1975; D. R. Johnson 1981). The **urban-dispersion theory** holds that many municipal police departments were created because other cities had them, not because there was a real need. In this view, police forces were considered an integral part of the governmental structure needed to stabilize communities (Monkkonen 1981).

No single theory provides an adequate explanation. Although some cities had major urban disturbances before they established new police departments, others did not. And although there was public concern about crime, the degree of concern varied among communities. Moreover, some cities established after the 1830s and 1840s did not have mob violence or serious crime. Yet police departments were created, because a governmental structure was assumed to include a police component similar to the ones that existed in older, larger cities.

Police were also used to control class-based economic unrest, but since many police officers came from the dissident groups or had friends or family members who were participants, some police officers and departments resisted brutal or excessive responses.

The police departments established from the 1830s to 1850s—Boston in 1837, New York in 1844, Philadelphia in 1854—were loosely based on the Peelian model of the London police. As noted previously, this model emphasized prevention more than apprehension. Prevention was accomplished by dispersing police throughout the community to keep crime from occurring and to intervene when it did. Apprehension, or arrest, was not stressed, because it was associated with secrecy, deceit, incitement, and corruption. Chapter 7 discusses the historical development of both the patrol and the investigation functions in law enforcement.

The London model also included an elaborate structure based on military principles, strict rules of conduct, and well-defined management practices. Great care was taken in the selection and retention of police officers. Since creating a new police force in England was controversial, the most important consideration was control of officer behavior. Community expectations and acceptance were the overriding concerns in the development and management of police.

The establishment of the new police was not as controversial in the United States. Departments were generally based on the Peelian prevention concept, but few similarities existed beyond that point. Differences were essentially the result of three factors: social context, political environment, and law enforcement policies. The United States was more violent than Britain, politicians were more meddlesome, and the police were more decentralized and were expected to be locally responsive (D. R. Johnson 1981).

## The County Sheriff

By the 1870s, most cities had a police department, even if it consisted of only one person. The county sheriff was the dominant law enforcement officer in more rural areas. The office of sheriff was first established in the eighth century in England. Individuals who occupied this position were both powerful and influential. They served as the chief magistrates of the courts under their jurisdiction, collected taxes, and attempted to apprehend criminals. American colonists adopted the idea of the county sheriff, but by the time all the colonies were settled, the duties of the office had been limited primarily to civil matters in the county and criminal law enforcement in areas where municipal police had no jurisdiction.

The sheriff became an elected official in the United States and, for many years, was paid based on fees received for serving summonses, subpoenas, and warrants and for looking after prisoners at the county jail. The sheriff became an important figure in western states where local law enforcement was the responsibility of the sheriff and of town or city police officers, called **marshals**. Sheriffs usually were elected to office as representatives of the most influential groups in the county. Only a small portion of the sheriff's time was spent pursuing criminals; other duties, such as tax collecting, inspecting cattle brands, punishing convicted felons, and serving court orders, proved to be more time-consuming.

Although the primary responsibilities of the modern sheriff vary somewhat by department, the most typical include the following: (1) collect some types of taxes (in some but not all counties) and serve civil processes; (2) provide personnel (bailiffs) and security for the court system; (3) operate jails and other correctional facilities (e.g., prison farms); (4) maintain peace and order; (5) provide general law enforcement service in unincorporated areas (i.e., those areas not in legally incorporated cities and towns); and (6) in some counties, provide contract law enforcement services.

### Vigilance Committees

Another form of policing that was important during the nineteenth century was the private, organized group known as a vigilance, or **vigilante**, committee. The word *vigilante* is of Spanish origin and means "watchman" or "guard." Although the term vigilante has several possible meanings, one definition of a vigilante group is a voluntary association of men (they rarely included women) who respond to real or imagined threats to their safety, protect their property or power, or seek revenge.

The behavior associated with vigilante movements ranges from attempts to provide reasonable due process to individuals suspected of criminal acts to arbitrary, discriminatory, and brutal acts of revenge. The term *lynching* was originally used to describe public whippings carried out by Colonel Charles Lynch, the head of a vigilante movement in the late 1700s in Virginia. Later, the term was used to mean hanging. In southern states between 1882 and 1951, approximately 4,700 persons were lynched by unorganized mobs, a form of vigilantism. Most of the victims were Black (Karmen 1983, 1616–1618).

Vigilante movements were most common in the American West during the nineteenth century. This was largely because the western frontier was undeveloped; hence, the need for established police to engage in social control was not efficient. Vigilante groups would form episodically as needed. Yet it is important not to confuse vigilantes with lawless mobs. Often, a vigilante group was composed of the social elite from that society to enforce conservative values of life, property, and law and order. Prominent figures who were either part of vigilante groups or supported their actions included two US presidents (Andrew Jackson and Theodore Roosevelt), five US senators, and eight governors (Brown 1991).

## Modern American Policing

The development of police in America was highly localized. In 2016, the Bureau of Justice Statistics estimated there were more than 12,000 different local police departments employing more than 468,000 sworn officers and more than 131,000 nonsworn personnel (Hyland and Davis 2021). County sheriffs' offices complement the local police function; the 369,000 sworn and nonsworn personnel across the 3,000 separate offices constitute about one-fifth of the general-purpose agencies in America (Burch 2012). The policing function is also carried out at state and federal levels (whose development will be discussed later in this chapter).

The fragmentation of modern police departments is directly related to the historical development, and the following discussion identifies and describes two models of policing: the political and the reform/professional (also called the reform, bureaucratic, or quasi-military model). Kelling and Moore (1988) noted that American policing evolved over the twentieth century across seven different dimensions: (1) authorization (where the police derive their power and legitimacy within society), (2) function (the role police play within society and the goals they have), (3) organizational design (how the police are bureaucratically structured), (4) relationship to environment (social distance from the public controlled by the police), (5) demand (how police services and activities are managed), (6) tactics (programs, activities, and output the police use to achieve their goals), and (7) outcomes (measures of success and failure). They argue that it is possible to identify distinct eras of policing by utilizing this framework.

### The Political Era

From about the middle of the eighteenth century to the 1920s, local policing was dominated by politics; consequently, this era saw the development of what was essentially a **political model** of policing oriented to special interests. Politics influenced every aspect of law enforcement during this period: who was employed, who was promoted, who was the chief of police, and who was appointed to the police commission, a group of citizens appointed to run the police department in a manner approved by elected officials. To some degree, even police arrest practices and services were determined by political considerations (Kelling and Moore 1988). An example of the political model is presented in Inside Policing 2.2.

---

**INSIDE POLICING 2.2**  **Political Era Policing**

An example of political-era policing can be found by examining the history of the Kansas City (MO) Police Department. Thomas Pendergast ran the Democratic political machine in Kansas City between the 1880s and 1930s. Although he was elected as a city alderman only once and his official occupation was the owner of a concrete business, "Boss Tom" levied great power and influence among local politicians. This influence enabled him not only to secure government contracts for his business but also to ensure protection for his other interests: gambling, prostitution, and bootlegging.

Pendergast did many favors for government officials and, over time, was able to place allies in key positions. Pendergast supporters occupied such offices as county prosecutor, mayor, and governor. One supporter was a relative unknown named Harry S. Truman, who (with Pendergast's support) became a county judge during this era. But controlling the Kansas City Police Department was critical to Pendergast's operation. Only with the assistance of the police would he be able to operate his illegal activities. By 1900, Pendergast had named 123 of the 173 officers within the police department, and later, he would also have influence over the majority of the Board of Police Commissioners. Because officers literally owed him their livelihood, Pendergast would routinely use the police to forward his interests. For example, during elections, officers would engage in intimidation and illegal arrests to ensure that supporters of anti-Pendergast candidates did not vote on Election Day. Police officers also would not investigate gambling, prostitution, and bootlegging operations affiliated with Pendergast, instead focusing their efforts on his rivals.

Pendergast's primary liaison to the police department was a gangster named Johnny Lazia. He too was a bootlegger and a gambler and routinely provided police officers with portions of his profits in exchange for their protection. Because of their control of the police, Kansas City had a reputation for being a safe place for out-of-town criminals. These criminals were required to pay Lazia for the right to hide out in Kansas City, and officers were directed to arrest those who did not pay him off.

During this time, Pendergast's concrete business built many city structures, including city hall, the county courthouse, the municipal auditorium, and a police station. But eventually, support for the political machine diminished, and in 1939, the state of Missouri took control of the Kansas City Police Department, eliminating "home rule." A newly appointed police chief discovered rampant corruption within the department, and half of the officers were dismissed. This arrangement, which is still in place today, permits the governor to appoint members of the Board of Police Commissioners.

Subsequent investigations into Pendergast's business practices revealed that he engaged in tax evasion between 1927 and 1937, for which he was sent to prison for 15 months. Vice President Truman was among those who attended Pendergast's funeral when he died in 1945. Truman was sworn in as the 33rd president of the United States several weeks later.

*SOURCE*: Adapted from https://www.kcpolicememorial.com/history/.

Political and economic corruption was commonplace in police departments during this period. Although some officers were honest and responsible, a large number were neither. Police work during this period became decentralized and neighborhood oriented. Individual officers had a great deal of discretion and tended to handle minor violations of the law on a personal basis. The nature of the offense, whether the suspect treated the officer with "respect," what was known about the person's family, and prior activities were all taken into consideration. Standards of enforcement often varied within cities, and local politicians played a more important role in determining enforcement priorities than did the chief of police.

Several trends converged in the mid-1800s that resulted in the creation of political machines that controlled cities, including the police department. As cities grew, there was an increasing need for municipal services, such as police, fire protection, and the collection of garbage. Upper- and middle-class citizens had the political influence to ensure that their needs were met, but many newly arriving immigrants, both native (from rural areas) and foreign-born, did not. As the number of new arrivals increased, those with political ambition attempted to gain the support of other newcomers. Often, the leaders of these groups were successful, and they took political control of many cities. Upper- and middle-class citizens in these cities did not give up their attempts to influence the political process or be elected to office, however. Even after they lost power, they acted as critics of the political machines that emerged (D. R. Johnson 1981, 17–55).

To be elected to public office, a candidate had to make promises to citizens. One of the most important promises was related to employment. Public jobs served as rewards for some individuals who supported the political party in power. Police jobs became an important part of this political **patronage system**. These jobs were popular because they required little or no skill and paid well compared with other jobs that also required minimal ability. Moreover, many officers did little but frequent bars and pool halls when they were supposed to be working. These officers considered a police job a reward for supporting the political machine more than a real job.

Police departments were also vital to the political machine's boss in terms of his ability to maintain political control. The police were particularly useful during elections, because they maintained order at polling booths and were able to determine who voted and who did not. Individuals who became police officers were often avid supporters of the political machine and would do anything to help keep it in power. After all, their jobs depended on it. But they also supported it because the machine often represented a point of view consistent with their own.

Another response to local political influence was for states to take control of local police governance. State control of the police occurred in "New York City in 1857, Detroit in 1865, Cleveland in 1866, New Orleans in 1868, Cincinnati in 1877, Boston in 1885, and Omaha in 1887" (Fogelson 1977, 14). In these circumstances, state authorities were appointed to manage or oversee municipal police, yet revenues for supporting the police remained a local function. This arrangement was short-lived in most places, in part because state control had neither removed the police from partisan politics nor improved the quality of law enforcement. Fogelson (1977, 14–15) noted that "state authorities not only abolished metropolitan policing in New York and Albany in 1870 but also reestablished local control in Cleveland in 1868, New York in 1870, New Orleans in 1877, Cincinnati in 1880, Detroit in 1891 and Omaha in 1897." Some large cities continued to be governed by state boards; however, local control across municipal lines returned in Baltimore and Boston in the twentieth century and in St. Louis in 2012, leaving Kansas City (MO) as the only major police department governed by a state-appointed board.

From the previous discussion, it is possible to summarize the political era utilizing the seven distinguishing features in Kelling and Moore's (1988, 2–4) framework. In this era, the police derived their authority from powerful local politicians who utilized the police to maintain the status quo and retain political power (like Thomas Pendergast as described Inside Policing 2.2). The police engaged in a variety of *functions* that included crime control, but arguably, providing social services was critical for the police to maintain legitimacy. A geographically decentralized organizational structure was necessary during this era to ensure the police were able to satisfy the needs of local politicians. These characteristics led to a close and personal relationship with citizens. Demands for police services were channeled through local politicians as well as personal contacts with citizens. These services were acquired through *tactics* that included foot patrol and rudimentary investigations. The police were evaluated mostly by the level of satisfaction of citizens and local politicians and not necessarily by their ability to engage in crime prevention.

## Criticism in the Political Era

By the 1890s, as cities grew larger and became more difficult to manage, the politically dominated, often corrupt police departments came under increasing criticism. This criticism applied not only to the police but also to all city services. All problems attendant to large cities appeared to become important during this period: an increase in crime, population congestion, inadequate housing, health problems, waste disposal, and so on. The period from the mid-1890s to the mid-1920s became known as the Progressive Era in the United States, because many of these types of problems, including poor working conditions and child labor, began to be addressed not only in the public sector but also in private enterprise.

Social critics began to argue that political power should change hands. These reformers were composed of religious leaders and civic-minded, upper- and middle-class businesspeople and professionals. They argued that the government should be managed efficiently, public officials should be honest, and there should be one standard of conduct for everyone. The recommended reform/professional model was based on the principles of industrial management, because these principles were given credit for making the United States an economic success. Efficiency meant providing the highest quality of service at the lowest cost. To become efficient, organizations had to have centralized control under a well-qualified leader, develop a rational set of rules and regulations, and become highly specialized, with duties and performance requirements specified for each specialized position.

The Progressive Era movement touched all aspects of American life. As it applied to government, it was based on three basic ideas: (1) honesty and efficiency in government, (2) more authority for public officials (and less for politicians), and (3) the use of experts to respond to specific problems. This movement and these ideas gained more and more credence as the United States moved into the twentieth century. These changes also applied to police departments, which gradually began to shift away from a political orientation to more of a bureaucratic, legalistic, or reform approach to policing (D. R. Johnson 1981; Kelling and Moore 1988).

## The Reform/Professional Era

It is necessary to pause here to clarify specific terms. As noted, Kelling and Moore (1988) identified particular eras within American policing, and we use their framework as a foundation for this chapter. In their original work (and in previous editions of this textbook), the term *reform era* was used to describe the period we are about to introduce. However, here and throughout this text, we have taken liberties to reposition this as the *reform/professional era*. We made this decision because we recognize there have been various policing reform movements throughout American history. Many would say the events surrounding the murder of George Floyd in 2020 have thrust the United States toward another reform movement. In short, there's a lot of talk about reform. The underlying reasons and the goals of reform movements may vary; however, we feel it is important to clarify that when we're discussing the era of policing between the 1920s and 1970s, referring to it merely as "the reform era" may be confusing. After all, which "reform" are we talking about? Therefore, this text will continue to discuss reform in general as well as specific reform movements in America, but when referencing this time in American history, we'll use the term *reform/professional era*.

By the 1920s, attempts to reform local policing—and, to some degree, state and federal law enforcement—were beginning to have an impact. The period from the 1920s to the 1960s was likely the most significant in the development of policing in the United States, because it established the foundations for the **professionalization** of law enforcement. The term *professionalization* has a number of possible definitions. As used here, it means an attempt to improve police behavior and performance by adopting a code of ethics and improving the selection, training, and management of police departments. It also means that the police, like other professions, would focus on a single core strategy rather than performing a kaleidoscope of loosely coupled services. For the police, this core strategy would become crime control. Professionalism is discussed in more detail in Chapter 11.

During this period, a **reform/professional model** (also called the professional, bureaucratic, legalistic, quasi-military, or semi-military model) of policing began to dominate thinking about police work. Essentially, this model posits that the police–community relationship should be based on law and departmental policy, because police (both as organizations and as individuals) should not be unduly influenced by politics or personal considerations when making decisions. One of the critical aspects of this model is related to the mission of the police. Advocates of this model thought that crime-fighting should be the primary purpose of the police, and they used this idea to mobilize support for their reforms and to improve the public image of the police (Kelling and Moore 1988). The police, in effect, began to emphasize the most dramatic aspects of their work (D. R. Johnson 1981).

Between about 1920 and the mid-1960s, many police departments changed dramatically in the United States. Political meddling was substantially, but not entirely, replaced by efficient and centralized management and a commitment to professionalism. This change was the result of (1) European developments in crime science, (2) changes in American society and politics, and (3) the growth of the police reform movement.

American society and politics also began to change in ways that affected the development of policing. As the economy emphasized industrial and consumer goods and as rail and automobile transportation improved, more and more people moved to the suburbs. Many of them were white and middle class. The population of cities began to change as increasing numbers of Spanish-speaking immigrants and Blacks from the rural South arrived. Many of these newcomers were unskilled, poor, powerless, and in great need of city services (D. R. Johnson 1981).

Extensive crime problems often plagued the Spanish-speaking and Black neighborhoods. Many police officers began to think of these neighborhoods as dangerous and troublesome areas in which to work. Given the fact that police forces, beginning with the slave patrols (slave patrols were created to apprehend runaway slaves and to ensure that slaves did not revolt against their masters), had a long history of racist behavior, the tension between minority groups and the police increased and became an important factor in the numerous urban riots of the twentieth century. These riots began in East St. Louis in 1917 and were followed by several in 1919, at least seven during World War II, and numerous others in the 1960s. There were 42 major to serious disorders in 1967 alone (National Advisory Commission 1968). Although there were many reasons for these riots, a significant factor was the behavior of police officers in minority neighborhoods.

In the newly established suburban communities, the mostly white, middle-class inhabitants expected that government services would be based on the principles of efficiency and quality. The police were expected to be well trained and courteous, use the best equipment, and employ the latest management techniques. Many of the reform ideas of the Progressive Era and the legalistic model of policing had a positive impact on these communities before they gained influence in larger, older cities, where a tradition of political interference was difficult to change.

Among the more important developments during this period was the emergence of the commission approach to reform. When there was sufficient concern about police behavior in a community, prominent citizens and experts were appointed to commissions to conduct investigations and to make recommendations for change. Commissions were formed at both the local and the national levels.

In 1919, the Chicago Crime Commission was established to supervise the criminal justice system in Chicago. Unlike most other commissions created during the following decade, the one in Chicago became permanent. By 1931, 7 local, 16 state, and 2 national crime commissions had been established to investigate the police. Perhaps the best known of these was the National Commission on Law Observance, known as the Wickersham Commission for the man who headed the investigation. In 1931, the commission published 14 volumes, two of which were about the police. The 12 other volumes concerned other aspects of crime and the criminal justice system. August Vollmer was the principal police consultant to the Wickersham Commission and the author of the major report on the police (Walker 1977).

Vollmer's report identified what he thought were the most important problems in law enforcement: excessive political influence, inadequate leadership and management, ineffective recruitment and training, and insufficient use of the latest advances in science and technology. By 1931, it was widely accepted these were the problems that needed to be addressed in police work. However, another report by the commission, on police lawlessness, overshadowed Vollmer's recommendations. The report identified widespread police abuses, including brutality, to secure confessions (Walker 1977).

After the Wickersham Commission published its reports, there was at least the beginning of a national consensus on the direction for professionalization of the police, essentially toward a legalistic model in which laws and rules were enforced without regard to politics by well-trained and scientifically proficient, dedicated, honest employees who worked in a centralized department that was primarily concerned with crime-fighting. Many police departments, however, remained substantially political well into the 1960s.

By the 1930s, the themes of reform—centralization, standardization of behavior through the development of policies and procedures, more education and training, selection and promotion based on merit, commitment to the goal of fighting crime, and use of the latest advances in science and technology—were well established. And one of the most significant events of the twentieth century—the Great Depression of the 1930s—actually made police reform easier. With reduced funds available, there was less opposition to centralizing the police, and in many cities, some local precinct stations were closed to save money. Centralization made it easier for chiefs of police to control their officers and also resulted in less meddling by politicians. In addition, for the first time, well-educated, middle-class Americans became interested in police work as a career, because it offered job security (D. R. Johnson 1981).

The police in America underwent a dramatic transformation during the first half of the twentieth century. In the reform era, the police derived their authority from the law and professionalism, which was critical to wrestle influence away from local politicians. Their primary function became crime control, and delivery of police services that were common in the political era became less frequent and devalued. The organizational design became centralized, which was necessary to manage police tasks consistently and even-handedly. The relationship the police had to the public became more distant, since close ties were seen as unnecessary or even counterproductive to their core strategy of crime control. Demand for police activities was guided from centralized dispatchers. The core tactics of the police were routine patrol, rapid response, and reactive investigations. Success and failure were measured by the ability of the police to control crime, particularly those serious crimes as defined by the FBI's Uniform Crime Reports (Kelling and Moore 1988).

By the 1960s, however, these reform ideas began to be questioned due to three important developments: (1) urban riots, (2) the civil rights movement, and (3) the perception of an increasing crime rate. As minorities, and later women, became increasingly active in trying to change their status in society and people began to be more concerned about crime, the police became one focal point for criticism. By the mid-1960s, this concern was so great that two other national commissions were established, in part to address problems concerning the police. These were the President's Commission on Law Enforcement and Administration of Justice (hereafter called the Crime Commission), established by President Lyndon Baines Johnson in 1965, and the National Advisory Commission on Civil Disorders (hereafter called the Riot Commission), established in 1967.

Like its predecessor the Wickersham Commission, the Crime Commission focused on crime and the entire criminal justice system. The Riot Commission examined the criminal justice system and many aspects of civil disorder, such as poor housing and unemployment. The recommendations of these two commissions concerning the police were a blend of previous reform suggestions and new ones intended to make the police more responsive to the community. In effect, the legalistic model of policing that had been the basis of reform for several decades began to be challenged. However, this does not mean that its tenets were abandoned; rather, some tenets were debated and gradually began to be replaced with new ideas about the role of the police.

Three of the most prominent spokesmen for early police reform were August Vollmer, O. W. Wilson (see Inside Policing 2.3), and J. Edgar Hoover (see Inside Policing 2.8). All were controversial during their careers, and they have remained so as historians have provided examples of their abuses of authority and their racist and sexist behaviors. Yet despite this criticism, their ideas about the police role and police management remain influential and have resulted in improved police performance in many areas.

The political era of often corrupt and inefficient policing was somewhat changed by the reform/professional era, which in turn also met criticism. The civic problems of the 1960s brought a new set of critics who wanted to overcome the isolation of a professionalized police force from citizen concerns and develop new strategies and methods to respond to problems of crime and order maintenance. These subsequent changes, along with others, resulted in the emergence of what is now called community policing. About the same time (the mid-1970s) that the reforms began to be implemented, the crime rate began a 40 year decline (although there are some indications this decline may be coming to an end). In

## INSIDE POLICING 2.3 | Reformers of the US Police

### August Vollmer

August Vollmer served first as town marshal and then as chief of police in Berkeley, California, from 1905 until 1932. One of the leading spokesmen for police professionalism in the first few decades of the twentieth century, he advocated the principles of merit associated with the Progressive Era as well as more education and training, adoption of the latest management techniques, and the use of science and technology. Vollmer was an advocate of the police officer as social worker, in the sense that he believed police should act to prevent crime by intervening in the lives of potential criminals, particularly juveniles.

Vollmer is often called the father of modern police administration. Some of his important contributions include the early use of motorized patrols, scientific use of modus operandi files, and the latest advancements in criminalistics. He suggested the development of a centralized fingerprint system that was established by the FBI; he established the first juvenile unit; he was the first to use psychological screening for police applicants and the first to emphasize the importance of college-educated police officers.

In the area of education, Vollmer was instrumental in the establishment of police-training classes and, later, a criminology degree program at the University of California at Berkeley. He became a professor of police administration at Berkeley in 1929, and he helped develop the first degree-granting program in law enforcement at San Jose State College (now San Jose State University) in 1930. As a result of his efforts, programs at institutions of higher-learning became increasingly acceptable.

### Orlando Winfield Wilson

O. W. Wilson worked in Berkeley, California, for August Vollmer from 1921 to 1925. At the same time, he completed his degree at the University of California. With Vollmer's recommendation, he became chief of police in Fullerton, California, in 1925 but lasted only until 1926, because his ideas about modern law enforcement were not acceptable to many citizens in the community.

Wilson was considering another career when Vollmer recommended him as a possible chief for the Wichita, Kansas, police department in 1928. Wilson was selected for that position and, over the next 11 years, turned what was considered an inefficient and corrupt department into what some called the West Point of law enforcement. He left Wichita in 1937, because his strict enforcement of vice laws had alienated too many powerful citizens. He resigned under pressure, but not before creating what became a model for other police departments. Visiting dignitaries from other countries who expressed a desire to visit a police department were taken to Wichita by the US State Department. After Wilson left Wichita, he became a professor in the School of Criminology at the University of California at Berkeley from 1939 to 1960. His service was interrupted during World War II, when he became a colonel in the US Army. His job was to develop plans to rebuild police departments in countries that had been occupied by the Axis Powers. After he left the Army, he returned to his teaching position.

In 1950, Wilson published the first edition of *Police Administration,* arguably one of the most influential books ever written about police in the United States. It describes in detail how police departments should be organized and managed. It was widely used in training programs, colleges, and universities and as a basis for organizing and managing police departments in the United States and other countries until the 1970s, when Wilson's ideas began to be criticized. Nevertheless, the basic structure of many present-day police departments is the result of Wilson's ideas.

*(Continued)*

**INSIDE POLICING 2.3** **Reformers of the US Police** *(Continued)*

In 1960, while still teaching at Berkeley, Wilson agreed to serve on the committee to select a new police commissioner in Chicago. When the committee could not find an acceptable candidate, they offered the job to Wilson. He agreed and served until 1967; during that time, he made many important changes that received widespread publicity and made Chicago a model of modern policing. One year after he retired, however, the Chicago police performed poorly in their attempts to manage the demonstrations at the 1968 Democratic Convention. This failure raised important questions about Wilson's effectiveness and the difficulty of changing police organizations. After his retirement, Wilson moved to California and spent his time writing and traveling until his death in 1972.

Wilson typified police leadership and management during the reform/professional era. He believed that politics had no place in policing and was a strong advocate of centralized police management and strict discipline. He was also an articulate spokesman for police professionalism as it related to more training and education, better salaries and benefits, and his definition of police management.

SOURCES: S. Walker, *A Critical History of Police Reform* (Lexington, MA: Heath, 1977), 21–165; G. E. Carte and E. H. Carte, *Police Reform in the United States: The Era of August Vollmer, 1905–1932* (Berkeley: University of California Press, 1975), 21–23; G. E. Caiden, *Police Revitalization* (Lexington, MA: Heath, 1977), 210–217; G. F. Cole, *The American System of Criminal Justice*, 5th ed. (Pacific Grove, CA: Brooks/Cole, 1989), 178; adapted from W. J. Bopp, *O. W. Wilson and the Search for a Police Profession* (Port Washington, NY: Kennikat Press, 1977).

Chapter 4, the development of and controversies about community policing and the extent to which it contributed to a decline in crime are discussed.

This chapter's "Voices from the Field" presents a brief historical and personal account of police history from the retired chief of police David C. Couper, who was an integral force in implementing quality management and problem solving in Madison, Wisconsin.

### Southern Colonial and Frontier Police Development: A Minority Perspective on the Development of American Police

There is a tendency to focus exclusively on the American history of the police as it developed in the northern colonies, but it is important to highlight other areas where different approaches to law enforcement emerged. Two particular areas included the southern colonies and the western American frontier.

In the southern colonies, slave patrols represented the first form of modern policing, existing as early as the mid-1700s. The need for slave patrols was premised on the fact that slaves represented a dangerous class that the economic elite (e.g., plantation owners) desired to control. Eventually, all southern states had statutes that created and legitimized slave patrols (Williams and Murphy 1990). Furthermore, slave patrols relied on private citizens to carry out their duties. Participation in slave patrols was part of a citizen's civic responsibility. This structure often led to great difficulties in accountability to the central government as well as great variation in the behavior of the various "policing" functions. When disorderly or runaway slaves were encountered, they were often immediately punished by the patrol; thus, recognizable due process was absent from this style of policing. Reichel (1999) commented, "In an ironic sense the resistance by slaves should have been completely understandable to American Patriots. Patrols were allowed search powers that the colonists later found so objectionable in the hands of British authorities." The level of fear and resentment on the part of slaves toward these patrols was high. Inside Policing 2.4

| INSIDE POLICING 2.4 | From Slave Patrols to Today |

Watch the video *From Slave Patrols to Today: What the History of Policing Teaches Us About the Present* (https://www.youtube.com/watch?v=ep7y6FM7yuQ), which further describes the early roots of policing and social control in southern traditions and includes commentary from David Couper (who is featured in this chapter's "Voices from the Field").

links to a YouTube video that starts with a conversation on slave patrols and policing in southern colonial traditions, noting how these early traditions influenced and evolved into modern policing.

Some argue that within urban environments, the development and function of the police was guided by a desire to maintain racial segregation and discrimination. The police are agents of governmental social control and legal order, and this was differentially applied toward minorities. For example, influential politicians within the political era were typically white males, and they utilized the police to maintain the status quo—often by controlling "outsiders," who were most likely to be Black. Minority groups were politically powerless and thus had less influence on policing than their white counterparts. During the reform/professional era, under the guise of equal application of the law, the police differentially applied the law within predominantly Black urban communities. At the same time, minority representation within police departments was stalled during this period. Civil service requirements that were designed to professionalize the police and remove political influence from hiring and firing officers became roadblocks for the integration of minorities. As late as the 1960s, at the peak of the reform/professional era, minorities who became part of the policing establishment were relegated to policing Black neighborhoods or not given full police power. In short, the policing experience in America varied considerably for people of different races and ethnicities (Williams and Murphy 1990). With this in mind, cultural diversity within police organizations will be more fully examined in Chapter 12.

## State Police

Before 1900, only Texas and Massachusetts had formed a **state police** force. Some states then began to develop their own law enforcement agencies in response to perceived inefficiencies of locally controlled police, but the idea was slow to catch on. Not until the 1960s did all states have some form of state police.

### Texas and Massachusetts

Many inhabitants lived in rural isolation in early Texas and faced dangerous problems such as widespread Indian raids. Consequently, the citizens decided to create a quasi-military force, called the Texas Rangers, to protect themselves. After Texas declared its independence from Mexico in 1836, the Rangers were well established. Originally designed for community defense, by the 1850s they were doing general police work. They pursued robbers, runaway slaves, and illegal immigrants from Mexico. Rangers tended to take the law into their own hands and to be brutal in their treatment of prisoners, particularly minorities. Such behavior was commonplace well into the twentieth century. In 1935, Texas created a larger state police, the Department of Public Safety, which was responsible for supervising Ranger activity, and their behavioral excesses were gradually reduced (D. R. Johnson 1981).

## VOICES FROM THE FIELD

### David C. Couper
*Chief of Police (Ret.), Madison Wisconsin Police Department*

In the spring of 1960, after serving four years with the Marines, I enrolled at the University of Minnesota and started to look for a night job. That's how I began my police career. When I retired, a good friend of mine, who spent most of her life researching the police, commented on how far the police had come in society. I remember saying, "Improving the police is like stretching a big rubber band. When you let go, it snaps right back to the way it was before you started." I think that statement is still true.

When Sir Robert Peel founded the Metropolitan Police Department in London, his basic principle for policing was that in order for the police to perform their duties they had to have public approval, and that approval would be diminished proportionally by their use of physical force. To Peel, "the police are the public and the public are the police." Even then, 150 years ago, someone knew that if the police were to be successful in preventing crime and disorder, they had to have the goodwill of the people—all the people.

I joined a large-city urban police department in the 1960s. Luckily, I had a four-week recruit academy taught by a police commander who was an unusual cop—he had a college degree. When I began police work by walking a beat, there were no portable radios; I "pulled," or checked in with, the dispatcher every hour on our beat. Many of us in that era saw (and often silently condoned) discrimination against Blacks and other minorities. It nevertheless impacted us. When our colleges and universities shut down during the days of the Vietnam War protest, we found ourselves on a police line facing our fellow students. And it changed us.

As chief of police of a medium-sized city in 1972, I found myself in the forefront of police change. My city found itself in a "war at home"; there was extreme tension not only with university students but with the minority community as well. Many young,

college-educated chiefs were able to implement community and problem-oriented policing, total quality management, a "softer" and negotiated approach to public demonstrations and civil disobedience, and effective controls on the use of deadly force. We committed ourselves to bring women, minorities, and college-educated young people into policing.

Today, in a post-9/11 world, I see the police in a very precarious position. Yes, they have compact portable radios, cell phones, computers, DNA identification methods, and lightweight body armor, but I believe they have lost the vision that sustained many of us before September 11. What I believe sustained the police from the 1960s to the 1990s was the understanding that they are the gatekeepers of a great democracy, that they are first and above all things "constitutional officers" committed to preserving and defending, on a daily basis, the Bill of Rights. It is easy to stray from a noble vision and to think that police work is about a life-and-death battle between "them" and "us." Fear has not only permeated our nation, but our nation's police as well. And a police department that is fearful of the public is a dangerous organization.

In the past the police were uneducated, corrupt, and abusive. They did not have the goodwill or cooperation of the public because of their lack of education, corruption, and use of brutality. This led to calls for police reform. Today, the police are better educated (yet a college degree is not universally required for employment), corruption is less a problem (but it still exists), and the use of deadly force has been constrained (although deadly mistakes still occur and police pursuit of fleeing motor vehicles remains a critical issue). But I will contend that the goodwill and cooperation of the public, especially among racial minorities and immigrants, is still severely lacking.

The Massachusetts experiment with a state police force was controversial. Rural residents and prohibitionists were disenchanted with the failure of city police to enforce laws against drinking, so the state legislature created a state police force and gave it general law enforcement responsibilities. Its primary task, however, was to enforce laws against vice. That was what it did in large cities, but it gradually won a reputation for effective detective work in robbery and murder cases in other areas. Nevertheless, controversy about its activities in cities continued, and the state police force was disbanded in 1875. A few state investigators were retained to work in rural areas.

### Pennsylvania

The next appearance of a state police force was in 1905, with the establishment of the Pennsylvania State Police. In the Midwest and Northeast, as early as the 1860s, certain problems arose that proved difficult for local police to resolve. These problems were related to economic development, particularly in the areas of mining and industrialization. An increasing crime problem in affluent rural areas coupled with the exploitation of workers and the workers' demands that such treatment stop resulted in levels of conflict and violence that were difficult to control.

Western Pennsylvania had more than its fair share of such problems. As a major mining region that attracted immigrant labor, it suffered ethnic and labor violence during the latter part of the nineteenth century. The violence became so extensive that President Theodore Roosevelt appointed a commission to look into a major coal strike in 1902. The result was the creation of the Pennsylvania State Police in 1905. This police force was unlike any other in the United States, because it emphasized a military approach. All officers had either National Guard or Army experience. Yet the state police proved to be even-handed in handling labor conflict, and the levels of violence began to decline. Like the Texas Rangers, however, state police officers tended to discriminate against "foreigners." In fact, officers were chosen in part because they had contempt for foreigners.

Gradually, the Pennsylvania State Police began to expand its duties and do routine police work in rural areas throughout the state. Between 1908 and 1923, 14 states, mostly in the north, created state police forces based on the Pennsylvania model. Not all state police, however, were as even-handed as those in Pennsylvania when it came to labor strife. In Nevada, Colorado, and Oregon, the state police tended to side with organized business interests (e.g., mining). This bias became such a problem in Colorado that the state police were disbanded in 1923 (D. R. Johnson 1981).

### Highway Patrol

Between the 1920s and the 1960s, state police forces began to take on new responsibilities. One of the most important was the enforcement of traffic laws. With the increasing use of automobiles, the number of related problems—the violation of traffic laws, accidents, and the regulatory requirements associated with vehicle registration and driver licensing—also increased. As the highway system grew, there was a need for a statewide authority, because many of the roads were outside the jurisdiction of cities. The automobile also gave criminals more flexibility: they could come and go more easily and avoid capture more readily.

This situation resulted in two approaches to the development of state law enforcement: a state police and a **highway patrol**. The former had broad law enforcement powers (similar to municipal police departments), while the latter was generally limited to traffic enforcement. The differences between state police forces and state highway patrols are important. State police have their own criminal investigators, may have their own patrol force, gather criminal intelligence, and usually have a forensic science laboratory. State highway patrols concentrate on traffic and accidents on the state's roads and highways (Borkenstein 1977).

The highway patrol approach became more common over time. For example, in the 1920s, eight state police departments and six highway patrol units were established. In the 1930s, 18 units were created to deal with traffic, but only eight to deal with general law enforcement (D. R. Johnson 1981). By the 1960s, nearly all states had some type of state police or highway patrol, or a combination of the two. They are usually responsible for traffic regulation on state roads and highways, and about two-thirds also have general police powers. State police often fill a void in rural law enforcement, because they provide services where there are none or their assistance is requested by other law enforcement units (Cole 1989). Inside Policing 2.5 briefly describes the development of the state police in Oregon, which was typical of other states during the 1920s and 1930s. Inside Policing 2.6 describes the evolutionary process of the Missouri State Highway Patrol.

---

**INSIDE POLICING 2.5**    **The Oregon State Police**

Discussions about the possibility of creating a state police force in Oregon began in 1918. During World War I, the state had created an Oregon Military Police to protect shipbuilding plants, but it was disbanded after the war ended. Concern about problems associated with state policing continued, however, because responsibilities were fragmented among several state departments. The State Traffic Department had already been established, but it was having a difficult time coping with the increasing number of automobiles on state highways. In 1929, it had only 50 officers to patrol the entire state. Prohibition was also proving to be a difficult problem. Increasingly, criminals were using cars and avoided local police, who had jurisdiction only within city limits.

In response to these concerns, the state senate established the state police force on March 1, 1931. The force was designed by a committee that examined the Royal Canadian Mounted Police, the Texas Rangers, and the state police of New Jersey, Pennsylvania, and Michigan. The new force began operations on August 1. It was given the law enforcement responsibilities of several older state agencies, including the State Highway Commission (which governed the State Traffic Department), the Secretary of State, the Fish and Game Commission, the State Fire Marshals, and the Prohibition Commissioner. The responsibilities of this new police force included the enforcement of traffic laws, game and fish codes, all laws relating to arson and fire prevention, and laws against illegal liquor and drugs. In addition, the department was given law enforcement responsibilities throughout the state so that the department could serve as a rural patrol force and assist local police.

The state police were given additional responsibilities in 1939 and 1941. In 1939, a crime detection laboratory was established at the University of Oregon Medical School; it was subsequently relocated in Portland. (By 1989 there were six regional crime detection laboratories, which provided assistance to local police.) In 1941, all fingerprint records and criminal photographs were transferred from the state penitentiary to the state police.

In the late 1970s, the state police force was reorganized into the present five districts. By 1989, the number of patrol stations had increased from 31 to 45. By 1996, the number of personnel had increased from the original 95 to more than 1,200.

*SOURCE*: Oregon Department of State Police. *Memorandum*. March 15, 1989.

## INSIDE POLICING 2.6  Missouri State Highway Patrol

The Missouri State Highway Patrol (MSHP) was officially created in 1931, although it took six years of political compromises to do so. While some states were comfortable with the creation of a state policing agency, the creation of state-level law enforcement was difficult in Missouri because of the general skepticism on the part of local politicians to relinquish control to the state government. State police agencies, in many ways, act in direct competition with lower levels of government, particularly county sheriffs. Yet there was a recognized need for a state-level department in Missouri at the beginning of the twentieth century. The development of state-level policing was partly because of the creation of an expanded highway system throughout the largely rural state, the difficulties associated with enforcing Prohibition's bootlegging laws, labor disputes in rural areas, and the decentralization of local law enforcement in the state. Thus, the creation of the MSHP represented a significant compromise between local and state politicians: the MSHP would have jurisdiction limited to the enforcement of traffic offenses and not be empowered to have general policing duties (e.g., search and seizure). Therefore, the MSHP had a narrowly defined mission. Over time, however, the MSHP slowly did evolve into a full-service state police agency, although their name remained "highway patrol." This evolutionary process was also experienced in other states, including Mississippi, Nebraska, Ohio, and Washington.

Missouri's experience demonstrates another type of state law enforcement evolution. Recognizing the rivalry between state- and county-level law enforcement, the state initially resisted creating a full-service state police agency. Thus, the only way the state was able to create a much-needed state-level agency was to limit its power. As social and political conditions changed over time, the mission of the highway patrol was broadened to reflect the general services department it is today.

SOURCE: D. N. Falcone, "The Missouri State Highway Patrol as a Representative Model." *Policing: An International Journal of Police Strategies and Management1* 24, no. 4 (2001): 585–594.

## Other Types of State Law Enforcement Agencies

Some states also have other types of law enforcement agencies. Just as with the federal government, any state agency that regulates behavior that is punishable by fine or imprisonment may have a law enforcement component. States that have a park system or environmental laws, any form of legalized gambling, or state income taxes will usually have law enforcement officers associated with that activity. Many states also have an agency whose responsibility is to regulate the selling and distribution of liquor. A few states even have agencies that respond primarily to drug-related problems.

In addition to state police, state highway patrols, and the other types of agencies noted earlier, many states also provide law enforcement services to local jurisdictions—for example, special investigation assistance and crime labs for the analysis of physical evidence. There may also be a statewide computer system to provide information about wanted persons and stolen property. Many states also gather and analyze crime-related information and provide the results to local police. All states also now have some type of organization to set standards for the selection and training of police—for example, the California Commission on Peace Officers Standards and Training.

## Federal Law Enforcement

The development of federal agencies tended to lag behind that at the local level, because the constitutional mandate for federal law enforcement was unclear. Prior to the Civil War, there were three types of federal law enforcement activities: the Revenue Cutter Service, the US Marshals, and the Post Office.

In 1789, the Revenue Cutter Service was created to respond to problems of smuggling. In that same year, the US Marshals Service was established so that the federal courts would have officers to perform police duties. Marshals investigated cases of mail theft and crimes against the railroad. They also investigated murders on federal lands, but the majority of their responsibilities were civil. One of the more interesting aspects of the marshal's role was law enforcement in the West, described in Inside Policing 2.7.

Crimes involving the mail were a significant problem in the nineteenth century. Often, these crimes were committed by postal employees, because many people sent money through the mail. Swindlers and confidence men also used the mail. Lotteries were a popular scam in which people were asked to send a small amount of money to be eligible for an expensive prize; those who sent in money never heard from the lottery sponsors again.

---

**INSIDE POLICING 2.7**  **Federal Marshals in the American West**

The US Marshals were among the first law enforcement officials in the West. In federal territories, they were often the only officials available to deal with criminals. Once a territory became a state, other law enforcement officials, such as the sheriff, town marshal, or city police, assumed responsibility for most law enforcement problems. However, because these local police officers had authority only in one jurisdiction, the US Marshal appointed some of them to be deputy marshals, which allowed them to pursue criminals outside the town or county.

Marshals usually had no law enforcement experience but were appointed because of their political connections. Often, they were criticized for being inefficient and corrupt, much like city police of the nineteenth century. Their payment—rewards and fees—strongly influenced their priorities. Because rewards for catching criminals were rare, most of a marshal's salary was determined by fees collected from serving civil processes. This system of payment lasted until 1896.

Marshals usually dealt with liquor smugglers, gun runners, and individuals who committed crimes involving the mail. The most infamous criminals were the train robbers. The railroads may well have been the most disliked industry in the nineteenth century; although railroads played an important role in the development of the United States, the owners treated many citizens callously and indifferently. Consequently, train robbers were considered to be heroes by some people. This status contributed to the rise of romantic legends about outlaws such as the James, Younger, and Dalton brothers and Bill Doolin. But train robbers were hardly heroes. Jesse James initiated the idea of wrecking a train to rob it. Or they might ambush a train at a water stop and use dynamite or gunfire to steal the money or gold it carried.

Marshals played an important role in the American West. They were effective in developing informants and isolating outlaws. Perhaps their most important contribution was developing a basis for cooperation between different law enforcement bodies (i.e., town marshal and police or county sheriff) as federal territories became states.

*SOURCE*: D. R. Johnson, *American Law Enforcement: A History* (St. Louis: Forum Press, 1981), 96–100.

In the states, the Post Office assumed responsibility for all mail-related crimes (US Marshals dealt with such crimes in the federal territories). At first, the postmaster used assistants to investigate crimes, but in 1836, the position of postal inspector was established. By the Civil War, postal inspectors were investigating robberies, embezzlements, and the counterfeiting of stamps, as well as Post Office employees involved in criminal activities.

## The Secret Service

Although counterfeiting money had always been a problem at local and state levels of government, it became a serious problem nationally when the federal government decided to issue standard paper currency in 1861, at the time of the Civil War. The first attempts to suppress the counterfeiting of national currency occurred in 1864, when the secretary of the Treasury employed a few private detectives. In June 1865, the Secret Service was established. The first director, William Wood, distributed his agents among 11 cities and instructed them to work undercover to penetrate counterfeiting rings.

By the late nineteenth century, the Secret Service provided investigative services to other agencies of government that needed them, including the postal service, customs service, and Bureau of Immigration. In 1901, the task of protecting the president was added to the Secret Service's responsibility. In 1908, its role was limited to two major activities: protective services and counterfeiting (D. R. Johnson 1981).

## The Federal Bureau of Investigation

To take over some of the duties the Secret Service had been performing for other agencies, the Bureau of Investigation was created within the Justice Department in 1908. This office began its work when the Secret Service transferred eight agents to the new bureau. It later became the FBI, the general investigative law enforcement agency of the federal government.

The primary reason the FBI eventually became so highly regarded was the publicity surrounding its crime-fighting role in the 1930s. The two most important crimes involving the FBI were the kidnapping of ace flier Charles Lindbergh's baby and the ambush murders of five people, including one FBI agent, that became known as the Kansas City Massacre. The Lindbergh incident was only one of several such cases in the late 1920s and 1930s. During this period, criminals abducted several wealthy individuals or members of their families and held them for ransom. However, the Lindbergh case received the most publicity, and the FBI was successful in identifying a suspect who was then convicted and executed. On June 17, 1933, in Kansas City, Pretty Boy Floyd and two companions tried to rescue a friend being transported to prison. Three police officers (a chief, Henry Reed, and detectives Frank Hermanson and William Grooms) and one federal agent (R. J. Caffrey) were killed. One of the criminals was captured, convicted, and executed. Floyd was killed by the FBI in a shoot-out, and the third was killed by other criminals.

Another event that added to the prestige and power of the FBI was the election of Franklin Roosevelt as president. He became a strong supporter of J. Edgar Hoover and the FBI and assisted in expanding the Bureau's powers. The most important expansion was its responsibility to investigate cases of domestic espionage, counterespionage, and sabotage (D. R. Johnson 1981, 172–181). The federal responsibility for enforcement of laws against drugs began in 1914 when the Harrison Narcotic Act was signed into law. The Bureau of Internal Revenue was given the responsibility for enforcing this act. It created a Narcotics Section, which within a few years became a major division. In 1930, the Federal Bureau of Narcotics was created; it became the Drug Enforcement Administration (DEA) in 1973.

By the 1920s, the US Marshals Service, the FBI, the Postal Inspectors, the Secret Service, and the Narcotics Division of the Internal Revenue Service were the established federal law enforcement agencies. The one that received the most attention, however, was the FBI.

Between the 1930s and the 1960s, the FBI became the premier law enforcement body in the United States. J. Edgar Hoover was appointed to serve as Director in 1924. He became a national law enforcement leader and advocate of police reform in the 1930s and maintained this role into the 1960s. He is profiled in Inside Policing 2.8. Information about the current role and selected activities of the FBI is presented in Inside Policing 2.9.

## INSIDE POLICING 2.8  J. Edgar Hoover

J. Edgar Hoover was director of the Federal Bureau of Investigation (FBI) from 1924 until his death in 1972. He first entered the Department of Justice in 1917 while attending law school. When he took over the Bureau in 1924, it had just experienced a scandal, and Hoover set out to reform the organization. Like O. W. Wilson and Los Angeles Police Chief, William Parker, Hoover believed in a centralized command structure and improved recruitment and training. Interestingly, Wilson and Parker did not have a high regard for Hoover, and vice versa. This mutual disdain was the result of competition over leadership in the police reform movement and the fact that the FBI under Hoover looked down on local law enforcement.

The FBI began to receive national attention during the 1930s in its well-publicized campaign to catch infamous criminals such as John Dillinger. After some successes, the FBI became a national symbol of effective crime-fighting. Hoover enhanced the Bureau's reputation by establishing a national fingerprint file, providing assistance to local departments in training their personnel, and providing criminalistics services in some important criminal cases. In the 1960s, the Bureau also established a national computer system that included important crime-related information.

Perhaps the most important contribution to local law enforcement was the development of the FBI National Academy, which trained police managers from all over the United States. For many years, this program was considered (and is still considered by some) the most prestigious in law enforcement. Another contribution to policing included the creation of the Uniform Crime Reports. These crime statistics were compiled annually by the FBI and were used as a method to evaluate the effectiveness of local police departments. This represented the first systematic attempt to evaluate how effective police were at reducing crime, and they continue to be used for this purpose today.

Hoover enhanced his reputation during World War II as the Bureau pursued and arrested several spies. A fervent anti-communist, Hoover was criticized after the war for his involvement with Senator Joseph McCarthy and in the 1950s and 1960s for his failure to respond effectively to the problems of organized crime. He was also criticized for his tactics in responding to civil rights issues. After Hoover's death, it was discovered that the FBI often used illegal methods (e.g., wiretaps) to secure information about such civil rights leaders as Martin Luther King and to gather intelligence on activist groups. Hoover believed that communists had infiltrated the civil rights movement with the intent of using the race issue to destabilize the country.

Hoover is a good example of how a person in law enforcement can become very powerful. As a result of the investigations of his agents, he had access to a large amount of information about many important people in Washington, DC, and throughout the United States. Some critics have suggested that such knowledge was a significant factor in his being able to stay in office until his death at the age of 77. Some critics have even suggested that some presidents were fearful of Hoover's power. Nevertheless, despite these criticisms, Hoover did make important contributions to law enforcement in developing the FBI.

SOURCES: D. R. Johnson, *American Law Enforcement: A History* (St. Louis: Forum Press, 1981), 171–180; G. E. Caiden, *Police Revitalization* (Lexington, MA: Heath, 1977), 242, 286, 333.

## INSIDE POLICING 2.9 The Federal Bureau of Investigation

Founded in 1908, the FBI is part of the US Department of Justice. In 2021, it employed more than 35,000 special agents and support personnel. This represents a 34 percent increase since 2001, and notably, the number of intelligence analysts has increased more than 200 percent in that time period. The mission of the FBI is to uphold the law through the investigation of violations of federal criminal law; protect the United States from foreign intelligence and terrorist activities; provide leadership and law enforcement assistance to federal, state, local, and international agencies; and perform these tasks in a manner that is responsive to the needs of the public and is faithful to the Constitution of the United States.

The Bureau's criminal investigation priorities include public corruption, civil rights issues, organized crime, white-collar crime, major thefts, and violent crime. Examples of investigations involving violent crimes and major offenders include searching for fugitives and escaped prisoners involved in FBI investigations; crime on Native American reservations; assaulting, kidnapping, or killing the president, vice president, and members of Congress; kidnapping and extortion; sexual exploitation of children; and tampering with consumer products. The FBI's national security priorities include counterterrorism (especially since September 11, 2001), counterintelligence, and cybercrime.

The headquarters of the FBI is in Washington, DC. In addition, there are field offices in 56 major cities, including Puerto Rico. There are also 400 satellite offices, known as resident agencies, which house from 1 to 12 special agents. Both field offices and resident agencies are located according to crime trends and available resources. The FBI's role in international investigations (e.g., drugs, terrorism, and financial crimes) has resulted in the establishment of 63 legal attaché offices in embassies around the world.

The FBI is also involved in numerous other activities, including managing several computer crime–related databases, providing crime laboratory services to agents and other law enforcement organizations, and training programs for FBI agents and employees and officers from state and local police.

SOURCE: https://www.fbi.gov/file-repository/the-fbi-story-2020-web.pdf/view and Today's FBI: Facts and Figures, 2013–2014.

## Response to Terrorism

The role and priorities of many federal law enforcement agencies shifted after September 11, 2001. A notable structural change was the creation of the Department of Homeland Security, which, among other things, involved reorganizing existing agencies, such as Immigration Services, Border Protection, Immigration and Customs Enforcement, the Secret Service, the Transportation Security Administration, and the Federal Emergency Management Agency, under a new cabinet-level position (Maguire and King 2011). Despite this reorganization and increased federal focus on terrorism, the majority of personnel in American policing remain at the local level. Shifting priorities have created many opportunities for federal, state, and local police agencies to collaborate on Joint Terrorism Task Forces designed to bring together local personnel and federal intelligence and resources.

**TABLE 2.1** Federal Law Enforcement Agencies (Selected List)

| AGENCY | DESCRIPTION | WEBSITE |
|---|---|---|
| Customs and Border Protection (DHS) | Primarily responsible for keeping terrorists and weapons out of the United States while facilitating lawful international travel and trade. | www.cbp.gov |
| Immigration and Customs Enforcement (DHS) | Created in 2003 as part of the Homeland Security Act; it promotes safety through criminal and civil enforcement of laws governing border control, customs, trade, and immigration. | www.ice.gov |
| Federal Bureau of Investigation (DOJ) | Priorities include terrorism, foreign intelligence operations and espionage, cyber and high-technology crime, and public corruption. | www.fbi.gov |
| Secret Service (DHS) | Primarily responsible for protection of the nation's leaders and protecting financial infrastructures. | www.secretservice.gov |
| Drug Enforcement Administration (DOJ) | Responsible for enforcement of controlled substances laws, including growing, manufacturing, or distribution of drugs. | www.dea.gov |
| Marshals Service (DOJ) | Primarily responsible for protecting the federal judiciary, apprehending federal fugitives, managing seized assets acquired through illegal activities, transporting federal prisoners, and operating the Witness Security Program. | www.usmarshals.gov |
| Internal Revenue Service, Criminal Investigation (Treasury) | Investigates criminal violations of the Internal Revenue Code, including tax crimes, narcotics-related financial crimes, and counterterrorism and espionage. | www.irs.gov/compliance/criminal-investigation/criminal-enforcement |
| Alcohol, Tobacco, Firearms and Explosives (DOJ) | Investigation and prevention of unlawful use, manufacturing, and possession of firearms and explosives; investigates arson and bombings; investigates illegal trafficking of alcohol and tobacco. | www.atf.gov |
| Postal Inspection (USPS) | Protection of US Postal Service and employees, and enforcement of laws related to the mail system. | postalinspectors.uspis.gov |

The exact role of local police in fighting terrorism remains unclear, and this shifting priority can create unintended consequences for crime prevention and police–community relations (Willis 2014). It is clear that federal law enforcement has experienced significant changes in structure, mission, and priorities after 9/11, but local policing has also been impacted in more subtle ways. For example, a study coordinated by the International Association of Chiefs of Police (2005) reported that local police executives reported organizational missions had shifted after the 9/11 attacks to include focusing on terrorism and domestic security. The report went as far as to suggest policing was shifting away from a community-oriented policing model and toward a homeland security or domestic security model. Federal support to aid local police in this mission shift has increased since 2001, and initiatives such as the 1033 program have forwarded the militarization of local policing. The 1033 Program makes excess Department of Defense property (from furniture to military vehicles and weaponry) available to local law enforcement. The militarization of the police is described further in Chapter 15.

Table 2.1 provides a list of federal law enforcement agencies, which includes a brief description, agency website, and estimated number of full-time officers. This is a partial list—most, if not all, federal departments maintain some law enforcement or investigative units, including the individual Office of Inspector General (OIG) who protect internal entities and processes of their departments related to fraud, waste, or abuse. Federal law enforcement exists across all three branches of the government—executive, legislative, and judicial. The agencies highlighted here were selected because they are either the largest agencies or the most visible or prominent.

## Summary

The police heritage in the United States can be traced to classical Greece and Rome and to developments in Europe, particularly England. The first form of policing in US cities was the constable–nightwatch system, which existed from the 1600s to the 1930s. When this system proved to be inadequate, it was replaced by modern, integrated day–night police departments. Modern police departments at the local level have moved through three distinct periods of development, each dominated by a different model of policing. These models are political, reform/professional, and community policing. Each model has a different conception of the police role and how police officers should interact with members of the community. Two of the models—the political and the reform/professional—are discussed in this chapter.

State and federal police forces also have an interesting history. State police forces were created to respond to law enforcement and traffic problems and provide related services to local police. Federal law enforcement agencies have existed since the eighteenth century but were not well established until the middle of the nineteenth century. Today, there are numerous federal law enforcement agencies and agencies with investigators working in a law enforcement capacity.

## Critical Thinking Questions

1. In what way did Sir Robert Peel and his ideas about policing influence the development of policing in the United States? How did English policing differ from early policing in the northern colonies?

2. Identify and explain the characteristics of political policing. Why did political policing develop in the United States?

3. Identify and explain the characteristics of reform/professional policing. Why did reform/professional-era policing develop in the United States?

4. Discuss the contributions of August Vollmer and O. W. Wilson to the reform and evolution of law enforcement.

5. Briefly discuss the evolution of policing in America, including slave patrols and frontier/vigilante policing.

6. How was it that state and federal law enforcement was able to emerge in American when, historically, there was a desire for local rule?

## References

Berg, B. L. 1992. *Law Enforcement: An Introduction to Police in Society*. Boston: Allyn & Bacon.

Borkenstein, R. 1977. "State Police." In S. H. Kadish (ed.), *Encyclopedia of Crime and Justice*, pp. 1131–1135. New York: Free Press.

Brown, R. M. 1991. "Vigilante Policing." In C. B. Klockars and S. D. Mastrofski (eds.), *Thinking About Police: Contemporary Readings*, 2nd ed., pp. 58–73. New York: McGraw-Hill.

Burch, A. M. 2012. *Sheriffs' Offices, 2007—Statistical Tables*. Washington, DC: Bureau of Justice Statistics.

Carte, G. E., and Carte, E. H. 1975. *Police Reform in the United States: The Era of August Vollmer, 1905–1932*. Berkeley: University of California Press.

Cole, G. F. 1989. *The American System of Criminal Justice*, 5th ed. Pacific Grove, CA: Brooks/Cole.

Cooper, L. 1975. *The Iron Fist and the Velvet Glove*. Berkeley, CA: Center for Research on Criminal Justice.

Fogelson, R. M. 1977. *Big-City Police*. Cambridge, MA: Harvard University Press.

Germann, A. C., Day, F. D., and Gallati, R. R. 1978. *Introduction to Law Enforcement and Criminal Justice*. Springfield, IL: Thomas.

Hyland, S. S., and Davis, E. 2021. *Local Police Departments, 2016: Personnel*. Washington, DC: Bureau of Justice Statistics.

International Association of Chiefs of Police. 2005. *Post 9-11 Policing: The Crime Control–Homeland Security Paradigm, Taking Command of New Realities*. Alexandria, VA: Author.

Johnson, D. R. 1981. *American Law Enforcement: A History*. St. Louis: Forum Press.

Karmen, A. A. 1983. "Vigilantism." In S. H. Kadish (ed.), *Encyclopedia of Crime and Justice*, Vol. 4, pp. 1616–1618. New York: Free Press.

Kelling, G. L., and Moore, M. H. 1988. "The Evolving Strategy of Policing." In *Perspectives on Policing*. Washington, DC: National Institute of Justice. Available at https://www.ojp.gov/pdffiles1/nij/114213.pdf

Lane, R. 1967. *Policing the City: Boston 1822–1882*. Cambridge, MA: Harvard University Press.

Lentz, S. A., and Chaires, R. H. 2007. "The Invention of Peel's Principles: A Study of Policing 'Textbook' History." *Journal of Criminal Justice* 35: 69–79.

Maguire, E. R., and King, W. R. 2011. "Federal-Local Coordination in Homeland Security." In B. Forst, J. R. Greene, and J. P. Lynch (eds.), *Criminologists on Terrorism and Homeland Security*, pp. 322–356. New York: Cambridge University Press.

Miller, W. 1977. *Cops and Bobbies*. Chicago: University of Chicago Press.

Monkkonen, E. 1981. *Police in Urban America*. Cambridge, UK: Cambridge University Press.

National Advisory Commission on Civil Disorders. 1968. *Report*. New York: New York Times Company.

President's Commission on Law Enforcement and Administration of Justice. 1967. *Task Force Report: The Police*. Washington, DC: US Government Printing Office.

Reichel, P. L. 1999. "Southern Slave Patrols as a Transitional Police Type." In L. K. Gaines and G. W. Cordner (eds.), *Policing Perspectives: An Anthology*, pp. 79–92. Los Angeles: Roxbury.

Walker, S. 1977. *A Critical History of Police Reform*. Lexington, MA: Heath.

Walker, S., and Katz, C. M. 2011. *The Police in America: An Introduction*, 7th ed. New York: McGraw-Hill.

Williams, H., and Murphy, P. V. 1990. "The Evolving Strategy of Police: A Minority Perspective." In *Perspectives on Policing*. Washington, DC: National Institute of Justice.

Willis, J. J. 2014. "A Recent History of the Police." In M. D. Reisig and R. J. Kane (eds.), *The Oxford Handbook of Police and Policing*, pp. 3–33. New York: Oxford University Press.

# Legal Issues

## CHAPTER OUTLINE

## KEY TERMS

- affidavit
- arrest
- battery
- bright-line rule
- Carroll doctrine
- color of law
- Compstat
- constitutional or federally protected rights
- criminal procedure

- custody
- depolicing
- exclusionary rule
- fruit of the poisonous tree doctrine
- hot-pursuit exception
- intentional torts
- interrogations
- Miranda warnings
- negligent torts

- open-fields doctrine
- plain-view doctrine
- pretextual stops
- probable cause
- protective sweep
- reasonable suspicion
- search incident to arrest
- *suspicion*
- stop and frisk
- wrongful death

LAW ENFORCEMENT IS AMONG the core roles of the police in America. The police are the primary government agency responsible for enforcing criminal law, initiating the formal criminal justice system, and assisting in prosecuting law violators. However, the police are also accountable to the rule of law, and the law acts as a mechanism to control and guide police behavior. This is because the police are responsible for public safety and protecting civil liberties. Legal issues identify what actions by the public are forbidden and provide the police with a basis to engage in law enforcement; however, the law also provides guardrails within which the police must operate while enforcing the law. Thus, criminal procedure and civil liability are mechanisms to ensure that police operate so as not to compromise citizens' individual liberties while engaging in law enforcement and to provide remedies for citizens when these liberties are compromised. This chapter will explore each of these legal aspects of policing.

## Criminal Procedure

**Criminal procedure** is how a person accused of a crime is processed through the criminal justice system (Worrall 2010). It consists of rules that the government must abide by to ensure that certain rights enjoyed by the public are not violated, and it ensures fairness in the processing of people accused of crimes. The most common rights related to policing addressed by the courts include those related to arrest, searches, seizures, and interrogations. Criminal procedure is also associated with the adjudication process, such as ensuring a fair trial, the right to retain counsel, and various pretrial procedures.

Before 1937, there were few important procedural rulings by the US Supreme Court. The individual safeguards found in the Bill of Rights had not yet been applied to the states. Between the 1930s and 1960s, the Court began to selectively incorporate some of these safeguards into the procedural requirements that local police had to follow. Not until the 1960s did the "due process revolution" begin. During this decade, the Court increasingly applied provisions of the Bill of Rights to the states. The 1960s were characterized by widespread support for the protection of the civil rights of individuals. The Warren Court of this period, named for Chief Justice Earl Warren, was associated with a liberal political philosophy, because most judges supported more legal restrictions on the police. From a politically conservative point of view (which included the views of a majority of police officers), the police were "handcuffed" in their ability to fight crime. Hence, the process of criminal procedure is concerned with two competing values: the need to protect the freedom of citizens from government tyranny while simultaneously ensuring a civil and ordered society that is free from disorder and crime.

An overview of case law related to criminal procedure is beyond the scope of this chapter, although Inside Policing 3.1 provides capsules of benchmark and contemporary decisions related to criminal procedure and police civil liability regarding search and seizure. Instead, we provide a description of laws and procedures related to common police practices of street-level officers. This chapter will present an overview of rights related to searches and seizures of persons and property and citizens' rights during custodial interrogations.

| INSIDE POLICING 3.1 | Selected Supreme Court Cases on Search and Seizure (1960 to the Present) |
|---|---|

*Mapp v. Ohio* (1961): The exclusionary rule used in federal trials is applied to the states. Evidence obtained illegally cannot be used in a trial or in subsequent proceedings.

*Katz v. United States* (1967): Fourth Amendment requirements for search and seizure apply to electronic surveillance even if there is no actual physical intrusion into the property of a defendant.

*Terry v. Ohio* (1968): Police officers are authorized to stop and frisk suspicious persons to conduct a proper investigation and to protect the officer from possible harm.

*Chimel v. California* (1969): When making arrests, police officers are allowed to search the defendant and the immediate area under the defendant's control (which, in effect, means that only the area within an arm's-length distance can be searched).

*Nix v. Williams* (1984): Illegally obtained evidence will not be excluded from a trial if it is inevitable that the evidence will be discovered anyway. This is the inevitability of discovery exception to the exclusionary rule.

*United States v. Leon* (1984): Evidence obtained using a search warrant that a police officer obtained from a detached and neutral judge can be used at trial even if it is later discovered that there was no probable cause to issue the warrant. This is one example of the good-faith exception to the exclusionary rule.

*Kyllo v. United States* (2001): A search warrant must be obtained in advance if officers want to use thermal imaging devices to scan homes for heat sources consistent with growing marijuana. Such devices may not be used to gather probable cause.

*Illinois v. McArthur* (2001): Police officers may detain an individual from re-entering his home to secure a search warrant if there is probable cause to believe he had hidden marijuana in the home and would destroy it on re-entry.

*Maryland v. Pringle* (2003): Discovery of drugs from the back seat of an automobile is probable cause to arrest all vehicle occupants even if all occupants deny ownership of the drugs.

*Hudson v. Michigan* (2006): Although officers are required to knock and announce their presence during the execution of a typical search warrant, failure to knock and announce properly will not result in the exclusion of evidence seized pursuant to the warrant.

*Georgia v. Randolph* (2006): All on-location cohabitants of a residence must provide consent for officers to search to make the search reasonable.

*Brendlin v. California* (2007): A passenger of a motor vehicle is considered seized under the meaning of the Fourth Amendment. A reasonable person would believe they are not free to leave when the car they are traveling in is stopped by the police.

*Herring v. United States* (2009): Evidence discovered pursuant to an arrest warrant is admissible in court even if it was later determined that the warrant clerk misinformed the officer and a valid warrant did not exist.

*Florence v. Board of Chosen Freeholders of the County of Burlington* (2012): A strip search of individuals being booked into jail, even for minor offenses, is reasonable and therefore constitutional.

*Florida v. Jardines* (2013): The use of a drug-sniffing dog at the front door of a home constitutes a search under the meaning of the Fourth Amendment.

*Missouri v. McNeely* (2013): There is a warrant preference for drawing and testing blood for alcohol content during stops for driving under the influence; however, local jurisdictions may adopt their own rules and guidelines regarding the warrant application procedure so as to not adversely impact law enforcement officers.

*Riley v. California* (2014): Police may not search the contents of a cell phone incident to arrest without a warrant.

*Fernandez v. California* (2014): Police may search a residence when one co-occupant provides consent, even if a second co-occupant refuses consent provided the second co-occupant is no longer present.

## Searches and Seizures of Persons

The Fourth Amendment provides safeguards from unreasonable searches and seizures. This amendment guides the Court in creating guidelines for when officers may stop or arrest citizens, because these actions constitute a seizure of that person. The two most common forms of seizure of a person are stops (and often "frisks" associated with the stop) and arrests, and the Court has provided roadmaps to ensure that these seizures are reasonable in scope or duration.

Before discussing stops and frisks or arrests, it is first important to understand the degree of certainty an officer must possess to avoid an unreasonable action. Stops and frisks must at a minimum be based on the legal standard of **reasonable suspicion**. This standard is difficult to quantify and perhaps explain, but del Carmen (2001) describes reasonable suspicion as that which is based on objective facts and logical conclusions that a crime has been or is about to be committed, based on the circumstances at hand. Although the Court has not clearly defined this standard, in *Alabama v. White* (1990) it acknowledged that reasonable suspicion is a lower standard than probable cause and may arise from information that itself has questionable reliability. In other words, reasonable suspicion is a standard that is lower than probable cause but more than a simple hunch. Since reasonable suspicion is somewhat less rigorous than other standards, the scope of officer behavior is necessarily limited to actions such as stopping a suspect or frisking a suspect. In contrast, arrests must be based on the standard of **probable cause**.

Probable cause is an incredibly important legal threshold, because various parts of the criminal justice system are formally initiated only after probable cause is established. Most notably, the police (and the government) must have probable cause to arrest someone (and file formal charges against that person), to secure a search warrant, or to conduct a search and seizure of citizens' "persons, houses, papers, and effects" (as stated in the Fourth Amendment).

Given the centrality that probable cause has in policing, what, exactly, is it? Probable cause "exists where the facts and circumstances within the officers' knowledge, and of which they have reasonably trustworthy information, are sufficient in themselves to warrant a belief by a man of reasonable caution that a crime is being committed" (*Brinegar v. United States* 1949). Hence, the officer has reason to believe that a particular individual has "more likely than not" committed a certain crime. Probable cause is when a crime is *likely* being committed, whereas reasonable suspicion is when a crime *may* be being committed. Probable cause is the minimum legal standard necessary to make a custodial arrest of a person, and it is a more rigorous standard than reasonable suspicion. In sum, the degree of certainty the officer has that criminal activity is afoot is inversely related to the scope, length, and intensity of the detention of the suspect.

Although the Fourth Amendment provides a right to be free from unreasonable searches and seizures, it does not address how this right should be enforced. The most recognized method for enforcing the reasonableness standard of the Fourth Amendment is called the **exclusionary rule**. This rule holds that evidence obtained by the government in violation of the Fourth Amendment's guarantee against unreasonable searches and seizures is not admissible in criminal prosecution to demonstrate guilt. The premise of this rule is that excluding illegally seized evidence from court will deter police officers from acting improperly. Although the birth of the exclusionary rule can be traced back to *Weeks v. United States* (1914), it was not until the decision in *Mapp v. Ohio* (1961) that the Court incorporated the rule to govern evidence collected by state and local police officers. Writing for the majority, Justice Tom C. Clark stated the Court had previously acknowledged that the "criminal is to go free because the constable has blundered," but also noted that "the criminal goes free, if he must, but it is the law that sets him free. Nothing can destroy a government more quickly than its failure to observe its own laws, or worse, its disregard of the charter of its own existence."

An extension of the exclusionary rule is the **fruit of the poisonous tree doctrine**, which indicates that not only evidence seized improperly but also any additional evidence seized after that police action must be excluded from criminal court. For example, assume the police improperly obtained a confession to a crime and that during the confession the suspect told the police where to find evidence (e.g., a knife). When the police locate the evidence, they find additional evidence (e.g., a handgun) of a different crime. In this hypothetical scenario, the confession and the knife would be excluded from court pursuant to the exclusionary rule. The handgun would also be excluded, because it was the "fruit" that was obtained from an initial improper confession.

American police interact with citizens hundreds of thousands of times each day. Issues of liability become important when officers wish to detain citizens against their will. To detain citizens, officers are required to have a certain level of proof that a crime has been committed or that the citizen was involved in criminal activity. In *United States v. Seslar* (1993), three different types of police-citizen encounters were identified:

1. **Consensual encounters**. These involve *voluntary interactions* between the police and the public, and the questioning by the officer is typically noncoercive. There is *no legal justification needed* in these encounters, and because the encounter is consensual, the citizen is free to terminate the encounter at any time. Thus, there is no seizure under the meaning of the Fourth Amendment.

2. **Investigative detentions**. These encounters involve a *temporary detention* of the citizen's movement by the police. Officers may detain citizens for questioning when there is *reasonable suspicion* to believe the citizen has committed, is committing, or

is about to commit a crime. This type of temporary detention has also been referred to as a Terry stop, after the landmark Court decision (*Terry v. Ohio* 1968).

3. **Arrests**. Arrests involve a *seizure of the citizen* by the police that are characterized as lengthy and highly intrusive, in which there is likelihood that the intent of the detention is to subject the citizen to criminal prosecution. Officers are required to have *probable cause* that a crime has been or is being committed to make an arrest (Klotter 1999).

Officers must understand these basic typologies of encounters to avoid exposing themselves and police organizations to civil liability, and they must be prepared to articulate the facts and circumstances available to justify a level of proof. Indeed, officers may consider the totality of circumstances when determining reasonable suspicion or probable cause. If an officer detains a citizen beyond that person's will without the requisite level of proof, then an illegal seizure under the Fourth Amendment or the intentional tort of false arrest may occur. In the "Voices from the Field" included in this chapter, prosecutor Jean Peters Baker further describes the historical foundation and modern application of the Fourth Amendment.

**Stops and Frisks.** The term **stop and frisk** often is confused so that people believe this is one continuous act. An officer may *stop* a person, temporarily depriving them of freedom of movement, if the officer has reasonable suspicion that the person is involved in a crime. Furthermore, the officer may *frisk* the person if there is reasonable suspicion to believe the citizen is armed and poses a threat to the officer for the duration of the stop.

The landmark case that outlined the parameters for stops and frisks was *Terry v. Ohio* (1968). In that case, the suspect (John Terry) was observed by a seasoned police officer to be engaging in suspicious behavior with others in front of a store in downtown Cleveland. Based on the officer's experience, he indicated that it was reasonable to believe they were casing the store for a robbery. On stopping the suspects to inquire of their intentions, the officer indicated that the suspects' mumbled responses to his questions led him to believe that the suspects were armed. He discovered a firearm on Terry after patting down his upper torso, and Terry was charged with carrying a concealed weapon.

Although the officer did not have enough information to elevate the legal standard to probable cause, he indicated there was reasonable suspicion to believe Terry was about to commit a crime and was armed at the time of the encounter. The Court indicated that a temporary stop of Terry, based on reasonable suspicion, did not violate the Fourth Amendment and that a limited pat-down or frisk of his outer garments was reasonable based on the circumstances. Since stops and frisks represent a limited intrusion on the citizen's liberty, these practices are permissible even if the officer does not have probable cause to believe a crime is about to be committed.

A more recent case further illustrates the scope of a stop and frisk. Lemon Johnson was a passenger in a vehicle that was properly stopped for traffic violations. Officers questioned the occupants of the vehicle regarding gang activity in the area and requested Johnson exit the vehicle, which he did. Suspecting Johnson was involved with gangs and armed, officers conducted a pat-down of his clothing and discovered a handgun and drugs. Johnson argued that the conversation was consensual and not a "stop," as required under *Terry*. Furthermore, he argued that officers did not have probable cause to believe he was involved with gang activity and were thus unjustified in their frisk. A unanimous Court rejected his argument. They indicated that, indeed, because he was a passenger in a lawfully detained vehicle, Johnson was lawfully seized. In addition, the Court said officers had suspicion to believe he was affiliated with a violent street gang, and thus the limited frisk of his clothing was reasonable to ensure officer safety (*Arizona v. Johnson* 2008).

The Court later indicated that evidence seized pursuant to a misapplication of the stop and frisk parameters is not always automatically excluded from trial. Detectives in Salt Lake City were conducting surveillance on a home based on an anonymous tip of drug trafficking. During surveillance, detectives noticed many people arriving at the home, staying briefly, and then leaving. One of these people was Edward Strieff. Detectives approached Strieff, stopped him, and asked for his identification. Detectives learned that Strieff had an outstanding warrant for a traffic violation and promptly arrested him. As part of the routine arrest, the detective searched Strieff and discovered methamphetamine and drug paraphernalia, which the detective seized, and they charged Strieff with unlawful possession. The initial stop by the detective was unreasonable, however, because he did not have reasonable suspicion that Strieff was engaged in criminal activity. Therefore, Strieff argued that the discovery of the drugs and paraphernalia was illegal and must be excluded from trial. The Supreme Court disagreed, noting that the drugs and paraphernalia were seized pursuant to a valid warrant, rather than pursuant to an unreasonable stop. While it is true that Strieff's identification could not be determined but for the stop and that the detective's decision to stop Strieff was negligent, these errors in judgment were not a flagrant violation of his rights. So while the stop in fact may have been unconstitutional, exclusion of the drugs and paraphernalia was not necessary, because Strieff was under arrest for the traffic warrants at the time of the discovery (*Utah v. Strieff* 2016).

Unprovoked flight from police officers may also constitute reasonable suspicion that legitimizes a temporary stop of the individual. The Court held in *Illinois v. Wardlow* (2000) that unprovoked flight from the police provides an officer with ample reasonable suspicion to temporarily detain that suspect. Furthermore, the Court indicated that this behavior, coupled with the fact that the encounter took place in a high-crime area, produced legal justification to stop and detain the citizen. Mere presence in a high-crime area would not substantiate reasonable suspicion, but flight coupled with the environmental characteristics of where the encounter took place provides additional rationale for suspicion. Suspicion is formed by taking both behavior and location into consideration.

Again, it is important to understand that stops and frisks are separate activities that must require reasonable suspicion. Not all stops necessitate a frisk. The officer must articulate separately which factors led to the stop and which factors led to the frisk. The purpose of a stop is to prevent criminal activity or determine whether a crime has taken place; the purpose of a frisk is to ensure officer safety. The extent of intrusion permissible in a frisk is limited to a pat-down of the suspect's outer clothing for weapons. Frisks may only be conducted if there is reasonable suspicion to believe the suspect is armed and may pose a physical threat to the officer during the encounter (del Carmen 2001). The duration of the encounter is to be no longer than permitted to achieve its purpose, and no physical force is permitted beyond that of the pat-down (del Carmen 2001).

A frisk may not be used as a "fishing expedition" for evidence or other contraband. For example, in *Minnesota v. Dickerson* (1993), the Court indicated that drugs found during a frisk must be excluded as evidence from trial. Timothy Dickerson was observed leaving a known crack house, and he was frisked by an officer pursuant to a stop. The officer felt a small object in Dickerson's pocket and, by manipulating it with his hands, believed it to be crack cocaine wrapped in cellophane. The officer retrieved the object and confirmed that it was drugs. This procedure went beyond the scope of a Terry frisk. The evidence was not admissible in court because the purpose of the frisk was to discover weapons, and since the officer had to manipulate the object to determine what it was, this manipulation constituted a second search that was beyond what was reasonable.

**Arrest.** An **arrest** is the act of depriving a person of their liberty by legal authority and is performed for interrogation or criminal prosecution (Zalman and Siegel 1997). Laws related to the reasonableness of an arrest also fall under the rubric of the Fourth Amendment, because arrest is the seizure of a person against that person's will by an agent of the government. Arrests are among the most critical activities police officers perform within the criminal justice system, because an arrest must typically be made before other system components may act. Following an arrest, administrative procedures are conducted; these include fingerprinting, photographing, and booking the person into jail. Unfortunately, the public does not completely understand when and under what circumstances an arrest can be made or the legal guidelines officers must follow when conducting a search for evidence during an arrest.

Officers must have probable cause to believe that a particular person has committed a specific crime to make an arrest. Since arrests are more intrusive than stops, it is necessary that the officer have a higher legal justification for depriving a person of their liberty. There is also a preference that arrests be made on issuance of an arrest warrant by a neutral and detached magistrate. In reality, however, most arrests are made without an arrest warrant. Obtaining a warrant to make arrests in many situations would unduly limit the crime-control function of the police. The courts have indicated that routine felony arrests made in public do not require a warrant, even if officers have an opportunity to obtain one (*United States v. Watson* 1976). However, if officers wish to make a felony arrest in a private home, they must first secure a warrant if there is an opportunity to do so or if exigent (emergency) circumstances are absent (*Payton v. New York* 1981). This demonstrates the expectation of privacy an individual enjoys in private places over public places.

It is not necessary to have reasonable suspicion to search an individual if they are under arrest and taken into custody. On arrest, officers may perform a comprehensive search of the suspect and the possessions in their immediate control. This **search incident to arrest** may be for weapons, but it can also include any contraband discovered during the search. Furthermore, officers may search the area in the suspect's immediate control to discover evidence or weapons without a search warrant (*Chimel v. California* 1969). The area in someone's immediate control has been understood to consist of the area within the person's wingspan, or their "lunge-and-reach" area. The purposes of the Chimel rule are to ensure officer safety and to prevent the destruction of evidence.

It is also permissible for officers to perform a limited **protective sweep** of a home to determine whether others could pose a safety risk for officers (*Maryland v. Buie* 1990). Jerome Edward Buie and an accomplice were wanted for armed robbery, during which one of the men was wearing a red running suit. Officers obtained an arrest warrant for Buie, entered his house, and saw Buie emerge from the basement. After placing him under arrest, officers proceeded to the basement to determine whether anyone else was there who could pose a threat to officer safety. Once in the basement, officers observed a red running suit that matched the description of the one used during the robbery. This running suit was seized (without a warrant) and used against Buie in court. The Supreme Court indicated that the search of Buie's basement was reasonable: the officers had reason to perform a cursory search of the area for protective purposes. However, a protective sweep is different from a full-blown search for evidence and allows only a cursory inspection of spaces

| INSIDE POLICING 3.2 | Comparing Searches Incident to Arrest to Protective Sweeps | |
|---|---|---|
| | **SEARCH INCIDENT TO ARREST** | **PROTECTIVE SWEEP** |
| Purpose | Officer safety <br> Prevent evidence destruction | Officer safety |
| Standard of Proof | Valid arrest | Reasonable suspicion |
| Scope | Person and area within immediate control | Cursory inspection of where threat may be |
| Duration | Contemporaneous with arrest | As long as it takes to achieve purpose |

where a person may be located. In this regard, protective sweeps are similar to frisks, in that they must be limited in nature to the discovery of weapons or people who could harm the officer and not evidence of a crime. In contrast to frisks, evidence of a crime discovered during a protective sweep is permissible in court.

Searches incident to arrest and protective sweeps may seem very similar; however, they are two different searches conducted under different circumstances and serve different purposes. Inside Policing 3.2 contrasts these two exceptions to the warrant requirement across purpose, legal standard of proof, scope, and duration.

### Searches and Seizures of Property

Similar to searches and seizures of persons, the courts have attempted to balance the need for public safety with adhering to expectations of privacy regarding searches and seizures of property. Also, there is a preference for searches and seizures of property to be conducted under a **search warrant**, which is a "written order, issued by a magistrate, directing a peace officer to search for property connected with a crime and bring it before the court" (del Carmen 2001, 181). Search warrants must demonstrate that there is probable cause that evidence of a crime exists in a particular place and must fully describe the place to be searched, thus eliminating the possibility of a general warrant. Probable cause must be supported under oath or affirmation, typically by a police officer, before a neutral and detached judge. During this oath (often called an **affidavit**, which is the same as an oath except that it is written), the officer describes what is to be seized and exactly what is to be searched. The judge may then issue a search warrant commanding law enforcement to search by signing the warrant (del Carmen 2001).

Historically, the police must knock and announce their presence when executing a search warrant on a citizen's house. Police must knock, identify themselves, announce their intent to search the house with a warrant, and allow the occupant a reasonable amount of time to comply. There are several reasons for this rule. It permits the person to answer the door, thereby avoiding unnecessary confrontations with the police and potential property damage; it is unnecessary and dangerous for the police to burst into a home. At the same time, there can be very reasonable justifications for not adhering to this requirement. For example, knocking and announcing could permit the occupant to destroy evidence or arm themselves to confront the police. Therefore, the police may request a "no-knock" warrant from the judge if they have reasonable suspicion to believe there is a risk of evidence destruction or the officer's safety could be jeopardized. The knock and announce requirement was viewed as part of the Fourth Amendment right that people enjoy—in other words, the method of entry had to be reasonable. But the Supreme Court decoupled the exclusionary rule from violations of the knock and announce requirement. Therefore, violations of this rule do not necessarily make the seizure of evidence unreasonable, and the evidence could still be introduced at criminal trials (*Hudson v. Michigan 2006*).

Two recent, high-profile encounters between the police and citizens have brought the utility of no-knock warrants to the center of public debate. In March 2020 (several months before the events in Minneapolis involving George Floyd), the Louisville Metro Police Department executed a no-knock warrant on an apartment to search for drugs. During the ensuing confrontation, Breonna Taylor was shot and killed by police. In 2022, the police were executing a similar no-knock entry in Minnesota. Amir Locke was asleep on the couch, and when the police burst in, he grabbed for his firearm. Locke too was shot and killed by the police. The method the police used to enter Taylor's and Locke's apartments are important from a legal perspective, but more importantly, these examples underscore the volatile and dangerous nature of no-knock warrants (under any circumstances). Indeed, many states and the Department of Justice have introduced measures to limit the practice of no-knock warrants to rare circumstances.

There are many circumstances where searches without a warrant are reasonable in their scope. For example, the **plain-view doctrine** falls beyond the warrant requirement. It is not unreasonable for the police to seize evidence of a crime if the evidence is in view of the officer. But the plain-view doctrine contains several important caveats. First, the police must have prior justification for being present at the scene; stated differently, the initial police intrusion must be lawful. Second, the evidence seized must be in plain view, and police may not take actions that expose to view concealed portions of the premises or its contents. Third, the objects seized must be immediately apparent as evidence or contraband.

The facts and circumstances in *Arizona v. Hicks* (1987) are instructive and provide an example of the plain-view doctrine in action. The police responded to James Thomas Hicks's apartment after a neighbor called complaining that someone in the apartment above had fired a bullet through their floor and into the neighbor's apartment. On arrival, the police entered Hicks's apartment and discovered several guns and a stocking mask. However, while inside, an officer observed several new pieces of expensive stereo equipment that appeared out of place in the otherwise squalid apartment. Having reasonable suspicion that the stereos were stolen, the officer moved the pieces, recorded the serial numbers, and confirmed via radio that, indeed, the equipment was stolen. Hicks was charged and convicted of receiving stolen property. Later, the Supreme Court indicated that the stereo equipment could not be used as evidence to prosecute Hicks, because the act of moving the stereo constituted a second search in which the officers did not have probable cause. Although the officers were legally present in the apartment and the stereo equipment was in plain view, it was not immediately apparent as evidence or contraband. Hence, the third criterion for the plain-view doctrine was not present.

Another exception to the warrant requirement includes items observed in open fields. The **open-fields doctrine** indicates that "items in open fields are not protected by the Fourth Amendment's guarantee against unreasonable searches and seizures, so they can properly be taken by an officer without a warrant or probable cause" (del Carmen 2001, 259).

In other words, people who leave items in public view do not enjoy a right to privacy; thus, the Fourth Amendment does not apply to these places. In *Oliver v. United States* (1984), the police were acting on a tip that marijuana was being grown in a field on Ray Oliver's farm. The police ignored the "No Trespassing" sign at the edge of the property and, without probable cause, entered the field to observe the marijuana. The Court indicated that this type of trespass was permissible and that the marijuana could be used as evidence to convict Oliver.

Similarly, warrants are not required for abandoned property (e.g., garbage left on private premises). The police may seize garbage bags left for removal and search the bags for contraband (often receipts of illegal activity or drug paraphernalia). Once a person abandons property and makes it available for public scrutiny, that person no longer enjoys an expectation of privacy in relation to that property (*California v. Greenwood* 1988).

Another common exception to the warrant requirement is the **hot-pursuit exception**. Police may follow a felon or otherwise dangerous criminal into a place typically protected by the Fourth Amendment, such as a home, or may cross jurisdictional boundaries. Hot pursuits must be based on probable cause, but the officer may develop probable cause via hearsay or direct observation. The gravity of the offense must be taken into consideration, and relatively minor offenses may not provide justification for warrantless pursuits. Once in a constitutionally protected area, the officer may search for the suspect and for weapons or evidence, but once the suspect is found, the search must cease. At this point, any search without a warrant must be based on other factors, such as those described previously in the *Chimel* or *Buie* rulings.

Another exception to the warrant requirement is when the citizen provides officers with *consent* to search. Officers may search a person or property if a person *voluntarily* consents to the search. Consent searches, therefore, do not require a warrant, and any evidence that is obtained during a consent search is permissible in court. Furthermore, officers do not need to advise citizens of their right to refuse consent (*Schneckloth v. Bustamonte* 1973); it must merely be demonstrated that consent was voluntarily given and not coerced by the officer. When searching a home, officers must have consent to search from all co-occupants present at the scene (*Georgia v. Randolph* 2006; *Fernandez v. California* 2014).

**Vehicle Searches.**  Court doctrines related to searches and seizures often rely on an individual's expectation of privacy when determining the reasonableness of police action. Generally, people enjoy a greater level of privacy in homes and private places than they do in public. But the lines between public and private spheres become difficult to disentangle when confronted with stops of citizens in motor vehicles. Are motor vehicles private places? Or because they are operated in public, do citizens enjoy a diminished expectation of privacy in vehicles? What can the police do when making a traffic stop? Because of the unique nature of motor vehicle searches, it is important to consider these searches and seizures separately from those conducted in other types of places.

The courts have recognized motor vehicles as having substantially fewer Fourth Amendment protections than fixed premises, because motor vehicles are highly mobile, allowing evidence to be moved and suspects to flee police custody. The contents of motor vehicles (including drivers and passengers) travel in plain view, thus exposing them to public review. Furthermore, motor vehicles are highly regulated by the government (e.g., driver's licenses, vehicle registration, and insurance). Together, these characteristics have led the courts to adopt relaxed standards regarding searches and seizures and the necessity of obtaining warrants for searches of motor vehicles.

Police officers may stop motor vehicles if they have reasonable suspicion that a crime has been committed. On stopping a vehicle, officers may investigate whether there is probable cause to arrest a driver (or passengers) or to issue a summons or ticket. In fact, officers have a great deal of discretion pursuant to traffic stops. Inside Policing 3.3 provides capsules of benchmark and contemporary decisions related to search and seizure involving automobiles.

May an officer stop a vehicle for a traffic violation under the pretext that the stop may elicit another, more serious violation? This was the question posed before the Court in *Whren v. United States* (1996). Two plainclothes officers observed Michael Whren and another occupant driving a vehicle with temporary tags in an area of high drug activity. The vehicle was stopped at an intersection for an unusually long period, and the driver was staring at the lap of the passenger. Suspecting the occupants to be involved with drug sales, the officers approached the vehicle at a red light, stopping them for a traffic violation. Whren was observed to be holding a bag of crack cocaine, for which he was arrested and subsequently convicted. Whren argued that the officers would not normally engage in traffic enforcement and were using the traffic violation merely as a pretext to determine whether he was involved with drugs (*Whren v. United States* 1996). The Supreme Court determined this practice to be permissible and that seizures incident to **pretextual stops** of vehicles are not unreasonable.

Circumstances exist where police officers may stop vehicles without reasonable suspicion. Sobriety checkpoints permit police officers to systematically stop vehicles without

## VOICES FROM THE FIELD

### Jean Peters Baker
*Prosecutor, Jackson County Missouri*

What constitutes a legal Fourth Amendment search? Can one use their cell phone in a public place without law enforcement intrusion tracking one's location?

Such questions will continue to arise as technology evolves and courts react. The lesson for law enforcement is that they must transform and adjust with each new court decision.

Our Fourth Amendment to the US Constitution was actually set in motion in England in 1604. Sir Edward Coke explained in the *Semayne* case, "The house of every one is to him as his castle and fortress, as well for his defen[s]e against injury and violence as for his repose."[1] The *Semayne* case was an early limitation on government power, in this case, the king's power, from intruding in one's home without justification. Hence, the adage remains true today: a man's home is his castle.

This evolution, beginning with limiting the king's absolute authority to invade a man's home, has

morphed into one's privacy concerns with the use of wireless technology such as cellular telephones and the Global Positioning System (GPS). Yet the basic tenets of the Fourth Amendment, requiring a warrant to be supported by probable cause and sanctioned by a judge, remain strong. One such case involved law enforcement officers placing a GPS tracking device on Antoine Jones's car.[2] In 2004, the FBI began investigating Jones for narcotics violations, including installing a GPS device on the undercarriage of a Jeep Grand Cherokee registered to Jones's wife; they continued to monitor the vehicle's whereabouts for 28 days. Law enforcement gathered more than 2,000 pages of information during that time and subsequently seized $850,000 in cash, 97 kilograms of cocaine, and 1 kilogram of cocaine base (crack), leading to Antoine Jones's conviction.[3] But the Supreme Court held that "the Government's installation of a GPS device on a

*(Continued)*

target's vehicle, was a 'search'" under the Fourth Amendment, and that search was found to be unconstitutional because the government failed to gain a proper search warrant.[4] In part, the Court relied on the fact that installation of the GPS device required the police to trespass onto the property (i.e., vehicle) without knowledge or consent of the owner and without judicial approval; therefore, parallels could be drawn between this modern case and *Semayne.* The convictions were thrown out.

As social norms and technology change, our courts must balance our constitutional protections against unreasonable searches and invasions of privacy with those emerging technological advances. Each judicial balance that is struck provides a roadmap for law enforcement to follow. Often, that roadmap is unclear, and law enforcement must decipher the court's meaning when new facts and technology emerge.

What impact will the *Jones* decision have on law enforcement practices? Maybe very little. Police only need to apply for a warrant through a prosecutor and a judge to gain approval for their investigations. However, the potential for real impact exists, because law enforcement may not use a hunch or an instinct to further an investigation through GPS technology. A warrant requires probable cause, which is much more than a hunch on the part of law enforcement. Hunches often lead to concrete information from which law enforcement may work, but *Jones* has curtailed that process. Disregarding a hunch as unreliable police practice fails to understand human interaction and the everyday happenings of ordinary police work. *Jones* also has an impact under Missouri

law, which allows law enforcement only 10 days to recover data without reapplying for a secondary warrant. Ten days does not allow much time to net the necessary intelligence to solve crimes, especially narcotics-related offenses.

*Jones* may have a lasting effect on collecting information using cell phone GPS systems. Historically, law enforcement accessed cell phone GPS data so long as officers demonstrated that the information was relevant and material to an ongoing investigation and the data uncovered could be gained by physical surveillance. After *Jones*, however, law enforcement use of cell phone data to track an individual's movements over a period of time may require a showing of probable cause, supported by a warrant. Since 2012, defense attorneys have argued—and at least one court (a Massachusetts Superior Court) has held—that police need a warrant to collect and use cell phone locational data.[5] Should these arguments become reflected in more decisions, defense lawyers may gain significant leverage to argue that the Fourth Amendment protects locational information broadly and that police require warrants for collecting locational data. Hunches or instincts on behalf of law enforcement become more limited, which restricts their ability to protect the public.

Police and prosecutors continue to explore the practical implications of *Jones*. The scope of the opinion is narrowly written, focusing only on a physical intrusion, which the Court called a trespass to property. Would the Court rule the same on thermal imaging and satellite technology advances? Maybe. Maybe not. For now, the ruling does not address surveillance data obtained without physical intrusion.

[1] Coke's Rep. 91a, 77 Eng. Rep. 194 (K.B. 1604).
[2] See *United States v. Jones*, 132 S. Ct. 945 (2012).
[3] Jones at 948–949.
[4] Jones at 945–954.
[5] See, e.g., *Commonwealth v. Pitt*, 29 Mass. L. Rptr. 445, *3, n. 5 (Mass. Super. Ct. 2012). I

reasonable suspicion, because the nature of the stop is limited. This issue was addressed in *Michigan Department of State Police v. Sitz* (1990). The sobriety checkpoint in question was highly publicized before initiation, and officers' actions were set by guidelines developed by the Checkpoint Advisory Committee. Officers stopped 126 vehicles passing a set location over the course of 75 minutes. Motorists were stopped, on average, for 25 seconds so that those officers could conduct preliminary investigations for intoxication. The Court determined that the stops were not unreasonable by adopting a balancing test of three factors: "the gravity of public concerns served by the seizure, the degree to which the seizure advances the public interest, and the severity of the interference with individual liberty"

| INSIDE POLICING 3.3 | Selected Supreme Court Cases on Search and Seizure Involving Automobiles (1960 to the Present) |
| --- | --- |

*New York v. Belton* (1981): Officers may search the contents of an automobile contemporaneous with an arrest. This search incident to arrest rule is similar to *Chimel* in vehicle contexts. The "Belton rule" was reconsidered in *Arizona v. Gant* (2009).

*United States v. Ross* (1982): Where probable cause exists to believe that an automobile contains evidence in a criminal case, police may conduct a warrantless search, including searching any closed containers that may be in the automobile (e.g., luggage).

*Michigan Department of State Police v. Sitz* (1990): Vehicles may be stopped at highway sobriety checkpoints even if there is no individualized suspicion the driver is committing a crime.

*Florida v. Bostick* (1991): This case expanded the meaning of "consent" in consensual searches. If an officer's request is not coercive and the passenger is free to refuse, the search satisfies consent, even if the passenger—Bostick, in this case, being on a bus—is not free to leave.

*Whren v. United States* (1996): Does a pretextual stop (a stop made for a legally valid reason such as a taillight violation but whose underlying purpose was altogether different, such as to examine the vehicle for drugs) made by a police officer invalidate a subsequent legal vehicular search for drugs? The Court ruled that the subjective intentions of police officers do not invalidate an objectively reasonable action.

*Illinois v. Caballes* (2005): Drug-sniffing dogs may search a vehicle stopped during a routine traffic stop even if there is no reasonable suspicion the vehicle contains drugs. However, the Court clarified this in *Rodriguez v. United States* (2015), indicating the use of a drug dog may not prolong the stop beyond the time necessary to issue a traffic ticket.

*Arizona v. Gant* (2009): The police may search the vehicle of an arrested recent occupant only if there is reasonable suspicion to believe the arrestee may access the vehicle (to procure a weapon or destroy evidence) or if it is reasonable to believe evidence of the crime for which the driver was arrested will be discovered. This limited the scope of vehicle searches previously outlined in *Belton.*

*United States v. Jones* (2012): Use of a GPS tracking device affixed to a car to monitor movement constitutes a search under the Fourth Amendment; therefore. a search warrant is required.

(del Carmen 2001, 221). *Sitz* does not permit random stops for sobriety checks, and such stops absent reasonable suspicion are restricted to fixed checkpoints.

Although officers may stop motorists at sobriety checkpoints without individualized suspicion of criminal behavior, the same rules do not apply for ordinary criminal wrongdoing. The City of Indianapolis conducted vehicle checkpoints to determine whether drivers had illegal drugs. Drivers were temporarily detained, similar to the process described in *Sitz*, but here, the Court felt there was not a compelling state interest to engage in drug interdiction that permitted such suspiciousness stops. Determining whether a driver is in possession of drugs does not represent the same level of immediate public safety risk as demonstrated in *Sitz*, and thus this practice is unconstitutional (*Indianapolis v. Edmond* 2000). Later, however, the Court did permit checkpoints designed to gather information about a specific crime. In Lombard, Illinois, a 70-year-old bicyclist was struck and killed by an unknown motorist. Shortly thereafter, the police set up a checkpoint where motorists were stopped and asked whether they knew anything about the hit-and-run accident, and police provided motorists with flyers containing information about the crime and ways to contact the police to share information. During this checkpoint, Robert Lidster lost control of his vehicle, hitting an officer, and was later determined to be driving while intoxicated. He contested this charge, indicating he was stopped at a checkpoint without reasonable suspicion and that the purpose of the checkpoint was to detect ordinary criminal wrongdoing (which was determined in *Edmond* to be unconstitutional). The Court disagreed, stating it was a reasonable investigatory tool to gather information regarding a death. Here, the Court recognized that the public interest of a death investigation outweighed any minor inconvenience or privacy concern experienced by individual drivers, making suspicionless stops reasonable (*Illinois v. Lidster* 2004).

The **Carroll doctrine** provides for warrantless searches of motor vehicles if the vehicle is, in fact, mobile and if there is probable cause. The Court's rationale in *Carroll v. United States* (1925) is that the inherent mobility of a vehicle may permit the destruction of evidence, allow the occupants to flee the jurisdiction, and make obtaining a warrant in this situation impractical for law enforcement. The scope of the search may extend to the entire car, including the trunk and closed containers, if there is probable cause to believe these locations contain evidence or contraband (*United States v. Ross* 1982). The Court also determined that searches of passengers' belongings with probable cause are reasonable (*Wyoming v. Houghton* 1999). Inside Policing 3.4 provides an overview of actions permissible during traffic stops.

---

**INSIDE POLICING 3.4**   What May an Officer Do After a Vehicle is Stopped?

1. **Order driver and passengers to get out of the vehicle.** Officer safety is often cited as a primary rationale for having occupants exit the vehicle.
2. **Ask driver to produce driver's license and other documents (as required by state law).**
3. **Ask questions of driver and passengers.** This may be done without providing Miranda warnings, and although occupants have the constitutional right not to respond, nonresponse may be taken into consideration when determining probable cause.
4. **Search passengers' belongings, if there is probable cause.** Passengers have a diminished expectation of privacy in a vehicle, and the government's interest in effective law enforcement would be impaired because of the mobility of the vehicle.
5. **Require drunk driving suspects to take a breathalyzer test.** These tests may not be administered to all drivers, only to those suspected of drunk driving.
6. **Locate and examine the Vehicle Identification Number (VIN).** The VIN is conveniently located on the dashboard on the driver's side and is visible from outside the vehicle. Officers may compare this number with the VIN registered to the plates of the vehicle to determine whether the car is stolen.
7. **Search vehicle if probable cause develops.**
8. **Search vehicle if consent is given.** If a person intelligently and voluntarily gives consent to search a vehicle, probable cause is not required.
9. **Search passenger compartment for weapons if there is reasonable suspicion of a threat to officer safety.**
10. **Seize items in plain view.**
11. **Arrest with probable cause.**

SOURCE: Adapted from R. V. del Carmen, *Criminal Procedure: Law and Practice* (Stamford, CT: Wadsworth, 2001), 221–225.

Traditionally, officers may search and seize evidence from the passenger's compartment of the vehicle incident to a valid arrest. In *New York v. Belton* (1981), the Court held that the passenger compartment of a vehicle may be searched if the occupant is under arrest. This is similar to the Chimel rule discussed earlier—the search of the vehicle is permissible when done contemporaneous with an arrest, and officers are not required to articulate probable cause for the search. The ruling in *Belton* is considered a **bright-line rule**, which is a clear, easily understood, and easily applied standard in a specific situation. The search incident to arrest rule was revisited in *Thornton v. United States* (2004). In this case, the officer was in the process of stopping a motor vehicle when the driver parked and exited the vehicle. Unlike most police–public contacts involving motor vehicles, the initial contact occurred after the driver had exited the car and closed the door behind him. The officer discovered drugs in Marcus Thornton's pocket and placed him under arrest. Then, pursuant to the arrest that occurred outside the vehicle, the officer used the Belton rule to search the vehicle, eventually finding a firearm that petitioner Thornton was not permitted to possess because of a prior felony conviction. The Court ruled that this search was permissible, and that the evidence discovered pursuant to the search was admissible in court. The majority relied on the fact that the petitioner was under arrest, so a search pursuant to the arrest was reasonable to protect officer safety and preserve evidence.

More recently, the Court has limited the scope of the Belton rule in *Arizona v. Gant* (2009). Officers learned Rodney Gant did not possess a valid license and further observed him driving a motor vehicle. Gant was arrested, handcuffed, and placed in the back of a police car. Then, officers searched his vehicle (consistent with the Belton rule). The search of the vehicle produced drugs and drug paraphernalia. In a 7-2 ruling, the majority found the scope of the search in *Gant* to be unreasonable. They reasoned that search of a vehicle pursuant to arrest is not necessarily automatic—officers must reasonably believe that the search will produce evidence related to the crime for which the person was arrested, or the person under arrest must be in close proximity to the passenger compartment where a weapon could be obtained or evidence destroyed. In this case, Gant was arrested for driving under a suspended license, so officers could not reasonably justify searching for physical evidence related to that offense. Furthermore, Gant was secured in a police car, so he was in no position to procure a weapon or destroy evidence. This recent ruling places real limitations on vehicle searches.

## Interrogations and Confessions

Policing, at its core, involves personal contact between the officer and the public. Although these contacts occur millions of times a year, there are certain circumstances in which the police must advise citizens of their constitutional rights regarding answering questions. These procedures stem from perhaps one of the best-known cases in the history of the Supreme Court—namely, *Miranda v. Arizona* (1966). Although most people can recite the **Miranda warnings** verbatim (largely from their popularized use in television dramas), far fewer people appreciate how these rights came about, when police must use them, and whether exceptions exist. Capsules of benchmark and contemporary Supreme Court decisions are provided in Inside Policing 3.5.

Ernesto Miranda, a poor Mexican immigrant, was arrested for rape and kidnapping. Police officers interrogated Miranda for two hours while he was in custody, during which time he confessed to the crimes. After his conviction, Miranda appealed, claiming his Fifth Amendment privilege from self-incrimination was violated. The Supreme Court agreed and indicated that the police must take appropriate safeguards to ensure that a defendant's rights are not violated during such procedures. Specifically, police must advise

## INSIDE POLICING 3.5 | Selected Supreme Court Cases on Interrogations (1960 to the Present)

*Escobedo v. Illinois* (1964): Defendants have "an absolute right to remain silent" during custodial interrogations; however, the ruling did not provide police sufficient guidance on when this occurs or whether police must advise a suspect of these rights. These issues were later clarified in *Miranda v. Arizona* (1966).

*Miranda v. Arizona* (1966): To prevent police from coercing confessions, the Court established a rule that a defendant must be informed of Fifth and Sixth Amendment rights and that the defendant must waive those rights before any police interrogation.

*New York v. Quarles* (1984): Miranda warnings do not apply when circumstances dictate to the police that public safety is an important and immediate necessity. This means that under certain circumstances the police can ask incriminating questions of suspects before giving the suspect the Miranda warning. This is the public safety exception to the exclusionary rule.

*Moran v. Burbine* (1986): A request for an attorney must come from the defendant. If another party calls an attorney and the attorney contacts the police about the defendant, the police are not obligated to delay or stop an interrogation of the defendant. This attempted contact has no bearing on the admissibility of the defendant's statement if the defendant waived the right to an attorney.

*Missouri v. Seibert* (2004): Strategically withholding Miranda warnings during a custodial interrogation may render a subsequent post-Miranda confession unconstitutional.

*Florida v. Powell* (2010): The Miranda requirement is satisfied when the police advise someone of the right to talk with a lawyer before answering any questions and that this right may be invoked at any time during questioning. The police do not have to explicitly advise the person of the right to have an attorney present during questioning.

*Berghuis v. Thompkins* (2010): Suspects in a custodial interrogation must explicitly exercise their right to be silent. Statements made at the end of an interrogation where the suspect was uncommunicative (but did not state the wish to exercise these rights) are admissible in court.

*J. D. B. v. North Carolina* (2011): Courts may take suspects' age into consideration when determining whether they would reasonably believe they were in "custody" for the purposes of Miranda warnings.

defendants that (1) they have the right to remain silent, (2) any statement made may be used against the defendant in court, (3) the defendant has the right to have an attorney present during questioning, and (4) if a defendant cannot afford an attorney, then the state will appoint one before questioning. The defendant must intelligently and voluntarily waive these rights before questioning, and although this waiver does not have to be written, many police organizations do require a written waiver by the defendant.

Police must advise defendants of these rights during all custodial interrogations. **Custody** occurs when a person is deprived of their freedom in a significant way, such as during an arrest. **Interrogations** are those circumstances when the police ask questions that tend to incriminate the citizen (del Carmen 2001). The Court required giving this advice, because it recognized that custodial interrogations could be so psychologically coercive that responses may not be completely voluntary during these encounters. What makes this case so unique (and perhaps so memorable) is that the Court created active procedural safeguards for the police to follow, which are similar to a recipe for ensuring that a person's rights are not violated. But it is interesting to note that Miranda warnings are not constitutional rights per se, and that it is possible for a law to be created that would make these familiar rights a thing of the past. As the author of the majority opinion, Chief Justice Warren indicated,

> We encourage Congress and the States to continue their laudable search for increasingly effective ways of protecting the individual's rights while promoting efficient enforcement of our criminal laws. However, unless we are shown other procedures that are at least as effective in apprising accused persons of their right of silence and assuring a continuous opportunity to exercise it, the following safeguards must be observed.

Congress appeared to rise to Chief Justice Warren's challenge and, two years after the *Miranda* decision, enacted 18 USC § 3501, which held in part that any voluntary confession may be admissible in evidence against the defendant. This statute went largely unutilized until the Court considered *Dickerson v. United States* (2000). Charles Dickerson made presumably voluntary incriminating statements to the FBI during a custodial interrogation before being advised of the Miranda warnings and, because of this, argued that his statements were inadmissible as evidence against him at criminal trial. The government argued that these voluntary statements were admissible as evidence under 18 USC § 3501. Chief Justice William Rehnquist, writing for the majority, held that in fact the Miranda procedure had become an "embedded" police practice and was now a "part of our national culture"; furthermore, "Miranda announced a constitutional rule that Congress may not supersede legislatively." Despite 18 USC § 3501, the *Dickerson* decision reaffirmed the Miranda requirement during custodial interrogations.

Once someone has exercised their desire to speak with an attorney, all questioning of the accused must stop. However, if there is a significant break in time between requesting an attorney and requestioning, statements made may be admissible in trial court. In *Edwards v. Arizona* (1981), the suspect exerted his desire to speak with an attorney. The next day, the police reinitiated questioning, and this time, the defendant waived his rights and made incriminating statements. The Court held that this waiver during the second interrogation was invalid and that he could not voluntarily waive his rights so soon after exerting them. But more recently, the Court said that a significant lapse in time between interrogations could create a situation where a waiver during the subsequent interrogation was considered voluntary. In *Maryland v. Shatzer* (2010), the Court held that a break of more than two weeks created a presumption of voluntariness in the second interrogation. The Court has subsequently outlined several exceptions to the Miranda requirements.

**Public Safety Exception.** The police may ask questions of a suspect who is in custody if there is a concern for public safety, and this exception to the Miranda warnings was outlined in *New York v. Quarles* (1984). In this case, officers were approached by a woman who claimed that she had just been raped by a man fitting the description of Benjamin Quarles and that the man had a firearm. Officers found Quarles in a supermarket, placed him under arrest, and found him in possession of an empty holster. Before he was advised of his Miranda warnings, the officer asked Quarles where the gun was, to which he responded by leading the officer to the gun. The Court indicated that although Quarles was clearly in custody and the officer's questions constituted an interrogation, there existed a significant, immediate threat to public safety that permitted the officer to ask these questions without first issuing Miranda warnings. The rationale was that the threat to public safety outweighed the suspect's right to be free from self-incrimination.

**Inevitable Discovery.** If the police do not advise suspects of their Miranda warnings during custodial interrogations, then the information given during an interrogation may not be used in criminal court, according to the exclusionary rule. Furthermore, if the suspect provides information during the interrogation that leads to the recovery of physical evidence, this evidence also may not be used in court—unless the police can demonstrate that the physical evidence would have been inevitably discovered without the benefit of the information provided during the improper interrogation.

This exception was outlined in a series of cases before the Court. First, in *Brewer v. Williams* (1977), the Court indicated that the admission by the defendant would be excluded from court, because the police engaged in what amounted to a functionally equivalent interrogation. On December 24, 1969, officers were driving the suspect (Robert Anthony Williams, a religious man under arrest for kidnapping a little girl) to meet his attorney, and the suspect had previously indicated he wished to remain silent until speaking with his attorney. The officers engaged in what has been known as the "Christian burial speech," telling Williams that it would be nice if the girl's body could be recovered before Christmas so that the family could provide her with a proper Christian burial. Williams then led the police to the body, which happened to be only a few miles away from where a search party was actively looking for evidence of the crime.

Initially, the Court indicated that the admission was inadmissible in court, because the "speech" was likely to elicit an incriminating response from Williams, in violation of his Miranda warnings. And since the discovery of the body was a "fruit" produced by an improper police action, it too must be eliminated from court. However, it was later argued in *Nix v. Williams* (1984) that the search party would inevitably have discovered the body, even if Williams had not led the police to the crime scene. The Supreme Court agreed, indicating that evidence that would have inevitably been discovered by the police is admissible in court. It is important to understand that the fact that an active search party was close to discovering the body was an integral component of the Court's rationale. The ruling might have been different if the search party had not been so close to the evidence.

This chapter has thus far concentrated on issues related to criminal procedure while highlighting current legal doctrines related to searches and seizures of persons, searches and seizures of property, and the rights of the accused during police interrogations. To ensure compliance with criminal procedure, improperly obtained evidence is excluded from criminal court. However, other legal remedies are available to ensure police compliance with criminal procedure as well as with the substantive law or organizational procedure. A common remedy is civil liability.

## Civil Liability

America is a litigious society, and the police are not completely immune from such action. Civil liability is a growing concern in American policing, and this trend is not likely to change in the foreseeable future. In many ways, civil liability is inherent in the awesome power that police have in a democratic society. Civil lawsuits often arise when police officers abuse this power, engage in negligent behavior, or otherwise violate a citizen's civil rights. The risk of being sued is part of the police presence, and officers, supervisors, managers, and other agents of government understand this. However, exactly *how, why,* and *under what circumstances* they may be held liable are not always as clear.

This section offers an overview of the laws that govern civil liability for police officers. It includes the actual (and potential) costs and pervasiveness of civil lawsuits against the police, various avenues for civil litigation (including state and federal laws), emerging trends in police liability, and the unintentional cost litigation may have on officers. Police administrators must be cognizant of the law as it relates to policing innovation, and ultimately, "police executives of the future will have to sift innovations through a civil liability filter" (Kappeler 2001, 200).

## Costs of Liability in Policing

Many costs are associated with police civil liability. Beyond the obvious monetary costs, there are often ancillary costs associated with retraining officers and purchasing new equipment, as well as personal costs for officers and supervisors who are targets of litigation.

The number of civil lawsuits against the police grew during the 1960s and 1970s. An early report by the International Association of Chiefs of Police indicated there were 1,741 civil suits against the police in 1967. This estimate grew to 3,897 in 1971, an increase of 123 percent. By 1975, the number of suits nearly doubled again (del Carmen 1991), and the frequency of such suits has continued to escalate since that time. Silver (1996) estimated that police face more than 30,000 suits per year. However, the true number of civil lawsuits filed against the police is largely unknown, and this has led some to call for the creation of a national, systematic data set to fully understand the dimensions of civil liability (Vaughn, Cooper, and del Carmen 2001). In 2014, the 10 largest cities in the United States paid $248.7 million to settle police misconduct lawsuits, and over the previous five years, these departments paid over $1 billion (Elinson and Frosch 2015). Kappeler (2001) estimated that the costs of liability could be as high as $780 billion annually. In examining a nonrandom sample of insurance claims for police behavior among 350 police departments, Ouss and Rappaport (2020) found that over the past 23 years, the number of claims against the police has remained pretty stable. However, they also found that the win rate and payout associated with these claims has risen dramatically. In other words, the police may not be sued more frequently, but the civil damages are higher when they are. They note that between 2013 and 2015, which intersects with the events in Ferguson, Missouri, annual payouts for police misbehavior rose 10-fold. Inside Policing 3.6 provides a brief discussion on how insurance reform can shape accountability within police departments (Ramirez et al. 2019).

---

**INSIDE POLICING 3.6** | **Insurance and Police Reform**

This column summarizes a longer paper that suggests ways insurance companies might help encourage police departments to adopt better practices, including training, policies, and accreditation. It provides current examples but indicates that states could strengthen the impact since they regulate the insurance industry.

**Discussion Question:** Sources of "police reform" often include changes from accrediting bodies or court litigation, are imposed by consent decrees, or come from within police departments themselves. This article outlines reform-pressured insurance companies. Is it appropriate for private industry to influence reform within police agencies?

SOURCES: *Modern Policing* blog, April 12, 2016, www.oup.com/cordner/insurance-police-reform/; *Criminal Injustice* podcast, August 25, 2020, https://www.criminalinjusticepodcast.com/blog/2020/08/25/123-can-require-insurance-tame-misconduct?rq=liability

What has changed in policing over the past three decades to warrant such profound increases in civil liability? One possible answer is "nothing"; instead, the propensity of the public and its lawyers to sue officers for their actions during encounters may have increased. The increase in lawsuits may be more a function of the public's view of the police (and of government in general) as having abundant resources with which to compensate citizens for even the most meager of transgressions. There may be some truth to this perception. Kappeler (2001) reported that the average jury award for litigation against municipal government is approximately $2 million. Awards resulting from civil litigation involving the police tend to be somewhat lower than this estimate. Ross (2000) analyzed federal lawsuits alleging failure to train between 1989 and 1999 and reported that the average award for the plaintiff was around $492,794, with an additional average of $60,680 in attorneys' fees. A survey of Texas police chiefs found the typical award in police civil liability cases to be approximately $98,100; however, these amounts are often significantly reduced on appeal (Vaughn et al. 2001).

Many of these cases are settled prior to going to court. Often, the decision to settle out of court is a tactical decision designed to avoid potentially paying more money in a jury-awarded decision. In their survey of Texas police chiefs, Vaughn et al. (2001) asked chiefs about their motivations to settle. Sixty percent reported that the decision was motivated by the desire to avoid paying more money later. Indeed, there was some truth to this motivation, in that the average settlement was approximately $55,411 per case (compared with $98,100 awarded by a jury). Other motivations included wanting to make the case go away (56 percent), to avoid losing in court (38 percent), to avoid embarrassment (37 percent), and to compensate for no police wrongdoing (22 percent). Only 17 percent of police chiefs indicated that their decision to settle was in part to compensate the plaintiff for some wrongful act by the police officer. In addition to paying less than if the case proceeded to court, the municipality would not have to devote scarce resources to other costs associated with the litigation, including attorney costs, costs associated with expert testimony, and officers' time testifying in court.

Although the number of lawsuits filed for improper police behavior has increased, what is seldom reported is the success rate for plaintiffs in their quests for compensation. In truth, most police lawsuits are decided in favor of the officers, although the exact number varies considerably. Early research indicated that only about 4 percent of all claims against the police were found in favor of the plaintiff. More recent research places this figure at about 8 percent (Kappeler, Kappeler, and del Carmen 1993). In their survey of Texas police chiefs, Vaughn et al. (2001) found that chiefs reported losing approximately 22 percent of all civil suits. In his examination of federal lawsuits decided in federal district courts between 1980 and 2000, Kappeler (2001) reported that plaintiffs prevailed in 45.7 to 53.4 percent of all cases; however, "prevail" does not necessarily mean the police were found liable—only that there were sufficient grounds to warrant a jury trial since there was found to be a substantive issue before the court. Nonetheless, these civil suits can cause significant damage to the reputations of police officers and the police departments involved. Furthermore, the cost associated with protecting officers and departments from lawsuits can be high, regardless of the final determination.

## Avenues of Liability

Police may be defendants in two different ways: They may be sued in state courts for violations of state laws, or they may be sued in federal court for violations of constitutional or federally protected rights. However, it is important to understand that defendants may be held liable simultaneously in both arenas for the same action if that action violates both state torts and civil liberties. Recall that this discussion revolves around civil law; therefore, double jeopardy claims are irrelevant. In other words, if the officer's actions are negligent under state tort laws and, at the same time, are a violation of federal civil rights, the plaintiff may seek relief in both state and federal courts. To make matters more confusing, if the action by the officer is also in violation of criminal law, then prosecutors may seek indictments in criminal court as well. To understand these different procedures, we will now explore the basics of state tort law and federal liability, with particular emphasis on Title 42 § 1983 of the US Code.

## Civil Liability in State Courts

Officers and supervisors may be defendants in state courts when state torts are violated. Most suits in state court allege wrongful police conduct in which a person is injured as a result of actions conducted by another person. Generally, there are three classifications of state tort laws: (1) strict liability torts, (3) intentional torts, and (3) negligent torts. Strict liability torts involve the creation of some condition that is so hazardous the person engaging in such an activity can be reasonably certain that injury or damage will occur (Kappeler 2001). Strict liability torts rarely involve the police and thus will not be discussed in detail here.

**Intentional Torts.** **Intentional torts** involve behavior specifically designed to cause some type of injury or harm. The key to intentional torts is the *culpable state of mind of the officer*, in that their actions were purposive and designed to bring about some type of injury or property loss. Although numerous different activities may be classified as intentional torts, among the most common for police officers are excessive use of force, wrongful death, assault, battery, and false arrest.

*Excessive use of force* entails the application of physical force that is not in line with the level of resistance faced by the officer. In other words, the application of force was unreasonable. Officers are trained to match resistance by citizens with a certain level of force, but this must be *proportional* to the level of resistance by the citizen. If officers use force that is not proportional, they may be sued for intentional use of excessive force. Effective training, supervision, and documentation of use-of-force encounters between the police and the public are essential to reduce exposure to civil liability. Similarly, **wrongful death** suits may arise when an unjustified police action results in the death of a citizen. The victim's family levies a civil suit, and compensation is sought for pain and suffering, medical and funeral expenses, and loss of future earnings (del Carmen and Smith 2001).

*Assault* involves the "intentional causing of an apprehension of harmful or offensive conduct; it is the attempt or threat, accompanied by the apparent ability, to inflict bodily harm on another person" (del Carmen 1991, 18). Assault occurs when officers intentionally cause a person to fear for their own safety. An example may be that, during a custodial investigation, an officer grabs and threatens a suspect with serious physical injury, such as throwing the person out the second-floor window (Kappeler 2001). In contrast, **battery** is harmful or offensive body contact between two people, such as when an officer applies any force to an individual without justification. The basic difference between the two is that assault involves menacing conduct, whereas battery must involve actual contact (del Carmen 1991).

Claims of *false arrest* arise from intentional, illegal detention of an individual for prosecution. Typically, these suits arise from warrantless arrests, a common event in modern policing. The legal standard for making an arrest is probable cause; that is, the facts and circumstances would lead a reasonable person to believe a specific person has committed a criminal act. If officers detain a person without sufficient probable cause, this may give rise to an allegation of false arrest.

Police officers, supervisors, organizations, and municipalities are often the targets of intentional tort violations, perhaps because of their very nature. The police occupy a unique role in society, whereby they are among the few government entities sanctioned to exercise control over the public through the use of force. Given the sheer number of encounters between the police and the public coupled with the legitimate right to use coercion, it is not surprising that these civil suits occur with some frequency. However, actions only become problematic under intentional tort laws when the action is unreasonable.

**Negligent Torts.** Whereas intentional torts focus on the mental state of an individual, **negligent torts** only require *inadvertent and unreasonable behavior resulting in damage or injury* (Kappeler 2001). Negligence is an injury that is the result of a lapse of due care where the ingredients for injury were the result of some action or inaction on the officer's part. Thus, negligence provides liability for unreasonably creating a risk (Levine, Davies, and Kionka 1993). Four criteria must be satisfied to prove negligence. First is *legal duty*, which involves those actions on the part of the defendant as prescribed by the courts that require some action. Thus, there must be a legal basis for the requirement of certain behavior or activity. Second is *breach of duty* (or failure to conform with duty), which is more complex. It must be demonstrated that a reasonably prudent person would believe the officer breached their duty to a plaintiff. Third is that this breach of duty must *cause* some type of injury; in other words, but for the officer's actions, the plaintiff would not have been injured or damaged. Finally, *actual damage or injury*, including mental, physical, or economic injury, must have resulted from this action (del Carmen 1991; Hughes 2001a; Kappeler 2001).

*Failure to arrest* may be negligent behavior if the plaintiff can prove the *officer's inaction caused injury or damage*. Discretion involves the ability to choose between a course of action or inaction. Officers often do not make arrests, even when there are sufficient legal grounds to do so. Whether discretion is a virtue or a vice is beyond the parameters of the current discussion; however, officers and supervisors should recognize liabilities associated with inaction. An example of negligence may be illustrated by the circumstances surrounding *Thurman v. City of Torrington* (1985). The plaintiff, Tracey Thurman, alleged that Torrington police officers failed to arrest her estranged husband for a pattern of domestic abuse even though officers observed the abuse in question. After officers failed to arrest the suspect, Thurman sustained significant and debilitating injuries that persist to this day. Although this case was settled in federal court, the ingredients for negligent failure to arrest were also present. The *Thurman* case, along with other factors, gradually led to police departments taking a more legalistic approach to domestic abuse (Sherman 1992).

## Civil Liability in Federal Courts

Recently, there has been a tremendous increase in the number of civil liability filings against the police in federal courts. The most typical avenue for redress has come through the "resurrection" of Title 42 of the US Code, § 1983 (Barrineau 1994). In § 1983, citizens can seek relief from officials who violate their constitutional rights under the guise of their governmental positions. Title 42 USC § 1983 reads in part:

> Every person who, under color of any statute, ordinance, regulation, custom, or usage, of any State or Territory or the District of Columbia, subjects, or causes to be subjected, any citizen of the United States or other person within the jurisdiction thereof to the

deprivation of any rights, privileges, or immunities secured by the Constitution and laws, shall be liable to the party injured in an action at law, suit in equity, or other proper proceeding for redress.

As such, 42 USC § 1983 does not create any substantive rights. Instead, it outlines a procedure that individuals can follow to seek compensation for violations of their constitutional rights. There are two essential components of § 1983: (1) the defendant must be acting under the color of law and (2) there must be a violation of a constitutional or federally protected right.

**Color of Law.**    **Color of law** translates into the misuse of power possessed by an individual who is a "state actor" and derives their power from the government. Police officers are given authority and power by the state. Thus, if officers are performing typical police duties (e.g., making arrests, enforcing traffic regulations, or conducting searches and seizures of property), they are acting under the color of law (Kappeler 2001). Worrall (1998) indicated that the courts often define the color of law by asking "Was police power used?" or "Did the department authorize the act?"

Is an officer working off-duty security acting under the color of law for the purposes of liability? Can police organizations be liable under § 1983 for their actions? In other words, are there circumstances in which police officers may not act under the color of law? Vaughn and Coomes (1995, 398) noted several important exceptions and caveats to this prong of the § 1983 requirements for liability. In their review of contemporary case law on the topic, they concluded that officers act "under the color of law if they invoke police power, if they discharge duties routinely associated with police work, or if they use their authority to lure potential plaintiffs into compromising positions." Officers act under the color of law if they perform certain activities typically associated with policing, including wearing a uniform, identifying themselves as police officers, placing people under arrest, and filing reports. This is subjective from the plaintiff's point of view and depends on whether the plaintiff believed the defendant was acting as a public official.

However, if an officer, even if in uniform, acts as a private citizen and does not invoke police powers, then that officer is not acting under the color of law for liability purposes. To answer the question posed earlier, if the officer is working an off-duty assignment under the auspices and direction of the police department, then that officer's actions may be carried out under the color of law. In contrast, if the officer is working off-duty security through a private contract with a private security firm, then the officer is not acting under the color of law. Table 3.1 provides a series of situations where officers are considered acting under the color of law as well as when they are not doing so.

**Violations of Constitutional or Federally Protected Rights.**    The second prong of § 1983 involves rights protected by **constitutional or federally protected rights**. Therefore, rights provided by the states are not covered in § 1983 actions. Typically, plaintiffs will seek redress for violations in one of the amendments outlined in the Bill of Rights or the equal protection clause of the Fourteenth Amendment.

An example of § 1983 in action may be instructive. The *Graham v. Connor* (1989) decision outlines the conditions under which officers (and, by extension, police departments and municipalities) may be held civilly liable for unreasonable force, while also outlining the conditions for immunity. The plaintiff (Dethorne Graham) asked a friend to drive him to a store to obtain orange juice for his diabetic condition. On arriving at the store, Graham observed too many people in line, so he hurried out and asked his friend to drive him to a friend's house instead. A police officer, observing Graham's suspicious behavior, stopped

**TABLE 3.1**  Factors to Determine Whether an Officer Acted under the Color of Law

| OFFICERS ACT UNDER THE COLOR OF LAW IF . . . | OFFICERS DO NOT ACT UNDER THE COLOR OF LAW IF . . . |
|---|---|
| They identify themselves as a law enforcement agent. | They do not invoke police power. |
| They perform the duties of a criminal investigation. | Their inaction does not constitute state action. |
| They file official police documents. | They commit crimes in a personal dispute without invoking police power. |
| They attempt or make an arrest. | They act as federal agents. |
| They invoke their police powers outside their lawful jurisdiction. | They report the details of alleged crimes as private citizens. |
| They settle a personal vendetta with police power. | |
| They display or use police weapons/equipment. | They work for a private security company and do not identify themselves as law enforcement personnel. |
| They act pursuant to a statute or ordinance. | The department removes the officers' lawful authority. |
| The department policy mandates they are "always on duty." | |
| They intimidate citizens from exercising their rights. | |
| The department supports, facilitates, or encourages the off-duty employment of its officers as private security personnel. | |

*Source*: Adapted from M. S. Vaughn and L. F. Coomes, "Police Civil Liability under Section 1983: When Do Police Officers Act Under the Color of Law?" *Journal of Criminal Justice* 23 (1995): 409.

the car driven by Graham's friend and detained the plaintiff until he could determine what had happened in the store (although Graham explained his medical condition). After the officer determined that no crime had been committed, he released Graham. However, while Graham was in police custody, he was denied access to treatment for his medical condition and sustained injuries as a result. Graham sued the officer for violating his Fourth Amendment rights that protected him from excessive use of force. The Court held that officers might be liable pursuant to § 1983 for excessive use of force. In doing so, they determined a standard of *objective reasonableness* is to be used in such cases, indicating the force must be considered from the view of the officer at the time of the event and not in 20/20 hindsight.

*Graham* is also important because it is foundational for understanding the legal parameter of police use of force and was a large component of the Department of Justice (DOJ) investigation into the Michael Brown shooting in Ferguson, Missouri (US DOJ 2015). Inside Policing 3.7 contains an excerpt from this DOJ report. Police departments craft

## INSIDE POLICING 3.7 Legal Analysis of the Michael Brown Shooting

On August 9, 2014, Officer Darren Wilson of the Ferguson (MO) Police Department encountered Michael Brown during a pedestrian stop. By the end of the encounter, Officer Wilson had shot and killed Brown, an unarmed, 18-year-old Black male. This event served as the impetus for a week of rioting, numerous arrests, and millions of dollars in property damage, and it renewed the national conversation surrounding police interactions with and use of force on people of color, particularly young Black males. In November 2014, a St. Louis County grand jury declined to indict Officer Wilson for any criminal wrongdoing.

Following are excerpts from the DOJ's independent investigation and legal analysis of this fatal shooting and whether Wilson's actions violated Brown's federally protected rights or were criminal.

> The federal criminal statute that enforces Constitutional limits on uses of force by law enforcement officers is 18 USC § 242, which provides in relevant part, as follows: "Whoever, under color of any law, . . . willfully subjects any person . . . to the deprivation of any rights, privileges, or immunities secured or protected by the Constitution or laws of the United States [shall be guilty of a crime]."

> Sufficient credible evidence supports Wilson's claim that he reasonably perceived Brown to be posing a deadly threat.

> Wilson has stated his intent in shooting Michael Brown was in response to a perceived deadly threat. The only possible basis for prosecuting Wilson under section 242 would therefore be if the government could prove that his account is not true—*i.e.*, that Brown never assaulted Wilson at the SUV, never attempted to gain control of Wilson's gun, and thereafter clearly surrendered in a way that no reasonable officer could have failed to perceive. Given that Wilson's account is corroborated by physical evidence and that his perception of a threat posed by Brown is corroborated by other eyewitnesses . . . there is no credible evidence that Wilson willfully shot Brown as he was attempting to surrender or was otherwise not posing a threat. Even if Wilson was mistaken in his interpretation of Brown's conduct, the fact that others interpreted that conduct the same way as Wilson precludes a determination that he acted with a bad purpose to disobey the law. The same is true even if Wilson could be said to have acted with poor judgment in the manner in which he first interacted with Brown, or in pursuing Brown after the incident at the SUV. These are matters of policy and procedure that do not rise to the level of a Constitutional violation and thus cannot support a criminal prosecution.

SOURCE: Adapted from US Department of Justice, *Department of Justice Report Regarding the Criminal Investigation into the Shooting Death of Michael Brown by Ferguson, Missouri Police Officer Darren Wilson.* (Washington, DC: Department of Justice, 2015).

policies and train officers based in large part on the guidelines provided in *Graham*, yet the public is likely unaware of (and unconcerned with) these legal precedents. This presents a consequential gap between how officers and the public understand and interpret use-of-force encounters, including the aforementioned shooting in Ferguson. The general public evaluate the reasonableness of officer-involved force based on 20/20 hindsight—exactly the method *Graham* forbids. "To put it simply, citizens will review specific incidents of force and determine on a case-by-case basis whether it passes the sniff test. Hence, it is imperative for policy makers at least to be aware of how the public will perceive the reasonableness of officer action during use-of-force encounters" (Novak 2009, 156). The risk of Ferguson-like incidents remains as long as gaps between the legal parameters and public perceptions exist.

**Defenses to § 1983.** There are four instances when defendants confronted with suits under § 1983 can offer defenses for their actions, thus negating the federal lawsuit. These involve absolute immunity, qualified immunity, probably cause, and good faith.

First, a civil action is brought against those protected by *absolute immunity* will be dismissed by the court. However, this form of immunity has little application to liability for police officers, and it is typically reserved for the judiciary. The lone exception to this rule is when an officer commits perjury in court. If the officer, while testifying in criminal court, gives incorrect information that violates a person's right, the officer may seek absolute immunity from § 1983 lawsuits. However, although it is immune from civil lawsuits, the act of perjury is a criminal offense with which officers may be charged and convicted in criminal courts (Kappeler 2001).

Second, *qualified immunity* extends to police officers performing duties that are discretionary in nature. This immunity analysis hinges on two questions posed in *Saucier v. Katz* (2001). First, did the officer's conduct violate a constitutional or federally protected right? Second, was this right clearly established at the time of the action? According to Kappeler (2001, 62), "If a court determined that the law was not clearly established or that the officer's conduct was reasonable, the officer is to be afforded immunity from liability."

Qualified immunity is explored in *Groh v. Ramirez* (2004), and that case may be illustrative of how this defense is exercised in practice. As a special agent for the Bureau of Alcohol, Tobacco, and Firearms, Jeff Groh prepared a warrant to search Joseph Ramirez's home for firearms and other contraband. The warrant was approved by a federal judge, and on executing the warrant, agents indeed discovered firearms. Search warrants, as described earlier in this chapter, are required to contain four separate elements: (1) probable cause, (2) support by oath or affirmation, (3) a description of what will be searched, and (4) a description of what will be seized. The warrant in *Groh* failed to indicate exactly what was to be seized. Based on this omission, Ramirez sought civil damages against Groh and other agents who executed the warrant, reasoning that the agent (while acting under color of law) violated his right to be free from unreasonable searches and seizures. Special Agent Groh sought qualified immunity, reasoning that the omission in the warrant was merely a negligent oversight. The Court agreed with Ramirez, noting that the warrant was so deficient that a reasonable officer should have known that it was invalid. The fact that a judge approved the warrant does not absolve the officer from civil liability. The Court applied *Saucier*, indicating that the agent's behavior violated a federally protected right and that this right was clearly established at the time. The special agent was not entitled to qualified immunity from civil liability.

Third, police officers may defend themselves from federal litigation if they can claim there was *probable cause* to believe their action was legal. This is particularly important for defenses against claims of false arrest or improper searches and seizures. For example, if officers can demonstrate probable cause that a person had committed a crime or that justified a search, then redress in federal court is barred (*Hunter v. Bryant* 1991; Kappeler 2001). Even if it is later determined that probable cause did not exist, but the officer was acting on good faith, the officer is immune from liability: "Probable cause is so strong a defense in arrest and search and seizure cases that some courts have held that if probable cause is present, the officer is not liable even if malice is involved in the officer's act" (del Carmen 1991, 57).

Finally, officers may be free from civil liability if they can demonstrate their actions were conducted in *good faith*. This means the officers could not have reasonably known that their actions were in violation of law or the Constitution, such as executing a warrant that they believed to be valid. The factors the court will consider good faith actions include the following:

1. The officer acted in accordance with agency rules and regulations.
2. The officer acted pursuant to a statute that was reasonably believed to be valid, but was later declared unconstitutional.
3. The officer acted in accordance with orders from a superior that were reasonably believed to be valid.
4. The officer acted in accordance with advice from a legal counsel that was reasonably believed to be valid. (del Carmen 1991, 55–56)

## Emerging Liability Issues for the Twenty-First Century

Policing in the twenty-first century may present new challenges to police officers, supervisors, and municipalities in the civil liability arena. Changes in technology, information systems, data analysis, and society provide a dynamic environment to which police officers must adapt. As stated earlier, people may become plaintiffs in civil liability suits for violating constitutional or federally protected rights. As such, it is important for officers and police managers to remain current on changes in criminal procedure. This section does not present an exhaustive discussion of these issues, but it does provide an overview of contemporary issues confronting modern police organizations.

**Community Policing and Zero-Tolerance Policing.** Community policing is designed to increase the level of discretion of the line officer as well as the frequency of officer–citizen encounters. Officers will have more ability to make decisions, engage in problem-solving activities, and facilitate partnerships with citizens. The changing role of the police has caused some to wonder whether community policing may alter the exposure of police officers and police managers to civil liability. On the one hand, Worrall (1998) found that an organization's level of commitment was related to fewer civil liability lawsuits. Recalling the characteristics of community policing, the idea that it may decrease liability makes sense theoretically, and Vaughn et al. (2001) outlined these arguments: (1) there is an increase in women's and minority voices in police organizations designed to reduce citizens' complaints, (2) there are improvements in attitudes toward the police, and (3) there are improvements in confidence in the police and the criminal justice system. In short, because the police and the public are working in partnership, there may be less antagonism and misunderstanding between them.

On the other hand, there are several reasons to believe community policing may increase civil liability for police. First, the number of contacts between the police and the public should increase; this may lead to more opportunities for civil liability. Community policing also exposes police to areas that were not considered public matters before the community policing model. Hughes (2000), for instance, argues that increased contact with the public in new and diverse matters will logically lead to more opportunities for civil suits against the police.

Second, discretion and policy creation are shifted to the lowest level of the organization. Therefore, officers will have more opportunity and responsibility for creating and implementing policies or customs on behalf of the organization "under the color of law." This may suggest that control and accountability of police officers will decrease and make direct supervision of these officers more difficult. Indeed, direct supervision and control of officers are counter to the community policing philosophy. Similarly, police departments may have to relax the number of policies influencing the behavior of officers.

Increased liability may be demonstrated by considering New York City's experience with its **Compstat** (Compare Statistics) procedure. The New York Police Department has realized reductions in crime since the 1990s, and some attributed to their aggressive broken windows model of police services (Kelling and Bratton 2015). This style encourages officers to be proactive in their problem solving and make arrests for relatively minor violations of the law. However, Greene (1999) also noted that the number of legal filings alleging violations of civil rights has increased dramatically during the same time. Many of these complaints involved police abuse of authority or brutality.

## Use of Force

Officers expose themselves and police organizations to civil liability when excessive physical force is used during interactions with the public. Excessive use of force is considered an unreasonable seizure of an individual and therefore a violation of the Fourth Amendment, which creates the potential for § 1983 action. This was introduced earlier in this chapter (*Graham v. Connor* 1989), and the use of force will be more fully explored in Chapter 10. However, an increasingly popular form of less-lethal force being adopted by police departments is conducted energy devices (CEDs), also known as Tasers. The Court has yet to fully examine under what conditions the application of CEDs is considered unreasonable, creating a potential for an emerging source of liability for police in America.

CEDs provide an attractive option for officers who are confronted with active resistance by citizens. CEDs release an electrical charge that temporarily incapacitates the suspect. Unlike other forms of less-than-lethal force, such as batons, PR-24 batons, or oleoresin capsicum spray (OC spray, Mace, or pepper spray), CEDs can be applied at a distance, reducing the need for officers to be in close proximity with the citizen; thus, it is a safer use-of-force alternative for officers. The availability of CEDs may also decrease the frequency of firearm use, which creates fewer lethal-force incidents. Because of this, many police departments have recently adopted CEDs into their use-of-force options for officers (White and Ready 2007).

However, debate exists regarding whether CEDs are truly safe alternatives during less-than-lethal police–public encounters. Amnesty International (2008) noted an unacceptable frequency of in-custody deaths during CED applications and called for police departments to either discontinue or significantly limit when they can be used. Research by Lee et al. (2009) found that in-custody deaths increased 6.4-fold in police departments in the year following the introduction of the use of CEDs, whereas firearm use decreased 2.3 times. However, in-custody deaths and firearm use returned to "normal" levels in two to five years, essentially regressing to the mean. No change in officer injuries was reported in the five-year follow-up. The researchers concluded that given the significant potential for death associated with CEDs, it may not be an appropriate less-than-lethal-force alternative. The dilemma for police is how to properly train officers on when CEDs should be used during interactions with resistant suspects and where in the use-of-force continuum it is appropriate to place CEDs. Some recommend that CEDs are properly placed below intermediate on the continuum (Hough and Tatum 2009). However, given the potential for unintended injury or death, it may be more appropriate to reserve CED application for more resistant suspects or when there is an immediate threat to officers or others and less intrusive tactics are unavailable.

A 2009 case from the Ninth Circuit Court of Appeals addresses the issue of civil liability and CED application. The case considered whether Officer Brian McPherson was entitled to qualified immunity during a use-of-force encounter when applying a CED. Carl Bryan was pulled over for a seatbelt violation. Bryan, reported to be quite agitated and clothed only in boxer shorts and tennis shoes, exited his vehicle despite Officer McPherson's directions to remain in the vehicle. Bryan was resistant in that he was not following verbal commands; however, he was neither assaultive nor attempting to flee. Officer McPherson discharged a CED without warning when Bryan was 20 feet from the officer and facing the opposite direction. The CED immobilized Bryan, and his subsequent fall caused facial contusions and fractured four teeth. Bryan filed for civil damages under 42 USC § 1983. The Court of Appeals held that the use of the CED in this circumstance was unconstitutionally excessive and denied Officer McPherson's request for qualified immunity. The Appellate Court reasoned that this was a minor offense, there was no immediate threat to the officer, and less intrusive tactics were more appropriate. The officer should have recognized the significant potential for unintended harm associated with using a CED under these circumstances, and a reasonable officer should have known that it was unreasonable to deploy this level of force during the encounter. The fact that the officer did not intend to cause the level of harm that was actually inflicted is irrelevant. The Appellate Court, in denying qualified immunity, concluded that the law was clearly established and that the officer should have realized the application of force was excessive (*Bryan v. McPherson* 2009).

In summary, CEDs are an emerging civil liability threat in American policing since they are becoming increasingly popular, but there is a lack of consensus among citizens, police administrators, and the legal community as to appropriate application.

## Impact on Officers

Officers and supervisors must accept the potential for civil liability as a part of policing. In a survey of police officers, Hughes (2001b) found that 18.5 percent of officers had been sued for a job-related matter, and that 74.8 percent of officers personally knew an officer who had been named in a lawsuit for a job-related matter. In the same survey, 86.4 percent felt that officers are sued even when acting properly. This has led some officers to view public complaints and lawsuits as just another part of policing.

Although the media tend to focus on plaintiff experiences, it is also important to consider the impact of a lawsuit from the officer's perspective. When officers and supervisors are sued for wrongdoing, there may be effects beyond the obvious loss of monetary resources. When named as a defendant in a civil lawsuit, an officer may experience heightened levels of stress and anxiety. Pursuant to citizen complaints or civil litigation, officers are often interrogated regarding the act in question as well as past behavior and disciplinary records. Officers often report administrative policies, discipline, and a perceived lack of support as important sources of stress. However, these organizational responses, at least in part, may be reactions by supervisors and municipalities to insulate themselves from litigation. Still, officers may interpret these reactions as the organization not "backing" them, citizens being out to "get rich" at the expense of officers, and "no one respecting what the police do." Not only does the stress of many officers increase, but these problems may also lead to increased cynicism among officers. Inside Policing 3.8 provides one officer's account of being the subject of a civil lawsuit.

## INSIDE POLICING 3.8    The Civil Lawsuit Experience

Civil lawsuits impact officers in significant ways, regardless of the outcome. Joan C. Barker conducted extended research with the Los Angeles Police Department that gave her unprecedented access to conversations and observations into the lives of police officers. Following is one officer's experience of being sued:

We were on loan to Hollywood because they were having the Christmas parade. So we were working the crowd, people were just arriving, and everyone was in a good mood. Lots of people. Families and such. And everything was fine when this citizen came over and told us that there was a man down and bleeding. We went to see this guy, and he was down and out. All bloody. He was passed out, and when I leaned over to talk to him, he woke and said he'd been in a bar and got in a fight and got himself beat up; and then he saw who we were, that we were police, and became all combative. Calling us "pigs" and that sort of thing. He was drunk and not hearing at all what we had to say. He was swearing and spitting at the [pedestrians]. And now there were lots of people, mothers and their children, all coming to this parade.

Here's this beat-up drunk swearing and carrying on. This guy was saying real foul things, bad language and spitting at the people . . . and we told him to "shut up," but we said it nicer at the time. The first time we did, then later it was just "shut up." But we handcuffed him, and he was spitting and kicking out at people, so we thought, "We can't have this." So we got out the restraints and tied him so he couldn't kick anymore. Had to pick him up and carry him to where we could get a car for transport. And the sergeant said we should take him to county and get him [treated] and absentee to book him, and we did. Eight hours, eight hours of paperwork because of this guy.

And that was it. We thought that was it, and then we get summonses. [My partner] and I got the summonses and we didn't even know what they were talking about. It had been five years since the incident. We didn't even recognize the name. It wasn't even familiar to me; I had to go through my officer's notebook to find out what had happened, and then I remembered the guy and what happened. Now, this is what he alleges. He alleges that my partner and I went into this gay bar, and pulled him out and beat him up, because he was gay, and then arrested him. He didn't even know what had happened to him, but that was his story. I actually think he really believes that we did it. I think he really didn't remember what really happened and thought we did it. He alleged this, brought this to a lawyer five years later. Five years! Half a decade. Where are you going to get the witnesses [even] three years later? Just [my partner] and me and the sergeant.

It was the worst time of my life, to be accused of something and not be able to prove myself innocent. To not even have the opportunity to prove myself because the city was busy covering its ass. [very agitated] I didn't do anything, and everybody knew it. I had a partner and a sergeant, and they took the deposition of [my partner], but didn't even call the sergeant in. They didn't even need us because they'd already decided. They just paid the fucker thirty-five hundred dollars, and it goes in my package that there was an action against me and the city paid. How does that look?

When the partner was interviewed, he stated,

After that time I did as little as I could and had as little contact with citizens as possible. I used to work the L car [a one-officer unit that handles reports most of the time], so I was only there if they asked me to be there. And there was a record of that. I didn't do anything else if I could help it. It didn't make any sense to do anything—any real police work. Not patrol. I didn't want to go through that again.

Based on this description, it is apparent the officers harbored resentment toward the city for settling the lawsuit. By settling out of court, the city avoided additional costs associated with the lawsuit, but it sent a message to the officers (and perhaps other officers in the department) that they had done something wrong. This also led to one officer seeking assignments not involving contact with citizens to avoid similar situations. It is important to recognize that civil lawsuits are stressful events for officers and that these lawsuits (regardless of the outcome) may increase the level of officer cynicism and stress.

SOURCE: Adapted from J. C. Barker. *Danger, Duty and Disillusion* (Prospect Heights, IL: Waveland, 1999), 128–129.

Even when they are not identified as defendants, civil lawsuits can impact other officers in the police organization. In the wake of a lawsuit, officers may feel the need to proactively engage in fewer interactions with the public, particularly officer-initiated encounters. Officers rationalize this as a normal response to what they feel is an unjust situation, and further rationalize that their own likelihood of being named as a defendant in a lawsuit decreases if they interact with fewer citizens. This phenomenon has been called **depolicing** or, more recently, the Ferguson effect. Some have cautioned that officers' hesitancy to engage in proactive behaviors (to avoid public scrutiny) will lead to increases in crime (Mac Donald 2015). Yet empirical evidence of the Ferguson effect is conflicting. Rosenfeld (2015) examined homicides and other violent crimes in St. Louis for several years and found no evidence that the highly publicized shooting of Michael Brown and subsequent civil unrest was significantly correlated with violence, and careful analysis fails to support the Ferguson effect. A comprehensive analysis of 53 large cities assessed the relationship between changes in arrest patterns to changes in homicides. The reasoning was that if, in fact, depolicing had occurred after Ferguson, then a strong negative relationship between arrests (particularly arrests of Blacks for minor offenses) and homicides would appear. While the research revealed declines in arrest rates, this trend had begun before the events in Ferguson—arrest rates had been trending downward for years, and this was not the result of a sudden, abrupt shift in 2014. More important, no relationship between arrest and homicide rates was observed, including in 2015 when homicide rates spiked. This calls into question the existence of depolicing in general, and the correlation between depolicing and homicide in particular (Rosenfeld and Wallman 2019).

There is some evidence indicating that the events in Ferguson have impacted officers' attitudes and behavior (Deuchar et al. 2019; Nix and Wolfe 2018). For example, Wolfe and Nix's (2015) examination of officers' attitudes provides some support for the notion that officers may be less motivated to engage in partnerships because of press within the media. However, this reluctance is mitigated among officers with a strong orientation toward organizational justice and self-legitimacy. Collectively, the evidence appears to suggest that high-profile events (and perhaps subsequent civil liability associated with these effects) can impact officers' attitudes and behavior; however, in contrast to Mac Donald's (2015) assertions, the direct link between any "depolicing" and crime is far from clear or inevitable (Capellan et al 2019).

Additional empirical research suggests that the phenomenon of depolicing may be limited to posttraumatic events, such as those described previously. Novak, Smith, and Frank (2003) examined whether officers who had experienced civil liability claims behaved differently than other officers. Their basic hypotheses were that officers will behave less aggressively (e.g., fewer proactive encounters with citizens, arrests, use of force, and searches) if they have previously been sued, known officers who have been sued, or are highly cognizant of liability during the course of their activities. In other words, officers who have more experience with litigation will subsequently avoid situations that increase their exposure to liability. However, the data did not support these hypotheses. It appeared that an officer's aggressive behavior was largely unaffected by personal experience with litigation. Although it is important not to confuse aggressive and proactive behavior with improper behavior, it appears that officers may not allow fear of litigation to hamper them from engaging in proactive law enforcement activities. Relatedly, Hickman, Piquero, and Greene's (2000) analysis of officers in Philadelphia indicated that officers assigned to community policing roles performed at parity with officers assigned to more traditional police roles regarding generation of citizen complaints. They found no difference between officers in proportion, type, or frequency of citizen complaints filed against them.

De-policing is a phenomena that continues to occupy public discussions. This is particularly true after the events in 2020, specifically, police responses to protests to the George Floyd murder. Mikdash and Zaiour (2022) noted that officer-initiated activities in Minneapolis decreased significantly after the Floyd murder. Additionally, the COVID-19 pandemic likely influenced officer-initiated activities in several ways (Nielson et al. 2022), depending on the jurisdiction. Around the same time, violent crime began to surge in the United States, and public protests were commonplace in many cities. Responding to increases in violence and protest likely taxed police personnel resources, providing less discretionary time for officers to engage in self-initiated behaviors.

Nevertheless, whether depolicing is real or imagined, the perceived threat of depolicing can have implications for police managers. The most effective way to avoid this phenomenon is to maintain an environment that does not allow it to occur in the first place. Supervisors who manage those engaged in depolicing must take additional steps to explain to officers that avoiding encounters with the public is not in line with organizational goals and comprises unethical behavior. Effective policing involves maintaining a healthy relationship with citizens. By engaging in depolicing, officers alienate not only citizens who are frustrated with the police but also citizens who support the police. Over time, depolicing likely will fade away, and police officer activity will regress to the mean (or return to previous levels). In the meantime, the department may sustain irreparable damage to public trust, public support, and the department's reputation. Building on the research by Wolfe and Nix (2015), police managers can mitigate officers' temptation to engage in depolicing by encouraging self-legitimacy and organizational justice. In other words, healthy organizations that promote (internal) distributive justice, procedural justice, and interactional justice can avoid depolicing and its potential negative consequences.

## Summary

Criminal procedure is the process by which a person accused of a crime is processed through the criminal justice system and outlines the rules that the government must follow to ensure the civil liberties of citizens. Police officers may stop a citizen only if there is reasonable suspicion to believe criminal activity is afoot, and they may frisk that citizen only if there is reasonable suspicion to believe that the person is armed, posing a threat to officer safety. Arrests can only occur if the legal threshold is elevated to probable cause. Pursuant to an arrest, officers may search the person and the area within that person's immediate control or may perform a protective sweep for others who may pose a threat to officer safety. Like arrests, searches of property must be conducted only with probable cause. Although there is a preference for obtaining a search warrant before engaging in a search of property, notable exceptions to this requirement include the plain-view doctrine, the open-fields doctrine, and the hot-pursuit exception. The courts have indicated that persons in motor vehicles enjoy a diminished expectation to privacy, and searches of motor vehicles are more relaxed than those of private homes. Before questioning suspects who are in custody, officers must advise them of their Miranda warnings, and these rights must be intelligently and voluntarily waived before questioning. Notable exceptions to the Miranda requirement include the public safety exception and inevitable discovery.

Civil litigation regarding police behavior increased, both in the number of suits filed and in the amount of money paid for damages or injury, in the 1960s and 1970s, however has remained relatively stable in recent decades. People who initiate lawsuits (called plaintiffs) against the police (called defendants) may do so in either state or federal courts. In state courts, torts may be brought for intentional as well as negligent behavior. In federal courts, plaintiffs may bring lawsuits against the police if there is a violation of constitutional rights or federally protected rights. Often, these lawsuits are filed under 42 USC § 1983. To be successful in a § 1983 lawsuit, the plaintiff must demonstrate that the officer acted under the color of law and that the act violated the plaintiff's civil rights. Acceptable defenses to § 1983 lawsuits include absolute immunity, qualified immunity, probable cause, and good faith. Although community policing may decrease the incidence of civil liability in policing, there is an equal chance that civil liability will increase. Regardless of whether plaintiffs prevail in their lawsuits against the police (and most do not), the process can cause negative consequences for police officers, including increased stress and cynicism.

## Critical Thinking Questions

1. Discuss the difference between reasonable suspicion and probable cause as well as the permissible behaviors associated with these legal thresholds.

2. Compare and contrast the criminal justice system with the civil system of justice.

3. Discuss the ways in which the police must balance the need for public safety with the need to ensure the civil liberties of citizens.

4. Does requiring the police to advise suspects of their Miranda warnings unduly handcuff the police? Support your answer.

5. What is more effective at controlling police behavior, the exclusionary rule or civil litigation? Why?

6. Describe 42 US § 1983. What key components are necessary for a claim under § 1983?

7. Under what circumstances do officers act "under the color of law," and why is it important to understand this?

8. Will community policing increase or decrease the number of civil liability claims? Support your answer.

# References

*Alabama v. White*, 496 US 325 (1990).

Amnesty International. 2008. "'Less Than Lethal'? The Use of Stun Weapons in US Law Enforcement." London: Amnesty International.

*Arizona v. Gant*, 556 US 332 (2009).

*Arizona v. Hicks*, 480 US 321 (1987).

*Arizona v. Johnson*, 555 US 323 (2008).

Barrineau, H. E. 1994. *Civil Liability in Criminal Justice*, 2nd ed. Cincinnati, OH: Anderson.

*Berghuis v. Thompkins*, 560 US 370 (2010).

*Brendlin v. California*, 551 US 249 (2007).

*Brewer v. Williams*, 430 US 387 (1977).

*Brinegar v. United States*, 338 US 160, 176 (1949).

*Bryan v. McPherson*, No. 08-55622, US Ninth Circuit (2009).

*California v. Greenwood* 486 U.S. 35 (1988).

Capellan, J. A., Lautenschlager, R., and Silva, J. R. 2019. "Deconstructing the Ferguson Effect: A Multi-level Mediation Analysis of Public Scrutiny, de-policing, and Crime." *Journal of Crime and Justice*, 43, 125–144.

*Carroll v. United States*, 267 US 132 (1925).

*Chimel v. California*, 395 US 752 (1969).

del Carmen, R. V. 1991. *Civil Liabilities in American Policing: A Text for Law Enforcement Personnel*. Englewood Cliffs, NJ: Prentice Hall.

del Carmen, R. V. 2001. *Criminal Procedure: Law and Practice*, 5th ed. Belmont, CA: Wadsworth.

del Carmen, R. V., and Smith, M. R. 2001. "Police, Civil Liability, and the Law." In R. G. Dunham and G. P. Alpert (eds.), *Critical Issues in Policing*, 4th ed., pp. 181–198. Prospect Heights, IL: Waveland.

Deuchar, R., Fallik, S. W. and Crichlow, V. J. 2019. "Despondent Officer Narratives and the 'Post-Ferguson' Effect: Exploring Law Enforcement Perspectives and Strategies in a Southern American State." *Policing and Society*, 29, 1042–1057.

*Dickerson v. United States*, 530 US 428 (2000).

*Edwards v. Arizona*, 451 US 477 (1981).

Elinson, Z., and Frosch, D. 2015. "Cost of Police-Misconduct Cases Soars in Big US Cities." *Wall Street Journal*, July 15. https://www.wsj.com/articles/cost-of-police-misconduct-cases-soars- in-big-u-s-cities-1437013834/.

*Escobedo v. Illinois*, 378 US 478 (1964).

*Fernandez v. California*, 571 US 292 (2014).

*Florence v. Board of Chosen Freeholders of the County of Burlington*, 565 US 318 (2012).

*Florida v. Bostick*, 501 US 429 (1991).

*Florida v. Jardines*, 569 US 1 (2013).

*Florida v. Powell*, 559 US 50 (2010).

*Georgia v. Randolph*, 547 US 103 (2006).

*Graham v. Connor*, 490 US 397 (1989).

Greene, J. A. 1999. "Zero Tolerance: A Case Study of Police Policies and Practices in New York City." *Crime and Delinquency* 45: 171–187.

*Groh v. Ramirez*, 540 US 551 (2004).

*Herring v. United States*, 555 US 135 (2009).

Hickman, M. J., Piquero, A. R., and Greene, J. R. 2000. "Does Community Policing Generate Greater Numbers and Different Types of Citizen Complaints Than Traditional Policing?" *Police Quarterly* 3: 70–84.

Hough, R. M., and Tatum, K. M. 2009. "Examining the Utility of the Use of Force Continuum: TASERs and Potential Liability." *Law Enforcement Executive Forum* 9: 37–50.

*Hudson v. Michigan*, 547 US 586 (2006).

Hughes, T. 2000. *Community Policing and Federal Civil Liability under 42 USC § 1983.* Unpublished doctoral dissertation, University of Cincinnati.

Hughes, T. 2001a. "*Board of the County Commissioners of Bryan County, Oklahoma v. Jill Brown*: Municipal Liability and Police Hiring Decisions." *Justice Professional* 13: 143–162.

Hughes, T. 2001b. "Police Officers and Civil Liability: 'The Ties That Bind'?" *Policing: An International Journal of Police Strategies and Management* 24: 240–262.

*Hunter v. Bryant*, 502 US 224, 112 S. Ct. 634 (1991).

*Illinois v. Caballes*, 543 US 405 (2005).

*Illinois v. Lidster*, 540 US 419 (2004).

*Illinois v. McArthur*, 531 US 326 (2001).

*Illinois v. Wardlow*, 528 US 119 (2000).

*Indianapolis v. Edmond*, 531 US 32 (2000).

*J. D. B. v. North Carolina*, 564 US 261 (2011).

Kappeler, V. E. 2001. *Critical Issues in Police Civil Liability*, 3rd ed. Prospect Heights, IL: Waveland.

Kappeler, V. E., Kappeler, S. F., and del Carmen, R. V. 1993. "A Content Analysis of Police Civil Liability Cases: Decisions in the Federal District Courts, 1978-1990." *Journal of Criminal Justice* 21: 325–337.

*Katz v. United States*, 389 US 347 (1967).

Kelling, G. L. and Bratton, W. J. 2015. "Why We Need Broken Windows Policing." *The City Journal.* Available at https://www.city-journal.org/html/why-we-need-broken-windows-policing-13696.html

Klotter, J. C. 1999. *Legal Guide for Police: Constitutional Issues*, 5th ed. Cincinnati, OH: Anderson.

*Kyllo v. United States*, 533 US 27 (2001).

Lee, B. K., Vittinghoff, E., Whiteman, D., Park, M., Lau, L. L., and Tseng, Z. H. 2009. "Relation of Taser (Electrical Stun Gun) Deployment to Increase in In-Custody Sudden Deaths." *The American Journal of Cardiology* 103: 877–880.

Levine, L., Davies, J., and Kionka, E. 1993. *A Torts Anthology.* Cincinnati: Anderson.

Mac Donald, H. 2015. "The New Nationwide Crime Wave." *The Wall Street Journal*, May 29. https://www.wsj.com/articles/the-new-nationwide-crime-wave-1432938425/.

*Mapp v. Ohio*, 367 US 643 (1961).

*Maryland v. Buie*, 494 US 325 (1990).

*Maryland v. Pringle*, 540 US 366 (2003).

*Maryland v. Shatzer*, 599 US 98 (2010).

*Michigan Department of State Police v. Sitz*, 496 US 444 (1990).

Mikdash, M. and Zaiour, R., 2022. "Does (All) Police Violence cause De-policing? Evidence from George Floyd and Police Shootings in Minneapolis." *AEA Papers and Proceedings* 112: 170-173.

*Minnesota v. Dickerson*, 508 US 366 (1993).

*Miranda v. Arizona*, 384 US 436 (1966).

*Missouri v. McNeely*, 569 US 141 (2013).

*Missouri v. Seibert*, 542 US 600 (2004).

*Moran v. Burbine*, 475 US 412 (1986).

*New York v. Belton*, 453 US 454 (1981).

*New York v. Quarles*, 467 US 649 (1984).

Nielson, K. R., Zhang, Y., and Ingram, J. R. 2022. "The Impact of COVID-19 on Police Officer Activities." *Journal of Criminal Justice* 82: https://doi.org/10.1016/j.jcrimjus.2022.101943

*Nix v. Williams*, 467 US 431 (1984).

Nix, J., and Wolfe, S. E. (2018), "Management-Level Officers' Experiences with the Ferguson Effect." *Policing: An International* Journal, 41, 262–275.

Novak, K. J. 2009. "Reasonable Officers, Public Perceptions and Policy Challenges." *Criminology and Public Policy* 8: 153–161.

Novak, K. J., Smith, B., and Frank, J. 2003. "Strange Bedfellows: Civil Liability and Aggressive Policing." *Policing: An International Journal of Police Strategies and Management* 26: 352–368.

*Oliver v. United States*, 466 US 170 (1984).

Ouss, A., and Rappaport, J. 2020. "Is Police Behavior Getting Worse? Data Selection and the Measurement of Policing Harms." *Journal of Legal Studies*, 49, 153–198.

*Payton v. New York*, 445 US 573 (1981).

Ramirez, D., Wraight, M., Kilmister, L., and Perkins, C. 2019. "Policing the Police: Could Mandatory Professional Liability Insurance for Officers Provide a New Accountability Model?" *American Journal of Criminal Law*, 45, 407–460.

*Riley v. California*, 573 US 373 (2014).

*Rodriguez v. United States*, 575 US (2015).

Rosenfeld, R. 2015. "Was There a 'Ferguson Effect' on Crime in St. Louis?" *The Sentencing Project*. https://www.sentencingproject.org/wp-content/uploads/2015/09/Ferguson-Effect.pdf.

Rosenfeld, R., and Wallman, J. 2019. "Does De-policing Cause the Increase in Homicide Rates?" *Criminology and Public Policy*, 1–25. doi:10.1111/1745-9133.12414.

Ross, D. L. 2000. "Emerging Trends in Police Failure to Train Liability." *Policing: An International Journal of Police Strategies and Management* 23: 169–193.

*Saucier v. Katz*, 533 US 194 (2001).

*Schneckloth v. Bustamonte*, 412 US 218, 219 (1973).

Sherman, L. W. 1992. *Policing Domestic Violence*. New York: Free Press.

Silver, I. 1996. *Police Civil Liability*. New York: Bender.

*Terry v. Ohio*, 392 US 1 (1968).

*Thornton v. United States*, 541 US 615 (2004).

*Thurman v. City of Torrington*, 595 F. Supp. 1521 (1985).

*Utah v. Strieff*, 579 US (2016).

*United States v. Jones*, 565 US 400 (2012).

*United States v. Leon*, 468 US 897 (1984).

*United States v. Ross*, 456 US 798 (1982).

*United States v. Seslar*, 996 F 2d. 1058 (10th Cir.) (1993).

*United States v. Watson*, 423 US 411 (1976).

US Department of Justice. 2015. *Department of Justice Report Regarding the Criminal Investigation into the Shooting Death of Michael Brown by Ferguson, Missouri Police Officer Darren Wilson*. Washington, DC: Department of Justice.

Vaughn, M. S., and Coomes, L. F. 1995. "Police Civil Liability Under Section 1983: When Do Police Officers Act Under the Color of Law?" *Journal of Criminal Justice* 23: 395–415.

Vaughn, M. S., Cooper, T. W., and del Carmen, R. V. 2001. "Assessing Legal Liabilities in Law Enforcement: Police Chiefs' Views." *Crime and Delinquency* 47: 3–27.

*Weeks v. United States*, 232 US 383 (1914).

White, M. D., and Ready, J. 2007. "The TASER as a Less Lethal Force Alternative: Findings on Use and Effectiveness in a Large Metropolitan Agency." *Police Quarterly* 10: 170–191.

*Whren v. United States*, 517 US 806 (1996).

Wolfe, S. E., and Nix, J. 2015. "The Alleged 'Ferguson Effect' and Police Willingness to Engage in Community Partnership." *Law and Human Behavior* 40: 1–10. doi:10.1037/lhb0000164.

Worrall, J. L. 1998. "Administrative Determinants of Civil Liability Lawsuits against Municipal Police Departments: An Exploratory Analysis." *Crime and Delinquency* 44: 295–313.

Worrall, J. L. 2010. *Criminal Procedure: From First Contact to Appeal*, 3rd ed. Boston: Pearson Prentice Hall.

*Wyoming v. Houghton*, 526 US 295 (1999).

Zalman, M., and Siegel, L. 1997. *Criminal Procedure: Constitution and Society*, 2nd ed. Belmont, CA: West/Wadsworth.

# CHAPTER 4

# Police Strategies

## CHAPTER OUTLINE

| **KEY TERMS** | | |

- broad function
- broken windows theory
- case screening
- citizen input
- community crime prevention
- community policing
- computer-aided dispatch
- crime analysis
- differential police response
- directed patrol
- evidence-based policing
- flexible operations
- geographic focus
- hot spots policing
- partnerships
- personal service
- police–community relations
- positive interaction
- prevention emphasis
- problem-oriented policing
- problem solving
- solvability factors
- SARA model
- team policing

CHAPTER 2 ("POLICE HISTORY") discussed the political era of American policing (the 1800s and early 1900s) and the reform/professional era that followed on its heels in the twentieth century. During each era, there was broad consensus about how police departments should be organized and what police officers should do; in other words, there was agreement about the best police strategy. That began to change in the 1960s and 1970s, however, partly because of changes in American society and partly because of improved knowledge about the effectiveness (or lack thereof) of different police practices. Initially, community policing (COP) became the next dominant model of policing, but of equal significance, it became clear that police departments could choose from among multiple strategies, each with their own strengths and weaknesses. This chapter explains how and why the contemporary police strategies of COP and problem-oriented policing (POP) developed. Subsequent police strategies, such as intelligence-led policing and predictive policing, along with a general framework for comparing and assessing the strengths and weaknesses of various strategic options are taken up later in Chapter 8.

## Evolving Strategies of Policing

Social upheaval and the drawbacks of the reform/professional model of policing, especially its legalistic orientation and its tendency to isolate the police from the public, continued to be of concern to many police, political leaders, and academics in the 1970s and 1980s (Kelling and Moore 1988). These concerns tended to focus heavily on unsatisfactory relationships between police and their communities, especially minority communities. At the same time, crime rates increased steadily throughout the 1970s, suggesting that the prevailing methods of policing associated with the professional model were failing on two important counts: public trust and crime control. These two key issues, together with new information from police research and ongoing trial and error within the police field, help account for the initial experimentation with COP in the 1980s and then its dramatic increase in popularity both during and after the 1990s.

In regard to research, major studies of three central components of police operations shook the foundations of the reform/professional model of policing. Beginning in the 1970s, studies cast doubts on (1) the effectiveness of reactive motorized patrol in controlling crime, (2) the need for a rapid response to every report of a crime and request for service, and (3) the effectiveness of criminal investigation. Although these studies had limitations, the research raised significant questions about whether the police were using the best methods to control crime. This inquisitive and questioning approach has become ingrained in modern policing, leading to continuous efforts to develop more effective tactics and strategies.

The police were also encouraged to broaden their use of research and analysis to solve crime and disorder problems. Goldstein (1990) recommended that the police begin to think in terms of problems rather than incidents; that is, they should change from an incident-based response strategy to a problem-oriented strategy by viewing groups of incidents as problems that might be caused by identifiable underlying conditions. Goldstein argued that officers should not only try to determine the relationship between incidents that might be occurring in the same family, building, or area, for example, but also consider alternatives other than law enforcement to try to solve problems, thereby decreasing the number of future incidents. The key to this problem-oriented approach is the use of data to analyze problems to discover exactly what they are and why they are occurring.

Data, analysis, and computers have also pushed police departments in the direction of becoming more data driven, intelligence led, and even predictive. Reactive policing, especially in the form of next-day investigations of reported crimes and weekly crime analysis briefings, is no longer considered viable. Instead, policing is expected to be smarter and more proactive. This proactive trend in modern police strategy was already underway before the events of September 11, 2001, but since then, the enormous pressure on police to discover and prevent terrorist attacks before they happen has given the approach significant additional momentum.

In Chapter 1, we mentioned that strategies are the broad approaches police agencies take in trying to accomplish their multiple goals. During the political era, the goal of maintaining order ("keeping a lid on things") in a growing and rambunctious new country with a still-developing legal system was the main policing priority. Then, in the reform/professional era, the goal of controlling crime through enforcement of the law took precedence. Today, however, there is greater awareness of the multiple goals of policing, but also less clarity about which of the goals should be top priorities. To be sure, controlling crime is still of great significance. However, we are more conscious of the necessity of good **police–community relations** to reinforce the legitimacy of the police in a free society, we are more aware of how important it is that people feel safe (regardless of the actual amount of crime), we are less tolerant when police fail to exercise their power and authority fairly, and we are increasingly adamant that police achieve all these goals at the lowest possible cost. In addition, there is greater awareness today of different programs and practices for achieving these various goals, along with more knowledge about how well those methods actually work.

In these modern circumstances, a police department is challenged to design and implement the strategy, or combination of strategies, that will work best in its community (Moore and Trojanowicz 1988). This is relatively new for policing—in the past, at any one time, there was only one strategy to use. Today's police leaders, in contrast, must think about strategies, make decisions about strategies, and then be held accountable for having implemented the most effective strategies.

## Landmark Studies of Police Effectiveness

Prior to the 1970s, a limited amount of research focused on police effectiveness. As a result, police organizations implemented programs and strategies based mainly on tradition and professional judgment, which are useful sources of wisdom but are also prone to the justification "we've always done it this way." Since the 1970s, however, a significant amount of research has been conducted on various aspects of police operations and police strategy, much of it yielding important policy implications. In "Voices from the Field," Darrel Stephens, the former police chief from Charlotte–Mecklenburg, North Carolina, reflects on the impact of this research during his career.

## Darrel Stephens

*Executive Director (ret.), Major Cities Chiefs Association; Chief of Police (ret.), Charlotte–Mecklenburg, North Carolina*

Policing in America has changed over my 50-year career. It is not the same institution that was chronicled in the series of Presidential Commission reports on crime and the administration of justice in the late 1960s and early 1970s—it is much better. A great deal more is known about the impact of the fundamental strategies the police have used for many years to address crime problems. We know more about the limitations of the police and how they might be more effective. Police departments are more diverse, educational levels of police officers have significantly increased, and both citizen oversight and community engagement are stronger.

Although policing has clearly improved over the years, there are continuing challenges. High-profile officer-involved deaths have eroded the confidence the public has in the police and highlighted gaps in trust between white and Black residents. There have been significant increases in homicide and aggravated assault in many urban areas in the last few years. Currently, the police are struggling to fill vacancies as officers leave the profession because they feel unappreciated and overworked. The COVID-19 pandemic exacerbated the staffing situation and reduced in-person contact with the community. Combined, these things contribute to an environment where it is difficult to provide basic services—many police agencies have stopped responding to some calls for service and have increased the use of telephone and online reporting for property crimes. And there are agencies contracting with private security companies to provide some services. Adding to these challenges are calls across the country for reforming and reimagining policing.

Community and problem-oriented policing have evolved over the years. These ideas called for a fundamental change in the way the police related to citizens and stakeholders. Citizens are more than the "eyes and ears" of the police feeding the criminal justice system—citizens are viewed as partners who have ideas, resources, and the ability to do things that can prevent crime as well as solve it. The police use problem-solving techniques to gain deeper insight into the issues that they are called on to address and to develop tailored solutions that have a longer-lasting impact on the problem. Moreover, these solutions are not confined to a law enforcement response. The response might be aimed at prevention or engaging other community or governmental resources that are in a better position than the police to deal with the problem.

But the status of community and problem-oriented policing remains a bit unsettled. The post-9/11 era added additional responsibilities to police and local government related to terrorism response and prevention. New ideas have competed for police attention and resources—Compstat, intelligence-led policing, evidence-based policing, predictive policing—creating confusion on how these ideas fit together and their actual operational focus. Staffing shortages have forced some departments to back away from engaging the community in problem-solving, relying instead on "the basics"—just responding to calls and assigning units to be visible at hot spots.

Despite these challenges, community and problem-oriented policing should continue to play an integral role in policing strategy. Reformers are calling for better police–community relationships, more accountability, and improved effectiveness in solving neighborhood problems. Achieving these objectives requires community engagement and transparency. A key aspect of engagement is collaboration between police, residents, and stakeholders in both understanding problems and responding to them. Community safety requires more than police and the criminal justice system.

Going forward, there will always be tension between those who believe the best response to crime is aggressive policing and long prison sentences and those who want to see solutions that include alternatives to the justice system. Community and problem-oriented policing can be an important part of reducing that tension.

## Patrol Studies

The most influential early study on police operations, both for its breakthrough in initiating large-scale experimental research in police departments and for the long-term impact of its findings, was the Kansas City Preventive Patrol Experiment (Kelling et al. 1974). Prior to this experiment, police departments had little interest in scientific observation or intellectual inquiry; many, in fact, were anti-research (Caiden 1977).

The purpose of the Kansas City experiment was to determine the effect of random patrol (i.e., officers patrolling randomly in their beats when not assigned to handle a call) on crime, citizens' feelings of security, and other outcomes. Traditionally, most police departments routinely tried to ensure that a certain percentage of an officer's time was devoted to random patrol, normally 40 to 60 percent, based on the expectation that such patrolling both deterred crime and increased the chances of intercepting crimes in progress.

For study purposes, one part of the city was divided into 15 areas, which were further divided into three groups, each containing five beats. Each group was matched with respect to crime, population characteristics, and calls for service and was assigned different levels of patrol as follows: *control beats* maintained the normal level of patrol (i.e., one car per beat); *proactive beats* were assigned two to three times the normal number of patrol units (i.e., two to three cars per beat); and *reactive beats* had no preventive patrol (i.e., no cars patrolling). In these reactive beats, patrol units would enter to answer calls, but then leave and do their patrolling in the proactive beats. Remarkably, these experimental conditions, including the absence of patrol in the reactive beats, were maintained for one full year.

The results indicated that the three patrol conditions did not affect (1) crime rates deemed suppressible by patrol (i.e., burglaries, auto thefts, larcenies involving auto accessories, robberies, and vandalism), (2) citizens' attitudes toward police, (3) citizens' feelings of security, (4) rates of reported crime, (5) traffic accidents, or (6) arrests. In fact, surveys indicated that residents of the proactive beats did not even notice the extra levels of patrol where they lived, and residents of the reactive beats did not notice the absence of patrol. The conclusions of the Kansas City study suggested that traditional preventive patrol was not as effective as most had believed and that the substantial amount of uncommitted time typically devoted to random patrol could be used more effectively.

There are several possible reasons why differing levels of patrol had no impact on either crime rates or citizens' attitudes during the one-year Kansas City study (Larson 1975; Feinberg, Kinley, and Reiss 1976). The most likely reason, however, is that because normal police patrol is spread so thinly to begin with, simply adding or eliminating a patrol car or two in a relatively large area is unlikely to have any measurable impact. And because it is not feasible to dramatically increase patrol strength across large areas for any length of time due to manpower and budgetary constraints, the Kansas City findings are as relevant today as they were in the 1970s.

Much of the research since the Kansas City study relates to how police can better manage their time or restructure their activities to reduce crime and provide better service to the community. In many respects, the strategies discussed later in this chapter and in Chapter 8 (COP, POP, intelligence-led policing, and predictive policing) are feasible only because the Kansas City study showed that patrol officers, who constitute the majority of personnel in almost all police departments, do not have to spend 40 to 60 percent of their time randomly patrolling assigned beats.

### Response Time Studies

Shortly after the preventive-patrol experiment, a follow-up study in the Kansas City Police Department raised serious questions about another common assumption of patrol: the effectiveness of *rapid response* times (Pate et al. 1976a). Before this study, the assumption was that the faster the police responded to calls, the more satisfied citizens would be, and the more likely that suspects would be apprehended. Based on these assumptions, police departments spent considerable money attempting to reduce response times by introducing new technology (e.g., the 911 telephone number, vehicle-locator systems, and **computer-aided dispatching**) and adopting sophisticated methods of patrol allocation and deployment (Caiden 1977).

Overall, the research revealed that two primary factors limit the effectiveness of rapid police responses. First, the time between when a crime occurs and when a citizen discovers that the crime has occurred is important. For example, it may be hours between when a burglary occurs and when the victim discovers the crime (Cordner, Greene, and Bynum 1983). Second, even when the crime directly involved the victim (e.g., as with violent crimes) or when there was a witness, citizens delay on average six minutes before calling the police—they often call a friend, relative, or insurance agent first. Thus, in many cases, there is virtually no chance to make an arrest at the crime scene, regardless of how quickly police respond once they are notified. One study in three jurisdictions found that arrests attributable to quick response were made in only 3 percent of reported crime cases (Spelman and Brown 1982). Furthermore, researchers discovered that *citizen satisfaction* with police service depends less on a quick response than on being told *when* to expect the officer to arrive (even if there is a delay) and then *what* the officer actually does on arrival. Other studies have confirmed these results (Spelman and Brown 1982; Sherman 1983).

The impact of this study was that police began to realize they could respond differentially to calls—that is, because not all calls have the same level of importance, they could be assigned different levels of priority. For example, noncritical calls can be responded to less quickly than critical calls. Moreover, "critical" is not simply a function of seriousness—an assault that occurred two days ago might be a relatively serious crime, but immediate police response for a two-day-old crime is not going to affect the outcome. By contrast, a parking violation is not a very serious offense, but if someone calls to say a car is blocking their driveway right now, a quick police response could make a big difference in a resident's ability to get to work on time or take their child to school—and in the citizen's satisfaction with the police service received.

Studies also found that as long as citizens are informed of approximate arrival times, their satisfaction levels with the police remain high, even though they may not see an officer right away (or, in some cases, at all if they use the option of telephone or Internet reporting). Naturally, for truly critical calls (e.g., crimes in progress or injuries), it remains important for the police to respond as quickly as possible (Coupe and Blake 2005). In reality, however, the vast majority of calls to police departments are not critical (Lum, Koper, and Wu 2021), so response can be managed more efficiently, saving time that can then be devoted to more effective activities.

### Criminal Investigation Studies

In the mid-1970s, as a result of research commonly referred to as the RAND study (Greenwood and Petersilia 1975), police investigative units were found to be rather ineffective and inefficient. In this study, operations in 25 detective units were observed, and surveys were completed in 156 agencies. The major findings of this study indicated that (1) only 20 percent of serious crimes are ever solved; (2) when serious crimes are solved, it is usually through information obtained from victims rather than through leads developed by detectives; (3) in 75 percent of cases that are eventually solved, the suspect's identity is known or easily determined at the time the crime is reported to the police; (4) the majority of detective time is devoted to reviewing reports, documenting files, and attempting to locate and interview victims for cases with low probability of ever being solved; and (5) police collect a great deal of physical evidence, but most of it is never subjected to forensic analysis and does not contribute to crime solving.

In some ways, this RAND study was the most surprising, because the fiction of Sherlock Holmes leads us to believe that all crimes can be solved and, in real life, detectives occupy higher-status positions than patrol officers and are presumed to be smart, cunning, and relentless (Eck 1992). To this "detective mystique" can be added, today, the *CSI* effect—our expectation that forensic science can be used to solve every crime in 60 minutes or less. The harsh reality, however, is that police still solve only 20 to 25 percent of reported serious crimes, and that most evidence still comes from witnesses, informants, and confessions (Cordner 2013). In addition, we have learned that the scientific validity of many long-accepted forensic science techniques is questionable (National Research Council 2009; see Inside Policing 4.1). Since the RAND study, police departments have looked for ways to release detectives from fruitless investigations so that they can concentrate more on cases with better probabilities of success and perhaps use their time more effectively in other ways as well.

The combined effect of these early landmark studies was, at first, depressing. Preventive patrol did not prevent crimes, rapid response did not catch many offenders, and detectives did not solve many cases. After the shock wore off, however, the impact was extremely positive. First, careful follow-up studies often produced more nuanced findings. Second, police departments developed more refined strategies that were often determined to be more effective. Third, as noted earlier, when police were freed from the need to perform time-consuming traditional activities, they had more time to try alternatives. A much greater spirit of trial and error, and even experimentation, developed in policing.

---

**INSIDE POLICING 4.1**   **Delaware Reviewing Hair Evidence Convictions**

The FBI determined in 2015 that its crime lab had a very high error rate in microscopic (non-DNA) hair comparison analyses completed prior to 2000, possibly contributing to mistaken convictions. Delaware has now joined several other states conducting independent reviews to identify any past convictions involving questionable hair evidence, as reported here. The announcement notes that use of such evidence "would not necessarily cast doubt on the case's resolution if additional evidence, such as confessions or DNA analysis, supported the conviction."

**Discussion Question:** Most crime labs are attached to law enforcement agencies, such as the FBI and state police agencies. Critics say they should be independent in order to avoid forensic analyses that are biased in favor of investigators and prosecutors. What do you think are the pros and cons of independent crime labs versus ones attached to law enforcement agencies?

*SOURCE: Modern Policing* blog, March 5, 2019, gcordner.wordpress.com/2019/03/05/delaware-reviewing-hair-evidence-convictions/.

## Strategic Developments

In the aftermath of the Kansas City patrol study, the response time studies, and the RAND study of criminal investigation, many police departments considered revising their basic operational strategies. Their efforts were aided by the federal Law Enforcement Assistance Administration (LEAA), an agency that offered grants throughout the 1970s to police departments willing to implement and evaluate innovative programs and practices (Feeley and Sarat 1981). Although the LEAA ceased to exist in 1980, successor federal agencies like the Bureau of Justice Assistance, the National Institute of Justice, and the Office of Community Oriented Policing Services (COPS Office) continue to promote and support police innovation to this day. Additionally, the National Policing Institute (originally named the Police Foundation), the Police Executive Research Forum, the International Association of Chiefs of Police, and other professional organizations and associations in the police field have come to play a large role in encouraging police experimentation and disseminating the latest information to police and sheriff departments throughout the country. Fifty years ago, each police department was like an island, heavily dependent on its own experience to determine the best way to operate. Today, police departments have access to a tremendous amount of information about new innovations, best practices, and the results of careful effectiveness studies.

In this section and in the rest of this chapter, we discuss the big picture of strategic developments in policing since the early landmark studies of the 1970s and 1980s. Later, in Chapters 7 and 8, we will look in more detail at a wide variety of specific police operational tactics and programs.

### Improving Crime-Control Effectiveness

The basic operational strategies of the reform/professional model of policing suffered a serious one-two punch, as described previously. First, during the heyday of the model in the 1960s and 1970s, crime increased dramatically in America, along with significant social unrest. Second, specific studies showed that preventive patrols, rapid response, and detective investigations, the three operational cornerstones of professional model policing, were not effective in controlling crime. Even staunch traditionalists had to concede the need to find better police operational strategies.

In the realm of patrol, the primary thrust was toward more directed and targeted strategies. The prevailing interpretation of the Kansas City study came to be that spreading police patrol thinly across a jurisdiction had little benefit. An alternative was to concentrate patrol. This simple insight had substantial consequences. Patrol might be concentrated in certain places, or at certain times, or even on certain specific behaviors or offenders (Pate, Bowers, and Parks 1976b). To guide the concentration of patrol, however, police departments needed better information about crime and calls for service, which led to more emphasis on **crime analysis** (Reinier et al. 1977). There was also the matter of how to get patrol officers to concentrate their efforts, which led to **directed patrol** (Cordner 1981) and, more recently, **hot-spots** policing (Weisburd and Braga 2006). The overall thrust has been away from random patrol toward directed, targeted, and concentrated patrol. Importantly, studies have consistently found that focused patrol has more impact on crime and disorder than unfocused patrol (Wilson and Boland 1979; Weisburd and Eck 2004; Braga 2008; Braga et al. 2019).

Similarly, police thinking has become more targeted in regard to response time and call handling, with an emphasis on how the police can best manage the public demand for their services. Essentially, managing demand requires categorizing requests for service and matching those requests with different police responses. Differential response programs classify calls according to their degree of seriousness and whether they are "happening now." Calls are subsequently responded to with (1) an immediate response by a sworn officer, (2) a delayed response by a sworn officer, (3) response by a nonsworn police employee, or (4) no direct police response, with reports taken instead by telephone, mail, or Internet or having the citizen come to the police station (McEwen, Connors, and Cohen 1986).

A substantial body of research on **differential police response** indicates that alternative response strategies significantly reduce costs and improve effectiveness, do not affect citizens' levels of satisfaction, and do not increase crime (Cahn and Tien 1981; Cohen and McEwen 1984; McEwen et al. 1986; Worden 1993). Citizen satisfaction is probably highest when the complainant (the person calling the police) is given the opportunity to choose which response option suits them best. Perhaps it should not be surprising that many people opt for telephone or online reporting rather than having a police car pull up in front of their residence, causing their neighbors to speculate what kind of trouble they are in. Interestingly, there is some evidence that nonwhite citizens are less likely to choose telephone, Internet, or mail-in reporting, instead preferring to come directly to a police station to report crime (Alarid and Novak 2008). This underscores the point that one-size-fits-all responses rarely work.

Criminal investigations have also become more targeted. One development was **case screening**, designed to "screen out" cases with a very low probability of being solved so that detectives can concentrate on more promising cases (Eck 1992). To properly determine which cases should receive more, or less, follow-up investigation, research identified **solvability factors** that best predicted which cases were more solvable (Greenberg et al. 1977; Eck 1979). Naturally, some crimes are so serious that they deserve full-fledged investigation whether or not they seem promising. The detective caseload of thefts, burglaries, and other property crimes, however, is so overwhelming in many police departments that a system for targeting the limited amount of investigative time is essential. Research also specifically examined what detectives do and found four activities that were most likely to produce additional information relevant to solving a case: (1) increased emphasis on locating additional witnesses, (2) using informants, (3) contacting other police officers, and (4) utilizing police records (Eck 1983).

A separate method for targeting investigations is to focus on offenders rather than offenses. This method can take the form of targeting groups of offenders, such as gangs or organized crime groups, or it can focus on individuals. The method is based on the awareness that some offenders commit crimes on a regular basis. Thus, for example, rather than investigating each burglary after it happens and trying to determine a suspect, a detective might focus on known active burglars with the objective of catching them in the act (Martin and Sherman 1986).

These enhancements to police patrol, response, and investigation, including high-tech modern versions associated with intelligence-led policing and predictive policing, all have the common theme of targeting and focusing limited police resources to improve police efficiency and productivity. What might not be obvious is that these enhancements mainly rely on unchanged reform model assumptions about how best to reduce crime—they simply try to work in a smarter and more targeted way. The primary crime-control mechanisms embedded in these enhancements continue to be enforcement and police presence.

Herman Goldstein (1979, 1990) was among the first to suggest a significantly different way of conceptualizing police crime control when he advanced the notion of problem-oriented policing (POP). His insight was fourfold: first, that crime and disorder are often clustered; second, that they often spring from some underlying condition, such as a poorly run motel or poorly designed apartment complex; third, that fixing the underlying condition often has a substantial impact on the amount of crime and disorder that occurs; and fourth, that enforcing the criminal law is only one of many tools, and not always the most effective, that might be used to fix the condition or problem.

POP is situated about halfway between the enforcement and deterrence approach of the reform/professional model on one end of a continuum and the approach of primary prevention on the other end. The latter is mainly outside the realm of policing and emphasizes education, housing, health care, and employment; in other words, create a fair and prosperous society to eliminate the root causes of crime, and people will have less reason to commit crime. POP does not attempt to address those root causes of crime, since they are generally far outside the jurisdiction of the police. Rather, POP targets mid-level conditions that are within the reach of the police, either directly or through collaboration with other agencies and partners. POP is explained in more detail in the final section of this chapter.

## Improving Police–Community Relations

The preceding discussion of the evolution toward more targeted policing, including the development of POP, was focused on improving police effectiveness in crime control. Controlling crime is one of the principal goals of the police, and as explained, it had become apparent by the 1970s and 1980s that prevailing police strategies were not working well.

Of equal importance, the state of police–community relations had become unsatisfactory. Efforts began as early as the 1950s to try to improve how police dealt with the public and how the public perceived the police (Radelet 1986). In a free society that prides itself on government "of the people, by the people, and for the people," positive police–community relations are important in their own right—a telling reflection of social harmony and democracy. In more practical terms, if the public does not trust and respect the police, the police's job becomes harder and more dangerous. Ultimately, police can only be successful if they are seen by the public as legitimate. If the community sees the police as an occupying army or a band of heavy-handed strangers, all aspects of policing become more difficult.

Historically, one of the most persistent and compelling problems confronting the police has been their relationship with minority groups. Depending on the time period, a minority group could consist, for example, of Irish Americans, Italian Americans, Hispanics or Latinos, African Americans, Asian Americans, Native Americans, or gays and lesbians. The police have a long history of discriminating against members of minority groups because of their own prejudices, ignorance, or official responsibility for enforcing laws that restricted some people's civil rights (e.g., segregation laws). Numerous civil disturbances in the United States have been precipitated by police behavior that was considered inappropriate or offensive by minority groups.

In addition, changes in society and in the routine nature of police work have tended to create more distance between the police and the public. The advent of police cars, for example, and later air conditioning in those cars, resulted in larger patrol beats for officers and less informal contact with citizens. Similarly, the development of 911 telephone systems made it easier for the public to summon the police in an emergency, but also made police patrol units much busier and more closely tethered to their patrol cars, further reducing informal police–public contact.

The reform/professional model of policing essentially saw the relationship with the community as a matter of legal and bureaucratic considerations. As tensions developed, this model attempted to be more responsive to the public by diversifying the police force and establishing community-relations programs. In the 1950s and 1960s, many police departments established community-relations units in response to perceived problems in police–community relations. Initially, these community-relations units engaged mostly in public relations by presenting the police point of view to the community. This one-sided approach was soon recognized as inadequate, however, and was expanded to provide the community with a forum for expressing its views to the police. The two-way police–community relations philosophy emphasized the importance of communication and mutual understanding. Police departments often formed advisory groups of citizens, held neighborhood meetings, started programs designed to improve relations with youth, and generally tried to reach out to the community.

In the 1970s, it became apparent that a few police–community relations officers or a small unit was not effective in guaranteeing smooth relations between a community and its police department. It was recognized that a community experiences its police department much more through the actions of patrol officers and detectives than through the speeches made by community-relations specialists. Efforts then began to train regular patrol officers in community-relations and crime prevention techniques and to make them more knowledgeable about community characteristics and problems (Boydstun and Sherry 1975).

In the 1970s and 1980s, the public became increasingly fearful of crime, especially violence, gang activity, and drug use, all of which were alarmingly portrayed by the media. Many police departments became more legalistic, proactive, and assertive in an effort to deal with these problems and to satisfy public and political pressure. They tended to rely on aggressive patrol, field interrogations, citations, arrests, and increased undercover activities. These approaches, although applauded by many minority leaders (because crime victimization tends to be disproportionately experienced by minority citizens), also increased the tension between police and minority citizens, particularly African Americans and Hispanics. The perception that some police officers were discriminating against minority citizens became widespread. In fact, this perception was often accurate, particularly as it applied to police use of excessive force. However, the degree to which such behavior was racially motivated or willful was much more difficult to determine. These issues, and how best to deal with them, continue today in the context of racial profiling (Fridell et al. 2001) and with regard to police use of force, especially deadly force.

Many police–community relations programs evolved into **community crime prevention** in the 1970s and 1980s. This approach is based on the assumption that if a community can be changed, so too can the behavior of those who live there. Attempts to change communities often include (1) organizing the community to improve and strengthen relationships among residents to encourage them to take preventive precautions and to obtain more political and financial resources; (2) changing building and neighborhood design to improve both public and police surveillance, which improves guardianship; (3) improving the appearance of an area to decrease the perception that it is a receptive target for crime; and (4) developing activities and programs that provide a more structured and supervised environment, especially for youth (e.g., recreation programs).

Also in the 1970s, a major reorganization effort toward decentralization and increased community participation, known as **team policing**, was attempted in several cities (Schwartz and Clarren 1977). In retrospect, team policing was an obvious precursor to community policing, but it did not succeed at the time (Sherman, Milton, and Kelley 1973). The approach was based on reorganizing the patrol force to include one or more quasi-autonomous teams, with a joint purpose of improving police services to the community and increasing job satisfaction for the officers. The team was normally stationed in a particular neighborhood and was responsible for all police services in that neighborhood. The team was expected to work as a unit and have a close relationship with the community to prevent crime and maintain order. On the whole, however, most team policing programs differed little from the traditional policing of the past, mainly because of resistance within the police culture, resistance from within the police bureaucracy, and lack of evidence that it was an effective police strategy. By the 1980s, team policing had disappeared, but the need to establish better police–community relations had not. Then, just in the nick of time, along came foot patrol.

Many observers now believe that the abandonment of foot patrol by most American police departments by the mid-1900s changed the nature of police work and negatively affected police–citizen relations (see Inside Policing 4.2). Officers assigned to large patrol car beats do not develop the intimate understanding of and cordial relationship with the community that foot patrol officers assigned to small beats develop. Officers on foot are in a position to relate more intimately with citizens than officers driving by in cars.

The results of two research studies, together with the development of small, portable police radios, boosted the resurgence of foot patrol starting in the 1980s. When two-way police radios were first developed, they were bulky, heavy, and mounted inside patrol cars. These radios enabled police headquarters to contact officers on patrol, which was a huge technological advancement, but this only worked if the officers were in their cars. Portable radios ("walkie-talkies") started to appear in the 1970s and became common by the 1980s. Today, foot patrol officers carry tiny, lightweight radios that enable them to handle calls promptly and request information or assistance whenever needed. They are never out of touch, even outside their patrol cars.

An experimental study conducted in Newark, New Jersey, found that neither adding nor removing foot patrol affected crime in any way (Police Foundation 1981). This finding mirrored what had been found seven years earlier in Kansas City regarding motorized patrol. However, citizens served by foot patrol were less fearful of crime and more satisfied with the police than citizens served only by motor patrol. Also, citizens were aware of

---

**INSIDE POLICING 4.2** | **Policing in Milwaukee**

Here's a nice, 18-minute audio interview with the late George Kelling, author of the book *Policing in Milwaukee: A Strategic History*. Kelling, who grew up in Milwaukee, gives an overview of 150 years of policing in the city and puts it in the context of the national scene and recent events.

**Discussion Question:** There was a time when nearly all social interaction, other than within the family, occurred in public places—sidewalks, streets, parks, and so on. Face-to-face policing was easier then, with some obvious benefits. Today, however, a lot of social interaction is virtual and electronic. How can police maintain close community ties in the modern world?

*SOURCE: Modern Policing blog, March 27, 2016, www.oup.com/cordner/policing-in-milwaukee/.*

additions and deletions of foot patrol in their neighborhoods, a finding in stark contrast to the results of the Kansas City study, in which citizens did not even notice changes in the levels of motorized patrol. A second major foot patrol research program in Flint, Michigan, reported findings that were similar to the Newark findings (Trojanowicz 1982).

These studies were widely interpreted as demonstrating that even if foot patrol did not decrease crime, at least it made citizens feel safer and led to improvements in police–community relations. Why the difference between motorized patrol and foot patrol? In what has come to be known as the **broken windows theory**, foot patrol officers pay more attention to disorderly behavior and minor offenses than do motor patrol officers (Wilson and Kelling 1982). Also, they are in a better position to manage their beats, to understand what constitutes threatening or inappropriate behavior, and to observe and correct it. Foot patrol officers are likely to pay more attention to derelicts, petty thieves, disorderly persons, vagrants, panhandlers, noisy juveniles, and street people, who, although they are not committing serious crimes, cause concern and fear among many citizens. Foot patrol officers have more opportunity than motor patrol officers to control street disorder and reassure ordinary citizens through the use of persuasion and other informal methods rather than overenforcement of minor laws and ordinances.

Foot patrol and broken windows policing, when properly applied (i.e., when not used as an excuse for "zero tolerance" overenforcement), have been shown to reassure the public, make people feel safer, and increase the community's trust and confidence in the police. These methods of policing are now widely associated with COP, described in more detail later in this chapter as well as in Chapter 8.

## Improving Professionalism

In discussions about the evolving strategies of policing, it is common to refer to policing in the reform/professional era as the professional model. Since this era gave way to COP and other strategies in the late twentieth century, it is natural to think that the professional model was replaced, but that is not the optimal view. Rather, it makes more sense to say that the best elements of the professional model formed the foundation on which COP and other modern strategies have since been built.

The professionalization movement that began in policing during the early 1900s emphasized higher standards for selection of police personnel, training to prepare police to perform their duties, modern equipment, sound management practices, and a code of ethics to guide police behavior and decision making (Kelling and Moore 1988). Few people today would argue strongly against these principles. Other characteristics of twentieth-century professional policing were more debatable, however, such as the emphasis on strict law enforcement and crime-fighting as core police strategies, the tendency of the police to want separation from the public, and the preference for highly centralized and autocratic styles of organization and management. These latter elements of police professionalization are the main reasons why police and community leaders began searching for alternative policing strategies. But they never intended to, and they did not, throw the baby out with the bath water (Stone and Travis 2011).

Over the past several decades, while COP and other strategies have vied for dominance, many strands of police professionalism have continued to develop behind the scenes. Standards for police hiring have risen, police departments have become much more diverse, and a higher proportion of police officers are college graduates. Police training is longer, better, and more realistic. Management and executive training for police leaders is more widespread and sophisticated. Police equipment and technology have improved dramatically, enhancing officer safety, police decision making, and coordination of police resources in the field.

Other contributors to police professionalization include standards, certification, and accreditation. Individual police officers generally must meet state standards to be eligible for hiring, and then they must complete state-mandated training to be sworn in as certified police officers. In many states, they can also lose their certification for misbehavior or for failing to meet continuing training requirements. At the organizational level, police departments, sheriffs' offices, and other law enforcement agencies can seek national accreditation from the Commission on Accreditation for Law Enforcement Agencies (CALEA) as well as state-level accreditation. To achieve accreditation, agencies must prove to assessors that they meet applicable standards, which can number more than 400 in the case of CALEA's advanced accreditation program. Accreditation does not guarantee effective policing, since it mainly applies to administrative and policy matters. However, it does provide a body of standards that is constantly updated to reflect best practices and legal requirements (Commission on Accreditation for Law Enforcement Agencies 2022). By going through the accreditation process, a police department can show its community that it is operating in accordance with professional standards—not just doing things "the way we've always done them."

Accreditation corresponds closely to the four elements of what Stone and Travis (2011) refer to as the "new professionalism" of policing. They concur that earlier models of police professionalism had many useful features that have continued to support good policing around the country. One of these elements is accountability—not only internal accountability but also external accountability to duly authorized elected and appointed officials, commissions, and community groups. Another element is national coherence, which includes meeting national standards through accreditation as well as engaging in the national and professional dialogue about best practices in policing. This element is the very antithesis of provincialism, which is the tendency in some police agencies to think that there is nothing useful to be learned from anyone who is not steeped in the local way of doing things.

The other two elements of the new professionalism are legitimacy and innovation. Legitimacy refers to the necessity of policing based on consent, cooperation, and collaboration. This element corresponds well with the significance of police–community relations, with COP, and with respectful policing and procedural justice (Tyler 2004). Innovation refers to a commitment to adopt the best available practices in the field as well as to contribute to ongoing scientific testing of police programs and strategies to advance the body of knowledge in police science and administration. The idea is that a true profession is based on a scientific body of knowledge, and that true professionals have a responsibility both to master the body of knowledge and to contribute to its growth and refinement.

These additional elements take the concept of police professionalism to another level. The older version was narrow, limited, and self-serving. It was appropriate for an occupation struggling to achieve acceptance and prestige, but it did not measure up to the criteria generally used to distinguish professions and professionals from other occupational categories. The expanded model of police professionalism is more complete and, if accepted and adopted, is likely to provide a more solid foundation for police strategies and police effectiveness.

### Developing Evidence-Based Practices

One consistent theme throughout the first part of this chapter has been the impact of research on police strategies. The Kansas City patrol study, the response time studies, and the RAND study of criminal investigation each revealed weaknesses in the strategies then being used, leading to experimentation with different alternatives in the hope of finding more effective methods for controlling crime, improving police–community relations, and achieving other important police goals. This experimentation has continued for the past 40-plus years. Today, there is an even stronger sense of how important it is to assess and evaluate police strategies and programs so that police departments can operate as effectively as possible.

This approach is now referred to as **evidence-based policing** (Sherman 1998; Lum and Koper 2017; Cordner 2020). The basic idea is that police departments should adopt the practices with the strongest evidence of effectiveness. Unless police departments follow this principle, they are (1) not being as effective as they could be and (2) wasting resources on ineffective strategies and programs. The first consequence matters because it translates into more crime, fewer cases solved, more fear of crime, and less-satisfied citizens—in other words, less accomplishment of the important goals of policing. The second consequence matters because the public and their political leaders are increasingly intolerant of wasteful spending and high taxes. As politically popular as the police were from the mid-1990s through the early 2010s (until the crisis of legitimacy of the post-Ferguson era and then the killing of George Floyd), there is a growing sense that policing has become too expensive. Police budgets are being scrutinized more closely than ever, and police departments are having a harder time proving that their need for additional personnel, equipment, or other resources is greater than the need for more or better education, social services, housing, and health care.

The police are not unique in facing pressure to demonstrate that their practices are evidence based. Criminal justice agencies in general are under the same microscope, especially the corrections sector, because of the explosive growth in the costs of incarceration over the past 25 years. The federal government's Office of Justice Programs has created a Crime Solutions website (see https://crimesolutions.ojp.gov/) to help officials determine which criminal justice programs are effective, which are promising, and which have no effects. The United Kingdom's College of Policing has a similar Crime Reduction Toolkit available on a website (see Figure 4.1). Beyond criminal justice, evidence-based practices are also being pushed in health care, education, and many other public and private endeavors.

Evidence-based policing requires not only a commitment to use the most effective practices but also a willingness to sponsor or conduct evaluation and research on a regular basis. This is important because many police practices have not been studied carefully, or the results of studies have been inconclusive. Also, police departments constantly adopt new practices. To be true to the evidence-based principle, scientific studies must be ongoing to keep the knowledge base up to date, and police executives must be dedicated to staying abreast of the knowledge base, using it in their decision making and contributing new knowledge whenever possible. As discussed previously in conjunction with the new professionalism, these are things that true professionals do: they work to master the body of knowledge in their field, and they also accept responsibility for helping to build the knowledge base.

The push for a more evidence-based approach to policing raises the issue of whether policing rests (or should rest) primarily on a foundation of scientific knowledge or professional

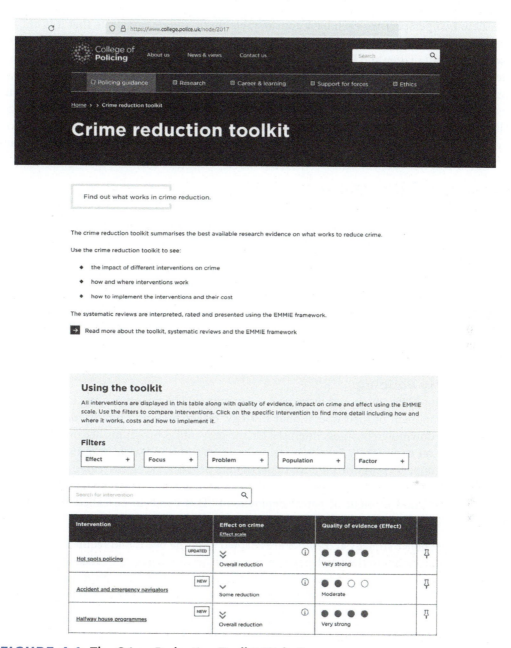

**FIGURE 4.1**  The Crime Reduction Toolkit Website.

*SOURCE*: https://whatworks.college.police.uk/toolkit/Pages/Toolkit.aspx.

opinion (Sparrow 2011; Weisburd and Neyroud 2011). The scientific approach emphasizes general principles based on careful testing of programs and strategies to determine their real effectiveness. The alternative view emphasizes that policing is more like a craft, and because the context and details of each situation are fundamentally different, the usefulness of general principles is limited. This perspective tends to give greater importance to professional opinion and accumulated experience than to science and research in deciding which police programs and strategies make the most sense for any particular jurisdiction.

These two perspectives each have considerable merit and demonstrate that it is not an either/or issue (Cordner and Alpert 2018). Police work has characteristics of both a profession and a craft (Tilley and Laycock 2016). The importance of scientific evidence in helping decide which police practices are most and least effective will likely continue to grow, making evidence-based policing a key feature of ongoing strategic developments in the field. At the same time, science is not the only source of reliable and useful knowledge (Fleming and Rhodes 2017). For now, and likely forever, the design and implementation of police strategies and programs will continue to rely on both professional police judgment and the body of scientific police knowledge.

## Strategic Alternatives

The preceding sections have described a host of strategic developments since the 1970s aimed at improving police effectiveness in controlling crime, improving police–community relations, and making policing more professional and scientific. These developments have coalesced around four contemporary strategies: COP, POP, intelligence-led policing (ILP), and predictive policing. COP and POP have been around the longest and are most fully developed, whereas intelligence-led policing and predictive policing are still in earlier stages of definition and elaboration. It is also important to note that the lines between these strategies are sometimes vague and elastic, so considerable overlap exists. The first two of these strategies, COP and POP, are described in the following sections. The discussion of ILP and predictive policing picks up in Chapter 8.

### Community Policing

Starting in the 1980s, more and more police departments began employing foot patrol as a central component of their operational strategy, rather than as a novelty or an accommodation to downtown business interests. Crime prevention programs became more and more reliant on community involvement, as in neighborhood watch, community patrol, and "crimestoppers" programs. Police departments began making increased use of civilians and volunteers in various aspects of policing and made permanent geographic assignment an important element of patrol deployment. This came to be called **community policing (COP)**, and it entailed a substantial change in police thinking,

> one where police strategy and tactics are adapted to fit the needs and requirements of the different communities the department serves, where there is a diversification of the kinds of programs and services on the basis of community needs and demands for police services and where there is considerable involvement of the community with police in reaching their objectives. (Reiss 1985, 63)

COP is the logical combination of more than 40 years of police effectiveness research and decades of experimentation with police–community relations programs, crime-prevention strategies, and team policing. It can be thought of as an attempt to harness the advantages of foot patrol and generalize them throughout all police field services, with an emphasis on broken windows theory and its focus on minor crime, disorder, and fear of crime. The Office of Community Oriented Police Services (2009, 1), formed in the US Department of Justice in the 1990s, defines COP as "a philosophy that promotes organizational strategies that support the systematic use of partnerships and problem-solving techniques to proactively address the immediate conditions that give rise to public safety issues such as crime, social disorder, and fear of crime." This definition includes several important components that have come to characterize modern COP—philosophy, organizational strategy, partnerships, and problem solving.

Still, COP remains many things to many people. A common refrain among proponents is "Community policing is a philosophy, not a program." Two equally common refrains among police officers are "This is what we've always done" and "Just tell me exactly what you want me to do differently." Some critics, echoing concerns similar to those expressed by police officers, argue that if COP is nothing more than a philosophy, it is merely an empty shell (Goldstein 1987). To flesh out more details, it is helpful to identify three major dimensions of COP and some of the most common elements within each dimension (Cordner 2014):

- The philosophical dimension
- The strategic dimension
- The tactical dimension

**The Philosophical Dimension.** Many of its most thoughtful and forceful advocates emphasize that COP is a new philosophy of policing, perhaps constituting even a paradigm shift away from professional-model policing. The philosophical dimension includes the central ideas and beliefs underlying COP. Three of the most important of these are citizen input, broad function, and personal service.

COP takes the view that in a free society, citizens should have open access to police organizations and input to police policies and decisions. Mechanisms for achieving greater **citizen input** vary, including the normal political process, systematic and periodic community surveys (Bureau of Justice Assistance 1994a), open forums, town meetings, radio and television call-in programs, and regular meetings with citizen advisory boards, ministry alliances, minority group representatives, business leaders, and other formal groups. Today, an increasing number of police departments also use websites, blogs, social networking, and social media (including Twitter and Facebook) to further enhance their communication with the public (Cordner and Perkins 2013; Tiry, Oglesby-Neal, and Kim 2019; Hu and Lovrich, 2020).

COP also embraces a broad view of the police function rather than a narrow focus on crime-fighting or law enforcement (Kelling and Moore 1988). This view recognizes the kinds of nonenforcement tasks that police already (and inevitably) perform and seeks to give them greater status and legitimacy. These tasks include order maintenance, social service, and general assistance duties. They may also include greater responsibilities in protecting and enhancing "the lives of those who are most vulnerable—juveniles, the elderly, minorities, the poor, the disabled, the homeless" (Trojanowicz and Bucqueroux 1990, xiv). In the bigger picture of the **broad function**, the police mission includes resolving conflict, helping victims, preventing accidents, solving problems, and reducing fear, as well as reducing crime through apprehension and enforcement.

COP supports tailored policing based on local norms and values and on individual needs. Ideally, citizens feel they have received **personal service**. Many citizens resent being subjected to "stranger policing" and would rather deal with officers who know them and whom they know. Of course, not every police–citizen encounter can be amicable and friendly. However, officers who generally deal with citizens in a friendly, open, and personal manner may be more likely to generate trust and confidence than officers who operate in a narrow, aloof, and/or bureaucratic manner.

**The Strategic Dimension.** The strategic dimension of COP includes the key operational concepts that translate philosophy into action. These strategic concepts are the links between the broad ideas and beliefs that underlie COP and the specific programs and practices by which it is implemented. They ensure that agency policies, priorities, and resource allocation are consistent with a community-oriented philosophy. Three strategic elements of COP are flexible operations, geographic focus, and prevention emphasis.

COP recommends less reliance on the patrol car and more emphasis on face-to-face interactions through **flexible operations**. One objective is to replace ineffective or isolating operational practices (e.g., motorized patrol and rapid response to low-priority calls) with more effective and more interactive practices. A related objective is to find ways of performing necessary traditional functions (e.g., handling emergency calls and conducting follow-up investigations) more efficiently to save time and resources that can then be devoted to more community-oriented activities. As described earlier in this chapter, many departments have now increased their use of foot patrol and other alternatives to traditional motorized patrol (Cordner and Trojanowicz 1992), differential responses to calls for service (McEwen et al. 1986), and more targeted investigation techniques (Eck 1992).

COP strategy emphasizes the geographic basis of assignment and responsibility by shifting the fundamental unit of patrol accountability from time of day to place. That is, rather than holding patrol officers, supervisors, and shift commanders responsible for wide areas, but only during their 8- or 10-hour shifts, COP seeks to establish 24-hour responsibility for smaller areas. A key ingredient of this **geographic focus** is permanency of assignment. COP recommends that patrol officers be assigned to the same areas for extended periods of time to increase their familiarity with the community and the community's familiarity with them. Ideally, this familiarity will build trust, confidence, and cooperation on both sides of the police–citizen interaction. Also, officers will become more knowledgeable about the community and its residents, aiding early intervention and timely problem identification and avoiding conflict based on misperception or misunderstanding.

COP strategy also emphasizes a more proactive and preventive orientation, in contrast to the reactive focus that characterized much of policing under the reform model. Officers are encouraged to look beyond the individual incidents that they encounter as calls for service and reported crimes to discover underlying problems and conditions (Eck and Spelman 1987). The **prevention emphasis** of COP also takes more of a social welfare orientation, particularly toward juveniles. An argument is made that police officers, by serving as mentors and role models and by providing educational, recreational, and even counseling services, can affect people's behavior in positive ways that ultimately result in decreased crime and disorder. In essence, police are asked to support and augment the efforts of families, churches, schools, and social service agencies. This kind of police activity is seen as particularly necessary by some to offset the deficiencies of these other social institutions in modern America.

**The Tactical Dimension.** The tactical dimension of COP ultimately translates ideas, philosophies, and strategies into concrete programs, practices, and behaviors. Even those who insist that COP is a philosophy rather than a program must concede that unless COP eventually leads to some action, some new or different behavior, it is all rhetoric and no reality (Greene and Mastrofski 1988). Indeed, many commentators have taken the view that COP is little more than a new police marketing strategy that has left the core elements of the police role untouched (see, e.g., Klockars 1988; Manning 1988; Weatheritt 1988). Three of the most important tactical elements of COP are positive interaction, partnerships, and problem solving.

Policing inevitably involves negative contacts between officers and citizens—for example, arrests, tickets, stops for suspicion, orders to halt disruptive behavior, and the inability to make things much better for victims. COP recognizes this fact and recommends that officers offset it by engaging in positive interactions whenever possible. Many opportunities for **positive interaction** arise in the course of call handling. Even more opportunities can be seized during routine patrol if officers are willing to exit their vehicles and take initiative. For example, officers can go in and out of stores and in and out of schools, talk to people on the street, or knock on doors. They can take the initiative to talk not only with shopkeepers and their customers but also with teenagers, apartment dwellers, tavern patrons, and anyone they run across in public places or who is approachable in private places. Police should insert themselves wherever people are and talk to those people, not just watch them.

Participation of the community in its own protection is one of the central elements of COP (Bureau of Justice Assistance 1994c). This participation can run the gamut from watching neighbors' homes to reporting drug dealers to patrolling the streets. It can involve participation in problem identification and problem-solving efforts, in crime prevention programs, in neighborhood revitalization, and in youth-oriented educational and recreational programs. Community-oriented police agencies are expected not only to cooperate with citizens and communities but also to actively solicit input and participation and build **partnerships** (Bureau of Justice Assistance 1994b). The exact nature of this participation can, and should, vary from community to community and from situation to situation. As a general rule, however, police should avoid claiming that they alone can handle crime, drug, or disorder problems, and they should encourage individual citizens, community groups, and other public and private agencies to work together and share the responsibility for controlling crime and disorder (Scott and Goldstein 2005).

Supporters of COP are convinced that the very nature of police work must be altered from its present incident-by-incident, case-by-case orientation to one that is more focused on **problem solving** (Goldstein 1990). Certainly, incidents must still be handled, and cases must still be investigated. Whenever possible, however, attention should be directed toward underlying problems and conditions. Following the medical analogy, policing should address causes as well as symptoms and should adopt the epidemiological public health approach as much as the individual doctor's clinical approach.

This element of COP, problem solving, provides a bridge to the POP strategy discussed later in this chapter. As discussed previously, POP developed as an alternative strategy for reducing crime, whereas COP developed mainly to address poor police–community relations. To emphasize this point, these two strategies developed separately and for different reasons. However, when COP was gaining popularity and widespread adoption in the 1990s, it was recognized that something was missing—COP was warm and fuzzy and well-grounded philosophically, but it lacked a coherent approach to dealing with crime and disorder, something the police are expected to have. At that point, the architects of COP seized on problem solving as the missing ingredient, and it has been a core element ever since.

**Implementing Community Policing.** The evidence today about the implementation of COP is mixed and somewhat contradictory. This is not surprising. Because COP is such a broad and flexible concept, it has been implemented differently in different places. In fact, what one jurisdiction calls COP another jurisdiction committed to COP might not even recognize. This has been both the greatest strength and the greatest weakness of the approach.

<table>
<tr><td>INSIDE POLICING 4.3</td><td>Arlington's Community Policing Story</td></tr>
</table>

The police department of Arlington, Texas, has had a sustained and serious commitment to community policing. This 26-minute video presents their story, including the department's response to a fatal officer-involved shooting of an unarmed man, the impact of the deadly ambush in nearby Dallas, and ongoing relationship building with youth, schools, and the community at large. A companion COPS Office document to facilitate conversation and discussion is available here as well.

**Discussion Question:** In the Arlington video, what examples do you see of the philosophical, strategic, and tactical dimensions of community policing? Since the precise form of COP varies from place to place, what seems to be the main emphasis in Arlington?

SOURCE: *Modern Policing* blog, August 21, 2018, https://gcordner.wordpress.com/2018/08/21/arlingtons-community-policing-story/.

Specific illustrations of successful COP implementation are readily available (see Inside Policing 4.3). The Chicago Alternative Policing Strategy (CAPS), which began in 1993, was the best big-city example of department-wide COP, with sustained implementation for 14 years and measurable effects on crime, public opinion, citizen involvement, problem solving, and citizens' views about neighborhood problems (Skogan and Steiner 2004; Skogan 2006). However, Chicago's commitment to COP subsequently faded following a change in administration (Skogan 2022), so much so that 10 years later, it stood out as a city in crisis (Madhani 2016). Inside Policing 4.4 highlights a podcast discussing the evolution of CAPS in greater detail.

Successful implementation in many smaller jurisdictions has also been documented (Office of Community Oriented Policing Services 2002). National surveys have consistently found a high level of COP implementation among police departments around the country. For example, in 2002 the Police Executive Research Forum (Fridell and Wycoff 2004) surveyed a sample of 282 police departments and found 16 different COP activities (from a total of 56 choices offered by the survey) claimed by at least 75 percent of responding agencies. A more recent survey found that the majority of police departments serving populations of 10,000 or more had written community policing plans, including 80 percent of agencies that served a million or more residents (Brooks 2020).

As positive as this picture seems, there is also evidence that COP is sometimes more rhetoric than reality (Mastrofski 2006). According to the 2002 Police Executive Research Forum survey (Fridell and Wycoff 2004), several specific COP activities had been implemented by less than 25 percent of the responding agencies. It seemed that most police agencies had adopted a relatively modest version of COP. Few police agencies had shown much interest in the most "radical" component of COP—real power sharing with the community (Brown 1985).

Information from other sources tends to corroborate the sometimes limited or modest nature of COP as implemented. For example, community police officers in cities seem to spend relatively little time actually interacting with or engaging citizens (Parks et al. 1999). Instead, they spend considerable time in the office doing administration and paperwork, and like their regular patrol colleagues, they spend considerable time on routine patrol

**INSIDE POLICING 4.4**

In this *Reducing Crime* podcast, Jerry Ratcliffe interviews Wesley Skogan, who was instrumental in evaluating CAPS and community policing in Chicago over the years. He discusses the origins of community policing, how it evolved over time, and contemplates its future in American policing.

**Discussion Question:** Wes Skogan talks about some of the reasons why community policing was successful in Chicago before budget cuts caused it to fade away. What were the reasons for its success?

*SOURCE:* https://soundcloud.com/reducingcrime/46-wes-skogan.

and conducting personal business. This pattern of time utilization also holds true for small-town and rural officers (Frank and Liederbach 2003). Similarly, although community police officers often develop higher job satisfaction and a more positive outlook toward the community than their patrol officer peers (Hayeslip and Cordner 1987), many other basic attitudes and beliefs related to traditional law enforcement practices remain unchanged (Pelfrey 2004). This suggests that the experience of doing COP has a strong, but not necessarily life-changing, impact on officers, perhaps because of the countervailing influence of the traditional police culture.

It has also been found that everyday problem solving by police officers typically does not conform closely to the analytical and collaborative problem-solving model promoted by the advocates of POP (Cordner and Biebel 2005). Typical street-level problem solving tends to focus on problems that are small in scope; officers analyze those problems primarily through personal observation and tend to draw on personal experience for responses, which almost always include enforcement, often in concert with one or two other responses (see Figure 4.2). The reality of street-level problem solving seems to be that it is often more thoughtful, analytical, collaborative, and creative than mere knee-jerk enforcement, but it is still a far cry from the ideal model of POP (also see Scott 2000).

Another limitation of COP is that little evidence shows the approach enhances community processes in ways that would be expected to subsequently produce long-term reductions in fear, disorder, and crime (Kerley and Benson 2000). This is likely because most COP is still *police centered*, with the police more often doing things directly to try to reduce crime and disorder rather than working to strengthen the community so that it might more successfully protect itself. This is not to say that many police agencies have not tried to increase public participation in crime prevention and other activities, but the ideal of police and citizen *coproduction of public safety* has not generally been realized to a significant degree. On a related issue, COP has clearly helped the police work more closely with some parts of the community, but other segments of the community have been more resistant or harder to engage (Skogan 2006).

Of equal concern is that the adoption of COP *strategies* at the managerial level does not always lead to the utilization of community-based *tactics* in the field (Bennett 1998). Implementation of any new program in a complex organization is a management challenge; implementation of such a far-reaching philosophical and strategic change as COP requires careful planning, systematic attention to detail, leadership, and patience (see Chapter 5). These capabilities are not always in great supply in police agencies, especially when

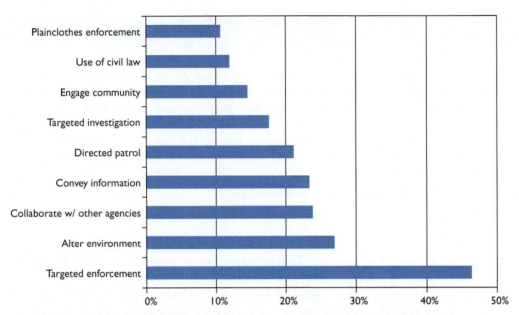

**FIGURE 4.2** Response Strategies Utilized in Problem-Oriented Policing Projects in San Diego (Top Nine Responses).

SOURCE: G. Cordner and E. P. Biebel, *Problem-Oriented Policing in San Diego: A Study in POP in Practice in a Big-City Police Department*. Report submitted to the National Institute of Justice, Washington, DC, 2002. Available at https://www. ncjrs.gov/pdffiles1/nij/grants/200518.pdf/.

agencies are buffeted by political pressures or frequent changes in top management, both of which are common. Consequently, many police departments have a much stronger commitment to COP at the top than at the street level.

One of the logical methods for enhancing COP implementation is training. Studies have indicated that this training is often successful in conveying knowledge about COP, developing skills, and changing attitudes (see, e.g., Scarborough et al. 1998). However, research also indicates that the effects of COP training do not always survive once the officer leaves training and enters (or re-enters) the police culture, where traditional values and practices tend to be held supreme (Haarr 2001). One step that many police agencies have overlooked is the necessity of revising their performance evaluation systems to incorporate COP and problem-solving activities (Lilley and Hinduja 2006). A common refrain in many organizations, including police departments, is "If you don't measure it, it won't happen."

Importantly, COP dramatically re-emerged in the post-Ferguson era as the primary reform strategy for improving police–community relations and police legitimacy (President's Task Force 2015). This raises the question: Had COP started to fade away or was it never implemented sufficiently? A generation of police has been hired since COP became commonplace, and a generation of community residents has experienced its benefits. One reason why COP might have seemed to fade is that many people began to take it for granted. Who would disagree that the police need the public's cooperation to control crime and disorder? Who would disagree that a police department that loses the public's trust finds itself in difficult straits?

That said, it is also true that many police agencies implemented COP only half-heartedly, federal financial support for COP fell significantly from the levels seen in the

1990s, and the 2008 recession tightly squeezed local governments and their police departments. Many police agencies cut back on the very tactics and programs that had won them so much public approval and trust beginning in the 1990s, not because they wanted to, but because their budgets were decimated. Other agencies never truly engaged, although they may have adopted the rhetoric of COP. In addition, the era of terrorism and homeland security that began in 2001 caused police to rethink their fundamental strategies, leading some agencies to shift away from COP and toward intelligence-led policing, a topic addressed in Chapter 8.

The picture that we are left with is mixed. Still, hardly any police agency that encounters a crisis fails to list community policing at the top of its plans to fix things. In the late 2010s, Chicago re-emphasized COP with initial success (Studenkov 2017; Queram 2018), Los Angeles appointed a new police chief with a strong commitment to community engagement (Stoltze 2018), and New York shifted substantial resources to neighborhood policing (O'Neill 2018). Today, cities overseen by consent decrees, such as New Orleans and Baltimore, are typically required to implement community policing, and federal funding for community policing has been increased. All indications are that public and political support for community policing remains strong, despite implementation challenges. More information about COP is available from the Office of Community Oriented Policing and can be found at https://www.cops.usdoj.gov/.

## Problem-Oriented Policing

**Problem-oriented policing (POP)** got its start in the 1980s in Madison (WI), Newport News (VA), and Baltimore County (MD). These police departments adopted concepts that had been developed by Herman Goldstein (1979, 1990), who taught at the University of Wisconsin and was able to test his ideas with the Madison Police Department. Police chief Darrel Stephens adopted POP to tackle burglaries, thefts, and domestic violence in Newport News (Eck and Spelman 1987), and police chief Neil Behan used the approach to address fear of crime in Baltimore County (Cordner 1988). Within a few years, POP was adopted by many other police departments, annual POP conferences were held to showcase the best work in the field, problem solving was incorporated as a core element of COP, and a Center for Problem-Oriented Policing was established.

The process of POP consists of four steps (see Inside Policing 4.5): (1) careful identification of the problem, (2) careful analysis of the problem, (3) a search for alternative solutions to the problem, and (4) implementation and assessment of responses to the problem. These four steps are commonly abbreviated as scanning, analysis, response, and assessment (SARA). Community input can be incorporated within any or all of the steps in the process. Identification, analysis, and assessment should rely on information from multiple sources. A variety of alternative solutions should be considered, including, but not limited to, traditional enforcement methods. Typically, the most effective solutions are those that combine several different responses, including some that draw on more than just the police department's authority and resources.

The problem-solving approach should be characterized by several important features: (1) it should be the standard operating method of policing, not an occasional special project; (2) it should be practiced by personnel throughout the ranks, not only by specialists or managers; (3) it should be empirical, in the sense that decisions are made on the basis of information that is gathered systematically; (4) it should involve, whenever possible, collaboration between police and other agencies and institutions; and (5) it should incorporate, whenever possible, community input and participation so that the community's

**INSIDE POLICING 4.5** | **The SARA Model**

A commonly used problem-solving method is the SARA model (scanning, analysis, response, and assessment). The SARA model contains the following elements:

**Scanning**
- Identifying recurring problems of concern to the public and the police.
- Identifying the consequences of the problem for the community and the police.
- Prioritizing those problems.
- Developing broad goals.
- Confirming that the problems exist.
- Determining how frequently the problem occurs and how long it has been taking place.
- Selecting problems for closer examination.

**Analysis**
- Identifying and understanding the events and conditions that precede and accompany the problem.
- Identifying relevant data to be collected.
- Researching what is known about the problem type.
- Taking inventory of how the problem is currently addressed and the strengths and limitations of the current response.
- Narrowing the scope of the problem as specifically as possible.
- Identifying a variety of resources that may be of assistance in developing a deeper understanding of the problem.
- Developing a working hypothesis about why the problem is occurring.

**Response**
- Brainstorming for new interventions.
- Searching for what other communities with similar problems have done.
- Choosing among the alternative interventions.
- Outlining a response plan and identifying responsible parties.
- Stating the specific objectives for the response plan.
- Carrying out the planned activities.

**Assessment**
- Determining whether the plan was implemented (a process evaluation).
- Collecting pre- and postresponse qualitative and quantitative data.
- Determining whether broad goals and specific objectives were attained.
- Identifying any new strategies needed to augment the original plan.
- Conducting ongoing assessment to ensure continued effectiveness.

*SOURCE*: https://popcenter.asu.edu/content/sara-model-1.

problems (not just the police department's) are addressed and the community shares in the responsibility for its own protection.

A crucial characteristic of the problem-oriented approach is that it seeks solutions tailored to specific community problems. Arrests and law enforcement are not abandoned; rather, an effort is made in each situation to determine which alternative responses best fit the problem. Use of criminal law is always considered, as are civil law enforcement, mediation, community mobilization, referral, collaboration, alteration of the physical environment, public education, and a host of other possibilities (see Inside Policing 4.6). The commonsense notion of choosing the tool that best fits the problem, instead of simply grabbing the most convenient or familiar one in the toolbox, lies close to the heart of the problem-solving method. A carpenter would not use a hammer when a saw would be more effective. Similarly, police should use criminal law when it is the most effective tool for the situation, but not when some other tool would work better.

---

## INSIDE POLICING 4.6   The Problem Analysis Triangle

While the SARA model is useful as a way of organizing the approach to recurring problems, it is often very difficult to figure out just exactly what the real problem is. The *problem analysis triangle* (sometimes referred to as the crime triangle) provides a way of thinking about recurring problems of crime and disorder. This idea assumes that crime or disorder results when (1) likely offenders and (2) suitable targets come together in (3) time and space in the absence of capable guardians for that target. A simple version of a problem analysis triangle is described as follows:

Offenders can sometimes be controlled by other people; those people are known as handlers. Targets and victims can sometimes be protected by other people as well; those people are known as guardians. And places are usually controlled by someone; those people are known as managers. Thus, effective problem solving requires understanding how offenders and their targets/victims come together in places and understanding how those offenders, targets/victims, and places are or are not effectively controlled. Understanding the weaknesses in the problem analysis triangle in the context of a particular problem will point the way to new interventions. A complete problem analysis triangle looks like this:

Problems can be understood and described in a variety of ways. No single way is definitive. They should be described in whichever way is most likely to lead to an improved understanding of the problem and effective interventions. Generally, incidents that the police handle cluster in four ways:

*(Continued)*

**The Problem Analysis Triangle**
*(Continued)*

- **Behavior.** Certain behaviors are common to the incidents—for example, making excessive noise, robbing people or businesses, driving under the influence, crashing vehicles, dealing drugs, or stealing cars. There are many different behaviors that might constitute problems.
- **Place.** Certain places can be common to incidents. Incidents involving one or more problem behaviors may occur at, for example, a street corner, a house, a business, a park, a neighborhood, or a school. Some incidents occur in abstract places such as cyberspace, on the telephone, or through other information networks.
- **Person.** Certain individuals or groups of people can be common to incidents. These people could be either offenders or victims. Incidents involving one or more behaviors occurring in one or more places may be attributed to, for example, a youth gang, a lone person, a group of prostitutes, a group of chronic inebriates, or a property owner. Or incidents may be causing harm to, for example, residents of a neighborhood, senior citizens, young children, or a lone individual.
- **Time**. Certain times can be common to incidents. Incidents involving one or more behaviors in one or more places caused by or affecting one or more people may happen at, for example, traffic rush hour, bar closing time, the holiday shopping season, or during an annual festival.

There is growing evidence that crime and disorder do cluster in these ways. It is not evenly distributed across time, place, or people. Increasingly, police and researchers are recognizing some of these clusters as the following:

- Repeat offenders attacking different targets at different places.
- Repeat victims repeatedly attacked by different offenders at different places.
- Repeat places (or hot spots) involving different offenders and different targets interacting at the same place.

*SOURCE:* https://popcenter.asu.edu/content/problem-analysis-triangle-0.

We have used the terms *problem solving* and *problem-oriented policing* somewhat interchangeably, but they can and should be differentiated. Problem solving refers to small scale, officer-level activity within the context of COP. For example, if an officer is trying to resolve a landlord–tenant dispute, the officer should first analyze the situation and then, based on what was found, possibly arbitrate the dispute, refer the tenant to legal aid, help the landlord develop a better and more binding rental contract, or all of the above. In any event, the response should be tailored to the specifics of the situation and should take advantage of handlers, guardians, and place managers whenever possible, instead of relying solely on police authority and the criminal law.

POP, as contrasted with problem solving, is broader in scope, with deeper analysis and more wide-ranging solutions. For example, an officer handling a landlord–tenant dispute might suspect that it is a recurring problem, not only at one location but also at many rental properties throughout the city. Further analysis by the officer or someone else in the police department would reveal the actual size of the whole problem, where it occurs (and where it does not), and so on. If it is a significant problem, then city-wide responses tailored to the nature of the problem would be devised and implemented. One possibility might be landlord training. The SARA process here would be the same as in smaller-scale problem solving, but it would be addressed to a bigger and broader problem. Similarly, attention would be focused on offenders and their handlers, victims and their guardians, and places and their managers, just as in problem solving. Hopefully, however, broader-scale POP would result in a bigger impact on the whole problem city-wide, compared with smaller-scale problem solving at just one location.

POP is consistent with COP, but conceptually separate. The principal aim of POP is to identify and reduce all kinds of chronic crime and disorder problems, whereas the principal aim of COP is to repair and improve one particular type of problem: police–community relations. They are both important developments in modern policing, and they are complementary.

The experience over 20 to 30 years of implementing POP has been mixed. Innovative and effective examples surface every year as candidates for the Herman Goldstein Award for excellence in POP (see https://popcenter.asu.edu/content/about-goldstein-pop-awards), testaments to the value and durability of the strategy. A comprehensive review of POP evaluations revealed that the majority of studies reported significant reductions in crime or disorder. In fact, the typical reduction in crime and disorder was about 34 percent (Hinkle et al. 2020). Collectively, this indicates there is strong evidence that POP approaches can have an impact on outcomes that are important to police and citizens.

Field studies, however, have shown that most police problem solving is shallow and narrow in scope (Cordner and Biebel 2005; also see Buerger 1994). The proposition that every police officer should always be engaged in full-fledged POP may be too idealistic—a department that has a few broad-scale POP projects going at any one time may be doing as well as can be expected. One specific challenge is that good problem solving requires in-depth analysis, which takes time and requires data and skills that are not available in every police organization. Another is that the mantra to consider a wide range of alternative responses, not just enforcement, conflicts with the styles and cultures of policing in many agencies.

One promising development is that several states—including Oregon, Illinois, and Wisconsin—have begun to hold their own annual POP conferences to encourage, highlight, and recognize good problem-oriented policing. In addition, on the international scene, the United Kingdom and New Zealand hold national competitions to identify their best examples of POP each year. And in 2018, the "inventor" of problem-oriented policing, Herman Goldstein, was awarded the Stockholm Prize in Criminology, signifying that his important work reconfiguring police strategy had been recognized by the wider scientific community.

The best source of information about POP is the Center for Problem-Oriented Policing, found online at https://popcenter.asu.edu/. Among the most practical and beneficial resources offered at this site are the *Problem-Specific Guides for Police* on topics such as false burglar alarms, drive-by shootings, hate crime, and prescription fraud (see Inside Policing 4.7). Each of these guides briefly summarizes research about the problem itself and various responses that have been used to deal with the problem around the world, and then offers realistic options tailored to the specific characteristics of the problem. There are currently 74 of these problem-specific guides; they are short and practical, with periodic updates. The website also offers 13 *Response Guides* (e.g., assigning police officers to schools, focused deterrence of high-risk individuals) and 14 *Tool Guides* (e.g., analyzing crime displacement and repeat victimization).

## INSIDE POLICING 4.7   Problem-Specific Guides for Police

The *Problem-Specific Guides for Police* summarize knowledge about how police can reduce the harm caused by specific crime and disorder problems. The guides are available in print versions and web versions. Guides are updated periodically on the basis of new research and police practice.

1. Assaults in and Around Bars, 2nd ed.
2. Street Prostitution, 2nd ed.
3. Speeding in Residential Areas, 2nd ed.
4. Drug Dealing in Privately Owned Apartment Complexes
5. False Burglar Alarms, 2nd ed.
6. Disorderly Youth in Public Places
7. Loud Car Stereos
8. Robbery of Automated Teller Machines
9. Graffiti
10. Thefts of and from Cars in Parking Facilities
11. Shoplifting
12. Bullying in Schools
13. Panhandling
14. Rave Parties
15. Burglary of Retail Establishments
16. Clandestine Methamphetamine Labs, 2nd ed.
17. Acquaintance Rape of College Students
18. Burglary of Single-Family Houses
19. Misuse and Abuse of 911
20. Financial Crimes Against the Elderly
21. Check and Card Fraud
22. Stalking
23. Gun Violence Among Serious Young Offenders
24. Prescription Fraud
25. Identity Theft
26. Crimes Against Tourists
27. Underage Drinking
28. Street Racing
29. Cruising
30. Disorder at Budget Motels
31. Drug Dealing in Open-Air Markets
32. Bomb Threats in Schools
33. Illicit Sexual Activity in Public Places
34. Robbery of Taxi Drivers
35. School Vandalism & Break-Ins
36. Drunk Driving
37. Juvenile Runaways
38. Exploitation of Trafficked Women
39. Student Party Riots
40. People with Mental Illness
41. Child Pornography on the Internet
42. Witness Intimidation

43. Burglary at Single-Family House Construction Sites
44. Disorder at Day Labor Sites
45. Domestic Violence
46. Thefts of and from Cars on Residential Streets & Driveways
47. Drive-By Shootings
48. Bank Robbery
49. Robbery of Convenience Stores
50. Traffic Congestion Around Schools
51. Pedestrian Injuries & Fatalities
52. Bicycle Theft
53. Abandoned Vehicles
54. Spectator Violence in Stadiums
55. Child Abuse and Neglect in the Home
56. Homeless Encampments
57. Stolen Goods Markets
58. Theft of Scrap Metal
59. Street Robbery
60. Theft of Customers' Personal Property in Cafes and Bars
61. Aggressive Driving
62. Sexual Assault of Women by Strangers
63. Export of Stolen Vehicles
64. Abandoned Buildings and Lots
65. Animal Cruelty
66. Missing Persons
67. as Drive-Offs
68. Chronic Public Inebriation
69. rug-Impaired Driving
70. Home Invasion Robbery
71. Elderly Abuse
72. Hate Crimes
73. Robbery of Pharmacies
74. Retaliatory Violent Disputes

SOURCE: https://popcenter.asu.edu/content/problem-specific-guides-0.

## Summary

Modern police organizations have a variety of strategies to choose from, including community policing, problem-oriented policing, intelligence-led policing, and predictive policing. These strategies have developed over the past 30 to 40 years for particular reasons, but one thing they have in common is landmark research demonstrating that previous police operational methods were not effective. Since the first effectiveness studies were completed in the 1970s, police departments have searched for alternative strategies that would be more effective in controlling crime, satisfying the public, making people feel safe, and achieving other important goals of the multidimensional police bottom line. Today, we have solid evidence on the strengths and weaknesses of each of these contemporary strategies, as well as an expectation that future studies will produce even more authoritative information to help police executives choose and design the most effective strategies for their communities.

## Critical Thinking Questions

1. The results of the Kansas City Preventive Patrol Experiment were surprising to the public and the police. What do you think were the main reasons why different levels of motorized patrol failed to impact crime or public perception?

2. According to the findings of the Newark Foot Patrol Experiment, crime was not reduced in neighborhoods that had foot patrol, but people in those areas felt safer anyway. How would you explain this apparent contradiction?

3. The relationship between the police and the community, especially minority communities, seems to be a chronic problem. Why do you think that is the case?

4. Getting police officers and police departments to emphasize crime prevention, as opposed to law enforcement and criminal investigation, has proven difficult. Why do you think this is the case?

5. Many police departments have encountered difficulties in implementing COP. Why do you think it has been so difficult to translate the rhetoric of COP into reality?

6. Both the federal government and thousands of America's local police departments embraced COP starting in the 1990s. Yet in the 2020s, American policing is experiencing a crisis of legitimacy. What happened?

## References

Alarid, L. F., and Novak, K. J. 2008. "Citizens' Views on Using Alternate Reporting Methods in Policing." *Criminal Justice Policy Review* 19: 25–39.

Bennett, T. 1998. "Police and Public Involvement in the Delivery of Community Policing." In J. P. Brodeur (ed.), *How to Recognize Good Policing: Problems and Issues*, pp. 107–122. Thousand Oaks, CA: Sage.

Boydstun, J. E., and Sherry, M. E. 1975. *San Diego Community Profile: Final Report*. Washington, DC: Police Foundation.

Braga, A. 2008. *Police Enforcement Strategies to Prevent Crime in Hot Spot Areas*. Crime Prevention Research Review No. 2. Washington, DC: Office of Community Oriented Policing Services.

Braga, A., Turchan, B., Papachristos, A., and Hureau, D. 2019. Hot Spots Policing of Small Geographic Areas Effects on Crime. *Campbell Collaboration*. https://www.campbellcollaboration.org/better-evidence/effects-of-hot-spots-policing-on-crime.html.

Brooks, C. 2020. *Local Police Departments: Police and Procedures, 2016*. Washington, DC: Bureau of Justice Statistics. https://bjs.ojp.gov/content/pub/pdf/lpdpp16.pdf.

Brown, L. P. 1985. "Police–Community Power Sharing." In W. A. Geller (ed.), *Police Leadership in America: Crisis and Opportunity*, pp. 70–83. New York: Praeger.

Buerger, M. 1994. "The Problems of Problem Solving: Resistance, Interdependencies, and Conflicting Interests." *American Journal of Police* 13(3): 1–36.

Bureau of Justice Assistance. 1994a. *A Police Guide to Surveying Citizens and Their Environment*. Washington, DC: Author.

Bureau of Justice Assistance. 1994b. *Neighborhood-Oriented Policing in Rural Communities: A Program Planning Guide*. Washington, DC: Author.

Bureau of Justice Assistance. 1994c. Understanding Community Policing: A Framework for Action. Washington, DC: Author.

Cahn, M. F., and Tien, J. 1981. *An Alternative Approach in Police Response: Wilmington Management of Demand Program*. Cambridge, MA: Public Systems Evaluation.

Caiden, G. E. 1977. *Police Revitalization*. Lexington, MA: Heath.

Cohen, M., and McEwen, J. T. 1984. "Handling Calls for Service: Alternatives to Traditional Policing." *National Institutes of Justice Reports* 187(September): 4–8.

Commission on Accreditation for Law Enforcement Agencies. 2022. *Standards for Law Enforcement Agencies: The Standards Manual for the CALEA Law Enforcement Accreditation Program*, 6th ed. as amended. Gainesville, VA: Author.

Cordner, G. 1981. "The Effects of Directed Patrol: A Natural Quasi-Experiment in Pontiac." In J. J. Fyfe (ed.), *Contemporary Issues in Law Enforcement*, pp. 37–58. Thousand Oaks, CA: Sage.

Cordner, G. 1988. "A Problem-Oriented Approach to Community-Oriented Policing." In J. Greene and S. Mastrofski (eds.), *Community Policing: Rhetoric or Reality?* pp. 135–152. New York: Praeger.

Cordner, G. 2013. "Science Solves Crime: Myth or Reality." In R. M. Bohm and J. T. Walker (eds.), *Demystifying Crime and Criminal Justice*, 2nd ed., pp. 157–165. New York: Oxford.

Cordner, G. 2014. "Community Policing." In M. D. Reisig and R. J. Kane (eds.), *The Oxford Handbook of Police and Policing*, pp. 148–171. New York: Oxford.

Cordner, G. 2020. *Evidence-Based Policing in 45 Small Bytes*. Washington, DC: National Institute of Justice. https://www.ncjrs.gov/pdffiles1/nij/254326.pdf.

Cordner, G. and Alpert, G. 2018. "Striking a Balance: Research, Science, and Policing." *The Police Chief* 8(August): 14–15.

Cordner, G., and Biebel, E. P. 2005. "Problem-Oriented Policing in Practice." *Criminology & Public Policy* 4(2): 155–180.

Cordner, G., Greene, J. R., and Bynum, T. S. 1983. "The Sooner the Better: Some Effects of Police Response Time." In R. R. Bennett (ed.), *Police at Work: Policy Issues and Analysis*, pp. 145–164. Thousand Oaks, CA: Sage.

Cordner, G., and Perkins, E. 2013. *E-COP: Using the Web to Enhance Community Oriented Policing*. Washington, DC: Office of Community Oriented Policing Service. https://cops.usdoj.gov/RIC/Publications/cops-w0706-pub.pdf.

Cordner, G., and Trojanowicz, R. C. 1992. "Patrol." In G. Cordner and D. C. Hale (eds.), *What Works in Policing? Operations and Administration Examined*, pp. 3–18. Cincinnati, OH: Anderson.

Coupe, R. T., and Blake, L. 2005. "The Effects of Patrol Workloads and Response Strength on Arrests at Burglary Emergencies." *Journal of Criminal Justice* 33: 239–255.

Eck, J. E. 1979. *Managing Case Assignments: The Burglary Investigation Decision Model Replication*. Washington, DC: Police Executive Research Forum.

Eck, J. E. 1983. *Solving Crimes*. Washington, DC: Police Executive Research Forum.

Eck, J. E. 1992. "Criminal Investigation." In G. Cordner and D. C. Hale (eds.), *What Works in Policing? Operations and Administration Examined*, pp. 19–34. Cincinnati, OH: Anderson.

Eck, J. E., and Spelman, W. 1987. *Problem-Solving: Problem-Oriented Policing in Newport News*. Washington, DC: Police Executive Research Forum.

Feeley, M. M., and Sarat, A. D. 1981. *The Policy Dilemma: Federal Crime Policy and the Law Enforcement Assistance Administration, 1978-1988*. Minneapolis: University of Minnesota.

Feinberg, S. E., Kinley, L., and Reiss, A. J., Jr. 1976. "Redesigning the Kansas City Preventive Patrol Experiment." *Evaluation* 3: 124–131.

Fleming, J., and Rhodes, R. 2017. "Experience Is Not a Dirty Word." *Policy & Politics Journal Blog*, June 20. https://policyandpoliticsblog.com/2017/06/20/experience-is-not-a-dirty-word.

Frank, J., and Liederbach, J. 2003. "The Work Routines and Citizen Interactions of Small-Town and Rural Police Officers." In Q. C. Thurman and E. F. McGarrell (eds.), *Community Policing in a Rural Setting*, pp. 49–60. Cincinnati, OH: Anderson.

Fridell, L., Lunney, R., Diamond, D., and Kubu, B. 2001. *Racially Biased Policing: A Principled Response*. Washington, DC: Police Executive Research Forum.

Fridell, L., and Wycoff, M. A. 2004. *Community Policing: The Past, Present, and Future*. Washington, DC: Police Executive Research Forum.

Goldstein, H. 1979. "Improving Policing: A Problem-Oriented Approach." *Crime & Delinquency* 25: 236–258.

Goldstein, H. 1987. "Toward Community-Oriented Policing: Potential, Basic Requirements and Threshold Questions." *Crime & Delinquency* 33: 6–30.

Goldstein, H. 1990. *Problem-Oriented Policing.* New York: McGraw-Hill.

Greenberg, B., Elliott, C. V., Kraft, L. P., and Proctor, H. S. 1977. *Felony Investigation Decision Model: An Analysis of Investigative Elements of Information.* Washington, DC: Law Enforcement Assistance Administration.

Greene, J., and Mastrofski, S. (eds.). 1988. *Community Policing: Rhetoric or Reality?* New York: Praeger.

Greenwood, P. W., and Petersilia, J. 1975. *The Criminal Investigation Process, Volume I: Summary and Policy Implications.* Santa Monica, CA: RAND Corporation.

Haarr, R. N. 2001. "The Making of a Community Policing Officer: The Impact of Basic Training and Occupational Socialization on Police Recruits." *Police Quarterly* 4: 402–433.

Hayeslip, D. and Cordner, G. 1987. "The Effects of Community-Oriented Patrol on Police Officer Attitudes." *American Journal of Police* 6(1): 95–119.

Hinkle, J. C., Weisburd, D., Telep, C. W., and Petersen, K. 2020. "Problem-Oriented Policing for Reducing Crime and Disorder: An Updates Systematic Review and Meta-Analysis." *Campbell Systematic Reviews* 16(2): e1089.

Hu, X., and Lovrich, N, 2020. *Electronic Community-Oriented Policing: Theories, Contemporary Efforts, and Future Directions.* Lanham, MD: Lexington Books.

Kelling, G. L., and Moore, M. 1988. *The Evolving Strategy of Policing: Perspectives on Policing.* Washington, DC: National Institute of Justice.

Kelling, G. L., Pate, T., Dieckman, D., and Brown, C. E. 1974. *The Kansas City Preventive Patrol Experiment: A Summary Report.* Washington, DC: Police Foundation.

Kerley, K., and Benson, M. 2000. "Does Community-Oriented Policing Help Build Stronger Communities?" *Police Quarterly* 3: 46–69.

Klockars, C. B. 1988. "The Rhetoric of Community Policing." In J. Greene and S. Mastrofski (eds.), *Community Policing: Rhetoric or Reality?* pp. 239–258. New York: Praeger.

Larson, R. C. 1975. "What Happened to Patrol Operations in Kansas City? A Review of the Kansas City Preventive Patrol Experiment." *Journal of Criminal Justice* 3: 267–297.

Lilley, D., and Hinduja, S. 2006. "Organizational Values and Police Officer Evaluation: A Content Comparison between Traditional and Community Policing Agencies." *Police Quarterly* 9: 486–513.

Lum, C., and Koper, C. S. 2017. *Evidence-Based Policing: Translating Research into Practice.* Oxford: Oxford University.

Lum, C., Koper, C., and Wu, X. 2021. "Can We Really Defund the Police? A Nine-Agency Study of Police Response to Calls for Service." *Police Quarterly.* https://journals.sagepub.com/doi/full/10.1177/10986111211035002.

Madhani, A. 2016. "Task Force Finds Chicago Police Department Plagued by Racism." USA Today, April 13. https://www.usatoday.com/story/news/2016/04/13/task-force-finds-chicago-police-has-been-plagued-racism/82996318/.

Manning, P. K. 1988. "Community Policing as a Drama of Control." In J. Greene and S. Mastrofski (eds.), *Community Policing: Rhetoric or Reality?* pp. 27–46. New York: Praeger.

Martin, S. E., and Sherman, L. W. 1986. "Selective Apprehension: A Police Strategy for Repeat Offenders." *Criminology* 24: 155–173.

Mastrofski, S. 2006. "Community Policing: A Skeptical View." In D. Weisburd and A. A. Braga (eds.), *Police Innovation: Contrasting Perspectives.* Cambridge, UK: Cambridge University Press.

McEwen, J. T., Connors, E. F., and Cohen, M. I. 1986. *Evaluation of the Differential Police Responses Field Test.* Washington, DC: National Institute of Justice.

Moore, M. H., and Trojanowicz, R. C. 1988. *Corporate Strategies for Policing.* Perspectives on Policing No. 6. Washington, DC: National Institute of Justice.

National Research Council. 2009. *Strengthening Forensic Science in the United States: A Path Forward.* Washington, DC: National Academies Press.

Office of Community Oriented Policing Services. 2002. *Community Policing in Smaller Jurisdictions.* Washington, DC: Authors.

Office of Community Oriented Policing Services (COPS Office). 2009. *Community Policing Defined*. Washington, DC: Author. https://cops.usdoj.gov/RIC/ric.php?page=detail&id=COPS-P157.

O'Neill, J.P. 2018. "How the NYPD Keeps Making the City Safer." *New York Post*, June 4. https://nypost.com/2018/06/04/how-the-nypd-keeps-making-the-city-safer/.

Parks, R., Mastrofski, S., DeJong, C., and Gray, K. 1999. "How Officers Spend Their Time with the Community." *Justice Quarterly* 16(3): 483–518.

Pate, T., Bowers, R. A., Ferrara, A., and Lorence, J. 1976a. *Police Response Time: Its Determinants and Effects*. Washington, DC: Police Foundation.

Pate, T., Bowers, R. A., and Parks, R. 1976b. *Three Approaches to Criminal Apprehension in Kansas City: An Evaluation Report*. Washington, DC: Police Foundation.

Pelfrey, W. V., Jr. 2004. "The Inchoate Nature of Community Policing: Differences between Community Policing and Traditional Police Officers." *Justice Quarterly* 21: 579–601.

Police Foundation. 1981. *The Newark Foot Patrol Experiment*. Washington, DC: Author.

President's Task Force on Twenty-First Century Policing. 2015. *Final Report*. Washington, DC: Office of Community Oriented Policing Services. https://www.ojp.gov/ncjrs/virtual-library/abstracts/final-report-presidents-task-force-21st-century-policing.

Queram, K. E. 2018. "How Gun Violence Decreased in Chicago." *Route Fifty*, June 4. https://www.routefifty.com/public-safety/2018/06/gun-violence-decreased-chicago/148694/.

Radelet, L. 1986. *The Police and the Community*, 4th ed. New York: Macmillan.

Reinier, G. H., Greenlee, M. R., Gibbens, M. H., and Marshall, S. P. 1977. *Crime Analysis in Support of Patrol*. Washington, DC: Law Enforcement Assistance Administration.

Reiss, A. J., Jr. 1985. "Shaping and Serving the Community: The Role of the Police Chief Executive." In W. A. Geller (ed.), *Police Leadership in America: Crisis and Opportunity*, pp. 61–69. New York: Praeger.

Scarborough, K. E., Christiansen, K., Cordner, G., and Smith, M. 1998. "An Evaluation of Community Oriented Policing Training." *Police Forum* 8: 11–15.

Schwartz, A. T., and Clarren, S. N. 1977. *The Cincinnati Team Policing Experiment: A Summary Report*. Washington, DC: Police Foundation.

Scott, M. 2000. *Problem-Oriented Policing: Reflections on the First 20 Years*. Washington, DC: Office of Community Oriented Policing Services.

Scott, M., and Goldstein, H. 2005. *Shifting and Sharing Responsibility for Public Safety Problems*. Response Guide No. 3. Washington, DC: Office of Community Oriented Policing Services. https://www.popcenter.org/responses/responsibility/.

Sherman, L. W. 1983. "Patrol Strategies for Police." In J. Q. Wilson (ed.), *Crime and Public Policy*, pp. 145–163. San Francisco: Institute for Contemporary Studies Press.

Sherman, L. W. 1998. "Evidence Based Policing." *Ideas in American Policing*. Washington, DC: Police Foundation.

Sherman, L. W., Milton, C. H., and Kelley, T. V. 1973. *Team Policing: Seven Case Studies*. Washington, DC: Police Foundation.

Skogan, W. G. 2006. *Police and Community in Chicago: A Tale of Three Cities*. New York: Oxford University Press.

Skogan, W. G. 2022. "Prospects for Reform? The Collapse of Community Policing in Chicago." *University of Chicago Law Review* 89(2): 1–23.

Skogan, W. G., and Steiner, L. 2004. *CAPS at Ten: Community Policing in Chicago*. Chicago: Criminal Justice Information Authority.

Sparrow, M. 2011. "Governing Science." *New Perspectives in Policing*. Washington, DC: National Institute of Justice. https://www.ojp.gov/pdffiles1/nij/232179.pdf

Spelman, W., and Brown, D. K. 1982. *Calling the Police: Citizen Reporting of Serious Crime*. Washington, DC: Police Executive Research Forum.

Stoltze, F. 2018. "Michel Moore Appointed LAPD Chief to Replace Charlie Beck." *KPCC Public Radio*, June 4. https://www.scpr.org/news/2018/06/04/83148/second-time-s-the-charm-garcetti-appoints-michel-m/.

Stone, C., and Travis, J. 2011. "Toward a New Professionalism in Policing." *New Perspectives in Policing.* Washington, DC: National Institute of Justice. https://www.ojp.gov/pdffiles1/nij/232359.pdf

Studenkov, I. 2017. "C.A.P.S. Programs May Receive More Funding and Staff after Years of Decline." *Chicago Gazette*, November 2.

Tilley, N., and Laycock, G. 2016. "Engineering a Safer Society. *Public Safety Leadership* 4. https://www. aipm.gov.au/wp-content/uploads/2016/08/Research-Focus-Vol-4-Iss-2-Engineering.pdf.

Tiry, E., Oglesby-Neal, A., and Kim, K. 2019. *Social Media Guidebook for Law Enforcement Agencies: Strategies for Effective Community Engagement.* Washington, DC: Urban Institute. https://www. urban.org/sites/default/files/publication/99786/social_media_guidebook_for_law_enforcement_ agencies_0.pdf.

Trojanowicz, R. C. 1982. *An Evaluation of the Neighborhood Foot Patrol Program in Flint, Michigan.* East Lansing: School of Criminal Justice, Michigan State University.

Trojanowicz, R., and Bucqueroux, B. 1990. *Community Policing: A Contemporary Perspective.* Cincinnati, OH: Anderson.

Tyler, T. R. 2004. "Enhancing Police Legitimacy." *Annals of the American Academy of Political and Social Science* 593(10): 84–99.

Weatheritt, M. 1988. "Community Policing: Rhetoric or Reality?" In J. Greene and S. Mastrofski (eds.), *Community Policing: Rhetoric or Reality?* pp. 153–176. New York: Praeger.

Weisburd, D., and Braga, A. 2006. "Hot Spots as a Model for Police Innovation." In D. Weisburd and A. Braga (eds.), *Police Innovation: Contrasting Perspectives*, pp. 225–244. Cambridge, UK: Cambridge University Press.

Weisburd, D., and Eck, J. E. 2004. "What Can Police Do to Reduce Crime, Disorder, and Fear?" *The Annals of the American Academy of Political and Social Science* 593: 42–65.

Weisburd, D., and Neyroud, P. 2011. "Police Science: Toward a New Paradigm." *New Perspectives in Policing.* Washington, DC: National Institute of Justice.

Wilson, J. Q., and Boland, B. 1979. *The Effect of the Police on Crime.* Washington, DC: Law Enforcement Assistance Administration.

Wilson, J. Q., and Kelling, G. L. 1982. "Broken Windows: The Police and Neighborhood Safety." *Atlantic Monthly* 249: 29–38.

Worden, R. E. 1993. "Toward Equity and Efficiency in Law Enforcement: Differential Police Response." *American Journal of Police* 12: 1–32.

**Part II**

# Police
# Administration

## CHAPTER 5

# Police Organization and Management

## CHAPTER OUTLINE

## CHAPTER OUTLINE (continued)

### KEY TERMS

- balance of power
- centralization
- chain of command
- classical principles
- contingency theory
- controlling
- decentralization
- generalists
- group norms
- inertia
- innovation
- leading
- learning organization
- management
- organizational change
- organizational design
- organizing
- paramilitary model
- planning
- research and development
- specialists
- systems theory
- total quality management
- winning hearts and minds

POLICING A DEMOCRATIC SOCIETY is complex. Indeed, because of this complexity, a police department is one of the most difficult public institutions to manage effectively, perhaps even more so today than in the past. Before 1980, police leaders did not have to contend with the 24-hour cable television news cycle; even 15 years ago, police departments had little worry over viral YouTube videos. As a further complication in the current environment, "What once may have been seen as a purely local matter involving a police department, a chief or an officer, is now seen as part of a national pattern or problem" (Johnson 2016).

It is important to have a fundamental understanding of both the historical and the present-day processes used in managing police departments. This chapter provides a basic overview of police organization and management, including the important topic of *managing change* in police agencies.

## The Managerial Process

**Management** is directing individuals to achieve organizational goals efficiently and effectively. The functions carried out by police managers include planning, organizing, leading, and controlling; how well these functions are performed determines, to a large degree, how successful a department will be.

Although managers perform each of these functions, the time involved in each one varies according to the manager's level in the department. For instance, managers at higher levels, such as assistant chiefs, spend a greater proportion of their time *organizing and planning*; those at lower levels, such as sergeants, spend more time on *supervision*, which focuses primarily on leading and controlling direct subordinates. The time spent in various functions is also influenced by the size of the department. For instance, in a small police department, a sergeant may function as both an assistant chief and a supervisor.

**Planning** is the process of preparing for the future by setting goals and objectives and developing courses of action for accomplishing them. These courses of action involve such activities as determining mission and value statements, conducting research, identifying strategies and methods, developing policies and procedures, and formulating budgets. Although all managers engage in planning, the scope and nature of the activity differ considerably, depending on the level within the department. For instance, whereas a patrol supervisor may develop work schedules and activities for the upcoming week, police chiefs may plan activities and changes for the next year or two. In general, the higher the managerial level, the broader the scope of planning and the longer the time frame for the plan.

**Organizing** is the process of arranging personnel and physical resources to carry out plans and accomplish goals and objectives, which includes designing the organization's structure, units, and jobs. Although all managers are involved in organizing, the degree and scope differ, depending on their level within the department. Whereas the patrol supervisor is concerned with daily work assignments, the chief is more concerned with the organization's overall structure and distribution of personnel and physical resources.

**Leading** is motivating and influencing others to perform the right tasks in the right way to contribute to accomplishing the organization's goals and objectives. Guiding the behavior of others is challenging and may entail leading by example, setting expectations, and influencing values and beliefs. Typically, to motivate employees, police managers must rely on persuasion and internal rewards, such as job satisfaction and feelings of accomplishment, since they do not control salaries or other financial incentives. The leadership role for top-level managers can also encompass managing the relationship between the police and the community as well as other important entities, including criminal justice and government agencies, not to mention the elected officials who set the police budget and ultimately oversee the police department.

**Controlling** is the process by which managers determine and improve the quality and quantity of departmental systems and services, including whether goals and objectives are being accomplished, whether operations are consistent with plans, and whether officers are following departmental policies and procedures. Both *efficiency* (the relationship between resources and outputs) and *effectiveness* (the degree to which goals and objectives are accomplished) are key concepts in this phase of management. If goals or objectives are not realized or plans, policies, and procedures are not being followed, managers must determine why and take action. Controlling can be troublesome, because it may be difficult to determine why performance failures occur and what action should be taken to improve or correct them.

As noted earlier, managers at various levels in the department perform their functions differently. Figure 5.1 depicts the various hierarchical levels found in medium to large police departments. Such organizational structures are termed *pyramids*, because the number of personnel decreases as one goes up in the hierarchy (i.e., there are fewer at the top). *Top managers* exercise the most organizational power and authority and control the most resources and rewards. *Middle managers* formulate objectives and plans for implementing decisions from above and coordinate activities from below. *Lower managers* implement decisions made at higher levels and coordinate and direct the work of employees at the lowest level of the organization. *Rank-and-file personnel* carry out specific tasks.

Formal communication in traditional organizational structures adheres to the **chain of command**, emanating from the top of the hierarchy down through the lower levels and back up. Strict adherence to the chain of command, however, can create problems with respect to both timeliness of decision making and accuracy of communication, so even in the most traditional organizations, *informal* communication channels usually develop and are invaluable for getting work done efficiently.

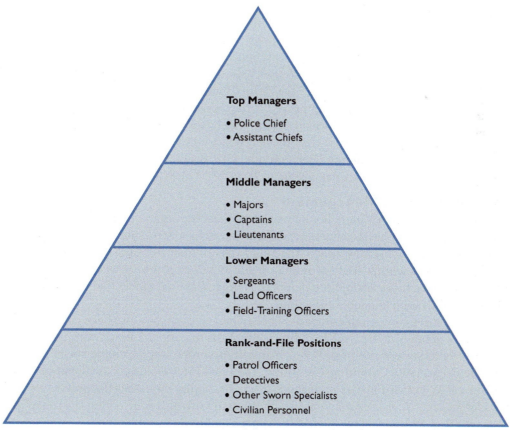

**Top Managers**

- Police Chief
- Assistant Chiefs

**Middle Managers**

- Majors
- Captains
- Lieutenants

**Lower Managers**

- Sergeants
- Lead Officers
- Field-Training Officers

**Rank-and-File Positions**

- Patrol Officers
- Detectives
- Other Sworn Specialists
- Civilian Personnel

**FIGURE 5.1** Organization Pyramid with Levels of Hierarchy.

## The Evolution of Police Management

The theory and practice of police management have evolved through three major perspectives—classical, behavioral, and contemporary. Each of these perspectives and its impact on police management are described next.

### Classical Police Management

The early writers on police management emphasized what is known as a classical approach to organization, including a rigid hierarchical structure, strong centralized control, and authoritarian leadership styles. A cornerstone of this approach was Max Weber's concept of *bureaucracy,* a term he coined at the end of the nineteenth century to identify characteristics that organizations needed to operate rationally. Following the introduction of the bureaucratic model, many writers began to develop what have become known as **classical principles** of organization, which were believed to be universal. Some of Weber's administrative principles that reflect this approach include *specialization* (division of work), *authority and responsibility* (the right to command and require obedience), *discipline* (necessary for effectiveness), *unity of command* (employees are to receive orders from only one superior), *scalar chain* (hierarchy of authority), and *centralization* (the extent to which decision making is retained by the top organizational levels) (Gerth and Mills 1946).

Early police theorists, in an attempt to create a more professional police force, placed great emphasis on the classical principles. The result was a highly bureaucratic structure with many hierarchical levels managed and organized along military lines in an attempt to insulate the police from partisan politics. Often called the **paramilitary model,** this approach emphasized a legalistic style of police work for controlling crime along with authoritarian managerial practices intended to control officers' behavior and minimize corruption.

Influential writers promoting these ideals first appeared in the United States during the early 1900s, continued to dominate into the 1950s, and still influence police management today. Bruce Smith's *Police Systems in the United States* (1940) emphasized that police departments could be significantly improved if they were properly designed and managed according to the "principles of organization" widely adopted in military and industrial circles. Another significant work that affected police practice was O. W. Wilson's *Police Administration* (1950, including later editions with Bruce McLaren). This text became known as the "bible" of police management.

### Behavioral Police Management

Beginning in the early 1970s, police management theorists began questioning the classical approach with its emphasis on bureaucracy and hierarchical structure, authoritarian managerial practices, and narrow view of the police role. In line with increased behavioral research (i.e., the scientific study of human behavior) during the 1950s and 1960s, these writers stressed a more flexible and democratic organizational model that might improve employee motivation and job satisfaction.

By the 1960s, a considerable amount of behavioral research had also been completed on what police actually do on the job, indicating that the majority of police work was related not directly to law enforcement, but to maintaining order and providing social services (e.g., see Bercal 1970; Cumming, Cumming, and Edell 1965; Goldstein 1968; Parnas 1967; Wilson 1968). Perhaps just as important, it was becoming clear that the police role was broader and more complex than many had originally suspected, involving the use of *discretion* to deal with a wide range of complex problems and situations.

These findings had serious implications for the well-entrenched paramilitary model. As Bittner (1970, 51) argued, "The core of the police mandate is profoundly incompatible with the military posture. On balance, the military–bureaucratic organization of the police is a serious handicap." He viewed the proper use of discretion as central to the professionalization of the police role, and he believed that overreliance on regulations and bureaucratic routine seriously inhibited such development. Bittner noted that the paramilitary model put more emphasis on a neat appearance and conformance to bureaucratic routine than on effective performance.

Similarly, Goldstein (1977) suggested that the *organizational climate* in police departments must change if the objective is to retain highly qualified officers and take advantage of their talents. Rank-and-file officers should be more involved in policy making and in determining methods of operation and should be able to realize their "full potential" in ways other than being promoted into management.

## Contemporary Police Management

Increased sophistication and findings from behavioral science research led to the development of systems theory and contingency theory and the movement toward private sector influences, including corporate strategy, total quality management, and reinventing government. These developments encouraged not only improved managerial practices but also more appreciation for the external environments of police organizations.

**Systems and Contingency Theory.**   Conceptually, **systems theory** means that all parts of a system (i.e., an organization) are interrelated and interdependent. The importance of applying systems theory to police departments is that it helps managers understand that any changes made in their unit will affect other units and the organization as a whole. Thus, police managers should ensure that the activities of their units are in agreement with the overall needs and goals of the department.

Police managers should also be aware that systems can be viewed as either open or closed. An *open system* interacts with, and adapts to, its environment; a *closed system* does not. The environment for police departments is essentially the community in which they operate, plus other organizations they interact with. Departments that are relatively more open are more effective, because they are more aware of external needs, expectations, opportunities, and threats and therefore can adapt their practices accordingly.

**Contingency theory** is based on open-systems theory and recognizes that many internal and external factors influence organizational behavior. Because these factors vary according to different circumstances, there is no "one best way" to organize and manage diverse types of organizations. The underlying theme for *contingency management* is that *it all depends on the particular situation*. The task for managers, then, is to try to determine in which situations and at what times certain methods and techniques are the most effective.

Roberg (1979) applied contingency theory to policing. He emphasized contingency concepts and the necessity of identifying *both* internal and external variables that affect police departmental behavior. Accordingly, such factors as the complex nature of the role, increasing educational levels of employees, and the relatively unstable nature of the environment (e.g., changing laws, cultural diversity, and political influences) must be considered in attempting to determine the most effective police management methods. When such factors are considered, "many of the simplistic classical prescriptions which have been applied to police organization design are clearly inadequate" (190).

---

**INSIDE POLICING 5.1**   Principles of Quality Leadership

1. Believe in, foster, and support teamwork.
2. Make a commitment to the problem-solving process, use it, and let data (not emotions) drive decisions.
3. Seek employees' input before making key decisions.
4. Believe that the best way to improve work quality or service is to ask and listen to employees who are doing the work.
5. Strive to develop mutual respect and trust among employees.
6. Have a customer orientation and focus toward employees and citizens.
7. Manage based on the behavior of 95 percent of employees, not on the 5 percent who cause problems; deal with the 5 percent promptly and fairly.
8. Improve systems and examine processes before placing blame on people.
9. Avoid top-down, power-oriented decision making whenever possible.
10. Encourage creativity through risk taking and be tolerant of honest mistakes.
11. Be a facilitator and coach; develop an open atmosphere that encourages providing for and accepting feedback.
12. With teamwork, develop with employees agreed-upon goals and a plan to achieve them.

SOURCE: D. C. Couper and S. H. Lobitz, *Quality Policing: The Madison Experience* (Washington, DC: Police Executive Research Forum, 1991), 48.

---

**Private-Sector Influences.**   Following World War II, a management system focusing on product quality, known as **total quality management**, was developed in Japan to help revitalize Japanese industries. It transformed a situation in which "Made in Japan" had become a symbol for inferior products to one synonymous with the highest-quality products in the world. The foundation for this approach lies in *quality-control* techniques and the process of *continuous improvement*. To maximize the use of human resources, total quality management stresses the importance of employee participation, teamwork, and continuous learning and improvement. Its quantitative dimension involves the use of research and statistical techniques to evaluate and improve the processes in an organization and to link those processes to results.

This approach spread rapidly to the public sector as well—including the police. *Quality Policing: The Madison Experience* (Couper and Lobitz 1991) describes one department's change away from a highly traditional, bureaucratic organization toward a quality-oriented organization (also see Couper 2021). The change process was demanding and took about 20 years to complete. The principles of quality management or "quality leadership" used by Chief Couper in transforming the department are listed in Inside Policing 5.1. More information about "The Madison Experience" is presented later in this chapter as a case study of organizational change.

## Organizational Design

**Organizational design** is concerned with the formal patterns of arrangements and relationships that link people together to accomplish organizational goals. It was traditionally assumed by the classical school that a pyramidal structure was the most appropriate for police departments. This design, characterized by many hierarchical levels and narrow spans of control (i.e., a small number of employees per supervisor), allowing close supervision and control of employees and operations, creates a *tall structure*. Conversely, a *flat structure* is characterized by fewer hierarchical levels with wider spans of control (i.e., a larger number of employees per supervisor), allowing greater employee autonomy and less control of operations. These differences between tall and flat structures are illustrated by the two organization charts depicted in Figure 5.2, both with 24 people at the rank-and-file (bottom) level. It is easy to see that the tall structure has two extra levels of hierarchy and narrower spans of control for closer supervision and control over subordinates.

Organizations with taller structures attempt to coordinate their activities through **centralization**; that is, authority and decision making are retained at the top levels. Organizations with flatter structures employ more **decentralization**, wherein authority and decision making are delegated to lower levels. This may be important in policing, since those at the lowest levels—police officers and their immediate supervisors—know their communities' needs better than anyone else in the organization. Tall structures also tend to have a greater degree of *specialization* with respect to the division of labor. The narrower the range of tasks performed by each employee, the greater the level of specialization; conversely, the greater the number of tasks performed, the lower the level of specialization. This explains why patrol officers, who perform a great number of diverse activities, including patrolling, responding to calls, problem solving, and investigation, are often referred to as **generalists**, as opposed to **specialists**.

Departments adopting community policing (COP) often flatten their structures (i.e., reduce the number of hierarchical levels). For example, when Austin, Texas, moved toward

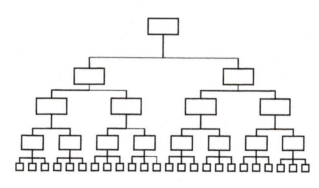

Tall Structure

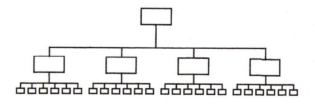

Flat Structure

**FIGURE 5.2** Tall and Flat Organizational Structures.

COP in the late 1990s, it was decided to gradually eliminate the rank of deputy chief (thus eliminating one hierarchical level) and one-third of the positions of captain. This restructuring allowed the department to become more flexible, move decision making down, and have more street-level officers to handle calls and be available for the expanded role of engaging the community (Watson, Stone, and DeLuca 1998).

Although some restructuring of the traditional paramilitary design is necessary when implementing COP and other policing innovations, major structural changes in traditional police departments have been difficult to come by. One study by Maguire (1997), which analyzed the characteristics of 236 large municipal departments (with 100 or more sworn members) throughout the country found no significant structural differences among those departments that reported adopting COP, those that reported they were in the planning or implementation stages, and those that reported having no plans for COP. A later study by Zhao, Ren, and Lovrich (2010, 224–225) of 195 police agencies in 47 states found that "while the rhetoric of community policing has been widely disseminated and putatively broadly implemented, COP practices *never have been* organizationally institutionalized. ... The structural changes in police organizations called for in the COP philosophy have not been accomplished despite widespread *adoption of the outward trappings of policing reform*" (emphasis added).

## Criticisms of the Paramilitary Design

As noted earlier, the traditional paramilitary design or model has been nearly indestructible in policing—attempting to do so has been described by some authors as bending granite (Guyot 1979; King 2003). In addition, this model has been criticized by scholars since the early stages of the behavioral police management era (Myren 1960; Angell 1971; Germann 1971). Auten (1981), for instance, suggested that the paramilitary organization treats the patrol officer like a *soldier* and thus is based on numerous inaccurate assumptions about police work and democracy. Ironically, one observer (Cowper 2000) with extensive experience in both policing and the military suggested that military leadership has evolved beyond strict adherence to the traditional model (e.g., reducing reliance on rules and increasing feedback from soldiers), whereas American police departments continue to adhere more closely to it.

An early study by Franz and Jones (1987) lent empirical support to the critics' charges. In this study, police officers were compared with employees in other city departments that had not been exposed to the paramilitary design. The researchers found that police employees perceived (1) greater problems with communications, (2) greater amounts of distrust, (3) lower levels of morale, and (4) lower levels of organizational performance. Franz and Jones concluded that "the data presented seriously question the capability of the quasi-military police organizational model to meet today's needs" (161).

Typically, today's police managers report that they have adopted modern and contemporary organizational approaches. For example, Vito, Suresh, and Richards (2011) surveyed 126 police managers from 23 states attending a management training course and found a strong preference for the *servant* leadership style, which emphasizes concern for the needs and welfare of organization members. Similarly, a National Institute of Justice report discussing what will be required of police leaders in the future identified a wide range of desirable knowledge and skills (Batts, Smoot, and Scrivner 2012; see Inside Policing 5.2).

| INSIDE POLICING 5.2 | Leadership Traits for Modern Policing |

- **Global perspective.** A knowledge and awareness of global history and issues and their impact on crime.
- **Creativity.** A thought process equipped to deal with problems that are outside the norm.
- **Change management and adaptivity.** An ability to adapt and change organizations based on global shifts and technology needs.
- **Comfort in the midst of independence.** An ability to remain comfortable in an organization in which workers demand autonomy.
- **Strong oral and written communication.** An ability to explain complex theories in understandable terms.
- **Mastering technological trends.** An ability to anticipate how technological changes will interact with constitutional law and prepare the agency to respond appropriately.
- **Architect of change.** An ability to act as a trendsetter and innovator.
- **An understanding of research methods.** Be comfortable with research analysis and interpretation, which may include holding progressive and advanced degrees; be able to develop stronger relationships with colleges and universities.
- **Striking a balance: integrating strategy, culture, and political influences.** An ability to incorporate numerous influences into an executive model to clarify the direction in which the organization must go to accomplish its mission and, possibly, what an organization must do to recover from crisis.

SOURCE: A. W. Batts, S. M. Smoot, and E. Scrivner. 2012. "Police Leadership Challenges in a Changing World." *New Perspectives in Policing* (Washington DC: National Institute of Justice). https://www.ojp.gov/pdffiles1/nij/238338.pdf.

## Influence of Community Policing

As noted earlier, over the past several decades police departments have been advised to flatten their organizational structures, decentralize authority, and de-specialize police functions to implement COP more effectively. Reflecting this, one of the three fundamental components of COP (in addition to partnerships and problem solving) is organizational change (Office of Community Oriented Policing Services 2009; Cordner 2014a). The basic logic is straightforward—if COP is a different approach to doing police work, then how police agencies are organized and managed might need to be different.

Besides organizational structure, three other implications of COP for police management can be noted. One is organizing and allocating resources based more on geography (i.e., beat teams and area commanders) rather than on function or time of day. Another is upgrading information systems and analytical capacities to support officers focused on community engagement and problem solving in specific geographic areas (Dunworth et al. 2000). Third is having police executives who expect their officers to follow the principles of procedural justice on the street realize that, within the police department, organizational justice is equally important (see "Voices from the Field" by Chief of Police Shon Barnes). Consequently, supportive, coaching, and mentoring styles of supervision and management are encouraged when the objective is to effectively implement COP.

## VOICES FROM THE FIELD

### Shon F. Barnes
*Chief of Police, Madison, Wisconsin, Police Department*

Procedural justice is a concept that has gained significant appeal in the ongoing effort to improve police–community relationships. Police managers are attempting to implement this concept as part of "cultural change" within police departments. Police managers must realize why citizens comply with authority (the central tenant of procedural justice) in order to better educate a police workforce that is intent on reducing the number of negative police–citizen encounters.

In order for police managers to promote *internal* procedural justice, there must be a change in the traditional police culture. Mangers can achieve a cultural change toward the procedural justice goal by practicing LEAD (Listen and give voice to all, Educate to create trust, Accept only absolute fairness in decision making, and Discipline with dignity).

Giving voice to all community stakeholders is an essential element in establishing a culture that supports procedural justice. COP asserts that police managers should give voice to citizens and stakeholders when determining police crime reduction objectives. This is an important aspect of strategic planning and must also include officers. Police leaders should spend as much time in police employee forums as they do in neighborhood and community forums. This strategy affords police managers the opportunity to send the positive message of procedural justice. Most important, managers who provide forums for effective communication are able to set and define worthwhile goals that are a vital element of effective leadership.

The only way to build trust within an organization is to establish a culture of fairness. To make the concept a reality, police managers must include line officers in the decision-making process, because when officers participate in the process, they are more likely to view decisions as fair. Departmental internal trust and fairness are directly correlated with the external application of community trust and fairness exhibited by officers who are in direct contact with our citizens. There can be no external community procedural justice practices, if police managers have not established procedural justice practices internally.

Discipline with dignity refers to any opportunity to provide "a teachable moment" when officers miss the mark. Police managers should be aware that culture change does not occur in a vacuum. Officers will make mistakes. Managers should immediately acknowledge officer mistakes, determine the cause, use the mistake as an opportunity for growth and development, and apply corrective action while maintaining the employee's dignity.

The implementation of procedural justice within a police department is contingent on the application of strategic leadership. The establishment of a vision and direction for procedural justice initiatives is an essential element of the implementation phase. In all organizations, the values and direction of the leader matter. Culture simply means we live by these values (voice, decision fairness, treatment with dignity and respect, and trust) and those who will join our ranks must be responsive to them. These are the values all police managers must set forth in order for citizens to recognize the presence of justice in all police interactions.

## Structuring Police Discretion

The way that police organizations are managed is also strongly affected by two realities of police work: (1) police officers have discretion, which means that they make decisions about how best to handle incidents, such as whether to issue citations and make arrests and whether to use force; and (2) because of situational exigencies (Bittner 1970), such as uncertainty, unpredictability, the need for quick decisions, and other peculiarities of policing, it is nearly impossible to prescribe in advance exactly what choices officers should make in each case. Thus, police managers have the difficult task of guiding and controlling subordinates who actually have a substantial amount of leeway in how they do their work (Scott and Cordner 2014). Moreover, supervisors are rarely present when quick decisions must be made in the field—decisions that sometimes have serious consequences.

Because of the nature of police work, the control function of management is largely exercised after the fact. Reports are reviewed by supervisors, and thanks to modern technology, dashboard camera and body-worn camera video can also be reviewed to determine whether officers performed properly. When officers use significant levels of force or complaints are received from the public, internal and sometimes outside investigations are undertaken, again to determine whether performance was proper. Of course, officers who are found to have performed improperly may be sent for additional training, disciplined, or even terminated, depending on the circumstances.

Guiding officers' exercise of discretion on the front end is an even more important responsibility of police management. One of the reasons for careful hiring of police officers is to select applicants who have qualities and characteristics associated with good judgment and decision making. Next, a primary aim of training is to give police the knowledge and skills they will need to make and carry out good decisions, along with practice in making quick decisions under stress. Then, building on careful selection and training, police departments establish policies and procedures that are designed to guide officer decision making in various situations, usually specifying factors that should be considered and sometimes either mandating or prohibiting specific actions. Because of the nature of police work described earlier, these policies and procedures almost always leave some room for discretion, and sometimes significant room, but the aim is to set boundaries and give officers as much guidance as feasible, given that it is impossible to anticipate every conceivable variable and situation that might arise.

## Managing Police Performance

Police management has the challenge of monitoring and optimizing performance on three levels: the entire organization, units within the organization, and individual police personnel. At each level, it is crucial to identify and measure the key dimensions of performance, which are those most connected to the police organization's goals and overall mission.

### Measuring What Matters

It is common for organizations to measure the wrong things, perhaps because they are fuzzy about their actual goals and mission or because goals have changed over time but measures and measurement systems have not. A particularly common weakness is the tendency to measure what is easy to measure, rather than what really matters the most. A related fault is the tendency to measure inputs and activities rather than outputs and outcomes. This approach confuses "How hard are we working?" with the more important question "What are we accomplishing?" For example, in the education field, this leads to a focus on the number of hours in the curriculum, rather than on the extent of students' learning.

It is vitally important to "measure what matters," because in organizations, "we get what we measure." People in organizations usually try to determine what they must do to be successful, or at least stay out of trouble, and knowing what aspects of performance are measured is a strong clue. In a police department, patrol officers are typically attuned to whether their sergeant counts their stops, citations, or arrests; the sergeant in turn tries to meet the lieutenant's expectations; and so forth. In modern times with computerized data systems, it is becoming easier to track all kinds of data about officer and unit performance, so knowing which "metrics" are being scrutinized is a key piece of knowledge for anyone hoping to be successful in the organization.

Many police agencies have run afoul of "measuring what matters" in recent years. On the broadest level, US police are still measuring crime according to Uniform Crime Report categories established more than 80 years ago so that, for example, cyberthefts are not counted in the serious crime tally each year, no matter how much is stolen. In the United Kingdom, the national government until recently set crime-related targets for each of its 43 local police forces, causing them to reallocate resources and pursue those targets regardless of whether they actually represented their region's biggest problems (Guilfoyle 2013). In the New York Police Department (NYPD), pressure from the top on precinct commanders to reduce crime levels resulted in widespread downgrading of reported crimes, such as recording burglaries as trespassing, and outright failure to record crimes such as sexual assaults and thefts (Eterno and Silverman 2012). More recently, the pressure shifted to stops and frisks in the NYPD, causing those numbers to skyrocket until a federal court ruled they were unconstitutional and discriminatory (Goldstein 2013). In Chicago, command pressure to produce "contact cards" (simple documentation of each public contact) apparently deflected attention away from the more important objectives of finding illegal guns, making arrests, and solving cases (Mitchell 2016; see Inside Policing 5.3).

## Police Organizational Performance

The case was made in Chapter 1 for monitoring and measuring seven dimensions of police organizational performance (Moore and Braga 2003):

- Reduce crime and victimization.
- Call offenders to account.
- Reduce fear and enhance personal security.
- Ensure civility in public spaces (ordered liberty).

---

### INSIDE POLICING 5.3 | Measuring What Doesn't Matter

This article/radio report describes the ups and downs of street stops, gun seizures, and gun crimes in Chicago over the last 20 years. Until recently, officially recorded stops had been increasing dramatically, yet fewer guns were being recovered. The suggestion is that administrative pressure had become more about the number of contact cards than about cases solved, crimes prevented, or intelligence gathered.

**Discussion Question:** There is a saying, "keep your eye on the prize," which means to keep focused on what you are trying to accomplish. Yet people and organizations routinely get distracted and confuse outputs with outcomes, sometimes just because the outputs are easier to count (measure). If you were a supervisor of five patrol officers, what outcomes would you emphasize, and how would you keep the officers focused on those end results rather than on how many tickets they wrote and how many calls they handled?

SOURCE: *Modern Policing* blog, May 10, 2016, www.oup.com/cordner/measuring-what-doesnt-matter/.

- Quality services/customer satisfaction.
- Use force and authority fairly, efficiently, and effectively.
- Use financial resources fairly, efficiently, and effectively.

Traditionally, most police organizations have systematically measured performance related to the first two dimensions only, typically by counting reported Part 1 crimes, arrests, and cases solved. In recent years, however, it has become more common for police agencies or their parent governments to conduct regular surveys to measure public satisfaction, legitimacy, perceptions of disorder, and fear of crime. Also, the public clamor during the past 20 years over racial profiling, the more recent focus on stops and frisks in several cities, and the current crisis related to police use of deadly force all point to a growing recognition that use of force "fairly, efficiently, and effectively" is a key aspect of police performance that must be measured and monitored much more carefully than in the past.

It is easier to list these dimensions of police performance than to accurately measure them. Nevertheless, it would be wise for every police agency to acknowledge these dimensions and report annually on them, even if only indirect indicators and qualitative assessments are available in some categories. Simply publishing and referring to them on a regular basis sends a clear message within the organization and to the community that each of these dimensions is an important component of how well or poorly the police organization is meeting its community's goals and needs. As a kind of annual report card, the framework can help identify areas of weakness that need more attention; equally important, the same framework should be used to monitor and measure the performance of subunits and individuals within the organization.

## Police Unit Performance

In the United States, most police agencies are small, so their focus is likely to be on the overall performance of the entire police organization, rather than on police unit performance. However, many police organizations are composed of multiple subunits, and these are important to consider because the overall performance of a medium-size or large police agency is, at least to a degree, the sum of the performance of its parts. Top-level police executives have the challenge of measuring the performance of their organizations' subunits to guide resource allocation, hold lower-level managers accountable, fix problems, and coordinate interunit activity. Lower-level police managers, especially if they are responsible for specific subunits, need information about how well their own units are performing to carry out their responsibilities of planning, directing, and controlling to maximize their units' performance.

The leading approach to police unit performance over the past 25 years has been Compstat, a process pioneered in the 1990s in the NYPD. In a nutshell, Police Commissioner William Bratton needed a method to get his 76 precinct commanders more focused on reducing crime. Compstat—weekly meetings of all precinct commanders and top brass to review current crime trends—provided that method. This was a new capacity in the NYPD, made possible by better computerization and more analytical staff. Instead of reviewing last month's or last year's crime data, Commissioner Bratton was suddenly able to quiz a precinct commander on the details of last week's crimes, which ones were going to be solved, what was the plan to interrupt any current patterns, and so forth. Armed with such information, the commissioner could hold those commanders accountable for being intimately knowledgeable about the crime in their precincts and for finding ways to reduce it. Precinct commanders who were not up to the task were quickly replaced, sending a strong message about "what mattered" in the NYPD.

Now that Compstat has been around for some time and has spread throughout the country, experience shows it can be viewed as a two-edge sword. On the positive side, it has helped police executives focus their agencies' attention squarely on reducing crime by targeting hot spots, thus elevating the role of crime analysis and crime mapping, making day-to-day policing more data-driven (Shane 2007) and more proactive (Henry 2002). The downside has been that it can lead to an excessively short-term and short-sighted approach to policing, deflecting attention from longer-term trends and patterns and putting substantial pressure on police commanders and police officers to show "positive" results—this sometimes leads to creative bookkeeping and manipulation of statistics (Rayman 2010; Eterno and Silverman 2012).

A well-rounded approach is to use the seven-dimension framework to measure and monitor police unit performance (Cordner 2014b). As an example, Table 5.1 illustrates how the framework could be used to measure and monitor the performance of police precincts or districts. A positive feature of using this approach is that it employs a breadth of measures to match the breadth of functions performed by the district/precinct unit. Also, the measures are mainly associated with outcomes. Arguably, this is both preferable and reasonable when focusing on a core operational unit—the district/precinct has the opportunity to reduce crime, solve crimes, make the public feel safer, and so forth, in contrast to support units that can only hope to accomplish these kinds of outcomes indirectly. Of course, the two specific measures listed for each performance dimension can certainly be debated, and better measures might be identified.

**TABLE 5.1  Unit Measures for a Police District or Precinct**

| DIMENSION | DISTRICT/PRECINCT MEASURES |
|---|---|
| Reduce crime | Reported violent crime per 100,000 population<br>Reported property crime per 100,000 population |
| Hold offenders accountable | Clearance rate for crimes investigated at the district/precinct level<br>Conviction rate for crimes investigated at the district/precinct level |
| Reduce fear | Personal fear of crime measured with community surveys<br>Perceived likelihood of being a crime victim measured with community surveys |
| Ensure civility | Number of injury and fatal traffic crashes<br>Perceived level of social disorder measured with community surveys |
| Services/satisfaction | Public confidence in the police measured with community surveys<br>Customer satisfaction with specific services measured with follow-up surveys |
| Use of force and authority | Percentage of custodial arrests that involve police use of force<br>Disproportionality index for vehicle and pedestrian stops (reflecting minority overrepresentation) |
| Use of financial resources | Percentage of annual district/precinct budget expended<br>Overtime expenditures per district/precinct employee |

By way of contrast, a much more abbreviated framework could be used to monitor and measure the performance of a police agency's communications/dispatching center. This unit normally answers telephone calls to the police agency from the public, including emergency calls, and uses the police radio system to dispatch police officers to incidents and respond to inquiries from police officers in the field. The center does interact directly with the public, mainly via the telephone, but otherwise, its performance is entirely in support of other units of the organization. Because the communication center's performance is only indirectly tied to accomplishment of a majority of the overall organization's desired outcomes (e.g., reducing crime), it is not reasonable to use most of those seven categories when measuring the performance of this unit. Still, connecting the unit to the overall effectiveness of the entire police agency by way of those dimensions that are applicable, such as providing quality services and providing those services in a fair and efficient manner, allows the best yardstick for gauging its performance and helps its members see how their work contributes to the big picture.

## Supervision and Police Performance

At the bottom of the hierarchy, effectiveness is largely determined by the degree to which the individual performance of police personnel is guided by the overall mission, values, and priorities of the department. And organizational goals are more likely to be accomplished if they are aligned with supervisory practices. In a study of the effects of 64 sergeants' supervisory styles on the behavior of 239 patrol officers in the Indianapolis, Indiana, and St. Petersburg, Florida, police departments, Engel (2003) found that the *style* of field supervision can significantly influence patrol officer behavior. Although four supervisory styles were discovered—traditional, innovative, supportive, and active—the active style was more likely to have an influence on officer behavior, either positively or negatively.

Another study found that supervisory styles can impact officer behavior for *integrity violations*. In a study of five regional police organizations in the Netherlands, Huberts, Kaptein, and Lasthuizen (2007) found that *role modeling* by police supervisors was significant in limiting unethical conduct relating to interpersonal relationships. It appeared that employees copy a leader's integrity standards in their daily interactions with one another. In addition, the authors found that leader *strictness* was especially effective in controlling fraud, corruption, and misuse of resources. Similarly, Wolfe and Piquero (2011), using a random sample of 504 officers in Philadelphia, reported that when police supervisors (1) developed fair policies, (2) communicated such policies to their subordinates, and (3) allowed the officers to express their opinions, officers were much less likely to be the subject of citizen complaints, Internal Affairs investigations, or disciplinary charges. Additionally, they were less likely to follow a code of silence or believe that noble-cause corruption was permissible (see Chapter 9 for further discussion of police misconduct).

Sholihin and Pike (2010) found that using performance evaluation measures deemed fair by police officers is positively related to organizational commitment. A survey of 670 uniformed officers in one police force in the United Kingdom concluded that the perceived *level of support* provided by both the organization and management was by far the most important predictor of organizational commitment, regardless of rank. These findings and others (see, e.g., Currie and Dollery 2006) suggest that the ability of police supervisors and managers to support and encourage their employees is a strong indicator of organizational success.

One aspect of police supervision that is sometimes overlooked is making sure that officers use their time effectively. When Famega, Frank, and Mazerolle (2005) conducted an observational study of more than 1,300 hours of Baltimore officers while on patrol, they found that more than three-quarters of an officer's time per shift was unassigned, on average. During this time, officers primarily self-initiated random patrol or backed up other officers on calls to which they were not dispatched. Only 6 percent of unassigned-time activity was directed by supervisors, dispatchers, or other officers. Furthermore, only 4 percent of all activities were part of a long-term initiative to deal with a problem. These results clearly indicated that patrol officers were not actively supervised and were substantially underutilized. The researchers suggested holding supervisors and officers more accountable for unassigned time; it may also be prudent to encourage and train police supervisors to adopt a more *active style* in managing their subordinates.

## Managing Group Behavior

Police managers must be well informed about managing group behavior and possible conflict between and among groups. Because today's police departments tend to be relatively diverse in age, sex, race, ethnicity, and experience, different groups will naturally have different—sometimes conflicting—demands on management.

### Police Subcultures

In addition to the formal structure of a police department, informal arrangements often greatly impact agency operations. Individual beliefs, values, and norms in police departments are strongly influenced by group behavior. As subsequent chapters will discuss in greater detail, *socialization* in policing occurs when recruits learn the values and behavioral patterns set by experienced officers. From this early socialization, police officers tend to develop a different view of their job from that of their managers. In a classic study, Reuss-Ianni (1983) observed that these divergent views can result in two distinct subcultures within the same organization: a *manager's culture* and a *street cop's culture*. Managers are concerned with departmental priorities, policies, and procedures, whereas officers are concerned with doing the job "according to the street," often acquired not from the department's official view of reality but from the officer's perspective, determined by trying to stay safe and out of trouble. These differing perspectives can result in an adversarial relationship where street cops maintain their own code, which can include the set of rules described in Inside Policing 5.4.

Recent studies have confirmed that street cops tend to have different perspectives than their bosses, but also that police cultures vary substantially among police organizations; that is, the so-called police subculture is not the same in every police department. The National Police Research Platform surveyed employees in 89 municipal and county law enforcement agencies in 2014 to 2015 and found that supervisors and managers had consistently more positive views of the community than patrol officers, were less likely to agree that officers need to stick together, and took a more serious stance toward misconduct. Among street-level officers, however, the range of variation in beliefs and perspectives was dramatic. As one example, only 23 percent of officers in one police department agreed that "most people respect the police," whereas 92 percent of officers in another

**INSIDE POLICING 5.4** | **Street Cop's Code**

1. Take care of your partner first, then the other officers.
2. Don't "give up" (inform on) another cop; be secretive about the behavior of other officers.
3. Show balls; take control of a situation and don't back down.
4. Be aggressive when necessary, but don't go looking for trouble.
5. Don't interfere in another officer's sector or work area.
6. Do your fair share of work and don't leave work for the next shift; however, don't do too much work.
7. If you get caught making a mistake, don't implicate anybody else.
8. Other cops, but not necessarily managers, should be told if another officer is dangerous or "crazy."
9. Don't trust new officers until they have been checked out.
10. Don't volunteer information; tell others only what they need to know.
11. Avoid talking too much or too little; both are suspicious.
12. Protect your ass; don't give managers of the system an opportunity to get you.
13. Don't make waves; don't make problems for the system or managers.
14. Don't "suck up" to supervisors.
15. Know what your supervisor and other managers expect.
16. Don't trust managers; they may not look out for your interests.

SOURCE: Adapted from E. Reuss-Ianni, *Two Cultures of Policing: Street Cops and Management Cops* (New Brunswick, CT: Transaction Books, 1983), 13–16.

agency agreed with that statement. Similarly, only 19 percent of officers in one department considered it very serious to fail to report a use of force, contrasted with 93 percent of officers in another agency (Cordner 2016). Clearly, police culture is a variable, not a constant.

## Employee Associations and Unions

Historically, the best-known police employee organization has been the *police union*, which is composed of police officers and is their official representative in collective bargaining with the employer. Police unions are generally local but often are connected to national umbrella organizations, such as the Fraternal Order of Police, the International Union of Police Associations (an affiliate of the American Federation of Labor and Congress of Industrial Organizations, or AFL-CIO), the Teamsters, the American Federation of State, County, and Municipal Employees, and others.

The police labor movement has gone through several stages. Police associations were evident as early as the 1890s, but they did not firmly establish themselves until the mid-1960s. Earlier, the Boston police strike of 1919 created a backlash against police unions throughout the country. Later, between 1943 and 1947, police unionization stalled because of unfavorable court decisions and strong resistance by police chiefs. Once established, police unions have bargained for higher salaries, better fringe benefits, more influence over working conditions, and more elaborate disciplinary procedures to protect employees. They have also tended to fight back against critics of the police, to the extent that employee organizations have become major obstacles to effecting change in some jurisdictions. This has become particularly evident since 2014 in the form of union resistance to demands for police accountability following fatal use-of-force incidents.

Research on police unions has been limited. Initially, Carter and Sapp (1996) found that police unions prioritized wages and benefits, leaving management issues in the domain of police executives. Later, however, Kadleck (2003) examined 648 police unions from across the country and found that union leaders reported having influence over policy creation and a general distrust of police managers. Walker (2008) suggested a research agenda for police scholars aimed at better understanding the nature of police unions and their impact on police management, discipline and accountability, police subculture, police–community relations, city or county finances, and politics. Levin (2020: 1333) recently noted that police unions "have become public enemy number one for commentators concerned about race and police violence" due to "their obstructionism and their prioritization of members' interests over the interests of the communities they police."

It is important to recognize that union leaders often have a strong informal influence over departmental members. Consequently, these union leaders should be treated with respect by police managers, and they should be kept abreast of managerial decisions so that they can share this information with the membership. To facilitate this process, union representatives should be encouraged to serve on committees and participate in management meetings. An open and participative relationship with the union may help to avoid the costly and unpleasant effects that often result from strikes, job actions (i.e., work slowdowns or speed-ups), refusals to negotiate, and media attention; perhaps most important, they may also help create an improved working environment.

Not all employee organizations are unions. As Walker (1992) pointed out, police officers have historically belonged to *fraternal organizations*. These groups are sometimes organized along ethnic lines. Nationally, for example, Latino officers are represented by the Latino Police Officers Association and Asian officers by the Asian Police Officers Association. Employee groups may also form their own local associations. In San Francisco, for example, the African American officers' association is known as Officers for Justice; in San Jose, California, it is known as the South Bay Association of Black Law Enforcement Officers.

As departments become more diverse in their makeup, other employee organizations often develop. For instance, many departments have women's organizations (e.g., the Women's Police Officer Association), and gay and lesbian officers are represented in California by the Golden State Peace Officers Association. It is apparent that if departments are to maintain a healthy work environment, police managers must deal effectively with the diverse needs of all these employee organizations. In general, it is best to establish a working relationship with each group and to share with them the department's expectations. Then, if there are conflicts, they can be dealt with in an open and honest manner.

## Managing Critical Incidents

An aspect of police management that has few parallels with other types of organizations has to do with critical incidents. Corporate and government leaders must indeed be prepared for *crisis management*, which usually means that something bad has happened and they must manage its impact on employees, customers/clients, and the organization's image. Police chiefs and sheriffs also have that responsibility, but in addition, their agencies are expected to respond to the critical incident itself and make things better. This calls for tactical knowledge and skill to command personnel in the field as they respond to active shooters, hostage situations, terrorism, natural and man-made disasters, civil disorder, and other dangerous and life-threatening incidents.

Police organizations have developed a great deal of critical-incident expertise over the past several decades. Special units (i.e., Special Weapons and Tactics [SWAT]) have been created to deal with highly dangerous situations; these units generally have their own command structure as well as extensive training, all designed to improve decision making and operational performance when it counts. Also, police departments learned the Incident Command System (ICS) from the fire service and now use it regularly when faced with large-scale emergencies. The ICS and related National Incident Management System developed by the US Department of Homeland Security are designed to clarify roles and authority, especially when multiple agencies are involved. One can easily imagine how complicated things can get in the midst of a hurricane or tornado or when searching for a violent terrorism suspect in a metropolitan area with multiple overlapping jurisdictions. Having an established ICS improves coordination and helps avoid conflicts and misunderstandings among police and other first-responder agencies.

## Media Relations and Strategic Communications

The relationship between the media and the police has often been one of uneasiness, with a lack of trust on both sides. In today's environment, police departments must become more transparent with the public they serve; police executives and managers must find ways to communicate in an open and honest way with the media to project their desired departmental image to the public. Of course, this is easier said than done, since the news media tends to focus on (and may even sensationalize) dramatic events, including violent crime and police misconduct, rather than on routine police activities or accomplishments. Consequently, it is important for departments to establish good working relationships with the media to "get the word out" on what they are doing to improve community relations and help reduce crime and community problems. In addition, increased transparency includes dealing forthrightly with the media and the public regarding high-profile events (e.g., police shootings) and cases of misconduct, detailing steps that will be taken to correct them.

One national study (Chermak and Weiss 2006) surveyed 239 law enforcement agencies and 420 media organizations (both television and newspaper) in large cities to determine police–media relationships and how COP strategies were being presented and covered. The results indicated that 80 percent of the departments had at least one full-time public information officer (PIO) who was responsible for managing the agency's public image, disseminating information, and interacting with the media; where a PIO was not designated, some other high-ranking official performed public information duties. Both sides agreed that police–media relations were positive (90 percent for the PIOs and 72 percent for the media). In terms of media coverage, the number of crime stories over a two-week period was significantly greater than the number of COP stories over an entire year. These results indicated that police departments and PIOs are not taking full advantage of their access to news organizations to promote COP. It was suggested that departments should work more closely with the news media in "devising and implementing broader marketing strategies to increase public awareness and involvement in community policing activities" (Chermak and Weiss 2006, 156).

In recent years, many police agencies have broadened their thinking from media relations to strategic communications (Stephens, Hill, and Greenberg 2011). In part, this reflects a more proactive approach to relationships with print and electronic news media, with more emphasis on disseminating positive stories and "shaping the narrative" related to policing issues. Of equal significance, however, is the explosion of social media. Police organizations have recognized that more and more people get their news online, rather than from newspapers or television, and police have realized that they can distribute their own stories via social media without needing the assistance of traditional news outlets. Many police departments now utilize their own web pages, Facebook pages, Twitter feeds, and YouTube channels to communicate directly with the public (Tiry, Oglesby-Neal, and Kim 2019). This has dramatically altered the police–media relationship and provided police organizations with almost unlimited opportunities to tell their stories.

Recent critical incidents in Chicago, Los Angeles, Columbus, and many other jurisdictions illustrate the challenges faced by police executives in today's rapidly evolving media environment. Immediately after such an incident, especially a police shooting, the pressure to speak quickly and to demonstrate transparency and accountability is enormous, yet often all the facts are not known. At the same time, police employees are watching to see whether their leaders will support them or will succumb to popular or political pressure. Perhaps of greatest significance at such moments is the amount of credibility and trust that the police department and its leaders have built up over the years, both with the community and within the police organization. In addition, careful attention to media relations and strategic communications is likely to pay dividends when critical incidents occur, which, in the world of policing, they will. (See Inside Policing 5.5).

## Organizational Change

Managing change is one of the most important responsibilities of police leaders. No organization can continue to operate in the same way over an extended period of time and expect to stay successful. Even effective police agencies that enjoy public trust and confidence must adapt to changing circumstances.

The focus of this section is on **organizational change** as distinguished from police reform. Reform specifically implies that something is wrong and needs to be fixed.

---

**INSIDE POLICING 5.5**   **Getting the Facts Out Quickly**

This article reports an incident in Prince George's County, Maryland, of a SWAT raid at a wrong apartment, resulting in two officers being shot (not critically) by the startled resident and one round being fired by police. Noteworthy is that the police chief held a full press conference in less than 24 hours, providing the facts, apologizing for the bungled operation, halting serving search warrants until the cause of the mistake is determined, and announcing that the resident would not be charged. The reporter comments on the rarity of such quick and full disclosure in the aftermath of a controversial incident.

**Discussion Question:** The public expects quick information from the police after a critical incident such as an officer-involved shooting. But it often takes time to establish the facts, and sometimes releasing information will interfere with an active investigation. What policy and practice would you put into place to balance these competing interests?

*SOURCE: Modern Policing Blog, September 26, 2018, www.gcordner.wordpress.com/2018/09/26/getting-the-facts-out-quickly/.*

Without a doubt, police reform is a major concern in America today, and the rest of this book addresses a variety of reform-related topics, such as use of force, racial profiling, diversity, and accountability. This chapter, however, takes a slightly different orientation. Regardless of whether anything is wrong, an organization must change because its environment changes, priorities change, personnel change, technology changes, and so forth.

While the focus here is not directly on police reform, it can be argued that few reforms are sustainable unless they are accompanied by organizational change. Police officers are members of organizations. When their behavior goes awry, whether biased decision making, unnecessary use of force, abuse of authority, or other forms of misconduct, it is *organizational* behavior. Preventing and minimizing such behavior is the job of police leaders and managers, and if misconduct is occurring at unacceptable levels, then organizational changes likely are needed. Externally imposed reform measures, such as consent decrees, lawsuits, and new legislation, may temporarily influence officers' behavior, but in the long run, they are likely to be ineffective unless they are supported by organizational changes.

As discussed earlier in this chapter, the police have traditionally been organized and managed according to classical principles. Typically, departments have been structured in a hierarchical, bureaucratic manner, where the leadership style is authoritarian and employees are tightly controlled. It can be extremely difficult to make and sustain changes to such traditional, paramilitary departments. Therefore, current thinking is that a less bureaucratic, less centralized orientation allows a department to more readily adapt to community needs and expectations.

Because organizations have many components, many "moving parts," there are several different ways that one might attempt to change an organization. This section briefly discusses some of the more common approaches to police organizational change.

## Reorganizing

Reorganizing, or changing the structure of the organization, is a logical and frequently employed method for police organizational change. In some ways, it is one of the easiest techniques to implement, since all it entails is moving lines and boxes on the organization chart. It is clearly within the purview of police executives and can be accomplished with the stroke of a pen.

On the plus side, reorganizing is a sensible approach if the current structure is illogical, inefficient, out of date, or out of synch with the organization's mission and strategies. A special unit may have been created years ago in response to a pressing problem, for example, but is no longer needed. The opposite may also be true—a new problem (e.g., identity theft) or a new capability (e.g., intelligence analysis) may necessitate a new organizational unit. Similarly, residential or commercial growth in a section of the jurisdiction that was previously undeveloped may create the need for a new district or precinct. More generally, successful implementation of a new strategy like COP might require changes to the organizational structure, such as flattening the hierarchy, reducing the number of special units, or switching the primary basis of patrol units from time of day (shifts) to geography (areas of responsibility).

There are two related caveats to consider with respect to reorganizing in order to effect change. First, it is not as easy as "the stroke of a pen." Because people in organizations have existing relationships, both formal and informal, simply redrawing lines on the organization chart will not necessarily change their behavior and performance and may very well cause consternation among personnel whose comfortable positions are affected. Second, reorganizing is sometimes utilized in isolation, without any complementary strategies, to give the appearance of change without much genuine effort or commitment to really making the organization better. In other words, reorganizing may be used to give the appearance of change, perhaps in response to political or public pressure, without much true expectation of or desire for change. These caveats do not invalidate reorganizing as a method for achieving organizational change; they simply serve as reminders to be realistic about, and even skeptical toward, any claims that reorganization, by itself, will result in substantial improvements in performance and effectiveness.

## Improving Leadership and Management

In American policing, perhaps the single most popular change strategy is to hire a new police chief, often from outside the agency. Much as in professional sports, when things are going poorly, it is often not practical to replace the whole team, so replacing the chief is more common, and sometimes is even accompanied by the same sports clichés—"we decided to go in a different direction" or "the officers needed to hear a different voice." In many places it is the tradition that a newly elected mayor (or governor) will appoint their own chief of police. In recent years, changing chiefs seems to have become even more common in response to crises (Johnson 2016).

Apart from hiring a new chief, improving the capabilities of current and rising leaders in the organization is a well-established approach to organizational change. Many states have police leadership development programs, such as the Law Enforcement Management Institute of Texas and California's Law Enforcement Command College. Programs ideally start with first-line supervisors, such as Kentucky's Academy of Police Supervision. There are also national-level leadership development programs offered by the FBI, the Federal Executive Institute, the International Association of Chiefs of Police, the Major Cities Chiefs Association, the Police Executive Research Forum, the Northwestern University Center for Public Safety, and the Southern Police Institute at the University of Louisville.

Modern approaches to improving leadership and management tend to draw a sharp distinction between those two activities, putting most of the emphasis on leading. The implied assumption is that managing (doing the job right) is the easy part, whereas leading (doing the right job) is more challenging. Leading somehow sounds more glamorous and sophisticated than managing. The reality, however, is that both are equally important and equally difficult (see Inside Policing 5.6). A police department that lacks coherent and effective planning, organizational structure, and control is unlikely to perform well or provide quality services to its community. Managing establishes the foundation on which leadership can then provide direction, guidance, and inspiration to obtain the best and most creative performance from employees.

## Revising Policies and Procedures

Another technique often used to change behaviors in police departments is to adopt or revise policies and procedures. Written directives are one of the core elements through which police managers exercise direction and control. They are particularly important in police organizations because of the reality and inevitability of discretion. Since police officers make many important decisions on their own, without direct supervision, and because "situational exigencies" make it nearly impossible to prescribe correct actions in advance, police agencies try to guide officer decision making by identifying the factors that should be considered, the range of acceptable options, and choices to be avoided.

Examples of policy adoption for organizational change include those regarding domestic violence and pursuits. In the case of domestic violence, many police departments

---

**INSIDE POLICING 5.6** | **Managing Versus Leading**

Overmanaged organizations have systems and processes with no passion. Overled organizations have heart with instability and chaos.

**Overmanaged**

1. Systems drain energy. You have three requisition forms for a box of paper clips.
2. People go through the motions but have forgotten their purpose.
3. Procedures turn into bureaucracy. You haven't deleted a procedure since the Great Depression.
4. No one challenges the way things are done.
5. People become cogs in the machine. Everyone is lost in the weeds.

**Overled**

1. Leaders struggle to keep all the balls in the air.
2. Passion runs high. Processes run low.
3. No one is really sure who does what.
4. Training is learn-as-you-go. "Go figure it out."
5. Systems are the enemy. "Just do it."

SOURCE: *Leadership Freak* blog, April 27, 2016, https://leadershipfreak.wordpress.com/2016/04/27/over-led-and-under-managed/.

---

implemented new policies in the 1980s and 1990s that reduced officer discretion, either by mandating arrest whenever probable cause was established or by specifying that arrest was expected unless the officer could articulate specific reasons, in writing, to justify an exception. In regard to vehicle pursuits, most departments have adopted policies that either prohibit lengthy high-speed chases or restrict them to situations that meet narrowly defined criteria. Some police agencies have also promulgated foot pursuit policies, recognizing how often foot chases result in injuries to officers and/or suspects and realizing that the practice was often ignored in training and written guidelines (Kaminski and Alpert 2013).

Even when policies and procedures are in place, police departments should review and revise them regularly to stay current and support organizational change. In the post-Ferguson era, for example, many police departments considered revisions to their use-of-force policies to place more emphasis on conflict management and de-escalation (Police Executive Research Forum 2016). Following the murder of George Floyd, many agencies strengthened their policies on peer intervention. The acquisition of new equipment, such as Tasers and body-worn cameras, generally leads to new or revised written guidelines. Similarly, new legislation or court cases might necessitate changes to existing policies and procedures.

## Changing Strategies and Tactics

The dominant organizational change initiative in policing over the past 25 years has been COP. As discussed in Chapter 4, the COP strategy has both philosophical and programmatic elements, making its implementation challenging and sometimes incomplete and half-hearted. It is an especially interesting case since (1) it was such a popular innovation throughout the 1990s, (2) seemed to wane after the 9/11 terrorist attacks and the economic Great Recession, and then (3) enjoyed a resurgence as a reform strategy in response to current crises in police legitimacy and accountability.

Debates over the rhetoric or reality of COP notwithstanding, one of the most direct routes to organizational change is to alter the way the organization's work is structured and carried out. Historically, police departments clearly changed during the early to mid-1900s, when vehicle patrolling replaced foot patrols and when quick response to reported crimes became a central tactic. In recent years, directed patrol, broken windows policing, and hot-spots policing have all been designed to influence what patrol officers do and where they spend their time when not answering dispatched calls. Similarly, repeat-offender programs aim to get detectives focused more on prolific offenders than on stacks of unsolved cases with low probability of success. These and other modern developments in police operations are described in more detail in Chapters 7 and 8.

## Changing Behavior and Culture

In one way or another, all organizational change boils down to changing behavior. In the industrial age, the focus was mainly on getting people in organizations to work harder, leading to an emphasis on rewards, punishment, and motivation. This approach has some applicability in policing, but police organizational change usually depends more on changing what officers do and how they do it, rather than merely how hard they work.

In particular, changing police behavior typically focuses more on how officers interact with the public. Through recruitment, selection, training, and supervision, police departments try to improve the way officers deal with victims, witnesses, suspects, violators, and others whom they encounter. In contemporary terms, they look for enhanced interpersonal skills and emotional intelligence, more awareness of unconscious bias, and greater emphasis on procedural justice in resolving incidents and encounters.

Another way to think about changing police organizational behavior is to conceptualize police work mainly as decision making. Looking at it this way, changing policing involves changing the decisions that officers make. This might occur by eliminating or mandating some choices through policies and procedures, as noted earlier, or by creating new choices, such as opening a detoxification center where substance abusers could be taken in lieu of arrest. Decision making is also affected by values. For police organizations, it is not only a matter of providing information to help officers make the most logical and efficient choices—it is also necessary to persuade them to pursue the right outcomes in the right ways. In other words, the police organization must find ways to influence the values, beliefs, and ethics of its members, with the hope that officers, in their daily work and decision making, will always be aiming to accomplish what the organization and the community want them to accomplish and doing so using methods that are proper and approved.

As discussed earlier, the street cop culture and the manager's culture often seem at odds within police departments, with officers resisting any changes that might make their work more difficult or make them more accountable to their bosses. The President's Task Force on Twenty-First Century Policing (2015, 12) noted the old saying that "organizational culture eats policy for lunch," and further observed that "if policies conflict with the existing culture, they will not be institutionalized and behavior will not change."

Police culture has two main components, an *occupational* culture and an *organizational* culture. The occupational culture reflects the role of the police and the realities of police work that are more or less universal. Discretion, uncertainty, authority, and danger are some of the characteristics of the work that influence the values and beliefs typically found in the police occupational culture. Organizational culture, in contrast, is not universal; it varies from one police department to another. We noted earlier that police officers' perspectives on the community, their tolerance of misconduct, and how strongly they feel the need to stick together vary tremendously among police agencies (Cordner 2016). In addition, the pervasiveness and strength of the organizational culture vary (Ott 1989). That is, in some police departments, the impact of the culture on officer behavior is strong, but in others, it is weak. When the culture is relatively weak, individual officers feel that they have more latitude to follow their own values and beliefs than those favored by their peers.

Recently, attention has focused on the warrior versus guardian aspects of police culture. Some experts believe that policing has become more militarized, especially since the 9/11 terror attacks, resulting in a stronger warrior mentality that, unfortunately, has spilled over into day-to-day policing and ordinary public encounters. Efforts began a decade ago to recruit new police "in the spirit of service" rather than "in the spirit of adventure" (Scrivner 2006), but when new recruits are brought into an existing police culture, they are often the ones who change, not the culture. Increased emphasis is now being placed on training by teaching de-escalation techniques, improving interpersonal communication skills, and reinforcing the guardian and protector roles of police (Hoban and Gourlie 2014; Rahr and Rice 2015). Changing training does not guarantee culture change either, however. Studies often find that the values and beliefs of new police change significantly after they leave the academy, join their more experienced colleagues, and begin doing the hard work of policing (Haarr 2001).

The leader has the challenge of encouraging and developing a positive, professional culture within the agency. In the meantime, if the culture is negative and corrosive, the leader must find a way to shield new employees from it by offering them a better alternative that promises a healthier, safer, and more satisfying career.

## The Change Process

Organizational change occurs when an organization adopts new ideas or behaviors (Pierce and Delbeq 1977). Usually, an innovative idea is introduced, such as a new patrol strategy or job design, and changes in employee behavior are supposed to follow. Of course, the greater the degree of change required, the more significant will be the behavioral changes required. For instance, COP requires a substantial change not only in the role of police officers but also of their supervisors and managers. Thus, a transition toward COP requires substantially greater behavioral change by personnel than simply changing a patrol tactic or procedure would require. The corollary is that the greater the degree of planned change, the greater the resistance to it will be.

### Resistance to Change

In general, people do not like to change their behavior. Adapting to a new environment or learning a new work method often results in feelings of stress and fear of the unknown (e.g., Will I like it? Will I be able to do it well?). Members of organizations tend to react to change emotionally, not rationally, and often respond with personal attacks against those who are promoting change. Figure 5.3 identifies the range of anti-change arguments frequently encountered—needless to say, the most common ones come from the bottom of the pyramid.

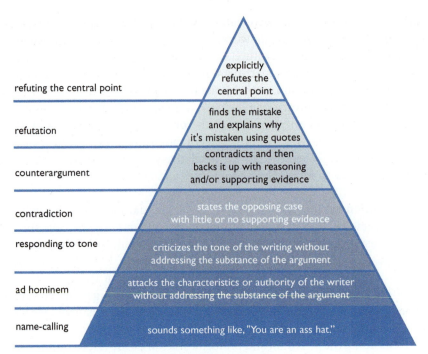

**FIGURE 5.3** Graham's Hierarchy of Disagreement.

SOURCE: "Working in Change in Policing," *The Thinking Blue Line* blog, April 16, 2016, thinkingblueline.com/2016/04/16/working-in-change-in-policing/.

**Inertia.**  A great deal of **inertia**, or "doing things as they have always been done," is strongly associated with traditional organizations. People have what is known as *sunk costs* in their jobs and routines, including time, energy, and experience; these are powerful forces in resisting change. Individuals or groups with many such investments sunk into a particular department or job may not want changes, regardless of their merit. COP, for example, requires officers to do many of their old tasks in new ways and to take on new tasks with which they are not familiar. They may be "asked to identify and solve a broad range of problems; reach out to community elements that previously were outside their orbit; and put their careers at risk by taking on unfamiliar and challenging responsibilities" (Skogan and Hartnett 1997, 71). These expectations are often beyond the officers' capabilities and the traditional roles for which they were initially selected and trained (Lurigio and Rosenbaum 1994). There is little doubt that most officers would rather do what they believe they were hired for and what they perceive to be the "real" police role: crime-fighting. COP approaches are often dismissed as "social work," which takes important time away from their crime-fighting activities.

Although inertia occurs at managerial levels too, the attitudes of sergeants are especially important. Because sergeants have the most direct influence over the day-to-day activities of street officers, it is crucial that they "buy into" the new program, promoting the department's new policies and procedures. To do so, sergeants must act as facilitators and trainers as well as supervisors.

**Misunderstandings.**  Resistance to change is likely to occur when officers do not clearly understand the purpose, techniques, or consequences of a planned change because of inadequate or misunderstood communication. A major problem concerns the uncertainty about consequences of change. If employees are not told how they will be affected by change, rumors and speculation will follow, and resistance (and even sabotage) may be strong enough to severely limit the change effort. When change is imposed on officers instead of occurring as a result of their participation, misunderstandings are more likely. For example, when police departments attempt to develop COP strategies, they frequently make the mistake of not clearly articulating what new roles will be created and the effect of those new roles on all involved. In addition, departments often do not allow officers to participate in the planning and development of the new program in order to gain a sense of "ownership."

**Group Norms.** As discussed earlier, groups have an important impact on the behavior and attitudes of their members. **Group norms**, or expected behavior from group members, can be a powerful factor in resistance to change. If individual officers follow the norms strictly (e.g., that only law enforcement activities are important), they will not easily perceive or readily accept the need for change. If significant departmental changes are to occur, police managers must consider group norms and influences and include group consensus and decision making in planning for change. The major way to achieve such involvement is to engage in participatory management.

**Balance of Power.** Changes that are perceived to threaten the autonomy, authority, power, or status of a group or unit will most likely encounter resistance, regardless of their merit. For instance, such resistance was well documented in the team-policing experiments of the 1970s, when departments attempted to decentralize their operations into neighborhood teams (Sherman, Milton, and Kelley 1973). Because this approach provided more control and autonomy for lower-level management (sergeants), middle managers (lieutenants and captains) resisted the change by subverting and, in some cases, sabotaging the plans for fear that they would lose authority, power, and status.

## Overcoming Resistance to Change

According to one leading management expert, "It is easy to talk about change, but the talk should never be divorced from the reality that this issue impacts people at a deeply personal level" (Petty 2016). He provides the following advice to leaders responsible for managing organizational change:

1. Show respect for your employees by providing advanced and in-depth context for internal or strategy changes.
2. Give people a voice in how changes will be implemented.
3. Solicit ideas that may minimize or eliminate the need for adverse changes.
4. Teach people about the business drivers behind change.
5. Change is a process, not an event.
6. Answer the burning question, "What does this mean for me?"

Several studies of change in police organizations provide support for these suggestions. One major factor in overcoming resistance to change is *officer involvement and participation* in the change process and program design. In a study of COP implementation in six small to mid-size agencies in North Carolina (Adams, Roche, and Arcury 2002), a major finding was that those who perceived a *participatory management style* were more supportive of the change toward COP. Importantly, the strongest support for a move toward

COP was found among officers in the city that allowed the most involvement in designing the program and showed the clearest support for COP by the command staff. In addition, compared with traditional officers, COP officers were found to be significantly more satisfied with their jobs. The importance of participatory management in bringing about constructive change is strongly supported in the research and should be utilized by departments of all sizes.

A study by Lord and Friday (2008) found results consistent with those just discussed. Their study took place in the Concord (NC) Police Department, where attitudinal measures of officers were taken both before (2002) and after (2005) COP was implemented. Concord made structural changes consistent with COP, such as permanent assignment to areas, decentralization of authority, partnerships with citizens, and use of problem-solving methods. However, findings from surveys and focus groups indicated that officer attitudes about their new job responsibilities were more negative toward COP after implementation, and officer attitudes about the effectiveness of COP did not change significantly. These negative outcomes were associated with (1) lack of feedback, (2) lack of job autonomy, (3) lack of preparedness (training), and (4) lack of adequate resources to take on new responsibilities.

What is important about these findings is that the major predictors in officer attitudes were all *under the control* of police administration, meaning that police managers can significantly influence officer attitudes toward organizational changes.

## Case Studies

In this section we provide snapshots about organizational change in six police departments. The information about Madison and Chicago is most comprehensive, because those experiences were fully documented and evaluated. The other snapshots are much shorter.

### Madison, Wisconsin

The most thoroughly documented transition from traditional policing to a COP paradigm was in the police department of Madison, Wisconsin, in the 1980s and 1990s (Wycoff and Skogan 1993). The use of what was called *quality leadership*, including participation at all levels, smoothed the transition process and helped to overcome resistance to change (Couper 2021).

The police chief at the time, David Couper, had been appointed in the early 1970s and operated initially with a high-control, central-authority model. This traditional style of police management resulted in distrust, grievances, complaining, and confrontations. The chief eventually realized that he needed to change his behavior. Following discussions with rank-and-file officers, it became clear that "lack of communication" was a primary concern, and that a new management or leadership style was necessary. Consequently, the chief decided to let employees participate more in organizational decisions while he, the chief, should act less like a commanding general and more like a facilitator.

This decision led to the establishment of the Officers' Advisory Council (OAC) to provide advice to the chief, and the OAC was critical in clearing the way for a major change in leadership style. The council consisted of 12 peer-selected employees who served for a two-year period. Over time, the OAC was given increased responsibility; it developed its ability to gather data and make recommendations using a problem-solving approach. The council learned that if it obtained data to support its recommendations, the recommendations would be put into practice; thus, it had significant input in departmental policies and procedures.

In 1984, the Committee on the Future was formed to look at trends and how they might affect the police department in the coming years. The committee was composed of a diverse group of members who had at least 15 years of service remaining; the intent was to engage members who had a vested interest in the future of the department. A member of the OAC was appointed to serve on this committee to link the two groups. After a year of meeting two to four times a month, the committee released a report of its findings listing three major recommendations:

1. Get closer to the people we serve.
2. Make better use of available technology.
3. Develop and improve health and wellness in the workplace.

Early in 1985, almost parallel with the developments in the department, the mayor's office initiated a city-wide effort to improve the quality/productivity (QP)—now known as total quality management—of the city's departments. A four-day seminar conducted by W. Edwards Deming, the "father" of the quality movement, was followed by a 15-day training seminar in QP principles and procedures for city employees. Five police employees attended the sessions, which covered team building, group processes, facilitator skills, and gathering and using data.

Following the QP training, the police department articulated the management philosophy of quality leadership, which included the following principles: (1) teamwork for planning and goal setting, (2) data-based problem solving, 3) a customer orientation, (4) employee input in decisions, (5) policies to support productive employees, (6) encouragement for risk taking and tolerance for mistakes, and (7) the manager as facilitator rather than commander. Quality leadership, and its emphasis on employee input, became the means to the goal of a healthier workplace and a necessary prelude to fully implementing COP.

A decision was then made to develop a prototype of the new design in one part of the department before attempting to redesign the entire organization; this prototype, the new experimental police district (EPD), was the first decentralized police facility in the department. Opened in 1988, the EPD housed approximately one-sixth of the department's personnel and served one-sixth of Madison's population. The charge of the EPD was to promote innovation and experimentation in three areas:

1. Employee participation in decision making about the conditions of work and the delivery of police services.
2. Management and supervisory styles supportive of employee participation and of COP and problem-oriented policing (POP).
3. The implementation of COP and POP.

To get citizens involved, eight community meetings were held in the project area and two in each alderman's (city council) district. The first set of meetings in each district was for people whom the department and alderman designated as community leaders. The second set of meetings was open to all concerned citizens. At the meetings, citizens were questioned about their knowledge of and satisfaction with police services, neighborhood problems and concerns, and how they felt police could work with them in responding to problems. The group process used at the meetings resulted in a listing of problems rated by priority.

In their evaluation of the Madison Police Department's change process, Wycoff and Skogan (1994, 88–89) found that "it is possible to change a traditional, control-oriented police organization into one in which employees become members of work teams and participants in decision making processes." Furthermore, some of the lessons learned in Madison for overcoming obstacles to change include the following:

1. It is possible to implement participatory management in a police department, and doing so is very likely to produce more satisfied workers.

2. Decentralization contributed significantly to the creation of the new management style. It also contributed to the development of team spirit and processes. Officers who worked in the EPD believed the decentralized station improved relationships with the public; they reported increased numbers of contacts with citizens in the community and an ever-increasing number of citizens who came to the station for assistance.

3. The managers of the Madison Police Department also thought that the best way to move toward decentralization was to change one part of the organization (i.e., the EPD) before proceeding with department-wide implementation.

Careful selection of new personnel was another element of the change strategy in Madison. During the long time frame for undergoing change and experimentation (over two decades), the police department continued to make efforts to recruit highly educated officers whose backgrounds, life experiences, and attitudes increased the likelihood that they would be supportive of change (Wycoff and Skogan 1994, 89–90).

### Chicago

From 1994 to 2006, Chicago was the nation's best example of largely successful implementation of COP in a big city (Skogan and Hartnett 1997; Chicago Community Policing Evaluation Consortium 2004; Skogan 2006). The Chicago Alternative Police Strategy (CAPS) started in five pilot districts before city-wide expansion. A total of 1,500 police personnel of all ranks went through orientation and skill-building sessions, and nearly 700 beat meetings, attended by 15,000 people, were held during the first year and a half of the program. The organizational change process incorporated six key elements:

1. **Involve the Entire Department and City.** Rather than forming special COP units, the whole department would change. Thus, COP roles were developed for all of the units, including the detective, tactical, gangs, and narcotics divisions, rather than just for uniformed officers.

2. **Permanent Beat Assignments.** To develop partnerships with the community and learn about the neighborhood, officers had to be assigned to one place long enough for residents to know them and learn to trust them. Additionally, officers had to have enough free time to allow them to engage in community work.

3. **Strong Commitment to Training.** The department invested a significant effort in training officers and their supervisors in the skills required to identify and solve problems in working with the community. By emphasizing training, a message would be sent to the rank and file that COP was real and upper management was committed to the program.

4. **Significant Role for the Community.** The foundation of CAPS was the formation of police–community partnerships, focused on identifying and solving problems at the

neighborhood level. One of the major problem-solving roles for the police was to engage community resources by drawing other city agencies into identifying and responding to local concerns. This community involvement was developed in two ways. First, beat meetings, usually monthly, involved small groups of residents and beat officers. The meetings were held in church basements and park buildings throughout the city. Second, advisory committees were formed at the district level to meet with upper management and district staff; committees included community leaders, school council members, ministers, business operators, and other institutional representatives.

5. **Link Policing to Delivery of City Services.** The police role was expanded to include a broad range of concerns outside the scope of traditional policing. The delivery of city services in the prototype districts was linked to the police department through the use of service-request forms. Requests for service generated by officers were closely monitored by city hall, which developed a system to prioritize and track each case.

6. **Emphasis on Crime Analysis.** A user-friendly crime-mapping system was developed, with printouts to be distributed at beat meetings and made accessible to the public at each district station. Other analytic tools included "beat planners," which were beat officers' notebooks filled with local information. New roll-call procedures were also developed to encourage officers on various shifts to share information about their beats and community resources.

In addition to the six key elements developed in the organizational plan, Chicago also used a number of other methods to help facilitate the organization-wide change process, especially with respect to **winning hearts and minds** of rank-and-file members. Supervisors were encouraged to serve as coaches and mentors and, eventually, were given additional training to help them adjust. Officers were reassured that traditional police work still counted and would be rewarded; in other words, they were not being asked to become social workers. And the initiative name, CAPS, intentionally avoided the label of COP.

The results in Chicago were impressive. Before CAPS was launched, public opinion of the police in Chicago was not positive, but for the most part, this opinion improved steadily for 10 years through 2003. The same was true for various measures of crime and disorder. Interestingly, the primary concerns of residents identified in beat meetings tended to be social disorder, drug problems, physical decay, and parking/traffic issues, not the violent crimes that police expected.

Yet despite achieving positive outcomes, CAPS continued to struggle with problem solving even after 10 years. Analysis of hundreds of beat-level plans found that efforts to solve local priority problems had not been effective; the same problems, in approximately the same locations, persisted year after year. Beat meeting effectiveness in setting problem-solving agendas for the public declined over time, and neither officers nor resident activists had refresher training in problem solving.

One of the problems in securing long-term change efforts and reforms in police departments relates directly to the tenure of the police chief, and often the mayor as well. A transition in leadership at the top is frequently followed by changes from the new chief, dismantling or discarding key ingredients of reforms and substituting their own agenda and policies. After more than a decade of CAPS success, this is precisely what happened within the department after a new police chief was selected (Skogan 2022). In 2003, the city's major newspaper created a crime scare during a period when the mayor was in the process of selecting a new chief. Politically, the most expedient response was to quickly appoint a candidate from the detective unit committed to tough enforcement. The new chief abruptly reorganized and refocused the department on "guns, gangs, and homicides." Observers at the time recommended keeping CAPS on life support, "perhaps to be resurrected when a crisis of legitimacy again haunts the police, and they have to rediscover community policing in order to rebuild again their credibility with the community" (Skogan 2008, 33). Needless to say, that day came, and Chicago's mayor and police today are once again trying to figure out how to rebuild their credibility.

### Cincinnati

Cincinnati serves as one of the best examples of court-imposed collaborative reform. Its story began in 2001 with a police shooting that touched off three days of rioting. The US Department of Justice eventually found a pattern of unconstitutional violations, resulting in a consent decree, federal monitor, and federal judge overseeing reforms. What makes Cincinnati stand out is that the city, the community, the police department, and the police union eventually became engaged partners in a collaborative process that included "all parties" meetings, POP and COP, an external-complaints authority, much greater transparency, and a genuine commitment to resolve the issues that got the city into trouble. The consent decree expired in 2008, but the city voluntarily extended its provisions. According to one community activist, the police department has experienced substantial change for the better: "Now, there's a growing sense that the police are partners in trying to build a stable environment where we can work, earn money, and live safely" (Sheil 2014).

### Camden, New Jersey

Organizational change in Camden, New Jersey, began with the unique opportunity to completely remake the police department. The city's police department was disbanded in 2013 and immediately replaced by a new Camden County Police Department. The city's police were all laid off and had to reapply for jobs with the county department. The agency's police chief was able to select his officers and had a free hand in making other changes: "I was able to do in three days what would normally take me three years to do. All of the barriers were removed. I was now driving on a paved road" (Landergan 2020). Policies were revised, performance measures were changed, and emphasis was placed on building and sustaining community relationships. The chief advocated a "slow but seismic shift from a warrior to a guardian mentality" and "the core elements of community-oriented policing: community partnerships, organizational transformation, and problem solving" (Tsuruoka 2018, 1).

### New Orleans

The New Orleans Police Department came under a federal consent decree in 2012, based on an investigation that found "a pattern or practice of excessive force, including stops, searches and arrests in violation of the Fourth Amendment. The investigation also found evidence of discriminatory policing based on race, ethnicity, gender and sexual orientation" (US Department of Justice 2012). Since then, the department has implemented a wide variety of changes to policies, training, and accountability, resulting in less use of force and less misconduct (Sledge 2020), although full compliance with the decree has not yet been achieved. Of particular note is EPIC (Ethical Policing Is Courageous), a training and monitoring program aimed at persuading all officers to intervene whenever they see another officer committing, or about to commit, misconduct (see https://epic.nola.gov/home/). While many departments have a policy that requires peer intervention, this program, based on the concept of "active bystandership," is an attempt to go a step farther by significantly altering the culture within the department.

### Baltimore

The Baltimore Police Department (BPD) came under a federal consent decree in 2016 for many of the same reasons as New Orleans. Since 2016, the department has methodically revised policies, trained officers on the new policies, and implemented audits and inspections to systematically determine whether officers are adhering to laws, policies, and procedural justice in interactions with the public. Because the agency had a history of zero-tolerance enforcement, a new standard of "most effective/least intrusive" was adopted to encourage more thoughtful decision making and greater use of informal options, referral, mediation, and problem solving. The department also adopted the EPIC program pioneered in New Orleans. In its most recent report, the Baltimore Consent Decree Monitoring Team (2022, 8) reported that "Tangible signs of change are emerging. BPD's training academy, once understaffed and listless, is becoming a national model. The number of potentially problematic arrests, particularly for low-level offenses, appears to be declining ... BPD was the only one of approximately a dozen major city police departments credited with handling the racial justice protests in the summer of 2020 in a competent, lawful manner."

## Institutionalizing Innovation and Change

We mentioned earlier that every organization must change to keep up with changing conditions. By the same token, people and organizations tend to resist change because of habits, inertia, fear of the unknown, and similar factors. A challenge, then, is to put organizational mechanisms in place that encourage rather than discourage change.

If constructive and timely change is to take place in police departments, mid-level and top-level managers must develop an organizational climate that fosters and encourages **innovation**—developing and using new ideas and methods. Such a climate should be open, trustworthy, and forward looking. In their study of police innovation in six American cities, Skolnick and Bayley (1986) pointed out that the need to sustain and defend innovation is critical, since the tendency to regress toward the traditional way of doing things is strong. They made several recommendations for successful innovation:

- The first, and most important, requirement is *effective and energetic leadership from the office of the chief.* It is not enough to espouse certain ideals and values; the chief must become an active, committed proponent of them.

- The second requirement is that *the chief must be able to motivate* (and sometimes manipulate) *departmental personnel* into supporting the values that the chief espouses.

- A third requirement is that the *integrity of innovation must be defended.* Once a new value system (one dedicated to the development of new concepts and methods) has been established, it must be protected from the pull to return to the status quo.

- The fourth requirement is *public support.* Innovative programs that are implemented with community input enjoy strong, and often unexpected, support from the public that can sway, or at least offset, resistance from within the organization.

"Measuring what matters" is also important for sustaining organizational change. Performance measures that are used to evaluate individual officers and subunits should be carefully crafted to reflect the behavior that is wanted, especially when changes are being sought. Aligning performance measures in this way helps management avoid sending mixed messages to officers about what is expected, helps in determining whether further efforts are needed to spur implementation of changes, and helps the agency identify and reward those officers whose behavior and performance are most in line with the new directions. Doing these simple things—sending clear messages, making adjustments when needed, and recognizing good performance—goes a long way toward encouraging organizational change. As Spitzer (2007, 54) notes, "if you don't measure the right things, you won't be able to manage the right things, and you won't get the right results."

### Continuous Improvement

An attitude of and commitment to continuous improvement are essential for long-term organizational effectiveness. If all members of an organization understand that they should always be looking for better ways to do their work, the threat that change represents loses some of its potency. The Madison case study captured this approach with its utilization of total quality management and quality leadership. Importantly, the concept is not that top executives are responsible for figuring out better processes and methods. Rather, every member of the organization is responsible, and the people actually doing the work are most likely to recognize shortcomings and be in a position to design improvements.

Continuous improvement and measuring what matters must be closely linked. Good measurement of what matters provides crucial information about processes and activities that are not being carried out correctly or are not having desired results. In this regard, Guilfoyle (2013) has written a useful book titled *Intelligent Policing: How Systems Thinking Methods Eclipse Conventional Management Practice*. His book details many fallacies about traditional performance measurement systems based on his experience in the British police service, as well as suggestions for more rational performance management.

### Research and Development

Continuous improvement cannot be accomplished without continuous learning, which is another way to sustain innovation in police departments. In other words, if management can develop an environment that promotes continuous learning, the department (and its members) benefits from its own and others' experiences, including both successes and failures. Such a learning environment leads to a **learning organization**, which is able to process what it has learned and adapt accordingly. Geller (1997) provided several structural and process ideas that would help police departments become learning organizations. He suggests that one of the best ideas is to create a **research and development (R&D)** unit (also known as research and planning unit (RPU]) that *actually does* R&D instead of only statistical descriptions of departmental inputs and outputs.

An R&D unit or RPU might help foster an appreciation for, and use of, the practical benefits of empirical research in the field, promoting the adoption of evidence-based practices. Unfortunately, R&D units in police departments today are often misused and underutilized. A study by Haberman and King (2011) found that most police RPUs spend the majority of their time on administrative support tasks, such as budget forecasting and updating the department's policy manual. Some time is spent on analytical tasks, such as analyzing statistics and crime mapping; however, the least amount of time is devoted to actual R&D tasks.

A study by Rojek, Alpert, and Smith (2012) examined whether law enforcement departments use published research to develop policies and operations, the areas of operations to which they apply this knowledge, and the types of sources on which they rely to obtain research. Only 24 percent said they used research to inform their decisions "very often." Agencies utilizing research were most likely to use it in decisions regarding use of force (74 percent), emergency/pursuit driving (59 percent), domestic violence (46 percent), and handling the mentally ill (46 percent). In terms of information sources, 85 percent used professional journals (i.e., *Police Chief Magazine* and the *FBI Law Enforcement Bulletin*), and 71 percent used other publications of the International Association of Chiefs of Police. Nearly 60 percent reported using publications from the National Institute of Justice, which are generally research reports, whereas only 34 percent of the agencies reported using research from academic journals. The conclusion reached by the authors was that "the utilization of science into practice requires decision makers to modify their behavior and be more thorough in their decision-making processes. It also requires researchers to modify their behavior and make their research findings available and understandable to the practitioners" (Rojek, Alpert, and Smith, 338–339).

A related idea that would help foster organizational learning would be to expand *police–researcher partnerships*. A random national sample of 871 state and local law enforcement agencies of all sizes was questioned regarding the prevalence and nature of their participation in any form of research partnership within the past five years (Rojek, Smith, and Alpert 2012). One-third of the agencies reported participating in a research partnership; this likelihood increased with agency size (agencies with 100 or more officers reported a participation rate nearly twice that of the second largest group of 50–99 officers). Of those reporting participation, 30 percent were engaged in a long-term formal collaborative form of partnership. When agencies that had *not* participated in a partnership were asked why, the main reasons were lack of funding, lack of contact by a researcher, and lack of confidence in the utility of a research partnership.

Academic researchers and police practitioners often have difficulty communicating and collaborating with one another—it has been called "the dialogue of the deaf" (Bradley and Nixon 2009). For instance, Fleming (2010) enumerates a number of difficulties, such as academics being required to deal with the command-and-control structure of police departments and frequent rotation among police staff. When police work with academics, they often feel they are not kept informed, do not receive what they expected or get it too late to be useful, and sometimes get blindsided when findings are published. Despite these challenges, some productive police–researcher partnerships are in place around the country.

## Education and Training

The previous discussion referred to turning police departments into learning organizations, but innovation and change are also likely to be enhanced when the people within police agencies personally engage in continuous learning. Police training is discussed in Chapter 6, and higher education is the topic of Chapter 14. Here, we will just make the point that police officers and police managers learn new information and skills through training and education. They may learn techniques that can be brought into the organization and applied directly, or they may simply have their horizons widened, making them more aware and receptive to new ideas and concepts.

The police field is gradually adapting to the reality that professionals bear some responsibility for their own learning and development; that is, professionals do not depend completely on their employer to keep up their skills and knowledge. This principle is crucially important for policing, both because police claim professional status and because the knowledge base of the field has expanded greatly over the past 30 to 40 years. There was a time when police could be confident they had learned everything (of a formal nature) that they needed to know during basic training, but that time is well past. In today's world, professional status carries with it serious responsibilities that mainly fall on the shoulders of individual police officers and police leaders. Included among them are the responsibility to be on the lookout for new information and evidence-based practices that can be added to the police department's repertoire to improve its performance and effectiveness.

## Summary

The history of police management theory begins with the classical theorists, who stressed a bureaucratic, paramilitary approach to organizational design. Beginning in the early 1970s, behavioral theorists started to question the classical approach, placing greater emphasis on worker participation, job satisfaction, more flexible designs, and recognition of the complex nature of the police role. Subsequent developments have emphasized police departments as open systems and the use of contingency theory. Private-sector processes also became influential, including the use of total quality management techniques. There has been much criticism of the traditional paramilitary design, while a continuing focus is on finding the best ways to structure and guide the discretionary decisions that police officers make in the field.

It is important to establish realistic and measurable police goals, including both quantitative and qualitative indicators. It is crucial to "measure what matters" in organizational, unit, and individual performance, rather than falling prey to measuring what is easy to measure. Police managers also have to deal with quite a few challenges, including the police culture, unions, critical incidents, the news media, and social media.

The process of organizational change in policing requires the development of a culture that encourages innovation. The primary obstacles to change include inertia, misunderstandings, group norms, and the **balance of power**. Each of these obstacles makes the change process more difficult and requires a sustained effort by management if it is to be overcome. In general, ways to overcome obstacles to change include taking a long-term view of the change process, participative management, community involvement, investments in research and development, commitment to education and training, measuring what matters thoughtfully, and inculcating an ethos of continuous improvement throughout the organization.

## Critical Thinking Questions

1. What aspects of classical and behavioral management theories have contributed the most to today's police organizations? What particular aspects should be discarded?

2. What influence does the paramilitary organizational design have on present-day policing? Why is it so hard to change? Is it still necessary?

3. As a mid-level manager, what steps would you take to implement new performance evaluation criteria for patrol officers?

4. Explain the difference between traditional media relations and strategic communications. If you were a police executive, how would you use social media?

5. Discuss four reasons why police officers tend to resist organizational change. Which obstacle do you believe is the most serious? How would you attempt to overcome this obstacle?

# References

Adams, R. E., Roche, W. M., and Arcury, T. A. 2002. "Implementing Community-Oriented Policing: Organizational Change and Street Officer Attitudes." *Crime & Delinquency* 48: 399–430.

Angell, J. E. 1971. "Toward an Alternative to the Classic Police Organizational Arrangements: A Democratic Model." *Criminology* 9: 185–206.

Auten, J. H. 1981. "The Paramilitary Model of Police and Police Professionalism." *Police Studies* 4: 67–78.

Baltimore Consent Decree Monitoring Team. 2022. *Seventh Semiannual Report.* https://static1.square-space.com/static/59db8644e45a7c08738ca2f1/t/620c205fdfa1535274047ae2/1644961899345/7th+Se miannual+Report.pdf.

Batts, A. W., Smoot, S. M., and Scrivner, E. 2012. "Police Leadership Challenges in a Changing World." *New Perspectives in Policing.* Washington DC: National Institute of Justice. https://www.ojp.gov/pdffiles1/nij/238338.pdf

Bercal, T. E. 1970. "Calls for Police Assistance." *American Behavioral Scientist* 13: 681–691.

Bittner, E. 1970. *The Function of the Police in Modern Society.* Washington, DC: US Government Printing Office.

Bradley, D., and Nixon, C. 2009. "Ending the 'Dialogue of the Deaf': Evidence and Policing Policies and Practices: An Australian Case Study." *Police Practice and Research* 10: 423–435.

Carter, D. L., and Sapp, A. D. 1996. "A Comparative Analysis of Clauses in Police Collective Bargaining Agreements as Indicators of Change in Labor Relations." In G. Cordner and D. Kenney (eds.), *Managing Police Organizations*, pp. 19–43. Cincinnati, OH: Anderson.

Chermak, S., and Weiss, A. 2006. "Community Policing in the News Media." *Police Quarterly* 9: 135–160.

Chicago Community Policing Evaluation Consortium. 2004. *CAPS at Ten: Community Policing in Chicago.* Chicago: Illinois Criminal Justice Information Authority.

Cordner, G. W. 2014a. "Community Policing." In M. D. Reisig and R. J. Kane (eds.), *The Oxford Handbook of Police and Policing*, pp. 148–171. New York: Oxford University Press.

Cordner, G. W. 2014b. "Measuring Police Unit Performance." In G. Bruinsma and D. Weisburd (eds.), *Encyclopedia on Criminology and Criminal Justice*, pp. 3037–3047. New York: Springer.

Cordner, G. W. 2016. "Police Culture: Individual and Organizational Differences in Police Officer Perspectives." *Policing: An International Journal of Police Strategies and Management* 40: 11–25.

Couper, D. C. 2021. *Arrested Development: A Veteran Police Chief Sounds Off About Racism, Protest, Corruption, and the Seven Steps Necessary to Improve Our Nation's Police*, 3rd ed. Madison, WI: Independently Published.

Couper, D. C., and Lobitz, S. H. 1991. *Quality Policing: The Madison Experience.* Washington, DC: Police Executive Research Forum.

Cowper, T. J. 2000. "The Myth of the 'Military Model' of Leadership in Law Enforcement." *Police Quarterly* 3: 228–246.

Cumming, E., Cumming, I., and Edell, L. 1965. "Policeman as Philosopher, Guide and Friend." *Social Problems* 12: 276–286.

Currie, P., and Dollery, B. 2006. "Organizational Commitment and Perceived Organizational Support in the NSW Police." *Policing: An International Journal of Police Strategies and Management* 29: 741–756.

Dunworth, T., Cordner, G., Greene, J., Bynum, T., Decker, S., Rich, T., Ward, S., and Webb, V. 2000. *Police Department Information Systems Technology Enhancement Project (ISTEP)*. Washington, DC: Office of Community Oriented Policing Services.

Engel, R. S. 2003. *How Police Supervisory Styles Influence Patrol Officer Behavior*. Washington, DC: National Institute of Justice.

Eterno, J. A., and Silverman, E. B. 2012. *The Crime Numbers Game: Management by Manipulation*. Boca Raton, FL: CRC Press.

Famega, C. N., Frank, J., and Mazerolle, L. 2005. "Managing Police Patrol Time: The Role of Supervisor Directives." *Justice Quarterly* 22: 540–559.

Fleming, J. 2010. "Learning to Work Together: Police and Academics." *Policing: A Journal of Policy and Practice* 4: 139–145.

Franz, V., and Jones, D. M. 1987. "Perceptions of Organizational Performance in Suburban Police Departments: A Critique of the Military Model." *Journal of Police Science and Administration* 15: 153–161.

Geller, W. A. 1997. "Suppose We Were Really Serious about Police Departments Becoming 'Learning Organizations'?" *National Institute of Justice Journal* 234: 2–8.

Germann, A. C. 1971. "Changing the Police: The Impossible Dream?" *Journal of Criminal Law, Criminology and Police Science* 62: 416–421.

Gerth, H. H., and Mills, C. W. 1946. *From Max Weber: Essays in Sociology*. New York: Oxford University Press.

Goldstein, H. 1968. "Police Response to Urban Crisis." *Public Administration Review* 28: 417–418.

Goldstein, H. 1977. *Policing a Free Society*. Cambridge, MA: Ballinger.

Goldstein, J. 2013. "Judge Rejects New York's Stop-and-Frisk Policy." *New York Times*, August 12. https://www.nytimes.com/2013/08/13/nyregion/stop-and-frisk-practice-violated-rights-judge-rules.html/.

Guilfoyle, S. 2013. *Intelligent Policing: How Systems Thinking Methods Eclipse Conventional Management Practice*. Devon, UK: Triarchy Press.

Guyot, D. 1979. "Bending Granite: Attempts to Change the Rank Structure of American Police Departments." *Journal of Police Science and Administration* 7: 253–284.

Haarr, R. N. 2001. "The Making of a Community Policing Officer: The Impact of Basic Training and Occupational Socialization on Police Recruits." *Police Quarterly* 4: 402–433.

Haberman, C. P., and King, W. R. 2011. "The Role of Research and Planning Units in Law Enforcement Organizations." *Policing: An International Journal of Police Strategies & Management* 34: 687–698.

Henry, V. E. 2002. *The Compstat Paradigm: Management Accountability in Policing, Business and the Public Sector*. Flushing, NY: Looseleaf Law.

Hoban, J. E., and Gourlie, B. J. 2014. *The Ethical Protector: Essays on Police Ethics, Tactics and Techniques*. Spring Lake, NJ: RGI Media and Publications.

Huberts, L. W. J. C., Kaptein, M., and Lasthuizen, K. 2007. "A Study of the Impact of Three Leadership Styles on Integrity Violations Committed by Police Officers." *Policing: An International Journal of Police Strategies & Management* 30: 587–607.

Johnson, K. 2016. "Amid Heightened Scrutiny, It's a Precarious Time for US Police Chiefs." *USA Today*, May 24. https://www.usatoday.com/story/news/nation/2016/05/23/police-chiefs-ferguson-san-francisco/84785128/.

Kadleck, C. 2003. "Police Employee Organizations." *Policing: An International Journal of Police Strategies and Management* 26: 341–351.

Kaminski, R. J., and Alpert, G. P. 2013. "Research in Brief: Recent Findings on Police Foot Pursuits." *The Police Chief* 80(January): 14.

King, W. R. 2003. "Bending Granite Revisited: The Command Rank Structure of American Police Organizations." *Policing: An International Journal of Police Strategies & Management* 26: 208–230.

Landergan, K. 2020. "The City that Really Did Abolish the Police." *Politico*, June 12. https://www.politico.com/news/magazine/2020/06/12/camden-policing-reforms-313750.

Levin, B. 2020. "What's Wrong with Police Unions?" *Columbia Law Review* 120: 1333–1401.

Lord, V. B., and Friday, P. C. 2008. "What Really Influences Officer Attitudes Toward COP: The Importance of Context." *Police Quarterly* 11: 220–238.

Lurigio, A. J., and Rosenbaum, D. P. 1994. "The Impact of Community Policing on Police Personnel: A Review of the Literature." In D. P. Rosenbaum (ed.), *The Challenge of Community Policing*, pp. 147–166. Thousand Oaks, CA: Sage.

Maguire, E. R. 1997. "Structural Change in Large Municipal Police Organizations During the Community Policing Era." *Justice Quarterly* 14: 547–576.

Mitchell, C. 2016. "Police Data Cast Doubt on Chicago-Style Stop-and-Frisk." *WBEZ News*, May 4. https://www.wbez.org/shows/wbez-news/police-data-cast-doubt-on-chicagostyle-stopandfrisk/d79738c6-b5a2-494d-acaf-e659969b3e6b/.

Moore, M. H., and Braga, A. 2003. *The "Bottom Line" of Policing: What Citizens Should Value (and Measure) in Police Performance*. Washington, DC: Police Executive Research Forum.

Myren, R. A. 1960. "A Crisis in Police Management." *Journal of Criminal Law, Criminology and Police Science* 50: 600–604.

Office of Community Oriented Policing Services. 2009. *Community Policing Defined*. Washington, DC: Author.

Ott, J. S. 1989. *The Organizational Culture Perspective*. Pacific Grove, CA: Brooks/Cole.

Parnas, R. 1967. "The Police Response to the Domestic Disturbance." *Wisconsin Law Review* (Fall): 914–960.

Petty, A. 2016. "The Human Cost of Mismanaging Change." *Leadership Caffeine*, February 29. https://artpetty.com/2016/02/29/leadership-caffeine-the-human-cost-of-mismanaging-change.

Pierce, J. L., and Delbeq, A. L. 1977. "Organization Structure, Individual Attitudes and Innovation." *Academy of Management Review* 2: 27–37.

Police Executive Research Forum. 2016. *Guiding Principles on Use of Force*. Washington, DC: Author. https://www.policeforum.org/assets/30%20guiding%20principles.pdf/.

President's Task Force on Twenty-First Century Policing. 2015. *Final Report*. Washington, DC: Office of Community Oriented Policing Services.

Rahr, S., and Rice, S. K. 2015. "From Warriors to Guardians: Recommitting American Police Culture to Democratic Ideals." *New Perspectives in Policing*. Washington, DC: National Institute of Justice. https://www.ncjrs.gov/pdffiles1/nij/248654.pdf/.

Rayman, G. 2010. "The NYPD Tapes: Inside Bed-Stuy's 81st Precinct." *Village Voice*, May 4. https://www.villagevoice.com/news/the-nypd-tapes-inside-bed-stuys-81st-precinct.

Reuss-Ianni, E. 1983. *Two Cultures of Policing: Street Cops and Management Cops*. New Brunswick, CT: Transaction Books.

Roberg, R. R. 1979. *Police Management and Organizational Behavior: A Contingency Approach*. St. Paul, MN: West.

Rojek, J., Alpert, G., and Smith, H. 2012. "The Utilization of Research by the Police." *Police Practice & Research: An International Journal* 13: 329–341.

Rojek, J., Smith, H. P., and Alpert, G. P. 2012. "The Prevalence and Characteristics of Police Practitioner–Researcher Partnerships." *Police Quarterly* 15: 241–261.

Scott, M., and Cordner, G. 2014. "Police Discretion and Its Control." In G. Bruinsma and D. Weisburd (eds.), *Encyclopedia on Criminology and Criminal Justice*, pp. 3587–3596. New York: Springer.

Scrivner, E. 2006. *Innovations in Police Recruitment and Hiring: Hiring in the Spirit of Service*. Washington, DC: Office of Community Oriented Policing Services.

Shane, J. M. 2007. *What Every Chief Executive Should Know: Using Data to Measure Police Performance*. Flushing, NY: Looseleaf Law.

Sheil, B. 2014. "Can Cleveland Learn from Cincinnati Police Reforms?" *Fox 8 Cleveland*, February 24. https://fox8.com/2014/02/24/i-team-can-cleveland-learn-from-cincinnati-police-reforms/.

Sherman, L. W., Milton, C. W., and Kelley, T. V. 1973. *Team Policing: Seven Case Studies.* Washington, DC: Police Foundation.

Sholihin, M., and Pike, R. 2010. "Organisational Commitment in the Police Service: Exploring the Effects of Performance Measures, Procedural Justice and Interpersonal Trust." *Financial Accountability & Measurement* 26: 392–421.

Skogan, W. G. 2006. *Police and Community in Chicago: A Tale of Three Cities.* New York: Oxford University Press.

Skogan, W. G. 2008. "Why Reforms Fail." *Policing & Society* 18: 23–34.

Skogan, W. G. 2022. "Prospects for Reform? The Collapse of Community Policing in Chicago." *University of Chicago Law Review* 89(2): 4.

Skogan, W. G., and Hartnett, S. M. 1997. *Community Policing, Chicago Style.* New York: Oxford University Press.

Skolnick, J. H., and Bayley, D. H. 1986. *The New Blue Line: Police Innovation in Six American Cities.* New York: Free Press.

Sledge, M. 2020. "New Orleans Police Department Seeks End to Consent Decree Despite Open Issues." *Nola.com*, December 17. https://www.nola.com/news/courts/article_196e0746-3ffe-11eb-8a7f-a3923b682aae.html.

Smith, B. 1940. *Police Systems in the United States.* New York: Harper & Row.

Spitzer, D. R. 2007. *Transforming Performance Measurement: Rethinking the Way We Measure and Drive Organizational Success.* New York: Amacom.

Stephens, D. W., Hill, J., and Greenberg, S. 2011. *Strategic Communication Practices: A Toolkit for Police Executives.* Washington, DC: Office of Community Oriented Policing Services.

Tiry, E., Oglesby-Neal, A. and Kim, K. 2019. *Social Media Guidebook for Law Enforcement Agencies: Strategies for Effective Community Engagement.* Washington, DC: Urban Institute. https://www.urban.org/sites/default/files/publication/99786/social_media_guidebook_for_law_enforcement_agencies_0.pdf.

Tsuruoka, S. 2018. *Camden's Turn: A Story of Police Reform in Progress; A Guide for Law Enforcement and Community Screenings.* Washington, DC: Office of Community Oriented Policing Services.

US Department of Justice. 2012. "Justice Department Announces Consent Decree with City of New Orleans to Resolve Allegations of Unlawful Misconduct by New Orleans Police Department." *Justice News*, July 24. https://www.justice.gov/opa/pr/justice-department-announces-consent-decree-city-new-orleans-resolve-allegations-unlawful.

Vito, G. F., Suresh, G., and Richards, G. E. 2011. "Emphasizing the Servant in Public Service: The Opinions of Police Managers." *Policing: An International Journal of Police Strategies & Management* 34: 674–686.

Walker, S. 1992. *The Police in America: An Introduction*, 2nd ed. New York: McGraw-Hill.

Walker, S. 2008. "The Neglect of Police Unions: Exploring One of the Most Important Areas of American Policing." *Police Practice & Research* 11: 95–112.

Watson, E. M., Stone, A. R., and DeLuca, S. T. 1998. *Strategies for Community Policing.* Upper Saddle River, NJ: Prentice Hall.

Wilson, J. Q. 1968. *Varieties of Police Behavior.* Cambridge, MA: Harvard University.

Wilson, O. W. 1950. *Police Administration.* New York: McGraw-Hill.

Wolfe, S. E., and Piquero, A. R. 2011. "Organizational Justice and Police Misconduct." *Criminal Justice and Behavior* 38: 332–353.

Wycoff, M. A., and Skogan, W. G. 1993. *Community Policing in Madison: Quality from the Inside Out*. Washington, DC: National Institute of Justice.

Wycoff, M. A., and Skogan, W. G. 1994. "Community Policing in Madison: An Analysis of Implementation and Impact." In D. P. Rosenbaum (ed.), *The Challenge of Community Policing: Testing the Promises*, pp. 75–91. Thousand Oaks, CA: Sage.

Zhao, J., Ren, L., and Lovrich, N. 2010. "Police Organizational Structures During the 1990s: An Application of Contingency Theory." *Police Quarterly* 13: 209–231.

# Selection and Development

## CHAPTER OUTLINE

## CHAPTER OUTLINE (continued)

### KEY TERMS

- andragogy
- bona fide occupational qualification
- career growth
- cognitive learning
- de-escalation
- disparate impact
- education

- field training officer
- four-fifths rule
- in-service training
- job task analysis
- lateral entry
- Peace Officer Standards and Training
- pedagogy

- police training officer
- problem-based learning
- procedural justice
- screening in
- screening out
- specialized training
- training

As NOTED IN THE previous chapters, the nature of policing and police departments is becoming more complex and challenging, necessitating hiring and developing the highest-quality personnel available. Although the quality of police personnel has always been important, with the increased complexity of the police role and the renewed movement toward community policing (COP) practices, the quality of personnel has perhaps become the key element in effective police operation. Indeed, a report by the Police Executive Research Forum (PERF; 2019, 7) concluded "the skills, temperament, and life experiences needed to succeed as an officer are becoming more complex."

The debate over the meaning of *quality*, however, is not easy to resolve. For instance, does an individual need a certain level of intelligence, and how is that level measured? Are certain physical characteristics a factor? Should higher education be required? What about ethical values? Considerations of quality also suggest that departments should select personnel, including women, who are representative of the communities they serve, because they help provide a greater understanding of issues related to gender, race, and ethnicity. Diversity issues in policing are discussed in depth in Chapter 12.

Police selection and development are also influenced by a city or county civil service system. For instance, civil service requirements may significantly influence a department's criteria for selection, promotion, and discipline. Civil service provisions were enacted in 1883 with the passage of the Pendleton Civil Service Act, which tried to eliminate the spoils system in which politicians could simply hire and fire police personnel based on their political affiliation or friendships. By establishing hiring standards for all applicants, police departments gained considerable autonomy against political influence. But civil service also had a number of negative side effects. For instance, Wilson and McLaren (1977, 28), who were early critics of the civil service, believed that civil service rules provided too much security for "incompetent and untrustworthy" officers, who are virtually impossible to "weed out." Today, although it is possible to terminate incompetent or dishonest police employees, it is an onerous and time-consuming effort as a result of civil service provisions.

A police department makes essentially three selection decisions: (1) entry, (2) reassignment, and (3) promotion. Decisions about police entrance are usually for the lowest-level position (patrol), but supervisory- and managerial-level entry are also possible. A few departments recruit for lower-level and middle-level managers (e.g., sergeants, lieutenants, and captains) from outside the department; this practice is known as lateral entry (discussed in the final section of this chapter). Some departments also select their chief of police from the outside. Because most sheriffs are elected, potential candidates may include persons outside the sheriff's department, or even outside the law enforcement field.

All states have created statewide standards for parts of the personnel process (e.g., selection, training, and promotion). For example, many states now have an organization called Peace Officer Standards and Training (discussed later). There is still considerable variation among states, however, and some departments do not adhere to the personnel standards that are established because they are not obligated by law to do so.

If high-quality police recruits are to be chosen, the selection process should be designed to screen in, rather than screen out, applicants. **Screening out** identifies applicants who are unqualified and removes them from consideration, leaving in the applicant pool all those who are minimally qualified. Recruits who may not be well qualified for police work are then selected from this pool. **Screening in** applicants, in contrast, identifies only the best-qualified candidates for the applicant pool. The department will select its recruits from these applicants, thus ensuring a relatively high-quality candidate. Interestingly, many police departments still rely on screening out applicants, but the process has been under attack since at least 1973, when the National Advisory Commission on Criminal Justice Standards and Goals noted the following:

> The selection of police personnel should be approached positively; police agencies should seek to identify and employ the best candidates available rather than being content with disqualifying the unfit. The policy of merely *eliminating the least qualified results in mediocrity* because it allows marginal applicants to be employed along with the most qualified. (italics added)

## Recruitment

The initial step in the selection process is recruiting *qualified candidates*. The relationship of the number of applicants to those who qualify (or meet standards) for positions is often a major factor in the quality of the personnel selected. Since at least the second decade of the twenty-first century, if not earlier, police agencies began reporting a shortage of qualified applicants. A RAND Corporation survey in 2008 found that the majority of police agencies surveyed reported problems with recruitment, specifically a lack of qualified applicants (Wilson, Rostker, and Fan 2010). Reviewing the literature on police staffing, J. M. Wilson (2012) summarized a number of trends that may be reducing the pool of interested and qualified applicants available for policing. One trend obvious to many police recruiters is the shrinking pool of applicants who meet minimum qualifications, specifically people without past criminal records who are financially stable and can pass physical fitness requirements (see, e.g., Raymond et al. 2005). For example, the amount of credit card debt (a potential disqualifier for some agencies) has grown significantly in recent decades, as has the rate of obesity among young Americans (see, e.g., Raymond et al. 2005).

In addition to the shrinking pool of qualified candidates, many young people today desire to work in settings that allow more rapid advancement and provide greater balance of work and family life than are available in policing (Wilson 2012). At the same time as the pool of qualified applicants may be dwindling, the opportunities for such individuals appear to be increasing. Private security and federal policing have grown significantly in the past two decades, increasing labor market competition (Wilson 2012).

In addition to these larger social and economic forces, recent increased public scrutiny, protests, and calls for greater police accountability have had a significant influence on the morale of police officers. A recent survey of police officers revealed that the majority of officers feel their job has become more difficult as a result of recent high-profile fatalities at the hands of police (Morin et al. 2017). Morale and increased job challenges may be contributing to higher officer resignations and retirements. At the same time, these events may be limiting interest in policing as a career choice for some young people (International Association of Chiefs of Police [IACP] 2019).

### The Great Resignation and Policing

The COVID-19 pandemic "churned" labor markets, with the quit rate hitting a 20-year high (Parker and Horowitz 2022). While state and local government agencies have been experiencing high quit rates since before the pandemic, the pandemic accelerated the problem, resulting in not only recruiting challenges but also "actual declines in workers" in state and local government, with police agencies experiencing some of the highest resignations and retirements (Farmer 2022). These problems were likely exacerbated by increased public scrutiny since the killing of George Floyd in 2020.

A survey of police agencies by the IACP in 2019 found that 78 percent of agencies reported difficulty recruiting qualified applicants, and the PERF (2021) found that overall hiring in police agencies declined by 5 percent from the previous year. More serious, they found that agencies experienced an 18 percent increase in resignations and 45 percent increase in retirements during the same period (PERF 2021). Fewer people are applying to police agencies, while at the same time, more police officers are resigning and retiring (PERF 2019). Thus, police agencies are faced with the challenge of more officers quitting policing for other careers and more officers retiring, leaving agencies with even more vacancies to fill while continuing to experience the trend of fewer qualified applicants. To counter these forces, police agencies may need to identify and pursue recruitment methods tailored to the new realities of the labor market.

Much information on the recruitment process can be gleaned from two national surveys on recruitment and hiring conducted by the PERF (Taylor et al. 2005; see also Jordan et al. 2009) and the RAND Corporation (Wilson et al. 2010). The PERF study included 985 agencies representing all state police agencies and random samples of county and municipal agencies. The RAND Corporation surveyed all agencies with 300 or more officers.

### Recruitment Methods

The most commonly reported recruitment methods in both the PERF and the RAND surveys were (1) newspaper ads, (2) career fairs, and (3) Internet advertising. In addition, a sizeable number of agencies reported using college outreach/internships, explorer programs, and school resource officers. The majority of agencies in the RAND survey also reported that they targeted specific groups for recruitment. The most commonly targeted groups for recruitment were those with previous police experience, college graduates, racial and ethnic minorities, and women.

### Recruiting for Diversity

In attempting to recruit diverse groups of qualified applicants, it is important that departments recognize that different *recruitment strategies* may be necessary. One of the more effective strategies to attract diverse applicants is to specifically *target* them for recruitment purposes.

The PERF and RAND surveys found that departments use specific strategies to increase the number of female and minority applicants. For example, some promising practices targeting females noted in the PERF survey included recruiting at events focusing on women, including women's trade shows, women's fairs, and women's fitness clubs. One department noted that they have a commitment to increasing opportunities for females so recruits can see women in positions of authority. Others use advisory committees to help determine effective ways to recruit women, whereas many use recruitment posters with females clearly present. For minorities, promising practices included the use of advisory groups or task forces to determine appropriate recruitment strategies; one agency reported bringing different minorities onto the task force and using a person from each group to recruit fellow minorities (e.g., a Hispanic member would go into the Hispanic community to find places to advertise and recruit, an Asian member would do the same in the Asian community, and so on). Several agencies also noted partnering with minority organizations such as the National Association for the Advancement of Colored People (NAACP) to help recruit. Posters with minority members prominently displayed were also used by many agencies.

The PERF results further indicated that significantly more Black and Hispanic officers, officers of other races, as well as females are working in law enforcement and that the proportion of white officers has declined (by approximately 9 percent). These changes are likely the result of targeted recruitment strategies described previously. Other highly targeted groups included four-year college graduates and people with prior police service. College graduates are recruited by 67 percent of the RAND respondent agencies, and 53 percent are recruiting those with prior experience.

Research by Jordan et al. (2009) revealed at least five significant findings on attracting and hiring female and minority candidates. First, only approximately 18 percent of agencies used a *targeted recruitment strategy*. A much larger percentage of state and large agencies targeted these populations compared with smaller agencies. Indeed, the RAND study found that 80 percent and 74 percent of large agencies made special efforts to recruit racial/ethnic minorities and women, respectively. Overall, the PERF results indicated that agencies using special recruiting strategies did receive more applicants and hire more people from these groups: the number of minority hires increased by 3.2-fold, whereas female hires increased by 2.2-fold.

A second finding, possibly associated with the first, was that a positive relationship was found between the annual *recruiting budget* and the number of applications from women and minorities and the number of women and minorities hired. In other words, the more resources put into the recruiting effort, the more successful the recruiting and hiring of women and minorities.

A third finding related to *special entry conditions*, where women and minorities may be allowed to have lower fitness standards or preferences on the waiting list; however, these conditions were actually used in less than 3 percent of agencies. Interestingly, even when such conditions were allowed, they did not affect the number of applications or hires from these groups.

A fourth finding indicated that *starting pay* was related to the number of both female and minority applicants, but it did not impact the hiring of either group. On average, a $7,300 increase in starting pay resulted in an 89 percent increase in female applicants and a 145 percent increase in minority applicants.

Last, a requirement of two years of college (i.e., 60 units) or a bachelor's degree did not impact the receipt of applications from or the hiring of women. For minorities, there was no impact on applications from requiring either two years of college or a college degree. And although there was no impact on hiring for a college degree requirement, there was a negative impact from the two-year requirement. In sum, as the authors noted, these results indicated a pattern that supports a proactive and targeted approach to attracting qualified female and minority candidates to policing instead of relying on more general recruiting strategies or providing preferential treatment.

In recent years, agencies have recognized diversity in much broader terms than simply race, ethnic, and gender diversity. The President's Task Force on Twenty-First Century Policing (2015, 2), for example, noted that "law enforcement agencies should strive to create a workforce that contains a broad range of diversity including race, gender, language, life experience and cultural background to improve understanding and effectiveness in dealing with all communities."

## Responding to the Recruitment Challenge

In 2009, the Office of Community Oriented Policing Services (COPS Office) partnered with the IACP in creating the Law Enforcement Recruitment Toolkit to assist agencies in understanding the challenges they faced and provide guidance in recruitment efforts. The publication identifies the recruitment needs of law enforcement agencies, challenges to law enforcement recruitment, and a number of innovative strategies some law enforcement agencies are using in their recruitment. Some of the more innovative strategies include collaboration with other police agencies in recruiting, engaging the community in recruitment efforts, streamlining the recruitment and selection process, and involving everyone in the department in recruiting. Inside Policing 6.1 provides an example of one strategy to engage the community in recruiting. The challenges identified by the COPS Office and IACP have only intensified over the past decade.

In response to the crisis in recruitment, the IACP, the PERF, and the COPS Office have all hosted forums to bring together experts to discuss the current situation and identify methods for responding (see, e.g., Copple 2017; IACP 2019; PERF 2019). All three organizations' forums identified a similar constellation of problems and possible solutions. The PERF, for example, held a conference that brought together police executives and police officers who were early in their career. The report that followed (PERF 2019) suggested ways to recruit people who might not otherwise consider applying to be a police officer. Specifically, they suggested that police agencies consider a number of changes to enhance recruitment and officer careers. First, emphasize service over excitement and avoid the traditional police advertising showing only the most adventurous and exciting work and, instead, provide realistic portraits of policing. Second, streamline the application process. It can take from four months to over a year for applicants to complete the police hiring process (IACP 2019), resulting in recruits dropping out of the process before completion for various reasons, including finding other employment. Third, adopt an approach to

| INSIDE POLICING 6.1 | Sacramento Community Recruiter Program |
|---|---|

The community recruiter program in Sacramento, California, adopts the same core principles and strategies that are part of COP. It arose from the recognition that community members, including community leaders, understood little about the department and its selection and recruitment processes. When instituted in 2004, the program represented a reinvention of the recruitment process, identifying interested community leaders and training them to be what the department calls community recruiters. Community recruiters undergo a three-hour orientation about the department and the qualifications and requirements for new recruits. They receive a handbook containing details about the written, oral, and physical agility examinations; job requirements; background checks; and job applications. The department produced a video that addresses each aspect of the testing process and life in the academy.

As the program grew, recruiters became more involved in the process. Instead of just providing names of possible candidates, these community members became involved in the process of screening acceptable candidates. Community recruiters now serve on entry-level and promotional oral panels. This involvement has enhanced the process and provided a valuable opportunity for the department to understand cultural differences, particularly as they relate to interviewing and testing. Through involvement in the interview panels, community recruiters learn about the department and become more effective recruiters and screeners.

SOURCE: COPS/IACP Leadership Project, *Law Enforcement Recruitment Toolkit* (Washington, DC: US Department of Justice, Office of Community Oriented Policing Services, 2009). https://cops.usdoj.gov/RIC/Publications/cops-p171-pub.pdf.

recruiting that is more intensive and personal. Fourth, change traditional incentives to align with what younger officers today want—for example, opportunities to learn new skills and try different assignments and more flexible scheduling for better work–life balance. Fifth, rethink traditional career trajectories of police employees. These approaches and others are designed not only to address the specific recruitment challenges, but also to adapt to a changing workforce and a new generation.

## Selection

Following recruitment, the selection process attempts to determine which candidates are best suited to the needs of the department. The process must decide whether candidates have the requisite skills and abilities to perform effectively. Various selection criteria are used to make such judgments, including preemployment standards and preemployment testing, to establish a ranking system from which candidates are hired.

It is crucial that these standards and tests be valid and reliable indicators of job performance. *Validity* is the degree to which a measure actually assesses the attribute it is designed to measure. For example, are the physical strength and agility criteria traditionally used for selection related to the ability to perform the job satisfactorily? If not, they are not valid criteria for selection. *Reliability* is a measure's ability to yield consistent results over time. In the physical strength and agility example, the measure would be reliable if a candidate taking the test on more than one occasion received the same or a similar score each time. Departments attempt to use criteria that are both valid and reliable; it is possible to have selection criteria that are valid but not reliable or reliable but not valid. For instance, although a physical strength score may be reliable, it may not be a valid criterion if it cannot be shown to be job-related.

In addition, validity is important because invalid criteria may have an adverse impact on groups that are protected by equal employment opportunity laws and regulations. The Equal Employment Opportunity Act of 1972 extended to public agencies the "anti-discrimination in employment" provision of Title VII of the 1964 Civil Rights Act. Title VII prohibits any discrimination in the workplace based on race, color, religion, national origin, or gender. In *Griggs v. Duke Power Company* (1971), the US Supreme Court held that an employer's requirement of a high school diploma and two standardized written tests for a position disqualified a higher percentage of Blacks than whites and could not be shown to be related to job performance. Consequently, the standards had a **disparate impact** on the plaintiff (Willie Griggs) specifically and on African Americans in general. A selection method can be considered to have a legally disparate impact when the selection rate of a group is less than 80 percent of the most successful group; this is also known as the **four-fifths rule**. Before *Griggs*, selection standards could be used as long as they did not intentionally discriminate; after *Griggs*, standards could not be used that were intended to be impartial but in fact were discriminatory in practice.

In another important decision, *Albemarle Paper Company v. Moody* (1975), the Supreme Court found that selection and promotion tests or standards must be shown to be related to job performance; that is, the standard must be *job-related*. This decision had far-reaching implications for police selection, because all selection criteria must be shown to be related to on-the-job performance. It is important to note, however, that departments can require a standard, even if it may have a disparate impact, if the standard can be shown to be a valid predictor of job performance. For example, in *Davis v. City of Dallas* (1985), the Supreme Court upheld the Dallas Police Department's requirement of 45 hours of college credit, although it discriminated against minorities, because of the professional and complex nature of police work. Legal precedent for higher-educational requirements had previously been established by other professions. Such a job-related standard, known as a **bona fide occupational qualification** (BFOQ), is permissible under Title VII even though it may exclude members of a protected group.

Police departments should attempt to use selection methods that not only are valid but also have no adverse impact. This means that departments must commit resources to validating their selection and testing methods, usually through a **job task analysis** that identifies the behaviors necessary for adequate job performance. Based on such identification, the *knowledge*, *skills*, and *abilities* required for on-the-job behaviors are formulated, after which procedures (e.g., tests and interviews) are developed to identify candidates who meet these requirements. The procedures are then tested relative to their effectiveness in predicting job performance.

## Preemployment Standards

Candidates are measured against a department's view of what is required to become an effective police officer. A number of minimum standards are established that must be met prior to employment. These standards are usually rigid and establish certain finite qualifications that, if not met, will most likely eliminate the candidate from further consideration. Such standards may include age, height and weight, vision, physical agility and strength, residency, education (general suitability, including background, psychological condition, and medical condition, will be discussed later). Although not all departments have all of these requirements, they are common to many. The specific standards themselves, however, vary considerably.

**Age.**  Traditionally, police departments have allowed applicants to be between the ages of 21 and 32 to 38, with some accepting applicants as young as 18. Many police experts and police managers believe that 18- to 21-year-olds may not be mature enough to perform police work satisfactorily and, if hired, should only be assigned service duties. For this purpose, some departments have police cadet or community service officer programs; when the person completes the educational requirement and meets the minimum age requirement, they apply to become a sworn officer.

**Height and Weight.**  Stringent minimum and maximum height and weight requirements were standards for most departments in the past. These requirements, however, have been changing over the past several decades because of legal challenges. For instance, minimum height requirements have been challenged successfully as being discriminatory against both women and minority groups, especially Asians and Hispanics. For example, in *Vanguard Justice Society v. Hughes* (1979), the Court noted that a 5-foot, 7-inch height requirement excluded 95 percent of the female population but only 32 percent of the male population and found this to be evidence of gender discrimination. Because of such rulings, the general standard has now become *weight in proportion to height*.

**Vision.**  Vision requirements were also traditionally stringent, ranging from 20/20 to 20/70 uncorrected in both eyes or 20/20 corrected with contacts or glasses. This standard has also been relaxed over the years, because such a requirement cannot be job validated and eliminates otherwise potentially strong candidates. Virtually all police departments, however, still maintain certain corrected and uncorrected vision requirements.

**Physical Agility and Strength.**  Testing of physical agility and strength has been related to an assumed need for physical strength and endurance. For example, candidates would be required to drag a dummy, scale a wall, perform an agility run, or run a certain timed distance (a half mile to two miles); if they fell below a certain minimum, they would be eliminated.

Many of these standards cannot be shown to be *job-related* and tend to be discriminatory in nature, especially against women. For example, Lonsway (2003), in her national study of 62 police agencies (38 city, 21 county, and 3 state), found that although the vast majority (89 percent) use some form of physical agility testing, in agencies that did not use such a test the representation of sworn female officers was 45 percent higher (15.8 to 10.9 percent). In an attempt to improve the pass rate of otherwise capable applicants, some departments, such as San Antonio, Texas, offer physical fitness workshops that help prepare applicants for the physical agility test; the San Antonio department also offers a workshop on the written exam (Taylor et al. 2005).

As Lonsway (2003) suggests, some less discriminatory alternatives include either no physical testing or health-based screening. No physical agility testing would eliminate the negative impact on female applicants in the selection process. Furthermore, there has been no evidence of an adverse impact on policing where this has been done. In Florida, for example, more than half of the local police agencies and sheriffs' offices use no physical agility test, and the FBI does not use an entry-level physical agility test. When no physical testing is used, departments typically require a medical examination and administer physical training *in the academy*. With this approach, the physical performance of recruits is tested after they participate in a conditioning program as part of the training academy, which not only mitigates the risk of discriminatory impact by allowing recruits to train for successful performance but also may allow better assessment of job-related tasks such as defensive tactics (Gaines, Falkenberg, and Gambino 1993).

**Residency.**  Whether a department has a residency requirement has a strong impact on those who may be recruited. There are essentially two types of requirements: (1) an applicant must reside within a geographic area (e.g., state, county, or city) for a specific period of time (one year is common) prior to application (preemployment), or (2) an applicant must relocate after being selected (postemployment). Proponents of such a requirement argue that it is important for individuals to have an understanding of the community in which they work and that those who live in the community have a greater stake in and concern for the community. Although an assumption may exist that a postemployment residency requirement would improve citizens' attitudes of the police because the officers are "more connected" to the community, there is no evidence supporting such an assumption. Opponents of residency requirements argue that they unnecessarily restrict the applicant pool, since the best candidates may not live within the geographic limits.

**Education.**  Although Chapter 14 includes a comprehensive discussion on higher education and policing, we will briefly discuss higher-education standards here. First, it should be recognized that overall, in local police departments, approximately 15 percent of agencies require at least some college credits. However, only 1 percent require a four-year degree for recruitment purposes, whereas 10 percent require a two-year college degree and 84 percent require only a high school diploma (Reaves 2015). Although there has been a trend of recruits entering the field with college degrees (up to one-third in some departments; Taylor et al. 2005), many departments are either reducing their minimum educational requirements to increase applicant pools or allowing officers to finish their education within a certain number of years after being hired (see Inside Policing 6.2). Another strategy that has been gaining favor in many departments is to allow military experience to substitute for college credit. In 2013, an estimated 54 percent of local police departments allowed military service to substitute for their degree requirement (Reaves 2015).

### General Suitability

Departments usually conduct an extensive investigation of an applicant's past experience, behavior, and work history in an attempt to assess the person's character and general suitability for police work. In general, this process is composed of a background investigation and a polygraph examination.

---

**INSIDE POLICING 6.2**   **Competition in Recruiting**

This article reports continuing recruitment challenges facing police agencies due to the strong economy, retirement of baby-boomers, and recent negative narratives about policing. One result is more competition between agencies for the best recruits and lateral hires, including bonuses for successful applicants and for current officers who refer them. Average police salaries have been raised 15 percent since 2010 to make them more attractive. Larger agencies continue to offer substantially higher salaries than smaller ones.

**Discussion Question:** What innovative approaches would you use to recruit younger candidates to policing?

SOURCE: *Modern Policing* blog, April 22, 2018, https://gcordner.wordpress.com/2018/04/22/competition-in-recruiting/.

**Background Investigation.** A thorough background investigation, based on the extensive personal history provided by the candidate, is one of the most important aspects of the selection process. The investigator attempts to determine whether the person is honest and reliable and would make a contribution to the department. Family background, employment and credit history, personal references, friends and neighbors, education records, criminal and possibly juvenile records, drug use, and when appropriate, military records are all checked to develop a general assessment of the person's lifestyle prior to applying for police work. In their landmark study of New York police applicants, Cohen and Chaiken (1972) found that applicants who were rated as excellent by the background investigators had the lowest incidence of misconduct (some 36 percent had personal complaints filed). In contrast, the applicants rated as poor had the highest incidence of misconduct (some 68 percent). Because these investigations are time-consuming and expensive, some police departments, especially smaller ones with limited resources, may not be thorough. Snowden and Fuss (2000) found this to be true; that is, in larger departments, more time was spent on training and background investigations, including greater use of secondary references and procedures. Because background investigations appear to be a good predictor of future police behavior, it is important that departments take no shortcuts at this stage.

Two important aspects of the background investigation relate to a candidate's *criminal record* and *history of drug use*. Generally, a criminal record does not automatically disqualify one from police service. With respect to misdemeanor convictions, departments vary widely, but the trend is to examine the type and extent of violations and make a determination based on the candidate's overall record. Several court cases have laid the foundation for what is a permissible drug-use standard for police employment practices. For instance, a Dallas Police Department standard requiring police applicants not to have recent or excessive histories of marijuana use was upheld (*Davis v. City of Dallas* 1985). And in *Shield Club v. City of Cleveland* (1986), the Court upheld drug-testing requirements and the rejection of applicants who tested positive for narcotics, amphetamines, or hallucinogens. In both rulings, the courts indicated that such requirements were job-related and therefore not discriminatory. It is also important to note that each of the departments utilized an objective testing system that prevented any form of individual discrimination.

The Bureau of Justice Statistics (BJS) survey (Hickman 2005) found that agencies today tend to be less strict concerning criminal history and drug use. According to the survey, only about 33 percent of agencies required a clean criminal record, compared with about 52 percent in 1989. Although the term *clean criminal record* may have been interpreted differently, the pattern is clear that screening standards relating to prior arrests, convictions, and drug use have been lowered in many departments.

**Polygraph Examination.** The polygraph, or lie detector, is used to check the accuracy of background information and to determine whether there has been any inappropriate behavior, past or present, on the applicant's part (e.g., criminal acts or illegal drug use). Although the polygraph has been touted by some as an effective tool in discovering problems with applicants, some research has suggested that it is not a reliable method to determine truth or falsehood of an individual's statements (see, e.g., Kleinmuntz and Szucko 1982; Hodes, Hunt, and Raskin 1985; Rafky and Sussman 1985). One problem with the polygraph is the amount of stress it puts on a candidate and the resulting false positives (i.e., when a candidate is falsely accused of lying). Therefore, some jurisdictions have made such testing illegal. Furthermore, some departments still ask questions about an applicant's lifestyle or sexual practices, which are private matters. If a polygraph examination is administered, all questions relating to the applicant's background should be job-related. Finally, the polygraph should never be used as a substitute for the background investigation, only as a supplement to it.

**Psychological Condition.** Psychological screening to determine a candidate's suitability for police work has become more common; this screening may be written, oral, or both. The most commonly used written tests are the Minnesota Multiphasic Personality Inventory (MMPI), the California Personality Inventory (CPI), and the Inwald Personality Inventory (IPI), developed specifically for police screening (TELEMASP 1994). The MMPI was originally designed to test a mental patient's psychological state and thus has been widely criticized for inappropriate questions and validity in assessing job performance. As a response to the criticisms, the test has been revised and renamed the MMPI-2. The IPI seeks to evaluate the psychological fitness of the applicant by measuring various behavioral patterns and characteristics; it further attempts to identify deviant behaviors that could impact job performance. The CPI, in contrast to the other two tests, attempts to measure personality traits only in normal individuals, as well as characteristics that are important in everyday life.

According to the results of a meta-analytic study (a synthesis of 78 research studies) regarding psychological testing in law enforcement agencies, the CPI was found to be the strongest predictor of future job performance when measured against the various forms of the MMPI and the IPI (Varela et al. 2004). The authors concluded that the CPI was the strongest predictor of job performance because it measures normal personality traits in comparison with the MMPI and the IPI, which measure, at least in part, traits relating to psychopathology. The authors of a recent review, however, concluded that research on the CPI was limited and that gaps existed in research on all of the instruments (Lough and Von Treuer 2013).

A statewide survey conducted in Texas to determine the type and extent of psychological testing used in the initial hiring process (Lee 2006) found that of the 43 responding agencies (including municipal and county agencies and the Department of Public Safety), 70 percent relied on the MMPI or the MMPI-2 as their psychological screening test. These findings are troubling, since the research indicates the MMPI is the least valid and useful of the three tests reviewed.

Considerable controversy surrounds the use of psychological testing for police screening; for example, an earlier review of the research by Burbeck and Furnham (1985) suggested that such tests may be useful for screening out people suffering from some mental abnormality, but not for predicting job performance. Metchik (1999) also cautions that the screening-out model has questionable validity and reliability, both because it cannot differentiate individuals who will become mediocre officers from those who will become superior ones and because the potential for false positives (i.e., incorrectly eliminating good candidates) is high. The Texas survey described previously also discovered that 95 percent of the agencies used psychological screening to *screen out unsuitable candidates*, rather than to *screen in the best available candidates*. Importantly, this suggests, as Metchik (1999) notes, not only are *mediocre candidates likely be selected, but superior candidates* are likely to *be screened out*.

A number of newer psychological instruments have been used for police screening. The Australian Institute of Forensic Psychology profiling system has been in use since the 1990s. This system is a battery of six tests designed to screen out applicants (Lough and Von Treuer 2013). The Revised NEO Personality Inventory (NEO PI-R) has garnered attention for its potential ability to predict top performers (Costa and McRae 1992). The NEO PI-R measures five general personality domains: (1) neuroticism, (2) extraversion, (3) openness, (4) agreeableness, and (5) conscientiousness. Although it has been part of the psychological testing process for New Zealand police applicants since 1996 (Black 2000), its use remains limited in the United States despite a growing body of evidence illustrating its potential. For instance, Detrick, Chibnall, and Luebbert (2004) found that several areas of police academy performance (academic, physical training and defensive tactics, firearms, and disciplinary action) were related to the NEO PI-R scores of a recruit. In addition, Detrick and Chibnall (2006) found that high scores on conscientiousness combined with low scores on neuroticism were predictive of high performance in both the police academy and field training. Although additional research is necessary, it would appear that including the NEO PI-R as a standard psychological measure in the police recruit screening process may be of value in the selection of superior candidates.

**Medical Condition.** Virtually all police departments have certain medical requirements an individual must meet before being hired. A medical examination is given by a physician either designated by the department or chosen by the candidate. The exam attempts to determine the general health of the candidate and to identify specific conditions, such as heart, back, or knee problems. In general, any weaknesses that may be aggravated by the requirements of police work will eliminate the candidate from further consideration—the costs of losing an officer to injury or illness, often with long-term disability compensation or a lawsuit, are too great. If a department requires some form of drug testing, it usually takes place during this phase of the process.

## Preemployment Testing

The preemployment standards for police departments, as well as the legal justifications, change periodically. This is an area in which departments need specific, as well as the most current, information to select the best-qualified candidates. Although preemployment standards are usually scored on a pass–fail basis and are used to eliminate candidates, preemployment tests are generally used to place candidates in order of rank. The two most commonly used tests are some form of written test and the oral interview. Some departments use the written test simply as a qualifier (i.e., on a pass–fail basis) and the oral interview as the only criterion for rank order.

**Written Exams and Performance.** Traditionally, departments have used some type of written civil service test, usually a standardized intelligence test or jurisdictionally specific knowledge test, to screen and rank order candidates. Few attempts, until recently, were made to determine whether these tests impact the applicants' ability to perform successfully as a police officer. Although it is easy to argue that police officers should be intelligent and knowledgeable, it is difficult to determine what kind and level of intelligence or knowledge is being measured.

In addition, some research suggests that minority citizens tend to score lower on police entry exams (see, e.g., Sproule 1984; Gaines, Costello, and Crabtree 1989). Thus, if a simple rank ordering of candidates is used, it will generally create an adverse impact. These problems have led to attempts to validate police written tests empirically since at least the late 1970s (see, e.g., Crosby, Rosenfield, and Thornton 1979) and, by departments, to seek exams that are more objective and job-related (Law Enforcement Assistance Administration 1973). Regarding validation, Gaines and Falkenberg (1998) reviewed the written exams of more than 400 police applicants representing one jurisdiction; the authors found that although males and females did not score differently, Blacks had significantly lower scores than whites. Moreover, exam scores were primarily a function of the *educational level* of the applicant and were unrelated to oral board scores. The exam had questionable validity in that it did not discriminate between highly qualified and less qualified applicants. Since the exam primarily measured educational level, the authors recommended simply adopting a minimum educational requirement; the authors argued that a more racially diverse pool of candidates would emerge using a two-year college requirement instead of the exam. Alternatively, police departments could institute a written exam aimed at the level of a two-year college student.

A study of more than 1,500 police recruits from a major metropolitan police department's training academy (White 2008) indicated that the main predictor of superior academy performance was a *reading test* score. Academy performance was measured by calculating an overall average score of four exams taken over the entire six-month academy, including a comprehensive final exam. The primary findings indicated that with respect to higher recruit exam scores, whites, Asians, and others scored higher than Blacks and Hispanics; males scored higher than females; as age increased, exam scores decreased; and as reading levels increased, exam scores increased. The most critical discovery appeared to be that of applicants who read at the *12th-grade level or higher*: 34.4 percent posted an average of 90 percent or higher on the recruit exams, compared with 11.5 percent of those with lower reading levels. Conversely, college education, military experience, and residency had no significant impact on academy exam scores. Similarly, in a study with a sample of 503 recruits accepted into the Baltimore County Police Academy, Wright, Dai, and Greenbeck (2010) noted that neither prior military experience nor police experience were predictors of academy success. Unlike the White (2008) study, however, recruits who had graduated from college were more likely to be successful than those with solely a high school diploma. Interestingly, the most significant predictor of academy success overall was some type of work experience *outside* of law enforcement.

In one of the few studies relating civil service exam scores to measures of police performance on the street, Henson et al. (2010) collected data on 486 police recruits who entered the Cincinnati Police Department's academy program from 1996 to 2006. The authors looked at the relationships among civil service exam scores and training academy success (measured by quiz, spelling, midterm and final scores, and note taking and overall score) and active service performance (measured by three supervisory performance ratings, use of force complaints, and commendations). In general, the findings suggested a positive correlation between high civil service scores and academy performance scores, although results were mixed for performance evaluation ratings. That is, the results were positive for an officers' second-year evaluation and three-year evaluation average, but no relationship existed for the first-year evaluation. In addition, no relationship existed between military experience and academy performance or active service performance; furthermore, a relationship existed between military experience and increased citizen complaints.

Finally, higher education did not impact any of the measured criteria. However, as Henson et al. (2010) pointed out, this finding was not unexpected in that only a simplistic measure of college education could be utilized because of lack of variation in the sample—that is, between those with some college and those with no college. In other words, no distinction was made among those with only a few units, an associate's degree, a college degree, or even a graduate degree.

Because literacy skills in police applicants have been markedly declining and written civil service tests do not adequately screen for literacy, some states require all candidates to pass one of any number of tests designed to measure reading and writing skills before they begin the academy (Clark 1992). Since 1988, for example, the regional training center for Miami-area police departments has required participants in its preservice program to take a test to ensure they can read at a 10th-grade level. The requirement was imposed because, according to the training center, earning a high school diploma does not guarantee that the graduate can read beyond the junior high school level (Clark 1992). Because the Miami-area example is undoubtedly reflective of a national concern, the arguments for moving toward requiring a college degree become even more evident.

One interesting example of eliminating otherwise capable applicants—in this case, one who was thought to be *too smart*—occurred in New London, Connecticut. Robert Jordan, who scored a 33 on IQ tests that measure a person's ability to learn and solve problems, was denied an interview under a city policy where candidates who score above or below a range of 20 to 27 are generally not interviewed for positions. The national average for police officers is 21 to 22, the same as for bank tellers, salespeople, and office workers (*Law Enforcement News* 1997, 4). The authors of the IQ exams had established a set of low and high markers for specific occupations (in the case of policing, 18 to 30), with the high marker eliminating people who would likely become bored with the job and soon resign (presumably leaving the city stuck with a high bill for training the officer). Jordan, who sued the city, lost the lawsuit in federal district court (*Jordan v. City of New London* 2000), because the city was following the standards set up by the exam's authors (Hughes 2003).

In a sample of 65 mid-level managers (comprising mostly sergeants, lieutenants, and captains) representing 23 states, Hughes (2003) found little support for the contention by the court and the testing agency in the *Jordan* case—specifically, that intelligent recruits become bored with their jobs and subsequently leave them. Although this was a small sample and must be replicated and enlarged, it nevertheless indicates the complicated issues with respect to testing intelligence and what level is appropriate to a specific field. In addition, as the author notes in this case, it suggests to the public that police departments are not attempting to hire the "best and brightest" for police service.

**Personal Interview.**  Virtually all police departments use some form of personal interview, usually at the end of the selection process. The interview allows police representatives (and sometimes community members) to observe the candidates directly with respect to their suitability for the department and to clear up any inconsistencies that may have developed in the earlier stages of the process. Candidates are measured on attributes that generally are not measured elsewhere, including motivation, verbal skills, confidence, potential for violence, decision-making skills, and demeanor.

The interview is not usually substantive, with specific questions about police policy or the department, but it can be. Typical questions might include the following: Why do you want to be a police officer? How have you prepared yourself for a career in law enforcement? What types of books or magazines do you read? Why do you want to work for this department? There are also usually questions about hypothetical situations and how the person would respond (i.e., make decisions). For COP departments, Campbelis (1999) proposes in-depth interviews designed to identify problem-solving skills and techniques that the candidate might possess. De Long (1999) further recommends the use of problem-solving scenarios to enable the evaluators to determine whether candidates have the needed attributes to adequately perform COP activities.

Some departments use only the oral interview to rank order candidates. This method has been useful in helping departments overcome potentially adverse impacts of other selection criteria and to increase the number of women and minority candidates. Although the interview is more flexible, it is also subjective, and there is no strong evidence that it is a useful predictor of future police performance (Burbeck and Furnham 1985). Other research indicates that the validity of the oral interview is also suspect and that the characteristics of the raters influence the ratings and, ultimately, the rankings of the candidates (Falkenberg, Gaines, and Cox 1990; Doerner 1997). Methods that help to improve the validity of the oral interview include using only those rating factors that are critical components of the job, training the raters so that they clearly understand the process and the way responses should be graded, and using set standards that raters can compare with candidate responses (Gaines and Kappeler 1992).

Table 6.1 presents a summary of the general steps of the police selection process and the most important concerns at each step.

### Recruit Screening Methods

Table 6.2 represents the findings of the BJS national surveys, which included screening methods for new officer applicants in more than 3,000 state and local police departments (Reaves 2010) and sheriffs' offices (Burch 2012) in 2007. As indicated in Table 6.2, nearly 100 percent of all local and sheriffs' offices used criminal record checks, background investigations, driving record checks, and personal interviews. In addition, almost 90 percent of officers were employed by departments that used medical exams and 80 percent by departments that used drug testing. Nearly 60 percent of all officers worked in agencies utilizing physical agility testing, with nearly 50 percent in agencies utilizing written aptitude tests and personality inventories (although sheriffs' offices were at 41 percent of the latter); one-quarter of all agencies used the polygraph exam. Finally, sheriffs' offices, in comparison

**TABLE 6.1** Process Summary of Police Selection

| STEPS | RELATED ISSUES |
|---|---|
| Recruitment | Advertising, requests, and referrals |
| Selection criteria | Age, height, weight, vision, criminal record, and possible residency requirement |
| Written examination | General intelligence or job content |
| Physical examination | Agility and endurance |
| Personal interview | Communication skills, interpersonal style, and decision-making ability |
| Psychological testing and interview | Emotional stability and psychological profiles |
| Background investigation | Character, employment/credit history, education, references, and criminal record |
| Polygraph examination | Character and background information |
| Medical examination and drug testing | General health and specific problems |

*Source*: Adapted from R. Roberg, J. Kuykendall, and K. Novak, *Police Management*, 3rd ed. (Los Angeles: Roxbury, 2002), 133.

**TABLE 6.2** Selected Screening Methods of Local Police Departments and Sheriffs' Offices, 2007

| SCREENING METHODS | PERCENTAGE OF DEPARTMENTS AND OFFICES REQUIRING | |
| --- | --- | --- |
| | POLICE DEPARTMENTS | SHERIFFS' OFFICES |
| Criminal record check | 100 | 99 |
| Background investigation | 99 | 98 |
| Driving record check | 99 | 98 |
| Personal interview | 99 | 99 |
| Medical exam | 89 | 88 |
| Drug test | 83 | 80 |
| Psychological evaluation | 72 | 62 |
| Credit history check | 61 | 50 |
| Physical agility test | 60 | 56 |
| Written aptitude test | 48 | 46 |
| Personality inventory | 46 | 41 |
| Polygraph exam | 26 | 24 |

*Sources*: Reaves, B. A. *Local Police Departments, 2007* (Washington, DC: Bureau of Justice Statistics, 2010), Appendix Tables 3–5, 35–36; Burch, A. M. *Sheriffs' Offices, 2007—Statistical Tables* (Washington, DC: Bureau of Justice Statistics, 2012), Tables 8–9, 9–11.

with local departments, required substantially fewer psychological evaluations (62 percent compared with 72 percent) and credit history checks (50 percent versus 61 percent).

The selection of candidates for police departments is time-consuming and expensive. Given the costs, the steps of the process are normally arranged from the least costly and most likely to eliminate the most candidates to the most expensive. Accordingly, when used, the written and physical agility tests are usually given at the beginning, followed by the medical exam, polygraph examination, psychological testing, background investigation, and finally, the personal interview. In "Voices from the Field," John P. Jarvis of the FBI discusses the need for screening methods that are informed by social science research.

Once candidates are selected, they are usually rank ordered and employed based on need. This ranking lasts for a given period—usually from six months to two years—before retesting is undertaken. Once selected, candidates start their developmental phase by attending a recruit training program.

## Americans with Disabilities Act

The purpose of the Americans with Disabilities Act (ADA) is to eliminate barriers to equal employment opportunity and to provide equal access to individuals with disabilities to the programs, services, and activities delivered by government entities (Rubin 1994). Thus, the ADA prohibits discrimination against qualified individuals with a disability. It does not

## John P. Jarvis
*Academic Dean, Academy, Federal Bureau of Investigation*

### Law Enforcement Personnel Selection and Development: The Promise of an Evidence-Based Strategy

The law enforcement profession continually seeks promising practices to recruit, select, train, and retain both sworn and civilian employees to protect and serve the communities within which they live and work. However, recurring debates surrounding strategies for attracting qualified and capable candidates

to perform effectively and efficiently in a policing role persist. Accompanying these entry-level debates are questions of basic versus advanced training and development of law enforcement officers not only for retention but also to serve as leaders within the departments or agencies they serve. This also extends to determining capacities to exercise supervision and oversight of police activities in increasing roles and responsibilities as administrators of police agencies rather than street officers. In order to achieve such goals, many singular issues relative to hiring, training, education, management, and leadership within the ranks emerge. However, few if any of these issues are addressed using systematic quantifiable evidence to support decision making that can complement all aspects of these personnel selection and development tasks. More commonly, hiring occurs when resources become available for such hiring and less attention is paid to how to hire the strongest candidates.

As noted previously, attracting applicants to apply for law enforcement positions is typically not a challenge, but attracting qualified personnel with potential to be trained to an adequate level of proficiency is a much greater hurdle to be traversed. Many apply, but few are viable candidates for service. Fortunately, law enforcement agencies are increasingly relying upon more thorough background checks, including established empirically based assessment tools to enable more sound selection and development decisions. Use of such an evidence-based strategy more effectively identifies behavioral backgrounds that are not conducive for successful outcomes in a law enforcement role. For example, one such behavioral factor which will commonly disqualify applicants is reported recent

and frequent drug use and/or abuse. This is inclusive of recreational use whether legal or not as many localities are now legalizing such uses. Prior felony arrests or other illegal activity also may disqualify an applicant. Even inappropriate social media postings or other related content either disclosed or discovered which are incongruent with positions of trust in police work can limit suitability for employment in law enforcement. Other issues that sometimes emerge include financial instability and or any history of mental health issues. Lastly, another major disqualifying factor is lack of candor on background interviews whereby candidates are found to be either deceptive or outright lie about their prior life experiences. Of course, many of these issues may also arise as challenges in retaining personnel if they should engage in such activities after being hired into the profession.

Police decision making that is devoid of utilizing validated hiring and promotional tests, deployment of psychological screenings (when appropriately applied), and cognizance of the legalities of fair hiring practices does so at some tangible risk. These risks noted, the promise of using such tools can and does provide an agency a return on the investment in these decisions. Development of personnel selection and development tools employing validated social science metrics, including psychological evaluations, holds promise for both assisting agencies to make hiring decisions but also may serve to safeguard employees assigned to high-risk roles such as special weapons and tactics, undercover operations, and other perils that sometimes emerge in the challenging landscape of public safety and policing. Such tools may also serve to mediate some legal liabilities to both agencies and communities if legal challenges to policing practices emerge, which also does occur with some frequency. Evidence-based hiring and data-driven decision making are not fail-safe, but such tools do provide an articulation of the basis for the difficult decisions that the police often have to make to protect and serve their communities.

mean that by having a disability one is entitled to protection under the law, but if a person meets the selection criteria for a job and has a disability, that person cannot be discriminated against for the job. Generally, blanket exclusions of individuals with a particular disability are not permissible. For instance, to exclude all persons with diabetes would ignore the varying degrees of severity and the ability to control the symptoms (Rubin 1994). Also, standards that tend to screen out individuals or groups of individuals on the basis of disability must be related to functions that are essential to the job. The ADA requires that applicants be given a conditional offer of employment prior to taking an exam or a test that may be disability related, including background investigations, psychological and medical exams, and polygraph tests. Although the full impact of the ADA on police selection is complicated and ongoing, departments must change some of their current procedures to ensure that selection criteria that screen out persons with disabilities are job-related and that questions relating to disabilities (unless job-related) are asked only after a conditional offer of employment has been made.

## Development

Development of a police department's human resources for successful careers in police work begins with training of the newly hired recruits, moves to a second phase of field training and evaluation, and continues into a third phase of long-term development or career growth. Each phase will be discussed in turn.

## Recruit Training

The initial training of the recruit is generally conducted through a police training academy, where the program content is determined by a state standards organization, often known as **Peace Officer Standards and Training** (POST). Although all police departments must meet minimum standards, some departments provide substantially more training than is minimally required. Larger departments often maintain their own academies, whereas smaller departments tend to send their recruits to regional or county academies.

Some states now require that people complete one of these basic training programs prior to being considered for employment. As a result, the department hires an already-trained employee and does not have to pay for the cost of that training, including the recruit's salary while attending the academy. Recruit training is influenced by program design and delivery. Some of the more important considerations in the design and delivery of a recruit training program include program orientation, philosophy and instructional methods, course content, and field training.

### Program Orientation

One of the important issues in police training is whether the orientation should be stressful or nonstressful. *Stressful training* is like a military boot camp or basic training; *nonstressful training* has a more academic environment. Many recruit programs continue to have a stressful orientation, expecting recruits to be obedient and subjecting them to both intellectual and physical demands in a highly structured environment. Discipline and even harassment have been an integral part of many of these programs. A comprehensive national survey of 681 recruit academies conducting basic law enforcement training—including state POST, state police, sheriff's office, county police, municipal police, college and university police, and multiagency police—by the BJS (Buehler 2021) found that half described their training environment as a balance of stress and nonstress. This is a significant change from the 2016 report, where only 32 percent described their training as a balance. The biggest changes were in agencies that had previously utilized mostly stress or more stress than nonstress, with sizable reductions in the number of academies in each category. Overall, 86 percent of recruits who started the training completed it.

Although stressful training has a long tradition, no evidence exists that this approach is a valid way to train recruits (Berg 1990) or that it is any more or less effective than a non-stressful approach. Probably the most comprehensive study in this area (Earle 1973) indicated that nonstressful training produces officers who receive higher performance evaluations, like their work more, and get along better with the public. Given the trend toward COP, problem solving, and higher-educational requirements, a stress-oriented approach is likely to be counterproductive and should be eliminated from training programs, to be replaced by a more academic approach.

## Philosophy and Instructional Methods

The philosophy of a program centers on two primary approaches: training and education. **Training** can be defined as the process of instructing the individual *how* to do the job by providing relevant information about the job; **education** can be defined as the process of providing a general body of knowledge on which decisions can be based as to *why* something is being done while performing the job. Training deals with specific facts and procedures, whereas education is broader in scope and is concerned with theories, concepts, issues, and alternatives. Many police training programs are heavily oriented toward teaching facts and procedures, to the exclusion of theories, concepts, and analytical reasoning. A strict reliance on this approach is problematic, because so much police work requires analysis and reasoning instead of applying specific procedures that supposedly fit all circumstances. Therefore, many academies are attempting to increase the percentage of time spent on an educational approach by employing professionals in the social sciences, especially criminal justice and criminology, psychology, and sociology, as instructors.

**Andragogy and Pedagogy.** Another important aspect of program development is the type of instructional methods to be used. In large part, this is determined by what teaching philosophy is going to be emphasized; two contrasting teaching philosophies are pedagogy and andragogy (Knowles 1970). Pedagogy involves a one-way transfer of knowledge, usually in the form of facts and procedures, from the instructor to the student (recruit). The primary concern is to promote "absolute solutions" to particular situations. An alternative teaching philosophy, which promotes the mutual involvement of students and instructors in the learning process and stresses analytical and conceptual skills, is known as andragogy.

Knowles (1970) describes pedagogy as the art and science of teaching children and andragogy as the art and science of helping adults learn. Although he does not suggest any fundamental differences between the way in which adults and children learn, he believes that significant differences emerge in the learning process as maturation takes place. Thus, where **pedagogy** involves *a one-way transfer of knowledge* between instructor and student through lectures, use of visual aids, student note taking, rote memorization, and taking factual tests, **andragogy** involves *a two-way transfer of knowledge* and active student participation through the use of problem analysis, role playing, group discussion and projects, independent student learning, and "acting out" to learn required skills in simulated situations. Thus, an instructor using andragogical teaching methods becomes a facilitator, helping to guide student learning through cognitive learning principles and critical thinking. At the same time, pedagogical teaching methods are also necessary, especially with respect to those activities that require memorization (e.g., laws and policies) and behavioral techniques (e.g., traffic stops and approaching a suspect).

Although the relevance of an andragogical approach to police training has been recognized since at least the late 1970s (Roberg 1979), programs still tend to emphasize pedagogical methods, emphasizing how to do a job rather than why or developing critical thinking and decision making. Recruits would most likely benefit from an andragogical approach with respect to topics that are relevant to contemporary policing concepts, including problem solving, cultural diversity, sexual harassment, conflict resolution, communication, and community organization skills (Birzer 1999, 2003). In addition, a small, qualitative study utilizing focus group and interview data from officers attending a law enforcement training facility in a southeastern state (Oliva and Compton 2010) found that, in general, officers displayed a strong preference for andragogical teaching methods. The four basic themes that emerged were (1) a desire for engagement (an intellectually stimulating classroom), (2) practicality (learning experience that focuses on real-world job demands), (3) affiliation (course allows social interaction), and (4) efficiency (a course that is well managed and addresses content within an appropriate period). These themes align with the tenets of adult learning and suggest that officers, in general, may be more satisfied by an andragogical approach to learning.

In this same context, it is worth noting that the research findings and themes with respect to andragogical learning and recruit training are just as applicable, if not more so, to in-service and specialized training (discussed later, in the "Career Growth" section), where officers are older and generally more mature. For example, Etter and Griffin (2011) estimate that there are nearly 200,000 officers at the state, county, and municipal levels who are over 40 years old and will require some type of annual in-service training to keep their law enforcement license or certification. Whereas the authors strenuously argue for adult learning andragogical principles to be used to more effectively train these older officers for in-service training, we suggest that andragogical concepts apply equally well to specialized career training, especially with respect to supervisory and managerial training.

**Cognitive and Problem-Based Learning.**   In a national survey of training academies, Bradford and Pynes (1999) analyzed course syllabi to determine the degree of cognitive versus task-oriented training. **Cognitive learning** can be defined as training that goes beyond learning a specific skill or task and instead focuses on the *process that establishes valid thinking patterns*. The authors found that less than 3 percent of basic training time listed in the curricula was spent in the cognitive and decision-making domain, with the remaining time spent in task-oriented activities. One exception to this finding was the Commonwealth of Massachusetts, where all subjects are taught in the cognitive domain, encompassing 90 percent of the curricula (720 of 800 hours). In 1997, the Massachusetts Criminal Justice Training Council realized that the goals of COP required new teaching methods and strategies. A new training curriculum was designed with a greater cognitive focus. Task skills and methodology are still taught, but from a cognitive perspective. According to the Massachusetts Criminal Justice Training Council, the objective of cognitive training is getting the officer to "understand how to speak to, reason with, and listen to people and learn to use communication skills to manage a wide range of problematic situations. Physical tactics and tools, though readily available, are secondary to the *primary response of communication*" (Bradford and Pynes 1999, 289; emphasis added).

Another approach to recruit training, which incorporates a cognitive perspective, is known as **problem-based learning** (PBL). PBL incorporates adult learning (andragogical) principles in attempting to help students develop problem-solving, critical-thinking, and self-directed skills with respect to subject matter; PBL also typically occurs in a collaborative environment where communication skills are stressed (Barrows 2002). A study of PBL learning strategies in Michigan police academies over a 16-year period found that recruits trained using PBL strategies had higher licensing exam test scores and reported more positive evaluations of their learning experiences (Queen 2016).

A study of a pilot program incorporating a portion of a PBL-based recruit curriculum was conducted in the POST academy at Meridian, Idaho (Werth 2009). In the program, recruits were divided into teams and assigned to a PBL activity involving various aspects of a mock homicide investigation. The exercise was evaluated by staff members and lasted throughout the 10-week academy, culminating in week 10 with each team participating in two days of practical exercises revolving around the investigation. In the final part of the exercise, each team gave a presentation to the evaluators and classmates for an overall assessment of their case management.

Data were collected in the spring through fall of 2007 from the three separate recruit classes who had participated in the pilot program. Of the 147 recruits participating in the program, 122 (83 percent) completed surveys asking questions related to the extent they believed the PBL program helped them to develop skills necessary to be effective officers. The results were overwhelmingly positive and statistically significant in all areas, including developing new skills, relating class material to field work, and building problem-solving, decision-making, and collaboration skills (i.e., working in a group and with other groups). These findings suggest that PBL methods can be introduced into training academies in stages, rather than attempting to change an entire academy curriculum and retrain an entire staff—both of which are expensive and time-consuming. The pilot program described constituted approximately 70 of the 525-hour basic Idaho patrol officer academy.

## Curriculum Development and Content

Police recruit training programs and curricula should be developed based on two criteria: first, the programs should incorporate the *mission statement* of the department and *ethical considerations*, and second, training should be based on what an officer *actually does* on a daily basis (Bayley and Bittner 1989; Alpert and Smith 1990). The subject matter should be based on a **job task analysis** if it is to be a valid indicator of the work performed by the recruits. The BJS survey (Reaves 2016) discovered that about 50 percent of academies use job task analyses to develop course content; the most common developmental methods used included mandates from the state POST organization. A majority also took input from academy staff (67 percent) and subject matter experts (54 percent).

As the complex nature of the police role has become more fully recognized (Roberg 1976), recruit training requirements, including the number of hours trained and the number of subjects covered, have increased significantly. The 2018 BJS study (Buehler 2021) found that the average number of hours of classroom or academy training was 833, or about 21 weeks. As Table 6.3 indicates, county police academies had the longest training programs (1,074 hours), followed by special jurisdiction (1,061 hours) and state police (944 hours) academies. In addition, 49.9 percent of the training academies included mandatory field training in their programs. The highest percentage of agencies requiring field training in their requirements for recruits to finish basic training were county (89 percent), state police (83 percent), and municipal police (81.8 percent). The average length of a field training program associated with the academy was 508 hours.

**TABLE 6.3**  Duration of Basic Recruitment Training by Type of Academy, 2018

| PRIMARY OPERATING AGENCY | CLASS | FIELD TRAINING | |
|---|---|---|---|
| | AVERAGE LENGTH | PERCENTAGE REQUIRING | AVERAGE LENGTH[a] |
| All types | 833 | 49.9 | 508 |
| State POST[b] | 667 | 17.2 | |
| State police | 944 | 83.9 | 462 |
| Sheriff's office | 731 | 53.7 | 364 |
| County police | 1,074 | 89.5 | 468 |
| Municipal police | 971 | 81.8 | 637 |
| Four-year college/ university | 755 | 23.8 | 307 |
| Two-year college | 767 | 30.3 | 264 |
| Technical school | 796 | 22.0 | 460 |
| Special jurisdiction | 1,061 | 100 | 422 |
| Multiagency | 894 | 50 | 252 |

[a]Excludes field training segments not overseen by academies.
[b]Peace Officer Standards and Training.
*Source*: E. D. Buehler, *State and Local Law Enforcement Training Academies, 2018* (Washington, DC: Bureau of Justice Statistics, 2021).

Based on the 2018 BJS survey results, the diverse topics covered in basic recruit training can be seen in Table 6.4. In terms of instruction time devoted to various topics, firearms skills received the longest training (with average instruction time of 73 hours), followed by defensive tactics (61 hours), patrol procedures (52 hours), and health and fitness (50 hours). Nearly all academies also provided basic first aid/CPR (24 hours), report writing (24 hours), and use of nonlethal weapons (20 hours). Training in the legal areas of criminal and constitutional law (51 hours) was also provided in nearly all academies, and nearly all included instruction on ethics and integrity (12 hours) and professionalism (12 hours), among other topics.

## Curriculum Updates

Departments must determine what subject matter is most important, because programs are constrained by time and resources. The amount of time devoted to any particular subject emphasizes to recruits the importance attached to that subject by the department. Table 6.4 indicates the varying amounts of hours devoted to certain topics, from a low of 9 hours (stress prevention/management) to a high of 73 hours (firearms skills). It should be noted that in police training there will always be debate regarding what topics should be covered and how much time they should receive. For example, given its importance to effective and just policing, should the area of ethics and integrity receive more time? And as new developments occur in policing, what new or increased coverage of topics should be added to the curriculum? Some topic areas that are new or could use more extensive training are addressed here.

**TABLE 6.4** Topics Included in Basic Training of State and Local Law Enforcement Training Academies, 2018

| TOPICS | PERCENTAGE OF ACADEMIES WITH TRAINING | AVERAGE NUMBER OF HOURS OF INSTRUCTION |
|---|---|---|
| **Operations** | | |
| Report writing | 99.5 | 24 |
| Patrol | 98 | 52 |
| Investigations | 97.2 | 36 |
| Basic first aid/CPR | 97 | 24 |
| Emergency vehicle operations | 97 | 40 |
| Computers/information systems | 63 | 12 |
| **Weapons/Defensive Tactics** | | |
| De-escalation/verbal judo | 88 | 18 |
| Defensive tactics | 99.5 | 61 |
| Firearms skills | 99 | 73 |
| Nonlethal weapons | 92 | 20 |
| **Legal** | | |
| Criminal/constitutional law | 99 | 51 |
| Traffic law | 97 | 26 |
| Juvenile justice law/ procedures | 97 | 11 |
| **Self-improvement** | | |
| Ethics and integrity | 99 | 12 |
| Health and fitness | 98 | 50 |
| Stress prevention/ management | 87 | 9 |
| Professionalism | 87 | 12 |

*Source*: Buehler, E.D., *State and Local Law Enforcement Training Academies, 2018* (Washington, DC: Bureau of Justice Statistics, 2021).

**Ethics and Integrity.** Since ethics and integrity are at the heart of fair and just police practices, as well as democratic ideals, it is crucial that training academies not only devote the proper amount of time to this topic but also, perhaps more important, incorporate it throughout the academy curriculum.

**De-escalation of Force.** As Table 6.4 indicates, virtually all departments provide training in self-defense, but fewer provide training in **de-escalation** of force to reduce violence between police and citizens. Indeed, a report by the PERF (2015) noted that too little training time was devoted to de-escalation tactics. And, the President's Task Force on Twenty-First Century Policing (2015) recommended that law enforcement agencies should emphasize de-escalation tactics in policy and training. Alpert and Moore (1993) have long advocated that *nonaggressive behavior that reduces violence should be reinforced and* *rewarded* by departments as the model for officers to copy. Importantly, this type of training would recognize and emphasize the use of nonaggressive behavior that, when appropriate, does not lead to an arrest. In other words, it must be recognized that many problems in the community can be solved without the need for an arrest or use of force. A fuller discussion of the evidence on de-escalation training is included in Chapter 10.

**Communication.** One of the most important—if not the most important—training topics police can use to de-escalate the use of force and to further **procedural justice** is the development and quality of *communication skills*. The PERF (2015, 556) advocated for "rigorous and ongoing training on communication skills." The elaboration of communication skills most likely should be taught as a standalone topic but also integrated with other topics where communication skills are especially important (e.g., domestic violence, human relations, and mediation skills/conflict resolution found in Table 6.4). Some contemporary research suggests that if greater attention were paid to enhancing officer communication skills, police–citizen interactions (especially with minorities) could be substantially improved, thus lessening the extent to which physical force may be needed (see, e.g., Giles et al. 2006; Hajek et al. 2006; Dixon et al. 2008). See Inside Policing 6.3 for an NYPD deputy inspector's perspective on the importance of communication skills in tense situations.

**Conducted Energy Devices.** The use of conducted energy devices (CEDs; more commonly referred to as Tasers) has become common practice in police departments. Although this "nonlethal" device has the potential to contribute to the de-escalation of force by police, it has also led to numerous high-profile deaths; thus, CEDs should be well regulated by departments that use them. Alpert and Dunham (2010), utilizing data from a national survey conducted by the PERF of 518 municipal, county, and state agencies in 2006, examined the current state of CED training and use. The authors found that 47 percent of agencies provided their officers with CEDs. Of these agencies, 47 percent required eight hours of initial training, whereas approximately 30 percent required four hours. Many, however, provided considerably less training. Nearly one in five agencies (17 percent) did not require any retraining of officers or deputies who carry a CED, while 64 percent required retraining every year, 13.5 percent every two years, and 4 percent every three years.

---

| **INSIDE POLICING 6.3** | **NYPD Deputy Inspector Matthew Galvin: Communication Brings the Subject to Us** |
| --- | --- |

**Wexler:** De-escalation begins with communication. . .   Why is communication so important?

  **Inspector Galvin:** Communication leads to negotiation, and it contributes to slowing the pace. If we slow the pace, we can buy some time and develop a plan. The communication, and talking in a de-escalating tone, brings the subject to us, rather than allowing ourselves to be brought up to the subject's escalated level of tension. If we can bring a feeling of calm to the situation, through time and communicating, and bring that subject to us, hopefully we can resolve it safely.

*SOURCE*: Police Executive Research Forum, *Guiding Principles on Use of Force* (Washington, DC: Author, 2015), 56.

With respect to location on a use-of-force continuum in policy or training, more than half (57 percent) place CEDs at the same level as chemical sprays (e.g., pepper spray), whereas one-third (36 percent) place CEDs higher on the force continuum. Alpert and Dunham (2010, 252) recommend that in addition to setting the use-of-force continuum appropriately—at active resistance—CED policies and training should require officers to "evaluate the totality of the circumstances before using a CED, which would include the environment, age, size, gender, apparent physical capabilities, and health concerns (e.g., obviously pregnant women) of suspects."

**Juveniles.** Although Table 6.4 indicates that nearly all departments (97 percent) include training on juveniles, most of this training likely relates to differences between juvenile and adult law and procedures to be used when formally dealing with teens. In addition, it is important that a good portion of juvenile training relates to how interacting with teens may need to differ from interacting with adults.

One study, for example, of nearly 900 students from 18 different high schools in Chicago (Friedman et al. 2004) found that of the 58 percent of youth surveyed who were stopped at least once by the police (the majority were African American and Hispanic), about 60 percent believed they were disrespected by being yelled at, cursed at, called names, and having a gun pulled on them. In addition, they felt that the police had a condescending attitude toward them. Another study using responses from a written survey of 14- to-16-year-old high school students (Hinds 2007) found that the student's attitudes toward police legitimacy were positively linked to police use of *procedural justice*—that is, being treated in a fair and just manner. Perceived unfair treatment was significantly associated with lowering judgments with respect to police legitimacy. Other studies on juvenile attitudes toward the police and legitimacy have found similar results (see, e.g., Geistman and Smith 2007; Sharp and Atherton 2007).

The state of Connecticut has developed and implemented a police training curriculum called Effective Police Interactions with Youth. This program is designed to reduce the likelihood that police interactions with juveniles, especially minority members, will lead to arrest. Using a pretest–posttest experimental design with a sample of 468 officers (from 33 local police departments) randomly assigned to either a training or a control group, LaMotte et al. (2010) examined the effectiveness of the program. A questionnaire administered to both groups before and after the training measured an officer's knowledge of and attitudes toward youth. The training group experienced a significant increase in their knowledge scores, from 46 percent correct before training to 77 percent correct after training. Attitudes also improved for confidence that they had the requisite skills to interact with youth, comfort in starting conversations with youth, and commitment to the belief that officers can positively impact youths' lives without detracting from other enforcement duties. Although a study of this nature cannot determine whether these improvements in knowledge and attitudes led to changes in actual behavior, it is nevertheless a useful model for other states to follow in improving training regarding juveniles.

**Mental Illness.** An increasingly important issue is how police deal with people with mental health issues. Some agencies have begun incorporating crisis intervention training (CIT) into their curriculum. This training is designed to provide officers with the ability to recognize mental illness, skills for responding to someone during a mental health crisis, and enhanced understanding and empathy toward people with mental health issues. A PERF (2015) survey found that CIT training was relatively limited in comparison with other areas of training. The report's authors suggested that attention to CIT should be

| INSIDE POLICING 6.4 | Seattle Chief of Police Kathleen O'Toole: Our Officers Use Crisis Intervention Skills to Calm Down People in Mental Health Crisis |
|---|---|

Like most police agencies, the Seattle Police Department (SPD) provides aid and service at a far greater frequency than engaging in enforcement. For instance, the SPD recognizes the need to harness community resources to address the complicated issue of behavioral crisis. The SPD partners officers with mental health professionals in the field and provides department-wide training on crisis intervention and tactical de-escalation.

Seattle police officers handled nearly 10,000 crisis interventions last year [2014], and very few resulted in enforcement or use of force. Most were routed to community mental health service providers, few subjects were arrested, none of the incidents required lethal force by police, and less than 2% of incidents involved de minimis or less-lethal force. The department has developed a streamlined referral system, allowing officers to easily divert those in crisis to important services provided by partner agencies.

I recall an incident just last month when police responded to a man with a knife at a laundromat. Officers recognized that the man was experiencing a mental health crisis, possibly exacerbated by the consumption of drugs. They talked to the man, calmed him down, and took him into custody, without jeopardizing their safety, his safety, or that of the public.

I'm proud the SPD has made great strides in this important area. We will continue to work with our community partners on innovative, multidisciplinary approaches to service the most vulnerable in our city.

SOURCE: Police Executive Research Forum, *Guiding Principles on Use of Force*, (Washington, DC:. 2016), 59.

increased. In Inside Policing 6.4, former Seattle Chief of Police Kathleen O'Toole discusses how her agency used crisis intervention training.

### Effectiveness of Recruit Training

How effective is the training provided to the recruits? What is the retention rate of recruits? One means of evaluation is to follow up on field performance to determine the areas in which recruits are having the most difficulty; methods used can include observation of recruits, evaluation of recruit performance, and surveys of recruits, trainers, and supervisors. In general, the validity of the measurement will be greater if more than one of these methods is used. Once problems are identified, a determination can be made regarding how to improve the program.

One study has indicated just how important it is for police agencies to incorporate newly acquired skills and attitudes from the academy into the *organization culture*. Haarr (2001), in a 16-month study, examined the attitudinal changes of recruits toward COP, problem solving, and public relations through basic training, field training, and their first year of probation. The training curriculum of the Phoenix Regional Police Training Academy was revised to educate officers in the theories and practices of COP and problem solving. The results indicated that the training academy had an initial positive impact on recruits' attitudes toward COP and problem solving. Over time, however, these positive attitudes dissipated as recruits returned to their respective departments for field training and were exposed to the work environment and organizational culture. In other words, field training processes and organizational environment factors (e.g., shifts, coworker attitudes, and whether the department requires officers to engage in COP practices) were more powerful forces than basic training, suggesting that police agencies failed to reinforce the positive impacts that the training provided.

Haarr (2005) further explored why police recruits drop out of police work. Recruits were followed through the Phoenix Regional Police Basic Training Academy to their respective police agencies, through field training and the completion of a one-year probationary period. The sample consisted of 113 dropouts from a total of 446 recruits, representing 25 cities. Qualitative data from phone interviews indicated that recruits who resigned during *basic training* did so for several reasons, including attitudinal differences with classmates toward interactions with the public; appropriate and inappropriate work behaviors; the paramilitary, stress-oriented nature of the academy; and strict standards of physical fitness. Those recruits who resigned during the **field training officer** (FTO) phase did so for reasons that related to the realities of police work and the organization—for example, conflict with their FTOs, conflict with their coworkers and how they interacted with the public, the phenomenon of running from call to call, the immense amount of paperwork, organizational policies and procedures, risks related to the job, and the possibility of being sued. In addition, several female recruits spoke of gender discrimination directed at them by their FTOs and supervisors. The recruits who resigned during the one-year probationary period indicated that they experienced continued conflict with the realization that their attitudes about police work and police–citizen interactions differed from those of their coworkers. In general, they realized that they would not be able to become involved in COP activities as they had expected and were conflicted over what they considered heavy-handed tactics used by coworkers (e.g., provoking subjects to fight and resist arrest), resulting in an escalation of the use of force.

These findings have significant policy implications for police executives with respect to the police role, image, and ethics and integrity. It is necessary to portray the police role in an honest way; for example, are COP practices really being practiced and rewarded? Furthermore, to hire quality, community-oriented officers with high ethical standards, an organizational culture must be developed that supports (including mandatory reporting of misconduct by peers or supervisors), rewards, and promotes people with these values. Otherwise, recruits with these values will continue to *self-select out* of the department, and perhaps out of policing altogether. In addition, the investments in recruiting, selecting, and training highly qualified recruits are lost when recruits voluntarily resign from the selection process. And since the recruits who drop out must be replaced, the costs to the agency are essentially doubled.

## Field Training

After successfully completing their work at the academy, recruits go through a final field training program to prepare them for the reality of police work. As noted previously, however, only a little over one-third of all types of police agencies include field training as part of their recruit training process. This on-the-job or apprentice training has been an integral aspect of the recruit training process for some time, but it has become much more expansive since the mid-1970s. As the BJS national survey on training academies (Buehler 2021) indicates in Table 6.3, 508 hours of field training is the average for those departments requiring it.

## Field Training Officer Program

The traditional method of new officers being broken in by experienced old-timers has given way to a highly structured FTO program, which uses experienced officers trained to act as mentors to new recruits. The importance of FTOs cannot be overstated, because they significantly impact the training of the recruit as well as imparting demeanor, values, and the department's culture. To this point, recruits have learned in the academy how to behave like police officers, but under the guidance of the FTO, the officer is exposed to the "real world" of policing. During this time, the FTO has the opportunity to subvert what has been taught by advising the rookie to "forget what you learned in the academy; I'll show you how we do it out here on the street."

With FTO programs, the probationary period is usually a highly structured experience in which new officers must demonstrate specific knowledge and skills. Frequent evaluations are made of the recruits' performance, usually by several FTOs who supervise their work in different areas and different shifts. The original FTO training model developed by the San Jose Police Department (known as the *San Jose model*) in 1968 (McCampbell 1987) was innovative in its time and is still widely used throughout the field today. FTOs evaluate 30 relatively traditional aspects of a trainee's performance using a 1-to-7 check-off scale.

Although most large policing agencies use some form of an FTO program, McCampbell (1987) reported that empirical evaluations of the San Jose model were lacking, and this continues to be true today. Although much of the research that exists is dated (see, e.g., McCampbell 1987), the little information available suggests FTO programs do not accomplish their intended goals (Hansen 1979), are more evaluative than learning-oriented (Warners and Williams 2010), and have failed to keep pace with the dynamic environment of policing over the past 40-plus years (Pitts and Peak 2007)—mainly, the failure to emphasize aspects of community-based and problem-oriented policing (POP) (Chappell 2007).

One study of the San Jose model (Chappell 2007) in a police department (275 sworn officers) that had revamped its training academy to reflect a problem-solving COP approach assessed whether COP-type training was integrated into the field training. Analyzing the formal check-off evaluations (and narrative descriptions where required) of field activities spread over a 14-week training period, the findings indicated, with few exceptions, that COP skills and tasks were not integrated into the field training experience. It appeared that although some of the daily observation tasks could have been modified to cover some COP-type activities, FTOs overwhelmingly stuck to evaluating the skills related to traditional policing practices. The implications of these findings suggest that if a police organization wants to integrate COP practices into its operations, it must first train FTOs in problem solving and COP principles, and the field training evaluation form must then be significantly revised to reflect the new philosophies and practices. Our attention now turns to one type of training program that has accomplished these changes.

## Police Training Officer Program

As a result of some of the San Jose model's deficiencies (Warners and Williams 2010), the *Reno model* of field training was created. The program was developed in 1999 by the COPS Office in partnership with the Reno Police Department and the PERF and was first tested in the Reno Police Department in 2001 (Pitts and Peak 2007). The Reno model was designed in part for initiating and training recruits with respect to the two main components of COP: community partnerships and problem solving. This model, referred to as the **police training officer** (PTO) program, differs significantly from traditional models.

The Reno model consists of an orientation phase and then 15 weeks of the curriculum in which probationary police officers (PPOs) go through five additional phases (COPS Office 2014). The Reno model also includes a midterm and final exam, which determine whether the PPO continues through and successfully completes the program. Although the Reno model has improved each phase of the process, the most significant advances are in the training phases, which are scenario-based rather than observation-based and are premised on PBL techniques (Pitts and Peak 2007; Warners and Williams 2010; COPS Office 2014). In the Reno model, PTOs assign "street" problems to trainees through which they learn about policing in the context of attempting to solve those problems. Trainees work through various responses with the help of their PTO. Within the four substantive topic areas, the curriculum covers 15 core competencies, many of which are not covered in the traditional model of after-academy training. For example, officers receive training in conflict resolution, problem solving, community-specific problems, cultural diversity and special-needs groups, communication skills, as well as lifestyle stressors, self-awareness, and self-regulation (COPS Office 2014). The scenario- and problem-based curriculum is meant to accustom PPOs to community-based policing practices and is designed to assist with a more fluid transition onto the streets, where officers use what they have learned in a real-life setting.

The four phases and 15 core competencies were developed from a survey by the department of more than 400 agencies who were asked to identify the important activities for a police officer working in a department where COP and POP are practiced (Hoover, Pitts, and Ponte 2003). The Reno PTO program is organized according to these four main phases and, as mentioned, is divided over a 15-week cycle. Although the training team is responsible for answering calls for service, the training objective for each phase will be addressed. In addition, a unique feature of the program is how each trainee is evaluated throughout the program. To avoid confusion over the role of trainer and evaluator, the PTO program separates the two roles. All training officers attend a 40-hour course on how to be a PTO. They are then assigned to a trainee as a trainer or an evaluator; that is, a PTO may be a trainer for one trainee but an evaluator for another. The evaluator reviews the training reports and interviews the trainer about the trainee's behavior and performance. After this review, the evaluator rides along with the trainee, comparing performance levels with the documented training reports and PTO interview, and then makes an independent assessment and recommendation. The recommendation is then forwarded to a board of evaluators for final recommendation to the police chief.

The board of evaluators is another unique feature of the PTO program. The board is made up of PTOs, training supervisors, and the training coordinator, who oversees the training process. The board's duties include reviewing performance of the trainees and PTOs, conducting evaluations of the program, and investigating training concerns. The board also reviews recommendations for termination submitted by training officers (evaluators) and, according to departmental needs, conducts exit interviews with trainees (Hoover et al. 2003).

Much like the San Jose model, evaluations of the Reno model are lacking. Pitts and Peak (2007) report that preliminary studies of PTO programs suggest PTO-trained officers are better prepared to engage in POP activities, be in leadership positions, and partner with local communities to address problems. It is worth mentioning, however, that most of the information to date comes from agency reports, and that the data have not been subjected to rigorous empirical testing (see, e.g., COPS Office 2014). Nonetheless, agency reports suggest PTO programs are beneficial. Anecdotally, police administrators generally indicate they favor PTO training programs, because they emphasize POP and COP practices.

After recruits have passed an FTO- or PTO-type program, they may become permanent, sworn police officers or work for an additional period in the field on probationary status. During this period, officers are evaluated several more times, and if their performance is acceptable, they become permanent employees.

## Career Growth

Once a person is recruited, selected, trained, and has completed probation in a police department, their career begins, and career growth becomes important. **Career growth** can involve individual development as well as a specific position within the department; it can involve training within or outside the department; and it attempts to match the needs of the individual with those of the department. Managers not only must be concerned with upgrading the knowledge and skills of officers in their current positions but also must plan to incorporate officers' interests with *career paths* that involve position enhancement, new assignments, and promotion.

In addition to improving the officer's knowledge and skills in each area of assignment, there is a need to develop career-path programs that will financially reward officers for staying in patrol and performing well. In many departments, the only way to obtain a pay increase after five or six years of service (other than cost-of-living adjustments) is to be promoted or transferred to a specialized position. This is not an effective system, because although they may wish to stay in patrol, good performers must be promoted or become specialists to receive increased compensation. Since the 1970s, the Los Angeles Police Department, for example, has had a career-path program that builds in several career-path levels below the rank of lieutenant, each with its own pay scale. This program allows officers to pursue police careers below the command level. All police departments should have *overlapping pay scales* in which patrol officers, if they are highly competent, could be paid at levels equal to those of management. Such a system would encourage many excellent officers to stay in patrol. This is the system in academe, for example, where the most highly regarded professors may be paid more than their managers (e.g., chairs and deans), and possibly even more than the college president.

### In-Service Training

The primary purpose of **in-service training** is the regular updating of all department members in a wide variety of subjects. It usually involves subject matter that all department members must know to function well. For example, officers must continually be aware of changing laws and ordinances, newly developed techniques, operating policies and procedures, and departmental changes and expectations.

In general, in-service training courses last from one to two weeks and therefore tend to offer relatively limited coverage of their subject matter. An interesting development in Kentucky, which requires 40 hours of approved in-service training each year, allows a college-level course to fulfill the requirement under the following conditions: (1) the course is taken from a regionally accredited college or university; (2) a minimum of three semester credit hours is earned; (3) a grade of C or higher is received; (4) approval is granted from the head of the officer's agency; and (5) a college course can be used only once every three years. Such a development is an important step in recognizing the benefit of college courses and may have a side benefit of enticing officers to enroll in college or to continue their college educations.

The vast majority (92 percent) of local police departments have an annual in-service training requirement for nonprobationary officers, including 100 percent of officers serving a population of 250,000 or more (Reaves 2010). For sheriffs' offices, the BJS reports that

94 percent of all agencies had an annual in-service training requirement for non-probationary deputies (Burch 2012).

## Specialized Training

**Specialized training** attempts to prepare officers for specific tasks (e.g., Special Weapons and Tactics [SWAT] or Hazardous Materials [HAZMAT]) or for different jobs throughout the department (e.g., investigator, supervisor, or FTO). Specialized training is essential if officers are to perform effectively outside the role of patrol officer.

Officers promoted to first-line supervisory positions (e.g., sergeant) should be provided with some form of *supervisory training*. Such training may be in-house or external and usually covers leadership behavior, specific job requirements, and policies and procedures. Once an officer is promoted to a managerial or executive-level position (e.g., lieutenant or higher), additional *management training* is necessary. The role of the police manager is even more complex than that of first-level supervisor and requires not only increased knowledge regarding management's role in the department but also long-range planning, policy development, and resource allocation. In California, for example, each of these types of training is required: police chiefs must complete an 80-hour executive-development course within two years of appointment; captains must complete an 80-hour management course within 12 months; lieutenants must complete an 80-hour management course (different in content from the captain's course) within 12 months; and sergeants must complete an 80-hour supervisory course within 12 months. As noted earlier in the chapter, supervisory and managerial training, with older and more mature officers, would generally work best under andragogical learning conditions. Since most of this type of training lasts for relatively short time frames (one to two weeks), andragogical practices could be utilized effectively for most, if not all, of the training period.

One of the most troublesome aspects of supervisory and management training for police is the evaluation procedure, or lack thereof. Although recruit training is often rigorously evaluated, training for experienced officers and managers rarely includes any meaningful evaluation. This lack of evaluation can be a serious problem, because many of the participants may not take the training seriously and thus will not attain the skills and knowledge necessary to be effective. Consequently, departments should require all supervisory and managerial training programs to include meaningful performance evaluations, because only in this way can they be sure that their future supervisors and managers are effectively trained for their new roles.

## Promotion and Assessment Centers

*Promotion* in police departments is usually based on one or more of several evaluative criteria, including an officer's (1) time on the job (seniority) or time in rank, (2) past performance, (3) written examination, (4) oral interview, and (5) college hours or degrees. In general, a percentage weight is assigned to each evaluative criterion used, and an overall promotional score is assigned. As openings at the next level of rank occur, individuals are promoted according to their score. Which criteria are used and what weight is assigned vary by department according to what the department or civil service commission regards as the most important. Often, police departments use only one or two criteria, although the criteria may have little, if any, relationship to the supervisory or managerial position for which the candidate is applying. Such a process can lead to selection of the wrong candidate for the position, which may have a long-term negative impact on the department and the officers being supervised.

In one of the few studies in this area, Roberg and Laramy (1980) analyzed the promotional results of a large midwestern police department that used a written exam (70 percent), performance evaluation (11.25 percent), seniority (10 percent), and college credits (8.75 percent) as criteria for promotion to sergeant. The results indicated that seniority (above the minimum requirement) should not be used as a criterion and that those with college hours scored higher on the written exam. The study concluded that the department needed to carefully *assess and validate the content of its promotional process* through analysis of the type of behavior required for effective job performance (e.g., supervisory ability).

Because it is difficult to measure supervisory or managerial potential based only on the type of criteria used in the aforementioned study, many departments are now using an assessment-center approach, which is perhaps the most promising method for selecting officers for promotion. An *assessment center* is a process that attempts to measure a candidate's potential for a particular managerial position. It uses multiple assessment strategies, typically spread over a two- or three-day period, which include different types of job-related simulations and possibly the use of interviews and psychological tests. Common forms of job simulations include in-basket exercises (e.g., carrying out simulated supervisory or managerial assignments like writing memos and reports or personnel matters), simulations of interviews with subordinates, oral presentations, group discussions, and fact-finding exercises. The candidate's behavior on all relevant criteria is evaluated by trained assessors, who reach a consensus on each participant. The primary advantage of this approach is that it evaluates all candidates in a simulated environment under standardized conditions, thus adding significantly to the validity and reliability of the selection process.

## Lateral Entry

**Lateral entry** refers to the ability of a police officer, at the patrol or supervisory level, to transfer from one department to another, usually without losing seniority. This concept is viewed by many as an important step toward increased professionalism through the improvement of career growth. Lateral entry is not a new concept, having been strongly endorsed by the 1967 President's Commission Task Force on Police:

> To improve police service, competition for all advanced positions should be opened to qualified persons from both within and outside of the department. This would enable a department to obtain the best available talent for positions of leadership . . . If candidates from within an agency are unable to meet the competition from other applicants, it should be recognized that the influx of more highly qualified personnel would greatly improve the quality of the services. (President's Commission on Law Enforcement and Administration of Justice 1967, 142)

Implicitly, this recommendation increases the competition for leadership positions; if those already within the department are not as well qualified, they must upgrade their skills and educational levels. This need is one of the primary obstacles to implementing lateral entry: older officers within the department feel that they, not "outsiders," should be provided the opportunity for advancement. Although this resistance can be a problem, probably of greater significance are the restrictions of civil service limitations, including retirement systems, which generally are not transferable. Because of these restrictions and lack of departmental support, lateral entry is still used sparingly today. Some legislative reforms that contribute to its implementation have been made; before lateral entry can become widely adopted, however, individual departments must openly, and perhaps aggressively, become its proponent. Undoubtedly, the expanded use of lateral entry would increase the quality of the applicant pool for most police departments, thus improving the selection of police supervisors and managers.

## Summary

With the increasing complexity of the police role and the movement of many agencies toward COP practices, the quality of police personnel has become perhaps the key factor to the effective operation of police departments. Thus, screening in, as opposed to screening out, candidates should be used so that only the best qualified are selected for the applicant pool. Candidates must meet a number of preemployment standards that attempt to depict a department's view of what is required to become an effective officer, usually including physical agility, educational, psychological, medical, and background qualifications. Preemployment selection tests are also used and usually include a written exam, personal interview, or both. Some departments, however, also require reading exams, because the reading ability of applicants has declined in recent years.

In preparing recruits for the job, decisions must be made about program orientation, philosophy, instructional methods, course content, and program evaluation. Furthermore, adult learning principles and concepts, known as andragogy (as opposed to pedagogy), should be introduced into the recruit, in-service, and specialized training curriculums.

Following academy training, recruits generally go through an on-the-job field training program prior to job assignment; many departments use an field training officer–type program or a more recently developed program related to a COP paradigm known as the police training officer program. The career growth of officers is important, because they must be prepared for changes not only in their current jobs but also in job assignments and promotions. Departments should establish career paths that allow employees at all levels to remain motivated throughout their careers. Finally, because promotions have long-term implications for the departments, administrators should carefully analyze the process and criteria used. Assessment centers may offer the greatest potential in this area.

## Critical Thinking Questions

1. Describe the meaning of *quality* with respect to police personnel. Explain what you consider the most important criteria with respect to quality in police recruits.

2. Why is the process of screening in police applicants important? How might this process relate to the potential for COP approaches and problem solving?

3. Should a college-degree requirement for recruit selection be defended as a bona fide occupational qualification? Why or why not?

4. Discuss whether you think that an andragogical teaching philosophy and cognitive PBL can become an integral part of recruit training in the near future.

5. Which five topics of the recruit training academy curriculum do you think should be assigned the greatest number of instructional hours, and why?

6. How might police training academies be changed in an attempt to improve the dropout rate of qualified individuals?

7. Discuss what you believe to be the most important criteria in the selection of FTOs or PTOs. Discuss differences between FTO and PTO programs. Which do you consider the most relevant to contemporary policing, and why?

# References

*Albermale Paper Company v. Moody,* 422 US 405 (1975).

Alpert, G. P., and Dunham, R. G. 2010. "Policy and Training Recommendations Related to Police Use of CEDs: Overview of Findings from a Comprehensive National Study." *Police Quarterly* 13: 235–259.

Alpert, G. P., and Moore, M. H. 1993. "Measuring Police Performance in the New Paradigm of Policing." In J. J. Dilulio, G. P. Alpert, M. H. Moore, G. F. Cole, J. Petersilia, C. H. Logan, and J. Q. Wilson (eds.), *Performance Measures for the Criminal Justice System*, pp. 109–140. Washington, DC: Bureau of Justice Statistics.

Alpert, G., and Smith, W. 1990. "Defensibility of Law Enforcement Training." *Criminal Law Bulletin* 26: 452–458.

Barrows, H. 2002. "Is It Really Possible to Have Such a Thing as PBL?" *Distance Education* 23: 119–122.

Bayley, D., and Bittner, E. 1989. "Learning the Skills of Policing." In R. Dunham and G. Alpert (eds.), *Critical Issues in Policing: Contemporary Readings*, pp. 87–110. Prospect Heights, IL: Waveland.

Berg, B. L. 1990. "First Day at the Police Academy: Stress-Reaction Training as a Screening-Out Technique." *Journal of Contemporary Criminal Justice* 6: 89–105.

Birzer, M. L. 1999. "Police Training in the 21st Century." *FBI Law Enforcement Bulletin* July: 16–19.

Birzer, M. L. 2003. "The Theory of Andragogy Applied to Police Training." *Policing: An International Journal of Police Strategies & Management* 26: 29–42.

Black. J. 2000. "Personality Testing and Police Selection: Utility of the 'Big Five.'" *New Zealand Journal of Psychology* 29: 2–9.

Bradford, D., and Pynes, J. E. 1999. "Police Academy Training: Why Hasn't It Kept Up with Practice?" *Police Quarterly* 2: 283–301.

Buehler, E. D. 2021. *State and Local Law Enforcement Training Academies, 2018—Statistical Tables.* Washington, DC: Bureau of Justice Statistics.

Burbeck, E., and Furnham, A. 1985. "Police Officer Selection: A Critical Review of the Literature." *Journal of Police Science and Administration* 13: 58–69.

Burch, A. M. 2012. *Sheriffs' Offices, 2007—Statistical Tables.* Washington, DC: Bureau of Justice Statistics.

Campbelis, C. 1999. "Selecting a New Breed of Officer: The Customer-Oriented Cop." *Community Policing Exchange* 25: 1, 4–5.

Chappell, A. T. 2007. "Community Policing: Is Field Training the Missing Link?" *Policing: An International Journal of Police Strategies & Management* 30: 498–517.

Clark, J. R. 1992. "Why Officer Johnny Can't Read." *Law Enforcement News* May 15: 1, 16–17.

Cohen, B., and Chaiken, J. M. 1972. *Police Background Characteristics and Performance.* New York: RAND Institute.

Copple, J. E. 2017. *Law Enforcement Recruitment in the Twenty-First Century: Forum Proceedings.* Washington, DC: Office of Community Oriented Policing Services.

Costa, P. T., Jr., and McRae, R. R. 1992. *NEO PI-R Professional Manual.* Odessa, FL: Psychological Assessment Resources.

Crosby, A., Rosenfield, M., and Thornton, R. F. 1979. "The Development of a Written Test for Police Applicant Selection." In C. D. Spielberger (ed.), *Police Selection and Evaluation*, pp. 143–153. New York: Praeger.

*Davis v. City of Dallas*, 777 F.2d 205 (5th Cir.) (1985).

De Long, R. 1999. "Problem Solvers Wanted: How to Tailor Your Agency's Recruiting Approach." *Community Policing Exchange, Phase VI* 25(2): 6.

Detrick, P., and Chibnall, J. T. 2006. "NEO PI-R Personality Characteristics of High-Performing Entry-Level Police Officers." *Psychological Services* 3: 274–285.

Detrick. P., Chibnall, J. T., and Luebbert, M. C. 2004. "The Revised NEO Personality Inventory as Predictor of Police Academy Performance." *Criminal Justice & Behavior* 31: 676–694.

Dixon, T. L., Schell, T. L., Giles, H., and Drogos, K. L. 2008. "The Influence of Race in Police–Citizen Interactions: A Content Analysis of Videotaped Interactions Taken During Cincinnati Police Traffic Stops." *Journal of Communication* 58: 530–549.

Doerner, W. G. 1997. "The Utility of the Oral Interview Board in Selecting Police Academy Admissions." *Policing: An International Journal of Police Strategies and Management* 20: 777–785.

Earle, H. H. 1973. *Police Recruit Training: Stress vs. Non-Stress.* Springfield, IL: Thomas.

Etter, G. W., Sr., and Griffin, R. 2011. "In-Service Training of Older Law Enforcement Officers: An Andragogical Argument." *Policing: An International Journal of Police Strategies & Management* 34: 233–245.

Falkenberg, S., Gaines, L. K., and Cox, T. C. 1990. "The Oral Interview Board: What Does It Measure?" *Journal of Police Science and Administration* 17: 32–39.

Farmer, L. 2022. "The Great Resignation's Impact on Local Government." *The Rockefeller Institute*, January 20. https://rockinst.org/blog/the-great-resignations-impact-on-local-government/

Friedman, W., Lurigio, A. J., Greenleaf, R., and Albertson, S. 2004. "Encounters Between Police Officers and Youths: The Social Costs of Disrespect." *Journal of Crime and Justice* 27: 1–9.

Gaines, L. K., Costello, P., and Crabtree, A. 1989. "Police Selection Testing: Balancing Legal Requirements and Employer Needs." *American Journal of Police* 8: 137–152.

Gaines, L. K., and Falkenberg, S. 1998. "An Evaluation of the Written Selection Test: Effectiveness and Alternatives." *Journal of Criminal Justice* 26: 175–183.

Gaines, L. K., and Kappeler, V. E. 1992. "Selection and Testing." In G. W. Cordner and D. C. Hale (eds.), *What Works in Policing: Operations and Administration Examined*, pp. 107–123. Cincinnati, OH: Anderson.

Gaines, L. K., Falkenberg, S., and Gambino, J. A. 1993. "Police Physical Activity Testing: An Historical and Legal Analysis." *American Journal of Police* 12: 47–66.

Geistman, J., and Smith, B. W. 2007. "Juvenile Attitudes Toward Police: A National Study." *Journal of Crime & Justice* 30: 27–51.

Giles, H., Fortman, J., Daily, R., Barker, V., Hajek, C., Anderson, M. C., and Rule, N. O. 2006. "Communication Accommodation: Law Enforcement and the Public." In R. M. Dailey and B. A. Le Poire (eds.), *Applied Interpersonal Communication Matters: Family, Health and Community Relations*, pp. 241–269. New York: Lang.

*Griggs v. Duke Power Company*, 401 US 424, (1971).

Haarr, R. 2001. "The Making of a Community Policing Officer: The Impact of Basic Training and Occupational Socialization on Police Recruits." *Police Quarterly* 4: 420–433.

Haarr, R. 2005. "Factors Affecting the Decision of Police Recruits to 'Drop Out' of Police Work." *Police Quarterly* 8: 431–453.

Hajek, C., Barker, V., Giles, S., Makoni, L., Peccioni, J., Louw-Potgieter, J., and Myers, P. 2006. "Communication Dynamics of Police-Civilian Encounters: South African and American Interethnic Data." *Journal of Intercultural Communication Research* 35: 161–182.

Hansen, G. 1979. *Field Training and Evaluation: Fresno Police Department.* Washington, DC: Bureau of Justice Statistics.

Henson, B., Reyns, B. W., Klahm, C. F., and Frank, J. 2010. "Do Good Recruits Make Good Cops? Problems Predicting and Measuring Academy and Street-Level Success." *Police Quarterly* 13: 5–26.

Hickman, M. J. 2005. *State and Local Law Enforcement Training Academies, 2002.* Washington, DC: Bureau of Justice Statistics.

Hinds, L. 2007. "Building Police–Youth Relationships: The Importance of Procedural Justice." *Youth Justice* 7: 195–209.

Hodes, C. R., Hunt, R. L., and Raskin, D. C. 1985. "Effects of Physical Countermeasures on the Physiological Detection of Deception." *Journal of Applied Psychology* 70: 177–187.

Hoover, J., Pitts, S., and Ponte, D. 2003. *Executive Summary: The Reno Model of Post-Academy Police Training.* Reno, NV: Reno Police Department.

Hughes, T. 2003. "*Jordan v. The City of New London*, Police Hiring and IQ." *Policing: An International Journal of Police Strategies & Management* 26: 298–312.

International Association of Chiefs of Police (IACP). 2019. "The State of Recruitment: A Crisis for Law Enforcement." https://www.theiacp.org/sites/default/files/239416_IACP_RecruitmentBR_HR_0.pdf

*Jordan v. City of New London.* 2000. Unreported case retrieved. https://www.aele.org/apa/jordan-newlondon.html.

Jordan, W. T., Fridell, L., Faggiani, D., and Kubu, B. 2009. "Attracting Females and Racial/Ethnic Minorities to Law Enforcement." *Journal of Criminal Justice* 37: 333–341.

Kleinmuntz, B., and Szucko, J. J. 1982. "Is the Lie Detector Valid?" *Law and Society Review* 16: 105–122.

Knowles, M. S. 1970. *The Modern Practice of Adult Education: Andragogy Versus Pedagogy.* New York: Association Press.

LaMotte, V., Ouellette, K., Sanderson, J. A., Anderson, S. A., Kosutic, I., Griggs, J., and Garcia, M. 2010. "Effective Police Interactions with Youth: A Program Evaluation." *Police Quarterly* 13: 161–179.

Law Enforcement Assistance Administration. 1973. *Equal Employment Opportunity Program Development Manual.* Washington, DC: US Government Printing Office.

Law Enforcement News. 1997. "Dumb-Da-Dum-Dum." *Law Enforcement News* June 15: 4.

Lee, C. B. 2006. "Psychological Testing for Recruit Screening." *Texas Law Enforcement and Administrative Statistics Program Bulletin* 13(2): 1–8.

Lonsway, K. A. 2003. "Tearing Down the Wall: Problems with Consistency, Validity, and Adverse Impact of Physical Agility Testing in Police Selection." *Police Quarterly* 6: 237–277.

Lough, J., and Von Treuer, K. 2013. "A Critical Review of Psychological Instruments Used in Police Officer Selection." *Policing: An International Journal of Police Strategies & Management* 36: 737–751.

McCampbell, M. S. 1987. *Field Training for Police Officers: State of the Art.* Washington, DC: National Institute of Justice.

Metchik, E. 1999. "An Analysis of the 'Screening Out' Model of Police Officer Selection." *Police Quarterly* 2: 327–342.

Morin, R., Parker, K. Stepler, R. and Mercer A. 2017. "Behind the Badge: Amid Protests and Calls for Reform, How Police View Their Jobs, Key Issues and Recent Fatal Encounters Between Blacks and Police." *PEW Research Center.* https://www.pewresearch.org/social-trends/2017/01/11/behind-the-badge/

National Advisory Commission on Criminal Justice Standards and Goals. 1973. *Report on Police.* Washington, DC: U.S. Government Printing Office.

Office of Community Oriented Policing Services (COPS Office). 2014. *PTO Manual.* Washington, DC: US Department of Justice.

Oliva, J. R., and Compton, M. T. 2010. "What Do Police Officers Value in the Classroom? A Qualitative Study of the Classroom Social Environment in Law Enforcement Education." *Policing: An International Journal of Police Strategies & Management* 33: 321–338.

Parker, K., and Horowitz, J.M. 2022. "Majority of Workers who Quit a Job in 2021 Cite Low Pay, No Opportunities for Advancement, Feeling Disrespected." *PEW Research Center,* March 9. https://pewrsr.ch/3hVWMfr.

Pitts, S. R., and Peak, K. 2007. "The Police Training Officer (PTO) Program: A Contemporary Approach to Postacademy Recruit Training." *The Police Chief* 74: 114–121.

Police Executive Research Forum (PERF). 2015. *Re-Engineering Training on Police Use of Force.* Washington, DC: Author.

Police Executive Research Forum (PERF). 2019. *The Workforce Crisis, and What Police Agencies are Doing About it.* Washington, DC: Author.

Police Executive Research Forum (PERF). 2021. *PERF Special Report: Survey on Police Workforce Trends.* Motorola Solutions Foundation. https://www.policeforum.org/workforcesurveyjune2021

President's Commission on Law Enforcement and Administration of Justice. 1967. *Task Force Report: The Police.* Washington, DC: US Government Printing Office.

President's Task Force on Twenty-First Century Policing. 2015. *Final Report of the President's Task Force on Twenty-First Century Policing.* Washington, DC: Office of Community Oriented Policing Services.

Queen, C. R. 2016. "Effectiveness of Problem-Based Learning Strategies within Police Training Academies and Correlates with Licensing Exam Outcomes." (PhD dissertation, Western Michigan University). https://scholarworks.wmich.edu/dissertations/1404

Rafky, J., and Sussman, F. 1985. "An Evaluation of Field Techniques in Detection of Deception." *Psychophysiology* 12: 121–130.

Raymond, B., Hickman, L. J., Miller, L. L., and Wong, J. S. 2005. *Police Personnel Challenges after September 11: Anticipating Expanded Duties and a Changing Labor Pool.* Santa Monica, CA: RAND Corporation.

Reaves, B. A. 2010. *Local Police Departments, 2007.* Washington, DC: Bureau of Justice Statistics.

Reaves, B. A.. 2015. *Local Police Departments, 2013: Personnel, Policies, and Practices.* Washington, DC: Bureau of Justice Statistics.

Reaves, B. A.. 2016. *State and Local Law Enforcement Training Academies*, 2013. Washington, DC: Bureau of Justice Statistics.

Roberg, R. R. (ed.). 1976. *The Changing Police Role: New Dimensions and New Perspectives.* San Jose, CA: Justice Systems Development.

Roberg, R. R. 1979. "Police Training and Andragogy: A New Perspective." *Police Chief* 46: 32–34.

Roberg, R. R., and Laramy, J. E. 1980. "An Empirical Assessment of the Criteria Utilized for Promoting Police Personnel: A Secondary Analysis." *Journal of Police Science and Administration* 8: 183–187.

Rubin, P. N. 1994. *The Americans with Disabilities Act and Criminal Justice: Hiring New Employees.* Washington, DC: National Institute of Justice.

Sharp, D., and Atherton, S. 2007. "To Serve and Protect? The Experiences of Policing in the Community of Young People from Black and Other Minority Groups." *British Journal of Criminology* 47: 746–763.

*Shield Club v. City of Cleveland*, 647 R. Supp. 274 (N.D. Ohio) (1986).

Snowden, L., and Fuss, T. 2000. "A Costly Mistake: Inadequate Police Background Investigations." *The Justice Professional* 13: 359–375.

Sproule, C. F. 1984. "Should Personnel Selection Tests Be Used on a Pass–Fail, Grouping, or Ranking Basis?" *Public Personnel Management Journal* 13: 375–394.

Taylor, B., Kubu, B., Friedell, L., Rees, C., Jordan, T., and Cheney, J. 2005. *The Cop Crunch: Identifying Strategies for Dealing with the Recruiting and Hiring Crisis in Law Enforcement.* Washington, DC: Police Executive Research Forum.

TELEMASP. 1994. "Background Investigation and Psychological Screening of New Officers: Effect of the Americans with Disabilities Act." *Texas Law Enforcement Management and Administrative Statistics Program Bulletin.* Volume 1, Issue 7: 1–7.

*Vanguard Justice Society v. Hughes*, 471 F. Supp. 670 (1979).

Varela, J. G., Boccaccini, M. T., Scogin, F., Stump, J., and Caputo, A. 2004. "Personality Testing in Law Enforcement Employment Settings: A Meta-Analytic Review." *Criminal Justice and Behavior* 31: 649–675.

Warners, R., and Williams, R. 2010. "The Field Training Experience: Perspectives of Field Training Offices and Trainees." *The Police Chief* 77: 58–64.

Werth, E. P. 2009. "Student Perception of Learning Through a Problem-Based Learning Exercise: An Exploratory Study." *Policing: An International Journal of Police Strategies & Management* 32: 21–37.

White, M. D. 2008. "Identifying Good Cops Early: Predicting Recruit Performance in the Academy." *Police Quarterly* 11: 27–49.

Wilson, J. M. 2012. "Articulating the Dynamic Police Staffing Challenge: An Examination of Supply and Demand." *Policing: An International Journal of Police Strategies & Management* 35: 327–355.

Wilson, J. M., Rostker, B. D., and Fan, C. 2010. *Recruiting and Retaining America's Finest: Evidence-Based Lessons for Police Workforce Planning.* Santa Monica, CA: RAND Corporation.

Wilson, O. W., and McLaren, R. C. 1977. *Police Administration*, 4th ed. New York: McGraw-Hill.

Wright, B., Dai, M., and Greenbeck, K. 2010. "Correlates of Police Academy Success." *Policing; An International Journal of Police Strategies & Management* 34: 625–637.

## CHAPTER 7

# Field Operations: Foundations

## CHAPTER OUTLINE

## CHAPTER OUTLINE (continued)

- Summary
- Critical Thinking Questions
- References

### KEY TERMS

- bias crime
- crackdowns
- Crime Gun Intelligence Centers
- crime suppression
- event analysis
- field operations
- follow-up investigation
- generalists
- law enforcement
- order maintenance
- police pursuit
- proactive arrests
- preliminary investigation
- proactive
- reactive
- social services
- specialists
- target oriented

POLICE FIELD OPERATIONS CONSIST of two primary functions: patrol and investigations. Although most departments have other operational functions (e.g., traffic, vice, juvenile, and crime prevention), a substantial majority of all police work involves either patrol or investigations. In local police departments, for example, about 65 percent of full-time officers perform patrol duties, whereas 16 percent primarily handle criminal investigations. In sheriffs' departments, 41 percent of full-time deputies are assigned to patrol duty and 12 percent to investigative duties; in addition, because most sheriffs' offices operate jail facilities and have court-related functions, 24 percent are assigned to jail- related duties and 17 percent primarily perform court-related duties (Reaves and Hickman 2002). These two operational units deal with the greatest diversity of problems and have the most influence on the public's perception of the police. Accordingly, the focus of this chapter is primarily on patrol work and secondarily on investigative or detective work.

In relatively small departments, patrol and investigations typically do not exist as separate units, because most police officers are **generalists**, meaning they perform a variety of activities—for example, conducting investigations that result from calls while on patrol that otherwise could be assigned to **specialists**. In contrast, most medium-size or large departments tend to *specialize* their investigative activities. In these departments, once a patrol officer is dispatched to the scene of a crime, that officer may conduct a preliminary investigation and then call in the detectives for follow up and further case development. In highly specialized departments, the patrol officer may call in the detectives as soon as it is ascertained that an investigation is necessary; once the detectives arrive, the officer returns to patrol duty.

## The Patrol Function

Police patrol has been referred to as the "backbone of policing" (Wilson and McLaren 1977), because most police officers are assigned to patrol and thus provide the greatest bulk of services to the community. Because patrol officers are also the most highly visible personnel in the department, the patrol unit forms the public's primary perception of any particular department. Thus, it is clear why patrol work is considered the backbone of policing.

In general, the *goals of patrol* include (1) crime prevention and deterrence, (2) apprehension of offenders, (3) creation of a sense of community security and satisfaction,

(4) provision of non-crime-related services, and (5) traffic control. For departments practicing community policing (COP), another important goal is (6) identifying and solving community problems concerning crime and disorder.

In attempting to achieve these goals, patrol officers perform essentially three functions: law enforcement, order maintenance, and social services. **Law enforcement** involves activities in which police make arrests, issue citations, conduct investigations, and attempt to prevent or deter criminal activity. **Order maintenance** may or may not involve a violation of the law (usually minor), during which officers tend to use alternatives to formal sanctions. Examples include loud parties, teenagers consuming alcohol, or minor neighborhood disputes. **Social services** involve taking reports and providing information and assistance to the public, everything from helping a stranded motorist to checking grandma's house to make sure she is all right. It is important to understand (as discussed in Chapter 1) that although police work is often viewed from a narrow, law enforcement perspective, research has continuously shown patrol work to be much broader in scope, and in practice, it is more likely to involve order maintenance and social service activities.

Some of these activities may overlap functional areas. For example, traffic control can fall under any of the categories; although traffic enforcement is a law enforcement function, directing traffic at the scene of an accident or providing medical assistance is a service function. Interestingly, traffic control accounts for the most contacts with the public (Eith and Durose 2011) and therefore has an important impact on how the public view the police. Attempting to solve community problems could also fall under different functions. For instance, planning with a citizen's group to establish a recreation center to keep at-risk juveniles off the street could be considered order maintenance, but it may also relate to law enforcement through crime prevention activities.

## Historical Development

Two critical developments of the 1930s helped change the nature of the patrol officer from a neighborhood cop who knew and who was known by the people on his beat: (1) the increased use of the patrol car and (2) development of the Uniform Crime Reports. By adopting the Uniform Crime Reports (i.e., Part I Crimes reported to the FBI) as their primary measure of performance, the police began to stress the crime-fighting dimension of their role and became less interested in what they defined as non-crime-related activities.

These two developments, along with the influence of O. W. Wilson's bureaucratic or paramilitary approach to police management, led to the new professionalized police department. This increased level of *professionalization* was concerned with portraying a proper police image and running things by the book—literally, Wilson's influential *Police Administration* (1950). The image of the patrol officer was one of a nonpolitical, incorruptible fighter of crime. It was believed that increased use of the police car would increase police efficiency through **crime suppression**, which had traditionally been regarded as the most important patrol function. In other words, because more area could be covered and response time would be shortened, crime could be better controlled or suppressed. According to Wilson and McLaren (1977, 320), patrol procedures should be designed to create the impression of a police "omnipresence," which would eliminate "the actual opportunity (or the belief that the opportunity exists) for successful misconduct." However, the increased use of patrol cars further isolated the officer from the community. And interestingly, some of the more professionalized departments took extra measures to *de-personalize* policing. For example, one strategy adopted to combat corruption was the frequent rotation of beat assignments.

The development of radio and the telephone also strongly impacted the relationship between the police and the community. Being able to call police and dispatch them to help citizens changed patrol work. Instead of watching to prevent crime, police began waiting to respond to crime; that is, they went from a **proactive** (police-initiated) to a **reactive** (citizen-initiated) approach. As a result, citizens tended to request police assistance more often (the development of the emergency telephone number 911 has significantly contributed to this tendency), which reinforced the all-purpose service orientation of the patrol function.

Poor people in particular began to use the police as lawyers, doctors, psychologists, and social workers. As Walker (1984, 88) notes, "While the patrol car did isolate the police in some respects, the telephone brought about a more intimate form of contact between police and citizen by allowing the police officer to enter private residences and involving him in private disputes and problems." What this meant was that the professional officer, who now knew less about the neighborhoods and people, was often ill-equipped to perform non-crime-related functions and did not tend to like the order maintenance and public service aspects of police work (Sherman 1983).

Because police have often become deluged with 911 calls—many of which are not emergencies and do not necessarily require the response of an officer—some cities are developing and promoting the use of a *311 nonemergency number*. For example, in the Baltimore Police Department, use of the 311 call system was credited with a 34 percent decrease in unnecessary calls to the 911 number, which represented a decrease of approximately 5,000 calls to 911 per week. Citizens had favorable views of the system, indicating that the 311 call system improved city services and police–community relations and reduced nonemergency calls to 911 (Mazerolle et al. 2002). A follow-up study of Baltimore's 311 system found that although the system appeared to free up time for patrol officers, most officers did not notice any increase in discretionary time (Mazerolle et al. 2005). The researchers thus recommended that 311 systems should also include a *dual-dispatching* policy, wherein patrol units would not be dispatched to 311 calls but instead would follow up with a community-oriented, problem-solving approach.

In some respects, patrol work has come full circle, and police departments are once again attempting to regain knowledge and awareness of the neighborhood context, although in a much more sophisticated fashion than in the past. As COP continues to develop, patrol officers must become increasingly aware of the neighborhood context by working with citizens and community groups in the coproduction of public safety to identify and solve crime and disorder problems. Along with this change in role emphasis, it is further suggested (Stephens 1996) that attitudes must change concerning the amount of time police spend on calls, including taking the time to ask a different set of questions on each crime report: Have we been here before? What is causing this situation to occur or reoccur? How can it be prevented? What should the police do? The callers? The victims? The community? The government? In this way, the police change their emphasis from *incident oriented* to *problem oriented* and from *responding to problems* to *solving problems* that relate to or cause crime.

## Terrorism and Patrol

In contemporary society, with a heightened awareness of potential terrorist acts, patrol work may need to change. De Guzman (2002), for instance, argues that patrol work will need to be more target oriented, with greater emphasis placed on event analysis in addition to crime analysis. **Target oriented** is the concept used by officers to assess likely targets in their districts; that is, they should be watching over not only obvious places and persons who might be of danger but also where disruption in "safe places" might occur. This suggests that the police should be able to "deconstruct the obvious" (Crank 1999). In other words, they should attempt to determine the vulnerability of people and places and how they may become targets of terrorism. **Event analysis** suggests that the police should be aware of important celebrations, ideologies, and anniversaries of known activists, terrorists, or groups and attempt to determine whether these events may be connected to a possible terrorist act.

Another change De Guzman (2002) believes may significantly impact terrorist acts is to intensify traffic enforcement. It is believed that no-nonsense (or even zero-tolerance) policies regarding traffic violations will limit the movement of terrorists. A number of US Supreme Court decisions have expanded the use of traffic stops for the purpose of stopping, searching, and investigating. Thus, the previously unreliable hunch or sixth sense of the police is slowly being acknowledged by the courts as legitimate grounds for police intervention. Although such an approach may, at least on the surface, appear better able to track and investigate certain people, there are important constitutional issues with respect to profiling and, perhaps just as important, police legitimacy (i.e., trust in the police). Chapter 8 includes a fuller discussion of police legitimacy.

Based on the earlier discussion, De Guzman (2002, 89) suggests that these activities call for the police to return to, or "lean" toward, a legalistic style and begin "to apply their innate talent for sensing change." Although undoubtedly more emphasis will need to be placed on anti-terrorist activities in the future, the police must be careful not to develop a "we versus they" attitude with respect to these activities. Thus, it seems more crucial than ever to promote a COP approach, where vital information can be gained through improved relationships with the community. In this way, the public plays an important role in helping to combat not only traditional criminal activity but also potential terrorist acts. Additionally, this should also lead to gains in police legitimacy, which in turn will lead to additional help and information in preventing crime and terrorism.

## Patrol Methods

The two most dominant methods of patrol are by automobile and by foot. As noted, the automobile had a revolutionary impact on policing, and it is now the most dominant method of patrol. Because it offers the greatest coverage and most rapid response to calls, it is usually considered the most cost-effective patrol method. However, along with this increased coverage came a trade-off in terms of isolation from the community. Suddenly, police officers lost contact with citizens in nonconflict and nonadversarial situations. The police, in the name of efficiency, essentially became outsiders in the communities they served. The urban riots of the early 1960s emphasized the problems that had developed in police–community relations. For instance, the President's Commission on Law Enforcement and Administration of Justice (1967, 53) suggested that "the most significant weakness in American motor patrol operations today is the general lack of contact with citizens except when an officer has responded to a call."

In recognition of the loss of contact with the community, there has been a resurgence of *foot patrol*, especially in downtown areas. The development of the portable radio vastly improved the capabilities of foot patrol officers, allowing constant communication with headquarters regarding conditions on their beat. However, foot patrol officers are severely limited in terms of mobility and response to calls. Consequently, they are sometimes paired with other forms of patrol, such as cars, horses, or bikes. Some departments use a combination of foot and car or foot and bike; that is, they allocate approximately half of their time to walking their beat and the other half to motor patrol. Departments that utilize such a patrol method feel they are getting the best of both forms of patrol—that is, a greater degree of citizen contact than that provided by motor patrol alone and greater mobility than that provided by foot patrol alone.

Two early comprehensive evaluations of foot patrol revealed that although foot patrol may effect a slight reduction in crime, it primarily reduces citizens' fear of crime and changes the nature of police–citizen interactions, toward more positive and non-adversarial exchanges. The major studies were the Newark Foot Patrol Experiment, which included data on foot patrol in Newark and 28 additional cities in New Jersey (Police Foundation 1981), and the Neighborhood Foot Patrol Program, which was conducted in 14 neighborhoods of Flint, Michigan (Trojanowicz 1982). Later reports of the Flint study (Trojanowicz and Banas 1985) discovered a decrease in the disparity between Black and white perceptions of crime and policing and an increased positive acceptance of the program and confidence in police services by Black members of the community.

Recent examinations of the effectiveness of more focused foot patrol initiatives have demonstrated some crime prevention benefit when implementing the strategy within smaller geographic areas. Newark, New Jersey, implemented Operation Impact in 2008, with pairs of officers and mid-level managers assigned to evening foot patrol shifts in roughly quarter-mile-size areas. Examination of crime trends in those areas before and after the foot patrol implementation reported that counts of violent crime had declined significantly during foot patrol activities, with foot patrol contributing to a 30 percent reduction in overall violent crime counts in the area (including murder, shootings, and aggravated assaults). The researchers suggested that offenders were aware of when and where foot patrol officers would be on duty, however, and that eventually made the foot beat predictable to potential offenders. At the same time, the researchers noted that robberies were being significantly displaced to surrounding catchment areas (Piza and O'Hara 2014).

To further examine the effectiveness of foot patrol, the Philadelphia Police Department identified hot spots for violent crime, particularly homicides, aggravated assaults, and outdoor robberies. The department paired rookie officers to work consecutive shifts in the summer months. During that time, those officers engaged in a variety of activities, from community-oriented work to aggressive enforcement. The results of the effort were noteworthy. Violent crime in the targeted foot patrol areas declined by 23 percent, whereas no measurable change was observed in the control areas, even when possible spatial displacement was taken into account. In addition, foot patrol treatment resulted in a reduction of 53 violent crimes. Kansas City, Missouri, implemented a similar foot patrol strategy and reported significant declines in violent crime during a 90-day intervention without displacing crime to surrounding areas (Novak et al. 2015). Other recent research in British Columbia suggests foot patrol impacted lower-level disorder or property crimes but not violent crime, and that it achieved this without spatial crime displacement (Andresen and Lau 2014).

Further analyses suggest foot patrol has an initial deterrence benefit, but also that effects decay rapidly. In Kansas City, the deterrent benefit lasted only about six weeks, with violent crime returning to normal levels even while foot patrol was still being implemented (Novak et al. 2015). Sorg et al. (2013, 88) concluded that although "it is premature to prescribe a specific length of deployment time, what can be gleaned is that staffing hot spots five days a week for 16 hours a day over a 3-month period did not result in initial deterrence decay, whereas the same dosage over 22 weeks did." This highlights the importance of identifying the appropriate dosage and duration level for the highest return on personnel investment. Issues of duration and dosage related to patrol are discussed in greater detail in the Chapter 8.

Departments may use numerous other patrol methods, depending on their particular needs and budgetary constraints. In general, *motorcycle patrol* is used for traffic control and enforcement in highly congested areas. However, one of the major problems with this form of patrol is that it is extremely dangerous, since just about any type of accident tends to cause harm to the rider. *Bicycles* are often used in parks and beach areas and in conjunction with stakeouts; they offer good mobility and interaction with the public. Because of these assets, bicycle patrols have increased in departments implementing COP. During the 1960s, *horse patrol* was used mainly for crowd control but today is being increasingly used in both downtown and park areas. *Planes* and *helicopters* are used primarily for traffic control, surveillance, and rescues. Their mobility and observation capabilities are excellent, but their cost and noise levels are high. Helicopters are increasingly being used in both automobile and foot pursuits. Cities surrounded by large bodies of water use *boat patrol* to enforce maritime laws, emergency assistance, and other law enforcement activities, including surveillance and narcotics control. In deciding what form of patrol should be used, police managers must consider speed, access, population density, visibility, cost, and community support. Table 7.1 indicates different types of patrol methods and their utilization in large police departments.

### Use of Patrol Resources

We now discuss how police resources are used, including patrol staffing (how many officers per car), resource determination (how many officers a department should have), and resource allocation (how officers should be distributed).

**Patrol Staffing.** When automobiles first began to be used for patrol purposes, two or more officers were often assigned to a car. Since the 1940s, however, many departments have begun to use single-person cars. There has been considerable controversy surrounding this issue. Do *one-officer* or *two-officer cars* do more work? Which method is safer for the officer? Which is safer for the citizen? The most comprehensive study on this issue was undertaken in San Diego in the mid-1970s (Boydstun, Sherry, and Moelter 1977). The findings indicated that one-person units produced more arrests, filed more formal crime reports, received fewer citizen complaints, and were clearly less expensive. A second study (Kessler 1985) replicating the San Diego analysis found the same results and further indicated that two one-officer cars responded to the scene of an incident faster than one two-officer car. One-officer units also had a safety advantage. Even considering the danger of the area and shift assignment, one-officer units had fewer resisting-arrest problems and approximately equal involvement in assaults on officers. A study of more than 1,000 officers in three Australian state police forces (Wilson and Brewer 2001) indicated that in all 12 patrol activities measured, two-officer cars encountered more resistance from citizens than one-officer cars; this suggests that officers working together may handle interactions with the public in a qualitatively different—perhaps less cordial—manner than single officers.

**Resource Determination.** Probably the most frequently used method for resource determination is the *comparative approach*, which involves comparing one or more

**TABLE 7.1** Types of Regularly Scheduled Patrols Other than Automobile Used by Local Police Departments, by Size of Population Served, 2007

| POPULATION SERVED | PERCENTAGE OF DEPARTMENTS USING EACH TYPE OF PATROL REGULARLY | | | | | | |
|---|---|---|---|---|---|---|---|
| | FOOT | BICYCLE | MOTORCYCLE | MARINE | TRANSPORTER | HORSE | AIR |
| All sizes | 55 | 32 | 16 | 4 | 2 | 1 | 1 |
| 1,000,000 or more | 92 | 100 | 100 | 69 | 31 | 77 | 100 |
| 500,000–999,999 | 81 | 100 | 94 | 52 | 29 | 61 | 71 |
| 250,000–499,999 | 78 | 89 | 91 | 26 | 24 | 50 | 57 |
| 100,000–249,999 | 59 | 71 | 90 | 12 | 15 | 17 | 14 |
| 50,000–99,999 | 56 | 69 | 74 | 12 | 6 | 5 | 5 |
| 25,000–49,999 | 52 | 58 | 55 | 6 | 4 | 2 | 1 |
| 10,000–24,999 | 50 | 44 | 25 | 5 | 2 | 1 | 1 |
| 2,500–9,999 | 58 | 36 | 8 | 4 | 1 | — | 0 |
| Under 2,500 | 54 | 15 | 4 | 1 | — | 0 | — |

—, less than 0.5 percent.

Transporter includes devices such as Segway.

Source: B. A. Reaves, *Local Police Departments, 2007* (Washington, DC: Department of Justice, 2010), 15.

**TABLE 7.2** Police–Citizen Ratios of Selected Major Cities

| CITY | SWORN OFFICERS PER 10,000 CITIZENS |
|---|---|
| Washington, DC | 53.97 |
| Chicago | 48.60 |
| Baltimore | 41.27 |
| Detroit | 37.94 |
| New York | 47.22 |
| Houston | 22.35 |
| Los Angeles | 24.91 |
| Seattle | 18.54 |
| San Antonio | 14.73 |
| San Jose, CA | 11.06 |

*Source*: Federal Bureau of Investigation, *Crime in the United States, 2019* (Washington, DC: US Department of Justice, 2019).

cities using a ratio of sworn officers per 10,000 population unit; if the comparison city has a higher police–citizen ratio, it is assumed that an increase in personnel is justified, at least to the level of the comparison city. Table 7.2 indicates the significant differences in police–citizen ratios between selected major cities. Large northeast cities such as New York, Chicago, Baltimore, and Washington, DC, all have more than 40 officers per 10,000 residents, whereas West Coast cities all have less than 30 per 10,000, with some having less than 20. This ratio is largely based on long-established staffing traditions.

Although comparison is frequently used, it is not necessarily a valid indicator of needed strength, since individual cities are extremely diverse in their needs for police services, expectations, crime rates, and levels of violence. For example, the diversity of major cities in the same state can be observed by comparing San Jose, with a police–citizen ratio of 11.06, to Los Angeles, with a ratio of 24.91, or by comparing San Antonio, with 14.73, to Houston, with 22.35. The most likely need for police resources relates to a department's managerial effectiveness, use of technology, competency of officers, and policing styles. For example, because Washington, DC, has almost three times the police protection of Seattle and more than six times as much as San Jose, one might assume that it would be the safest of the three cities, which is not the case.

It should be noted that the comparison method is perhaps most useful to a department and the community's political structure as a yearly gauge for its own needs and progress. In other words, compared with last year's level of police services provided to the city (or that of several years ago), how does the department measure up? If, for example, it can be shown that a department significantly increased its services to the community, a strong case could be made to the mayor or city manager and the city council that the ratio, and thus the resources for the department, should be increased.

A number of studies have attempted to address the following straightforward question: Does police department size impact crime? It makes intuitive sense that there should be an inverse relationship—more cops, less crime. But over the last several decades, empirical research has produced inconsistent results. Lee, Eck, and Corsaro (2016) systematically examined 62 separate studies that explored the size–crime relationship. They concluded that the influence of police department size on crime is small and insignificant. This is not to say that police force size doesn't matter whatsoever; instead, fluctuations in size seem to be unrelated to crime. This suggests that *how many* police officers a department has is less important that *what strategies* are being implemented.

Additional experimental research on this topic is necessary, however, before too much emphasis is placed on the quick fix of simply adding more police to reduce crime, although it may be politically expedient. Adding more police entails immense financial costs, since police departments operate 7 days a week, 365 days a year. Indeed, Bayley (1994) noted that, on average, when accounting for sick time, vacations, and days off, a police department must hire approximately 10 additional police officers to be able to add 1 police officer to every patrol shift, 7 days a week, 365 days a year. Thus, a city would need to hire 100 police officers to place 10 additional officers on every patrol shift 7 days a week, 365 days a year. Despite the costs, research suggests police–citizen ratios have little, if any, direct impact on crime rates. As noted earlier, managerial effectiveness, competency of officers, policing methods, and technology all appear to be factors in how the police affect crime. Accordingly, how the police are used and what they do are probably more important than adding a limited number of new officers to a department.

**Resource Allocation.**  Traditionally, police resources have been allocated equally over a 24-hour time period of three 8-hour shifts: the day shift, 8 am to 4 pm; the evening or swing shift, 4 pm to midnight; and the graveyard shift, midnight to 8 am. During these shifts, officers patrol geographic areas of approximately equal size. Of course, such an allocation method does not account for the fact that police calls vary by time of day, day of the week, area of the community, and even time of year.

Because the workload distribution is not equal across periods, days, or patrol areas, the equal allocation of police resources would mean that some officers were being overused (some would say overworked) whereas others were being underused. Such an arrangement presents operational problems not only in attempting to respond to calls for service, but also in not being able to perform directed or preventive patrol duties. Underused officers are likely to become bored and unmotivated, while overworked officers are likely to become fatigued and stressed. Accordingly, allocation plans should be based on need rather than resource equalization.

The two most important variables for determining allocation in these need-based plans are location and time. Knowing the location of problems assists departments in dividing up a community into geographic areas (i.e., *beats,* sectors or districts) of approximately equal workload. Time of occurrence is critical, because it determines how officers will be grouped into working periods, or *shifts.* As a general rule, the greater the number of problems or calls for service, the *smaller* the beat size should be. The time it takes to service a call is also important, since the resource being allocated is a skilled officer's time, which must be managed as effectively as possible. Once data on these variables have been collected and analyzed, beat boundaries, number of officers, and shift times are determined. Because of population shifts and changes in demand for service, it is important that departments continually re-evaluate patrol beat boundaries and assignment of personnel.

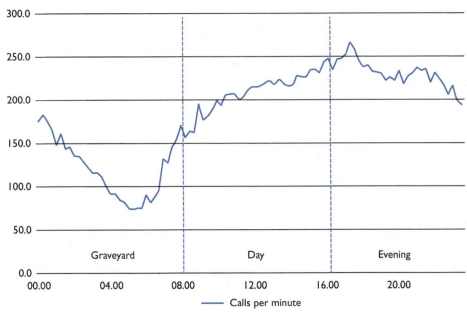

**FIGURE 7.1**  **Average Number of Dispatched Calls for Service by Time of Day (2015).**

*SOURCE*: Kansas City (MO) Police Department, Calls for Service Data, January 1–December 31, 2015.

Figure 7.1, showing the Kansas City, Missouri, Police Department's dispatched calls for service by time of day, indicates the evening shift has the greatest number of calls, with approximately 45 percent, followed by the day shift, with approximately 35 percent, and the graveyard shift with approximately 20 percent. Figure 7.1 further depicts the wide variation of calls concerning the time of day. Because of such wide variation of calls by time of day, departments often develop an overlapping shift to cover the increased workload; for instance, in Figure 7.1, such a shift might overlap the evening and graveyard shifts from approximately 2 pm to 10 pm, when the workload for calls is the highest.

To overcome the inherent problems in the equal time-allocation of resources, many medium-size and large departments have adopted alternate scheduling, such as a 4-10 or 12-4 plan; smaller departments generally do not have adequate personnel to utilize this schedule. With a 4-10 plan, for example, officers work four days a week, 10 hours per day, with three days off in a row. Officers tend to like the 4-10 plan because it allows increased leisure time, and the department gains increased coverage because of overlapping shifts. However, there may be fatigue problems with such a compacted schedule. Chapter 13 includes a discussion of the research on shift schedules and officer fatigue.

The development of computerized crime analysis and, more recently, computerized mapping allows the police to more precisely identify patterns of crime and disorder. This increased precision allows **field operations** to be directed to primary crime areas at primary crime times. Directing what officers do rather than allowing uncommitted random patrol time became increasingly popular after the Kansas City Preventive Patrol Experiment, discussed in Chapter 4. These new computerized crime-analysis techniques allow a variety of resource allocation strategies adapted to the spatial and temporal distributions of specific types of crime. These types of place-based approaches have become increasingly popular and sophisticated. They are discussed in detail in Chapter 8.

### Proactive Arrests and Crackdowns

**Proactive arrests**, which are initiated by the police, focus on a narrow set of high-risk targets. The theory is that a high certainty of arrest for a narrowly defined set of offenses or offenders will have a greater deterrent effect than will a low certainty of arrest for a broad range of targets (Sherman 1997). One of the most widespread developments in the use of proactive arrests in the mid-1980s was the use of police crackdowns. **Crackdowns** can be defined as an *intensive, short-term increase* in officer presence and arrests for specific types of offenses or for all offenses in specific areas. Drunk driving, public drug markets, street-walking prostitutes, domestic violence, illegal parking, and even unsafe bicycle riding have all been targets for publicly announced crackdowns (Sherman 1990a). The theory behind this approach is that the use of such crackdowns makes the risks of apprehension far more uncertain than in any fixed level of police-patrol activity.

One of the early reviews of crackdowns covered 18 case studies of various target problems and attempted to analyze what is known to date regarding crackdowns (Sherman 1990b). The evidence appears to support the notion of an initial deterrent effect on some offenses, as well as support for the notion of *residual deterrence*; that is, some crime reduction continues even after the crackdown has ended. Interestingly, the case studies revealed that short-term crackdowns suffered less from *deterrence decay* (i.e., a lessening of the crime deterrent effect) than did longer-term crackdowns. This suggests that the use of crackdowns might be more effective if they are limited in duration and rotated across crime targets or target areas. With respect to deterrence decay, the cost-effectiveness of crackdown strategies should also be evaluated. For example, an experimental study of raids on crack houses (Sherman and Rogan 1995) found that although crime on the block dropped sharply after the raid, the deterrent effect decayed after only seven days. Because of the labor-intensive nature of drug crackdowns, the strategy does not appear to be cost-effective in the long run.

Operation Safe Streets (Lawton, Taylor, and Luongo 2005) in Philadelphia stationed officers at 214 of the highest drug activity locations in the city 24 hours a day, 7 days a week. Crime data were compared for approximately 30 months before the intervention and 4 months after; the results revealed significant impacts on both violent and drug crimes within one-tenth of a mile of the target sites. However, because of the increased costs for additional patrol coverage (up to a half million dollars a week in overtime), program tactics had to be shifted to a single officer patrolling multiple high-crime areas (Moran 2002). Lawton et al. (2005) concluded that although crackdowns appear to be effective, they are rarely sustainable and thus are not long-term solutions because of high costs. The goal in the future would be "to engineer more cost-effective crackdowns, which can be sustained over time" (Lawton et al. 2005, 449).

## Police Pursuits

A long-standing controversy in police field operations is the issue of police pursuits. A **police pursuit** is an event in which a suspect attempts to flee from police, typically to avoid arrest. Police can chase suspects either on foot or by motor vehicle. Estimates on the number of police pursuits yearly run as high as 50,000, with the number of injuries they cause at approximately 20,000 (Charles, Falcone, and Wells 1992). A national survey of some 436 police departments (Alpert 1997), combined with case studies of approximately 1,250 pursuits in three departments (Metro-Dade, Miami; Omaha, Nebraska; and Aiken County, South Carolina), found that most pursuits are initiated for traffic violations: in Miami, 45 percent (448), in Omaha, 51 percent (112), and in Aiken County, 36 percent (5). A large percentage of pursuits, however, were also initiated for felonies: in Miami, 35 percent (344), in Omaha, 40 percent (89), and in Aiken County, 43 percent (6).

In addition, the survey indicated that 41 percent of the chases in Miami ended in personal injury (428) and 20 percent ended in property damage (213); in Omaha, 14 percent ended in personal injury (31) and 40 percent in property damage (91); in Aiken County, 12 percent ended in personal injury (2) and 24 percent in property damage (4). Arrests were made in 75 percent of the chases in Miami (784), 52 percent in Omaha (118), and 82 percent in Aiken County (14). Separate studies revealed that pursuits led to deaths of at least one person in 0.7 percent of all chases (a little less than 1 in 100 chases) in the Miami area (Alpert and Dunham 1988) and 0.2 percent in Minnesota (Alpert and Fridell 1992). Moreover, Alpert and Fridell (1992) suggest that a vehicle pursuit is at least as dangerous to the public as the use of a firearm.

These numbers are significant and suggest that the police must pay careful attention to the development of proper policy, training, and enforcement of guidelines. In this regard, Alpert's (1997) survey revealed that although 91 percent of the responding departments had written policies governing pursuits (meaning nearly 10 percent did not), many of them were implemented in the 1970s. Forty-eight percent of the departments reported having modified their pursuit policy within the past two years, with most (87 percent) making the policies more restrictive. The strong effects of policy changes were evident in the findings from both the Metro-Dade and the Omaha departments.

In 1992, Metro-Dade adopted a *violent felony-only* pursuit policy, and the number of pursuits decreased by 82 percent (from 279 to 51) the following year. In 1993, Omaha changed to a more permissive policy, allowing pursuits for offenses that were previously prohibited, and pursuits increased more than 600 percent the following year (from 17 to 122). In a follow-up study analyzing 1,049 pursuit-driving reports over a four-year period from the Metro-Dade Police Department, Alpert and Madden (1999) discovered that the more police cars that were involved, the more likely the pursuit was to result in a dangerous crash. Furthermore, the odds of injury increased at higher speeds, at night, and in commercial rather than residential areas.

A Bureau of Justice Statistics national survey (Hickman and Reaves 2003) found that nearly all (93 percent) local police departments had a written policy on pursuit driving. Specifically, 57 percent had a *restrictive policy* (i.e., based on criteria such as offense type or maximum speed); 27 percent had a *judgmental policy*, leaving the decision to the officer's discretion; and 5 percent *discouraged* all vehicle pursuits.

In addition, in Alpert's survey (1997), most departments reported that routine follow-ups to pursuits were mandated (89 percent). Most also indicated that they were either informal supervisory reviews (33 percent) or incident reports prepared by pursuing officers (47 percent). With respect to training, although 60 percent of the departments reported providing entry-level driver training at their academies, virtually all training focused on the mechanics of defensive and pursuit driving rather than on questions of when or why to pursue. Based on these findings, Alpert (1997) suggests that state and local police departments consider the following approaches:

1. Create and maintain systems to collect information on pursuit driving.

2. Review and update pursuit policies.

3. Evaluate the need for pursuit-specific training.

4. Support written policies with training and supervision.

5. Require that officers justify their actions or have a supervisor evaluate the pursuit (i.e., after-action reports and meaningful discipline for problem pursuits).

Alpert (1997) concluded that a balance must exist between the public's safety and the need to enforce the law, and that an appropriate policy balancing these perspectives would

## VOICES FROM THE FIELD

### Charles Fitzgerald
*Assistant Chief, Detroit Police Department*

The continued use of vehicular pursuits by law enforcement to stop a fleeing suspect has been studied and modified many times over the past two decades. The risks associated with vehicular pursuits have continued to escalate, and law enforcement agencies are making the criteria used to determine whether to chase or not more and more inflexible. When engaging in a police pursuit, many factors must be considered by the officer before even beginning the pursuit: the seriousness of offense, time of day, road conditions, population of area, weather conditions, speed of travel, and many other factors. With so many factors for officers to consider during a police pursuit, police organizations have made changes to their vehicular police pursuit policies to make them more stringent. High-speed police pursuits have resulted in numerous fatalities across the country, not only of the suspect(s) being pursued but also of innocent bystanders. The risk of an accident, and the consequences of an accident, resulting from a police pursuit should outweigh the professed need to maintain public order for minor violations, and only the most serious violations should be considered to initiate a police pursuit.

In June 2015, officers from the Detroit Police Department were attempting to pull over a Chevy Camaro for speeding. The officers believed the suspect was in possession of a weapon and were attempting to get the vehicle to stop when the vehicle jumped a curb on the city's east side and struck five small children playing in front of their house. Two of the children (ages 3 and 6) died instantly, while the other three children suffered serious injuries. The suspect was arrested at the scene, but no weapon was ever located in the vehicle. At time of this accident, officers were only allowed to pursue a vehicle if they had probable cause to believe the person driving the vehicle (or a passenger) has committed or was in the commission of felony crime. Possession of a weapon is a felony in Michigan, but when no weapon was found in the vehicle or at the crash site, the officer's story was heavily scrutinized for suspicion of fabricating their observations of the weapon in order to engage and continue their pursuit. This incident started the first of many manual revisions for vehicle pursuits in Detroit.

In October 2017, two Detroit Police Officers gave chase to a Pontiac Grand Prix in the early evening hours on mere suspicion the vehicle was stolen. The 19-year-old man behind the wheel drove off at a high rate of speed to avoid apprehension. He struck another vehicle that was proceeding through an intersection with the right of way. The 19-year-old died in the accident, and the other motorist suffered serious (but not life-threatening) injuries. The vehicle was later determined to be stolen. The vehicle pursuit policy in Detroit was once again revised to add the language that officers must have reasonable suspicion the subject in the fleeing motor vehicle committed a *violent* felony. Crimes such as stolen vehicle, possession of a weapon, or felony drug charges no longer are permissible to justify a police vehicle pursuit.

The sad and unfortunate truth is I can list plenty of other accidents that started with a police pursuit and ended in a fatality. Some of the accidents killed the driver of the fleeing vehicle, but many others killed an innocent victim/bystander. Police policies have changed over the years to become more rigorous about when an officer may give chase to a fleeing vehicle. Policies can become stricter, but many of them still leave wiggle room for an officer's interpretation of the policy. Officers argue that without the ability to pursue those who break the law, they will be unable to maintain law and order in their community. The community argues that citizens are being killed by overzealous officers who should exercise more care and control of the situation to safeguard uninvolved citizens. The policy in Detroit has changed three times since 2014, and while it appears to be stringent enough, it still hasn't deterred vehicle chases where the officer should have erred on the side of caution.

*limit chases* to the pursuit of *violent felons.* In addition, Alpert believes that officers need more training and direction through policy to know when they can and cannot pursue. Finally, he suggests that pursuit policies should be similar to shooting policies, in which it has become reasonably clear when one can and cannot fire a weapon. In "Voices from the Field," Assistant Chief Charles Fitzgerald discusses the changes in pursuit policy he has witnessed in Detroit.

Foot pursuits of suspects have received relatively little attention compared to vehicle pursuits; however, Dunham et al.'s (1998) study indicates approximately one-third (30 percent) of the vehicle pursuits ended when the suspect stopped and either ran on foot or gave up. And as an examination of assaults on officers (Pinizzotto, Davis, and Miller 1997) indicates, a significant number of officers assaulted during foot pursuits had no plan of action other than arresting the suspect. However, one department in Collingswood, New Jersey, developed a foot-pursuit policy as a result of an annual safety committee review indicating that several officers had been injured during foot chases (Bohrer, Davis, and Garrity 2000). Subsequently, the department established restrictions delineating when officers should not conduct foot pursuits, a review procedure for compliance with foot-pursuit policy, and twice-yearly foot-pursuit training coinciding with use-of-force training and the firearms requalification process. Within two years after the new policies were established, significant changes in how officers handled foot pursuits were noted—especially with respect to improved communications and using a team concept to set up a perimeter area rather than simply chasing fleeing suspects—which has led to fewer injuries. See Inside Policing 7.1 for an article on pursuit policies and practices.

## The Investigative Function

*Investigators* or *detectives* (the terms can be used interchangeably) are specialists who respond to crimes serious enough to warrant an investigation. The primary goal of criminal investigation is to increase the number of arrests for crimes that are prosecutable and will result in a conviction. As byproducts of this goal, detectives recover stolen property and produce information that may be useful in solving other crimes, often through the development and manipulation of informants (Cawley, Miron, and Araujo 1977; Forst 1982;

---

**INSIDE POLICING 7.1** | **To Chase or Not to Chase**

This article provides a balanced discussion of police pursuit policies and practices. According to a 2015 analysis, chases account for over 300 deaths per year in the United States, nearly half being bystanders or passengers. Many agencies have adopted stricter guidelines, limiting pursuits except in serious violent crime cases and putting decisions in the hands of supervisors. But other agencies continue to pursue and give officers discretion, not wanting offenders to believe that it's easy to escape.

**Discussion Question:** Balancing the risk of injury against allowing people to flee from the police, what type of policy would you create for vehicle pursuits?

*SOURCE: Modern Policing* blog, June 30, 2018, https://gcordner.wordpress.com/2018/06/30/to-chase-or-not-to-chase/.

Waegel 1982; Wycoff 1982). As discussed previously, crime investigation responsibilities are usually specialized, especially in medium-size to large police departments. The most common specialization is to have separate detective units for crimes against persons (e.g., homicide, robbery and assault, sex crimes, vice, and narcotics) and crimes against property (e.g., arson, auto theft and burglary, and larceny; Greenwood and Petersilia 1975). Many departments today also have specialized detective units for juveniles, gangs, intelligence, arson, and computer and bias crimes.

Police departments with 100 or more officers allocate, on average, 27 percent of their personnel to detective and investigative function, while smaller agencies assign 13 percent on average (Prince, Lum, and Koper 2021). The criteria most often used to determine a department's needs for investigative personnel include whether detectives work in pairs or alone; the extent of patrol participation in investigations; level of training, experience, and competency of the investigators; and the technological assistance available.

Patrol officers conduct the initial or **preliminary investigation**, which is generally for the purposes of establishing that a crime has been committed and for protecting the scene of the crime from those not involved in the investigation. Once this has been done, detectives generally conduct a **follow-up investigation** and develop the case. In some jurisdictions, the development phase involves working with the prosecuting attorney to prepare a case for trial; in others, this phase is the responsibility of investigators employed by the prosecuting attorney's office.

The basic responsibilities of the detective are (1) determine whether a crime has been committed, (2) identify the perpetrator, (3) apprehend the perpetrator, and (4) provide evidence to support a conviction in court. Police consider a case *solved* if the first three objectives are successfully attained. Other outcomes, such as recovering stolen property, deterring criminal behavior, and satisfying crime victims, may also be part of the process (Brandl 2002). The final phase may or may not involve a prosecution or a conviction. Investigations can be terminated if the police determine that no crime has been committed, if they have insufficient evidence to proceed, or if there is no longer a suspect available (e.g., a murder-suicide).

## Historical Development

Kuykendall (1986) analyzed the historical role of the police detective, which in the mid-1850s to early 1900s was more like a "secretive rogue" whose methods were as unscrupulous as those of the private detectives preceding them. Although some of their exploits were romanticized, the detectives were mostly inefficient and corrupt. They often had a close association with criminals, used and manipulated stool pigeons (i.e., snitches), and even had "deadlines" that established areas of a city in which detectives and criminals agreed that crime could be committed. Nineteenth- and early twentieth-century detectives believed that their work should be essentially clandestine. They were considered members of a secret service whose identity should remain unknown lest the criminal become wary and flee. Some detectives wore disguises, submitted court testimony in writing, and even used masks when looking at suspects. Although they did investigate crimes, detectives functioned primarily as a nonuniformed patrol force. They tended to go where persons congregated (e.g., beer gardens and steamboat docks) to look for pickpockets, gamblers, and troublemakers.

Just as police reformers of the early twentieth century hoped to replace the neighbor patrol officer with the soldier crime-fighter, they also hoped to replace secretive rogues with scientific criminal investigators. The detectives' relationships with criminals and snitches were criticized as corrupting and undesirable for a professional police officer. Furthermore, it was believed that the use of science would make such relationships unnecessary. The reformers stressed the importance of the detective as a perceptive, rational analyst, much like Sherlock Holmes. By the 1920s and 1930s, detectives were mostly investigating crimes after the fact rather than using clandestine tactics. Although many were ill prepared to utilize the newly developed scientific methods, this was less of a problem than it first appeared, because the use of scientific evidence proved to be of value in only a few cases and rarely aided the police in identifying suspects. Consequently, the information that became most important in making arrests and ensuring successful prosecutions was derived from witnesses, informers, and suspects. As detectives stopped being secretive rogues, they gradually became inquisitors, who often coerced information from suspects to solve cases.

By the 1960s, important changes in criminal procedural laws (e.g., search and seizure, evidence, and Miranda warnings), known as the *due process revolution*, and the continuing emphasis on efficiency in police departments had created a detective who was essentially a bureaucrat, or case processor. Although some detectives continued to work undercover, the majority were reactive and infrequently identified suspects who were not obvious. These detectives spent a greater proportion of their time processing information and coordinating with other criminal justice agencies than they did looking for suspects.

All the elements of the detective's role described previously are present to some degree today. Some detectives are secretive, some are skillful in obtaining confessions without coercion, and all must invest considerable time in processing information. Whereas the emergence of the legalistic model of policing tended to produce a detective who was more bureaucrat than sleuth, subsequent approaches and models of policing (e.g., team and community) tend to have a broader view of the detective's role. As a result of crime-analysis techniques, the detective has continued to evolve, becoming somewhat less reactive (since the 1960s) and more proactive, with an emphasis on criminals rather than on crimes. Of course, this is not a new role for the detective, and thus far, police departments have been able to make these changes without the extensive corruption problems historically associated with them (Kuykendall 1986).

Detectives today have multifaceted roles: they work undercover; they may operate sting programs; they may be involved in career-criminal programs, in breaking up organized gang activity, in Crime Gun Intelligence Centers, and in other intelligence-gathering operations. Detectives involved in such activities, however, constitute a relatively small percentage of those involved in investigative work, with the substantial majority functioning more as bureaucrats than as sleuths. Characterizing the detective as a bureaucrat is not intended to demean the role, but rather to suggest the perspective from which most detectives should be viewed. Detectives spend a considerable amount of their time talking to witnesses, suspects, and victims and completing the necessary paperwork to prepare cases for prosecutors. They are primarily information processors, not the Sherlock Holmes or Dirty "Make My Day" Harry of fiction.

### Terrorism and Investigation

Just as patrol work may need to change in response to the contemporary threat of terrorism, so too may investigative work. De Guzman (2002) suggests two potential areas of concern regarding investigation and terrorism. First, as noted previously, police investigation has become primarily reactive in nature; it may need to again become more proactive.

This means that evidence of a crime should not only be connected to a certain suspect but also examined for some connection to possible terrorist activity. This would be especially true if there were evidence that seemed not to fit with the nature of the crime committed; that is, could there be other motives attached to the offense under investigation? Second, for the most part, investigation remains highly individualized and disjointed from the rest of the department. Investigative units themselves tend to be highly fragmented. And although COP, along with its push for greater internal coordination, is being implemented in many departments, investigation remains in general untouched by the process. These conditions hamper the ability to solve cases and will be especially troublesome in cases involving terrorism. Consequently, it seems prudent for investigative units to integrate themselves with the rest of the department and redirect their functional focus, especially with respect to COP practices.

## Selected Research on Investigative Operations

Several important investigative issues are discussed in this section, including Crime Gun Intelligence Centers, advances in physical evidence, bias/hate crimes, and detective–patrol relationships.

### Crime Gun Intelligence Centers

An evolving investigative strategy involves the use of **Crime Gun Intelligence Centers** (CGICs). Supported by the Bureau of Alcohol, Tobacco, Firearms and Explosives (ATF), CGICs are collaborative efforts to collect, manage, and analyze crime gun violence data in a timely manner. Firearm violence, like many other types of criminal activity, tends to be concentrated among small numbers of people, and similarly, guns used during crimes are concentrated. In other words, very few guns are used in criminal activity, and when a crime gun is used, it is likely to be used across multiple crimes. One challenge associated with investigating and preventing gun crimes is identifying when and whether gun crimes are connected to each other and, when connections are found, using this information to enhance investigations and prevention strategies (Police Executive Research Forum 2017).

CGICs are positioned to enhance crime gun investigations and prevention in two ways. First, CGICs utilize two technology systems maintained by the ATF. The National Integrated Ballistic Information Network (NIBIN) is a database managed by the ATF that records and identifies ballistic evidence that can aid in connecting criminal events. The NIBIN utilizes information from spent shells and spent bullets. Because each firearm creates a unique marker on a shell where the firing pin strikes, it is possible to analyze these markings to determine whether shells recovered at different crime scenes were fired from the same gun. An additional, related database is eTrace. Investigators submit information (including "test fires") from firearms recovered to the National Tracing Center at the ATF, and when coupled with the NIBIN, these databases create a national clearinghouse of firearms and ballistics used in gun crimes (King et al. 2013; Police Executive Research Forum 2017). Second, CGICs rely on partnerships between agencies, particularly local police and the ATF, but also can include local and federal prosecutors and other state and federal law enforcement agencies. Partnerships are important, because information collected and uploaded to the NIBIN and eTrace comes from a variety of different sources and different jurisdictions. Partnerships encourage intelligence sharing as well as collaboration in investigations (Police Executive Research Forum 2017). CGICs are best thought of as an approach that can be coupled with other innovations, including focused deterrence, problem-oriented policing, and hot-spots policing (these strategies are discussed further in Chapter 8).

The CGIC approach is positioned to significantly contribute to crime gun investigations by linking otherwise random crimes, which can contribute to identifying serial shooters and clearing gun crime. To accomplish this, it is necessary for police to engage in comprehensive collection of evidence (meaning all ballistic information must be collected and analyzed through the NIBIN); the information must be collected and analyzed in a timely manner; follow up with investigators is important to identify shooters quickly; and an effective feedback loop is needed with analysts, officers on the street, investigators, lab technicians, prosecutorial partners, and other police departments (Police Executive Research Forum 2017). The CGIC concept has a lot of moving parts and relies on a number of different groups to be successful. Although there are only a few studies on the topic, early results on CGIC processes are promising. There is evidence indicating that the CGIC structure increases the number of leads or connections between shootings (Koper, Vovak, and Cowell 2019; Mei et al. 2019; Flippin, Katz, and King 2022), which provides detectives with more actionable intelligence, and that CGICs significantly reduce the time associated with analyzing evidence (Novak and King 2020; Katz et al. 2021). The research evidence strongly suggests that processes, inputs, and activities associated with the CGIC model were collectively enhanced, but whether this improves public safety is still unknown (Koper et al. 2019; Katz et al. 2021; Flippin et al. 2022).

### Advances in Physical Evidence: The Automated Fingerprint Identification System and DNA

Two developments in physical evidence are likely to have a significant impact on investigative effectiveness. These are the automated fingerprint identification system (AFIS) and the use of DNA evidence in criminal investigations.

The AFIS allows fingerprints recovered at a crime scene to be compared with thousands of other prints on file in a department's computer system. The computer will match fingerprints that are close to those found at the scene, and a suspect can be identified. Modern AFIS programs search hundreds of thousands of scanned prints and identify possible matches in minutes (Brandl 2008). The flagged prints can then be checked by a fingerprint examiner to see whether they match. Unfortunately, many of these systems are local and often do not include prints from other jurisdictions. To overcome the limitations of local AFIS systems, the FBI maintains the Next Generation Identification System, which includes the Advanced Fingerprint Identification Technology, among other biometric identification services to law enforcement nationwide (https://le.fbi.gov/science-and-lab-resources/biometrics-and-fingerprints/biometrics/next-generation-identification-ngi).

The use of DNA evidence in criminal investigations is a more recent development, and one that may prove more influential than fingerprints. *DNA testing* allows the comparison of human cell materials found at a crime scene (usually blood, semen, or hair) in an attempt to find a match between two samples. Since no two individuals, except for identical twins, have the same DNA makeup, it is essentially irrefutable evidence—that is, if it is properly collected, stored, and analyzed (serious mistakes in all of these areas have occurred). As with fingerprint identification, it used to be that the police first needed to identify a suspect to make a match; however, technology has allowed the development of DNA banks through which comparison matches can be made, thus potentially saving the police enormous amounts of time in investigative follow-ups. The FBI currently operates a DNA bank for the purpose of identifying suspects in cases. The Combined DNA Index System (CODIS) includes profiles on more than 20 million offenders (FBI 2021). Using databases such as CODIS, DNA evidence may prove useful to police in investigations where no suspect has been identified, and is not likely to be identified, through traditional means—sometimes referred to as no-suspect cases.

Advances in forensic techniques have the potential to improve the ability of police to solve some crimes. However, unlike television portrayals, these techniques have not radically transformed the work of detectives. A study of homicide investigations between 1996 and 2003 in Manhattan revealed that DNA evidence was used in only 6.7 percent of prearrest homicide investigations. In fact, it was not collected in 54.5 percent of investigations and was collected and submitted but not available before the case was cleared in 38.8 percent of cases. According to Schroeder and White (2009, 326), "the results clearly suggest that DNA evidence was largely irrelevant to prearrest homicide investigations conducted by the NYPD during the study period." However, they also noted that the collection of DNA from crimes increased between 1996 and 2003.

Although it was still not used in most cases, the researchers suggested that the increased collection of DNA may eventually translate into greater use of the evidence to solve crimes. A review of the research on forensic evidence and criminal justice case processing concluded that the potential impact of forensic evidence is constrained by its limited collection and examination (Peterson et al. 2013). A national survey of state and local law enforcement agencies revealed that in approximately 7.3 percent of unsolved rape cases and 5.6 percent of unsolved homicides, law enforcement agencies obtained DNA forensic evidence related to the crime but did not send it to a laboratory for testing (Strom and Hickman 2010). In an estimated 12,548 unsolved homicide and rape cases, agencies had untested DNA evidence. The nation's largest police departments accounted for the majority of untested evidence in unsolved cases.

A number of barriers may limit the use of DNA in investigations. Police agencies may lack knowledge regarding the use and potential of DNA (Pratt et al. 2006; Schroeder and White 2009; Strom and Hickman 2010). Strom and Hickman (2010), for example, found that the most common reason for not submitting forensic evidence for analysis was the lack of a suspect. Yet as noted earlier, forensic databases such as CODIS provide a means of checking samples against all DNA profiles in a database. Ideally, if a match is found, law enforcement will be provided information on the suspect (Beaver 2010). Another barrier involves the backlog at many crime laboratories. The time it takes for DNA results to be returned to police, in part because of case backlogs at many crime laboratories, may discourage police from sending DNA evidence for testing (Pratt et al. 2006; Schroeder and White 2009). In addition, some crime laboratories prioritize cases and place no-suspect cases lower on the priority list.

In addition to criminal justice system constraints, forensic evidence has inherent limitations to solve crime. Many crimes involve no physical evidence of any kind, let alone DNA or fingerprints (Cole 2010). Even in cases where DNA or fingerprints are found, the perpetrator's profile or fingerprints may not be in a database. And in many cases, detectives may not need DNA evidence to make an arrest and clear a case. In fact, DNA evidence is sometimes collected and sent for testing while detectives, who may be under pressure to solve a case, continue with their investigation rather than wait on results, thus collecting DNA for prosecutors more so than for their own investigations. Traditionally, physical evidence was used to confirm a known suspect rather than to identify an unknown person (Bayley 1994). It may take time for police agencies to view forensic evidence as a means of solving cases rather than as a means of confirming their work.

As mentioned, however, DNA evidence has not significantly changed detective work, and most crimes are solved through the identification of a suspect by witnesses or victims. Moreover, in a democracy, it is important to keep in mind that although the development of fingerprint and DNA banks is a significant breakthrough, we must be careful not to interfere with individual rights (i.e., the Fourth and Fifth Amendments) when collecting samples for these banks. Nonetheless, DNA may prove increasingly valuable in solving no-suspect cases, particularly as DNA databases become more extensive and police expand their use of DNA evidence. Research, however, suggests that many law enforcement agencies are unaware of the potential benefits of DNA testing or the testing resources available to them. Indeed, Pratt et al. (2006) concluded that law enforcement agencies view DNA as useful to prosecutors but not detectives. Schroeder and White (2009, 338) suggest that "the value of DNA may be overestimated for police investigations but underestimated for later stages of the adjudication process." The future of DNA evidence in solving crimes may rest on issues related to funding, knowledge among police, agency policies, and the inherent limitations of physical evidence. Strom and Hickman (2010) suggest police need improved training to encourage the use of forensic testing for investigation, including in no-suspect cases.

## Bias/Hate Crime Programs

Hate crimes motivated by bias against particular groups of people are a continuing concern for police. Members of minority groups that are targets of criminal activity because of their race, ethnicity, or sexual orientation are potential victims of bias crimes.

Unfortunately, we do not have accurate official statistics regarding these types of crimes, despite widespread reporting by advocacy groups (Lantz, Gladfeiter, and Ruback 2017). If police departments are to adequately respond to these crimes, they need a mechanism to identify and record these crimes and develop specific responses. The training of officers about the possibility of such hate crimes is an important first step. When such crimes occur, the department must make a concerted response involving investigation, traditional patrol, and communication with the group that has been the target of the crime.

Research suggests that bias crimes reported to the police are significantly less likely to result in a police report or arrest than other crimes (Lantz et al 2017). One study on bias crimes (Garofalo and Martin 1995) found that bias crime clearances were higher in departments where police responses to these crimes emphasized specialized investigations and arrest. It was further suggested that departments provide some type of motivation for inducing patrol officers to recognize and report bias crime when they encounter it. Unfortunately, most law enforcement officers receive minimal training on bias crimes or bias crime investigation, and most departments do not have bias crime units (Lantz et al. 2017). A study of 19 departments in the central United States by Walker and Katz (1995) found that 4 (25 percent) had separate bias-crime units with written procedures for handling bias crimes. Six (37.5 percent) of the departments did not have a separate bias-crime unit, but either designated specific officers in an investigative unit to handle bias crimes or had special policies and procedures that all officers would follow, and another six (37.5 percent) had neither a special unit nor special procedures. Of the 12 departments that did not have a special bias-crime unit, 8 provided no special training regarding hate crimes. More recently, the Bureau of Justice Statistics survey of local police departments found that about 38 percent of agencies with 100 or more sworn officers had personnel designated at least part-time to address bias/hate crime issues, although only 10 percent had personnel assigned full-time (Reaves 2015). Clearly, more effort must be exerted in this area of law enforcement, especially with respect to developing specialized investigative units or training personnel. Inside Policing 7.2 provides some examples of hate crime investigations and prosecutions.

## Detective–Patrol Relationships

The relationship in a police department between detectives and patrol officers is both extremely important and a source of potential conflict. This potential conflict must be addressed by the department, because effective communication between the two is vital to

---

**INSIDE POLICING 7.2** | **Investigating Hate Crimes**

This article reports several examples of successful investigation and prosecution of hate crimes. Reporting and documentation of hate crime is inconsistent around the country and federal prosecution is rare, so local police action is usually the key to success or failure. One reason that bias crimes often get overlooked is the element of the offender's motivation: "Police officers, for most crimes, are not rigorously trained to look at motive. They apprehend; they take reports; they do some investigation."

SOURCE: *Modern Policing* blog, August 26, 2018. https://gcordner.wordpress.com/2018/08/26/investigating-hate-crimes/

the success of many investigations. Investigators must make an effort to develop and maintain a good rapport with patrol officers. This relationship should be based on frequent personal contacts, acknowledgment of patrol officers' contribution to investigations, seeking out patrol officer advice when appropriate, and keeping officers informed as to the status of cases.

One of the major problems that continues to exist in many departments is related to the different statuses of detectives and patrol officers. Investigators tend to dress in civilian clothes, are often perceived to have more status in the department, and may even be of a higher rank or receive a higher salary. There are several ways to address this problem. One possible solution relates to the basic structure of the department—that is, using a COP model, in which detectives and patrol personnel work together as a team. Another solution is creating a personnel system that gives equal status and financial rewards to patrol officers and investigators. Rotating personnel through various investigative slots, so that the position is not thought of as being "owned" by anyone, is also a constructive approach. The Cedar Rapids, Iowa, Police Department has eliminated the position of detective and instead selects qualified patrol officers to rotate into the investigative division as they would any other specialty. Police departments must also be alert to the manner in which detectives and patrol officers are treated. Patrol officers must not be given the impression that, when compared to investigators, they are second-class citizens (Bloch and Weidman 1975).

## Summary

The primary activities of police field operations include patrol (the backbone of policing) and investigative work. Research indicates that patrol activities related to law enforcement are more substantial than past research has shown, whereas detective work is primarily concerned with information processing rather than sleuthing. Patrol work is attempting to regain the neighborhood contextual knowledge that was lost during efforts to professionalize the police in the early 1960s and 1970s. Since the 1960s, as a result of crime-analysis techniques, investigative work has become more proactive, with an emphasis on criminals rather than on crimes. The majority of police officers are assigned to foot or automobile patrol. Resources for these activities are largely determined by intuition and comparison.

Selected research on patrol operations emphasizes the growing use of data in resource allocation decisions, whereas the research on investigative operations emphasizes new technologies and collaborative efforts (e.g., CGICs). Although research suggests that some patrol strategies are effective in reducing crime, they are also resource intensive, with crime reductions that decay after these interventions take place. Thus, agencies have continued to explore more sophisticated approaches, discussed in Chapter 8.

## Critical Thinking Questions

1. Describe the three primary functions of patrol work, and provide an example of each.

2. What major policies would you formulate for vehicle pursuits? For foot pursuits?

3. How might advances in forensic analysis change detective work?

4. What are the benefits and drawbacks of DNA databases?

# References

Alpert, G. P. 1997. *Police Pursuit: Policies and Training, May*. Washington, DC: National Institute of Justice.

Alpert, G. P., and Dunham, R. 1988. "Research on Police Pursuits: Applications for Law Enforcement." *American Journal of Police* 7: 123–131.

Alpert, G. P., and Fridell, L. 1992. *Police Vehicles and Firearms: Instruments of Deadly Force*. Prospect Heights, IL: Waveland.

Alpert, G. P., and Madden, T. J. 1999. "Toward the Development of a Pursuit Decision Calculus; Pursuit Benefits Versus Pursuit Costs." *Justice Research and Policy* 1: 23–41.

Andresen, M. A., and Lau, K. A. 2014. "An Evaluation of Police Foot Patrol in Lower Lonsdale, British Columbia." *Police Practice and Research* 15: 476–489.

Bayley, D. 1994. *Police for the Future*. New York: Oxford University Press.

Beaver, K. M. 2010. "The Promises and Pitfalls of Forensic Evidence in Unsolved Crimes." *Criminology & Public Policy* 9: 405–410.

Bloch, P. B., and Weidman, D. R. 1975. *Managing Criminal Investigations*. Washington, DC: US Government Printing Office.

Bohrer, S., Davis, E. F., and Garrity, T. J. 2000. "Establishing a Foot Pursuit Policy: Running into Danger." *FBI Law Enforcement Bulletin*. Washington, DC: Department of Justice.

Boydstun, J. E., Sherry, M. E., and Moelter, N. P. 1977. *Patrol Staffing in San Diego*. Washington, DC: Police Foundation.

Brandl, S. G. 2002. "Police: Criminal Investigations." In J. Dressler (ed.), *Encyclopedia of Crime & Justice*, pp. 1068–1073. New York: Thomson.

Brandl, S. G. 2008. *Criminal Investigation*, 2nd ed. Boston: Allyn & Bacon.

Cawley, D. F., Miron, H. J., and Araujo, W. J. 1977. *Managing Criminal Investigations: Trainer's Handbook*. Washington, DC: University Research Corporation.

Charles, M. T., Falcone, D. N., and Wells, E. 1992. *Police Pursuit in Pursuit of a Policy: The Pursuit Issue, Legal and Literature Review, and an Empirical Study*. Washington, DC: AAA Foundation for Traffic Safety.

Cole, S. A. 2010. "Forensic Identification Evidence: Utility Without Infallibility." *Criminology & Public Policy* 9: 375–379.

Crank, J. 1999. *Understanding Police Culture*. Cincinnati, OH: Anderson.

De Guzman, M. C. 2002. "The Changing Roles and Strategies of the Police in Time of Terror." *ACJS Today* 22(3): 8–13.

Dunham, R. G., Alpert, G. P., Kenney, D. J., and Cromwell, P. 1998. "High-Speed Pursuit." *Criminal Justice and Behavior* 25: 30–45.

Eith, C., and Durose, M. R. 2011. *Contacts Between Police and the Public, 2008*. Washington, DC: Bureau of Justice Statistics.

Federal Bureau of Investigation (FBI). 2021. *The FBI's Combined DNA Index System (CODIS) Hits Major Milestone*. Washington, DC: FBI National Press Office. https://www.fbi.gov/news/pressrel/press-releases/the-fbis-combined-dna-index-system-codis-hits-major-milestone.

Flippin, M. R., Katz, C. M., and King, W. R. 2022. Examining the impact of a crime gun intelligence center. *Journal of Forensic Sciences* 67: 543–549.

Forst, B. 1982. *Arrest Convictability as a Measure of Police Performance*. Washington, DC: US Government Printing Office.

Garofalo, J., and Martin, S. E. 1995. *Bias-Motivated Crimes: Their Characteristics and the Law Enforcement Response*. Carbondale: Southern Illinois University.

Greenwood, P., and Petersilia, J. 1975. *The Criminal Investigation Process*. Santa Monica, CA: RAND Corporation.

Hickman, M. J., and Reaves, B. A. 2003. *Local Police Departments, 2000.* Washington, DC: Bureau of Justice Statistics.

Katz, C. M., Flippin, M., Huff, J., King, W. R., and Ellefritz, J. 2021. *Evaluation of the Phoenix Crime Gun Intelligence Center: Final Report.* Center for Violence Prevention & Community Safety, Tempe, AZ: Arizona State University.

Kessler, D. A. 1985. "One- or Two-Officer Cars? A Perspective from Kansas City." *Journal of Criminal Justice* 13: 49–64.

King, W. R., Wells W., Katz C., Maguire E., and Frank J. 2013. *Opening the Black Box of NIBIN: A Descriptive Process and Outcome Evaluation of the Use of NIBIN and Its Effects on Criminal Investigations, Final Report.* Washington DC: National Institute of Justice.

Koper, C., Vovak, H., and Cowell, B. 2019. *Evaluation of the Milwaukee police department's crime gun intelligence center.* Arlington, VA: National Police Foundation.

Kuykendall, J. 1986. "The Municipal Police Detective: An Historical Analysis." *Criminology* 24: 175–201.

Lantz, B., Gladfelter, A. S. and Ruback, R. B. 2017. "Stereotypical Hate Crimes and Criminal Justice Processing: A Multi-Dataset Comparison of Bias Crime Arrest Patterns by Offender and Victim Race." *Justice Quarterly* 36(2): 193–224. https://doi.org/10.1080/07418825.2017.1399211

Lawton, B. A., Taylor, R. B., and Luongo, A. J. 2005. "Police Officers on Drug Corners in Philadelphia, Drug Crime, and Violent Crime: Intended, Diffusion, and Displacement Impacts." *Justice Quarterly* 22: 427–451.

Lee, Y., Eck, J. E., and Corsaro, N. 2016. "Conclusions from the History of Research into the Effects of Police Force Size on Crime–1969 through 2013: A Historical Systematic Review." *Journal of Experimental Criminology* 12: 431–451.

Mazerolle, L., Rogan, D., Frank, J., Famega, C., and Eck, J. E. 2002. "Managing Citizen Calls to the Police: The Impact of Baltimore's 3-1-1 Call System." *Criminology and Public Policy* 2: 97–124.

Mazerolle, L., Rogan, D., Frank, J., Famega, C., and Eck, J. E. 2005. "Managing Calls to the Police with 911/311 Systems." *National Institute of Justice Research for Practice.* Washington, DC: US Department of Justice.

Mei, V., Owusa, F., Quinney, S., Ravishankar, A., and Sebastian, D. 2019. *An Evaluation of Crime Gun Intelligence Center Improvements Implemented in Washington, DC, 2016–2019.* Washington, DC: The Lab @ DC. https://crimegunintelcenters.org/wp-content/uploads/2019/12/DC-CGIC-Final-Evaluation-Report_10.30.19.pdf

Moran, R. 2002. "City's Anti-Drug Effort May Be Cut Back. Operation Safe Streets Cost Phila. up to Half-Million Dollars a Week in Police Overtime." *The Philadelphia Inquirer*, June: A1.

Novak, K. J., Fox, A. M., Carr, C. M., McHale, J., and White, M. D. 2015. *Kansas City, Missouri Smart Policing Initiative: From Foot Patrol to Focused Deterrence.* Washington, DC: Bureau of Justice Assistance.

Novak, K. J., and King, W. R. 2020. *Evaluation of the Kansas City Crime Gun Intelligence Center—Final Report.* Washington, DC: Bureau of Justice Assistance.

Peterson, J. L., Hickman, M. J., Strom, K. J., and Johnson, D. J. 2013. "Effect of Forensic Evidence on Criminal Justice Case Processing." *Journal of Forensic Sciences* 58: 78–90.

Pinizzotto, A. J., Davis, E. F., and Miller, C. E., III. 1997. *In the Line of Fire: A Study of Selected Felonious Assaults on Law Enforcement Officers.* Washington, DC: Department of Justice.

Piza, E. L., and O'Hara, B. A. 2014. "Saturation Foot-Patrol in a High-Violence Area: A Quasi- Experimental Evaluation." *Justice Quarterly* 31: 693–718.

Police Executive Research Forum. 2017. *The "Crime Gun Intelligence Center" Model: Case Studies of the Denver, Milwaukee, and Chicago Approaches to Investigating Gun Crime.* Washington, DC: Police Executive Research Forum.

Police Foundation. 1981. *The Newark Foot Patrol Experiment.* Washington, DC: Police Foundation.

Pratt, T. C., Gaffney, M. J., Lovrich, N. P., and Johnson, C. L. 2006. "This Isn't CSI: Estimating the National Backlog of Forensic DNA Cases and the Barriers Associated with Case Processing." *Criminal Justice Policy Review* 17: 32–47.

President's Commission on Law Enforcement and Administration of Justice. 1967. *Task Report: The Police*. Washington, DC: US Government Printing Office.

Prince, H., Lum, C., and Koper, C.S. 2021. "Effective Police Investigative Practices: An Evidence-assessment of the Research." *Policing: An International Journal* 44 683–707.

Reaves, B. A. 2015. *Local Police Departments, 2013: Personnel, Policies, and Practices*. Washington, DC: Department of Justice.

Reaves, B. A., and Hickman, M. J. 2002. *Census of State and Local Law Enforcement Agencies, 2000*. Washington, DC: Department of Justice.

Schroeder, D. A., and White, M. D. 2009. "Exploring the Use of DNA Evidence in Homicide Investigations." *Police Quarterly* 12: 319–342.

Sherman, L. W. 1983. "Patrol Strategies for Police." In J. Q. Wilson (ed.), *Crime and Public Policy*, pp. 145–163. San Francisco: Institute for Contemporary Studies Press.

Sherman, L. W. 1990a. "Police Crackdowns." *National Institute of Justice Reports*. Washington, DC: National Institute of Justice.

Sherman, L. W. 1990b. "Police Crackdowns: Initial and Residual Deterrence." In M. Tonry and N. Morris (eds.), *Crime and Justice: A Review of Research*, pp. 1–48. Chicago: University of Chicago Press.

Sherman, L. W. 1997. "Policing for Crime Prevention." In L. W. Sherman, D. Gottfredson, D. MacKenzie, J. Eck, P. Reuter, and S. Bushway (eds.), *Preventing Crime: What Works, What Doesn't and What's Promising*, pp. 364–429. Washington, DC: Office of Justice Programs.

Sherman, L. W., and Rogan, D. P. 1995. "Deterrent Effects of Police Raids on Crack Houses: A Randomized, Controlled Experiment." *Justice Quarterly* 12: 755–781.

Sorg, E. T., Haberman, C. P., Ratcliffe, J. H., and Groff, E. R. 2013. "Foot Patrol in Violent Crime Hot Spots: The Longitudinal Impact of Deterrence and Post-treatment Effects of Displacement." *Criminology* 51: 65–102.

Stephens, D. W. 1996. "Community Problem-Oriented Policing: Measuring Impacts." In L. T. Hoover (ed.), *Quantifying Quality in Policing*, pp. 95–129. Washington, DC: Police Executive Research Forum.

Strom, K. J., and Hickman, M. J. 2010. "Unanalyzed Evidence in Law-Enforcement Agencies: A National Examination of Forensic Processing in Police Departments." *Criminology & Public Policy* 9: 381–404.

Trojanowicz, R. C. 1982. *An Evaluation of the Neighborhood Foot Patrol Program in Flint, Michigan*. East Lansing: National Neighborhood Foot Patrol Center, Michigan State University.

Trojanowicz, R. C., and Banas, D. W. 1985. *The Impact of Foot Patrol on Black and White Perceptions of Policing*. East Lansing: National Neighborhood Foot Patrol Center, Michigan State University.

Waegel, W. B. 1982. "Patterns of Police Investigation of Urban Crimes." *Journal of Police Science and Administration* 10: 452–465.

Walker, S. 1984. "'Broken Windows' and Fractured History: The Use and Misuse of History in Recent Police Patrol Analysis." *Justice Quarterly* 1: 57–90.

Walker, S., and Katz, C. M. 1995. "Less Than Meets the Eye: Police Department Bias-Crime Units." *American Journal of Police* 16: 29–48.

Wilson, C., and Brewer, N. 2001. "Working in Teams: Negative Effects on Organizational Performance in Policing." *Policing: An International Journal of Police Strategies and Management* 24: 115–127.

Wilson, O. W. 1950. *Police Administration*. New York: McGraw-Hill.

Wilson, O. W., and McLaren, R. C. 1977. *Police Administration*, 3rd ed. New York: McGraw-Hill.

Wycoff, M. A. 1982. "Evaluating the Crime Effectiveness of Municipal Police." In J. R. Greene (ed.), *Managing Police Work*, pp. 15–36. Thousand Oaks, CA: Sage.

## CHAPTER 8

# Innovations in Field Operations

## CHAPTER OUTLINE

## KEY TERMS

- accountability
- broken windows theory
- community-based approaches
- directed patrol
- focused deterrence
- formal social control
- general deterrence
- informal social control
- intelligence-led policing
- hot spots
- legitimacy
- person-based approaches
- place-based approaches
- predictive policing
- problem-based approaches
- procedural justice
- quality-of-life policing
- specific deterrence
- transparency

THIS CHAPTER BUILDS UPON Chapter 7's discussion of foundations in police field operations, including patrol and investigative functions. Recognizing the history and origins of various attempts to reduce crime and disorder while promoting public safety, this chapter picks up where that conversation left off by highlighting policing innovations from the latter part of the twentieth century and the beginning of the twenty-first century.

There is no consensus on how to define *innovation* (King 2000); however, we borrow the term "from Weisburd and Braga (2006), in that we recognize field operations by the police seemed to experience great change and diffusion over the past 30 years. This chapter also borrows heavily from the detailed discussions in Chapter 4 on evolving policing strategies, particularly community policing (COP) and problem-oriented policing (POP), but since those approaches are presented in detail elsewhere in this text, we will not go into sufficient depth here, preferring to place COP and POP into their appropriate context given other innovations presented. When possible, this chapter emphasizes the current state of understanding on the effectiveness and efficiency of policing approaches (National Research Council 2004; National Academies of Sciences, Engineering, and Medicine 2018).

The need to innovate field operations comes from various pressures, both internal and external, to the police. These pressures include the recognition that traditional and standard models have limited effectiveness. Traditional models emphasize reacting to crime; therefore, their crime prevention value is limited. There is also the perceived need to respond to the lingering issue of race and inequalities in criminal justice and crime, and ever-shrinking municipal budgets require police (like other public service entities) to rethink how to achieve the greatest return on investment (Bayley 1994; National Research Council 2004; Weisburd and Braga 2006). Throughout much of the twentieth century, the police have applied a one-size-fits-all approach to public safety—this "standard model" of policing is described at length in Chapter 7, and it will have limited impact due to its heavy reliance on law enforcement as a public safety tool and low level of focus (Weisburd and Eck 2004). In contrast, COP, POP, and the innovations described here utilize a range of tools to address crime and disorder and have a much greater focus— concentrating efforts on certain people, in certain places, at certain times, using a variety of interventions. Additionally, innovations are more likely to be guided by intelligence and local data that shape police interventions with the public and include information gathered from the public (treating citizens as partners in crime prevention rather than passive recipients of policing services). Yet the degree to which the police utilize diverse approaches, how or why they focus attention and resources, and the level of public involvement will vary by approach. Furthermore, innovations in practice may look very different from innovations in theory (or "textbook" policing innovations). This must also be kept in mind when making sweeping generalizations about the utility of some approaches versus others.

The National Academies of Sciences, Engineering, and Medicine (2018) identified broad approaches the police utilize to enhance public safety. **Community-based approaches** involve the community in identifying and defining crime and problems, and they leverage the public as "hidden allies" in crime prevention (Spelman and Eck 1989). We have previously used the term *community crime prevention* to describe this type of approach. Examples of community-based approaches include COP, procedural justice, and broken windows policing. **Problem-based approaches** attempt to understand and address underlying causes of crime and disorder, and to draw solutions to eliminate these underlying causes of crime. In this type of approach, crime and disorder are symptoms of larger social problems, and simply responding to crime without treating the underlying cause will produce a limited impact over time. An obvious example of this, detailed in Chapter 4, is POP. **Place-based approaches** capitalize on geographic crime concentration to focus policing resources in small places at specific times. Examples of place-based approaches include hot-spots policing, intelligence-led policing, and predictive policing. Finally, **person-based approaches** recognize that a small proportion of individuals are involved in a disproportionate amount of crime; therefore, differentially focusing resources on high-risk offenders will produce a large crime prevention impact overall. An example of person-based approaches includes focused deterrence.

This chapter will not provide comprehensive overviews of each of these innovations, but we encourage students to consult the National Academies of Sciences, Engineering, and Medicine (2018) report for more detail. Rather, our goal is to utilize their framework to explore innovations systematically and to highlight twenty-first-century trends in policing. Table 8.1 provides an adaptation of the National Academies of Sciences, Engineering, and Medicine approaches, highlighting the logic, objective, ways to accomplish the objective, and key policing innovations that come from each approach. This table provides a framework for this chapter.

Both COP and POP are examined in Chapter 4; therefore, they will not be detailed here. However, at the end of this chapter, we will layer these innovations into discussing police innovations in general.

## Community-Based Approaches

The logic behind community-based approaches is to "enlist and mobilize people who are not police in the prevention of crime and the production of public safety" (National Academies of Sciences, Engineering, and Medicine 2018, 61). The police purposely engage the public in crime prevention, and implementing COP often requires shifts in organizational philosophy, strategy, and tactics. COP came to fruition in part because of the noted limitations of the standard model, but equally important, due to a perceived lack of trust and relationship between the police and the communities they served; this is especially true for disenfranchised groups (e.g., racial and ethnic minorities). Within community-based approaches, it is important to recognize both how and why policing is done.

This section picks up where Chapter 4 left off. Two additional police innovations are detailed here that are consistent with the community-based approach—namely, procedural justice policing and broken windows policing.

**TABLE 8.1  Approaches to Proactive Policing**

| | PROBLEM-SOLVING | COMMUNITY-BASED | PLACE-BASED | PERSON-BASED |
|---|---|---|---|---|
| Logic | Identify problems as patterns across criminal events and identify underlying causes | Capitalize on community resources to identify and control crime | Capitalize on the law of crime concentration and focus efforts geographically | Capitalize on the concentration of crime among a small, chronic portion of the criminal population |
| Objective | Solve recurring problems to prevent crime | Enhance collective efficacy and collaboration with police | Prevent crime in geographic areas | Prevent and deter specific crimes by known offenders |
| Ways to accomplish objective | Use the SARA model | Engage community or change the way that police and public interact | Identify high-crime areas and focus resources | Identify and apply strategies to high-rate offenders |
| Policing strategies | Problem-oriented policing, third-party policing | Community policing, procedural justice, broken windows policing | Hot-spot policing, predictive policing | Focused deterrence |

*Source:* Adapted from National Academies of Sciences, Engineering, and Medicine, *Proactive Policing: Effects on Crime and Communities* (Washington DC: National Academies Press, 2018), p. 2.

### Procedural Justice and Police Legitimacy

The shooting of Michael Brown in Ferguson, Missouri, and events in other cities since 2014 led to the appointment of a blue-ribbon President's Task Force on Twenty-First Century Policing. The first page of that group's report, issued in 2015, made the following observation:

> Building trust and nurturing legitimacy on both sides of the police/citizen divide is the foundational principle underlying the nature of relations between law enforcement agencies and the communities they serve. Decades of research and practice support the premise that people are more likely to obey the law when they believe that those who are enforcing it have authority that is perceived as legitimate by those subject to the authority. The public confers legitimacy only on those whom they believe are acting in procedurally just ways. In addition, law enforcement cannot build community trust if it is seen as an occupying force coming in from outside to impose control on the community.

George Floyd was murdered by a Minneapolis police officer in May 2020. Unlike Michael Brown's shooting, Floyd's killing was captured on video and quickly spread around social and mainstream media. The magnitude of public reaction, including protests and demonstrations, were unlike what we have seen since the civil rights protests of the 1960s. Floyd's murder fueled conversations about the role of policing in America and a democratic society, and organized groups like Black Lives Matter stimulated conversations about defunding or even abolishing the police.

Both the Task Force and the demonstrations after the George Floyd murder were in response to what is now seen as a crisis of police legitimacy. The concept of **legitimacy** is not a new invention, but rather corresponds directly to two of the seven dimensions of police performance discussed in Chapters 1 and 4: one dimension sometimes identified as quality services, customer satisfaction, or public trust, and the other stipulating that the police must use force and authority fairly, efficiently, and effectively. Legitimacy is also directly related to several of the Peelian principles enumerated when the London Metropolitan Police were established in 1829, such as "The ability of the police to perform their duties is dependent upon public approval of police actions" and "Police must secure the willing cooperation of the public in voluntary observance of the law to be able to secure and maintain the respect of the public" (*New York Times* 2014). In a free society, the police get their authority from the people, and the police cannot be effective unless they have the trust and confidence of the people. Events like Brown in Ferguson, Floyd in Minneapolis, and others around this period (Tamir Rice in Cleveland; Freddie Gray in Baltimore; Duante Wright in Brooklyn Center, MN; Eric Garner in New York; and Sandra Bland in Walker County, TX) created a legitimacy crisis for police.

Perhaps the three most significant contributors to police legitimacy are procedural justice, transparency, and accountability. **Procedural justice** is related to process and fairness—studies have found that people, in their dealings with the police and the rest of government, are as concerned with how they are treated as with the outcome of the interaction (Tyler 1990; Sunshine and Tyler 2003). Procedural justice focuses on the quality of treatment citizens receive and the quality of decision making during police–public encounters. The procedural justice framework includes our common dimensions:

1. Treating people with *dignity* and *respect*.
2. Giving citizens *voice* during encounters.

3. Being *neutral* and *transparent* in decision making.

4. Conveying *trustworthy motives*. (President's Task Force on Twenty-First Century Policing 2015; see also Tyler and Huo 2002; Tyler 2008; Mazerolle et al. 2013)

Thus, for example, vehicle drivers who are stopped by the police come away with more positive feelings if the officer is polite, listens to them, and explains what is happening—even if they get a ticket. Similarly, crime victims report more satisfaction when the police seem to care about their situation, even if the crime is never solved. The bottom line seems to be that people want to be treated justly, even when the outcome is not ideal from their point of view. Moreover, when people believe that the police behave justly, they are more inclined to support the police and obey the law because the system seems fair and trustworthy.

The President's Task Force on Twenty-First Century Policing (2015) highlighted the importance of building trust and legitimacy between the police and the public, particularly in light of the events in Ferguson. The Task Force offered 51 separate recommendations and dozens of action items to move the police forward. Their first recommendation was as follows:

> Law enforcement culture should embrace a guardian mindset to build public trust and legitimacy. Toward that end, police and sheriffs' departments should adopt procedural justice as the guiding principle for internal and external policies and practices to guide their interactions with the citizens they serve. (President's Task Force on Twenty-First Century Policing 2015, 11)

The **transparency** of police actions and decisions has received substantial attention since 2014, mainly following police shootings when police departments or prosecutors have delayed releasing officers' names, video, and investigative findings. The connections between legitimacy and transparency are obvious—if a police department is widely viewed as legitimate, the public is more trusting and less demanding of complete transparency; if a police department is not regarded as transparent, the public is more likely to become suspicious, dragging down legitimacy. The situation is complicated. Police officers, crime victims, and others deserve due process and some degree of privacy. Also, active investigations of all kinds might be harmed by the premature release of sensitive information. An underlying factor is the deep-seated American skepticism toward government, which often leads us to assume the worst when the full story is not revealed.

A main purpose of transparency is to make it more likely that police departments and individual police officers can be held accountable for their performance. Especially if public trust is low, any lack of transparency is often interpreted as an attempt to evade **accountability**. The topic of police accountability is covered in detail in Chapter 11, but it is a crucial consideration in the post-Ferguson era. If the public believes, correctly or not, that police officers are not being held accountable for their decision making, and especially for their use of force, then police legitimacy suffers, which leads to an erosion of public support and less voluntary compliance with the law.

One tangible response to these issues of legitimacy, procedural justice, transparency, and accountability has been to equip police officers with body-worn cameras. As seen in Chapter 11, studies have not yet firmly documented all the pros and cons of body-worn cameras, but they are being widely adopted anyway. Common sense supports the view that having video of police–citizen encounters is better than not having it, even if it is not a panacea.

Purposely infusing elements of procedural justice (voice, neutrality, respect, and trust-worthiness) is a way of "paying it forward"—the logic is that if citizens view encounters with the police as procedurally just, then they will be more likely to obey the law moving forward, in addition to being less combative with the police during future encounters. This creates a climate of trust between the police and the public, and this trust is a necessary component for citizens to work collaboratively with the police on crime prevention strategies (or fully participating in the criminal justice process if they are the victim of or witness to a crime). While citizens may not always agree with the outcome of the encounter—a citizen would certainly prefer a warning over a citation during the typical traffic stop—perceiving the officers' motives as neutral and respectful is far preferred to biased and disrespectful.

Research on procedural justice suggests this innovation is effective. Mazerolle et al. (2012, 2013) systematically examined published research on legitimacy and procedural justice, ultimately synthesizing results from 41 independent evaluations. They concluded when police purposely infuse legitimacy and elements of procedural justice during interactions with the public, citizens are significantly more likely to report increased satisfaction, confidence, compliance, and cooperation with the police. Clearly, strategies that include elements of procedural justice are more likely to have satisfied and cooperative constituents, which are important elements to a community-based approach. What remains less clear is whether citizens are less likely to reoffend and whether (or how much) public safety is achieved through procedural justice strategies.

### Broken Windows Policing

The **broken windows theory** was first proposed as a policing innovation by James Q. Wilson and George Kelling (1982) in an article in *The Atlantic* by observing that policing had de-emphasized disorder and other quality-of-life offenses, and that communities where these incivilities were prevalent suffered from low levels of **informal social control**. When incivilities go unchecked by the police, communities may be more susceptible to serious crime (or "criminal invasion").

The logic model associated with broken windows policing is displayed graphically in Figure 8.1. Disorder and incivilities go untreated, which leads to citizens becoming more fearful and withdrawing from the community. This means that citizens are less likely to be

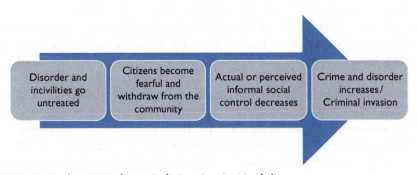

**FIGURE 8.1** Broken Windows Policing Logic Model.

*SOURCE*: Adapted from J. R. Green and R. B. Taylor, "Community-Based Policing and Foot Patrol: Issues of Theory and Evaluation." In J. R. Green and S. D. Mastrofski (eds.), *Community Policing: Rhetoric or Reality* (Westport, CT: Praeger, 1988), 195–223; J. C. Hinkle and D. Weisburd, "The Irony of Broken Windows Policing: A Micro-Place Study of the Relationship between Disorder, Focused Police Crackdowns and Fear of Crime." *Journal of Criminal Justice* 36 (2008): 503–512.

involved with social life within their community, and less likely to intervene when they see minor incivilities, decreasing informal social control. Where informal social control is low, the need for **formal social control** (e.g., law enforcement and the criminal justice system) is high. Communities that cannot police themselves are fertile grounds for more serious, predatory crime, like violent crime. This sets up a spiral of decay, in that serious crime encourages more incivilities, and the process repeats itself. Sousa and Kelling (2006, 77–78) used the "broken windows metaphor" to illustrate this phenomenon: "[Just] as a broken window left untended is a sign that nobody cares and invites more broken windows, so disorderly behavior left untended is a sign that nobody cares and leads to fear of crime, more serious crime and, ultimately, urban decay."

Wilson and Kelling (1982) argued it is appropriate for the police to focus attention on maintaining order in communities that cannot maintain order for themselves. One of the measuring rods for effective policing has been the ability of the police to address serious crime, including crime that is defined as a Part I offense in the FBI's Uniform Crime Reports (e.g., murder, rape, burglary, robbery, aggravated assault, larceny, motor vehicle theft, and arson). Obviously, these offenses are important because of the harm they inflict on victims. However, by prioritizing these offenses, the police may de-emphasize incivilities. The broken windows approach recognizes incivilities cause harm to communities, and therefore tending to these incivilities is a legitimate use of policing resources in their own right. But the tempting extension of the metaphor of the broken window is that if the police address incivilities, then these activities will have an impact on the more serious crimes they seek to reduce. Tending to incivilities (often through enforcement of incivilities, although this is not necessarily the only path available) became a way to legitimize formal intervention of the police for minor offenses. The New York Police Department's use of Compstat-based zero-tolerance policies, aggressively targeting minor violations of traffic laws, ordinances, and misdemeanors in designated areas, has been credited by some with significant crime reductions (Bratton 1996; Kelling and Bratton 1998).

The broken windows approach became quite popular starting in the mid-1980s, and there are several reasons for the appeal and diffusion of this innovation. First, the broken windows approach was credited with contributing to the crime drop in New York City, though the causal relationship was more anecdotal (Bratton and Kelling 2015) than empirical. Second, this approach is easily applied in practice, in that it encourages greater enforcement regarding common minor crimes. Whereas some approaches like COP or POP require comprehensive analysis, community partnerships, and organizational change, broken windows can be applied more quickly and seamlessly, without significant increases in resources.

Questions remain, however, concerning how much of this reduction can be attributed to zero-tolerance arrests and whether the cost was merited (citizen complaints of police abuse increased 60 percent). On closer scrutiny, the evidence strongly suggests that crime had been decreasing—sometimes as dramatically, but without the use of zero-tolerance tactics—in other major cities over the same time period (see, e.g., Greene 1999; Harcourt 2001; Herbert 2001; Rosenfeld, Fornango, and Baumer 2005). To be fair, neither Wilson nor Kelling utilized the term *zero tolerance* to describe broken windows, instead recommending incivilities be enforced following community tolerance levels. They advocated community engagement to understand what incivilities are of greatest importance and permit the community to set thresholds for behavior. For example, a community may tolerate drinking in public so long as the bottle is in a bag and out of sight. Or a community may tolerate panhandling, but not approve of panhandling in certain places (e.g., bus stops) or of certain people (e.g., elderly or families with young children) or aggressive panhandling. Over time, this important detail in the metaphor was overlooked for the simple-to-understand "zero-tolerance" label. It would be disingenuous to equate broken windows as zero tolerance, though it may be difficult to tell the two apart in practice.

Another related strategy based on broken windows theory, known as **quality-of-life policing**, targets the reduction of physical (e.g., graffiti) and social (e.g., prostitution) disorder to reduce serious crime. This tends to be a less aggressive strategy and assumes that as disorder is reduced, community members will work together to promote neighborhood safety, which in turn will help reduce crime. As with zero-tolerance policing, the better-controlled research has not been supportive of narrow, enforcement-oriented quality-of-life strategies with respect to reducing serious crime. For instance, Novak et al. (1999) found that increased enforcement of joyriding and liquor laws did not affect robbery and burglary rates. Katz, Webb, and Schaefer (2001) examined the effects of a quality-of-life initiative focused on social and physical disorder. They found a significant decline in calls for service regarding physical disorder and public morals (e.g., prostitution), but not in calls for serious crime. Similarly, Worrall (2002), in his analysis of misdemeanor arrests relative to total arrests in 58 counties in California, found that felony property crime, but not felony violent crime, declined. One way the broken windows approach has been translated into practice is through stop, question, and frisk (SQF). This is particularly true in cities like New York, where pedestrian traffic is high. Research from New York City reports that SQF was associated with reductions in crime within micro spaces where this practice occurred (Weisburd et al. 2015).

In a comprehensive observational analysis of social and physical disorder in 196 neighborhoods in Chicago, Sampson and Raudenbush (1999) found that, in general, serious crime (e.g., homicide, robbery, and burglary) was uncorrelated with public disorder. Robbery, however, had a low-level correlation with disorder, most likely because disorder increases the pool of potential victims with less recourse to police protection—especially those involved in prostitution and drug trafficking—who have cash on hand and therefore are more vulnerable to robbery offenders. Thus, they concluded that there is no evidence social or public disorder causes serious crime to increase, indicating that police targeting of low-level public offenses will have little, if any, impact on serious crime.

The available research on broken windows strategies suggests that with respect to serious, violent crimes, police should focus their available resources on directed and hot-spot patrol activities, in particular multistrategy, problem-oriented approaches. However, they should avoid a narrow, zero-tolerance model focused mainly on social incivilities and misdemeanor arrests, which is not as promising and "may undermine relationships in low-income, urban minority communities where coproduction is most needed and distrust between the police and citizens is most profound" (Braga and Bond 2008, 600).

## Place-Based Approaches

Crime is not distributed equally across time and space. This phenomenon has been described as the law of crime concentration (Weisburd 2015). Because of this reality, policing has developed into geographically defined areas to distribute police equitably across cities. Police departments, especially larger organizations, are sliced up into ever-decreasing geographic areas, such as precincts, sectors, beats, or reporting areas. But if crime and disorder are not equally distributed geographically, then it makes little sense to distribute police resources equally. To that end, concentrating policing resources in smaller areas has become a common-sense response to this reality.

It is important to compare and contrast the logic between community-based approaches and place-based approaches. Both involve focusing policing innovations geographically. However, community-based approaches tend to identify larger areas than do place-based. Communities or neighborhoods can range wildly in size, structure, and composition. Communities or neighborhoods may be defined by local government and have political relevance for allocating city services, voting districts, council districts, school district boundaries, homeowners associations, and so forth. Communities, in this sense, are more like areas identified by the Chicago School of Sociology or the Chicago Area Project (Schlossman and Sedlak 1983), where communities had relevance and structure for residents and businesses. Obviously, the concept of communities is central to approaches like COP.

In contrast, place-based approaches focus on much smaller areas within communities, including specific addresses, street segments, or clusters of streets (Weisburd 2015). Even in "high-crime communities," there are many areas that are relatively crime-free, whereas other, smaller places within communities tend to experience chronic and persistent levels of crime, disorder, and deviance. Therefore, focusing resources on a community as a whole may dilute the desired effect. Place-based approaches tend to focus on hot spots of crime, which are micro places of crime.

Weisburd et al. (2012, 5) described the logic as follows:

1. Crime is tightly concentrated at "crime hot spots," suggesting that we can identify and deal with a large proportion of crime problems by focusing on a very small number of places.

2. These crime hot spots evidence very strong stability over time, and thus present a particularly promising focus for crime prevention efforts.

3. Crime at places evidences strong variability at micro levels of geography, suggesting that an exclusive focus on higher geographic units, like communities or neighborhoods, will lead to a loss of important information about crime and the efficient focus of crime prevention resources.

4. Not only crime varies across very small units of geography, but also the social and contextual characteristics of places. The criminology of place in this context identifies and emphasizes the importance of micro units of geography as social systems relevant to the crime problem.

5. Crime at place is very predictable. Therefore, it is possible not only to understand why crime is concentrated at place, but also to develop effective crime prevention strategies to ameliorate crime problems at places.

## Directed Patrol

Early place-based approaches included **directed patrol**, which is proactive and uses officers' uncommitted time for a specified activity and is based on crime and problem analysis. The proactive dimension of the directed activity is essential, be it making arrests, issuing citations, conducting field interrogations, or educating the public about crime. Proactivity produces more information, heightens citizen awareness of police, perhaps creates an impression of greater police watchfulness, and most certainly requires police to be more alert and active.

## Hot-Spots Policing

Targeting **hot spots** for crime developed out of research analyzing 911 calls in Minneapolis (Sherman, Gartin, and Buerger 1989), where researchers discovered that 5 percent of the addresses in the city accounted for 64 percent of all 911 calls. Thus, a few locations, which were labeled hot spots, required a highly disproportionate amount of police time and resources. Following this research, the Minneapolis Hot Spots Patrol Experiment was designed to test the crime prevention effects of extra patrol officers directed at hot spots for crime during *hot times* for crime over a one-year period (Sherman and Weisburd 1995). Of the worst 110 hot-spot street corners in the city, 55 were randomly selected to receive increased police presence. The remaining 55 received normal patrol coverage, primarily in response to citizen calls for service. Results indicated that increased police presence failed to reduce serious crime, but did have a modest effect on disorder. Mere visibility seemed to have caused the modest effect on disorder, because the officers' activities at the hot spots were unstructured and not substantial. Additionally, officers do not need to spend much time in a hot spot to produce a measurable effect (Koper 1995). In "Voices from the Field," Renée Mitchell discusses her involvement in a hot-spots project in Sacramento, California.

One of the defining characteristics of hot spots is that they are relatively small areas of crime concentration. This can include repeat houses, street segments, intersections, or small collections of streets. The value of defining hot spots (or micro places) is that smaller micro units represent a more important "behavior setting" for social activities—certainly more appropriate than arbitrary, governmentally defined areas like beats, neighborhoods, or Census tracts. Implementing crime prevention strategies in larger areas runs the risk of diluting the effects of the intervention. Also, crime tends to concentrate even further in small segments within beats or neighborhoods that officers agree are "bad" or dangerous areas (Weisburd 2018). Therefore, to maximize crime prevention strategies, there is value in identifying the smallest areas as possible (or in research methods lingo, small units of analysis). For illustrative purposes, Figure 8.2 provides a visual image of hot spots in Kansas City, Missouri. These areas were determined by careful analysis of violent calls for service and reports taken for violent offenses over a two-year period. Each of these hot spots is approximately 0.25 square miles, or about 4 × 4 city blocks. The hot spots depicted in Figure 8.2 represent less than 1 percent of the city's total area.

Over time, a large body of research points to the effectiveness of policing strategies that are focused within hot spots (Braga, Weisburd, and Turchan 2018). The value lies in focusing resources and strategies on small geographic places with a disproportionate amount of crime, disorder, calls for service, or problems. Lum, Koper, and Telp (2011, 5) stated, "police strategies are more effective when they are place-based, proactive and focused." Two elements are important to remember. First, hot spots must be small. Traditionally police have defined problem places as beats or neighborhoods, resulting in dilution of efforts and resources, which is ultimately ineffective. Second, hot spots are identified using careful data analysis. Utilizing police records (e.g., call-for-service data or reports of criminal activity) assists greatly in objectively identifying small places to concentrate efforts.

There is significant value in focusing police resources in hot spots, but what remains unclear is *what* the police should be doing in those areas. There are a range of options—from increasing presence to conducting proactive strategies (e.g., stop, question, and frisk; Weisburd et al. 2015), problem-solving strategies, foot patrol (Novak et al. 2016), or

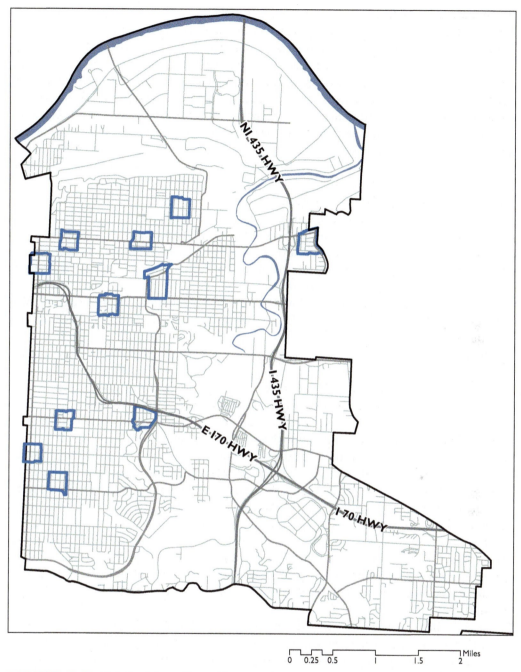

**FIGURE 8.2**  Hot Spot Locations (Kansas City, MO).

*SOURCE*: Kansas City (MO) Police Department.

offender-focused strategies (Groff et al. 2015). In other words, hot-spots strategies can include a hybrid of approaches. A multistrategy hot-spot study in Jersey City, New Jersey (Braga et al. 1999), evaluated the impact of using a *problem-oriented* approach in violent crime areas. The experiment included violent crime locations that made up 6 percent of the total of Jersey City but accounted for 24 percent of the assaults and 20 percent of the robberies. The violent crime locations were matched in pairs (a treatment and a control). The treatment areas were analyzed according to need and received several interventions that could be categorized as a "policing-disorder" strategy Almost all areas, however, received (1) a number of aggressive order-maintenance tactics, including repeat foot and radio car patrols, dispersing loiterers, issuing summonses for public drinking, and stops and frisks of suspicious persons, and (2) investigations into drug sales and drug enforcement. Slightly less than half required storefront cleanups by owners and trash removal on streets by the public works department; several areas also used increased lighting and housing-code enforcement.

The effects of the intervention were measured by analyzing six crime-incident categories (robbery, nondomestic assault, property, disorder/vandalism, narcotics arrests, and total incidents) and six citizen-call categories (robbery, street fighting, property, disorder/nuisance, narcotics, and total calls). The findings indicated that the total number of both criminal incidents and calls for service was significantly reduced at the treatment areas relative to the control areas. The results of this experiment indicate that a problem-oriented approach, focusing on aggressive patrol and drug enforcement, may have a significant impact on reducing violent behavior.

An experiment in Lowell, Massachusetts, modeled on the Jersey City program, also used a multistrategy, problem-oriented approach and focused on reducing disorder and calls for service in violent crime hot spots (Braga and Bond 2008). Similar to the Jersey City program, the researchers matched 34 violent crime locations (encompassing 2.7 percent of Lowell but generating 23.5 percent of crime and disorder calls and 29.3 percent of violent crime calls) into 17 pairs (treatment and control). After a one-year intervention involving strategies similar to those used in Jersey City, they discovered that the 17 treatment areas had a decreased number of calls for service and showed decreased signs of social and physical disorder compared with the control areas.

A recent multicity evaluation examined the efficacy of exercising procedural justice strategies in hot spots. Officers received extensive training on procedural justice techniques and then were assigned to high-crime hot spots. Among other things, researchers learned that officers receiving procedural justice training were significantly more likely to give citizens voice, show neutrality, and demonstrate respectful behavior during encounters, and were considerably less likely to engage in disrespectful behavior themselves. Citizens living in hot spots where officers were assigned were less likely to perceive officer misbehavior. Finally, hot spots where officers trained in procedural justice were assigned saw a 14 percent reduction in crime compared to similar areas (Weisburd et al. 2022).

These studies appear to have important implications for reducing drug problems and, concomitantly, for reducing violent and other crime and disorder problems using multiple patrol strategies, enhancing procedural justice, and working with other government officials to enforce civil code violations.

### Gun Violence

Several proactive arrest strategies have been used to reduce crime, particularly gun-related violence and often with a special focus on gang violence. The first major study in this area, known as the Kansas City Gun Experiment (Sherman, Shaw, and Rogan 1995), indicated that increased seizures of illegal guns in a high-crime area can reduce violent gun crimes. The experimental area contained extra gun-unit officers working overtime shifts who concentrated on detecting and seizing illegally possessed guns, whereas a control area had

## Renée J. Mitchell

*Senior Police Researcher with RTI International; Sergeant (Ret.), Sacramento Police Department*

In the fall of 2010, the Sacramento Police Department (SPD) was facing budget cuts that would require the reduction of the police force by 150 officers. In the face of the layoffs, SPD began looking for ways to increase the efficacy and efficiency of their patrol department. At that time, I was the crime analysis sergeant for the department. Having studied with Dr. Larry Sherman of the University of Cambridge as a Fulbright scholar, I had a basic understanding of hot-spots policing and randomized controlled trials (RCTs). Knowing hot-spots policing to be an effective tool to reduce crime, I reached out to a research team from George Mason University for guidance on how to design a hot-spot RCT. With their guidance, we decided to run a RCT based on the "Koper curve," asking the question, "Will visiting hot spots in random, intermittent order for 12- to 16-minute increments reduce crime and calls for service in Sacramento?"

Our experiment was a 90-day RCT, with 21 experimental and 21 control areas, with officers visiting hot-spot areas in a random order every two hours for 12- to 16-minute visits. When comparing the 2011 calls for service to the same three-month period in 2010, the results suggested a strong treatment effect. On average, each treatment hot spot had a decline of 3.57 calls for service, while each control hot spot had an average increase of 4.43 calls. Part I crime incidents showed a somewhat similar pattern to calls for service. During the experimental period, treatment hot spots experienced fewer total Part I incidents (105) than the control hot spots (121). In the same period in 2010, the treatment hot spots had 140 Part I incidents, compared to 95 in the control hot spots. The experiment was effective at reducing crime and calls for service, and this was accomplished efficiently during officers' normal work day, with no additional personnel or overtime.

When conducting this experiment, convincing police managers to implement a project was not a challenge; winning the officers over was. Anecdotally, I have found police executives to be open to the idea of implementing innovative projects—they usually want to find a new way of approaching an old problem. The challenges arise because managers decide the direction of the organization, but the officers do the work. In other words, policy is made at the top of the hierarchy, but implemented by those at the bottom. My challenge arose from imparting new processes and procedures on working cops, some of which have spent a lifetime policing in a particular manner, stressing the importance of adhering to the research protocols. When asked how it was managing an experiment as a practitioner, I would often describe it as riding a tsunami while trying to guide it between two buildings. I think in the end we were successful due to my crime analysis staff working very closely with patrol lieutenants, sergeants, and the officers. We had weekly communication with the sergeants and lieutenants and attended all of the patrol roll calls at least once a week. Updating everyone involved in the study on a continuous basis kept everyone actively engaged in the experiment.

In the end, the experiment didn't just give the organization outcome measures about the effectiveness of hot-spots policing; it also offered a thorough process analysis of the organization. Research can test an agency's ability of both managers and officers to implement a new strategy in a systematic way using disciplined methods. The hot-spots experiment forced SPD to examine their internal workings from their ability to gather and extract data to implementing procedural changes to creating flexibility within their hierarchy. This process allowed the organization to learn where their strengths and weakness lay. Research can be a benefit for both the greater good of police research and for the organization individually.

only regular activity levels. Over a 29-week period, gun crimes declined by 49 percent in the experimental area, but by only 4 percent in the control area. There appeared to be little evidence of a displacement effect to neighboring beats. In addition, there was also a high degree of community support for aggressive patrol tactics. This support was attributed to two important considerations: (1) police managers met with community leaders before implementation and secured their endorsement, and (2) police officers were told by their supervisors to treat citizens with respect and to explain the reasons for vehicle stops. This finding has important implications for virtually all strategies of police patrol. Unfortunately, as with other types of crackdowns, this program was extremely expensive and not sustainable over the long term.

Using the Kansas City Gun Experiment as a model, McGarrell, Chermak, and Weiss (2001) evaluated a 90-day patrol project in Indianapolis that was intended to reduce violent crime involving firearms. The study compared two opposing police strategies: **specific deterrence**, where the goal was to focus on the seizure of illegal weapons from targeted offenders (i.e., suspicious-looking pedestrians and motorists), and **general deterrence**, where the goal was to maximize motor vehicle stops as a sign of increased police presence. A third comparison group area, where police activity was unchanged, was also evaluated. Significantly, gun-related crime declined by 29 percent compared with the prior year in the targeted offender–specific deterrence area, whereas increases occurred in the general deterrence and comparison areas. Furthermore, there was little indication of displacement of violent crime to the five beats surrounding the targeted area.

Cohen and Ludwig (2003) evaluated the impact of Pittsburgh's Firearm Suppression Patrol (FSP) strategy. FSP was focused on specific target areas, where officers were relieved from responding to calls for service to focus on proactively seizing guns from citizens. Similar to Kansas City, police did this by engaging in traffic enforcement and pedestrian stops. The researchers found that FSP reduced shots fired by 34 percent in the target areas and reduced gunshot-related injuries by 71 percent in these areas. This occurred despite a small number of gun seizures, suggesting that the decreases resulted not from incapacitation, but rather from the deterrent value of this type of patrol activity. A variation on these initiatives was a program, known as Project Exile, that targeted the use of guns in violent or drug crimes (Rosenfeld et al. 2005). Implemented in Richmond, Virginia, the program involved sentence enhancements through the use of federal prosecutions, which generally provide longer sentences than those in state courts (as advertised extensively in print and electronic media, city buses, and business cards: "An illegal gun will get you five years in federal prison"). The evaluation found that Richmond's firearm homicide rate was significantly lower than the average rate among the nation's 95 largest cities after the implementation of Exile. In general, these findings support those of Kansas City with respect to the effectiveness of specific deterrence strategies over general deterrence strategies.

## Intelligence-Led Policing

Beginning in the late 1990s, some police leaders began calling for the adoption of **intelligence-led policing** (ILP). Like the Compstat process pioneered in the New York City Police Department in the 1990s (discussed in Chapter 5), this policing strategy emphasizes the use of real-time crime analysis, but it also incorporates intelligence analysis in the deployment of both specialized units and regular patrol officers (Carter 2009). In principle, a police department's resources should be targeted *each day* on the most serious immediate *and* long-term threats and problems facing the jurisdiction, based on careful analysis of calls for service, crime data, intelligence, and information from a variety of other sources.

This is a far cry from the traditional police strategy of simply deploying one patrol unit to each beat on each shift with no more tactical direction than "be careful out there."

The ILP model of policing was first developed in the United Kingdom and Australia (Ratcliffe 2016) with the following characteristics (Ratcliffe and Guidetti 2008): (1) it is managerially centered and top-down in decision-making format; (2) it is proactive; (3) it is informant and surveillance focused, with heightened attention directed toward recidivists and serious crime offenders; and (4) it provides a central crime intelligence mechanism to facilitate objective decision making. ILP is not a bottom-up model that relies primarily on patrol officers partnering with the community or identifying and analyzing neighborhood crime and disorder problems. Rather, it is a model in which headquarters uses intelligence to figure out what crimes and problems are threatening the jurisdiction and then deploys officers and detectives to intercept and eliminate them.

ILP tends to demand more centralization of information and decision making than is common in American policing, and more analytical capacity than most US police departments can muster (Scheider, Chapman, and Schapiro 2009). So far, ILP has appealed mostly to large departments such as the New York Police Department, the Los Angeles Police Department, and the New Jersey State Police (Fuentes 2006). However, many other police agencies are upgrading their analysis capabilities, and the states have developed fusion centers, with encouragement and some funding from the US Department of Homeland Security, to provide analysis services and products to local agencies (Rollins and Connors 2007). ILP likely is destined to become more popular and more widespread as police departments improve the efficiency and effectiveness of their systems for collecting, analyzing, and disseminating information and intelligence to field officers and commanders.

Three factors seem to account for the development and expansion of ILP since the 1990s: (1) technological improvements in police data systems (including computer systems, data mining, and surveillance cameras) that have vastly improved the capacity to collect and analyze information, and to do it more quickly; (2) the terrorist events of 9/11, which were seen as an intelligence failure (a failure to "connect the dots"), resulting in major new investments in police and homeland security intelligence analysis capabilities; and (3) the "new managerialism" philosophy that emphasizes top-down direction and control in organizations, including police departments, based on metrics, analytics, and performance measurement (Loveday 2008). This new managerialism and ILP developed hand in hand in the United Kingdom and can be understood as their central government's mechanism for controlling the 43 local police forces in the country, as well as the 43 chief constables' mechanism to control their own forces in line with central government demands.

In US policing, intelligence analysis has traditionally focused on various forms of organized crime, including drug cartels, gangs, and terrorist groups. This kind of intelligence work aimed to identify the people involved in these crimes, their methods, and their plans so that specialist police units could disrupt and interdict their criminal activities. The main thrust of ILP today is to expand this kind of approach to the entire police organization, not just a few specialist units. It is being encouraged by the federal government's Bureau of Justice Assistance through its Smart Policing Initiative (see https://bja.ojp.gov/program/smart-policing-initiative-spi/overview) and the National Highway Traffic Safety Administration through its Data-Driven Approaches to Crime and Traffic Safety program (see https://www.nhtsa.gov/sites/nhtsa.gov/files/811185_ddacts_opguidelines.pdf)). Both of these major national initiatives emphasize the value of data-driven police deployment and tactics and encourage the use of sophisticated analytical methods, such as risk terrain modeling (Kennedy, Caplan, and Piza 2011) and social network analysis (Johnson et al. 2013; Fox, Novak, and McHale 2015).

It is too soon to tell whether ILP as a department-wide strategy will be practical and what side effects might be felt. In the United Kingdom, however, some observers found that the implementation of ILP deflected police energy away from problem solving, and that it also had a tendency to leave the community out of the equation (Maguire and John 2006). As a result, since the mid-2000s the United Kingdom has given renewed emphasis to neighborhood policing and reassurance policing and has continued to look for ways to better integrate POP and COP. This now includes an emphasis on "community intelligence," which is more "bottom up" and depends as heavily on close connections between police officers and neighborhood residents as it does on surveillance technology or analysis of databases (Thomas 2016).

### Predictive Policing

The newest police strategy is **predictive policing**, a spin-off from ILP. The aim of predictive policing is anticipation—using data to react to incidents and patterns more quickly and to predict them in the hope of taking preventive or proactively. Prediction has been the ultimate objective of crime analysis for many years. Still, the current argument is that modern technology and data systems make it more than just a dream (see Inside Policing 8.1). Private-sector examples have been offered to demonstrate the power of data. Amazon suggests products to us based on our previous purchases, for example, and Walmart knows what items to stock when severe weather is forecast (Beck and McCue 2009). In a more sophisticated way, police agencies might be able to combine their own historical data about crimes and incidents with other information—such as transportation data or data from entertainment venues and special events—to anticipate crime, disorder, congestion, or other problems before they occur (Bachner and Lynch 2016).

Another approach is to speed up predictions. In the past, crime analysis might have examined a pattern of reported burglaries to guide patrol deployment or directed patrol over the ensuing week or two. The presumption was that the time between the crimes was days, if not weeks. Current predictive policing looks more closely at crimes committed in tighter time proximity—robbers who might commit two or three robberies in a night or within a very few days, for example (Haberman and Ratcliffe 2012). If an accurate prediction could be made after the first or second robbery, it might be possible to intercept the third one, still in the same night or the following day.

---

**INSIDE POLICING 8.1** | **Predictive Policing**

Here is an article that takes an in-depth look at PredPol, the software application for predictive policing featured in articles and videos about the LAPD. The article questions PredPol's effectiveness and describes the public relations frenzy and political connections associated with the product.

**Discussion Question:** Can predictive policing lead to more racial disparities in the criminal justice system? Why (or why not)?

SOURCE: *Modern Policing* blog, November 2, 2013, www.oup.com/cordner/predictive-policing/.

One element of predictive policing in some jurisdictions is the real-time crime center. These centers operate more in reacting to crime, but reacting *very quickly*. The centers incorporate some of the types of analytical capability mentioned in conjunction with Compstat and ILP, but they focus specifically on incidents occurring at the moment. They try to use real-time call-for-service information, real-time intelligence, video feeds from public and private surveillance cameras, data from mobile and fixed Automated License Plate Reader devices, and various other real-time data to provide immediate input to patrol officers, detectives, and commanders in the field. These real-time crime centers are a cross between an analysis unit or fusion center and an emergency communications center. Their development likely owes as much to modern technology as to police strategizing—they take advantage of things we *can* now do, technically, without a completely clear rationale or justification for why we *should* do them. In particular, the proliferation of surveillance cameras has created an avalanche of new data in the form of pictures. Real-time crime centers are one police response to the challenge of trying to keep up with that avalanche and make tactical use of it.

Predictive policing is an ambiguous concept at this point, still in its early stages of development. It is one of those phrases that sounds modern and appealing but does not come with many details. It also raises philosophical and legal concerns, since our criminal justice system is designed to hold people accountable for things they have already done, not things they might do in the future. Along this line, descriptions of predictive policing have been careful to avoid any suggestion that data would be used to predict a particular individual's future behavior, with assurances that the movie *Minority Report* is not the model being followed. It has also been noted, however, that predictions about crime or disorder that might occur in a geographic area could lead to police actions that still affect individuals or entire communities, perhaps unfairly (Casady 2011; Erbentraut 2014). Police strategists and civil libertarians alike will be watching carefully as this predictive policing concept continues to develop.

## Person-Based Approaches

Previously, we recognized that some places have a disproportionate amount of crime compared with others. Because of this reality, police can be more effective and efficient if they identify these places and shift resources accordingly. The same logic holds true for persons: most people do not commit crime, while a small number of chronic offenders are responsible for a large proportion of crime. Wolfgang, Figlio, and Sellin (1972) reported approximately 6 percent of individuals within a birth cohort were involved in about 55 percent of all juvenile crime, which is a ratio roughly similar to what was reported by Sherman et al. (1989) regarding hot spots. The logical policy from this concentration is to prioritize police resources on those most likely to be repeat or chronic offenders.

### Focused Deterrence Initiatives

Growing out of the earlier hot-spots gun projects, a series of strategic, **focused deterrence** initiatives targeting violent crime areas and groups demonstrate promise. These approaches focus on deterring the relatively small number of individuals involved in a disproportionate amount of gun violence, particularly gang or group members, while simultaneously providing services for anyone wanting to avoid violence.

These initiatives, commonly referred to as focused deterrence, or *pulling-levers policing*, are based on the premise that conflict within and between street groups over issues of respect is responsible for a large portion of urban violence, and that reaching out to these groups and their members with a specific deterrent message and offers of assistance to escape a violent lifestyle can reduce violence (Engel, Tillyer, and Corsaro 2013). Focused deterrence approaches include six common features:

1. Selecting a particular crime problem.
2. Pulling together an interagency enforcement group.
3. Conducting research, with help from front-line officers, to identify key offenders.4. Framing a special enforcement operation directed at key offenders if they commit further violence.
5. Matching enforcement with supportive services and community encouragement to embrace nonviolence while challenging the street code of retaliatory violence.
6. Communicating directly and repeatedly with offenders, letting them know they are under close scrutiny. (Kennedy 2019)

Team members identify individuals involved in violence, the groups they belong to, and the interrelationships among these groups. The individuals identified through this process are brought together with law enforcement, social service agencies, and community members at what are referred to as offender notification meetings, call-in sessions, or forums, where a specific deterrent message is conveyed. They are offered alternatives to their current lifestyle through social services, informed of the damage done to the community from their actions, encouraged to avoid violence, and warned of the consequences of violent acts: not only will the individuals involved in violence be pursued by law enforcement, but also the group or gang will be targeted for enforcement (Engel et al. 2013). In other words,

> individuals and groups are put on notice that law enforcement is mobilized to take out any group that engages in violence and help is available to those who want it. This advertising is done through offender notification meetings, probation and parole officers, and gang outreach workers. Individuals are notified that if any member of their group commits a homicide, the entire group will become the focus of a coordinated law enforcement effort. In essence, focused deterrence exploits the existing group structure to encourage these groups to police themselves in order to avoid becoming the priority of law enforcement. (Tillyer, Engel, and Lovins 2012, 975)

The most well-known of these initiatives is the Boston Gun Project (Kennedy, Piehl, and Braga 1996). What became known as the *ceasefire strategy* was an attempt to reduce gang-related violence. This strategy emphasized a team approach involving local and federal police and other justice system agencies, as well as private and community organizations. If gangs refrained from violent activity but committed other crimes, the normal approach of police, prosecutors, and the rest of the criminal justice system came into play. If the gangs hurt people, however, ceasefire members intervened (Kennedy 1998).

The overall Ceasefire strategy also included community and private-sector strategies, such as educational and employment opportunities. Community centers, the clergy, and gang-outreach workers also played a role in spreading the anti-violence message to young offenders and attempted to help them to enter mainstream society. The results were startling, with gang- and gun-related homicides in the 24-and-under age category significantly reduced from 1990 to 1995; during one 28-month period, there were *no* homicides in this

**INSIDE POLICING 8.2** | **Focused Deterrence**

In this two-part podcast, David Kennedy discusses the logic behind focused deterrence with the Center for Court Innovation. He describes the Boston Gun Project, Operation CeaseFire, and the Drug Market Initiative.

**Discussion Question:** The model described by Kennedy has been implemented to reduce homicides, drug markets, and intimate partner violence. How might this model be adapted to address other crimes?

*Source:* David Kennedy, "The Story Behind the Drug Market Initiative (Part I)," November 2010, https://www.courtinnovation.org/publications/david-kennedy-story-behind-drug-market-initiative-part-i-podcast; David Kennedy, "New Approaches to Justice (Part II)," November 2010, https://www.courtinnovation.org/publications/david-kennedy-new-approaches-justice-part-ii-podcast.

age group (Clark 1997). An evaluation of the project found a 63 percent reduction in youth homicide (Braga et al. 2001). Inside Policing 8.2 dives deeper into the logic, early formulation, and expansion of the focused deterrence approach.

A systematic review and meta-analysis of the empirical evidence on focused deterrence initiatives concluded that these programs are "very promising" (Braga et al. 2018), as does the National Institute of Justice's crimesolutions.gov program (https://crimesolutions.ojp.gov/ratedpractices/11). After a comprehensive review of a variety of crime prevention strategies, Abt and Winship (2016, 13) concluded "focused deterrence . . . has the largest direct impact on crime and violence, by far, of any intervention in this report." The success of these programs may rest on the specific deterrence effect of identifying and focusing on a particular problem and sustaining a cooperative team effort among criminal justice and public social-service agencies. Other police departments have adopted similar types of ceasefire deterrence strategies. For example, evaluations of ceasefire strategies in Minneapolis (McGarrell et al. 2006); Lowell, Massachusetts (Braga, McDevitt, and Pierce 2006); Kansas City, Missouri (Fox and Novak 2018); and New Orleans (Corsaro and Engel 2015) also reported significant results in reducing homicides. Also notable is the Cincinnati Initiative to Reduce Violence, which began in 2007. Recognizing the difficulties of sustaining violence reductions over time, the team focused on developing a comprehensive organizational design to ensure sustainability and institutionalize the initiative. Assessment shows that violence among group members involved in the program has declined significantly—homicides by group members involved in the program declined by more than 41 percent during the 42 months after the program was implemented (Engel et al. 2013).

In contrast, a focused deterrence strategy evaluated in Los Angeles (Tita et al. 2005), also patterned heavily after the Boston program, did not produce significant results with respect to gang violence. It is important to understand, however, that there are significant differences between the two cities. In Los Angeles, the government is not as centralized as in Boston; there are a variety of diverse, often conflicting political structures that overlap one another. The gangs were also different in their makeup—larger, more entrenched, and mostly Latino in Los Angeles but smaller, greater in number, and mostly African American in Boston. In addition, because of increased gang violence, the program was started before it could be properly organized and was never fully carried out as designed. The Los Angeles results provide an important policy lesson regarding the need to take differences between cities and departments into account when attempting to implement a program that has been successful elsewhere. Moreover, Weisburd et al. (2010) stress that failure to fully plan and implement a program often results in weaker program effects. In addition to these initial implementation problems, it is difficult to maintain these collaborations and the related reductions in violence over time. Tillyer et al. (2012) note:

> The success in violence reduction across some of these cities, however, appears to be short-lived. This lack of sustainability has been attributed to implementation issues by some involved in these initiatives. Failure to institutionalize the roles and processes leads actors to abandon the strategy over time, and thus, the results are only temporary. (977)

Related, focused deterrence approaches may struggle with sustainability. This is perhaps due in part to the multiagency, collaborative nature of the innovation. Berman and Fox (2010) outline how the Boston Ceasefire (also known as the Boston Gun Project)—the iconic example of focused deterrence's success that was referenced as the "Boston Miracle"—struggled to keep momentum over time, perhaps due to changes in personnel. Research in Kansas City (MO) noted significant reductions in homicides, group member–involved homicides, and gun-involved aggravated assaults after the implementation of a focused deterrence strategy. In fact, homicides in Kansas City dipped to a 42-year low. However, after about a year, significant treatment decay was detected despite the fact the approach remained operational. By the second year, violent crime had crept up to pre-project levels, and by the third year, gun-involved aggravated assaults had increased significantly (Fox and Novak 2018). One of the hallmarks of focused deterrence is certainty of punishment—if groups or group members involved with violence are told formal sanctions are forthcoming should they continue to engage in criminal activity, then the police and other partners must be prepared to follow through on those promises. Once certainty of detection and punishment declines, the continued success of focused deterrence is jeopardized.

These evaluations, when taken in totality, suggest focused deterrence is a promising approach to reducing group member–involved violence. However, they also point out that efforts can fall apart without careful planning and thoughtful attention to sustaining these multiagency collaborations.

## What Works in Policing

Evidence pertaining to the effectiveness of the four police approaches discussed in this chapter is limited, for several reasons. Some of the strategies, like COP, are so multifaceted that it is hard to separate out their effects. On a related point, both COP and POP are explicitly designed to be flexible and tailored—which makes it difficult to determine consistent effects since the strategies themselves take different forms in different places. ILP and predictive policing are so new that solid evidence is not yet available. In addition to these challenges, assessing the effectiveness of police strategies is complicated by the fact that the policing bottom line is multidimensional, as discussed in Chapter 1. This makes it likely that any strategy may have positive impacts on some police goals, but not others.

"What works" in policing is an easy question to ask; however, the answer is very complicated. Throughout the text, we strive to answer questions like this by relying on the research evidence. In other words, what does the research say? We purposely adopted this approach with the faith that good science will inform good policy, and we continue to believe this is true. However, one of the frustrations associated with answering this straightforward question is that these archetypes of policing innovation are often not subjected to rigorous evaluation. Police departments implement versions of these innovations (and versions not detailed here) on a regular basis, but too often, they are not evaluated adequately, if at all. Each time the police implement an approach but do not evaluate its effectiveness, efficiency, or fairness, we miss an opportunity to learn. Fortunately, a large volume of research has accumulated over time that helps us address this seemingly simple question.

Another complication in answering this question is that, in practice, policing innovations often are hybrid approaches of many of the innovations discussed earlier. As innovations become diffused across American police departments, there is a tendency to pick and choose certain characteristics and elements of several innovations when implementing an approach. This makes sense from a pragmatic perspective, but it also makes it difficult or impossible to responsibly evaluate the impact of an innovation if it is not implemented with fidelity. When approaches are cobbled together across innovations, it is difficult to determine which part of the approach "worked," or whether the benefit was seen only when multiple elements of innovations occur simultaneously. This should not be construed as criticism—it is just an observation of reality. Indeed, many innovations evolve as offspring of other innovations. Kennedy (2006) noted that lever-pulling and focused deterrence in Boston was a form of POP, and early iterations of focused deterrence were clearly viewed as a form of POP. Over time, focused deterrence has been viewed as a separate, unique entity in its own right; nevertheless, it may have been conceived as a form of POP. Moreover, police departments utilize a variety of innovations simultaneously.

Table 8.2 reports results from surveys received from nearly 200 large police departments. Nearly all respondents indicated they engage in COP, POP, hot-spots policing, directed patrol/focused deterrence, targeting known offenders, and targeting specific known addresses. Almost three-quarters indicated they engaged in ILP. While this demonstrates a high degree of innovation adoption already, many police departments further indicated they would either adopt each of these strategies or will increase implementation. Very few departments were entertaining elimination or decreasing use of these innovations. Meanwhile, only 38.2 percent of police departments were using predictive policing; however, over 70 percent planned to increase or implement predictive policing in the near future. Several conclusions may be drawn from these results. First, there is great diffusion of innovation across American police departments, and departments indicate they are more likely to enhance their use of innovation rather than eliminate it. This suggests that once departments adopt an innovation, they are more likely to continue using it. Second, it is likely that innovations are used either in conjunction with one another, or that innovations are being used for some places, people, or problems at the same time. If this is the case, elements from one innovation may be informing the use of others, though it is difficult from these results alone to fully understand what is happening on the streets.

Two words of caution when interpreting these results are warranted before proceeding. First, it is not possible to determine the level of commitment or fidelity to these innovations simply by examining survey data. While many police executive departments *say* they are implementing COP (Wilson 2006), it is not possible, from these data, to determine the level of implementation among street-level officers, or what the innovation looks like at the street level. Second, the Police Executive Research Forum survey combined directed patrol with focused deterrence, which are two very different innovations (a place-based approach and a person-based approach, respectively). The double-barreled nature of this question makes it impossible to understand whether responding departments are doing either directed

**TABLE 8.2** Innovative Strategies Used by Police

| INNOVATION | CURRENTLY USE (%) | WILL IMPLEMENT OR INCREASE IN NEXT 2–5 YEARS (%) | WILL ELIMINATE OR DECREASE IN NEXT 2–5 YEARS (%) |
|---|---|---|---|
| Community Policing | 93.7 | 31.7 | 2.6 |
| Problem-Oriented Policing | 88.9 | 34.9 | 1.6 |
| Hot-Spots Policing | 79.9 | 41.3 | 2.6 |
| Directed Patrol/Focused Deterrence | 92.1 | 35.4 | 2.1 |
| Targeting Known Offenders | 79.3 | 47.3 | 2.1 |
| Targeting Specific Problem Addresses/Locations | 91.5 | 39.2 | 1.1 |
| Information/Intelligence-Led Policing | 72.7 | 54.0 | 1.6 |
| Predictive Policing | 38.2 | 70.4 | 2.2 |

*Source:* Adapted from Police Executive Research Forum, *Future Trends in Policing* (Washington, DC: Department of Justice, Office of Community Policing Services, 2014).

patrol, focused deterrence, or both separately. It seems unlikely that over 90 percent of police departments are implementing focused deterrence as described in this chapter.

With these caveats in mind, the four strategies are compared in the report card presented in Table 8.2. The National Research Council's report (2004) indicated that the scientific evidence on whether COP reduces crime is weak. Systematic reviews of the best, most rigorous studies have concluded that diffuse police strategies such as COP have not been shown to reduce crime, whereas more specific strategies (e.g., neighborhood watch and targeted hot-spots policing) do consistently lead to crime reductions (Weisburd and Eck 2004; Braga 2010; Holloway, Bennett, and Farrington 2008). However, crime reduction is not the only objective of the police or the sole criterion by which they are judged. Evaluations have generally found that sincere COP efforts improve public trust in the police, which is an important outcome in a free society and can promote legitimacy in policing. In addition, COP has often led to public reassurance and reductions in fear of crime (Cordner 2010). These are important outcomes with real consequences for individuals and communities.

POP is one of the targeted approaches to policing that has been found to be effective in reducing crime (Hinkle et al. 2020). There is also limited evidence that POP can improve public confidence in the police and public reassurance, but few rigorous studies of POP have carefully examined these potential outcomes.

Procedural justice policing has been demonstrated to have positive outcomes on enhanced legitimacy and satisfaction with the police (Mazerolle et al. 2012, 2013); however, less is understood about whether there is a relationship between systematically exercising procedural justice and reducing crime and victimization. Focused deterrence has consistently demonstrated beneficial impacts on crime and victimization (Abt and Winship 2016; Braga et al. 2018), yet the capacity for sustainability remains challenging. ILP and predictive policing show the same two positive outcomes: crime reduction and holding offenders accountable. The conclusion about crime reduction is based on the consistent finding that targeted policing, including hot-spots policing, leads to crime reduction (Braga 2010). Although these kinds of studies have not explicitly focused on ILP or predictive policing, the primary focus of these two strategies is specifically targeting. Research on hot-spots policing demonstrates consistent benefits across the matrix. Similarly, the assignment of positive outcomes for holding offenders accountable is based on studies of targeted investigations, such as repeat-offender programs (Martin and Sherman 1986). These positive outcomes for ILP and predictive policing should be regarded as somewhat tentative, however, because they are based on a certain degree of logic given that current empirical evidence is sparse.

It is important to also discuss the potential weaknesses associated with various strategies. The question mark for COP is related to cost—some versions of COP do require extra personnel, and experience showed that it was most popular when supported with federal grants during the 1990s, whereas it is now under duress because of tight budgets. Focused deterrence, while effective, can have substantial costs and requires in-kind contributions from other parts of the criminal justice system and community. The question for ILP is whether its top-down, police-driven approach is destined to leave the community feeling left out, as seemed to happen in the United Kingdom. And the question for predictive policing, not surprisingly, is whether it can be implemented in a way that does not abuse police power and authority to the detriment of civil liberties and personal privacy. Hot-spots policing can enhance satisfaction and legitimacy; however, it may depend on how interventions within hot spots are implemented. Aggressive, broken windows styles of intervention within hot spots could exacerbate citizens' fear (Hinkle and Weisburd 2008) and compromise citizens' satisfaction. These potential weaknesses might be avoidable, but it is important to recognize them as warning signs deserving of careful attention.

The bottom line is that solid evidence exists about the relative effectiveness of modern police innovations, although confidence will increase when more evidence becomes available. In the meantime, it is apparent that all of the strategies each have their strengths and that most have some weaknesses, or at least potential concerns. It is tempting to conclude that a police department should adopt a blend of all of the strategies, but that is likely to be unrealistic and not affordable. In the absence of a complete blend, police departments would be smart to select the one or two strategies closest to meeting their communities' needs. Additionally, innovations would need to be selected while considering factors such as the nature and type of crime or problems to be addressed, the community agreement with the innovation, and organizational buy-in

Some innovations may be most impactful when addressing crime and victimization in public space (e.g., hot-spots policing or ILP) but less impactful at addressing crimes in private (e.g., intimate partner violence, where POP or focused deterrence may be more suitable). Also, democratic policing suggests that the people should influence how they are policed. Certain innovations, such as broken windows policing or certain treatment associated with hot-spots policing, could give the perception the police are an occupying force within the community, which may compromise citizens' willingness to partner with the police. As the President's Task Force on Twenty-First Century Policing (2015, 16) noted,

"Crime reduction is not self-justifying. Overly aggressive law enforcement strategies can potentially harm communities and do lasting damage to public trust."

Finally, some innovations may be more in line with existing organizational culture than others. If, for example, organizational culture is consistent with Wilson's (1968) legalistic typology, then innovations that department members may perceive as being soft on crime (e.g., COP or POP) may be more challenging to implement fully. Therefore, it may also be wise to pick and choose particular elements of certain strategies when they correspond to a community's specific needs.

## Summary

Field operations have evolved over the past several decades. Shortcomings of the standard model of policing have encouraged police to innovate their approaches to reducing crime and serving the public. A defining characteristic of these innovations is proactivity—strategic and police-initiated approaches to confront crime and disorder. Modern innovations also are more focused on crime prevention than the standard model. Innovations may be broadly categorized into several different categories, including problem-based approaches, community-based approaches, place-based approaches, and person-based approaches. As the police continue to engage in innovation, a healthy body of empirical examinations on these approaches have developed. Some approaches are more effective than others; however, great variation exists across crime type, context, and the ability of organizations to fully implement innovations. While these approaches may appear to be distinct and mutually exclusive, the reality is that many of these innovations borrow logic and strategies from others, and in practice, police implement hybrids of these approaches. National surveys confirm the police have embraced a variety of these innovations over time.

## Discussion Questions

1. How are place-based approaches similar to the standard model of policing? How are they different?

2. What is the difference between informal and formal social control?

3. Discuss the advantages and disadvantages of implementing "hybrid innovations."

4. What is the future of predictive policing? Does this innovation show promise?

5. If you were to recommend that a police executive implement one innovative strategy, which innovation would it be? Why?

## References

Abt, T., and Winship, C. 2016. *What Works in Reducing Community Violence: A Meta-Review and Field Study for the Northern Triangle*. Bethesda, MD: Democracy International.

Bachner, J., and Lynch, J. 2016. "Is Predictive Policing the Law-Enforcement Tactic of the Future?" *Wall Street Journal*, April 24. https://www.wsj.com/articles/is-predictive-policing-the-law-enforcement-tactic-of-the-future-1461550190/.

Bayley, D. 1994. *Police for the Future*. New York: Oxford University Press.

Beck, C., and McCue, C. 2009. "Predictive Policing: What Can We Learn from Wal-Mart and Amazon about Fighting Crime in a Recession?" *The Police Chief* 76(November): 18–24.

Berman, G., and Fox, A. 2010. *Trial and Error in Criminal Justice Reform: Learning from Error*. Washington, DC: Urban Institute Press.

Braga, A. A. (2010). *Problem-Oriented Policing and Crime Prevention*. Second edition. Boulder, CO: Lynne Rienner Publishers.

Braga, A. A., and Bond, B. J. 2008. "Policing Crime and Disorder Hot Spots: A Randomized Controlled Trial." *Criminology* 46: 577–607.

Braga, A. A., Kennedy, D. M., Waring, E. J., and Piehl, A. M. 2001. "Problem-Oriented Policing, Deterrence, and Youth Violence: An Evaluation of Boston's Operation Ceasefire." *Journal of Research in Crime and Delinquency* 38: 195–225.

Braga, A. A., McDevitt, J., and Pierce, G. L. 2006. "Understanding and Preventing Gang Violence: Problem Analysis and Response Development in Lowell, Massachusetts." *Police Quarterly* 9: 20–46.

Braga, A. A., Weisburd, D. L., and Turchan, B. 2018. "Focused Deterrence Strategies and Crime Control: An Updated Systematic Review and Meta-Analysis of the Empirical Evidence." *Criminology and Public Policy* 17: 205–250.

Braga, A. A., Weisburd, D. L., Waring, E. J., Green Mazerolle, L., Spelman, W., and Gajewski, F. 1999. "Problem-Oriented Policing in Violent Crime Places: A Randomized Controlled Experiment." *Criminology* 37: 541–581.

Bratton, W. J. 1996. "Remark: New Strategies for Combating Crime in New York City." *Fordham Urban Journal* 23: 781–785.

Bratton, W. J., and Kelling, G. L.2015. "Why We Need Broken Windows Policing: It Has Saved Countless New York Lives—Most of Them Minority—Cut the Jail Population, and Reknit the Social Fabric." *City Journal*. https://www.city-journal.org/html/why-we-need-broken-windows-policing-13696.html.

Carter, D. L. 2009. *Law Enforcement Intelligence: A Guide for State, Local, and Tribal Law Enforcement Agencies*, 2nd ed. Washington, DC: Office of Community Oriented Policing Services. https://it.ojp.gov/documents/d/e050919201-IntelGuide_web.pdf/.

Casady, T. 2011. "Police Legitimacy and Predictive Policing." *Geography & Public Safety* 2(4): 1–2.

Clark, J. R. 1997. "LEN Salutes Its 1997 People of the Year, the Boston Gun Project Working Group." *Law Enforcement News* 23(1): 4–5.

Cohen, J., and Ludwig, J. 2003. "Policing Crime Guns." In J. Ludwig and P. J. Cook (eds.), *Evaluating Gun Policy: Effects on Crime and Violence*, pp. 217–239. Washington, DC: Brookings Institution Press.

Cordner, G. 2010. *Reducing Fear of Crime: Strategies for Police*. Washington, DC: Office of Community Oriented Policing Services. https://www.popcenter.org/library/reading/pdfs/ReducingFearGuide.pdf.

Corsaro, N. and Engel, R. S.. 2015. "Most Challenging of Contexts: Assessing the Impact of Focused Deterrence on Serious Violence in New Orleans." *Criminology and Public Policy* 14(3): 471–505.

Engel, R. S., Tillyer, M. S., and Corsaro, N. 2013. "Reducing Gang Violence Using Focused Deterrence: Evaluating the Cincinnati Initiative to Reduce Violence (CIRV)." *Justice Quarterly* 30: 403–439.

Erbentraut, J. 2014. "Chicago's Controversial New Police Program Prompts Fears of Racial Profiling." *The Huffington Post*, February 25. https://www.huffingtonpost.com/2014/02/25/chicago-police-home-visits-_n_4855319.html/.

Fox, A. M., and Novak, K. J. 2018. "Collaborating to Reduce Violence: The Impact of Focused Deterrence in Kansas City." *Police Quarterly* 21(3): 283–308.

Fox, A. M., Novak, K. J. and McHale, J. 2015. "Using Social Network Analysis to Guide Law Enforcement Strategies." *Translational Criminology* 9: 6–8.

Fuentes, J. R. 2006. *Practical Guide to Intelligence-Led Policing*. New York: Manhattan Institute, Center for Policing Terrorism. https://www.manhattan-institute.org/pdf/NJPoliceGuide.pdf/.

Greene, J. 1999. "Zero Tolerance: A Case Study of Police Policies and Practices in New York City." *Crime and Delinquency* 45: 171–187.

Green, J. R., and Taylor, R. B. 1988. "Community-Based Policing and Foot Patrol: Issues of Theory and Evaluation." In J. R. Green and S. D. Mastrofski, *Community Policing: Rhetoric or Reality*, pp. 195–223. Westport, CT: Praeger.

Groff, E. R., Ratcliffe, J. H., Haberman, C. P., Sorg, E. T., Joyce, N. M. and Taylor, R. B. 2015. "Does What Police Do at Hot Spots Matter? The Philadelphia Policing Tactics Experiment." *Criminology*, 53(1), 23–53.

Haberman, C. P., and Ratcliffe, J. H. 2012. "The Predictive Policing Challenges of Near Repeat Armed Street Robberies." *Policing: A Journal of Policy and Practice* 6: 151–166.

Harcourt, B. 2001. *Illusion of Order: The False Promise of Broken Windows Policing.* Cambridge, MA: Harvard University Press.

Herbert, S. 2001. "Policing the Contemporary City: Fixing Broken Windows or Shoring Up Neo-Liberalism?" *Theoretical Criminology* 5: 445–466.

Hinkle, J. C., and Weisburd, D. 2008. "The Irony of Broken Windows Policing: A Micro-Place Study of the Relationship between Disorder, Focused Police Crackdowns and Fear of Crime." *Journal of Criminal Justice* 36: 503–512.

Hinkle, J. C., Weisburd, D., Telep, C. W., and Petersen, K. 2020. "Problem-Oriented Policing for Reducing Crime and Disorder: An Updated Systematic Review and Meta-Analysis." *Campbell Systematic Reviews* 16(2): 1-86.

Holloway, K., Bennett, T., and Farrington, D. P. 2008. "Does Neighborhood Watch Reduce Crime?" *Crime Prevention Research Review.* Washington, DC: Office of Community Oriented Policing Services.

Johnson, J. A., Reitzel, J. D., Norwood, B. F., McCoy, D. M., Cummings, B., and Tate, R. R. 2013. "Social Network Analysis: A Systematic Approach for Investigating." *FBI Law Enforcement Bulletin*, March 5. https://leb.fbi.gov/2013/march/social-network-analysis-a-systematic-approach-for-investigating/.

Katz, C. M., Webb, V. J., and Schaefer, D. R. 2001. "An Assessment of the Impact of Quality-of-Life Policing on Crime and Disorder." *Justice Quarterly* 18: 825–876.

Kelling, G. L., and Bratton, W. 1998. "Declining Crime Rates: Insiders' Views of the New York City Story." *Journal of Criminal Law and Criminology* 88: 1217–1231.

Kennedy, D. M. 1998. "Pulling Levers: Getting Deterrence Right." *National Institute of Justice Journal* 236(2): 8.

Kennedy, D. M. 2006. "Old wine in new bottles: Policing and the lessons of "pulling levers."" In D. Weisburd & A. A. Braga (Eds.), Police innovation: Contrasting perspectives (pp. 155–170). Cambridge, England: Cambridge University Press.

Kennedy, D. M. 2019. "Policing and the Lessons of Focused Deterrence." In D. Weisburd and A. Braga (eds.), *Police Innovation: Contrasting Perspectives*, 2nd ed., pp. 205–226. Cambridge, UK: Cambridge University Press.

Kennedy, D. M., Piehl, A. M., and Braga, A. A. 1996. "Youth Gun Violence in Boston: Gun Markets, Serious Youth Offenders, and a Use Reduction Strategy." *Law and Contemporary Problems* 59: 147–196.

Kennedy, L. W., Caplan, J. M., and Piza, E. 2011. "Risk Clusters, Hotspots, and Spatial Intelligence: Risk Terrain Modeling as an Algorithm for Police Resource Allocation Strategies." *Journal of Quantitative Criminology* 27: 339–362.

King, W. R. 2000. "Measuring Police Innovation: Issues and Management." *Policing: An International Journal of Police Strategies and Management* 23: 303–317.

Koper, C. S. 1995. "Just Enough Police Presence: Reducing Crime and Disorderly Behavior by Optimizing Patrol Time in Crime Hot Spots." *Justice Quarterly* 12: 649–672.

Loveday, B. 2008. "Performance Management and the Decline of Leadership within Public Services in the United Kingdom." *Policing: A Journal of Policy and Practice* 2: 120–130.

Lum, C., Koper, C. S., and Telp, C. W. 2011. "The Evidence-Based Policing Matrix." *Journal of Experimental Criminology* 7: 3–26.

Maguire, M., and John, T. 2006. "Intelligence Led Policing, Managerialism, and Community Engagement: Competing Priorities and the Role of the National Intelligence Model in the UK." *Policing & Society* 16: 67–85.

Martin, S. E. and Sherman, L. W. 1986. "Selective Apprehension: A Police Strategy for Repeat Offenders." *Criminology* 24: 155-174.

Mazerolle, L., Bennett, S., Davis, J., Sargeant, E., and Manning, M. 2012. "Legitimacy in Policing: A Systematic Review." *Campbell Collaboration Library of Systematic Reviews.* https://campbellcollaboration.org/lib/project/141/.

Mazerolle, L., Bennett, S., Davis, J., Sargeant, E., and Manning, M. 2013. "Procedural Justice and Police Legitimacy: A Systematic Review of the Research Evidence." *Journal of Experimental Criminology* 9: 245–274.

McGarrell, E. F., Chermak, S., and Weiss, A. 2001. "Reducing Firearms Violence through Directed Police Patrol." *Criminology & Public Policy* 1: 119–148.

McGarrell, E. F., Chermak, S., Wilson, J. M., and Corsaro, N. 2006. "Reducing Homicide Through a 'Level Pulling' Strategy" *Justice Quarterly* 23: 214–231.

National Academies of Sciences, Engineering, and Medicine. 2018. *Proactive Policing: Effects on Crime and Communities.* Washington, DC: National Academies Press. doi:10.17226/24928

National Research Council. 2004. *Fairness and Effectiveness in Policing: The Evidence.* Washington, DC: The National Academies Press. doi.org/10.17226/10419

*New York Times.* 2014. "Sir Robert Peel's Nine Principles of Policing." April 15. https://www.nytimes.com/2014/04/16/nyregion/sir-robert-peels-nine-principles-of-policing.html.

Novak, K. J., Fox, A. M., Carr, C. M., and Spade, D. A. 2016. "The Efficacy of Foot Patrol in Violent Places." *Journal of Experimental Criminology* 12: 283–308.

Novak, K. J., Hartman, J. L., Holsinger, A. M., and Turner, M. G. 1999. "The Effects of Aggressive Policing of Disorder on Serious Crime." *Policing: An International Journal of Police Strategies and Management* 22: 171–190.

President's Task Force on Twenty-First Century Policing. 2015. *Final Report of the President's Task Force on 21st Century Policing.* Washington, DC: Office of Community Oriented Policing Services.

Ratcliffe, J. H. 2016. *Intelligence-Led Policing,* 2nd ed. London: Routledge.

Ratcliffe, J. H., and Guidetti, R. 2008. "State Police Investigative Structure and the Adoption of Intelligence-Led Policing." *Policing: An International Journal of Police Strategies and Management* 31: 109–128.

Rollins, J., and Connors, T. 2007. *State Fusion Center Processes and Procedures: Best Practices and Recommendations.* New York: Manhattan Institute, Center for Policing Terrorism. https://www.manhattan-institute.org/html/ptr_02.htm/.

Rosenfeld, R., Fornango, R., and Baumer, E. 2005. "Did Ceasefire, Compstat, and Exile Reduce Homicide?" *Criminology and Public Policy* 4: 419–450.

Sampson, R. J., and Raudenbush, S. W. 1999. "Systematic Social Observation of Public Spaces: A New Look at Disorder in Urban Neighborhoods." *American Journal of Sociology* 103: 603–651.

Scheider, M. C., Chapman, R., and Schapiro, A. 2009. "Towards the Unification of Policing Innovations Under Community Policing." *Policing* 32: 694–718.

Schlossman, S. and Sedlak, M. 1983. "The Chicago Area Project Revisited." *Crime and Delinquency* 29, 398–462.

Sherman, L. W., Gartin, P. R., and Buerger, M. E. 1989. "Hot Spots of Predatory Crime: Routine Activities and the Criminology of Place." *Criminology* 27: 27–55.

Sherman, L. W., Shaw, J. W., and Rogan, D. P. 1995. *The Kansas City Gun Experiment.* Washington, DC: US Government Printing Office.

Sherman, L. W., and Weisburd, D. A. 1995. "General Deterrence Effects of Police Patrol in Crime 'Hot Spots': A Randomized, Controlled Trial." *Justice Quarterly* 12: 625–648.

Sousa, W. H., and Kelling, G. L. 2006. "Of 'Broken Windows,' Criminology, and Criminal Justice." In D. Weisburd and A. Braga (eds.), *Police Innovation: Contrasting Perspectives,* pp. 77–97. Cambridge, UK: Cambridge University Press.

Spelman, W., and Eck, J. E. 1989. "Sitting Ducks, Ravenous Wolves, and Helping Hands: New Approaches to Urban Policing." *Public Affairs Comment,* 35(2): 1–9.

Sunshine, J. and Tyler, T. R. 2003. "The Role of Procedural Justice and Legitimacy in Shaping Public Support for Policing." *Law and Society Review,* 37(3): 513-548.

Thomas, G. 2016. "A Case for Local Neighbourhood Policing and Community Intelligence in Counter Terrorism." *Police Journal: Theory, Practice and Principles* 89(1): 31–54.

Tillyer, M. S., Engel, R. S., and Lovins, B. 2012. "Beyond Boston: Applying Theory to Understand and Address Sustainability Issues in Focused Deterrence Initiatives for Violence Reduction." *Crime & Delinquency* 58: 973–997.

Tita, G. E., Riley, K. J., Ridgeway, G., and Greenwood, P. W. 2005. "Reducing Gun Violence: Operation Ceasefire in Los Angeles." *National Institute of Justice Research Report.* Washington, DC: US Department of Justice.

Tyler, T. R 1990. *Why People Obey the Law*. Princeton, NJ: Princeton University Press.

Tyler, T. R. 2008. "Psychology and Institutional Design." *Review of Law and Economics* 4: 801–887.

Tyler, T. R., and Huo, Y. J. 2002. *Trust in the Law*. New York: Russell Sage.

Weisburd, D. 2015. "The Law of Crime Concentration and the Criminology of Place." *Criminology*, 52: 133–157.

Weisburd, D. 2018. "Hot Spots of Crime and Place-Based Prevention." *Criminology and Public Policy* 17: 1–25.

Weisburd, D., and Braga, A. A. 2006. *Police Innovation: Contrasting Perspectives*. Cambridge, UK: Cambridge University Press.

Weisburd, D., and Eck, J. E. 2004. "What Can Police Do to Reduce Crime, Disorder and Fear?" *Annals* 593: 42–65.

Weisburd, D., Groff, E. R., and Yang, S. M. 2012. *The Criminology of Place: Street Segments and our Understanding of the Crime Problem*. New York: Oxford University Press.

Weisburd, D., Telep, C. W., Hinkle, J. C., and Eck, J. E. 2010. "Is Problem-Oriented Policing Effective in Reducing Crime and Disorder? Findings from a Campbell Systematic Review." *Criminology & Public Policy* 9: 139–172.

Weisburd, D., Telep, C. W., Vovak, H., Zastrow, T., Braga, A. A. and Turchan, B. 2022. "Reforming the Police Through Procedural Justice Training: A Multicity Randomized Trial at Crime Hot Spots." *Proceedings of the National Academy of Sciences* 119: 1–6.

Weisburd, D. L, Wooditch, A., Weisburd, S., and Yang, S. M. 2015. "Do Stop, Question, and Frisk Practices Deter Crime? Evidence at Microunits of Space and Time." *Criminology and Public Policy* 15: 31–56.

Wilson, J. Q., and Kelling, G. L. 1982. "Broken Windows: The Police and Neighborhood Safety." *Atlantic Monthly* 249: 29–38.

Wilson, J. Q. 1968. *Varieties of Police Behavior: The Management of Law and Order in Eight Communities*. Harvard University Press: Cambridge, MA.

Wilson, J. M. 2006. *Community Policing in America*. New York: Routledge.

Wolfgang, M. E., Figlio, R. M, and Sellin, T. 1972. *Delinquency in a Birth Cohort*. Chicago: University of Chicago Press.

Worrall, J. L. 2002. *Does "Broken Windows" Law Enforcement Reduce Serious Crime?* Sacramento, CA: California Institute for County Government.

**Part III**

# Police Behavior

## CHAPTER 9

# Behavior and Misconduct

## CHAPTER OUTLINE (continued)

- Organizational Responses
- Summary
- Critical Thinking Questions
- References

### KEY TERMS

- abuse of authority
- code of silence
- crisis intervention team
- discretion
- economic corruption
- grass eaters
- gratuity
- in-group solidarity
- legalistic style
- meat eaters
- noble-cause corruption
- occupational deviance
- particularistic perspectives
- police corruption
- police culture
- police deviance
- police misconduct
- police violence
- predispositional theory
- racial profiling
- rotten-apple theory of corruption
- service style
- socialization theory
- subjugation of a defendant's rights
- symbolic assailant
- systemic theory of corruption
- universalistic perspectives
- use corruption
- watchman style

JOHN ADAMS, when commenting on the virtues of the separation of powers, noted that ours is a "government of laws, and not of men." And as we said in Chapter 1, a principle of constitutional democracies is that the government exercises power based on laws, not on an individual. Yet we also recognize that all actors in the criminal justice system, especially the police, have the latitude to invoke legal sanctions. In other words, police officers have the discretion to invoke the law. This can seem counterintuitive—how can a democracy of laws and not men embrace individual discretion?

Police officers make daily decisions using their discretion, such as whether to stop a motorist for a traffic violation or to look the other way. If the motorist is stopped, are they given a ticket (and for what) or perhaps merely a warning? Does the officer perform a search? Does the officer make inquiries or engage in some other activity? Does an officer make an arrest, thereby initiating the formal criminal justice process? Does the officer make demands of the citizen, and if the citizen makes requests or demands of the officer, how does the officer respond? Does the officer use coercion or physical force? Officers have a great deal of discretion on whether and how to interact with citizens, and these decisions can have consequences for both the police and the public.

Is officer discretion a good thing or a bad thing? In reality, it is probably both. Neither the police nor the criminal justice system is equipped to engage in full enforcement, meaning there are insufficient resources to enact "zero tolerance" for every violation of the law. Therefore, discretion permits officers and police departments to prioritize strategies and perhaps circumvent outdated or unpopular laws. Discretion also permits officers to individualize justice and consider contextual cues. On the other hand, there is something undemocratic in enforcing some laws but not others, or by enforcing the law selectively. Discretion is different for some people and some communities, leading to abuse.

This chapter discusses police behavior, with a focus on understanding how officers learn to exercise discretion and what factors influence decision making. It considers many different perspectives on the conduct of the police in terms of both the way police make decisions and the factors that motivate their decisions. It is concerned with a general discussion of both appropriate and inappropriate (deviant) police behavior. This chapter considers two particular forms of deviance: the acceptance of gratuities and police corruption. Chapter 10 addresses other forms of police deviance related to the exercise of police authority, physical force, and the use of coercion. Issues and strategies for controlling and guiding police behavior are discussed in Chapter 11.

## Perspectives of Police Behavior

Police behavior may be described from universalistic or particularistic perspectives. **Universalistic perspectives** consider the ways officers are similar. These perspectives are widely used by police researchers, because they provide ways to distinguish police work from other occupations. **Particularistic perspectives** emphasize how police officers differ from one another.

### Universalistic Perspectives

A wide variety of research has sought to explain police behavior in universalistic terms. This research has been conducted from three perspectives: sociological, psychological, and organizational (Worden 1989).

**Sociological Perspective.** The sociological perspective emphasizes the social context in which police officers are hired and trained and in which police–citizen interactions occur. Police officers, as a result of their training and work experience, tend to view situations in a certain manner and act accordingly. Most of the research in this area has attempted to identify external or contextual factors that influence an officer's discretion (Black 1980). Research on women in policing has discussed the absence of role models for female officers and the problems women have adapting to male expectations (Martin 1990).

**Psychological Perspective.** The psychological perspective is concerned with the nature of the "police personality." Officers may have a certain type of personality prior to employment, or their personality may change due to their police experience. One of the enduring issues in research on police behavior is whether the values and attitudes of police officers stem from their backgrounds and upbringing or result from the experience of police work. Between the 1970s and the 1990s, researchers considered experience in police work to be the most important determinant of the police personality. However, more recent research has questioned this assumption, contending that predispositional factors (discussed later) may be more important than previously thought (Caldero 1997).

**Organizational Perspective.** The organizational perspective suggests that organizational (departmental) factors play an important role in police behavior. These factors can be formal, informal (cultural), and institutional.

Research on the influence of formal factors examines the ways the department structures police activity. For example, Greene and Klockars (1991) studied the caseloads of officers to assess the overall importance of law enforcement, order maintenance, and service activity in the daily work of the police. They discovered that police spend more time on law enforcement than had been previously thought. As discussed in Chapter 8, most of the research in the 1960s and 1970s discovered that law enforcement activities accounted for only between 10 and 30 percent of an officer's workload. Greene and Klockars, however, found that police officers spend about 43 percent of their time on law enforcement, 24 percent on traffic, only 21 percent on maintaining order, and 8 percent on service. Furthermore, recent research indicates that the amount of time spent on different core activities, including law enforcement, problem solving, order maintenance, service, investigations, and patrol, varies by assignment and that COP officers have very different workloads from their traditional officer counterparts (Smith, Novak, and Frank 2002; Famega 2009).

Research on informal factors studies **police culture**. In some ways, policing is both a culture and a subculture. As a culture, police work is characterized by its own occupational beliefs and values that are shared by officers across the United States; for example, police everywhere value their assigned beats. Their territories and the way they deal with their territories define to a great extent their reputations in the department (Herbert 1997). Police organizations often have their own local cultures as well, variations of the broader occupational culture (Manning 1997). As a subculture, police work has many values imported from the broader society in which officers live. Subcultures often develop within police organizations among working groups of officers, where values and norms for behavior are set and enforced among subgroups (e.g., a particular police precinct or unit or officers on a particular shift).

Research on institutional factors is concerned with how the department adapts to its environment. Policing is inherently local, and police departments adjust to local norms, politics, economics, crime, and problems. Though police behavior may vary from city to city, it also fluctuates within cities (especially large cities). For example, Klinger (1997) noted that officers' understanding of workload norms and level of crime, problems and deviance within a patrol district influences how officers behave when interacting with citizens. "Place" is not a neutral backdrop when understanding human behavior, and it is important to recognize how the environment may shape institutions.

## Particularistic Perspectives

Instead of emphasizing similarities among police, particularistic perspectives focus on decision-making differences among officers. Particularistic perspectives include typologies and other officer classification schemes, which are perspectives that identify different officer types or styles of policing.

Worden's (1989) research on police behavior suggests that officers, contrary to conventional wisdom, are not psychologically homogeneous; that is, they are not always intensely loyal to one another or preoccupied with order. Nor are they all suspicious, secretive, cynical, or authoritarian. The police socialization process does not necessarily result in officers having the same outlook.

Worden identified five ways in which police officers differ from one another. First is their view of human nature. Cynical police, for example, tend to be pessimistic, suspicious, and distrustful. The important issue here is the extent to which a person is cynical before employment, how that cynicism changes over time, and how it influences their behavior.

Second, officers have different role orientations. Some see themselves as crime-fighters who deter crime by making arrests and issuing citations. Others believe that the police role involves fighting crime as well as problem solving, crime prevention, and community service.

Third, officers have different attitudes toward legal and departmental restrictions. Some officers think that the ends justify the means in policing, often because they think that legal and policy guidelines are too restrictive, resulting in a criminal going free and thereby increasing crime and the suffering of victims. In addition, some officers believe that the criminal justice system is not punitive enough and that it is up to them to guarantee punishment through "street justice."

Fourth, officers' clientele influences their beliefs and their behavior. Preferences of particular judges, for example, or pressure on patrol enforcement practices from Mothers Against Drunk Driving, can influence patterns of police enforcement. The influence of particular groups can lead to selective enforcement of particular laws and alienate other groups with whom the police interact.

Fifth is the relationship between management and peer group support. Theoretically, police departments reward desired behavior and punish undesired behavior. Many observers, however, have noted that police departments are punishment-oriented. They do not have many ways to reward good behavior, so they tend to control the behavior of line officers by setting up elaborate standard operating procedures and punishing officers for infractions. Consequently, officers often turn to their peer group members for aid—that is, to other officers of the same rank in the department. The peer group is very influential in policing. Officers depend on it for physical protection and emotional comfort. This dependency in turn can result in increased secrecy in the department.

## Socialization Versus Predisposition

Policing is in the midst of broad change. The most visible changes are occurring under the umbrella of community policing (COP), which emphasizes police discretion, problem solving, decentralization of authority, and community involvement. Departments are increasingly seeking personnel who have the attitudes, values, and skills for COP.

COP-related concerns about hiring the "right" kind of officer have rekindled the debate about where officers' attitudes and values come from. If they come from the way officers adapt to their occupational environment, commanders will have to change the department or how it does its work in order to change officers' attitudes and values. If they come from the background characteristics of officers, then administrators will have to change their hiring policies. These two ways of thinking about police officers' values and attitudes are the socialization theory and the predispositional theory.

**Socialization Theory.** Beginning in the 1960s, as the body of knowledge about police behavior increased, social scientists suggested that police behavior was determined more by work experiences and peers than by preemployment values and attitudes. This was called the **socialization theory**—that is, individuals are socialized as a result of their occupational experiences. If a police officer becomes corrupt, it is because the police occupation contributes in some way to weaken values; in other words, corruption is learned within the department. This theory applies to any type of police behavior, good or bad.

Two socialization processes take place in police organizations. *Formal socialization* is the result of what transpires in the selection process and training program, what is learned about policies and procedures, and what officers are told by supervisors and managers. *Informal socialization* takes place as new recruits interact with older, more experienced officers. One's peers play an important role in determining behavior not only in the police occupation but also in other jobs. An understanding of informal socialization processes is important, because what one learns on the job and from one's peers may contradict what is learned during the formal socialization process.

In many police departments, the selection process attempts to eliminate individuals who may be prone to unnecessary violence or dishonest behavior. Therefore, police behavior—both good and bad—is seen as a consequence of behavior that is learned after employment. The police experience, and how individuals adjust to that experience, is the most important consideration in determining how "good" police behavior is to be achieved and how "bad" police behavior is to be avoided.

Van Maanen (1973) conducted participant-observation research within a small city police department in California and identified four stages of officer socialization. The first stage is *preentry choice*. Most individuals who choose a police career select it from among various career choices. They tend to go into police work believing they are entering an elite occupation. Many already know someone or something about police work and already tend to identify with the goals and values of the police, at least as they understand them. Their motivation for entering police work is often related to doing something important in society.

The second stage is *admittance/introduction*, which includes the police academy experience. All officers, after being hired, must take some form of academy training, where they learn the necessity of adhering to the rules and regulations of the department. The academy Van Maanen attended had a military atmosphere in which officers followed a rigid routine and were punished for deviating from it (e.g., being late). Officers spent much time studying the technical aspects of police work, and instructors elaborated on these aspects with police war stories. These stories provided important insights about the traditions and values of the department and what was considered "good" police work. Recruits learned that they must stick together and protect one another. Today, many academies are less stress oriented and more academically oriented, yet many of the lessons Van Maanen described are still applicable.

Once the police academy has been completed, new officers enter the third stage, *encounter*, in which they go to work in the patrol division, each being assigned to a training officer. Once they are in the field, they are taught what the work is really like. During this phase, the new officers are "tested" by the older officers. Can they perform? Can they operate the equipment effectively? Do they have common sense? Are they willing to take risks? Officers are always tested about their willingness to "back up" other officers. Perhaps the most crucial test new officers must pass is related to their dependability in helping fellow officers when they are in trouble.

In the final stage, *continuance/metamorphosis*, new officers adjust to the reality of police work. In effect, this reality involves a large number of routine problems and bureaucratic tasks, with only an occasional exciting or adventurous activity. However, for some officers, the possibility of an exciting or adventurous call continues to be an important motivating factor. As they progress in police work, many officers learn that the public does not understand or support them. And they often decide that the police system—meaning managers and supervisors and how they enforce rules and regulations—is unfair. Perhaps the most common adjustment made by officers, at least in the city Van Maanen studied, was to "lie low and hang loose." That is, they did as little work as possible to avoid getting into trouble.

**Predispositional Theory.** In recent years, there has been a renewal of interest in the **predispositional theory**, which suggests that the behavior of officers is primarily explained by the characteristics, values, and attitudes that they had before being employed as police. If an officer is dishonest or honest, or brutal or temperate in the use of force, those positive or negative traits likely existed before the individual was hired. Predispositional theory focuses on the idea that the policing occupation attracts people with certain attitudes and beliefs; thus, socialization has less explanatory value. Caldero and Larose (2003, 162) summarize the central principles of these research efforts are as follows:

1. Police have distinctively different values from other groups in American society.
2. Police values are highly similar to the values of the groups from which they are recruited.

3. Police values are also determined by particular characteristics of personality that set police officers apart from the groups from which they are recruited.

4. Police values are unaffected by occupational socialization.

5. The values carried by police officers are stable over time.

6. Regardless of racial or ethnic differences, police officers hold similar values.

7. Education has little impact on values held by police officers.

8. The police socialization process has little effect on the values of individual officers.

Crank and Caldero (1999) found that values consistent with police culture were already in place when police were hired. Moreover, police values changed little over an individual officer's career after hiring. Finally, screening processes ensured that police recruits held similar values, regardless of their ethnicity or gender. The perspectives developed by Crank and Caldero can be described as a *subcultural* theory of police attitudes and behavior, meaning that police values in general are not learned on the job but are already inherent when a recruit applies for police work. Police work then selectively accents some of these values; for example, working-class values are reflected and intensified in the strong loyalties officers have for one another.

## Early Examinations of Police Behavior

This section reviews important classic studies of police behavior, many of which were written years ago. However, these studies are as important today as they were when they were written. In many ways, the fundamental issues facing the police, the problems they confront on their beats, and the people they must work with have not changed significantly. Indeed, one of the fundamental problems is that despite truly staggering organizational changes over the past half-century, what officers do on the street has changed little. Assign an officer to walk a beat and the officer will view that work in much the same way as officers did 100 years ago, only with the addition of technological gadgets. Keep in mind that it is not important when the studies were written; it is the currency of the ideas.

The first social science–oriented study of the police was conducted in 1949 by William Westley (1970) in Gary, Indiana. Westley identified the importance of socialization as a significant factor in police behavior. He found that old-timers indoctrinated recruits believing that if the recruits were to be good cops, they must take charge of situations in which they became involved. Being in charge of a situation meant that citizens, particularly those in the lower classes, had to respect the officer. If a citizen failed to show respect or challenged an officer's authority, officers felt compelled to react. Officers believed that they could not back down when faced with challenges to their authority. Doing so only encouraged citizens to challenge the police more often, thus making the police officer's job more difficult. Many officers stated that it would be appropriate to "punish" the citizen using some type of physical force.

Westley also found that the police believed that the public did not support them. Consequently, many police officers were secretive about their daily routines. A concern for secrecy and protecting fellow officers was grounded in the fundamental belief that the public could not be trusted to fairly evaluate the appropriateness of police behavior. This research and analysis underscore the importance of **in-group solidarity**, or closeness and loyalty among officers, which results from a perception that the public cannot be trusted. In-group solidarity and officer secrecy make it difficult to determine what police officers actually do. Solidarity is often accompanied by a code of silence in which officers will not discuss inappropriate police behavior or may lie about it to protect a brother officer, creating what has been called "the blue wall of silence."

In an important analysis of two police departments, Jerome Skolnick (1966) provided many important insights about the activities and behavior of police officers. One of these was related to the *production orientation* of a police department, meaning that police behavior was influenced by the goals or objectives that the department emphasized. For example, if a department was concerned about making arrests and issuing traffic citations, officers were likely to be aggressive in making arrests and issuing tickets.

Skolnick also discussed the significance of danger in police work. He coined the phrase **symbolic assailant** to represent the person the police officer thinks is potentially dangerous or troublesome. Who is a dangerous person? Those "types" of people with whom the officer has had the most dangerous or troublesome experiences become, in effect, that officer's symbolic assailant. From their experiences, and from stories told by other officers, police develop a repertoire of danger signifiers, such as a person's actual behavior, language, dress, area, and in some situations, age, sex, and ethnicity. Such signifiers can be interpreted by the police as challenges to their authority. The person who is perceived to challenge that authority may be verbally or physically abused. Of course, such abuse confirms an officer's belief that a particular kind of person or a particular area is troublesome or potentially dangerous. Furthermore, it convinces the person abused, and others who witness the abuse, that the police are repressive and brutal. Finally, the symbolic assailant has implications for the perception that racial minorities may be more dangerous or predisposed to trouble, which can contribute to our understanding of the modern phenomenon of racial profiling (Rice 2010).

Perhaps the most important study of police behavior conducted in the 1960s was the one conducted by James Q. Wilson (1968). Wilson studied eight police departments and reported that in many respects they were quite different. Since Wilson's study, there have been many other attempts to identify different styles of police behavior in terms of both departments and individuals, but what makes Wilson's perspective an important contribution to our understanding of officer behavior is that he was able to identify and create typologies of behaviors within different organizations. Thus, although individual street officers continued to enjoy a great deal of discretion, their discretionary decisions were influenced by the larger organizational culture of the police department. Organizational culture in turn was largely influenced by the political climate of the local city government.

Wilson found that there were two general categories of problems confronting police departments. *Law enforcement problems* were those behaviors considered serious enough to warrant a citation or arrest, such as serious traffic violations and most felonies and major misdemeanors. *Order maintenance problems* involved less serious violations of the law, such as misdemeanors or problems that police usually handled without resorting to issuing citations or making arrests. Wilson stated that differences in policing styles were found primarily in how order maintenance problems were handled, and he identified three different organizational styles: *watchman*, *service*, and *legalistic*. Wilson suggested that the larger organizational values and cultural norms will influence individual officers' behavior and their exercise of discretion.

To illustrate, assume that police discover a group of teenagers drinking beer in a public park, a problem in maintaining order. In the **watchman style**, police officers are given substantial latitude as to how they handle such problems. Often, there are no policies or procedures to guide them. Consequently, officers are free to devise their own response or solution. The officers might take the beer and tell the teenagers to go home. They might even provide a lecture about excessive drinking, or they might do nothing at all. And if different officers observed the same problem, there would probably be several different responses to that problem.

In the **service style**, police see themselves as providing a product that the community wants. Such departments tend to be found in homogeneous communities with a common idea of public order. They train officers in what to do and how to do it. The police intervene frequently. However, many do so informally, and an arrest is not an inevitable outcome. The officers might refer the beer-drinking teenagers to a department program involving teenage drinking or to a community program. Or they might call the parents to come and get their children. Of course, police in the service style do not proceed this way for all order maintenance problems, but do so for those problems the community or the department considers important.

In the **legalistic style**, police try to enforce the law—write a citation or make an arrest— if possible. Police view themselves as law enforcers, and they would probably arrest the teenage beer drinkers. Of course, police in the legalistic style do not always make arrests, but they tend to make more arrests and issue more citations than do police using the other two styles.

Later empirical replications of his theory have supported much of Wilson's observations (Langworthy 1985), although recent research questions whether a link exists between political culture and organizational behavior (Hassell, Zhao, and Maguire 2003; Zhao and Hassell 2005; Liederbach and Travis 2008). Michael K. Brown's (1981) study of policing styles was conducted in three southern California cities. Individual officer styles, Brown suggested, depended on a combination of their aggressiveness and selectivity of crime problems. *Aggressiveness* was the degree to which they actively sought out problems. *Selectivity* was the extent to which they were concerned only about serious crime problems.

Using these two factors, Brown identified four styles of police behavior. *Old-style crime-fighters* are aggressive and tend to be selective, concentrating primarily on felonies. These officers develop extensive knowledge of the area in which they work, use informants, and tend to be coercive. They are sometimes willing to act illegally to get results. *Clean-beat crimefighters* believe in the importance of legal procedures. These officers are proactive and legalistic but do not tend to be selective. Almost all violations of the law are considered significant. *Service-style officers* do the minimum amount of work necessary to get by; that is, they are not aggressive but are selective. Only the most serious problems will result in their enforcing the law. Such officers tend to rely on informal solutions to problems rather than legalistic ones. *Professional-style officers* engage in limited self-initiated activity and are not selective. They are situationally oriented, although tough when necessary, and at other times, they may be service-minded.

It should be apparent that the observations by Wilson and Brown contributed to distinct understandings of officer behavior. Each offered different levels of analysis when considering discretion (i.e., organizational factors, situational factors, and individual officer factors). Each perspective is incomplete, however, because it forsakes the other correlates of behavior. Thus, a more complete model for understanding police behavior can be found by including each of these levels of analysis when attempting to understand street-level discretionary behavior.

Finally, John P. Crank's (1998) book *Understanding Police Culture* integrates many writings about police work and shows present-day trends in thinking about the police. It is an effort to develop a middle-range theory about the police and show how it can provide new insights into police work. Middle-range theory attempts to integrate findings from a broad body of research into a more general perspective. Crank suggests that police culture emerges from the daily practice of police work. Culture, he argues, does not make the police different from the public. Rather, it humanizes the police by giving their work meaning. Rejecting the notion that police culture is a "dark force," he argues that culture is carried in police common sense, in the way that everyday activities are celebrated, and in the way that police deal with death and suffering. Consequently, to understand police culture, one must examine the physical setting in which police work occurs and the groups with which police interact, such as wrongdoers, the public, the courts, the press, and the department's administration. Because these groups tend to be similar everywhere, police culture tends to take on similar characteristics in different departments, and one can speak of a police culture generally.

Elements of police culture are organized around four central principles. The first and most central principle is *coercive territorial control*. The police are trained formally and socialized informally to view their work in terms of the use of force to control specific territories to which they are assigned. Police learn about the use of force both in terms of a use-of-force continuum or policies (see Chapter 10) and in terms of informal tactics that enable them to control the public in police–citizen encounters. The use of force is more than a set of skills, however. Force is acted out as a moral commitment to control their assigned territories. Herbert (1997) echoed the importance of territoriality. In his observations of Los Angeles officers, he found that the ability of the police to control behavior in an assigned geographic area was a central factor that influenced officer behavior.

The second principle is *the unknown*. Police activity routinely puts officers in circumstances that are unpredictable and may have outcomes beyond their control. Such unpredictability makes police work interesting. However, the common unpredictability of everyday encounters may mask significant danger. Police officers have a wide repertoire of skills to ensure that unknown situations do not deteriorate into dangerous life-threatening encounters.

The third principle is *solidarity*, or the intense bonding and sense of occupational uniqueness that officers feel for one another. It is produced by the dangers and unpredictability of their work and from the intense individualism that is part of the police ethos. Central to solidarity is conflict with other groups: police officers often feel alienated from the courts and the public and from outsiders and different ethnic groups. The greater the conflict with outside groups, the greater the degree to which the police feel united in a sense of solidarity.

The fourth principle is *loose coupling*—the idea that police develop strategies and tactics to protect themselves when department goals and policies are perceived to undermine their ability to do their work. At the core of the police morality is the idea that they have to do something about "bad guys." Efforts by administrators to control police behavior and the courts to hold them accountable for due process are often met with distrust by line officers when such efforts interfere with their sense of occupationally driven morality. Lying in court, keeping information from administrators, and circumventing due process are all ways in which some police officers carry out their work despite administrative rules limiting what they are permitted to do.

It is unclear, however, whether a single police culture actually exists. Cochran and Bromley (2003) and Paoline (2003, 2004) argued that the reality of a single set of occupational attitudes, values, and norms for behavior might be overstated. Paoline identified several arenas where there may be variation in culture within the policing occupation, including variation between organizations and officer styles. He also noted that cultural variation exists between ranks within an organization. Specifically, upper management, middle management, and line officers may all adhere to different norms, attitudes, and values that shape their behavior. His assertions are supported by research that has identified different values between management and street officers (Reuss-Ianni 1983) and different supervisory styles among middle managers (Engel 2001). Finally, a single police culture might be less prevalent in the future as police departments continue to diversify. With the inclusion of more college-educated officers (see Chapter 14), more racial and ethnic minorities, and more women (see Chapter 12), considering police culture as a monolithic entity may become less useful when describing police behavior.

## Decision Making and Police Discretion

Decision making is different from the use of discretion. **Discretion** is more narrowly defined. The most commonly used definition is the decision not to invoke legal sanctions when circumstances are favorable for the sanctions (Goldstein 1998). Davis (1969, 4) described discretion as "whenever the effective limits on his power leave him free to make a choice among courses of action or inaction." In encounters with suspects, for example, police may be presented with a situation in which they have the legal basis for an arrest. They do not, however, always make an arrest. The decision not to make an arrest when it is legally justifiable is sometimes called *nonenforcement discretion*.

One key point in this process is the decision to initiate the criminal justice process—for example, make an arrest, file a report, issue a ticket, or exercise force. This decision-making point has been widely examined (and scrutinized) primarily because the officer's decision sets the other components of the criminal justice system in motion. But it is also important to recognize that officers routinely make other, low-visibility decisions regularly. Bittner (1974, 30) said that the role of the police is to address "something-that-ought-not-to-be-happening-and-about-which-somebody-had-better-do-something-now,"   and often the initial "something" is make an arrest. However, the police are often asked to do something when it is not completely clear whether a crime has been committed or whether it is appropriate for the criminal justice system to become formally involved. Officers use their discretion to maintain order and preserve the peace, often without exercising the law, and make decisions based on situational exigencies.

Herbert (1997, 57) describes an example of order maintenance where an officer was exercising discretion:

> A senior lead officer on regular patrol on a Friday night is especially attuned to various groups of teenagers gathered on sidewalks and street corners. He has no legal means to arrest or detain any of these youths, but he is bothered by their presence. He stops whenever he sees such a group and declares, "There is no hanging out around here." He never threatens to arrest them, because he has no basis for doing so. He merely hopes that his ongoing presence and harassment will convince the teenagers to gather someplace else, preferably inside.

In this example, the youths were committing no crime, although in other jurisdictions, they may have been engaged in some minor offense, such as loitering, disorderly conduct, or curfew violations. Nevertheless, the officer depicted here observed a situation where something ought not to be happening and something should be done to maintain order. The officer had a range of options at his disposal, from doing nothing to waiting until the youth committed an actionable offense. But here, he used his discretion by ordering them off the corner. The officer bluffed the youths to believe that if they did not follow his

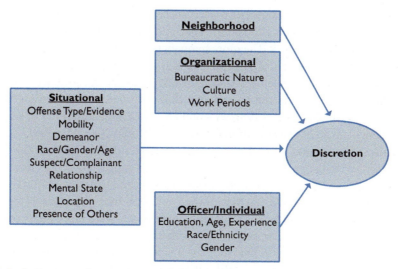

**FIGURE 9.1** Factors that Impact Police Discretion.

direction, formal action would occur, but never said so. He implied that their behavior was criminal. This notification from an authority figure was enough to encourage the youths to comply with his request, thereby accomplishing his goal of maintaining order. This was done without initiating the criminal justice system; scenarios like this likely occur countless numbers of times every day in America.

There has been a considerable amount of research concerning factors that influence police decision making and discretion. Sherman (1985), Brooks (1989), Riksheim and Chermak (1993), and Skogan and Frydl (2004) have summarized research in this area. Their observations are grouped into four categories of factors: organizational, neighborhood (or community), situational, and officer/individual. Figure 9.1 provides a visual depiction of how these factors simultaneously impact the discretion and decision making of street-level police officers.

## Organizational Factors

To what extent do the characteristics of police organizations affect officers' decisions? Several organizational (departmental) factors are worth discussing.

**Bureaucratic Nature.** The bureaucratic nature of a police department is an important factor affecting police behavior, as discussed in Chapter 5. The purpose of bureaucratic procedure is to guide and direct police behavior (Auten 1988; Alpert and Smith 1998). Various researchers have questioned the effectiveness of the bureaucratic "control principle" (see, e.g., Alpert and Smith 1998), however, and Cordner (1989) challenged the notion that written policy always contributes to the quality of police service. The discretionary demands of street activity may undermine bureaucratic efforts to control behavior (Adams 1990). Bureaucratic controls can backfire, contributing to police secrecy and undermining bureaucratic control. For these reasons, the effectiveness of bureaucracy to stimulate some behaviors and dampen others is certainly limited. Highly bureaucratic departments also tend to be impersonal and may overemphasize punitive discipline to control officers' behavior. This tendency may result in officers doing as little as possible to avoid getting into trouble.

**Work Periods, Areas, and Assignments.** Another important organizational variable is the frequency with which officers change work periods (shift or tour) and the areas (beat, district, or sector) in which they work. The more frequent these types of changes, the more distant the relationship between citizen and officer. There may be less communication and less understanding about community problems. Also important is the size of the area in which the officer works: the smaller the area, the more likely that a service rather than an enforcement orientation will prevail (Mastrofski 1981). A small area with a high quantity of serious crime, however, is more likely to have a law enforcement style (Brooks 1989, 126–130).

There is also some indication that discretionary choices differ based on the assignment of the officer within the organization. Novak et al. (2002) compared the decision making of officers assigned to COP tasks with that of officers assigned to traditional 911 duties. Although these officers used similar factors in their decision making, several important differences were observed. The authors found that COP officers were more likely to use victim preference when making an arrest decision than their more traditional counterparts, indicating that COP officers may be more responsive to citizens' demands. They also found that COP officers were less likely to arrest hostile citizens and that traditional officers were much more likely to arrest intoxicated citizens. This appears to indicate that officers assigned to COP tasks may be more tolerant of nonconforming behavior than their counterparts.

## Neighborhood Factors

To what extent do neighborhood characteristics or social context affect officers' decisions? Clearly, the kind of beats police patrol affect the work they do. As early as 1968, James Q. Wilson noted that in watchman-style departments, officers adapted their work to the kinds of problems that characterized their beats. This practice resulted in uneven delivery of service. Wilson and Kelling (1982) extended this idea to argue that police should tailor their work to the kinds of problems they encounter.

Characteristics of neighborhoods may also affect police behavior. One of the most interesting characteristics is racial composition. Research supports the view that the police write more reports, make more arrests, engage in more abusive behavior, and receive more citizen requests for police intervention in minority areas. As a result of this increased activity, police get to know the people in these areas better than in other areas. In addition, police tend to view minority areas as places where violent crimes are more likely to occur, and where they more likely to have their authority challenged. As a result, police are more suspicious and alert and more concerned for their own safety. Data consistently show that police arrest more individuals in minority areas than in other areas, although arrest rates are highly correlated with criminal activity (Sampson and Lauritsen 1997).

Another aspect of neighborhoods is their racial and ethnic heterogeneity. The greater the racial and ethnic diversity, the more likely the police will become involved in encounters with citizens whom they think are troublesome. Police often exercise a great deal of discretion in these areas, may feel more insecure, are often more aggressive, and tend to make more arrests. They are much more likely to arrest and threaten the use of force in racially mixed neighborhoods (Smith 1986).

Klinger (1997) outlines a theory to conceptualize the impact that neighborhood context has on officer behavior. He argues that officer decisions fall along a continuum of vigor (more formal actions or application of the law, like arrests) or leniency (less formal response) and that these responses vary by neighborhood. Officers who work together in particular patrol divisions develop in-group norms for behavior. Generally, officers react with greater vigor when the offense seriousness increases; however, this varies across space depending on how much crime and deviance occurs within the area. On the one hand, in areas with lower levels of crime and deviance, officers will respond with greater vigor for relatively less serious offenses. On the other hand, areas characterized by higher rates of crime and deviance will be met with officer leniency. This is because, among other reasons, crime and deviance are "normal" and to be anticipated in high-crime areas; thus, any particular offense must be more serious to elicit a vigorous reaction by officers. Klinger (1997) argues that the workload norms developed by officers within patrol divisions may offer more explanation for officer behavior than community characteristics and expectations, because communities exist within larger patrol divisions. Officers within patrol divisions create unique norms and expectations for each other.

Officers exercise higher levels of force during encounters with suspects in disadvantaged neighborhoods. Terrill and Reisig (2003) found that officers use higher levels of force in high-crime neighborhoods and neighborhoods with higher poverty rates, high unemployment, high rates of female-headed families, and high proportions of African Americans. At the same time, they found that racial minorities experienced higher levels of force than whites. However, their analysis clearly revealed that neighborhood context was far more important than a suspect's race at explaining the use of force by officers. They concluded that "race is confounded by neighborhood context: minority suspects are more likely to be recipients of higher levels of police force because they are disproportionately encountered in disadvantaged and high-crime neighborhoods" (Terrill and Reisig 2003, 306).

## Situational Factors

To what extent do situational characteristics affect officers' decisions? Many elements in a situation affect police behavior, the most salient of which are discussed next.

**Mobilization.** How the police are mobilized, or enter into a situation, is important in determining their conduct. In proactive or police-initiated encounters, officers are more likely to face antagonism from citizens. Proactive police behavior is more intrusive and less likely to be supported by victims and bystanders. As a result of the increased likelihood of a negative citizen response, police are more likely to make arrests and treat citizens harshly (Sherman 1985, 187). Consequently, proactive encounters are more likely to result in police–citizen antagonisms and conflict.

**Demeanor and Attitude.** The characteristics of both suspects and complainants are important factors in the discretion of police officers. Disrespectful, resistant, or uncooperative suspects are more likely to receive a more punitive officer response than those who are respectful, compliant, and cooperative. Disrespect toward an officer is a form of deviance itself that mobilizes officers to act more harshly, and officers' actions are compelled by the resistant citizens because this is viewed as a threat to the officer's legitimacy (Engel 2003) or competency (Herbert 1997). However, Klinger (1994) contends that legal factors, specifically the criminal conduct of suspects after coming into contact with police, outweigh demeanor considerations.

The attitude of the complainant is another widely cited factor influencing police decisions to arrest, according to the research by Smith (1987); Worden (1989); Engel, Sobol, and Worden (2000); and others. Black (1980), for example, observed that arrests were more likely to occur in both felony and misdemeanor situations when the complainant wanted the suspect to be arrested, but officers are less likely to do what the complainant wants if the complainant shows disrespect. Inside Policing 9.1 features an interview with Justin Nix, the lead researcher on an experimental study examining officers' perceptions and reactions to hostile demeanor.

| INSIDE POLICING 9.1 | Demeanor, Citizen Hostility and Police Behavior |

In this podcast, Jerry Ratcliffe interviews Justin Nix about his experiment on officers' perceptions of citizens' hostility (see Nix, Pickett, and Mitchell 2019 for the full study). Van Maanen's (1978) conceptualization of "The Asshole" is central to their study. Ratcliffe and Nix also discuss a variety of issues in policing that are highlighted in other chapters of this textbook, including officer retention and recruitment, body-worn cameras, and police-researcher partnerships.

   **Discussion Question:** Citizen hostility is an extralegal factor that can influence officer behavior. Most hostility is not illegal or criminal in and of itself. How can officers deescalate hostile citizens?

*SOURCE:* https://soundcloud.com/reducingcrime/justin-nix.

The demeanor of suspects and the attitude of complainants may interact with individual officer styles. For example, a widely cited test that many police officers apply to suspects is called the attitude (or personality) test. Many officers believe that they cannot allow a citizen to challenge an officer's authority (Herbert 1997). The challenge can include a question about being stopped, too many questions in general, criticism of the officer, or failing to comply promptly with a police request for information. Of course, any physical resistance would also be included. Research suggests that citizens who flunk such tests are more likely to be verbally and physically abused, given a traffic citation, or arrested (Van Maanen 1978).

**Race.** Research on the importance of race in police behavior is mixed. A large body of research supports the contention that African Americans are treated more harshly than whites or are more likely to be arrested (Maurer 1993; Kappeler, Sluder, and Alpert 1994; Chambliss 1997). Some researchers contend that this situation results because African Americans, and possibly other minorities, may be more likely to resist police authority or display a "bad" attitude or outright hostility from an officer's point of view. Others respond that hostility to the police derives from a history of police mistreatment. Kochel, Wilson, and Mastrofski (2011) examined 40 separate scientific studies to understand the race effect on officers' decisions to arrest. They write:

> From our findings, we can conclude more definitively than prior nonsystematic reviews that racial minority suspects experience a higher probability of arrest than do whites. We report with confidence that the results are not mixed. Race matters. Our finding is consistent with what most of the American public perceives, and that finding holds over time, research site, across data collection methods, and across publication types. Furthermore, controlling for demeanor, offense severity, presence of witnesses, quantity of evidence at the scene, the occurrence or discovery of a new criminal offense during the encounter, the suspect being under the influence of drugs or alcohol, prior record of the suspect, or requests to arrest by victim does not significantly reduce the strength of the relationship between suspect race and arrest . . . Thus, the most credible conclusion based on the evidence examined is that race does affect the likelihood of an arrest. (Kochel et al. 2011, 498)

Despite the centrality of race on officer decision making and the fact that disparate treatment of racial minorities can compromise fairness, ethical, and equitable justice within a democratic society, there is no consensus within the academic or practitioner communities as to *why* this disparity is observed. The reality is that disparity develops for a variety of reasons, including systemic racism, implicit bias, individual discrimination, or over-policing communities of color. Identification of the sources of disparity is an important step in correcting the problem. In other words, it is important to understand *why* a problem exists before taking steps on *how* to correct it.

Recently, the issue of racial profiling has captured the attention of citizens and police administrators. **Racial profiling** refers to proactive police actions that rely on race or ethnicity, rather than behavior that leads the police to identify a particular person as being, or having been, engaged in criminal activity (Ramirez, McDevitt, and Farrell 2000). The key component of this concept is that the encounter is police-initiated and not part of some other source of information (e.g., a wanted person who fits the citizen's description). The second component is that police use race, rather than behavior, to initiate the encounter. Racial profiling might occur in the context of traffic stops, but it can also be involved in other arenas (e.g., pedestrian checks).

A belief exists among citizens that profiling is common among police agencies (Reitzel and Piquero 2006). The Gallup Organization conducted a survey of Americans that indicated 59 percent felt racial profiling was widespread; among Blacks, 77 percent felt it was widespread (Newport 1999). Furthermore, 42 percent of Blacks indicated that they have been stopped by the police because of their race or ethnicity. This corresponds with lower ratings of citizen satisfaction with police services among racial and ethnic minorities. In fact, in a survey by the Bureau of Justice Statistics, fewer Blacks and Hispanics reported that police used "legitimate" reasons for stopping them than whites did (Durose and Langan 2007). At the same time, numerous examinations of police departments have been conducted across the nation to determine whether racial bias exists in police traffic enforcement patterns. These inquiries have often been conducted voluntarily by police departments, but they have also been conducted pursuant to lawsuits and mandated by state law (Tillyer, Engel, and Cherkauskas 2009).

Examinations into racial profiling tend to concentrate on whether racial and ethnic minorities are stopped more frequently than whites or whether poststop outcomes differ across racial groups (e.g., arrests, citations, searches; Fridell 2004; Pickerill, Mosher, and Pratt 2009; Tillyer et al. 2009; Barnum and Perfetti 2010; Engel, Klahm, and Tillyer 2010; Rice and White 2010). Results are far from consistent (Higgins, Vito, and Walsh 2008; Fallik and Novak 2012). Again, what remains largely unknown is exactly *why* racial and ethnic minority contacts with police vary in quantity and quality. One possible explanation is bigoted or racist police officers, consistent with the "rotten-apple" theory discussed later in this chapter. Another rationale may be differential traffic offending by racial minorities—although on closer inspection, this reason does not seem to hold up to empirical scrutiny. Perhaps it is cognitive stereotyping, in which officers believe minorities are more likely to possess guns and drugs than whites. It might also be differential officer deployment in predominantly minority communities by higher rates of crime and calls for police service (Withrow 2006). Inside Policing 9.2 discusses a re-examination of New York's stop-and-frisk policy, where the New York Police Department (NYPD) differentially deployed this tactic in predominately minority areas of the city, resulting in higher proportions of people of color coming into contact with the police. Additionally, it would logically follow that there will be disparity in police–minority contacts when examining city-wide

**INSIDE POLICING 9.2** Federal Judge Rules NYPD Stop and Frisk Unconstitutional

A federal district court judge has ruled that NYPD's stop-and-frisk tactics are unconstitutional. She found that the standard of reasonable suspicion was not being met in the half-million annual stops and that the practice amounted to indirect racial profiling. City and NYPD officials have strongly defended the practice in the past and seem likely to appeal the ruling.

**Discussion Question:** How can police departments monitor officer behavior (including stop-and-frisk, traffic stops, arrest, or use of force) to ensure officers are not behaving in a disparate manner?

SOURCE: *Modern Policing* blog, October 12, 2013, www.oup.com/cordner/nypd-stop-and-frisk-unconstitutional/.

traffic enforcement and pedestrian stop patterns. Further research is necessary to determine how widespread these disparities are and what causes them.

**Gender.** The effects of gender on police behavior regarding arrests are relatively understudied. The masculine predispositions of police departments are widely cited (Martin 1980, 1990). Visher (1983) found that females were less likely to be arrested than males who engage in similar behavior, especially when females act in an appropriate, "ladylike" fashion. However, the opposite could be true as well. When females act outside of their gender role, they may be more likely to be sanctioned by the police, because they are deemed more deserving of arrest. Furthermore, the extent to which these predispositions affect police–citizen encounters is unclear. Kraska and Kappeler (1995) suggest that sexual violence by the police may be more widespread than previously thought. Opportunity, power, authority, and isolation increase the likelihood of sexual harassment of citizens (Sapp 1994). Attractive women are also more likely to be stopped by police officers for traffic violations, with the intent not to issue a traffic citation but to make personal contact (see, e.g., Kappeler et al. 1994).

**Age.** The age of the citizen encountering the police can influence police–citizen encounters in several ways, particularly when the citizen is a juvenile (under 18 years old). Black (1976) stated that juveniles are less "respectable" than adults in that they hold a lower social standing in American society. Hence, they pose a greater threat to officers and are more likely to receive formal application of law, such as arrest (Visher 1983; Novak et al. 2002; Brown 2005; Brown, Novak, and Frank 2009). Brown et al. (2009) also reported that environment influences officers' arrest decisions—all else being equal, juveniles encountered in economically and socially disadvantaged neighborhoods were significantly more likely to be arrested than adults encountered in these same environments. If, indeed, officers treat juveniles more harshly than adults, this observation may explain why juveniles often hold less favorable attitudes toward police than adults do (Hurst and Frank 2000). However, the movement toward COP may impact how officers interact with juveniles. As Mastrofski, Worden, and Snipes (1995) noted, officers who expressed negative attitudes toward COP were more likely to arrest juvenile offenders than their pro-COP counterparts. Other researchers found that COP officers may be more disposed to informal sanctioning when encountering juveniles, and the role of the community police officer may be as mentor and role model rather than law enforcer (Cordner 1995). In short, juveniles may hold a unique position in police–citizen encounters, and the true influence of suspect age may be unknown.

**Suspect–Complainant Relationship.** Another interesting situational variable is the relationship between the suspect and the complainant. In general, if the relationship is close, the police may be reluctant to take official action (i.e., make an arrest), because they believe that it would be difficult to gain testimony from the victim in the courts. But the relationship has been, and remains, influential in the manner in which some police departments respond to calls about domestic violence or a family fight. In addition, when the relationship between the complainant and the suspect is close, the complainant may not wish the police to take official action. The preference of the complainant substantially influences the officer's decisions. Although officers do not always do what complainants want, they are more likely to take official action, such as writing a report, if the complainant requests such action.

**Seriousness of the Offense.** The type of offense also impacts police discretion—the more serious the crime, the greater the possibility of a formal response (Skogan and Frydl 2004). Violent crimes are more likely to result in an arrest for a simple reason: the victim is a witness to the crime. Consequently, about 50 percent of all violent crimes result in an arrest, whereas only about 20 percent of property crimes do. Police are more likely to arrest in felony encounters than in misdemeanor situations. This may seem like common sense, but in fact, it is not (Friedrich 1980). As Black (1980) noted, the legal decision to arrest is based on probable cause, not the seriousness of the act. Because the legal standard of proof is probable cause, officers tend to make arrests when there is greater and more prohibitive evidence, regardless of the type of crime. Evidence sufficiency is often more likely to be present for serious offenses.

**Mental State of the Citizen.** Recently, greater attention has been focused on treatment by the police of suspects with mentally disorders. Some have indicated that suspects who demonstrate symptoms of mental deficiency are treated more harshly by police while observing a disproportionately higher number of mentally disordered people coming into contact with the criminal justice system. Teplin (1984) found the arrest rates for mentally disordered citizens to be 46.7 percent, compared with 27.9 percent for those not displaying such deficiencies, suggesting that arrest, rather than other discretionary choices available to officers, was used with this special population to resolve conflict. However, research conducted by Engel and Silver (2001) did not find support for this "criminalization hypothesis." They reported that factors such as the seriousness of offense, seriousness of a weapon, and victim–offender relationship offered greater explanatory value than mental capacity of the citizen. They indicated that citizens with mental deficiencies were significantly less likely to be arrested than others—the opposite of what Teplin found.

Novak and Engel (2005) conducted a similar inquiry using a different set of data, and they too found that officers were significantly less likely to arrest citizens who were believed to be mentally disordered. This was observed even though mentally disordered suspects were significantly more likely to be hostile and disrespectful during interactions with police. Recall the previous discussion that hostile demeanor typically increases the likelihood of arrest; Novak and Engel (2005), however, reported that hostility and disrespect exercised by mentally disordered persons did not produce similar dispositions. They interpreted this finding by indicating that officers recognized persons with mental disorders were likely less in control of their actions and less likely to appreciate the possible consequences of their hostility, leading officers to conclude arrest was an inappropriate outcome for this population. This appears to indicate that the relationship between mental deficiencies and police behavior deserves greater examination.

In response to this problem, many jurisdictions have implemented programs to share responsibility by creating formal networks between law enforcement and social service agencies. A National Institute of Justice study of such network arrangements indicated that benefits accrue to the agencies involved and individuals who need help (Finn and Sullivan 1988). Networks that focus on the mentally ill have special units, on call 24 hours a day, that screen individuals for the most advisable disposition, identify the most appropriate facility to refer them to, and provide on-the-scene emergency assistance when necessary. These units consist of specially trained police officers or social workers hired by the department to perform these functions; in addition, some networks utilize social service agencies to provide the special unit.

One successful **crisis intervention team** can be found in Memphis. Following a police shooting of a mentally ill citizen, a crisis intervention team was created that consisted of police officers (with special crisis intervention training), emergency medical and psychiatric services, hospitals, and families of people with mental illness. These partners are more effective in determining nonconfrontational outcomes of encounters with the mentally ill and in determining whether evaluation of citizens taken into custody is necessary. For example, if citizens are identified as displaying mental illness, they may be taken to the hospital for evaluation rather than to jail and placed in the general population there. This program has had beneficial results, including reduced use of deadly force, fewer injuries to both officers and citizens, lower arrest rates, and reduced stigma and perception of danger attached to mental illness (Vickers 2000). Research also indicates that officer-reported crisis intervention training can improve awareness of support programs and improved attitudes toward citizens with schizophrenia, which in turn can improve and sensitize the manner in which officers interact with these special populations (Compton et al. 2006). Crisis intervention teams and additional officer training can improve interactions with the mentally ill overall and reduce the likelihood of injury for both citizens and officers (Skeem and Bibeau 2008). But intervention programs are not one-size-fits-all, and police departments must identify approaches that best fit their environment to improve the effectiveness of public safety initiatives (Cordner 2006; Reuland, Draper, and Norton 2010) and reduce the likelihood of officer injury.

**Environmental Context.** Police are also influenced by the location of the encounter. Officers are more likely to respond harshly in public settings than in private settings. This difference is the result of several factors: the type of crime (usually perceived as more serious crimes), the need to appear in control of the situation in public, the ambiguous role of the police in situations that occur in private places, and the fact that there are more police-initiated, or proactive, calls in public. As noted previously, proactive police interventions with citizens are more likely to result in arrests and citizen resistance than are reactive police responses. Proactive interventions tend to result from the police witnessing illegal behavior, usually at the misdemeanor level. Thus, as Black (1973) observed, police tend to be more proactive when a crime is not legally serious.

**Presence of Others.** The presence of other police officers and bystanders has a slight influence on what police officers do (Parks 1982). If officers think other police officers expect them to be harsh or punitive, write a report, or make an arrest, then they are more inclined to do so. Behaving in a manner that other officers believe to be appropriate is an important part of being accepted into the police subculture. Crank and Caldero (1999) suggest that officers who "wolf-pack" stops—that is, congregate in high numbers during routine stops—are more likely to create a variety of problems for managers. These problems include due process violations, violence, and increased levels of line-level secrecy.

Officers who work alone also tend to behave differently from officers who work in pairs. There is some support for the belief that officers working by themselves are more likely to make arrests, because they are more concerned about taking control of a situation when working alone. Although two-person units may be less likely to make arrests, they are more likely to treat suspects harshly, possibly because each officer is concerned about what the partner will think, particularly if a suspect challenges police authority (e.g., asks questions, talks back, fails to follow police direction, or fights; Brooks 1989; Sherman 1985).

Discretionary decisions are difficult to bring under departmental control. The ability of the police to use discretion enables them to adapt their responsibilities to the characteristics of public-order problems on their beat (Sykes 1986), and efforts to control discretion have sometimes backfired, creating line-level resistance and secrecy (Crank 1998). Perhaps the best to be hoped for is stated by Guyot (1991, 96): "The challenge for departmental leadership is to reduce the vindictive decisions and increase the wise ones."

## Individual (Officer) Factors

Decision making and discretion may also be influenced by the characteristics of the individual officer, but to what extent? Over the past several decades, there have been calls to diversify policing (particularly across education, race, and gender), because it has been assumed that officers with different traits will also make different discretionary choices. These individual factors will be introduced here and explored more fully in subsequent chapters of this text.

**Education, Age, and Experience.** It is difficult to separate age and experience, because most individuals entering police work are young—typically in their twenties—and grow older as they are gaining experience. In general, younger officers may work harder and be more aggressive and punitive than older officers. However, the quality of the older officers' work may be superior. Although some older, more seasoned officers may do less work and become less punitive, others may actually become more punitive if they become excessively cynical.

**Race.** The race of the officer is also important to consider. The bulk of the research on race has been about African American officers. Some evidence indicates that they are more respected by the African American community, but they may also be stricter in dealing with African American citizens. When compared with white officers, African American officers tend to be more aggressive and to make more arrests in African American neighborhoods (Brooks 1989, 138–140). However, this may be partly because of differential assignment of nonwhite officers to African American communities.

Overall, the race of the officer has less explanatory power than many might assume, because when individuals don a police uniform, they tend to become "blue" versus Black or white, thus supporting the socialization process. However, the true impact of officer race on decision may be more complex than previously characterized, and recent research demonstrates that Black and white officers may behave differently depending on

(1) the type of behavior being considered, (2) characteristics of the environment, and (3) characteristics of the individual with whom the officer is interacting. For example, Sun and Payne (2004) examined racial differences in how officers engaged in coercive actions or supportive actions. They found that Black officers were more likely than their white counterparts to be coercive during encounters with the public. At the same time, they also found that Black officers offered more support to citizens, but only in predominantly Black communities. They further found that the race of the citizen was unrelated to the exercise of coercion among Black officers and that environmental factors did not impact the level of coercion of officers. Meanwhile, Brown and Frank (2006) also examined racial differences in the decision to arrest suspects. They reported that white officers were significantly more likely to arrest citizens in general than Black officers. But interesting interactions were reported depending on the race of the officer and the race of the citizen. It appears that officers were more likely to arrest citizens when the encounter was intraracial (e.g., Black officer–Black citizen; white officer–white citizen). In fact, they reported the probability that a Black officer would arrest a Black citizen was 98 percent. If nothing else, a review of these two studies indicates that racial differences in officer behavior are complex and may vary across behavior, contexts, and racial characteristics of participants.

**Gender.** The gender of the officer is also presumed to be influential in the exercise of police discretion. There is some evidence to suggest that women are less aggressive. Early studies that support this observation, however, were conducted during the first decade of women's involvement in patrol work (see Martin 1989, 312–330, for a summary of these studies). Other, recent research by Paoline and Terrill (2004) failed to find significant behavioral differences between males and females. Based on observations of police officers in two cities, they found that male and female officers exercise coercion in similar ways. The only exception to this assertion is that male officers were significantly more likely to use coercion during encounters with male citizens. They hypothesize this lone difference as being a function of male officers viewing male suspects as more threatening than female suspects and thus employing more coercive strategies during these interactions. Furthermore, they found that male and female officers apply verbal and physical coercion at parity. These results appear to indicate that there are few measurable differences between male and female officers in how or whether they use coercion. If females as a group tend to be less aggressive or use force less often than men, this finding may be either desirable or undesirable, depending on one's preference in policing styles. For the most part, however, the less aggressive (i.e., less forceful and abusive) the police, the more likely they are to have a positive relationship with the community.

Research examining the influence of officer gender in decision making is conflicting. DeJong (2004) reports that female officers are less likely to provide comfort to citizens during encounters. Rabe-Hemp (2008) as well as Schuck and Rabe-Hemp (2005) reported that females used fewer extreme controlling behaviors, and that women were less likely to use supporting behaviors than male officers. Others report that behavioral dispositions do not vary much between male and female officers (Lundman 2009), although decision making of female officers may differ based on other contextual factors during the encounter (Novak, Brown, and Frank 2011). It may be intuitive to believe that female officers engage in different behaviors than male officers, but Skogan and Frydl (2004, 151) conclude that the body of research is "too small and the findings too variable to draw firm conclusions about the effects of officer sex on police practice.".

# Police Deviance

Not all police behavior is legal or proper. Sometimes, police officers engage in inappropriate acts, and occasionally, they do things that are illegal. Many people believe police officers should be held to a higher standard than ordinary citizens. They hold the police as symbols of the moral fabric of society and their behavior as a standard for the public to emulate. Consequently, the police must display the image and the substance of propriety. They must be above reproach, and also appear to be above reproach, in both their professional and personal lives.

**Police misconduct** can be defined as "a police act or omission that violates legal rules" (Kutnjak Ivokovic 2014, 304). This definition contains three distinct parts. First is the subject, which also involves an individual officer. However, this definition also allows the subject to be several officers working in concert with each other, as noted in the Knapp Commission's report (Knapp Commission on Police Corruption 1972) on misconduct in the NYPD. Second, misconduct involves violations of legal rules. These rules can include violations of local or federal law (including criminal, civil, and procedural laws) but also violations of organizational policies and standard operating procedures. Officers who ignore, usurp, or otherwise do not conform to established department policies are engaging in misconduct. Similarly, police departments often have codes of ethics (described more in Chapter 11), and officers who do not adhere to these codes are also engaged in misconduct. Third, this definition includes acts or omissions (i.e., failure to act).

Imagine the following scenario: Officers Bob and Janet perform a search of the home of a suspected drug dealer. They do not have a warrant, but they enter the home anyway. While inside, they find the suspect and large amounts of cash; however, they cannot find drugs. They take the suspect into custody and interrogate her without giving Miranda warnings. Frustrated, Bob plants drugs in the home, "discovers" them, and seizes it as evidence. The cash is also seized as evidence, but Bob puts $100 in his pocket, rationalizing that no one will miss it. Janet participates in or observes all of this behavior, but she does not report Bob.

Exactly how did the officers engage in misconduct? First, they satisfy the subject component of the definition, because the action was by the individual officer or the officers working in concert with each other. Second, they violated several laws, including procedural laws (entering the home) and perhaps the suspect's civil rights (interrogation without Miranda). These are likely also violations of department policies and its code of ethics and/or oath of office. Bob's behavior of planting the drugs and shaking down the drug dealer are clearly criminal acts; however, Janet's failure to report Bob for these acts is omission and therefore also misconduct.

Similarly, **police deviance** is behavior that does not conform to the standards of norms or expectations. How are such standards determined? Three major categories exist: *ethical*, *organizational*, and *legal*. Ethical standards are principles of appropriate conduct officers carry internally. Ethical behavior is an expression of personal values. Organizational (departmental) standards can be both formal and informal; they are derived from policy, procedures, rules, and regulations of the department (formal) and from the expectations of one's peers (informal). Legal standards are represented by the laws that officers are sworn to uphold and by due process, which establishes the means officers may use to achieve good ends.

Clearly, many of these standards carry the potential for conflict with others. Formal departmental policies may clash with informal cultural norms. The expectations surrounding the enforcement of the law may conflict with the principles of due process.

And a police officer's personal values may differ from the ethical principles established by the department. In short, the standards expected of a police officer are extraordinarily complicated, and deviance, in one form or another, is almost impossible to avoid.

It is difficult to determine how frequently police engage in deviant behavior as officers are not always forthcoming about their own inappropriate behavior—partly because of the blue code of silence, partly because citizens are reluctant to report police deviance, and partly because it is not always easy to distinguish between inappropriate and appropriate behavior. Given the many conflicting expectations facing police, it is likely that deviance is widespread; however, this is challenging to quantify empirically. In fact, many police departments have so many rules and regulations that it is difficult not to violate some of them.

## Types of Deviance and Misconduct

Identifying a commonly embraced definition of police deviance and misconduct is challenging; however, Kane and White (2009) provide a variety of different possible dimensions. Their categorization of misconduct comes from examining 21 years of information about officers in the NYPD who were involuntarily separated from the department. They recognize that officers may be disciplined for actions that occur while on duty as well as off duty. Unlike many occupations, police officers may be held accountable for behavior committed while off duty. An individual's occupational status of "police officer" can make a relatively ordinary crime (e.g., drunk driving or intimate partner violence) suddenly newsworthy and create situations where police departments can discipline officers for off-duty misconduct or deviance.

Kane and White (2009, 745) classify misconduct as follows:

1. Profit-motivated crimes: nondrug offense by on- or off-duty officers with the goal of generating profit.

2. Off-duty crimes against persons: assaults by off-duty officers (except for robberies).

3. Off-duty public order crimes: offenses against public order, including drunk driving and disorderly conduct.

4. Drugs: drug possession or sale and failing or refusing to submit to department drug tests.

5. On-duty abuse: actions by officers in their line of work, including excessive force, psychological abuse, or discrimination.

6. Obstruction of justice: attempts to subvert justice, such as conspiracy, perjury, and official misconduct.

7. Administrative/failure to perform: actions in conflict with department policy related to attendance, performance, obedience, or reporting.

8. Conduct-related probationary failures: terminations related to misconduct for those on probationary status.

These categories overlap with prior characterizations of deviance and misconduct. For example, Kappeler et al. (1994, 21) identify police crime as the "officer's use of the official powers of his or her job to engage in criminal conduct." In other words, an officer uses police authority to engage in violations of the criminal code: **occupational deviance**, an activity that does not conform to standards and is committed during the course of normal work activities or under the guise of the police officer's authority (Kappeler et al. 1994, 22; see also Barker and Carter 1994, 6); **police corruption**, which involves the use of police power and authority for personal gain (see also Goldstein 1977; Sherman 1978); and **abuse of authority**. Finally, Kappeler and his colleagues observe that Carter's (1985, 22) definition of the term abuse of authority contains three different elements:

1. Officers may physically abuse others through the use of excessive force.
2. Officers may psychologically abuse citizens through verbal assault, harassment, or ridicule.
3. Officers may violate a citizen's constitutional, federal, or state rights. (Kappeler et al. 1994, 24)

### The Prevalence of Police Deviance

It is challenging to gauge the extent of deviant behavior among the police. This is not surprising: people who commit illegal acts tend to keep them secret. In police departments, where peer support and loyalty are high, assessments of the level of deviance will always be difficult and are likely to underestimate its true extent. There are no national statistics or clearinghouse on the prevalence or extent of police deviance (Chappell and Piquero 2004).

A few authors have assessed the prevalence of deviance in particular departments, however, and this may provide some perspective on the extent of deviance overall. Barker (1994) looked at five categories of deviance in what he called "South City." Using a questionnaire, he asked each officer to judge the extent to which individuals in the department engaged in, or had engaged in, each pattern while on duty. These activities included sleeping on duty (39.58 percent), brutality (39.19 percent), sex on duty (31.84 percent), perjury (22.95 percent), and drinking on duty (8.05 percent). A review of these data shows that deviance in some categories was high. Four of 10 officers were thought to be sleeping on duty by their fellow officers, and the same number to be indulging in police brutality. Slightly more than one in five were believed to engage in police perjury. It is unreasonable to assume that these numbers represent police everywhere; generalizing from one research setting to the entire population is bad science. However, because they represent a seemingly normal department, Barker's findings are troubling. And there is evidence that other forms of deviance may be widespread.

Crank (1998) discussed two surveys to assess police deviance in one department in Illinois (Knowles 1996) and two in Ohio (Martin 1994). His overview presents two types of deviance not yet considered: racial and sexual harassment. Crank's discussion extends Sykes's (1996) analysis of these two surveys. Officers were asked in both surveys whether they had seen another officer harass a citizen-based on race (see Inside Policing 9.3).

When these surveys are considered together, they present a disturbing picture of police deviance. The findings suggested that deviance was widespread, and there appeared to be strong peer support to cover up deviant activities. These were typical police departments—none had a particularly negative record of police corruption. When compared with findings presented in the previous discussion, these findings suggest that police corruption may indeed be diverse in its types, widespread across departments, and hidden behind the secretive screen of department loyalties.

Kane and White (2009) provide descriptive statistics of officers in the NYPD who were terminated between 1975 and 1996, represented in Table 9.1. Although these data cannot provide adequate information regarding the prevalence of misconduct overall, they do provide good detail regarding the frequency of misconduct across their eight categories relative to each other. The analysis provided by Kane and White (2009) reveals that 1,543 officers were terminated from the NYPD during the 21-year period. Although this

**INSIDE POLICING 9.3    Racial Harassment**

One of every four officers (26.2 percent) in the Illinois survey (Knowles 1996) and one in six (14.9 percent) in the Ohio survey (Martin 1994) stated that they had witnessed racial harassment by their fellow officers. If one extrapolates these percentages back to the base populations from which they were drawn, one can appreciate the magnitude of the harassment and its potential for the alienation of minority citizens. According to the 1994 crime reports, Ohio had 18,721 sworn local or municipal officers, and Illinois, outside the Chicago Police Department (which declined to participate in the Illinois survey), had 16,131. Certainly, not all of these officers were active on the streets. One can allow a generous estimate that 50 percent of a police department is in administrative support. This would reduce the street-officer populations to 9,360 in Ohio and 8,065 in Illinois. Calculating the population estimates from these reduced figures, one arrives at 2,113 instances of police harassment in Illinois and 1,395 in Ohio in a single year's time, excluding the largest department in either state. Thus, in the two typical states, dominated by smaller police departments but with a sprinkling of big-city departments as well, police racism is by any reasoning a pervasive phenomenon. Nor are these figures in some way inflated by groups that harbor ill will against the police; keep in mind that these are numbers that the police are reporting about themselves.

*SOURCE*: Adapted from J. Crank, *Understanding Police Culture* (Cincinnati, OH: Anderson, 1998), 212.

estimate appears high, they note that the NYPD employed approximately 78,000 different people during this period—officers terminated for misconduct only represent about 2 percent of the total. Although it is challenging to estimate the prevalence of misconduct and deviance, these data suggest relatively few officers are ever terminated because of this behavior. Furthermore, the most common form of misconduct is administrative in nature. Police crime (as defined by Kappeler et al. 1994) is far rarer.

**TABLE 9.1   Charge Specifications against Officers Terminated for Misconduct in the NYPD, 1975–1996**

| CHARGE SPECIFICATION | PERCENTAGE |
|---|---|
| Administrative/failure to perform | 30.1 |
| Drugs | 19.0 |
| Profit-motivated crime | 15.7 |
| Off-duty crime against persons | 11.6 |
| Obstruction of justice | 10.8 |
| Off-duty public order crimes | 5.8 |
| On-duty abuse | 4.8 |
| Conduct on probation | 2.2 |

*Source*: Adapted from Kane, R. J., and White, M. D. 2009. "Bad Cops: A Study of Career-Ending Misconduct among New York City Police Officers." *Criminology and Public Policy* 8(4): 751.

## Deviant Officers

Police officers vary in their vulnerability to corruption. Most do not become involved in corrupt activities—they are morally committed to their work and are not psychologically capable of illegal activity. Only a small percentage become "bent" to the extent that they commit illegal activity. What should society think about those who do? And can police deviance be explained using a theoretical lens similar to understanding criminality?

One of the more important insights into police corruption was presented by the Knapp Commission on Police Corruption (1972), which conducted an investigation into the activities of the NYPD in the late 1960s and early 1970s. One of the most enduring elements of the Knapp Commission's report was the categorization of deviant officers into grass eaters and meat eaters. **Grass eaters** are police officers who accept graft when it comes their way but do not actively solicit opportunities for graft. **Meat eaters** are officers who actively and aggressively solicit opportunities for financial gain and are involved in more widespread and serious corruption. Inside Policing 9.4 provides a summary of Knapp Commission's findings, which remain comprehensive and influential.

A casual reader might think that meat eaters are a more serious problem than grass eaters, because they commit more serious crimes. Yet that is not so. The Knapp Commission found that the grass eaters were a more significant problem. They outnumbered meat eaters by a considerable margin, and although they did not solicit illegal opportunities, they took advantage of them when opportunity was provided. Their illegal involvement created a "wall of silence" behind which meat eaters could operate with impunity. The Commission found that the problem confronting efforts to clean up corruption was the **code of silence**, the secrecy that line-level officers maintain about their activities, both from the public and from police administrators, which they could not penetrate.

Barker (1996) expanded the Knapp Commission's typology of deviant officers, identifying five types. *White knights* are totally honest and may take an extreme stance in ethical issues. These officers are in the minority and are not deviant. *Straight-shooters* are honest but willing to overlook some of the indiscretions of other officers. They suffer in silence or seek out corruption-free assignments. *Grass eaters* engage in corrupt activities if the opportunity arises. *Meat eaters* actively seek out opportunities for corruption. Finally, *rogues*, at the far end of the scale, are considered an aberration even by meat eaters. They engage directly in criminal activities and in high-visibility shakedowns of citizens.

Research has provided some insight into the individual- and community-level correlates of misconduct and deviance. As presented previously, Kane and White (2009) examined the prevalence of misconduct in the NYPD that resulted in officer termination. They randomly selected officers from the same academy classes and collected data on both sets of officers to identify factors correlated with job-ending misconduct. They reported that risk factors associated with misconduct included officer minority race/ethnicity (Black, Hispanic, and Asian)—minorities were significantly more likely to be terminated because of misconduct than their white counterparts. However, they suggest a caveat associated with this finding; namely, Black officers became more represented within the NYPD yet the rates of misconduct for Blacks declined. They also note, perhaps not surprisingly, that prior criminal histories or problems with previous employers were correlated with misconduct in the policing occupation. They suggest that quality recruitment and screening tactics can reduce the likelihood of hiring officers who will later engage in misconduct. They further report that officers with higher levels of preemployment education and who scored better in the academy were less likely to be terminated because of misconduct.

---

**INSIDE POLICING 9.4**   **The Knapp Commission**

The Knapp Commission was established in May 1970 by Mayor John V. Lindsay as a result of an article that appeared in the *New York Times* on April 25, which stated there was widespread corruption in the New York City Police Department. The commission was given the task of determining the extent and nature of police corruption. Judge Whitman Knapp was appointed to head the investigation, which issued its final report in 1972.

The investigation found corruption to be widespread in the police department and many officers, both investigators and patrol officers, to be involved. Corruption was most extensive among investigators (what the commission called plainclothes officers) in the area of gambling. The plainclothes officers participated in what was known as a "pad." For example, each illegal gambling establishment in a precinct would contribute a certain amount of money (as much as $3,500 per establishment once or twice a month) to the officers. The total amount collected would be divided among the officers, each one receiving his "nut" (which was usually $300 to $400 per month, but at least one precinct had a nut of $1,200 per officer). Newly assigned officers had to wait two months before receiving a nut, but all plainclothes officers who left the precinct were given two months' severance pay.

Corruption in the narcotics area was less organized but was also extensive. Many of the payments came from shakedowns of narcotics dealers. Such payments were known as "scores"; the highest payoff uncovered was $80,000. There was some evidence to suggest that such large payments to police officers were not uncommon. Since the 1980s, corruption scandals in police departments have been primarily related to narcotics.

Uniformed patrol officers did not receive the large sums of money that went to plainclothes officers, but many patrol officers were involved in corrupt activities. Some participated in small gambling pads and often collected money from construction sites, bars, grocery stores, parking lots, and other business establishments. They could also get money from traffic violators, tow trucks (for business given to the company), prostitutes, and defendants who wanted their court cases fixed. These types of businesses were subject to a number of city laws, which if violated could result in a fine. To get around some of these laws, patrol officers were paid to "look the other way." Most often, the payoffs were $20 or less, but many officers were able to collect a large number of such payoffs in a month, adding substantially to their salary.

Ranking officers, sergeants, lieutenants, and even others above this level participated in corrupt activities, but the evidence was difficult to obtain above the level of lieutenant. This is because when ranking officers were involved, they used a "bagman," usually a patrol officer, to collect the payoffs. He received a percentage of the payoff. If he was discovered, he had to be willing to take the fall.

Although the Knapp Commission was careful to point out that not all police officers in New York City were corrupt, those who were not corrupt were aware of the corruption problems and, for the most part, did nothing about them.

*SOURCE*: Adapted from Knapp Commission, *Report on Police Corruption* (New York: Braziller, 1972), 1–11.

---

This supports strategies to increase training quality and recruit individuals with higher levels of education into policing (an issue that will be discussed further in Chapter 14).

Other research utilizing the same data suggests that misconduct is more prevalent in communities characterized by structural disadvantage (i.e., high poverty rates, female-headed households, households receiving public assistance, unemployment, and low educational attainment) and population mobility (Kane 2002). This appears to suggest that certain environments are more suitable and provide more opportunities for officers to engage in misconduct. Research has also examined social aspects of misconduct. Just as crime is disproportionately concentrated among small groups of individuals and within hot spots (as discussed in Chapter 8), occupational deviance is also concentrated within police departments. Specifically, deviance is concentrated within social networks of police officers. Inside Policing 9.5 highlights a social network analysis of deviance and misconduct within the Chicago Police Department, noting small proportions of officers are repeatedly involved in misconduct.

This social aspect is interesting to note for several reasons. First, deviance need not be rampant throughout an organization in order for departments themselves to be considered corrupt. This observation is consistent with the "bad apple" perspective presented earlier. Second, if deviance is concentrated within the social networks of officers, this would support the socialization hypothesis discussed earlier in this chapter in that all behavior—good and bad—is learned and socialized within groups. Police officers are no different in this regard. Third, careful tracking and monitoring of social networks of deviant cops could be a viable organizational strategy for identifying "bad apples" and intervening formally in order to curtail the spread of deviance throughout a police department.

## The Persistence of Corruption

Corruption has been and continues to be one of the most frequent problems faced by police departments in the United States. Consider the NYPD. It was found to have serious corruption problems in 1895 (by the Lexow Committee), in 1900 (by the Mazet Committee), in 1913 (as a result of the Curran investigations), in 1932 (by the Seabury Committee), in 1942 (as a result of the Amen investigation), and in 1952 (by the Brooklyn Grand Jury; Caiden 1977, 159). The Knapp Commission followed with a new corruption expose in the 1970s. In the mid-1980s, the department was rocked by the Buddy Boys scandal (*Law Enforcement Journal* 1986, 1). In 1994, the Mollen Commission noted widespread drug extortion among members of the 75th Precinct.

---

**INSIDE POLICING 9.5** | **Social Networks of Bad Cops**

This article reports a social network analysis of 23,000 complaints against Chicago police from 2000 to 2018. Not surprisingly, officers in certain assignments, such as the gang unit, generated more complaints. Most interesting was the tendency for problematic officers, regardless of assignments, to work together and, apparently, contaminate others—"The same cops who are exposed to other high complaint officers go on to be listed on four times as many uses of force per year in the next few years. They also commit shootings at rates more than five times higher than their colleagues who weren't exposed to misbehaving officers."

**Discussion Question:** Criminology notes that criminals are connected socially, and it appears here that deviant officers may also be connected socially. How can we apply criminological theory to understanding, identifying, and intervening in deviant cop networks in the same way we intervene in criminal networks?

SOURCE: *Modern Policing* blog, August 8, 2018, gcordner.wordpress.com/2018/08/23/social-networks-of-bad-cops/.

New York City has a large police department, with approximately 45,000 officers. It is unreasonable to assume, on the one hand, that all these officers will be honest or, on the other hand, that any particular incident indicates that the entire department is tainted. Yet the NYPD displays the persistence of corruption that characterizes many American police departments, large and small, and some of the most infamous corruption scandals in American police history originated in New York.

Why does corruption continue to recur in police departments? There are essentially four reasons. First, police officers are powerful and operate with autonomy and little direct supervision. By virtue of their authority, they encounter widespread opportunities for corruption. They are constantly exposed to situations in which the decisions they make can have a positive or negative impact on a person's freedom and well-being, and citizens may try to influence this discretion by offering free coffee and meals, money, sex, property—any item of value that will result in a favorable decision. Sometimes, an offer can be extraordinarily tempting. The Knapp Commission identified payoffs as high as $80,000 in drug cases, and that was in the late 1960s. Once officers begin to accept payoffs, they may become "addicted"—that is, they begin to depend on the extra income and spend accordingly.

Second, the community and political environment influence attitudes toward corrupt activities. Corruption in other government agencies, among prominent politicians, and in the business world enables police officers to rationalize their own behavior. Murphy and Caplan (1991, 248) make this point:

> Operating in this larger environment, it is not surprising that police become cynical about their work and feel that "nothing is on the level." When they meet citizens from every walk of life who are willing to pay them to overlook the law . . . some officers come to see themselves as "operating in a world where [money is] constantly floating about, [and they would be] . . . stupid and . . . fainthearted . . . not to allow some of [that money] to stick to their fingers."

Police departments employ many standards of behavior for officers to follow; in fact, there are so many standards that it is difficult to adhere to all of them. This multiplicity is also true of society in general. There are many laws, some of which (particularly traffic laws) are often violated by citizens. Officers see instances of such behavior all around them, in both the public and the private sector, among both the poor and the rich. Many officers even come to believe that if they are to be good police officers (e.g., to help people, maintain order, keep citizens from being afraid, make arrests, and ensure a successful prosecution), they must violate some of the rules they are supposed to follow. Furthermore, recall Kane's (2002) finding that communities characterized by structural disorganization have a higher incidence of misconduct, suggesting that these areas may have decreased social capital and be more suitable environments for officer misconduct.

Third, there is widespread tolerance among citizens of some kinds of police deviance. Citizens encourage the police to violate due process and citizens' rights to arrest felons. Television regularly displays "good" policing as that which inflicts pain on suspected felons, even when their guilt or innocence is as yet undecided. Businesses encourage small corruptions by giving officers gratuities and other perks for preferential treatment. In sum, it is unclear whether citizens always want police to "play fair," thus encouraging their moral and economic corruption.

Fourth, patterns of deviance can themselves become standards of behavior. Officers may be introduced by their training officers, for example, to restaurants that provide discounted meals for police. When standards encompass deviant behavior, line officers become secretive. Enormous pressure is put on all officers not to discuss police behavior outside police ranks. Even nondeviant officers will not break the code of silence for fear of reprisal, and this belief can carry over to the chief executive and managers in the department. In addition, executives and managers may be blamed and lose their jobs if the deviance is exposed, even if they are not involved. Caiden (1977) refers to such departments as being systematically corrupt. The "Voices from the Field" section of this chapter further discusses the role police management has in mitigating officer misconduct.

## VOICES FROM THE FIELD

### Michael S. Harrison
*Police Commissioner, Baltimore Police Department*

As our cities continue to advocate for police reform due to failed policing and the deaths of people at the hands of officers, we must look to push the needle in changing the culture within the policing profession. The peer intervention program, Ethical Policing Is Courageous (EPIC), not only educates but empowers officers to step-in to prevent misconduct and mistakes—potentially saving careers and lives in the process.

In 2014, as the superintendent of the New Orleans Police Department, my team and I, with the help and support of the Consent Decree Monitor, created EPIC as part of our commitment to transforming the department into a premier law enforcement organization. For many, EPIC is a catalyst for culture change, progress toward tangible reform efforts, and a pledge to self-improvement. I have attended EPIC training in both New Orleans and Baltimore, where I turned off my cell phone and gave the training my undivided attention, making it clear that I fully support this program. Not only do I believe that EPIC is one of the most important aspects of police reform, but it is also equally important that our leadership teams share in the same vision and capacity to see it become a reality in our department.

While peer intervention is nothing new in many different professions, in policing the lack of peer intervention was seen as loyalty. Historically, loyalty was viewed as "If I confide in you, you keep my secret." It had been perverted by having officers cover for one another when things went wrong. The consequences of this can be both profound and tragic. EPIC helps to redefine what it means to be loyal and to provide that loyalty on the front end before something bad happens. This is also known as active bystandership, where officers intervene to prevent misconduct from happening, avoid potential mistakes, and ultimately, promote officer health and wellness.[1]

EPIC is just one pillar to reforming the policing profession, but the results can lead to improved police–community relations and more collaborative work with our communities in building safer neighborhoods. Here in Baltimore, EPIC was developed in collaboration with various units within the department and our community partners.

Even with all of this, it will take more than just EPIC to change the culture of policing. It must include all of us and be done from the inside out and from top to bottom. We must move away from the "warrior" mentality and shift toward a "guardianship" philosophy that invests and cares deeply about protecting all those in our community, including fellow officers. We all have witnessed too many painful tragedies and endured the devastating consequences of all that is wrong with policing in America for too long.

Policing reform efforts are not just a professional motivation for me; it's a personal one. We must get it right now as we work to continue writing a new chapter of reform for the policing profession.

[1] Georgetown Law, "Active Bystandership for Law Enforcement (ABLE) Project," accessed March 30, 2022, https://www.law.georgetown.edu/cics/able/.

Caiden (1977, 169–171) argues that real progress in dealing with corruption was made in the 1950s and 1960s, because the police began to understand that the basic problem was systemic, not just the result of a few "rotten apples.". The **systemic theory of corruption** is that corruption stems from the nature of police work, and if anti-corruption protocols are inadequate, corruption will spread throughout a police department. The **rotten-apple theory of corruption** is that corruption is limited to a small number of officers who were probably dishonest prior to their employment. The term *rotten apple* stems from the metaphor that a few rotten apples will spoil the barrel; in other words, a few bad officers can spoil a department. The rotten-apple theory was the most prevalent theory of corruption prior to the 1960s and 1970s. This explanation is compatible with the predispositional theory of police behavior. A systemic theory of corruption tends to support the sociological perspective of police behavior.

Although police deviance and misconduct may be particularly problematic because of the position of power and trust within a democratic society, understanding why officers engage in deviance may be no different than understanding criminality in general. For example, research reported by Pogarsky and Piquero (2004) indicates that for officers who perceive sanctions for deviance to be certain and swift, the likelihood of misconduct is lower, which is consistent with the hypotheses of deterrence theory. Also, research by Chappell and Piquero (2004) indicates that police misconduct may be learned behavior, and that peer influence may be particularly important in shaping and reinforcing deviance.

Some research has found support for the rotten-apple theory. Lersch and Mieczkowski (1996) suggested that particular kinds of officers are more likely to be involved in questionable use-of-force incidents. They noted that 7 percent of sworn personnel in a large southeastern police department accounted for more than one-third of the use-of-force complaints from 1991 to 1994. These officers were younger than their peers and had less experience, and the incidents were more likely to result from proactive contacts with citizens. Although understanding of the extent and causal factors of police deviance is developing, it seems that a productive way to conceptualize misconduct may be through a traditional criminological lens.

### Are Gratuities a Type of Misconduct?

One of the most perplexing areas of police deviance concerns gratuities. A **gratuity** is the acceptance of something of value, such as coffee, meals, discount-buying privileges, free admission to athletic or recreational events or movies, gifts, and small rewards. Most commonly, it is coffee, beverages, or meals for free or at a reduced cost. Gratuities do not seem to be harmful, and they are often offered under the friendliest of circumstances. A beer on the house is, for many young people, an indication of their social worth, that their friends and colleagues value them. Yet officers who accept gratuities may unknowingly undermine the legitimacy of the police department, endanger a future promotion, and possibly lose their jobs. Although acceptance of gratuities is a common practice in many police departments, it is considered unethical by the International Association of Chiefs of Police. Although many departments have an explicit policy that precludes accepting gratuities, these policies are frequently ignored by officers. Many police managers also view violations of such policies to be a minor problem and may not enforce departmental regulations against them. Indeed, many officers view gratuities as normal and not a form of misconduct (Chappell and Piquero 2004).

Although a police officer may enjoy gratuities at first, they have a way of unpleasantly complicating life. For example, in a survey of citizens in Reno, Nevada, a majority of citizens polled did not think police should accept any gratuities. Almost half of the respondents stated that if they provided a gratuity, they would expect special consideration (e.g., extra patrol or a warning instead of a citation if stopped for traffic violation) from police officers (Sigler and Dees 1988).

Business owners may offer gratuities to encourage the police to spend more time at their establishment. Assume, for example, that an officer goes to the same restaurant every day to eat, because a free meal is provided. The value of the meals, over a month's time, is equal to about $180. The restaurant owner likes having police officers around, because she thinks it will decrease the likelihood of a robbery or unruly customers. However, if the owner offered to give the officer $180 in cash every month to spend the equivalent amount of time at the restaurant, the officer would probably not accept the money, and the police department would most certainly consider the acceptance of money a more serious problem than acceptance of the free meals. But there is no real difference in the two acts; both involve giving something of value for the express purpose of obtaining a private service—extra police protection or preferential treatment—from a public official.

DeLeon-Granados and Wells (1998) explored this gratuity exchange principle in a medium-size Midwestern city. An outcome of the acceptance of gratuities is that the business offering the "perk" receives a disproportionate amount of police service compared with businesses that do not engage in such behavior. After all, to receive a free cup of coffee, the officer must actually be at the location. Therefore, businesses that provide gratuities to police receive additional police presence, service, and safety compared with their counterparts. Their unique research found, perhaps not surprisingly, that officers were much more likely to be observed at establishments offering gratuities than at those that did not. This raises ethical issues regarding whether police presence should (in any part) be linked to whether the business provides free items or services to police officers.

## Police Sexual Misconduct

Police sexual misconduct is defined as behavior by an officer who takes advantage of their authority and power to commit sexual violence or initiate a sexually motivated cue for the purpose of sexual gratification (Maher 2003). The research cited previously provides insight into a poorly understood area of police behavior in sexual deviance. A similar view is provided by Kappeler (1993). In a review of litigation on police sexual misconduct, he found that the police lost 69 percent of the cases brought against them, a high number when one considers the average 10 percent loss rate for all other forms of civil litigation.

Many police have argued that much of this litigation stems from misunderstandings about police work. Many departments tended to justify sexual misconduct as a boys-will-be-boys attitude among their male personnel within the male-dominated workforce (see, e.g., Sapp 1994). Maher (2008) indicates police sexual misconduct is related to a variety of factors inherent to the policing industry, including authority, power, unsupervised (low-visibility) work environment, and secluded contact with citizens. A police culture that encourages solidarity and secrecy provides conditions suitable for deviant behavior.

Measuring the extent of police sexual misconduct is difficult, because similar to other forms of deviance, the behavior is rarely reported. However, McGurrin and Kappeler

(2002) attempted to generate a greater understanding of the prevalence and characteristics of these incidents by examining newspaper articles over an eight-year period. They found 501 reported cases of police sexual misconduct. The majority of incidents involved rape, attempted rape, sexual assault, or attempted sexual assault. Yet they found that more than 8 percent of cases involved sexual abuse of a child. Officers tended to be male, on-duty, municipal line officers, with a modal age of 25. Numerous officers had been previously convicted of sex offenses. More than 40 percent of the incidents commenced with a traffic stop, and about half of these involved physical force. Of those that involved force, more than half indicated that the officer's physical presence was sufficient to coerce the victim.

Maher (2003) attempted to estimate the prevalence of police sexual misconduct by providing self-administered surveys to 40 officers from 14 different jurisdictions, supplemented with face-to-face interviews. Officers reported what appears to be an alarmingly high rate of sexual misconduct, by either firsthand or secondhand knowledge. Maher concluded that police sexual misconduct is common. For example, these 40 officers collectively recalled 213 incidents of nonsexual contacts (e.g., making a traffic stop to get a closer look at the occupant) within the previous year. They also reported 161 officer-initiated sexual contacts (e.g., an officer initiates consensual sexual contact with a citizen), 122 instances of voyeurism (e.g., officers seeking opportunities to see nude or partially clad citizens by looking in windows or parked cars where the occupants are engaged in sex), and 110 instances of citizen-initiated sexual contacts. Although far less frequent, officers also reported 27 instances of sexual contact with offenders (e.g., unnecessary searches, frisks, and pat-downs of a suspect for the purpose of sexual gratification). On average, officers reported firsthand knowledge of 16.77 sexual misconduct instances per year. Secondhand knowledge of sexual misconduct was far higher than what is discussed earlier. Maher also interviewed police chiefs regarding the extent of sexual misconduct. Chiefs believe sexual misconduct to be "common and very serious" (Maher 2008, 243) and indicate that behavior such as unwanted flirtation, consensual sex, and voyeurism is far more common than behavior that may be criminal (i.e., rape or sexual assault). Chiefs also indicated that in their view sexual misconduct is less prevalent in policing today because of the industry's commitment to professionalism, better officer selection strategies, and more education on sexual harassment.

The results reported by Maher (2003, 2008) differ from other research in that officers indicated violent or "serious" misconduct was rare; in fact, the officers Maher interviewed indicated that serious forms of misconduct should not be tolerated. Maher also reported some of what may appear to be consensual liaisons between officers and citizens. However, as both Maher (2003) and Kraska and Kappeler (1995) note, consensual sexual relationships are an illusion. The substantial power differential that police have in exchanges with the public may initially appear to be consensual, but in fact, sexual relations may stem from a citizen's fear of the consequences if they fail to submit to an officer's implied or direct demands.

Police departments attempting to deter this type of deviance should consider a number of different strategies. Departments should proactively create policies prohibiting sexual misconduct, and personnel should receive formal and in-service training on what constitutes police sexual misconduct. Although this appears to be a basic response (and one that may not be overly effective), it is worth noting that in Maher's (2008) study, only 30 percent of police chiefs indicated their officers receive any such training on sexual misconduct.

Also, some chiefs Maher spoke to were reluctant to adopt such policies until they perceived it was a problem within their department. This is alarming given that most police sexual misconduct goes unreported. Thus, departments should ensure that citizens have opportunities to report sexual misconduct. This may include strategies such as complaints being filed with a nongovernment entity that addresses police misconduct in general or through other actors within their local government. Policies such as requiring citizens to file a misconduct complaint with the police department itself might discourage citizens from doing so. Maher (2008) suggests that victims alleging police sexual misconduct should be able to make formal complaints in writing only, rather than being required to report misconduct in person. Departments must make efforts to encourage citizen complaints about misbehavior, and then take these complaints very seriously. Complaints should be fully investigated in the same manner and with the same vigor as any other crime, and departments should adopt a zero-tolerance approach when complaints are substantiated. Such misconduct, although perhaps rare, is positioned to erode the public trust that the police must have in a democratic society.

## The Drug War and Police Deviance

Police deviance is a persistent problem, and some forms of deviance may be intensifying. Drug corruption, in many different forms, appears to be on the increase among police. Our concern is with the negative impact of the current drug interdiction on US police.

Kappeler et al. (1994) identify four types of corruption:

1. **Use corruption** is when officers use drugs. Kraska and Kappeler (1988) found that about 20 percent of the officers they studied in a medium-size department admitted that they smoked marijuana.

2. **Economic corruption** occurs when officers seek personal gain. Officers might, for example, keep drug money that is confiscated from dealers.

3. **Police violence** is the use of force to extract confessions.

4. The **subjugation of a defendant's rights** to obtain a drug conviction includes police perjury and "flaking," or the planting of drugs on a suspect by a police officer to acquire evidence.

Use of violence and subjugation of rights have been described by Crank and Caldero (1999) as **noble-cause corruption**, which occurs when police abandon ethical and legal means to achieve so-called good ends (see also Klockars 1983; Delattre 1996, 190–214). Both violence and subjugation of rights may be used by police who are more concerned about the noble cause—getting bad guys off the street, protecting victims and children—than about the morality of "technically" legal behavior. Noble-cause corruption occurs when officers break the law to do something about the drug problem.

According to Crank and Caldero (1999), noble-cause corruption and economic corruption may be inversely related. They argue that police departments during the twentieth century have been somewhat successful in combating economic corruption among the police. This success has been accomplished in large part by instilling police with a mission to do something about crime. The consequence is that, as police economic corruption decreases, noble-cause corruption seems to increase. Police today may be less likely to commit crime for personal gain, but they also may be more likely to commit crime to carry out ends-oriented justice.

## Organizational Responses

Controlling and reducing officer misconduct can be a daunting task for police organizations, but doing so can be critical in maintaining trust and legitimacy among the public. Traditionally, reform strategies include hiring and recruitment strategies as well as training (and retraining) officers to ensure "bad apples" are not brought into the department. Additionally, disciplining officers for misconduct (including dismissal) is used in an effort to deter existing officers from engaging in misconduct. These all appear to be common-sense measures.

Procedural justice is discussed elsewhere in this text, and that discussion focuses mainly on how citizens perceive officers' actions. Recently, however, a subtler internal strategy has emerged that could reduce misconduct—organizational justice, which is related to the practices within police departments and the relationships between officers and their supervisors. Wolfe and Piquero (2011) suggest that citizens who perceive they are treated procedurally justly will be more compliant with authorities and obey the law. Using this same logic, officers who feel internal organizational justice is fair and just will be less likely to engage in rule breaking, including misconduct.

To examine this further, Philadelphia police officers were surveyed about their perception of internal organizational justice (e.g., the extent to which they felt special assignments depend on who you know rather than on merit; whether rules dealing with officer conduct were fair; level of genuine interest of supervisors in subordinates; and their attitudes toward the code of silence and noble-cause corruption), and these perceptions were then compared with officers' complaints by citizens, internal affairs investigations, and discipline by the department. Wolfe and Piquero (2011) conclude that officers' perception of organizational justice was highly associated with officer misconduct. Officers who viewed internal decisions as fair and just were less likely to be involved with misconduct and have more favorable views of the code of silence. In other words, police departments

> that engage in organizational justice may reduce the chances of their officers engaging in these forms of misconduct. Police supervisors need to pay particular attention to developing agency policies that are procedurally fair, communicating with subordinate officers about specific policies and why they are in place, and allowing officers to voice concerns about such policies. This suggestion applies to policies concerning departmental rules, disciplinary processes, hiring and firing practices, and promotional procedures, to name a few. (Wolfe and Piquero 2011, 346)

The President's Task Force on Twenty-First Century Policing (2015) notes the importance of internal procedural justice in that officers who feel respected and valued by supervisors were more likely to accept department policies and initiatives. It appears there is also value in promoting organizational justice in that it also acts as a protective measure for officers by reducing their involvement in misconduct.

## Summary

Universalistic perspectives of police behavior are sociological, psychological, and organizational. Two particularistic theories are predisposition and socialization. The former explains police behavior in terms of the type of individual employed, whereas the latter is concerned with what happens after employment. Some of the more important studies of police behavior were made by William Westley, Jerome Skolnick, James Q. Wilson, and Michael K. Brown. These studies tend to support the importance of the socialization theory, because the influential factors they have identified all relate to the experiences of being a police officer. More recent research has suggested that predispositional factors are important as well.

There have also been attempts to relate police behavior and discretion to a number of specific factors: organizational, neighborhood, situational, and officer. Legal factors tend to determine the decision to arrest, but extralegal factors sometimes play a role. Despite substantial research on extralegal factors, their actual contribution to the use of police discretion is unclear.

Police deviance includes abuse of authority and deviant acts (contrary to standards) committed in the normal course of the job. The latter can be misconduct in terms of rules or corruption, such as accepting gratuities, which the authors consider inappropriate. Police corruption is marked by periodic scandals in some departments, and corruption involving drugs appears to be increasing.

## Critical Thinking Questions

1. Do you believe the predispositional or the socialization theory offers greater explanatory value in understanding police behavior? Why?

2. What contributions have Westley, Skolnick, Wilson, and Brown made to understanding police behavior? How do the perspectives of these authors differ?

3. Explain Van Maanen's stages of socialization. Why is understanding police socialization important to understanding officer behavior? Officer culture?

4. Discuss organizational (departmental) and neighborhood variables considered important in police behavior.

5. What are meat eaters and grass eaters? Which is the greater problem in controlling police corruption? Why?

6. What is a police gratuity? Is acceptance of gratuities a serious problem for American police? Why or why not?

7. What is meant by noble-cause corruption? Provide an example.

8. Why do you think certain police departments (e.g., the NYPD) have a long legacy of corruption? Do you think some departments are more corrupt than others? If so, why do you believe this to be the case?

## References

Adams, T. 1990. *Police Field Operations*. Englewood Cliffs, NJ: Prentice Hall.

Alpert, G., and Smith, W. 1998. "Developing Police Policy: An Evaluation of the Control Principle." In L. Gaines and G. Cordner (eds.), *Policing Perspectives: An Anthology*, pp. 353–362. Los Angeles: Roxbury.

Auten, J. 1988. "Preparing Written Guidelines." *FBI Law Enforcement Bulletin* 57: 1–7.

Barker, T. 1994. "Police Deviance Other Than Corruption." In T. Barker and D. Carter (eds.), *Police Deviance*, 3rd ed., pp. 123–138. Cincinnati, OH: Anderson.

Barker, T. 1996. *Police Ethics: Crisis in Law Enforcement*. Springfield, IL: Thomas.

Barker, T., and Carter, D. 1994. "A Typology of Police Deviance." In T. Barker and D. Carter (eds.), *Police Deviance*, 3rd ed., pp. 3–12. Cincinnati, OH: Anderson.

Barnum, C., and Perfetti, R. L. 2010. "Race-Sensitive Choices by Police Officers in Traffic Stop Encounters." *Police Quarterly* 13: 180–208.

Bittner, E. 1974. "Florence Nightingale in the Pursuit of Willie Sutton: A Theory of the Police." In H. Jacob (ed.), *The Potential for Reform of Criminal Justice*, pp. 17–44. Thousand Oaks, CA: Sage.

Black, D. 1973. "The Mobilization of Law." *Journal of Legal Studies, The University of Chicago Law School* 2: 125–144.

Black, D. 1976. *The Behavior of Law*. New York: Academic Press.

Black, D. 1980. *The Manners and Customs of the Police*. New York: Academic Press.

Brooks, L. W. 1989. "Police Discretionary Behavior: A Study of Style." In R. G. Dunham and G. P. Alpert (eds.), *Critical Issues in Policing: Contemporary Readings*, pp. 121–145. Prospect Heights, IL: Waveland.

Brown, M. K. 1981. *Working the Street: Police Discretion*. New York: Russell Sage Foundation.

Brown, R. A. 2005. "Black, White and Unequal: Examining Situational Determinants of Arrest Decisions from Police–Suspect Encounters." *Criminal Justice Studies* 18: 51–68.

Brown, R. A., and Frank, J. 2006. "Race and Officer Decision Making: Examining Difference in Arrest Outcomes Between Black and White Officers." *Justice Quarterly* 23: 96–126.

Brown, R. A., Novak, K. J., and Frank, J. 2009. "Identifying Variation in Police Officer Behavior Between Juveniles and Adults." *Journal of Criminal Justice* 38: 200–208.

Caiden, G. E. 1977. *Police Revitalization*. Lexington, MA: Heath.

Caldero, M. 1997. "Value Consistency Within the Police: The Lack of a Gap." Paper presented at the annual meeting of the Academy of Criminal Justice Sciences, Louisville, KY, March.

Caldero, M., and Larose, A. P. 2003. "Value Consistency Within the Police: The Lack of a Gap." *Policing: An International Journal of Police Strategies and Management* 24: 162–180.

Carter, D. 1985. "Police Brutality: A Model for Definition, Perspective, and Control." In A. S. Blumberg and E. Niederhoffer (eds.), *The Ambivalent Force*, pp. 321–330. New York: Holt, Rinehart & Winston.

Chambliss, W. 1997. "Policing the Ghetto Underclass: The Politics of Law and Law Enforcement." In B. Handcock and P. Sharp (eds.), *Public Policy: Crime and Criminal Justice*, pp. 146–165. Upper Saddle River, NJ: Prentice Hall.

Chappell, A. T., and Piquero, A. R. 2004. "Applying Social Learning Theory to Police Misconduct." *Deviant Behavior* 2: 89–108.

Cochran, J. K., and Bromley, M. L. 2003. "The Myth(?) of the Police Sub-Culture." *Policing: An International Journal of Police Strategies and Management* 26: 22–117.

Compton, M. R., Esterberg, M. L., McGee, R., Kotwicki, R. J., and Oliva, J. R. 2006. "Crisis Intervention Team Training: Changes in Knowledge, Attitudes and Stigma Related to Schizophrenia." *Psychiatric Services* 57: 1199–1202.

Cordner, G. 1989. "Written Rules and Regulations: Are They Necessary?" *FBI Law Enforcement Bulletin* July: 17-21.

Cordner, G. 1995. "Community Policing: Elements and Effects." *Police Forum* 5: 1–8.

Cordner, G. 2006. *People with Mental Illness: Problem-Oriented Guides for Police, Problem-Specific Guides Series No. 40*. Washington, DC: US Department of Justice.

Crank, J. 1998. *Understanding Police Culture*. Cincinnati, OH: Anderson.

Crank, J., and Caldero, M. 1999. *Police Ethics: The Corruption of Noble Cause*. Cincinnati, OH: Anderson.

Davis, K. C. 1969. *Discretionary Justice*. Baton Rouge: Louisiana State University Press.

DeJong, C. 2004. "Gender Differences in Officer Attitude and Behavior: Providing Comfort and Support." *Women and Criminal Justice* 15: 1–32.

Delattre, E. J. 1996. *Character and Cops: Ethics in Policing*, 3rd ed. Washington, DC: American Enterprise Institute.

DeLeon-Granados, W., and Wells, W. 1998. "'Do You Want Extra Police Coverage with Those Fries?' An Exploratory Analysis of the Relationship Between Patrol Practices and the Gratuity Exchange Principle." *Police Quarterly* 1: 71–85.

*Law Enforcement Journal.* 1986. "Drug Corruption—The Lure of Big Bucks."December 30: 1, 4.

Durose, M. R., and Langan, P. A. 2007. *Contacts Between Police and the Public, 2005.* Washington, DC: Bureau of Justice Statistics.

Engel, R. S. 2001. "The Supervisory Styles of Patrol Sergeants and Lieutenants." *Journal of Criminal Justice* 29: 341–355.

Engel, R. S. 2003. "Explaining Suspects' Resistance and Disrespect Toward Police." *Journal of Criminal Justice* 31: 475–492.

Engel, R. S., Klahm, C. F., and Tillyer, R. 2010. "Citizens' Demeanor, Race, and Traffic Stops." In S. K. Rice and M. D. White (eds.), *Race, Ethnicity and Policing: New and Essential Readings,* pp. 287–308. New York: New York University Press.

Engel, R. S., and Silver, E. 2001. "Policing Mentally Disordered Suspects: A Reexamination of the Criminalization Hypothesis." *Criminology* 39: 225–252.

Engel, R. S., Sobol, J., and Worden, R. E. 2000. "Further Exploration of the Demeanor Hypothesis: The Interaction Effects of Suspects' Characteristics and Demeanor on Police Behavior." *Justice Quarterly* 17: 235–258.

Fallik, S. W., and Novak, K. J. 2012. "The Decision to Search: Is Race or Ethnicity Important?" *Journal of Contemporary Criminal Justice* 28: 146–165.

Famega, C. N. 2009. "Proactive Policing by Post and Community Officers." *Crime and Delinquency* 55: 78–104.

Finn, P., and Sullivan, M. 1988. "Police Handling of the Mentally Ill: Sharing Responsibility with the Mental Health System." *Journal of Criminal Justice* 17: 1–14.

Fridell, L. A. 2004. *By the Numbers: A Guide for Analyzing Race Data from Vehicle Stops.* Washington, DC: Police Executive Research Forum.

Friedrich, R. J. 1980. "Police Use of Force: Individuals, Situations, and Organizations." *Annals* 452: 82–97.

Goldstein, H. 1977. *Policing a Free Society.* Cambridge, MA: Ballinger Books.

Goldstein, J. 1998. "Police Discretion Not to Invoke the Criminal Justice Process: Low Visibility Decisions in the Administration of Justice." In G. F. Cole and M. G. Gertz (eds.), *The Criminal Justice: Politics and Policies,* 7th ed., pp. 85–103. Belmont, CA: Wadsworth.

Greene, J. R., and Klockars, C. B. 1991. "What Police Do." In C. B. Klockars and S. Mastrofski (eds.), *Thinking About Police: Contemporary Readings,* pp. 273–285. New York: McGraw-Hill.

Guyot, D. 1991. *Policing As Though People Matter.* Philadelphia: Temple University Press.

Hassell, K. D., Zhao, J. S., and Maguire, E. R. 2003. "Structural Arrangements in Large Municipal Police Organizations: Revisiting Wilson's Theory of Local Political Culture." *Policing: An International Journal of Police Strategies and Management* 26: 231–250.

Herbert, S. 1997. *Policing Space: Territoriality and the Los Angeles Police Department.* Minneapolis: University of Minnesota Press.

Higgins, G. E., Vito, G. F., and Walsh, W. F. 2008. "Searches: An Understudied Area of Profiling." *Journal of Ethnicity in Criminal Justice* 6: 23–40.

Hurst, Y. G., and Frank, J. 2000. "How Kids View Cops: The Nature of Juvenile Attitudes Toward the Police." *Journal of Criminal Justice* 28: 189–202.

Kane, R. J. 2002. "Social Ecology of Police Misconduct." *Criminology* 40(4): 867–896.

Kane, R. J., and White, M. D. 2009. "Bad Cops: A Study of Career-Ending Misconduct Among New York City Police Officers." *Criminology and Public Policy* 8: 737–769.

Kappeler, V. E. 1993. *Critical Issues in Police Liability.* Prospect Heights. IL: Waveland.

Kappeler, V. E., Sluder, R. D., and Alpert, G. 1994. *Forces of Deviance: Understanding the Dark Side of Policing.* Prospect Heights, IL: Waveland.

Klinger, D. 1994. "Demeanor on Crime: Why 'Hostile' Citizens Are More Likely to Be Arrested." *Criminology* 32: 475–493.

Klinger, D. 1997. "Negotiating Order in Patrol Work: An Ecological Theory of Police Response to Deviance." *Criminology* 35: 277–306.

Klockars, C. 1983. "The Dirty Harry Problem." In C. Klockars (ed.), *Thinking About Police: Contemporary Readings*, pp. 428–438. New York: McGraw-Hill.

Knapp Commission on Police Corruption. 1972. *Report on Police Corruption.* New York: Braziller.

Knowles, J. J. 1996. *The Ohio Police Behavior Study.* Columbus, OH: Office of Criminal Justice Services.

Kochel, T. R., Wilson, D. B., and Mastrofski, S. D. 2011. "Effect of Suspect Race on Officers' Arrest Decisions." *Criminology* 49: 473–512.

Kraska, P. B., and Kappeler, V. E. 1988. "Police On-Duty Drug Use: A Theoretical and Descriptive Explanation." *American Journal of Police* 7(1): 1–28.

Kraska, P. B., and Kappeler, V. E. 1995. "To Serve and Pursue: Exploring Police Sexual Violence Against Women." *Justice Quarterly* 12: 85–112.

Kutnjak Ivokovic, S. 2014. "Police Misconduct." In M. D. Reisig and R. J. Kane (eds.), *The Oxford Handbook of Police and Policing*, pp. 302–336. New York: Oxford University Press.

Langworthy, R. H. 1985. "Wilson's Theory of Police Behavior: A Replication of the Constraint Theory." *Justice Quarterly* 3: 89–98.

Lersch, K., and Mieczkowski, T. 1996. "Who Are the Problem-Prone Officers? An Analysis of Citizen Complaints." *American Journal of Police* 15: 23–44.

Liederbach, J., and Travis, L. F. 2008. "Wilson Redux: Another Look at Varieties of Police Behavior." *Police Quarterly* 11: 447–467.

Lundman, R. J. 2009. "Officer Gender and Traffic Ticket Decisions: Police Blue or Women Too?" *Journal of Criminal Justice* 37: 342–352.

Maher, T. M. 2003. "Police Sexual Misconduct: Officers' Perceptions of Its Extent and Causality." *Criminal Justice Review* 28: 355–381.

Maher, T. M. 2008. "Police Chiefs' Views on Police Sexual Misconduct." *Police Practice and Research* 9: 239–250.

Manning, P. 1997. *Police Work: The Social Organization of Policing*, 2nd ed. Prospect Heights, IL: Waveland.

Martin, C. 1994. *Illinois Municipal Officers' Perceptions of Police Ethics.* Chicago: Illinois Criminal Justice Information Authority, Statistical Analysis Center.

Martin, S. E. 1980. *Breaking and Entering: Policewomen on Patrol.* Berkeley: University of California Press.

Martin, S. E. 1989. "Female Officers on the Move?" In R. G. Dunham and G. P. Alpert (eds.), *Critical Issues in Policing: Contemporary Readings*, pp. 312–330. Prospect Heights, IL: Waveland.

Martin, S. E. 1990. *On the Move: The Status of Women in Policing.* Washington, DC: Police Foundation.

Mastrofski, S. 1981. "Policing the Beat: The Impact of Organizational Scale on Patrol Officer Behavior in Urban Residential Neighborhoods." *Journal of Criminal Justice* 4: 343–358.

Mastrofski, S. D., Worden, R. E., and Snipes, J. B. 1995. "Law Enforcement in a Time of Community Policing." *Criminology* 33: 539–563.

Maurer, M. 1993. *Young Black Men and the Criminal Justice System: A Growing National Problem.* Washington, DC: The Sentencing Project, US Government Printing Office.

McGurrin, D., and Kappeler, V. E. 2002. "Media Accounts of Police Sexual Violence." In K. Lersch (ed.), *Policing and Misconduct*, pp. 121–142. Upper Saddle River, NJ: Prentice Hall.

Murphy, P. V., and Caplan, G. 1991. "Fostering Integrity." In W. A. Geller (ed.), *Local Government Police Management*, pp. 239–271. Washington, DC: International City Management Association.

Newport, F. 1999. "Racial Profiling Seen as Widespread, Particularly Among Young Black Men." *Gallup Organization*, December 9. https://www.gallup.com/poll/3421/racial-profiling-seen-widespread-particularly-among-young-black-men.aspx/.

Nix, J., Pickett, J. T. and Mitchell, R. J. 2019. "Compliance, Noncompliance and the In-Between: Causal Effects of Civilian Demeanor on Police Officers' Cognitions and Emotions." *Journal of Experimental Criminology* 15: 611–639.

Novak, K. J., Brown, R. A., and Frank, J. 2011. "Women on Patrol: An Analysis of Difference in Officer Arrest Behavior." *Policing: An International Journal of Police Strategies and Management* 34(4): 566–587.

Novak, K. J., and Engel, R. S. 2005. "Disentangling the Influence of Suspects' Demeanor and Mental Disorder on Arrest." *Policing: An International Journal of Police Strategies and Management* 28: 493–512.

Novak, K. J., Frank, J., Smith, B. W., and Engel, R. S. 2002. "Revisiting the Decision to Arrest: Comparing Beat and Community Officers." *Crime and Delinquency* 48: 70–98.

Paoline, E. A. 2003. "Taking Stock: Toward a Richer Understanding of Police Culture." *Journal of Criminal Justice* 31: 199–214.

Paoline, E. A. 2004. "Shedding Light on Police Culture: An Examination of Officers' Occupational Attitudes." *Police Quarterly* 7: 205–236.

Paoline, E. A., and Terrill, W. 2004 "Women Police Officers and the Use of Coercion." *Women and Criminal Justice* 15: 97–119.

Parks, R. 1982. "Citizen Surveys for Police Performance Assessment: Some Issues in Their Use." *Urban Interest* 4: 17–26.

Pickerill, M., Mosher, C., and Pratt, T. 2009. "Search and Seizure, Racial Profiling and Traffic Stops: A Disparate Impact Framework." *Law and Policy* 31: 1–30.

Pogarsky, G., and Piquero, A. R. 2004. "Studying the Reach of Deterrence: Can Deterrence Theory Help Explain Police Misconduct?" *Journal of Criminal Justice* 32: 371–386.

President's Task Force on Twenty-First Century Policing. 2015. *Final Report of the President's Task Force on Twenty-First Century Policing*. Washington, DC: Office of Community Oriented Policing Services.

Rabe-Hemp, C. E. 2008. "Female Officers and the Ethic of Care: Does Officer Gender Impact Police Behaviors?" *Journal of Criminal Justice* 36: 426–434.

Ramirez, D., McDevitt, J., and Farrell, A. 2000. *A Resource Guide on Racial Profiling Data Collection Systems: Promising Practices and Lessons Learned*. Washington, DC: Bureau of Justice Assistance.

Reitzel, J., and Piquero, A. R. 2006. "Does It Exist? Studying Citizens' Attitudes of Racial Profiling." *Police Quarterly* 9: 161–183.

Reuland, M., Draper, L., and Norton, B. 2010. *Improving Responses to People with Mental Illness: Tailoring Law Enforcement Initiatives to Individual Jurisdictions*. New York: Council of State Governments Justice Center.

Reuss-Ianni, E. 1983. *Two Cultures of Policing*. New Brunswick, NJ: Transaction.

Rice, S. K. 2010. "Introduction to Part 1." In S. K. Rice and M. D. White (eds.), *Race, Ethnicity and Policing: New and Essential Readings*, pp. 11–14. New York: New York University Press.

Rice, S. K., and White, M. D. 2010. *Race, Ethnicity and Policing: New and Essential Readings*. New York: New York University Press.

Riksheim, E. C., and Chermak, S. M. 1993. "Causes of Police Behavior Revisited." *Journal of Criminal Justice* 21: 353–382.

Sampson, R., and Lauritsen, J. 1997. "Racial and Ethnic Disparities in Crime and Criminal Justice in the United States." In M. Tonry (ed.), *Ethnicity, Crime, and Immigration: Comparative and Cross-National Perspectives*, pp. 311–374. Chicago: University of Chicago Press.

Sapp, A. D. 1994. "Sexual Misconduct by Police Officers." In T. Barker and D. Carter (eds.), *Police Deviance*, 3rd ed., pp. 187–200. Cincinnati, OH: Anderson.

Schuck, A. M., and Rabe-Hemp, C. 2005. "Women Police: The Use of Force By and Against Female Officers." *Women and Criminal Justice* 16: 91–117.

Sherman, L. W. 1978. *Scandal and Reform: Controlling Police Corruption*. Berkeley: University of California Press.

Sherman, L. W. 1985. "Causes of Police Behavior: The Current State of Quantitative Research." In A. S. Blumberg and E. Niederhoffer (eds.), *The Ambivalent Force*, 3rd ed., pp. 183–195. New York: Holt, Rinehart & Winston.

Sigler, R. T., and Dees, T. M. 1988. "Public Perception of Petty Corruption in Law Enforcement." *Journal of Police Science and Administration* 6: 14–19.

Skeem, J., and Bibeau, L. 2008. "How Does Violence Potential Relate to Crisis Intervention Team Responses to Emergencies?" *Psychiatric Services* 59: 201–204.

Skogan, W., and Frydl, K. 2004. *Fairness and Effectiveness in Policing: The Evidence*. Washington, DC: National Academies Press, National Research Council of the National Academies.

Skolnick, J. H. 1966. *Justice Without Trial*. New York: Wiley.

Smith, B. W., Novak, K. J., and Frank, J. 2002. "Community Policing and the Work Routines of Street-Level Officers." *Criminal Justice Review* 26: 17–37.

Smith, D. 1986. "The Neighborhood Context of Police Behavior." In A. Reiss and M. Tonry (eds.), *Communities and Crime*, pp. 313–342. Chicago: University of Chicago Press.

Smith, D. 1987. "Police Response to Interpersonal Violence: Defining the Parameters of Legal Control." *Social Forces* 65: 767–782.

Sun, I. K., and Payne, B. K. 2004. "Racial Differences in Resolving Conflicts: A Comparison Between Black and White Police Officers." *Crime and Delinquency* 50: 516–541.

Sykes, G. 1986. "Street Justice: A Moral Defense of Order-Maintenance Policing." *Justice Quarterly* 3: 467–512.

Sykes, G. 1996. "Police Misconduct: A Different Day and Different Challenges." *Subject to Debate: A Newsletter of the Police Executive Research Forum* 10(3): 1, 4–5.

Teplin, L. A. 1984. "Criminalizing Mental Disorder: The Comparative Arrest Rates of the Mentally Ill." *American Psychologist* 39: 794–803.

Terrill, W., and Reisig, M. D. 2003. "Neighborhood Context and Police Use of Force." *Journal of Research in Crime and Delinquency* 40: 291–323.

Tillyer, R., Engel, R. S., and Cherkauskas, J. C. 2009. "Best Practices in Vehicle Stop Data Collection and Analysis." *Policing: An International Journal of Police Strategies and Management* 33: 69–92.

Van Maanen, J. 1973. "Observations on the Making of Policeman." *Human Organization* 32: 407–418.

Van Maanen, J. 1978. "The Asshole." In P. K. Manning and J. Van Maanen (eds.), *Policing: A View from the Streets*, pp. 221–238. Santa Monica, CA: Goodyear.

Vickers, B. 2000. "Memphis, Tennessee, Police Department's Crisis Intervention Team." *Bulletin from the Field*. Washington, DC: Department of Justice, Office of Justice Programs.

Visher, C. A. 1983. "Gender, Police Arrest Decisions, and Notions of Chivalry." *Criminology* 21: 5–28.

Walker, S. 1984. "Broken Windows and Fractured History: The Use and Misuse of History in Recent Patrol Analysis." *Justice Quarterly* 1: 57–90.

Westley, W. A. 1970. *Violence and the Police*. Cambridge, MA: MIT Press.

Wilson, J. Q. 1968. *Varieties of Police Behavior*. Cambridge, MA: Harvard University Press.

Wilson, J. Q., and Kelling, G. 1982. "Broken Windows: The Police and Neighborhood Safety." *Atlantic Monthly* 127: 29–38.

Withrow, B. L. 2006. *Racial Profiling: From Rhetoric to Reason*. Upper Saddle River, NJ: Pearson Prentice Hall.

Wolfe, S. E., and Piquero, A. R. 2011. "Organizational Justice and Police Misconduct." *Criminal Justice and Behavior* 38: 332–353.

Worden, R. 1989. "Situational and Attitudinal Explanations of Police Behavior: A Theoretical Reappraisal and Empirical Assessment." *Law and Society Review* 23: 667–711.

Zhao, J., and Hassell, K. D. 2005. "Policing Styles and Organizational Priorities: Retesting Wilson's Theory of Local Political Culture." *Police Quarterly* 8: 411–430.

## CHAPTER 10

# Force and Coercion

## CHAPTER OUTLINE

# CHAPTER OUTLINE (continued)

## KEY TERMS

- coercion
- command voice
- conducted energy devices
- continuum of force
- deadly force
- de-escalation
- defense-of-life policy
- excessive force
- extralegal police aggression
- fleeing-felon rule
- less-lethal weapons
- mere presence
- officer survival
- physical force
- police brutality
- psychological force
- third degree
- trauma-informed policing
- use of force
- verbal force

THE USE OF FORCE is central to the police role. Police carry the legal authority to maintain order, demand compliance, stop and detain people, and even kill, if necessary. They are granted this authority to shield victims from dangerous felons; to control unruly, hostile, or physically abusive citizens; and to protect against immediate threats to human life.

**Use of force** is the most controversial aspect of the legal authority of police, yet its necessity is inescapable. It is a skill and a means to an end—the preservation of orderly social relations in accordance with societal laws and norms. Consequently, police use of force in the United States should be considered in the broader context of how it contributes to democratic relations among citizens.

Where does the right to use force come from? How can society reconcile the use of force with the democratic principles of freedom and equality? In 1970, Egon Bittner, briefly discussed in Chapter 1, provided important insights into the use of force. According to Bittner, the use of force can be justified in two ways. The first is self-defense: people can use force to defend themselves if they have a real belief that they are in danger. The second is based on the inherent police power to address health, welfare, order, and safety; that is, the police are a "mechanism for the distribution of situationally justified force in society" (Bittner 1995, 129).

Why does society need a police mechanism for the distribution of force? Over its history, US society has moved away from the use of force and toward the use of democratic, rational processes for solving problems and disagreements among citizens. Yet it is impossible to abandon altogether the use of force in the pursuit of democratic justice. To preserve democratic processes, society grants to police an exclusive right that is not permitted to other citizens: the use of force to achieve democratic ends.

Many students of police behavior think that "force" refers only to violent behavior by the police. That is incorrect. Force, or **coercion**, occurs any time the police require citizens to act in a particular way. Even a request is coercive, because it carries with it the authority of the state to back up the request with greater force and the implicit recognition, by citizen and officer alike, that "no" is not an acceptable answer. Because the police carry the governmental authority to intervene in a citizen's activities, all police–citizen interactions carry elements of coercion, even when officers are not consciously trying to be forceful.

Two factors determine police use of force and its justification. The first is formal training based on state law, local departmental regulations, and due process constraints. The second is local police cultures, which represent understandings of police territorial responsibilities, danger, and the control of unpredictable situations. This chapter examines how often police use force, police training on the use of force, and police culture before turning to the most difficult and controversial topics: excessive use of force and deadly force.

## Police–Citizen Interactions

How often do encounters between police and citizens become situations in which force is used? Information is provided by a number of scholarly studies, including a series of surveys conducted by the Bureau of Justice Statistics (BJS).

### Context of Force

One of the most extensive and important studies of police–citizen encounters was conducted more than 40 years ago by Reiss (1967). He reported on more than 5,000 observations of police–citizen interactions in areas that were racially diverse and had different crime rates. About 86 percent of the encounters were reactive, resulting from citizen requests. About 14 percent of the encounters were proactive, initiated by police officers. Police were more likely to experience antagonism or injury in proactive encounters, primarily because unlike in reactive situations, the person or persons they stopped did not request assistance from the police.

During the 5,000-plus encounters observed, the police made only 225 arrests (less than 5 percent). About 50 percent of the persons arrested openly challenged police authority; the challenge, however, was more likely to be verbal than physical. Of those arrested, 98 (42 percent) were treated "firmly," whereas only 21 (9 percent) were handled with "gross" force. These figures mean that only about 2 percent of all the police–citizen encounters observed involved any type of **physical force**, and none involved the use of lethal, or deadly, force. Overall, police officers infrequently made arrests, and when they did, they rarely used physical force.

Another important study of police–citizen encounters was conducted by Sykes and Brent (1983), who analyzed more than 3,000 such encounters. They identified three approaches to interacting with citizens, which they referred to as methods of regulation or supervision. The three methods of regulation are as follows:

1. **Definitional.** Officer asks questions or makes accusations. Serves to define the situation as an officer chooses by compelling citizens to focus on officer's question or accusation. Can also divert citizens' attention as a form of "cooling off."

2. **Imperative.** Officer gives order. Officer acts in a commanding way and "his force is in his grammatical form, his tone of voice, his emphasis" (Sykes and Brent 1983, 63).

3. **Coercive.** Officer threatens or uses force, such as display of readiness, drawn weapon, holding someone back, or actual use of force.

Sykes and Brent found that the most common initial police response was definitional, occurring about 83 percent of the time. Police almost always spoke first when dealing with citizens; thus, they had the opportunity to direct the discussion with their questions. The second most common initial response was imperative, occurring in about 17 percent of encounters. The researchers did not find the coercive response to be used initially in any police–citizen encounter; it was eventually used, however, if citizens did not cooperate with the officers. Even then, the most common officer response was to repeat the initial approach one or more times to obtain cooperation. From Sykes and Brent's research, it is clear that officers first try the definitional approach and will frequently repeat it if a citizen does not cooperate. If cooperation is not forthcoming or the citizen's behavior becomes threatening or too abusive, officers will become imperative and coercive.

Bayley (1986) studied police officer tactical choices in interactions with citizens in Denver. Bayley divided police–citizen interactions into three stages: the *contact stage* describes tactical choices made when officers first approach citizens; the *processing stage* is concerned with decisions made during the interaction between contact and exit; and the *exit stage* describes strategies used to end contact with the citizen. Bayley also identified several contact actions by police officers in traffic stops. In some situations, more than one action was used; many are similar to the findings of Sykes and Brent (1983). Asking drivers or passengers questions or for documents (the definitional approach) was the initial police action in most cases. Giving orders (the imperative approach) was also sometimes used.

Bayley's (1986) findings revealed the complicated nature of police–citizen transactions. In the three areas—contact, processing, and exit—officers used at least 28 different actions. By carefully reviewing the first actions, it becomes clear that the use of coercion is part and parcel of police work, even when it is not directly used. The initial acts all involve various levels of coercion, from the relatively mild "asked passengers for documents," which is not coercive but carries the potential for a stronger response, to the more significant "ordered driver to remain in the vehicle." Under processing actions, coercive behavior includes "body search." Exit actions range from the mildly coercive "gave admonishment" to the quite serious "arrested driver." Moreover, the original stop itself represents a seizure, an aggressive intervention of the state into the affairs of citizens.

These studies provide an understanding of how practical applications of force are integral to police work. This realization may be uncomfortable for citizens. Yet if we fail to see how force is intertwined with the daily routines of police work, we will not understand what the police are about.

Bayley and Garofalo (1989) studied 62 police officers in New York City to determine the extent to which they used some type of violence, including verbal aggression. They identified 467 potentially violent situations, of which 168 were proactive. Although reports suggested possible violence, such as a fight or the reported presence of weapons, only 78 (17 percent) of these situations involved visible conflict when the police arrived. In 70 (15 percent) of these cases, the violence was not physical, but involved only verbal threats or gestures. Police used physical force against citizens 37 times (8 percent), and citizens used it against the police 11 times (2 percent). Police force was almost always limited to "grabbing and restraining." Police use of deadly force was not observed.

Klahm, Frank, and Brown (2010) studied police use of force in police encounters with suspected offenders/disputants in Cincinnati. They found that police used verbal force in

30 percent of encounters, restraint force (pat-downs, handcuffing, and firm grip) in about 30 percent of encounters, and greater levels of force in about 2.5 percent of encounters. About 7.2 percent of all police–suspect encounters involved some form of citizen resistance.

What these studies from the 1960s to modern times indicate is that although police work rarely involves the use of significant levels of violence, the use or threat of force is ever present. The use of violence is one of the most important areas of study. The potential consequences to both the victim and the officer can be severe, including emotional trauma and the possibility of either physical injury or death, particularly when the police use deadly force. Yet despite the significance of police use of force, the US government does not collect official data on the use of force by police officers. As discussed later in this chapter, some organizations have attempted to collect data on fatal uses of force, but even these collections have problems.

## National Estimates on Police Use of Force

In an attempt to address the gap in our understanding and assess overall use of force by the police during police-citizen contacts, the BJS developed a national questionnaire (Greenfeld, Langan, and Smith 1997). Known as the Police–Public Contact Survey (PPCS) and conducted every three years since 1996, it surveys a nationally representative sample of residents age 16 or older, asking about their contacts with the police during the 12 months prior to the interview. In the 2018 survey (the most recent available), a total of 104,324 individuals were interviewed (Davis, Whyde, and Langton 2018). The survey asked about the prevalence of citizen contacts with the police, reasons for citizen contacts, and police actions during citizen contacts, including police threats and use of nonfatal force (Harrell and Davis 2020). Researchers estimated from the interviews that more than 61.5 million citizens had face-to-face contact with a police officer during the previous year. Traffic stops were the most likely reason for contact with police.

From the survey, the BJS also estimated that about 1.3 million people had force used or threatened against them during their most recent contact with the police. Although this number may seem large, it represents only 2 percent of the citizens police came into contact with the prior year. Additional survey findings from 2018 are presented in Table 10.1.

Although the PPCS is an important and useful step forward in collecting data on police use of force, Hickman, Piquero, and Garner (2008) argue that it likely underestimates the amount of force used by police. They point out that the PPCS does not survey individuals who recently had contact with police but were incarcerated during the time of the survey, a high-risk use-of-force population. To overcome this limitation, Hickman et al. combined the 2002 PPCS data with data from the 2002 Survey of Inmates in Local Jails, which involved surveys of a nationally representative sample of 6,982 local jail inmates. Using the combined data, they found that police used force in 20 percent of arrests, compared with about 19 percent using the PPCS alone. In total, they estimated that police officers used force 760,000 times in 2002, compared with 664,458 times using the PPCS alone, for an undercount of 95,542 uses of force. Despite the survey of inmates only accounting for 1 percent of all police contacts, they represented 13 percent of force incidents. Clearly, the PPCS alone underestimates the use of force by police officers.

In summary, the studies discussed in this section, covering different police departments over a 30-year period and including national estimates, show that police employ verbal force and the threat of physical force relatively often, but their use of actual physical force is much less common.

**TABLE 10.1** Highlights from the 2018 Police–Public Contact Survey

**Incidence and Prevalence of Contact with Police**

- An estimated 61.5 million US residents age 16 or older (about 24 percent of all persons of this age) had at least one face-to-face contact with a police officer during 2018.

- Of the 61.5 million persons with police contact during 2018, 46.9 percent of contacts were involuntary or police initiated.

**Reasons for Contact with Police**

- The most common reason for police contact was being the driver of a motor vehicle that was pulled over by police, accounting for over 18 million contacts.

- About 1.4 percent of involuntary contacts were street stops by police.

- Over 3 percent indicated the reason for the contact was a traffic accident.

**Police Threats or Use of Force During Contacts**

- Of the 61.5 million persons who had contact with a police officer during 2018, 1.3 million (2 percent) experienced threats or use of force by police.

- Blacks (4 percent) and Hispanics (3 percent) were more likely than whites (2 percent) to experience threats or use of force by police.

- Younger people were more likely to experience threats or use of force than older people who had contact with police.

*Source*: E. Harrell and E. Davis, *Contacts Between Police and the Public, 2018—Statistical Tables* (Washington, DC: Bureau of Justice Statistics, 2020).

## Learning to Use Force

The police learn about threats to their safety and the use of force both formally and informally. Formally, police are given direction by their department, including through training. Informally, police officers learn, from other officers on the job, the accepted methods and ways of thinking about their safety and the use of force. This section examines these two different but related ways in which police departments provide direction in the use of force: formal training in levels of force and informal, and cultural standards about the use of force in routine encounters.

### Training

Most officers are trained to use a **continuum of force**, from the least to the greatest, to match the intensity of a suspect's resistance (Terrill 2001). Ideally, an officer employs the least force necessary to solve a problem, restrain a suspect, or control a situation. These models are based on officers responding to the level of resistance from subjects. Some professional trainers have called for the discontinuation of force continuums in officer training, although their criticisms have been forcefully rejected by others (see, e.g., Fridell, Ijames, and Berkow 2016). More recently, some scholars have argued for a move away from the focus on the level of citizen resistance and instead suggested "a model that considers the risks presented by subjects and the necessity of force" (McLean and Alpert 2021, 131). Nonetheless, linear use of force continua focused on citizen resistance are still the most commonly used training tools, with one survey finding more than 80 percent of agencies using them (Terrill and Paoline 2013). Figure 10.1 presents the use-of-force continuum

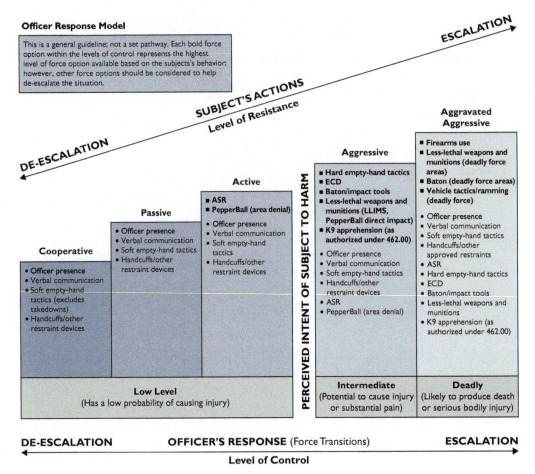

**FIGURE 10.1** St. Paul Police Department Use of Force Continuum.

*SOURCE*: By permission of the St. Paul Police Department. Adapted from the Las Vegas Model.

used by the St. Paul Police Department. The various levels of force incorporated into these continua were succinctly described by Skolnick and Fyfe (1993), and their descriptions are adapted as follows:

1. **Mere presence**. At the lowest level of force, the simple presence of an officer is usually enough to control most situations. **Mere presence** operates on the assumption that the visible authority of the state is sufficient to deter criminal wrongdoing. As demonstrated by a wide body of research, however, the passive authority of the state alone is insufficient to deter all illegal behavior or gain compliance from everyone. As Wilson (1968) observed, officers must become personally involved—they must develop personal skills in the use of coercion to control some kinds of problems.

2. **Verbalization**. This stage is sometimes called **verbal force**. When officers speak, they are taught to do so persuasively. Officers verbalize their commands in "adult-to-adult" communications. That is, they communicate on the presumption that they are

talking to adults who will understand and comply with their requests. *Example*: "Sir, would you please step out of the car."

3. **Command voice**. The **command voice** is more vibrant and is issued in the form of an order. Skolnick and Fyfe (1993) provide the following example: "Sir, I asked you for your vehicle papers once. Now I'm *telling* you to give them to me *now*."

4. **Firm grips**. Physical grasps of the body direct a suspect when and where to move. They are intended to control a suspect's physical movements but not to cause pain. They can be restraining, holding, or lifting. *Example*: Two people are attempting to fight. An officer grabs one person to hold him back, or two or more officers working as a team may separate the two people or "swarm" one person.

5. **Pain compliance**. A suspect's compliance is gained by causing pain. Various techniques are taught that enable officers to cause pain without lasting injury. *Example*: A person the officer is attempting to handcuff pulls away, and the officer twists the suspect's arm to put on the cuffs.

6. **Impact techniques**. Impact techniques involve physical contact between the suspect and an officer's body or less-lethal device. They are intended to knock down or incapacitate a dangerous suspect who has not responded to other techniques. Sometimes included among impact techniques are increasingly popular **less-lethal weapons**, including beanbags shot from a shotgun, oleoresin capsicum (OC) pepper spray, and conducted energy devices (also known as Tasers). *Example*: A suspect under the influence of drugs resists the police so vigorously that she cannot be controlled. She is struck with a baton, or sprayed in the face, or stunned with a conducted energy device. More technologically advanced, less-lethal weapons are currently being developed. For example, sticky foams may be fired from a large gun from 35 feet away. They act like contact cement, sticking the suspect to the floor or to whatever he or she touches (Miller 1995, 485–486). More recent adaptations of military technology may also be available to police in the future. For example, the Active Denial System uses directed energy radio frequency that rapidly heats skin and causes intense pain (Hager 2015).

7. **Deadly force**. The highest level is force that is capable of killing a suspect. The purpose is usually to incapacitate a suspect who presents an immediate and potentially deadly threat to another person, not to kill. Death, however, is a frequent byproduct. Skolnick and Fyfe (1993) describe three uses of deadly force: the carotid hold (or sleeper hold), which induces unconsciousness in a suspect and can be deadly in practice; the bar arm-control hold, in which the forearm is squeezed against the neck to cut off the flow of air; and the use of a firearm. *Example*: A suspect vigorously resists arrest, and the officer gets behind him and "chokes him out" to gain control of the suspect and place him in handcuffs.

As discussed earlier, there are often differences of opinion concerning what is and is not appropriate when police force is used. One important factor in determining appropriate use is the actual or perceived threat posed by the person resisting police authority (Terrill 2005). This threat potential is assessed not only in terms of the nature of the threat or actual resistance. but also by the physical size of the person in question and whether that person is under the influence of drugs or alcohol or might have a weapon.

In addition, any prior knowledge about the person and the potential for danger would be important.

### Re-engineering Training

In recent years, highly publicized videos of police officers using force have drawn intense scrutiny of police methods. Controversies surrounding a number of particularly high-profile deaths (e.g., George Floyd, Eric Garner, Michael Brown, and Tamir Rice) have ignited worldwide protests and a public discussion over how and under what circumstances police should use force. As a result, current methods and policies related to police training on the use of force are being questioned, and a number of changes in training and tactics have been proposed. The Police Executive Research Forum (PERF), for example, has stated that training on use of force is inadequate in most departments and proposed extensive changes in police training and tactics, including a greater emphasis on de-escalation and the incorporation of crisis intervention training (Wexler 2015). Although some agencies already use many of these methods, whether they will become widespread across the country is unclear. More importantly, we have limited evidence on the effectiveness of these methods for reducing the frequency and level of force, and for minimizing officer risk. We discuss some of these proposals here, along with the more traditional and widespread practices.

### Areas of Training

The training regimen for the use of force is elaborate. Particular areas of training related to the use of force include firearms, OC spray, conducted energy devices, self-defense, de-escalation, trauma-informed policing, flashlights, and canines.

**Firearms.** For most police trainees, the most popular training is in firearms (Marion 1998). This training is frequently the highlight of the academy, although continuing (in-service) firearms training for veteran officers has been less systematic and probably less effective (Morrison 2003). Traditional firearms training is gradually giving way to situationally based training, which includes simulated firearms scenarios and the use of mobile targets. "Shoot–don't shoot" scenarios are used to teach officers to exercise restraint when using deadly force. Among the most popular of these are Firearms Training Systems and Professional Range Instruction simulators, which present trainees with scenarios whose outcomes are manipulated by a specialist. Scenarios are presented in which outcomes are uncertain and typically call for the unholstering of a weapon. Many outcomes, however, do not call for the discharge of a weapon, and officers learn to react quickly so as *not* to shoot. The recent PERF (2016) report argues for moving beyond simple shoot–don't shoot scenarios, pointing out that these are somewhat unrealistic because officers face situations that involve more than the option to shoot or not shoot, including the ability to de-escalate situations or use less-lethal weapons.

**OC Spray.** Officers are required to train in the use of OC spray. Some departments require that trainees submit to being sprayed; in others, being sprayed is voluntary. OC's location on the force continuum also varies. In some agencies, it is considered intermediate force and can be used in response to subjects perceived as aggressive. However, some departments allow its use in response to passive resistance. The North Carolina Justice Academy, for example, locates OC spray just above Mace and below hard hands, the PR-24 (baton), and swarming techniques (Lamb and Friday 1997). According to this perspective, officers are taught to use OC spray when they think a person is about to become belligerent, to prevent the escalation of force (Trimmer 1993). The PERF (2016) has recently suggested that agencies consider the adoption of newer chemical sprays (e.g., pelargonic acid vanillylamide) that minimize cross-contamination and are not flammable.

**Conducted Energy Devices.** The so-called Taser fits in the category of **conducted energy devices (CEDs)**, which are defined as weapons "primarily designed to disrupt a subject's central nervous system by means of deploying electrical energy sufficient to cause uncontrolled muscle contractions and override an individual's voluntary motor responses" (PERF 2005). These weapons have become extremely popular in recent years and have largely superseded OC/pepper spray in many departments as the preferred option for dealing with belligerent and resisting subjects. Policies and practices vary, however, in regard to where the CED or Taser should be placed on the use-of-force continuum (Terrill and Paoline 2013).

**Self-Defense.** Officers are taught a variety of techniques for self-defense. Marion (1998, 68) describes self-defense training as follows:

> Recruits may be taught some "come-along" or "hand holds" (Peak 1993) as well as pressure points. By the end of the University Academy, recruits learn the Infra-Orbital [under the base of the nose], the Mandibular Angle [behind the ear] and the Hypoglossal [under the jaw] pressure points (Faulkner 1994). They also learn take-downs and proper handcuffing techniques. The force continuum is stressed in self-defense training, where cadets are taught to use no more force than necessary to subdue a subject. But once again, officer safety is the primary concern of all the training. (68)

**De-escalation.** Techniques of **de-escalation** involve the use of communication and tactics designed to provide officers with time when dealing with combative suspects (PERF Forum 2016). For example, by keeping a safe distance and/or finding cover, officers have time to begin calmly communicating with suspects without placing themselves at risk. These techniques to "slow things down" may be especially useful for dealing with mentally ill or distraught persons. However, we have almost no research evidence on the effectiveness of these programs (White 2021). The few studies conducted so far have produced mixed findings, with one showing no impact and one finding reductions in force and injuries to citizens and officers (Engel et al. 2020). However, as White (2021, 125) notes, the content of these trainings varies considerably: "In plain terms, we know little about what it is, what it includes, and whether it is effective." Clearly, more research is needed to identify the most effective approaches to de-escalation. In Inside Policing 10.1, Matthew Pontillo, assistant chief of the New York Police Department (NYPD), discusses their training on de-escalation techniques.

**Trauma-Informed Policing.** Many of the people police encounter in their work are the victims of trauma. More police agencies are beginning to recognize the importance of understanding how trauma influences the behavior of citizens who encounter the police. Training for **trauma-informed policing** focuses on educating officers on trauma—specifically, its prevalence, influence on citizens they encounter, how to recognize it, and how to respond to citizens with trauma. The goal is to integrate this knowledge in police practices and policies. By doing so, proponents hope that officers will be more effective at dealing with citizens, be able to avoid or de-escalate potentially volatile encounters, avoid retraumatizing citizens, as well as be safer in the course of their work (Scallon and Peckerman 2017; Haas 2018).

**INSIDE POLICING 10.1** | **Assistant Chief Matthew Pontillo: NYPD De-escalation Techniques**

We focus on the impact of high-emotion, high-stakes encounters and what that does to an officer's stress level, what the flow of adrenaline does, what they can expect, and how they can mitigate against that.

One of the things the program stresses is that police work is not personal. If someone curses you out or is agitated, you shouldn't take it personally. You have to be professional. You're not going to resolve anything; in fact you'll only make it worse, if you escalate the encounter and go up to the same level of agitation and aggression that the subject is displaying. If you humiliate someone, it will often lead to problems.

We also stress that respect begets respect, and disrespect begets disrespect. You get what you give. And it's in your best interest, and it goes to officer safety, if you can de-escalate something, as opposed to escalating to the point where you have to use force.

We stress during training the use of cover, concealment, containment, and communication with the subject. That's really the bedrock of the whole thing. Don't put yourself in a position where you have to use force.

And we tell officers that they do not always need to "stand their ground." They can move back and tactically reposition themselves in order to de-escalate a situation. This is not giving up; it is trying other avenues to solve the problem. We are pushing officers to read the situation, to take their time, to use their critical thinking skills, and not to rush it.

We also incorporate the negotiation skills we have learned from NYPD's top hostage negotiation teams: "active listening" skills, body language and nonverbal communication, gaining control through influence, showing empathy, and so on.

SOURCE: Police Executive Research Forum, *Re-Engineering Training on Police Use of Force* (Washington, DC: Author, 2015), 51.

**Officer Survival.** Central to many training programs are classes on **officer survival**. Such classes deal with the major risks faced by police officers—officer stress, suicide, and threats. Officers are taught how to deal with the murder of a partner; about the police officers' memorial in Washington, DC; and about the federal pension their spouse will receive if they are killed. They are exposed to the bureaucratic paperwork associated with death. Extremely violent encounters, although rare in practice, are central to training. Officer survival is also a component of many other classes. For example, classes on police procedure instruct officers that concerns about safety provide a legal justification for a wide variety of actions, including pat-downs. Finally, it is not unusual for officers to see training films emphasizing the hazards of police work.

**Flashlights.** A flashlight is infrequently thought of as a weapon, yet many officers use flashlights in just that way. For example, about two-thirds of 365 impact weapon incidents in the Los Angeles County Sheriff's Department over a five-year period involved flashlights rather than batons (Anderson 2003). As McEwen (1997) noted, policies on the use of flashlights are often ambiguous. Some departments have policies forbidding the use of flashlights as weapons. And when a flashlight is considered a weapon, it is regarded only as a backup.

The policy in one department McEwen (1997, 51) assessed stated that "the department does not recognize the flashlight as a formal policy weapon." Recognizing that it may be needed in some circumstances, the policy further observed that "when a flashlight is utilized in an application of force, whether to restrain or to effect an arrest, or in defense against an attack, it will be considered a weapon and all requirements pertaining to the use of force and the reporting of such force will be applicable." McEwen concludes that flashlights will be used as less-lethal weapons and that policy must recognize this fact and bring flashlights under use-of-force policy.

**Canines.** Many police departments use canines for a number of purposes: to search for drugs, explosives, and individuals who might be trying to avoid or escape from the police as well as to control individuals and crowds (Golden and Walker 2002). Many officers also believe that the use of dogs to search for suspects who might be armed reduces the possibility that officers will be injured or killed. Although they are not trained to do so, some handlers permit their dogs to bite as a "reward."

The use of canines varies by department. Some departments do not recognize them as a level of force; others do. The use of dogs is common, though. Moreover, dog bites are frequently severe. Campbell, Berk, and Fyfe (1998) argue that the widespread use of canines in some departments requires a revision in thinking about the use of force. In their study of the Los Angeles Police Department (LAPD) and the Los Angeles Sheriff's Department, the authors found that the use of canines was routine, and that encounters often ended with bites, many of them serious. Over a two-year period in the 1990s, the LAPD reported 44 percent of the 539 suspects who were apprehended with the assistance of dogs were bitten. Eighty-six of those suspects were injured badly enough from the bites to be admitted to the hospital. They observed that the use of canines frequently lacks the rigor of policy that accompanies the use of other kinds of less-lethal and lethal weaponry. When policies were in place, they were enforced in an incomplete and perfunctory way. Moreover, minority group members suffered a disproportionate number of dog bites, raising the specter that they might be used in a discriminatory way (see also Beers 1992). Campbell et al. (1998) concluded that because of the hazardous and injurious consequence of dog bites, the implementation and review of department policy regarding canines should be conducted in a rigorous manner with other uses of force.

Inside Policing 10.2 describes a more recent analysis of police canine bites in Richmond, CA.

## Police Culture and the Use of Force

The use of force is also affected by informal standards of police culture. As noted in Chapter 1, police organizational culture refers to the assumptions police have developed in learning to cope with the problems they confront, including when and how to use force. These assumptions include accepted practices and rules of conduct under different situations as well as the way of interpreting their work. Police culture provides officers with common-sense ways of thinking about activities (McNulty 1994). Reuss-Ianni (1983, 8) refers to this as "precinct street cop culture," which carries the "values, and thus the ends, toward which officers individually and in task groups strive." Although each department has its own culture (Paoline 2003), Crank (1998) has identified a wide variety of cultural themes, or building blocks of culture, that are so similar across departments that police officers generally can be described as participating in police culture.

Arguably the best illustration of how culture influences the use and interpretation of force is provided by the work of Jennifer Hunt (1985), who described how police rely on informal, cultural standards in the use of force. By focusing too much on legal definitions of force, society tends to overlook the "understandings and standards police officers

## INSIDE POLICING 10.2 | Use of Force and Injuries by K-9s

An analysis of use of force incidents in Richmond, California, indicates that dog bites accounted for 60 percent of the department's significant use of force injuries over a multiyear period, as reported by the *East Bay Times*.[1] In a three-year comparison with 20 large cities, Richmond's rate of 34 canine bites per 100,000 population easily topped the list, while three-quarters of the cities had rates below 10. The newly available data came as a complete surprise to the city's Community Police Review Commission—"That wasn't even on our radar. None of these cases made the light of day." All of the K-9 activations were deemed justified, and despite the injuries, officers point out that dog bites do less harm than bullets.

**Discussion Question:** Should police canines be used in the apprehension of suspects? If so, should they be restricted to certain types of situations?

[1] J. P. Sulek, "One Bay Area City, 73 Police Dog Bites, and the Law that Made Them Public." *East Bay Times*, December 19, 2021. https://www.eastbaytimes.com/2021/12/19/one-bay-area-city-73-police-dog-bites-and-the-law-that-made-them-public/.

SOURCE: *Modern Policing* blog, December 21, 2021, https://gcordner.wordpress.com/2021/12/21/use-of-force-injuries-by-k-9s/.

actively employ in the course of their work" (Hunt 1985, 316). Hunt observed that police have *working notions of normal force*, which are standards of acceptable force learned on the street. They are different from what police learn in training; for example, they should not hit a person on the head or neck because it could be lethal.

> On the street, in contrast, police conclude that they must hit wherever it causes the most damage in order to incapacitate the suspect before they themselves are harmed. New officers also learn that they will earn the respect of their veteran coworkers by not observing legal niceties in using force, but by being "aggressive" and using whatever force is necessary in a given situation. (Hunt 1985, 319)

Force is normal and acceptable under two circumstances. First, it is normal because it is the natural outcome of strong, even uncontrollable emotions normally arising from certain routine police activities. Second, it is justifiable if it establishes police authority in the face of a threat or is morally appropriate for the type of crime encountered by the officer. When officers use too much force, or when they do not use enough, they are the subject of reprimand, gossip, and avoidance. Hunt (1985) described how normal levels of force are learned in day-to-day practice and the psychological mechanisms that justify the use of force. By carefully considering the influence of culture, the reader can begin to understand how the difference between justified force and excessive force—so important in legal and administrative reviews of police behavior after an incident—is balanced by the ways street officers confront danger and gauge forceful responses.

Recent proposals designed to reduce instances of force by police typically acknowledge the role of culture. The PERF's (2015) report on re-engineering training highlighted the role of informal culture in police use of force, stressing the need to modify police cultural norms surrounding the use of force. The report notes, for example, that

> these concepts of slowing a situation down, calling for a supervisor to respond to the scene, bringing in additional resources, de-escalating, and disengaging tactically are sometimes seen as antithetical to police culture. Some officers, with the best intentions,

think that their job is to go into a situation, take charge of it, and resolve it as quickly as you can. Sometimes there is a feeling of competitiveness about it. If an officer slows a situation down and calls for assistance; there is sometimes a feeling that other responding officers will think, "What you couldn't handle this yourself?" (PERF 2015, 5).

Clearly, any attempts to modify how police use force will require more than simply changes in policy and training. Agency leaders must convince officers on the street to accept new ways of dealing with situations. In "Voices from the Field," the former president of the National Police Foundation (now the National Policing Institute), Jim Bueermann, discusses guiding principles on police use of force that he believes police leaders should adopt; additional information on PERF's recommendations can be found in Inside Policing 10.3.

## Controversy and the Use of Force

On occasion, the use of force by police officers may conflict with community standards, legal factors, or departmental policy.

**Type 1: Conflicts with the Community.** In Type 1 conflicts, the law and departmental policy may consider the police use of force to be appropriate, but a substantial segment of the community does not. Such conflict occurs most often in minority neighborhoods. The relationship between police and some minority citizens may be one of suspicion and distrust, so when the police, particularly officers who are not members of that minority group, use coercion, they have a substantial burden placed on them to prove that the use was appropriate. In these circumstances, incidents of force, even seemingly minor ones, feed into an accumulated reservoir of grievances in which any additional incident, however justified, can provoke community violence. The widespread availability of video technology has increased the number of incidents of police force coming under public scrutiny, highlighting disagreements over definitions of appropriate force. Controversial videos now appear regularly on television and social media.

An obvious recent example of a Type 1 conflict occurred in Ferguson, Missouri, in 2014. On August 9 at about noon, Michael Brown, an 18-year-old African American, and his friend left a neighborhood market. Brown had just shoplifted cigarillos from the store, an action caught on video cameras. About 5 minutes after leaving the store, a police officer drove up alongside Brown and his friend, both of whom were walking in the middle of the street, and instructed them to use the sidewalk. As the officer later testified, he noticed cigarillos in Brown's possession and thought Brown fit the description from the store. Moments later, the officer pulled his SUV in front of both men, blocking their path. At this point, an altercation ensued between Brown and the officer, who was still seated in his vehicle. According to the officer's later testimony, he claimed Brown struck him in the face and attempted to take his weapon (Cave 2014). Witness accounts of what occurred are less clear (Cave 2014). At some point in the altercation, Officer Wilson fired two shots, striking Brown once in the thumb (Buchanan et al. 2015). Brown then turned and ran. Officer Wilson exited the vehicle and pursued Brown (Buchanan et al. 2015). Witness accounts of what happened next conflict with one another (Bosman et al. 2014). According to Officer Wilson's testimony, Brown turned and charged the officer, ignoring his commands to get down on the ground (Cave 2014). Other witnesses' accounts are conflicting, with some providing accounts mostly consistent with Officer Wilson, some claiming Brown put his hands up in surrender, others saying Brown did turn but "staggered toward him, wounded, his arms outstretched in a gesture of surrender" and still others expressing uncertainty about Brown's actions (Cave 2014). What is clear is that Officer Wilson fired 10 shots at

# VOICES FROM THE FIELD

## Jim Bueermann

*President (ret.), National Police Foundation; Chief of Police (ret.), Redlands, California*

Perhaps nothing has a greater potential for fracturing the relationships between the police and the communities they are paid to protect than a contentious use-of-force incident. Police use-of-force controversies have rocked community trust and confidence in the police across the nation—in New York; Baltimore; Ferguson, Missouri; Pasco, Washington; Albuquerque; Cleveland; Cincinnati; North Charleston, South Carolina; and Los Angeles, to name just a few.

There are no easy answers when it comes to police use-of-force issues. Police officers are the only class of public employees in America that, without prior judicial review, are authorized to use force against members of society to carry out their duties—up to and including the taking of a life. As problematic as this issue is, our government has committed surprisingly few resources to understanding this phenomenon. Not only is there little science about this, but America's "official" repository of fatal police use-of-force cases captures only about 50 percent of those occurring each year. This database is maintained by the FBI as part of the Uniform Crime Reporting system and is entirely voluntary (which may be the principal cause of its low reporting rate).

While there is no magical formula for preventing tragic incidents, policing leaders can adopt a set of guiding principles regarding the use of force by their officers. These are as follows:

1. Develop and articulate a set of organizational values, in conjunction with the community, that clearly express the organization's commitment to the respect for human dignity and for doing everything possible to reduce the use of force.
2. Craft recruiting, hiring, reward, accountability, and training systems that are in alignment with the organizational values and maintain a constant focus on reducing the use of force.
3. Draft clear policies that outline legal guidelines and constraints on using force, articulate the organizational leader's position, and reflect the community's expectations. These policies should be reviewed on a regular basis to ensure they are legally compliant and continue to reflect community expectations. They should be made easily available to the public.
4. Conduct refresher training on the use of force policy on a regular basis to ensure officers continue to understand it and problematic areas are identified and clarified.
5. Invest adequate time and money in reality-based training in dealing with persons suffering from mental illness, brain diseases such as autism, deafness, and so on.
6. Develop a use-of-force tracking system that captures sufficiently specific information to allow a subsequent scientific analysis of the organization's use of force. Such an analysis by an outside entity such as university researchers should be conducted and the results of the analysis made public. Such a system should also allow the organization to track and monitor individual officers' use of force as part of an early warning system for officer misconduct.
7. Develop an internal use-of-force investigative process and review board that examines each use of force for necessity, preventable error, policy and legal compliance, and training issues. The board should report to the organizational leader on each significant use of force.
8. Communicate quickly to the public when a serious or high-profile use-of-force incident occurs, explaining as much as possible, as fast as possible. In the absence of credible official information, people will fill the information void with a narrative informed by their own experiences or perceptions.

> ### INSIDE POLICING 10.3 | Higher Standard on Use of Force
>
> In conjunction with a large group of chiefs and other officials, the PERF has published 30 guiding principles designed to minimize police use of force. The principles address policy, training, tactics, and equipment. The document, which emphasizes that implementation of the principles will require retraining and changes to police operations and culture, is available at https://www.policeforum.org/assets/30%20guiding%20principles.pdf
>
> **Discussion Question:** Which of the 30 principles is likely to have the most impact on reducing police use of force?
>
> SOURCE: Modern Policing blog, February 3, 2016, https://gcordner.wordpress.com/2016/02/03/higher-standard-on-use-of-force/.

Brown, striking him multiple times, including twice in the head (BBC 2014). Brown's body was left, only partially covered, in the street for four hours (McDermott 2015). The incident generated outrage in the Black community in Ferguson and elsewhere. The day after the shooting, initially peaceful protests turned volatile that evening, with rioters damaging buildings and reports of looting (Bosman and Fitzsimmons 2014). Protests continued for weeks after the shooting. Americans followed the protests and police response daily on television and social media. The police response to protestors drew widespread criticism and ignited a national debate over police crowd control tactics and the use of force.

In November, a grand jury decided not to indict Officer Wilson, inciting more unrest (McDermott 2015). "All told, it resulted in a dozen nights of violence, dozens of injuries, hundreds of arrests and millions of dollars in property damage" (McDermott 2015). The incident and resulting unrest triggered a national debate, a US Department of Justice investigation (2015) into police practices in Ferguson, and a consent agreement with the Department of Justice to overhaul police policies and practices.

**Type 2: Conflicts over Policy.** A Type 2 conflict occurs when there are differences between law and departmental policy. For example, a department might decide to overlook illegal immigration, because it thinks that enforcement will lead to loss of public support. Policy–law conflicts tend to involve the public. Some segments may favor the law, whereas others favor the department. An area of considerable concern involves high-speed police chases (Alpert et al. 2000; Welch 2002).

Consider that in 1994, more than 11,000 cars were stolen in Tampa, Florida. In 1995, officers began to chase car thieves, and the number of auto thefts was cut in half. Furthermore, the rate of overall crime dropped, and officers attributed this to the use of stolen cars by felons to commit other crimes. However, police officers involved in chases also were involved in several accidents. In one of these, officers careened into a utility pole. In another, they knocked a house off its foundation. More troubling, a car driven by a suspect crashed into another car and killed the two German tourists inside. This accident happened less than three weeks after a suspected car thief, followed by another sheriff's deputy, hit a car and killed two occupants (Navarro 1995, 18).

Since the 1980s, departments nationally are increasingly restricting high-speed pursuits. Chases require a police department to balance public safety with law enforcement.

Unfortunately, these two goals move at cross-purposes sometimes, and increases in law enforcement sometimes threaten the public safety. Chases are dangerous; the suspect, police officers, and innocent bystanders are sometimes injured and killed. Police chases are the "most deadly force" (Alpert and Anderson 1986). Yet many officers balk at the notion that they should withdraw from a chase and permit a suspected felon to escape. As Alpert (1989b, 229) observes, "few would argue that police should not initiate a chase, but that is where the consensus disappears." Wide controversy exists regarding if and when a chase should be curtailed.

The consequences of a Type 2 conflict are usually twofold: some segments of the community would be pleased by the pursuit policy, whereas others would not. In Tampa, residents facing higher insurance costs and economic loss supported the policy restricting pursuits. Within the police department, however, many officers were probably angry and upset.

**Type 3: Conflicts Between Norms.**   In a Type 3 conflict, an officer's behavior meets the expectations of some community segments but is inconsistent with both law and departmental policy. For example, assume that two police officers are working in a neighborhood that has extensive drug problems. They decide to harass and physically abuse individuals suspected of drug dealing. Such action is clearly illegal and in violation of departmental policy, but many persons in the neighborhood may applaud it. In such a situation, the police department might discipline the officers, perhaps terminate them, and possibly even recommend criminal prosecution. But the residents of the neighborhood might protest the action of the department, perhaps vigorously.

Type 3 conflict is most likely to occur when the police department and officers get too close to residents in a particular area and begin to enforce what they consider "neighborhood norms" rather than following the law. Community policing could result in this type of conflict if not carefully monitored. It remains to be seen whether the police can resist citizen pressure to "go outside the law to get the job done."

**Conflicting Expectations.**   The examples provided in the three types of conflict illustrate important problems in determining the appropriateness of police behavior. Officers are sometimes required to make choices that will alienate part of their public. There are also many less dramatic examples concerning the exercise of police authority and the use of coercion, and there are many gray areas. For example, a police officer might stop a citizen for a traffic ticket. If the citizen refuses to give the officer a driver's license, the officer must decide how to treat the citizen. At what point in this police–citizen encounter should the officer begin to use coercion? When should verbal threats be made? In many police departments, the guidance provided to police officers in these areas is vague or nonexistent. Officers, police managers, and members of the community are likely to have opinions about appropriate behavior in these situations, and at times, there will be conflicting expectations among these groups.

A contemporary example involves police use of CEDs. From the police perspective, CEDs contribute to officer safety and are useful for controlling suspects who are resisting arrest or otherwise threatening officers or others. One study, for example, documented an 80 to 85 percent effectiveness rate for subduing suspects (White and Ready 2007). From the general public's perspective, CEDs similarly seem beneficial if police can use them instead of baton strikes or deadly force (firearms) to make arrests and control violent suspects. In this perspective, police are seen as more effective while resorting to lesser levels of force and coercion.

If, however, police utilize CEDs preemptively or in place of lesser force (e.g., command voice or firm grips), it may lead to an increase in overall police use of force, an outcome that might not be regarded as favorable. Minority groups in particular may feel that police use CEDs too freely against them. Also, experience has shown that while CEDs are effective in controlling suspects, they may contribute to increased risk of injuries to citizens compared to other forms of force (Terrill and Paoline 2012). It is easy to see how police, legal experts, community leaders, and others might have conflicting opinions about the appropriateness of police use of CEDs.

The recognition that some decisions will have no good outcome may be frustrating for young adults interested in a career in policing. Many individuals approach police work with a clear notion of "good guy versus bad guy" fixed in their minds. Unfortunately, policing is not like that, nor can it be. In a democratic society, as Wilson (1968) observed long ago, the use of force will always be controversial.

## Inappropriate Force

In a democracy, police authority is constrained by democratic ideas of fair play. On the one hand, due process laws provide the legalized means that police are permitted to use to pursue suspected criminals and to deal with citizens and suspects. Department policy provides the administrative means, such as the use-of-force continuum, that police are supposed to follow in their day-to-day activities (Terrill et al. 2003). On the other hand, many police officers are ends-oriented. That is, they are more focused on the ends of criminal justice—arresting dangerous felons or acquiring information about criminal activity—than on following legally acceptable means to achieve those ends. Also, police culture seems to give more emphasis to "good" ends than to legal means, and it sometimes justifies questionable means in the pursuit of these good ends (Klockars 1980; Crank 1998).

The use of questionable and illegal force, as well as the use of unacceptably high levels of force and police brutality, has been a problem for the police throughout history. But what is meant by inappropriate force? And what constitutes brutality? Clearly, these questions must be at the center of any investigation into police misuse of force.

### Brutality and Excessive Force

Police brutality is difficult to define. It means different things to different people. Two common approaches to defining brutality distinguish between brutality and excessive force. Kania and Mackey (1977, 28) define **excessive force** as violence "of a degree that is more than justified to effect a legitimate police function." According to Carter (1994, 270), **police brutality** is excessive force, but to a more extreme degree, and includes violence that does not support a legitimate police function. An officer who beats a suspect who has already been handcuffed, for example, is committing police brutality.

This definition, however, does not fully address some aspects of police behavior that are widely seen as brutal but that are not violently forceful. As noted earlier, police use of force may range from verbal commands to physical force, and the majority of force incidents involve lesser forms of force. Although these actions may be taken legally to accomplish a legitimate police task, they may also be used inappropriately (e.g., racial slurs, threats, or insults). Citizens tend to define brutality and excessive force broadly to include these lesser forms of aggression. Yet brutality and excessive force refer specifically to physical forms of force. The more general term, *use of force*, covers the range of behaviors from verbal to physical force but also includes both legal and extralegal force. Holmes and Smith (2012, 345), in dealing with this problem, focus on **extralegal police aggression**, arguing that

> the concept *extralegal police aggression* is preferable for several related reasons. First, there is broad agreement on the definition of aggression, which generally refers to "*any form of behavior that is intended to injure someone physically or psychologically*" (Berkowitz 1993, 3, emphasis in original). Second, excessive force and brutality are sometimes defined to include only willful actions on the part of police officers (e.g., Griffin and Bernard 2003), but aggression may or may not entail conscious deliberation on the actor's part … both unconscious and conscious mental processes may trigger extralegal aggression by the police. Finally, the concept of aggression captures the critical point that these behaviors specifically aim to injure citizens.

Extralegal police aggression occurs whenever a police officer engages in behavior that is intended to injure someone physically or psychologically, but serves no legitimate police function. Included within this definition are a wide variety of behaviors, such as physical violence (e.g., brutality) and lesser forms (e.g., verbal threats and insults).

### Physical and Psychological Force in Police History

Both physical and **psychological force** were commonplace well into the 1930s. Hopkins (1931, 212–215) reported on a study of the New York City Police Department in 1930, finding that in 166 cases (23.4 percent of the total cases studied), some type of physical force was employed. The most frequently used method was to strike the suspect one or more times with a fist (67 cases). Other methods included use of a rubber hose (19 cases) and a blackjack (12 cases). One suspect was "hung out the window, kicked and dragged by the hair" (Hopkins 1931, 215). Larson (1932, 95–100) also discussed some of the coercive methods commonly used by police during this period. These methods became associated with the term **third degree**. Various third-degree methods historically employed by the police are listed in Inside Policing 10.4.

Most police officers of this period tended to deny any use of physical force. However, Bruce Smith, a prominent police consultant of that era, commented about the third degree in this regard: "In every police station in this country about which I know anything, there is a room remote from the public parts of the building where prisoners are questioned" (Hopkins 1931, 195). The Wickersham Commission (National Commission on Law Observance and Enforcement 1931), discussed in Chapter 2, found that the police use of such methods was widespread.

Continued problems with coercive psychological techniques resulted in famous decisions of the Warren Court in the 1960s. In *Miranda v. Arizona* (1966), the US Supreme Court decision observed that psychologically coercive techniques interfered with constitutional ideas of fair play. Consequently, the court issued its now famous requirement that suspects be advised of their right to an attorney and that the police's right to question suspects be restricted, except when that right has been waived or after an attorney has advised the suspect whether to talk to the police. As Vaughn (1992) has noted, other court rulings have expanded the rights of the police to use trickery and deception. However, by permitting open deception, several observers of the police have contended that the courts are encouraging the police to emphasize "good" ends over legal means (Skolnick and Fyfe 1993).

## INSIDE POLICING 10.4 | Historical Methods of Psychological and Physical Force

**Psychological Force**

Suspects are placed on "the Loop"—that is, moved from station to station to deny them access to family, friends, and attorneys.

Suspects are placed in very small, completely dark cells. Rats are placed in women's cells to "exhaust their nervous energy." A prisoner in an adjoining cell is told to "moan" and "yell" during the night. A large stove is placed next to a cell, and the stove is filled with items (e.g., bones, vegetable matter, or old tires) designed to give off a foul odor and increase the heat in the cell to unbearable levels (i.e., to create a "sweat box").

Suspects are interrogated for long periods under bright lights and without food or water, and/or they are denied access to substances like tobacco to which they are addicted. Suspects are threatened with various weapons; for example, a gun with blank shells is fired at the subject.

Murder suspects are required to touch or hold the hand of the murder victim.

Police pretend to beat prisoners in an interrogation room adjoining that of the suspect. One police officer is "hard" and "tough" and threatens the suspect; the other officer is sympathetic and supportive and pretends to protect the suspect from harm in exchange for information or a confession (also known as "good cop, bad cop" and the Mutt and Jeff technique).

Police officers make false promises about what will happen to the suspect.

**Physical Force**

Suspects are beaten on all parts of their body (usually except for the head) with rubber hoses, clubs, blackjacks, fists, telephone books, straps, brass knuckles, pistol butts, and whips. Arms and legs are twisted. Testicles are kicked, twisted, squeezed, and used to lift suspects upward, and testicles are also burned with acid. Suspects are tortured with electric shocks, dental drills, and lighted cigars. Suspects are dragged or pulled by their hair.

Suspects are drenched with cold water from a hose, their heads are held under water, water is forced into their noses, they are hung out the window, they are choked with neckties and ropes, and they are required to go without shoes until their feet are bleeding. Chemicals such as tear gas, scopolamine, and chloroform are employed.

*SOURCES*: Adapted from J. A. Larson, *Lying and Its Detection* (Chicago: University of Chicago Press, 1932), 95–121; E. J. Hopkins, *Our Lawless Police* (New York: Viking Press, 1931), 25, 128, 215.

Police today continue to rely on deception, a form of psychological coercion, to secure information. The following are examples of contemporary uses of deception:

1. The person, or suspect, is not told the truth about why they are being questioned.

2. The suspect is not told that the person asking the questions is a police officer.

3. The suspect is told that they are being interviewed rather than interrogated and are free to leave at any time.

4. The police misrepresent the circumstances of the crime the suspect is alleged to have committed; for example, a suspect might be told there was an eyewitness or that other available evidence that ties the suspect to the crime.

5. The police may make the crime seem more serious (carrying a more severe punishment) than it is to induce the suspect to make a bargain to confess to a less-serious crime.

6. The police provide a justification to the suspect for the act; for example, "the victim got what she deserved."

7. The police may make some type of promise that later can be denied or modified.

These examples illustrate that there are sometimes differences between what is legal and what is ethical. Generally, the police can *legally* use trickery and deception as long as their methods do not involve coercion or improper promises (e.g., the police cannot promise a light sentence, since that is the judge's prerogative, but they can promise to speak to the prosecutor on behalf of the suspect). Although it is legal, however, is it right to lie? Is it right for an investigator to tell a suspect that his fingerprints have already been found at the scene of a crime if they have not? Is it right for a police officer to pretend to be a drug dealer and offer to sell drugs to a suspect? These are not clear-cut cases, of course. Such behavior by the police may seem unethical to some but merely clever to others. Some citizens would have their confidence in the police shaken if they thought the police did not use such methods; others are shocked that they do.

The matter of police ethics, and the role of ethics in guiding and controlling police behavior, is discussed at greater length in Chapter 11.

## Frequency of Excessive Force and Brutality

How widespread is extralegal police violence and aggression? Unfortunately, this is an extremely difficult question to answer, particularly given the lack of sufficient data. Nevertheless, researchers have attempted to quantify the problem, relying primarily on perceptions of either police officers or citizens. Barker (1986), for example, studied the extent of police brutality, along with other types of police deviant behavior, in a city of moderate size in the southern United States. Based on questionnaire responses from 43 of 45 officers in that department, he found that about 40 percent used excessive force at times. Officers tended to believe that lying in court (committing perjury), sleeping on duty, and having sex or drinking on duty were more serious forms of deviant police behavior than the use of excessive force. This was particularly true when excessive force was used against persons in custody. Almost half the officers said they would rarely, if ever, report another officer if they used excessive force.

In another study, Carter (1985) surveyed 95 police officers in McAllen, Texas. He found that 23 percent believed that excessive force was sometimes necessary to demonstrate an officer's authority, and 62 percent believed that an officer had a right to use excessive force in retaliation against anyone who used force against the officer. In the areas of verbal abuse, slightly more than half of the officers believed that it was permissible to talk "rough" with citizens, and that rough talk was the only way to communicate with some citizens.

Friedrich (1980), in his comprehensive analysis of research on the use of force, found that police used force in only about 5 percent of encounters with offenders or suspects. In about two-thirds of these encounters, the force was considered excessive. Because only a small percentage of all police–citizen encounters are with offenders or suspects and only about 5 percent of these types of encounters involve the use of force, his findings suggest that both the use of force and the use of excessive force are rare in police work.

As part of its continuing efforts to acquire data about excessive force by law enforcement officers, the Law Enforcement Management and Administrative Statistics survey of police agencies included questions on formal citizen complaints about use of force. The 2007 survey included questions about the number of citizen complaints regarding the use of force, the disposition of complaints, and information regarding policies and procedures relating to the processing of complaints (US Department of Justice, Bureau of Justice Statistics 2011). The survey found that in 2006, local law enforcement agencies with 100 or more sworn officers received 22,447 citizen complaints about the use of force. Large agencies received the majority of complaints. In addition, the complaint rate was greater for larger agencies than for smaller agencies. For example, agencies with between 100 and 249 officers had 5.9 complaints per 100 officers responding to calls, whereas agencies with 1,000 or more officers had 9.47 complaints per 100 officers responding to calls. The Police Public Contact Survey, discussed earlier, asked citizens about force threatened or used against them in an encounter with police; the majority of the respondents perceived the force as excessive (Harrell and Davis 2020).

Research on extralegal police aggression, especially brutality, is extremely difficult to conduct. Police agencies are reluctant to study the issue or release data to researchers. Police officers engaged in these acts attempt to hide their actions from supervisors and the public. Moreover, offending officers believe that many, if not all, of the other officers (including supervisors and managers) who may be aware of this behavior will not report the brutality and will lie about the incident if it is investigated by the department or other individuals. As a result, the limited number of studies include a small number of jurisdictions, often rely on weak research designs, and use various, often imprecise measures. Moreover, the evidence from the limited number of studies is not entirely consistent. Nonetheless, we are beginning to piece together a picture of the problem and, as discussed in Chapter 11, devise approaches to deal with this important issue.

Perhaps the most infamous case of police brutality in modern history was the killing of George Floyd by Minneapolis police officers in 2020. Inside Policing 10.5 describes this incident and some of the subsequent events connected with it. The killing of Mr. Floyd ignited protests across the country and spurred an already growing call for police reform.

## INSIDE POLICING 10.5    How George Floyd Died, and What Happened Next

The death of George Floyd, a 46-year-old Black man, drew widespread outrage in May 2020 after a video circulated online showing Office Derek Chauvin holding his knee on Mr. Floyd's neck on a Minneapolis street corner as he gasped for breath. Mr. Floyd's death spurred nationwide protests against police brutality and a reckoning over everything from public monuments to sports team names.

### A Video of the Arrest Shocked the World and Led to Weeks of Protests

Mr. Floyd died on May 25 after being handcuffed and pinned to the ground under the knee of Mr. Chauvin, who is white, for more than nine minutes. Bystander video of the encounter quickly went viral. The disturbing video incited large protests against police brutality and systemic racism in Minneapolis and more than 150 American cities in the months that followed, leading to a nation-wide racial justice movement not seen since the civil rights protests

*(Continued)*

of the 1960s. The National Guard was activated in at least 21 states, and cities announced curfews as protesters filled the streets. The protests sometimes turned destructive. Law enforcement was criticized for responding to the protests—a majority of which were peaceful—with force, by spraying tear gas and shooting rubber bullets at protesters, and conducting mass arrests. After the video of the arrest surfaced, the Minneapolis Police Department fired Mr. Chauvin and the three other officers involved. The explosive video also prompted an FBI civil rights investigation.

### Video from Police Body Cameras Shows How a Call About a $20 Bill Turned Fatal

Around 8 pm on May 25, Minneapolis police officers responded to a call from a store clerk who claimed Mr. Floyd had paid for cigarettes with a counterfeit $20 bill, the Police Department said in a statement. In an initial statement, the police said that Mr. Floyd "appeared to be under the influence." It said that officers ordered him to step away from his car, and that he resisted them after he got out. Officers "noted he appeared to be suffering medical distress," the statement read, after which they called an ambulance. The statement lacked critical details about the fatal encounter, and bystander video and officer body camera footage released in August helped to fill in the blanks.

The body camera footage shows police officers approaching a car in which Mr. Floyd is sitting in the driver's seat. In the footage, Mr. Lane, one of the officers, taps his flashlight on the window and asks Mr. Floyd to show his hands. After being asked several times, Mr. Floyd eventually opens the car door, while apologizing. Six seconds after the door opens, Mr. Lane draws his gun, points it at Mr. Floyd and says, "Put your [expletive] hands up right now." Without explaining the reason for the stop, he pulls Mr. Floyd out of the car. After removing Mr. Floyd from the vehicle, Mr. Lane and Mr. Kueng handcuff him and walk him across the street to their squad car. Mr. Floyd protests and resists sitting in the back seat, saying he is claustrophobic, and officers try to force him in. He pushes himself out the other side of the vehicle, saying he is going to lie on the ground. Three officers pin Mr. Floyd facedown—Mr. Chauvin kneeling on his neck, Mr. Kueng kneeling on his upper legs and holding his wrist, and Mr. Lane holding Mr. Floyd's legs. (Mr. Than was keeping bystanders away). Mr. Floyd began saying repeatedly that he could not breathe. Mr. Chauvin kept his knee on Mr. Floyd's neck for nine and a half minutes. Six minutes after the officers put Mr. Floyd facedown, and only after bystanders shouted at them to attend to him, Mr. Kueng checks for Mr. Floyd's pulse and says he cannot feel it. All three of the officers continue to hold Mr. Floyd in a position that restricts breathing. Two minutes later, emergency responders arrive, and the medics load him into an ambulance. He was pronounced dead that night.

### The Officers Were Fired, and Then All Charged with Crimes

On May 26, the day after the killing, large protests erupted in Minneapolis and Mayor Jacob Frey announced that the four officers involved in the case had been terminated. Mr. Frey said he had asked the FBI to investigate, and in a statement posted on social media, he said, "Being Black in America should not be a death sentence."

Mr. Chauvin was arrested on May 29 and initially charged with third-degree murder. Within days, he had agreed to plead guilty, The New York Times reported in February, but William P. Barr, then the US attorney general, stepped in to reject the agreement, which had also included an assurance that Mr. Chauvin would not face federal civil rights charges.

Mr. Chauvin had said through his lawyer that his handling of Mr. Floyd's arrest was a reasonable use of authorized force. The officer was the subject of at least 22 complaints or internal investigations during his more than 19 years at the department, one of which resulted in discipline. After a weeks-long trial, Mr. Chauvin was found guilty on April 20 of second-degree murder, third degree murder and second degree manslaughter. The three other former officers involved in Mr. Floyd's death were charged with aiding and abetting second-degree murder and aiding and abetting second-degree manslaughter. They had been scheduled to stand trial together ... but on May 13 Judge Cahill announced during a pretrial hearing that the trial would be delayed ... to allow a federal case against the former officers to move forward.

### The Aftermath

Derek Chauvin was sentenced to 22½ years in state court and later pleaded guilty in a separate federal case on civil rights charges. The other three officers were found guilty of federal charges for failing to intervene (Arango, Bogel-Burroughs, and Senter 2022). Since the incident, the City of Minneapolis agreed to pay a $27 million settlement to the Floyd family and held a referendum on whether to dissolve the police department and create a department of public safety with a more holistic approach to crime. While a majority (56 percent) of voters did not support the proposal to dissolve the police (Brooks 2021), it nonetheless reflects the frustration among residents with the status quo (Smith and Senter 2021). In addition, more than 200 police officers have left the Minneapolis Police Department since the killing (Raguse 2021).

*SOURCE:* Adapted from "How George Floyd Died, and What Happened Next," *New York Times*, May 19, 2022 https://www.nytimes.com/article/george-floyd.html.

The aftermath in Minneapolis included days of unrest that resulted in significant damage to a five-mile stretch of the city, including the burning of a police precinct (*New York Times* 2021). The police response, televised around the world, drew additional public condemnation for their highly militarized approach and use of tear gas and rubber bullets. The incident provides a case study in police excessive force, training, policy, and crowd control techniques (an often overlooked issue in police use of force).

## Deadly Force

The term **deadly force** is defined as that force used with the intent to cause great bodily injury or death. Such deadly force is almost always limited to those situations when police use firearms in encounters with suspects. As noted, there are other times when citizens may be seriously injured or killed as the result of the use of other types of force, but that is rarely, if ever, the intent of the police. Some police scholars have suggested that chokeholds be defined as deadly force, because deaths do occur when such holds are employed and many departments have banned the practice. When the police engage in a high-speed pursuit that results in an accident and someone dies, this may also be seen as use of force in which the outcome involved death. This fact does not mean that deaths resulting from these and other police activities are unimportant, but that they are not included in the definition and therefore will not be considered.

Based on the definition provided earlier, there are three categories for which data are required if the extent of the use of deadly force is to be determined:

1. **Category 1: Death.** The police use a deadly weapon, and as a result, the person dies.
2. **Category 2: Injury.** The police use a deadly weapon, and the person is wounded but does not die.
3. **Category 3: Noninjury.** The police use a deadly weapon, but the person against whom it is directed is not injured.

### Category 1: Death

Sources of data for Category 1 use of deadly force can be found in a number of places: the National Center for Health Statistics (NCHS), FBI reports, and journalistic and crowd-sourcing data sets. The NCHS runs the National Vital Statistics System (NVSS), which reports data from coroners and medical examiners. Under the "homicide" cause-of-death category, there has been a "police or legal" intervention subcategory since 1949.

Research consistently demonstrates, however, that the NVSS underestimates the number of citizens who die from legal intervention. An analysis of the records of 36 large police departments conducted by Sherman and Langworthy (1979) suggested that the center's statistics were approximately 25 to 50 percent too low because of reporting problems. Loftin et al. (2003) found that NVSS data recorded 29 percent fewer instances of police homicides than the FBI's Supplemental Homicide Reporting program, and Feldman et al. (2017) estimated that NVSS data only captured about 45 percent of law enforcement-related deaths. After analyzing data from 1976 to 2013, Loftin, McDowall, and Xie (2017) concluded that misclassification is the primary cause of underreporting of deaths by legal intervention in the NVSS data.

The FBI collects data on killings of civilians by police but does not publish the statistics. The data are based on what are called Supplemental Homicide Reports (SHRs) submitted to the FBI by police departments, and the submission of such reports is voluntary. As a result of nonreporting, the SHRs also undercount citizens killed by police (Loftin et al. 2017). Although the data may be useful for comparisons across large cities, the reports do not provide an accurate national overview (Loftin et al. 2003). In short, the US government has no accurate official data to determine the number of citizen deaths that have resulted from the use of deadly force by police.

In 2003, the BJS attempted to collect more accurate data on deaths through the Arrest-Related Deaths Program, although the system suffered from a number of problems, was redesigned (Banks et al. 2016), and then suspended in 2014. In 2019, the FBI started collecting data in its National Use-of-Force Data Collection program. This program collects data on police uses of force that either result in death or serious injury, or whenever a firearm is discharged at a person. Unfortunately, the program is voluntary and suffers from a lack of reporting by law enforcement agencies. In 2019, only 5,043 agencies (representing less than 50 percent of the total law enforcement officer population) submitted data to the program. The FBI will not report aggregate use of force data until agencies representing 80 percent of law enforcement officers participate. As a result, the program has yet to report any actual data on use of force. Inside Policing 10.6 provides an overview of the failure of the Department of Justice to publish data on use of force as well as the failure of the FBI's Use-of-Force Data Collection program. Whether this or other government data collection systems can overcome the fragmented nature of policing in the United States and collect complete and accurate data remains to be seen.

In recent years, journalists and others have attempted to count the number of people killed by police. These attempts involve using multiple methods to identify incidents, including using official data, media reports, and in some cases, having researchers investigate individual cases. For example, FatalEncounters.org has attempted to use these methods to produce a national database of officer-involved homicides from 2000 to the present. The Fatal Encounters database includes any death that results from an interaction with law enforcement (e.g., police shooting or vehicular crash)—a definition that, as Renner (2019, 23) notes, "limits comparisons with SHR and NVSS data." The majority of these crowdsourced efforts rely primarily on media reports. As a result, cases not reported

| INSIDE POLICING 10.6 | Department of Justice Reporting on Police Use of Force Falling Short |

The US Department of Justice failed to publish annual summaries of police use of excessive force between 2016 and 2020 as required by law, and the FBI's new national data collection on police use of force has fallen short due to insufficient participation by law enforcement agencies, according to a new GAO report (available at https://www.gao.gov/products/gao-22-104456). The latter initiative was begun in 2016, with actual data collection starting in 2019. So far, agencies representing about 50 percent of sworn US law enforcement officers have been submitting use of force data. Based on criteria established when the initiative was launched, the FBI has to reach a threshold of agencies accounting for 60 percent of all officers before the end of 2022 or end the data collection.

   **Discussion Question:** How do you think the FBI will overcome the challenges of getting law enforcement agencies to voluntarily report data on police use of force?

SOURCE: *Modern Policing* blog, December 10, 2021, https://gcordner.wordpress.com/2021/12/10/doj-reporting-on-police-use-of-force-falling-short/

by the news are unlikely to be included in the counts. Nonetheless, as Zimring (2017, 33) notes, these "media accounts can provide a more accurate estimate of the volume of killings than any of the existing official aggregations." These new crowdsourcing methods provide estimates of approximately twice the number of police killings as official sources, at around 1,000 per year (Zimring 2017).

## Category 2: Injury

Category 2 data (i.e., a person is shot and injured) are more difficult to acquire for the entire United States, because there is no national reporting requirement. Fyfe (1988), however, provides some interesting insights into this category of data. He summarizes several studies conducted over varying time periods (2 to 9 years) from a total of 14 large cities in the United States. Although some variation exists among departments, these studies suggest that in general, when the police shoot an individual, that person is approximately twice as likely to be wounded as killed.

## Category 3: Noninjury

Data for Category 3 (i.e., a person is shot at but not injured) are even more difficult to obtain. However, there are some indications of the frequency of police actions in this area. In studies of four large cities, the percentage that officers shot and missed, as a percentage of total times they used their firearms, was 48.6 percent in Los Angeles during the period 1971 to 1975 (Fyfe 1978), 73.1 percent in Chicago for the period 1975 to 1977 (Geller and Karales 1981), 74.1 percent in Detroit for the period 1976 to 1981 (Horvath and Donahue 1982), 51.0 percent in Philadelphia for the period 1987 to 1992 (White 2006). Research indicates that police officers miss with about 60 to 85 percent of the bullets they fire (Geller and Scott 1992). As Donner and Popovich (2019, 245) note, "Prior research demonstrates that shooting accuracy is noticeably low and has not improved much over the years." If these data are indicative of practices throughout the United States, it means that depending on the city, police officers shoot at and miss many more people than they shoot at and either injure or kill.

The prior discussion includes some general projections about the use of deadly force in the United States. There is a need to determine how changes in training, departmental policy, programs (like community or problem-oriented policing), and new laws affect frequency of deadly force incidents. For example, as a result of changes in the policies concerning the use of Category 1 deadly force, there was an apparent decline in the number of citizens killed in the early 1980s ("Big Decline in Killings" 1986; Fyfe 1988). These policy and legal changes will be discussed later.

There has been substantial research concerning the circumstances in which police use deadly force. The research on police use of deadly force generally focuses on four important areas: (1) individual and situational factors, (2) environmental and departmental variations, (3) racial considerations, and (4) changes in law and policy.

## Individual and Situational Factors

Researchers have explored a variety of individual-level characteristics related to police killings of citizens, including characteristics of officers, characteristics of citizens, and the circumstances of shootings. For example, research reveals that individuals who are killed by police are disproportionately male and African American (Zimring 2017). Research also finds that the majority of victims posed a real or eminent threat to police and, in many cases, that the victim was armed and police believed the person posed a danger (see Smith 2004 for review).

The decision to use deadly force appears primarily to be the result of the officer's perception of whether a threat exists and how frequently the officer is exposed to threats. As used here, *threat* could mean any situation in which the department permitted the use of deadly force. An analysis of 2015 crowdsourced data revealed that 66 percent of people killed by police were armed with a firearm and 16.5 percent were armed with a knife, although 11.3 percent had no weapons (Zimring 2017). An officer's assignment appears to be a much more important predictor of the use of deadly force than an officer's age, intelligence, and educational background. Officers with riskier assignments are more likely to use deadly force.

Off-duty officers are also involved in many shootings. As many as 15 to 20 percent of incidents of police use of deadly force involve an officer who is off duty. The more aggressive the off-duty officer is in intervening in potentially violent situations, whether or not encouraged to do so by the department, the higher the rates for the use of deadly force.

The race of the officer also appears to be important, largely because of the assignment and living practices of officers. For example, African American officers are more likely to use deadly force, and to be the victims of its use, than are other officers, because they are more likely to live in, frequent, and be assigned to areas with high crime rates. Therefore, they are exposed to more situations in which they might have to use deadly force or become its victim (Fyfe 1988; Geller and Scott 1992).

## Environmental and Departmental Variations

The frequency with which police use Category 1 deadly force varies considerably across the United States. Zimring (2017) found that between 2009 and 2012, the rates per million residents varied from 1.36 in New York City to 8.53 in Philadelphia. Two categories of factors that may explain this variation in the frequency with which police use deadly force are environmental and organizational (departmental).

Environmental factors—factors having to do with the community and neighborhood where the police do their work—include, among others, the level of poverty, the proportion of minority residents, the homicide rate, the overall arrest rate, violent-crime arrest rate, and gun density (i.e., ratio of gun ownership to total population). Generally, the police are more likely to shoot and kill citizens in cities with higher concentrations of impoverished minority residents and higher rates of violent crime, although these relationships may not be consistent across cities of different sizes. For example, Smith (2004) found that police killings were related to the proportion of Black residents and violent crime in medium-size cities (100,000 to 249,999 residents), but in our nation's largest cities (250,000 or more residents), the proportion of Black residents took on greater significance. Based on the findings, Smith (2004, 158) suggested that

> Blacks in urban America are highly segregated and impoverished (Massey and Denton 1993). These large "threatening" populations concentrated in the nation's largest cities may produce much higher levels of antagonism between disadvantaged groups and the police. In smaller cities and large suburbs, on the other hand, ghetto communities are not as extensive or insular, and minorities may not be seen as a general threat. Thus a more generalized perception of threat may be less pervasive; rather, officers may respond to more specific threats from crime.

In addition, in any area where there are higher poverty and divorce rates, the police often may be called on more to intervene in potentially dangerous situations (Kania and Mackey 1977; Fyfe 1980, 1988; Sherman and Langworthy 1979). However, these factors do not by themselves explain all of the variation that may exist.

Departmental values, policies, and practices of political leaders and police managers also affect the frequency with which police use deadly force. Current research suggests that more restrictive shooting policies reduce the frequency with which deadly force is employed (discussed in more detail later). In addition, some evidence suggests that the leadership attitude in the city and department influences the frequency of use (Carmichael and Jacobs 2002). For example, the increase in the use of deadly force in Philadelphia during the 1970s appeared to result from the aggressive policing attitude of leaders in the city and the department. Zimring (2017) argues that police administrators are key to reducing shootings of civilians by police, although he also suggests that deaths of civilians are not a serious consideration among law enforcement leaders in the United States. The Guiding Principles report from PERF mentioned earlier advocates strongly for a renewed emphasis on "the sanctity of all human life—the lives of police officers and the lives of the people they serve and protect" (Wexler 2016, 4). The training that officers receive may also be influential. Some departments may encourage officers to intervene aggressively in potentially dangerous situations rather than wait until adequate backup support is available. On their own initiative, officers may also engage in such behavior (Fyfe 1988).

What is not known about neighborhood and department variation is more striking than what is known. As difficult as determining how often deadly force *fatalities* occur, it is even harder to know how many deadly force *incidents* occur (Blumberg 1997) involving injuries, misses, and mere threats. The proportion of deadly force incidents, rates of justifiable homicide, and firearms discharge rates vary dramatically across jurisdictions (Geller and Scott 1992) and departments (Fridell 1989). Blumberg's (1997, 521) observations about the state of our knowledge, made more than 20 years ago, still hold true today:

> The inescapable conclusion one must draw from the available evidence is that nobody knows how many times each year law enforcement officers in the United States fire their weapons at citizens, how many citizens are wounded, or how many are killed as the result of police bullets.

## Racial Considerations

African American and Hispanic citizens are more likely to be shot by the police than are whites. One explanation for this disproportion is that such disparities in shooting incidents simply mirror ethnic and racial involvement in criminal activity. When compared with rates of police–citizen contacts, arrest rates, and resistance to or attacks on the police, there is no apparent racial disparity in police use of deadly force. That is, in communities in which Blacks are shot at a high rate from the percentage of contacts with police, their arrest rates and the likelihood that they will resist the police tend to be similarly high (Fyfe 1988; Geller and Scott 1992). Yet Fyfe (1988), for example, found that police officers in Memphis were 15 times as likely to shoot at African American offenders who had committed property crimes as at white property-crime offenders.

Another explanation is that stereotypes portraying ethnic and racial minorities as dangerous may heighten officers' fear and influence shooting decisions (see, e.g., Holmes and Smith 2008). Recent evidence suggests that part of the disproportion in shooting rates may be attributable to the influence of cultural stereotypes on our behavior. A number of experimental studies of weapon recognition (Payne 2001) and shoot–don't shoot decisions (Correll et al. 2002) demonstrate that stereotypes can influence our perceptions of and responses to people of different racial identities. In these studies, participants responded more quickly and made more mistakes (i.e., misperceived a weapon or shot unarmed persons) when the target was African American (compared with a white target), although none of the participants was a trained police officer. In a follow-up experiment, Correll et al. (2007) included both citizens and police officers as participants. They found that the participants made video-game shoot–don't shoot decisions more rapidly for unarmed whites and armed Blacks and more slowly for armed whites and unarmed Blacks. This tendency was most pronounced among officers who worked in areas with large populations, high rates of violent crime, and greater concentrations of minorities. Police officers were not more likely to mistakenly shoot unarmed Blacks. Other experimental research using trained police officers and more realistic video simulators, however, found police officers took longer to shoot armed Blacks than armed whites and were less likely to shoot unarmed Blacks than unarmed whites (James, James, and Vila 2016). These experimental studies challenge previous research and suggest the need for additional research to reconcile these conflicting results. One of the problems is that none of the video formats entails the fatigue, stress, and real dangers of street-level work (Holmes and Smith 2008). A more recent study of almost 1,000 fatal police shootings from 2015 collected by the *Washington Post* "suggest evidence of implicit bias in real-world scenarios" (Nix et al. 2017, 329). Specifically, they found that Black citizens were more than two times as likely to be unarmed when shot and killed by police. And whites were significantly more likely to have been attacking officers than other racial/ethnic groups.

## Legal and Policy Changes

Blumberg (1997, 507–508) identified five changes in laws and departmental policy regulating the use of deadly force:

1. Many states modified the fleeing-felon rule and tightened the legal basis for use of deadly force.

2. The shooting of unarmed, nonviolent suspects has been ruled by the Supreme Court to be a violation of the Fourth Amendment of the Constitution.

3. Almost all urban police departments have enacted restrictive administrative policies regarding the use of deadly force.

4. The courts have made it much easier for a citizen to file a lawsuit and collect civil damages as a result of a police action.

5. Social science research has facilitated greater understanding of the reasons for, and policy implications of, the use of deadly force.

As late as 1967, few police departments had policies to guide officers in the use of deadly force. The state laws that existed at that time, and that still exist in some states, tended to broadly define occasions when officers could use deadly force. Perhaps the broadest of these legal guidelines was the **fleeing-felon rule**, which authorized the use of deadly force when attempting to apprehend individuals who were fleeing from a suspected serious crime. This rule dates from the early Middle Ages, when almost all crimes considered felonies were punishable by the death penalty; consequently, killing individuals fleeing from suspected felonies did not seem inappropriate.

An alternative to the fleeing-felon rule was first developed and tested in New York. Responding to concerns over the high number of officer and civilian shootings, the NYPD formulated a restricted policy permitting the use of deadly force only under circumstances of immediate danger to an officer or the public. The policy resulted in a nearly 30 percent reduction in shootings of citizens by officers. No increase in the number of officers shot was observed (Fyfe 1979). Similar policy changes resulted in decreases in officer use of deadly force in Atlanta, Kansas City, Los Angeles, Miami, and Philadelphia, among other cities (see, e.g., Meyer 1980; Sherman 1983; Alpert 1989a; White 2001; Zimring 2017).

Changes in departmental policies have had more influence than changes in the law in determining when police officers use deadly force. Once police departments began to develop policies in this area, they often were more restrictive than state law. Initially, departments limited the number of situations in which police could use deadly force; for example, a policy might indicate that a person who was fleeing from a certain property crime could no longer be shot at.

By the 1980s, more and more police departments began to adopt what is often called a **defense-of-life policy**. Generally, such policies restrict the use of deadly force situations to those in which the officer's or another person's life is in jeopardy or to prevent the escape of a person who is extremely dangerous. In some departments, even under these circumstances, deadly force can be employed only when other, less deadly means seem inappropriate (Geller and Scott 1992).

Since the adoption of more restrictive deadly force policies, the number of citizens killed by police has declined. This decline is understandable when one considers that prior to the adoption of a defense-of-life policy, in some communities as many as 25 percent of the victims of police use of deadly force posed no threat to a police officer or another person when they were shot. Despite the fears of many officers, more restrictive guidelines have not resulted in an increased number of police injuries or deaths (Fyfe 1988). In addition, no evidence either confirms or refutes the belief of some police officers that more restrictive policies encourage suspects to try to run from the police.

## Summary

Force is central to the police role and, as such, is an inherent part of police–citizen interactions. Yet its use is often controversial. Police are trained to act in terms of levels of force. However, local police cultural standards for the use of force often differ considerably from formal departmental policy and are more likely to support greater force than formal training and policy do.

Most uses of force are legal, but some are questionable and even illegal. The public's definitions of excessive force and brutality often differ from those of the police. There are two views of police brutality. The first is that brutality is widespread because rogue police officers are permitted to hide behind lax accountability mechanisms. The second is that brutality is not a major problem and must be considered in the context of overall high levels of violent crime. Although the frequency of illegal police violence or brutality is low, its importance should not be understated.

Police use of deadly force has been extensively studied, but its frequency is difficult to determine because of reporting problems. Research has examined the factors that contribute to the use of deadly force and attempted to explain why its frequency varies from community to community. Policy guidelines for the use of deadly force have changed, and many police departments have adopted strict policies governing the use of such force. The result has been fewer citizens killed by the police.

## Critical Thinking Questions

1. To what extent is police use of force and coercion inevitable? To what extent is police brutality inevitable?

2. Where should canines be placed on the use-of-force continuum? OC spray? Tasers?

3. How frequent is the police use of illegal violence? Why do police sometimes use illegal violence? Do you think it can ever be justified?

4. Why is it so difficult to measure the amount of force, including deadly force, the police use? What kind of a system could be developed to do a better job of measuring this important aspect of police behavior?

5. Many police departments have enacted deadly force policies that are more restrictive than the law in their states. Why do you think they have done this? Do you think it is proper for them to do this?

## References

Alpert, G. P. 1989a. "Police Use of Deadly Force: The Miami Experience." In R. G. Dunham and G. P. Alpert (eds.), *Critical Issues in Policing: Contemporary Readings*, pp. 480–497. Prospect Heights, IL: Waveland.

Alpert, G. P. 1989b. "Questioning Police Pursuits in Urban Areas." In R. G. Dunham and G. P. Alpert (eds.), *Critical Issues in Policing: Contemporary Readings*, pp. 216–229. Prospect Heights, IL: Waveland.

Alpert, G. P., and Anderson, P. 1986. "The Most Deadly Force: Police Pursuits." *Justice Quarterly* 2: 1–14.

Alpert, G. P., Kenney, D. J., Dunham, R. G., and Smith, W. C. 2000. *Police Pursuits: What We Know*. Washington, DC: Police Executive Research Forum.

Anderson, D. C. 2003. *Managed Force*. Ford Foundation Report.

Arango, T., Bogel-Burroughs, N. and Senter, J. 2022. "3 Former Officers are Convicted of Violating George Floyd's Civil Rights." *New York Times*, February 24. https://www.nytimes.com/2022/02/24/us/guilty-verdict-george-floyds-rights.html.

Banks, D., Ruddle, P., Kennedy, E. and Planty, M. 2016. *Arrest-Related Deaths Program Redesign Study, 2015–2016, Preliminary Report*. Washington, DC: Bureau of Justice Statistics.

Barker, T. 1986. "Peer Group Support for Police Occupational Deviance." In T. Barker and D. L. Carter (eds.), *Police Deviance*, pp. 9–21. Cincinnati, OH: Pilgrimage.

Bayley, D. H. 1986. "The Tactical Choices of Police Patrol Officers." *Journal of Criminal Justice* 14: 329–348.

Bayley, D. H., and Garofalo, J. 1989. "The Management of Violence by Police Patrol Officers." *Criminology* 27: 1–12.

BBC. 2014. "Ferguson Protests: What We Know about Michael Brown's Last Minutes." November 25. https://www.bbc.com/news/world-us-canada-28841715/.

Beers, D. 1992. "A Biting Controversy." *Los Angeles Times Magazine*, February 9: 23-26, 43–44.

Berkowitz, L. 1993. *Aggression: Its Causes, Consequence, and Control*. Philadelphia: Temple University Press.

Bittner, E. 1995. "The Capacity to Use Force as the Core of the Police Role." In V. Kappeler (ed.), *The Police and Society: Touchstone Readings*, pp. 127–137. Prospect Heights, IL: Waveland.

Blumberg, M. 1997. "Controlling Police Use of Deadly Force: Assessing Two Decades of Progress." In R. G. Dunham and G. P. Alpert (eds.), *Critical Issues in Policing*, 3rd ed., pp. 507–530. Prospect Heights, IL: Waveland.

Bosman, J., and Fitzsimmons, E. G. 2014. "Grief and Protests Follow Shooting of a Teenager." *The New York Times*, August 10. https://www.nytimes.com/2014/08/11/us/police-say-mike-brown-was-killed-after-struggle-for-gun.html/.

Bosman, J., Robertson, C., Eckholm, E., and Oppel, A. 2014. "Amid Conflicting Accounts, Trusting Darren Wilson." *The New York Times*, November 25. https://www.nytimes.com/2014/11/26/us/ferguson-grand-jury-weighed-mass-of-evidence-much-of-it-conflicting.html/.

Brooks, B. 2021. "Minneapolis Voters Reject Disbanding Police in Wake of George Floyd Murder." *Reuters*, November 3. https://www.yahoo.com/video/george-floyd-minneapolis-voters-weigh-100900856.html.

Buchanan, L., Fessenden, F., Lai, R., Park, H., Parlapiano, A., Tse, A., Wallace, T., Watkins, D., and Yourish, K. 2015. "What Happened in Ferguson?" *The New York Times*, August 10. https://www.nytimes.com/interactive/2014/08/13/us/ferguson-missouri-town-under-siege-after-police-shooting.html/.

Campbell, A., Berk, R., and Fyfe, J. 1998. "Deployment of Violence: The Los Angeles Police Department's Use of Dogs." *Evaluation Review* 22: 535–561.

Carmichael, J. T., and Jacobs, D. 2002. "Violence by and against the Police." In R. G. Burns and C. E. Crawford (eds.), *Policing and Violence*, pp. 25–51. Upper Saddle River, NJ: Prentice Hall.

Carter, D. L. 1985. "Police Brutality: A Model for Definition, Perspective, and Control." In A. S. Blumberg and E. Niederhoffer (eds.), *The Ambivalent Force: Perspective on the Police*, pp. 321–330. New York: Holt, Rinehart & Winston.

Carter, D. L. 1994. "Theoretical Dimensions on the Abuse of Authority by Police Officers." In T. Barker and D. Carter (eds.), *Police Deviance*, 3rd ed., pp. 269–290. Cincinnati, OH: Anderson.

Cave, D. 2014. "Officer Darren Wilson's Grand Jury Testimony in Ferguson, MO, Shooting." *The New York Times*, November 25. https://www.nytimes.com/interactive/2014/11/25/us/darren-wilson-testimony-ferguson-shooting.html?_r=0/.

Correll, J., Park, B., Judd, C. M., and Wittenbrink, B. 2002. "The Police Officer's Dilemma: Using Ethnicity to Disambiguate Potentially Threatening Individuals." *Journal of Personality and Social Psychology* 83: 1029–1314.

Correll, J., Park, B., Judd, C. M., Wittenbrink, B., Sadler, M. S., and Keesee, T. 2007. "Across the Thin Blue Line: Police Officers and Racial Bias in the Decision to Shoot." *Journal of Personality and Social Psychology* 92: 1006–1023.

Crank, J. P. 1998. *Understanding Police Culture*. Cincinnati, OH: Anderson.

Davis, D., Whyde, A., and Langton, L. 2018. *Contacts Between Police and the Public, 2015*. Washington, DC: Bureau of Justice Statistics.

Donner, C. M. and Popovich, N. 2019. "Hitting (or Missing) the Mark." *Policing: An International Journal* 42 474–489.

Engel, R. S., McManus, H. D., and Herold, T. D. (2020). "Does de-escalation training work? A Systematic review and call for evidence in police use-of-force reform." *Criminology & Public Policy* 19: 721-759.

Faulkner, S. 1994. "A Ralph Nadar Approach to Law Enforcement Training." *Police Studies* 17: 21–32.

Feldman, J. M., Gruskin, S. Coull, B. A., and Krieger, N. 2017. "Quantifying and Underreporting of Law-Enforcement-Related Deaths in United States Vital Statistics and News-Media-Based Data Sources: A Capture-Recapture Analysis." *PLoS Medicine* 14(10): e1002449. doi:10.1371/journal.pmed.1002399.

Felkenes, G. T. 1991. "Affirmative Action in the Los Angeles Police Department." *Criminal Justice Research Bulletin* 6: 1–9.

Fridell, L. 1989. "Justifiable Use of Measures in Research on Deadly Force." *Journal of Criminal Justice* 17: 157–165.

Fridell, L., Ijames, S., and Berkow, M. 2016. "Taking the Straw Man to the Ground: Arguments in Support of the Linear Use-of-Force Continuum." *Police Chief* 78: 20–25.

Friedrich, R. J. 1980. "Police Use of Force: Individuals, Situations, and Organizations." *Annals of the American Academy of Political and Social Sciences* 452: 82–97.

Fyfe, J. J. 1978. "Shots Fired: An Examination of New York City Police Firearms Discharges." PhD dissertation, University of New York at Albany.

Fyfe, J. J. 1979. "Administrative Interventions on Police Shooting Discretion." *Journal of Criminal Justice* 7: 309–323.

Fyfe, J. J. 1980. "Geographic Correlates of Police Shooting." *Journal of Research in Crime and Delinquency* 17: 101–113.

Fyfe, J. J. 1988. "Police Use of Deadly Force: Research and Reform." *Justice Quarterly* 5: 165–205.

Geller, W. A., and Karales, K. J. 1981. *Split-Second Decisions: Shootings of and by Chicago Police.* Chicago: Chicago Law Enforcement Study Group.

Geller, W., and Scott, M. 1992. *Deadly Force: What We Know.* Washington, DC: Police Executive Research Forum.

Golden, J. W., and Walker, J. T. 2002. "That Dog Will Hunt: Canine-Assisted Search and Seizure." In J. T. Walker (ed.), *Policing and the Law*, pp. 71–89. Upper Saddle River, NJ: Prentice Hall.

Greenfeld, L., Langan, P., and Smith, S. 1997. *Police Use of Force: Collection of Statistical Data.* Washington, DC: Bureau of Justice Statistics.

Griffin, S. P., and Bernard, T. J. 2003. "Angry Aggression Among Police Officers." *Police Quarterly* 6: 3–21.

Haas, B. 2018. "Trauma-Informed Policing." *ACEs Connection*, June 25. https://www.pacesconnection.com/blog/trauma-informed-policing-1.

Hager, E. 2015. "Alternatives to Bullets." *The Marshall Project*, September 23. https://www.themarshallproject.org/2015/09/23/alternatives-to-bullets.

Harrell, E., and Davis, E. 2020. *Contacts Between Police and the Public, 2018—Statistical Tables* Washington, DC: Bureau of Justice Statistics.

Hickman, M. J., Piquero, A. R., and Garner, J. H. 2008. "Toward a National Estimate of Police Use of Nonlethal Force." *Criminology & Public Policy* 7: 563–604.

Holmes, M. D., and Smith, B. W. 2008. *Race and Police Brutality: Roots of an Urban Dilemma.* Albany: State University of New York Press.

Holmes, M. D., and Smith, B. W. 2012. "Intergroup Dynamics of Extra-Legal Police Aggression: A Theory of Race and Place." *Aggression and Violent Behavior* 17: 344–353.

Hopkins, E. J. 1931. *Our Lawless Police.* New York: Viking.

Horvath, F., and Donahue, M. 1982. *Deadly Force: An Analysis of Shootings by Police in Michigan, 1976–1981.* East Lansing: Michigan State University.

Hunt, J. 1985. "Police Accounts of Normal Force." *Urban Life* 13: 315–341.

James, L., James, S. M., and Vila, B. J. 2016. "The Reverse Racism Effect: Are Cops More Hesitant to Shoot Black Than White Suspects? *Criminology and Public Policy* 15: 1–23.

Kania, R. R. E., and Mackey, W. C. 1977. "Police Violence as a Function of Community Characteristics." *Criminology* 15: 27–48.

Klahm, C. F., Frank, J., and Brown, R. A. 2010. "Police Use of Force: Tales from Another City." *Journal of Crime and Justice* 34: 205–220.

Klockars, C. 1980. "The Dirty Harry Problem." *Annals* 452: 33–47.

Lamb, R., and Friday, P. 1997. "Impact of Pepper Spray Availability on Police Officer Use-of-Force Decisions." *Policing* 20: 136–148.

Larson, J. A. 1932. *Lying and Its Detection*. Chicago: University of Chicago Press.

Loftin, J. A., McDowall, D., and Xie, M. 2017. "Underreporting of Homicides by Police in the United States, 1976–2013." *Homicide Studies* 21: 159–174.

Loftin, C., Wiersema, B., McDowall, D., and Dobrin, A. 2003. "Underreporting of Justifiable Homicides Committed by Police Officers in the United States, 1976–1998." *American Journal of Public Health* 93: 1117–1121.

Marion, N. 1998. "Police Academy Training: Are We Teaching Recruits What They Need to Know?" *Policing* 21: 54–79.

Massey, D. S., and Denton, N. A. 1993. *American Apartheid: Segregation and the Making of the Underclass*. Cambridge, MA: Harvard University Press.

McDermott, K. 2015. "Ferguson, One Year Later: From a City to a Symbol." *St. Louis Post Dispatch*, August 2. https://www.stltoday.com/news/special-reports/multimedia/ferguson-one-year-later-from-a-city-to-a-symbol/article_9869eee5-e3ea-5e9d-810c-8b383d91c41c.html/.

McEwen, T. 1997. "Policies on Less-Than-Lethal Force in Law Enforcement Agencies." *Policing* 20: 39–59.

McLean and Alpert. 2021. In Bennell, C., Alpert, G., Anderson, J. P., Arpaia, J., Huhta, J., Kahn, K. B., Khanizadeh, A., McCarthy, M., McLean, K., Mitchell, R. J., Nieuwenhuys, A., Palmer, A. and White, M. D. 2021. "Advancing Police use of Force Research and Practice: Urgent Issues and Prospects." *Legal and Criminological Psychology* 26: 130–131.

McNulty, E. 1994. "Generating Common-Sense Knowledge Among Police Officers." *Symbolic Interaction* 17: 281–294.

Meyer, M. 1980. "Police Shootings at Minorities: The Case of Los Angeles." *Annals of the American Academy of Political and Social Science* 452: 98–110.

Miller, M. R. 1995. *Police Patrol Operations*. Placerville, CA: Copperhouse.

*Miranda v. Arizona*. 384 US 436, 466 (1966).

Morrison, G. B. 2003. "Police and Correctional Department Firearm Training Frameworks in Washington State." *Police Quarterly* 6: 192–221.

National Commission on Law Observance and Enforcement. 1931. *Report on Lawlessness in Law Enforcement*, no. 11. Washington, DC: US Government Printing Office (also known as the Wickersham Commission).

Navarro, M. 1995. "The Debate over High-Speed Police Chases." *New York Times National*, December 17: 18.

*New York Times*. 2021. "How George Floyd Died, and What Happened Next." November 1. https://www.nytimes.com/article/george-floyd.html.

Nix, J. Campbell, B. A., Byers, E. H. and Alpert, G. P. 2017. "A Bird's Eye View of Civilians Killed by Police in 2015: Further Evidence of Implicit Bias." *Criminology & Public Policy* 16 309–340.

Paoline, E. A. 2003. "Taking Stock: Toward a Richer Understanding of Police Culture." *Journal of Criminal Justice* 31: 199–214.

Payne, B. K. 2001. "Prejudice and Perception: The Role of Automatic and Controlled Processes in Misperceiving a Weapon." *Journal of Personality and Social Psychology* 81: 181–192.

Peak, K. 1993. *Policing America: Methods, Issues, Challenges*. Englewood Cliffs, NJ: Prentice Hall.

Police Executive Research Forum (PERF). 2005. "Conducted Energy Device: Development of Standards for Consistency and Guidance." https://www.bja.gov/Publications/ced_standards.pdf.

Police Executive Research Forum (PERF). 2015. *Re-Engineering Training on Police Use of Force*. Washington, DC: Author.

Police Executive Research Forum (PERF). 2016. *Use of Force: Taking Policing to a Higher Standard*. Washington, DC: Author.

Raguse, L. 2021. "Changes to MPD Policy Since George Floyd's Death." *KARE11,* May 25. https://www.kare11.com/article/news/special-reports/power-to-change/changes-to-mpd-policy-since-george-floyds-death/89-c9b87a71-2fde-408f-ade0-376de018e70d

Reiss, A. J., Jr. 1967. *The Police and the Public.* New Haven, CT: Yale University Press.

Renner, M. L. 2019. "Using Multiple Flawed Measures to Construct Valid and Reliable Rates of Homicide by Police." *Homicide Studies* 23: 20–40.

Reuss-Ianni, E. 1983. *The Two Cultures of Policing: Street Cops and Management Cops.* New Brunswick, NJ: Transaction.

Scallon, C. J., and Peckerman, T. 2017. "Trauma-Informed Policing: Addressing the Prevalence of Trauma in Law Enforcement Encounters." *The Council of State Governments,* August 16. https://www.citinternational.org/resources/Documents/Trauma%20Informed%20Policing.pdf.

Sherman, L. 1983. "Reducing Police Gun Use: Critical Events, Administrative Policy and Organizational Change." In P. Maurice (ed.), *Control in the Police Organization.* pp. 98–125. Cambridge, MA: MIT Press.

Sherman, L., and Langworthy, R. 1979. "Measuring Homicide by Police Officers." *Journal of Criminal Law and Criminology* 9: 317–331.

Skolnick, J., and Fyfe, J. 1993. *Above the Law: Police and the Excessive Use of Force.* New York: Free Press.

Smith, B. W. 2004. "The Impact of Police Officer Diversity on Police-Caused Homicides." *The Policy Studies Journal* 31: 147–162.

Smith, M., and Senter, J. 2021. "In the City where George Floyd Was killed, Voters Decide the Police Department's Fate." *New York Times,* November 2. https://www.nytimes.com/2021/11/02/us/elections/minneapolis-police-vote.html.

Sykes, R. E., and Brent, E. E. 1983. *Policing: A Social Behaviorist Perspective.* New Brunswick, NJ: Rutgers University Press.

Terrill, W. 2001. *Police Coercion: Application of the Force Continuum.* New York: LFB Scholarly.

Terrill, W. 2005. "Police Use of Force: A Transactional Approach." *Justice Quarterly* 22: 107–138.

Terrill, W., Alpert, G. P., Dunham, R. G., and Smith, M. R. 2003. "A Management Tool for Evaluating Police Use of Force: An Application of the Force Factor." *Police Quarterly* 6: 150–171.

Terrill, W., and Paoline, E. A., III. 2012. "Conducted Energy Devices (CEDs) and Citizen Injuries: The Shocking Empirical Reality." *Justice Quarterly* 29: 153–182.

Terrill, W., and Paoline, E. A., III. 2013. "Examining Less Lethal Force Policy and the Force Continuum: Results from a National Use-of-Force Study." *Police Quarterly* 16: 38–65.

Trimmer, R. 1993. "Pepper Spray After Concord: Legal Issues for Policy Makers." *North Carolina Justice Academy,* July.

US Department of Justice. 2015. *Investigation of the Ferguson Police Department.* Washington, DC: Civil Rights Division, Department of Justice.

US Department of Justice, Bureau of Justice Statistics. 2011. *Law Enforcement Management and Administrative Statistics (LEMAS), 2007.* Computer file. ICPSR31161-v1. Ann Arbor, MI: Interuniversity Consortium for Political and Social Science Research.

Vaughn, M. 1992. "The Parameters of Trickery as an Acceptable Police Practice." *American Journal of Police* 11: 71–95.

Welch, M. 2002. "Police Pursuits: Just One Form of Police Violence." In R. G. Burns and C. E. Crawford (eds.), *Policing and Violence,* pp. 147–166. Upper Saddle River, NJ: Prentice Hall.

Wexler, C. 2015. "Summary: What You Will Find in This Report." In *Re-Engineering Training on Police Use of Force,* pp. 3–10. Washington, DC: Police Executive Research Forum.

Wexler, C. 2016. "Why We Need to Challenge Conventional Thinking on Police Use of Force." In *Guiding Principles on Use of Force,* pp. 4–32. Washington, DC: Police Executive Research Forum.

White, M. D. 2001. "Controlling Police Decisions to Use Deadly Force: Re-examining the Importance of Administrative Policy." *Crime and Delinquency* 47: 131–151.

White, M. D. 2006. "Hitting the Target (or Not): Comparing Characteristics of Fatal, Injurious, and Noninjurious Police Shootings." *Police Quarterly* 9: 303–330.

White, M. D. 2021. "Can Training Change Officer Perceptions and use of De-Escalation?" In Bennell, C., Alpert, G., Anderson, J. P., Arpaia, J., Huhta, J., Kahn, K. B., Khanizadeh, A., McCarthy, M., McLean, K., Mitchell, R. J., Nieuwenhuys, A., Palmer, A. and White, M. D. 2021. "Advancing Police Use of Force Research and Practice: Urgent Issues and Prospects." *Legal and Criminological Psychology* 26 125–128..

White, M. D., and Ready, J. 2007. "The TASER as a Less Lethal Force Alternative: Findings on Use and Effectiveness in a Large Metropolitan Police Agency." *Police Quarterly* 10: 170–191.

Wilson, J. Q. 1968. *Varieties of Police Behavior: The Management of Law and Order in Eight Communities.* Cambridge, MA: Harvard University Press.

Zimring, F. E. 2017. *When Police Kill.* Cambridge, MA: Harvard University Press.

## CHAPTER 11

# Accountability and Ethics

## CHAPTER OUTLINE

## CHAPTER OUTLINE (continued)

### KEY TERMS

- accreditation
- body-worn cameras
- certification
- civilian review board
- Commission on Accreditation for Law Enforcement Agencies
- early warning system
- early identification system
- ethical formalism
- ethical relativism
- ethical utilitarianism
- exoneration
- false complaints
- Garrity interview
- grievance arbitration
- internal affairs
- office of professional standards
- police auditor systems
- professionalism
- reliability
- sustained complaints
- unfounded complaints
- unsubstantiated complaints
- validity

THE POLICE ARE THE most visible representatives of the criminal justice system in the United States. Yet in important ways, the police stand apart from society. Their special dispensation is the use of force so that citizens can live together in peace. Nevertheless, by virtue of the authority granted to them to use force, they have the potential to undermine due processes of law (Skolnick 1994). This may occur infrequently, but citizens are nonetheless concerned about police abuse of authority.

The police are both respected and feared. They are respected by many citizens who highly regard the commitment police make to their work, but they are also feared because of the enormous life-and-death authority that they carry. The accountability of the police to democratic processes continues to be one of the central issues confronting the police throughout modern times (McMullan 1998).

To whom are the police accountable? One might be tempted to answer that they are accountable to elected and appointed officials, the general public, people who receive police service (e.g., victims and suspects), and other parts of the criminal justice system (e.g., prosecuting attorneys and judges). Yet this answer overlooks important issues of accountability. Do citizens understand police work well enough to judge the behavior of the police? Should police agencies be responsible for assessing the behavior of their own officers? And what happens when the public encourages the police to break the law in order to do something about lawbreaking people? In short, the issues of accountability are complicated, and there is little agreement on who has the authority to hold the police accountable, the means by which they should be held accountable, and for what they should be held accountable (Geller 1985).

The control of police behavior occurs in two fundamentally different ways. The first is through mechanisms of oversight, which are based on the idea that if a police officer's behavior can be tracked, then illegal or inappropriate behavior can be identified and corrected or punished. Oversight mechanisms are both internal and external to a police department. Internally, oversight is through departmental investigation, early warning systems, body-worn cameras, and the restraints of bureaucratic organization and management. Externally, oversight occurs through citizen review, external auditing, and legal remedies for police misconduct.

The second way is through standards, which will be considered in the second half of this chapter. According to this view, officers can be hired with, or trained in, standards of conduct by which they can gauge their behavior. Both professional and ethical standards of "right behavior" fortify them with an appropriate way of thinking about their work and thereby control their behavior.

## Internal Accountability Mechanisms

Several oversight mechanisms within police departments will be considered here: bureaucratic organization and management, internal complaint reviews, early warning systems, and body-worn cameras.

### Bureaucratic Organization and Management

The most important day-to-day source of accountability for police officers is in the way their department is organized and managed (Walker 2005). Accountability is carried out through the design and operation of principles of bureaucratic organization, as extensively discussed in Chapter 5. This idea will be reviewed here primarily in terms of management–employee relations.

**Written Directives.**  In police departments, bureaucratic standards are omnipresent. As Alpert and Smith (1999, 353) observe, "law enforcement is a paradigm of operational control. Virtually every aspect of policing is subject to some combination of either policy, guideline, directive, rule, or general order." The organization of rules and regulations takes on a specific language in a bureaucracy. Principal terms are listed here. These terms provide the statements that guide the behavior of the department and indicate the responsibility of officers within it.

1. A *departmental policy* is not, as often thought, a rule, but rather the statement of a guiding principle that should be followed. A policy should be thought of as a guide to thinking rather than a fixed outcome. A policy is a general statement that gives guidance to police officers as to the proper course of action (e.g., a use-of-force policy).

2. A *goal* is a general statement of purpose that is useful in identifying the role and mission of the police (e.g., to apprehend criminals).

3. An *objective* is a more specific and measurable statement of purpose that is related to a goal (e.g., make arrests in 25 percent of burglary cases).

4. A *procedure* identifies a method or series of steps to be taken when performing a task or attempting to solve a problem (e.g., how to investigate a traffic accident).

5. Finally, a *rule* or *regulation* is a specific statement that identifies required or prohibited behavior by officers (e.g., all officers must dress in a certain manner). The terms *rule* and *regulation* are often used interchangeably.

Administrative guidance focuses on a wide variety of topics. Under principles of departmental supervision, managers' responsibilities aim to ensure that officers' behaviors are consistent with bureaucratic policies and standards. Written directives (policies, procedures, rules, and regulations), as Carter and Barker (1994, 22–23) have observed, are important for the following reasons:

1. They inform officers of expected standards of behavior.
2. They inform the community of the departmental mission, goals, values, policies, procedures, and expected standards of officer behavior.
3. They establish a common foundation for executing the police process to enhance operational consistency, equal protection, and due process.
4. They provide grounds for disciplining and counseling errant officers.
5. They provide standards for officer supervision.
6. They give direction for officer training.

Within a bureaucratic environment, standards are expressed in written terms as departmental policy and guidelines. Yet in a police department, managers may not follow policies and standards to the letter. In practice, managers may react in a variety of ways when officers deviate from those written standards. They may (1) ignore it, (2) act formally or informally, or (3) protect the officer.

A manager's formal responses to improper behavior may include counseling or training (advising or teaching the person how to improve) or some type of disciplinary action (reprimand, suspension, demotion, or termination). The more public criticism there is of certain types of police behavior, the more likely managers are to use some form of punitive discipline. Some managers like to make an example of an employee, to send a signal to other officers that certain types of behavior will not be tolerated. Employees, however, may consider this type of managerial response politically motivated and unfair. From the employees' point of view, they are being made a scapegoat to satisfy political interests.

If a manager believes a deviation exists but has insufficient evidence to act formally, the manager might respond informally, perhaps by transferring the employee to a new work area or assignment. Certain types of assignments can be used so often in a department that they become known as punitive assignments (e.g., the jail or foot patrol during the winter). Sometimes, for instance, if the problem is related to the behavior of the officer when interacting with the public, the officer may be assigned to a job with minimal public contact. In addition, the manager may hope that this type of informal, punitive control will result in a resignation or retirement.

The effectiveness of written standards rests in part on the willingness of supervisors to hold officers accountable. Given that supervisors are recruited from the ranks of patrol officers, it seems likely that they will sometimes choose not to punish subordinates (Holmes and Smith 2008). A manager may be aware of a deviation but elect to protect the officer for at least five reasons. The manager may (1) approve of the "deviant" activity or behavior, (2) believe that the most likely official departmental response would be too punitive, (3) be influenced by the so-called code of silence in policing, (4) believe that acknowledging the deviation would result in criticism of their own management ability, or (5) simply want to avoid dealing with the problem by denying that it exists.

**Limitations of Written Directives.** Policies, procedures, rules, regulations, and objectives are written standards against which an officer's behavior is judged by supervisors. Officers are expected to conform to these standards. In many police departments, standards number in the hundreds and are printed in thick manuals. Standards tend to accumulate over time as police departments are faced with a wide variety of situations. It is not uncommon for police officers to be unfamiliar with many of these standards, because some are rarely used.

Why do police departments have so many policies? Part of the reason lies in the unpredictable nature of the police function. Police work is highly varied and carried out in a diverse array of circumstances. Policies attempt to provide direction in unclear situations. Auten (1988, 1–2) notes that the absence of policy leaves officers "in the dark in the expectation that they will intuitively divine the right course of action in the performance of their duties."

Policies, while providing a standard for behavior, suffer from significant limitations. In practice, they are sometimes rule oriented and tell officers what not to do rather than suggesting a possible course of action. This can have an alienating effect on individual officers. Some researchers contend that the rigid bureaucracy characteristic of many police departments is principally responsible for the alienation of line officers and the intensification of more secretive elements of police culture. Consider the following statement Manning (1978, 79) recorded during an interview:

> 140 years of fuck-ups. Every time something goes wrong, they make a rule about it. All the directions in the force flow from someone's mistake. You can't go eight hours on the job without breaking the disciplinary code . . . the job goes wild on trivialities.

A related issue is that police work, by its nature, requires officers to make quick discretionary decisions in varied, unpredictable situations. It has proven difficult, if not impossible, for police managers to formulate written guidelines that effectively cover all the varied situations police officers encounter on the street. Consequently, policing continues to require officers to act based on "an intuitive grasp of situational exigencies" (Bittner 1970, 46). Officers learn much of what they need to know to make good decisions and do good police work on the job by apprenticeship and trial and error, rather than by referring to the manual of policies, procedures, rules, and regulations. In this context, written guidelines can seem irrelevant at best and an impediment to effective policing at worst (Cordner 1989).

## Internal Investigation

All police departments have some way of responding to citizen complaints or internal concerns about police behavior. In many small and moderate-size departments, this response may be the part-time responsibility of only one officer, probably a supervisor or manager. In larger departments, it has been the practice to establish a unit, often called **internal affairs** or **office of professional standards**, to respond to complaints.

Police officer misconduct may come to the attention of police administrators or internal affairs units in a number of ways. Citizens may file a complaint about a particular police officer (an issue we will explore later in the chapter). Fellow police officers may file a formal complaint or provide an anonymous tip to supervisors or an internal affairs unit, or police supervisors or internal affairs units may uncover misconduct through proactive means (e.g., early warning systems). Finally, a police agency may be alerted to misconduct from other external agencies (e.g., other police departments).

**The Investigative Process.**  When police officers are being investigated as suspects in a crime, they have the same legal procedural rights as any other suspect. But what rights should they have when they are being investigated administratively by supervisors, managers, or internal affairs units? States vary in the rights afforded police officers facing discipline. Many states have adopted a Law Enforcement Officer's Bill of Rights (LEOBR). These statutes detail the rights afforded officers and the internal administrative process for

> ## INSIDE POLICING 11.1    Police Officer's Bill of Rights
>
> When any police officer is under investigation and subjected to interrogation that could lead to punitive action, the interrogation shall be conducted under the following conditions. These rights do not apply to an interrogation in the normal course of duty, which might involve counseling, instruction, or informal verbal admonishments.
>
> 1. The interrogation shall be conducted at a reasonable hour, preferably when the police officer is on duty, or during normal waking hours, unless the seriousness of the investigation requires otherwise. If the interrogation takes place during off-duty time, the officer shall be compensated in accordance with regular departmental procedures.
> 2. The persons to be present at the interrogation must be identified in advance, and the officer will not be interrogated by more than two investigators at one time.
> 3. The police officer will be informed of the charges against him or her prior to any interrogation.
> 4. The interrogation will be for a reasonable period of time.
> 5. The police officer shall not be subjected to any offensive language or threats of punitive action, except that an officer refusing to respond to questions or submit to interrogation shall be informed that failure to answer questions that are directly related to the investigation may result in punitive action. There will be no promise or reward offered as an inducement to answer any question.
> 6. The interrogation may be recorded by either the persons conducting the interrogation or the officer under investigation or both. The officer in question is entitled to written or recorded copies of the interrogation if additional action is contemplated by the department or if there is to be a continuing investigation.
> 7. If prior to or during the interrogation it is decided that the officer may be charged with a criminal offense, the officer will immediately be informed of his or her constitutional rights.
> 8. If a formal written statement of charges is filed against a police officer by the department, the officer has a right to request that a representative of his or her choice be present during any interrogation.
>
> SOURCE: Adapted from the *California Government Code*, Section 3303.

investigating officers accused of misconduct. In recent years, provisions in some state's laws have come under scrutiny for potentially impeding investigations of alleged misconduct by providing "a special layer of employee due process protections when faced with investigations of official misconduct" (Keenan and Walker 2010, 185). Recent reform efforts often include calls to repeal LEOBRs. Maryland became the first state to repeal its officers' Bill of Rights (Editorial Board 2021). Inside Policing 11.1 provides a summary of the rights provided by California's version of the law.

The process for investigating complaints against officers tends to be similar to that used in other types of investigations. The steps used by many police departments are briefly summarized as follows (D'Arcy 1990):

1. Review the complainant's allegation to determine what departmental standard was violated.
2. Contact and interview all witnesses, and re-interview the complainant, if necessary.

3. Collect all other evidence, such as photographs, medical reports, police reports, and so on.

4. Obtain background information on the complainant (e.g., criminal history and any prior allegations against officers).

5. Obtain background data concerning the officer (e.g., prior complaints, personnel evaluations, or prior disciplinary actions by the department).

6. Interview all departmental members who may be involved.

Although internal investigations and criminal investigations are similar, there are important differences. Carter (1994) identifies several pertinent differences in internal investigations:

1. The Fourth Amendment guarantees apply to police officers at home and off duty, as they do to any citizen.

2. Lockers at the police station, a police car, and other elements of on-duty performance are unlikely to be protected by the Fourth Amendment.

3. If an unlawful search occurs, the fruits of that search may be used during a disciplinary hearing but not in a legal proceeding. This may not apply to departments that have elaborate policies on the internal investigation process.

4. Under *Garrity v. New Jersey* (1967), statements compelled during an internal investigation cannot be used later in a court of law. Such compelled testimony for internal investigations is routine practice and is not protected by the Fifth Amendment from use within administrative processes and hearings, but it cannot be used in a criminal prosecution for the very reason that it was in fact compelled (i.e., not voluntary). This type of compelled testimony is frequently referred to as a **Garrity interview**.

**Complaint Outcomes.** Investigations into citizen complaints are typically classified in one of four possible ways. **Sustained complaints** are ones that, as the result of an investigation, are determined to be justified. **Unsubstantiated complaints** are ones that, in the opinion of those making the decision, have no supporting or exonerating evidence and so cannot be considered either true or false. The majority of citizen complaints against officers are classified in this manner, because it is often difficult to determine with reasonable certainty that the complainant's allegation is true. **Unfounded complaints** are those that the investigation determines did not occur as alleged by the complainant. **Exoneration** of an officer occurs when the investigation results in a finding that the alleged complaint is essentially true but the officer's behavior is considered justified, legal, and within organizational policy (Perez 1994).

If an officer is found guilty of the complaint, the officer can appeal the outcome. Avenues of appeal typically include the parent government's civil service system and the courts. If the complaint is sustained, the officer may receive some sort of punishment. Carter (1994, 367–368) identifies several kinds of punishments:

1. **Termination of employment.** This is complete severance, including loss of salary and benefits.

2. **Demotion/loss of rank.** Loss of rank is a significant action, because it represents loss of salary and liability in career growth. It may not include "grades," which are salary increments within ranks.

3. **Punitive suspension.** An officer is barred from work and denied salary for a designated period, usually not exceeding four weeks. In many jurisdictions, the officer cannot even work off duty in positions that require police authority.

4. **Punitive probation.** An officer stays on duty with full salary and benefits. A subsequent sustained misconduct allegation may result in dismissal.

5. **Reassignment.** This is often used in conjunction with some other kind of punishment. An officer may be taken out of a specialized position or moved to another shift or location.

6. **Mandatory training.** An officer may receive training on the issue related to the misconduct.

7. **Reprimand.** An officer is officially admonished for the behavior. It is in written form, usually from a division commander, with a copy placed in the personnel file.

8. **Supervisory counseling.** This is a discussion with the officer concerning a problem usually related to some performance factor or procedure. It is intended to be both instructive and corrective. It does not typically become a part of the employee's personnel file.

Research concerning the number, types, and dispositions of complaints against police is limited; however, several studies (Wallace 1990; Dugan and Breda 1991; Independent Commission on the Los Angeles Police Department 1991; Petterson 1991; Walker 1998; Arthur 2015) provide useful insights. A summary is presented here:

1. Although less than 1 percent of citizens complain about police methods and behavior, as many as 10 to 15 percent may think that they have something to complain about—either what officers did or failed to do.

2. The rate of complaints varies among police departments, from about 6 to 81 complaints per 100 officers per year.

3. The percentage of sustained complaints also varies among police departments, from about 0 to 50 percent.

4. Complaints concerning the excessive use of police force are usually sustained less often than other types of complaints.

5. It appears that a small number of police officers account for a disproportionate number of complaints. Although the research varies, a reasonable estimate is that approximately 10 percent of the officers in a police department receive at least 25 or 30 percent of the complaints by citizens.

6. It also appears that a disproportionate number of complaints are filed against younger, less-experienced officers. As many as two-thirds or more of all complaints in some departments may involve officers who are 30 years of age or younger and who have less than 5 years of experience.

Table 11.1 presents data on citizen complaints about excessive force in 10 of the nation's largest cities and reveals widespread differences between rates of complaints per 100 officers and the percentage of sustained complaints. The frequency of complaints varies sharply from city to city. To understand these differences, several factors must be considered. The number and types of complaints against the police in general are the result of actual differences in police behavior, the perceived receptivity of a police department to

**TABLE 11.1** Citizen Complaints about Police Use of Force

| CITY | NUMBER OF COMPLAINTS | COMPLAINTS PER 100 OFFICERS | % SUSTAINED |
|---|---|---|---|
| New York City | 7,663 | 21.76 | 3.45 |
| Los Angeles | 582 | 6.12 | 0.86 |
| Houston | 118 | 2.41 | 1.69 |
| Philadelphia | 243 | 3.59 | 34.57 |
| Phoenix | 19 | 0.59 | 0.00 |
| San Antonio | 38 | 2.12 | 0.00 |
| San Diego | 66 | 3.43 | 3.03 |
| Dallas | 166 | 5.32 | 1.81 |
| Austin | 31 | 2.19 | 6.45 |
| Jacksonville | 69 | 4.24 | 10.14 |

*Sources*: US Department of Justice, Bureau of Justice Statistics, *Law Enforcement Management and Administrative Statistics, 2007* (Ann Arbor, MI: Interuniversity Consortium for Political and Social Science Research, 2007), ICPSR31161-v1 (computer file).

accepting and acting on complaints, and a political climate that either discourages or encourages citizens to complain. Worden et al. (2013), for example, argue that an officer's "exposure to risk" varies by their activity level (e.g., number of stops or arrests). That is, officers who engage in more of these types of activities increase their chances for complaints to be filed. In some communities, citizens do not complain about the police either because they do not think it will do any good or because they are afraid the police will retaliate. Some departments make it difficult for citizens to complain by creating a cumbersome complaint process and by the negative (e.g., unfriendly, rude, curt, or discouraging) behavior of officers when citizens attempt to complain.

The political climate in a community may be particularly important in encouraging or discouraging complaints against the police. On the one hand, a new mayor or other elected official who calls for an aggressive crackdown on crime or talks about the police as the "thin blue line" between citizens and criminals may be indicating to citizens that their concerns about police excesses will not be taken seriously. On the other hand, a new mayor or chief of police might encourage citizens to come forward with complaints about the police. Such encouragement, however, may result in increased frivolous as well as legitimate complaints.

The reasons for variations in sustained complaints are also related to the degree to which departments have well-defined standards for police behavior, take those standards seriously, and conduct thorough investigations into complaints. Low rates of sustained complaints may result from a departmental culture that implicitly encourages officers to engage in aggressive police work and fails to thoroughly investigate accusations of misconduct.

## Issues in Internal Investigations

Several controversies surround the internal investigation of police officers. These include the physical location of the internal affairs unit, the personnel assigned to work in internal affairs, whether complaints should be encouraged, whether internal affairs units should be proactive or reactive, what should be done about false complaints, the type and severity of discipline for officers who have sustained complaints, and whether the police can effectively police themselves.

**Location and Personnel.** Does the location of internal affairs units influence the number of citizen complaints? It is possible that citizens who believe that they have been abused by the police will be reluctant to go to the police department to file a complaint. As Perez (1994, 103) observes:

> The uniforms, badges, guns, and paramilitary carriage of police officers at a station house might be too much to confront for more passive complainants. A system that requires complaints cannot be made exclusively for those citizens having the audacity to confront the government.

As a result of this possibility, some police departments have placed the internal affairs unit in another location away from police headquarters. This change of location may also have a positive impact on the public perception of the police, because citizens may believe that the police are taking their complaints seriously.

Most often, the personnel who conduct internal investigations are sworn police officers, but some departments also use civilians for investigations on the assumption that some citizens who want to complain will be more comfortable with a civilian than with a police investigator. Also, the use of civilians creates the public perception that complaints will be taken more seriously and be more thoroughly investigated.

Assignment to internal affairs is often controversial. Internal affairs investigators are rarely popular with other officers. The term *headhunter*, or some other uncomplimentary nickname, is sometimes used by officers to describe internal affairs investigators. As a result, some police chiefs and sheriffs have made it clear that assignment to, and effective performance in, an internal affairs unit is a fast track to advancement and promotion within the agency.

**Orientation of Internal Affairs Units.** Should citizen complaints against the police be encouraged? Encouraging citizens to come forward—either openly or anonymously—has several possible consequences. On the one hand, it may increase the trust between police and citizens and provide managers with valuable information about officer behavior (Walker and Graham 1998). On the other hand, it may also result in more complaints, justified or otherwise. Unfortunately, in departments that encourage complaints, a morale problem may develop as an increasing number of officers must endure investigations into complaints. Whether or not complaints are sustained, internal affairs investigations are often stressful for the officers involved and unpleasant for officers throughout the department.

Should internal affairs units be reactive or proactive? A reactive unit investigates only those complaints that are brought to its attention. A proactive unit seeks out officers involved in deviant behavior. For example, an internal affairs investigator might purposely commit traffic violations and, when stopped by an officer, offer a bribe to avoid a citation. If the officer takes the money, that officer is usually terminated and may be criminally prosecuted. Such a proactive approach may be strongly resented by officers, because it

---

**INSIDE POLICING 11.2** | **Police Misconduct: On Our Watch**

In this podcast, reporters Sukey Lewis and Sandhya Dirks discuss police disciplinary processes and the lack of transparency involved.

   **Discussion Question:** Why is transparency important for accountability in police misconduct cases?

*SOURCE: Criminal (In)Justice* podcast, July 6, 2021, https://www.criminalinjusticepodcast.com/blog/2021/07/06/141-on-our-watch?rq=141.

---

creates a climate of mistrust between them and managers. Although some authorities recommend that internal affairs units be proactive (Murphy and Caplan 1991, 261–263), managers must be aware of the possible adverse consequences of such action. See Inside Policing 11.2 for a podcast on the lack of transparency of internal police investigations and discipline.

Although it is not clear how often it occurs, citizens do make **false complaints** about police officers. How should the police respond? In some jurisdictions, persons suspected of filing a false report can be criminally prosecuted. Police officers can also sue the person for defamation if the person falsely accuses an officer of criminal conduct, misconduct, or incompetence.

Although it is the officer involved who decides whether to file a civil suit against a citizen who made a false complaint, the police department decides whether to file criminal charges. Should they have that right? Although filing criminal charges may act as a deterrent against false complaints, it may also have a chilling effect on citizens with legitimate grievances, making this a most difficult question to resolve.

**Responding to Sustained Complaints.** When complaints against officers are sustained, what should be done? The alternatives include counseling, retraining, verbal reprimands, written reprimands, demotions, suspension without pay, and termination. Unfortunately, there is no standard to follow. Generally, the more serious the behavior of the officer, the more severe the punishment.

After their examination of 171 sustained complaints involving excessive force or improper police tactics in the Los Angeles Police Department (LAPD), the Christopher Commission (Independent Commission of the LAPD 1991) concluded that the type of disciplinary measures taken against the officers were too lenient. Only about 12 percent of the officers were terminated or resigned or retired. Approximately 58 percent were suspended without pay for a period of time, and the remainder received some type of reprimand.

Officers do not have to accept the recommended disciplinary action if they believe it is inappropriate. Many police departments have an appeals process that allows the officer in question to challenge the type of discipline recommended. Officers can challenge in court what they perceive to be extreme forms of discipline. In unionized agencies, another option for officers may be to file for **grievance arbitration**. One study found that grievance arbitration typically reduces the amount of discipline that is ultimately imposed by 50 percent (Iris 2002). Consequently, disciplinary actions by managers may be based, at least in part, on an assessment of whether the officer will appeal or file a grievance. The authors of this book are aware of instances in which police managers knew of inappropriate behavior but took no action, because they believed that the appeals process would undermine any effort to punish the officer.

Another factor affecting the complaint process is the likelihood of civil litigation (discussed in Chapter 3) if the complaint is sustained. Some departments may be reluctant to discipline officers for fear that it will be interpreted as an admission of negligence on the part of the department. In some instances, citizen complaints cannot be investigated, because the complainant will not cooperate until the civil suit is resolved. Consequently, the investigation of a citizen complaint may not be completed for a long time, possibly a year or more.

### Early Warning/Early Identification Systems

A modern approach to police officer accountability that combines the bureaucratic and internal investigation methods is the use of an **early warning system** (EWS), also called an **early identification system** (Walker 2003c). These systems track specific types of officer behaviors and then alert management when individual officers exceed the threshold for such behavior. For example, Alpert and Walker (2000) found that 73 percent of agencies responding to a survey reported that they identified officers for intervention who had three or more use-of-force reports in one year. These data-based management systems provide a centralized means of tracking supposed risk indicators, such as citizen complaints against officers, internal rule violations, use-of-force reports, charging of suspects with resisting arrest, sick days, and accidents. Using these systems, supervisors can look for patterns indicating problems in officer behavior (Walker and Archbold 2014).

These systems are based on the premise, noted earlier, that a small percentage of officers, sometimes referred to as "repeaters" (Arthur 2015), are responsible for a large percentage of improper behavior. For instance, Lersch and Mieczkowski (1996), in their study of a large police department in the Southeast, found that 2.9 percent of the officers in their study accounted for about 25 percent of the complaints. Brandl, Stroshine, and Frank (2001) found that 10 percent of the officers in a large Midwestern police department accounted for 25 percent of citizen complaints of excessive force. Similarly, an analysis of excessive force complaints in the LAPD revealed that 10 percent of officers accounted for 27.5 percent of complaints (Independent Commission of the LAPD 1991; see, however, Worden et al. 2013).

An EWS attempts to identify such officers quickly, so that discipline or other corrective action can be taken sooner rather than later. Walker (2005) argues that an EWS can also help to alter the behavior of line-level supervisors who may wish to ignore the misbehavior of their subordinates. By providing information that cannot be ignored, since it can also be reviewed by higher-level supervisors, line-level supervisors may be forced to address the misbehavior of officers identified by the system.

These systems suffer from a number of limitations (see, e.g., Holmes and Smith 2008; Worden et al. 2013). They are dependent on official records of behavior that officers may actively hide from supervisors. In addition, since citizen complaints are often a primary indicator in these systems, they are dependent on effective citizen complaint mechanisms (Walker 2005). As such, agencies that discourage citizen complaints will be unable to operate an effective EWS. Most important, the performance indicators used in these systems are based largely on assumptions rather than research. Although the indicators make intuitive sense, we have very few empirical evaluations assessing the ability of these indicators to properly identify "problem" officers. In addition, few studies have evaluated the follow-up interventions with identified officers (Worden et al. 2013; Helsby et al. 2018). Moreover, the majority of studies utilize weak research designs and provide mixed results regarding effectiveness (Worden et al. 2013; Helsby et al. 2018). Clearly, we must await further research before we know whether these systems will live up to the promises.

It goes without saying that an EWS must be used with due regard for the rights of officers as well as citizens. An officer might come to the attention of the EWS because that officer is highly productive (i.e., makes a large number of arrests) or works a particularly tough assignment (Lersch, Bazley, and Mieczkowski 2006). In fact, proponents of the EWS encourage agencies to use a variety of indicators and consider the productivity of officers. The EWS indicators identify officers who might be engaging in a pattern of improper conduct; investigation and judgment are still required to determine whether a problem exists and corrective action is needed. Also, if intervention is needed, the initial response is often counseling or retraining, unless the improper conduct has been very serious.

## Body-Worn Cameras

Recently, recorded and highly publicized incidents of police use of force have instigated a national dialogue about police accountability. One of the most prominent and popular policy recommendations arising from these discussions over accountability is the use of **body-worn camera** (BWC) systems. In 2016, a survey by the Bureau of Justice Statistics showed that 48 percent of local police departments had BWCs, although only 60 percent of those agencies had fully deployed the cameras in the field (Hyland 2018).

The use of cameras by police is touted to improve police transparency and accountability, among other things. More specifically, the video recording of interactions between police and citizens is suggested as a means of improving evidence gathering, reducing assaults on officers, reducing citizen complaints (including false complaints), and reducing use-of-force incidents. Indeed, when police and citizens alike know they are being recorded, it may improve the behavior of all parties involved (White 2014; Ariel, Farrar, and Sutherland 2015; President's Task Force on Twenty-First Century Policing 2015).

Although BWCs have the potential to alter interactions between police and citizens, a number of important questions remain unanswered regarding the use of this new technology. Early evidence suggested that BWCs decrease citizen complaints (Ariel et al. 2015, 2017; Jennings, Lynch, and Fridell 2015) and use-of-force incidents (Ariel et al. 2015; see also White 2014), but more recent research has shed additional light on two of the most important measures of police–citizen interactions. A review of the studies on BWCs by Lum et al. (2019) reported most studies found that officers wearing BWCs received fewer complaints than officers without BWCs. They concluded, however, that the studies on BWCs' influence on officer use of force are inconclusive. That is, some studies find officers wearing BWCs use less force than officers without BWCs, whereas other studies find no differences in various use-of-force measures between officers with and without BWCs. The differences may be a result of differing agency polices and officer compliance with rules governing activation of their BWCs (Ariel et al. 2016). On the other hand, a recent randomized controlled study comparing New York Police Department (NYPD) officers with BWCs to officers without BWCs found a 21 percent reduction in complaints against officers assigned to wear cameras compared to those without (Braga, MacDonald, and McCabe 2021).The researchers concluded that not only did the cameras reduce complaints against officers, but that officers wearing cameras were more likely to comply with agency requirements requiring reports on stops of citizens compared to officers without BWCs. This finding suggests BWCs may improve the collection of important data, including stops and frisks of citizens. Without accurate reporting of stops, police agencies in the U.S. are unable to assess disparities in officer stops.

While research on BWCs has accelerated, many questions remain. For example, is the reduction in complaints against officers a result of changes in police behavior toward citizens or simply a change in citizen reporting? Officers tend to believe BWCs reduce frivolous or unfounded complaints, yet others suggest that officers may be using footage to discourage complaints (Lum et al. 2019). For example, police may use the footage to suggest that a citizen could have been cited for their behavior, implying that they may be cited should they follow through with the complaint. These claims and others still need additional rigorous evaluation. In addition, there is still much to be learned about such things as privacy and implementation issues. For example, do BWCs lead to more sustained complaints or decrease the amount of time agencies devote to investigating complaints? These are important issues for police legitimacy, because many citizens who file complaints are often dissatisfied with the process and litigation related to complaints is costly (Ariel et al. 2015).

Many of the allegations in citizen complaints involve behavior that is difficult to verify without independent evidence. For example, a large portion of complaints involve issues regarding officer demeanor and complaints about procedure-related issues, in addition to complaints related to use of force. BWCs hold the promise of alleviating these problems, among others, by providing independent evidence with which to make determinations on complaints.

Although the limited evidence suggests the technology decreases complaints against officers who wear them, it is too soon to know how effective BWCs will be at increasing accountability. Unfortunately, because of recent high-profile officer-involved police shootings, the adoption of BWC systems has outpaced empirical research on the effects of this new technology. Innovative ergonomic research on BWCs and the limits of BWCs are highlighted in Inside Policing 11.3 and 11.4, respectively.

### Effectiveness of Internal Investigations

Can the police effectively regulate the behavior of their own? Historically, a recurring debate has surrounded this question.

Proponents of internal (departmental) review argue that the police can conduct fair investigations of other officers, that internal review is necessary to maintain police morale, that external review interferes with the authority of the chief executive, and that other methods (e.g., elected and appointed officials or the courts) are available to citizens if they are not satisfied. In addition, many police officers do not believe that external review of police conduct is likely to be impartial. They believe that such reviews and recommendations for discipline will often be politically motivated.

External review proponents argue that internal investigations of police complaints are the actions of a system closed to outsiders and favorably predisposed toward police officers. As such, they argue that citizen input will result in more thorough and fair investigations of complaints that, in turn, will result in more sustained complaints and more discipline for guilty officers, which will better deter misconduct than internal mechanisms (Walker 2001). Furthermore, proponents argue that external mechanisms are more likely to be perceived as independent and fair, resulting in greater satisfaction for those who complain and improved perceptions of the police generally (Walker 2001). If the public perceives that the police are unresponsive and unfair in their investigation of complaints,

---

**INSIDE POLICING 11.3**    Science and Body-Worn Cameras

This article discusses several aspects of police body-worn camera usage that may be informed by science. Ergonomics and human factors analysis, for example, can help determine the pros and cons of different camera placement, such as head, shoulder, or chest. And neuroscience can help understand the "perspective bias" introduced by video recorded from a particular angle—not a new phenomenon, as film directors learned long ago "how to manipulate what people see."

**Discussion Question:** How might body camera footage be used by police agencies to improve training and agency policies?

SOURCE: *Modern Policing* blog, April 28, 2018, https://gcordner.wordpress.com/2018/04/29/science-bwc/.

---

**INSIDE POLICING 11.4**    Police Body-Worn Cameras and Their Limits

In this podcast, host David Harris discusses the issue of perspective in body camera footage and the implications for police accountability.

**Discussion Question:** What factors are important to consider when reviewing body camera footage?

SOURCE: *Criminal (In)Justice* podast, May 16, 2021, https://www.criminalinjusticepodcast.com/blog/2021/05/16/bonus-body-cams-limits?rq=camera.

---

public confidence in the police will erode. Consequently, involving citizens in the complaints process has the capacity to restore trust and confidence in police–citizen relations (West 1988).

## External Accountability Mechanisms

The second set of oversight mechanisms includes those outside the police department. These mechanisms have emerged primarily in response to concerns that police departments do not hold their members sufficiently accountable. Two external oversight mechanisms—civilian review and police auditors—are considered here. Although legal remedies also exist as a form of external accountability, they were discussed in detail in Chapter 3 and so will not be considered here.

### Civilian Review

A **civilian review board** is an effort to control police behavior by establishing an external form of review for allegations of police misconduct. It should be noted, however, that even in those communities with some type of external review, the police department usually continues to conduct its own investigations of complaints.

Research indicates that about 80 percent of the 50 largest cities in the United States have some type of external review of citizen complaints against the police (Walker and Bumphus 1991; Walker 2001, 2003a), and about 140 external oversight agencies are now in existence (De Angelis, Rosenthal, and Buchner 2016). The creation of an external review board is usually related to a political perception that the police are out of control and typically follows in the wake of a police scandal.

**A Brief History of Civilian Review.** Citizen participation in the review of complaints against the police can be traced to the progressive era (1890–1913), when reformers wanted to reduce the influence of corrupt politicians (Caiden 1977). Yet throughout the first half of the twentieth century, there was little progress in establishing citizen review. In its 1967 report, the President's Commission on Law Enforcement and Administration of Justice noted the problems faced by citizens when they tried to complain about police brutality. Such citizens might be arrested, or the police might file criminal charges against them for making a false report. Many police departments had no formal internal investigations unit or procedure. The commission found that less than 10 percent of citizen complaints were substantiated, and even when they were, officers were infrequently or too lightly punished. Both the National Advisory Commission on Civil Disorders (1968) and the National Commission on the Causes and Prevention of Violence (1969) reached similar conclusions. These studies found that police departments had inadequate investigative procedures and resisted efforts to make complaint procedures more meaningful.

Terrill (1991; see also Walker 2001) divides the discussion about civilian review into three time periods, which he calls "climates of opinion." The first era was the late 1950s and 1960s, during which various forms of civilian review boards were initially suggested. These early proposals, considered politically controversial, were vigorously resisted by the police. Several cities, such as Chicago and New York, struggled to establish some form of civilian review. Only Philadelphia established a review process that lasted for several years, but it too was eventually abandoned, in part for political and legal reasons but also in large measure because the police department's internal affairs unit processed many more cases and meted out much harsher punishments than did the civilian review board (Caiden 1977; Terrill 1991).

The second era, the 1970s, was distinguished by increases in public concern about the criminal justice system. Urban riots, the civil rights movement, the President's Commission on Law Enforcement and Administration of Justice (1967), and the National Advisory Commission on Civil Disorders (1968) all called attention to troubling behavior on the part of the police. This period was marked by increased public support for civilian review, and several communities (e.g., Detroit and Miami-Dade County, Florida) established some type of civilian oversight of the police. However, these civilian review processes were not without problems and resistance. The city of Detroit, over the opposition of the Detroit Police Department, established a board of police commissioners, which continues today. Its role includes supervisory control and oversight of the department, including the development of policies and procedures in consultation with the chief of police and approval of the police budget. The board also oversees the Office of the Chief Investigator, who has a staff of civilian investigators. The chief investigator is responsible for coordinating the receipt, investigation, and resolution of complaints. The board has the authority not only to receive complaints but also to review the investigation of complaints undertaken by the police department and either affirm or change any disciplinary action taken against officers.

During the third era, the 1980s and 1990s, several major cities established review processes, including the San Francisco Office of Citizen Complaints, the San Diego Police Review Commission, and the Dallas Citizens' Police Review Board. Police opposition to civilian review did not change, however, nor did their principal arguments. Although the police no longer considered civilian review part of a communist plot to overthrow the government, as they had in the 1960s, police executives, departments, and unions continued to argue that it undermined managerial authority and the professionalism of the police. To strengthen their argument, many departments worked hard to improve their internal investigations of citizen complaints.

Petterson's (1991) survey of 19 communities with some type of civilian review board indicated the diversity of approaches in this area. One of the boards was established in the 1960s, four in the 1970s, and 14 in the 1980s. Fourteen of the boards conducted their own investigations, whereas the others relied on investigations by the police department. Only one of the boards, however, was actually authorized to determine the discipline to be imposed on officers. The others could only recommend disciplinary measures that the police department may or may not use.

Today, civilian review boards encompass many different types of organizational designs and purposes. Walker and Kreisel (1996) identified five dimensions along which civilian review boards vary. They are discussed in Inside Policing 11.5.

**The Limits of Civilian Review.**  The decision by a community to establish some form of civilian review of police behavior is usually based on the assumption that it will be more effective and more fair than an internal investigation by the police. The limited research in this area, however, tends not to support this assumption (Holiday and Wagstaff 2021). Caiden (1977) concluded that attempts to institute civilian review in the 1970s failed because the police resisted such attempts and used both political and legal means to limit their potential effectiveness.

West (1988) found that complaint procedures (internal or external) were not related to the number of complaints filed or the seriousness of those complaints. When complaints were encouraged by either the police or the civilian review boards, however, they were less likely to be sustained. Similarly, Hickman (2006) found more complaints for use of force were filed in agencies with citizen review but that fewer complaints were sustained. Both these studies suggest that unjustified and minor complaints occurred more frequently when complaints were encouraged. Terrill and Ingram (2016), on the other hand, found that citizen complaint processes significantly increased sustained complaints. Overall, the limited evidence on the effectiveness of citizen review of complaint mechanisms is inconclusive. This is likely because the types of external citizen review vary considerably and many factors influence their effectiveness (Lum et al. 2016).

Perez (1994) has identified several problems associated with civilian review. First, civilian review boards do not tend to find problems more frequently than internal affairs units do. He observes that no fair system will find the police guilty of misconduct very often, because in a legalistic sense, the police are not guilty of misconduct very often. One must also consider a sociological reality. Most civilian review board members develop an appreciation for the police and for police work. Over time, they are less and less prone to be tough on officers, and they actually begin to find fault with complainants. (Perez 1994, 146). Consequently, civilian review is unlikely to change the efficiency or effectiveness of police review. Finally, as Perez (1994, 147) notes,

> members of civilian review boards . . . seem to have a sort of "boys will be boys" attitude toward truthfulness. . . . When a lie is discovered by civilian systems, it is considered to be a part of the "playing of the game," a natural product of a system designed to investigate misconduct. . . . Thus, while chiefs take lying very seriously, civilian review boards largely do not.

## INSIDE POLICING 11.5  Organizational Features of Citizen Review

### The Nature of Citizen Input

How are citizens involved in the review process? There are three ways:

1. Citizens conduct the initial fact-finding investigation.
2. Citizens have input into the review of complaints but do not conduct the investigation.
3. Citizens monitor the process but do not review individual complaints.

### The Complaint-Review Process

Review boards may have two purposes:

1. They review individual complaints. Virtually all boards do this.
2. They review department policies and make recommendations for changes. About 66 percent of the boards also do this.

### Jurisdiction

Do boards monitor police officers only, or are they also responsible for other public employees? Seventeen percent of the boards studied also set up other boards with the authority to monitor other public employees.

### Organizational Structure

Review boards have two types of organizational structure:

1. The majority (85 percent) had a multimember board. Boards ranged in size from 3 to 24 members. Twenty-seven percent of these boards included sworn police officers. This structure deals with one of the most important questions affecting civilian review: Who has representation on the civilian review board? Many minority group members, while seeking advocacy, are concerned with the issue of tokenism.
2. The remainder (15 percent) are administrative boards with a single administrative director. These boards presume that administrative procedure, rather than representation, is the best way to conduct a review of police behavior.

### Operating Policies

There are four different operating policies, each of which has direct implications for police accountability:

1. Independent investigative powers are held by about 33 percent of all review boards.
2. Subpoena power is held by 38 percent.
3. Public hearings are conducted by about half (46.2 percent).
4. About 32 percent provide legal representation for the officer, for the citizen, or both. Each of these four policies may be described as a different element of a "criminal trial" model.

Only 11 percent of the boards studied had all four elements. Two of the review boards had none.

SOURCE: Adapted from S. Walker and B. W. Kreisel, "Varieties of Citizen Review," *American Journal of Police* 15 (1996): 65–88.

Perez notes three additional limitations of civilian review. First, it is too far removed from the day-to-day existence of the line officer to understand and respond to the dynamics of illegal behavior. Second, civilian review can take away opportunities for the immediate supervisor to deal creatively with problems. Inadvertently, civilian review undermines the ability of the police department to "generate genuine humility and acceptance of error on the part of young, developing police officers" (Perez 1994, 161). Finally, civilian review tends to discourage the use of internal socialization processes. Perez believes that the role of peers and their contribution to the socialization of recruits is an inevitable and essential part of police work, and that it should be encouraged, not discouraged.

While these concerns may have some merit, proponents of citizen review hold that police investigating themselves is a conflict of interest, and that police have historically not done so in a transparent or effective manner (Holiday and Wagstaff 2021). In addition, research does suggest that citizen review improves citizen satisfaction with the complaint process. Moreover, it may improve legitimacy and police–community relationships (Holiday and Wagstaff 2021).

### Police Auditor Systems

**Police auditor systems** have developed more recently than civilian review board systems. The most important difference is that police auditors do not usually investigate or even monitor individual citizen complaints—that is left to the internal processes of the police department. Instead, the auditor model focuses on the police organization and its policies and practices. In the fashion of the US Government Accountability Office, police auditors examine different aspects of the ongoing operation of the police department to ensure that legal requirements are being met and that the most efficient and effective practices are being followed. As noted by Walker (2003a, 6–7), the auditor model

> seeks to identify problems in the complaint process or other police policies and recommend corrective action to the chief executive. . . . The underlying assumption is that these recommendations will have a preventive effect, reducing the likelihood of certain forms of misconduct occurring in the future.

Jurisdictions with well-established police auditors include the San Jose Police Department (Nurre 2008) and the Los Angeles County Sheriff's Department (Bobb 2007). Others include Austin, Boise, Omaha, Philadelphia, Portland, Reno, Sacramento, Seattle, and Tucson. Among the principles that seem to make this model most effective are independence from the law enforcement agency, free access to internal police data and documents, public reporting of findings and recommendations (see Inside Policing 11.6), and direct access to the chief or sheriff (Walker 2003b).

## The Limits of Oversight Mechanisms

Oversight of police in a democracy is clearly necessary. Many proponents of vigorous police oversight have argued that police agencies can create a culture of rule following. Walker (2005) argues that a combination of proper rules, reporting procedures for officers, citizen complaint mechanisms, and early intervention systems can make the formal and informal culture of police organizations more accountable. Proper supervision and external oversight, vigorous investigations, and appropriate interventions (e.g., training or punishment) may influence officer behavior to some degree, yet the discretion and autonomy officers have in their work allows them to disregard rules and avoid reporting requirements. Moreover, the low visibility of police work and the self-protective aspects of police culture make supervision of officers and investigation of misbehavior inherently difficult

| INSIDE POLICING 11.6 | Core Principles for an Effective Police Auditor's Office |

**Independence**

A police auditor's office must be fully independent of the law enforcement agency under its jurisdiction.

**Clearly Defined Scope of Responsibility**

The scope of the responsibilities of a police auditor's office must be clearly defined by ordinance (or contract).

**Adequate Resources**

The size of an auditor's office staff should be based on a formula reflecting the size of the law enforcement agency under the auditor's jurisdiction, as measured by the number of full-time sworn officers.

**Unfettered Access**

A police auditor must have unfettered access to all documents and data in the law enforcement agency.

**Full Cooperation**

A police auditor must have the full cooperation of all employees of the law enforcement agency under its jurisdiction.

**Sanctions for Failure to Cooperate**

The enabling ordinance of an auditor's office must specify sanctions for failure to cooperate with the work of an auditor on the part of any law enforcement agency employee.

**Public Reports**

A police auditor must issue periodic public reports (at least once a year).

**No Prior Censorship by the Police Department**

Reports by the police auditor shall not be subject to prior censorship by the law enforcement agency.

A police auditor may reject any and all demands by the law enforcement agency to see draft copies of public reports.

**Community Involvement**

A police auditor must have the benefit of community involvement and input.

**Confidentiality/Anonymity**

The work of a police auditor must respect the confidentiality of public employees as defined in the applicable state statute.

**Access to the Police Chief/Sheriff**

A police auditor must have direct access to the chief executive of the law enforcement agency under its jurisdiction.

**No Retaliation**

The enabling ordinance of an auditor's office must specify that there shall be no retaliation against the auditor for work done as a part of the auditor's responsibilities, including statements made in public reports.

SOURCE: Adapted from S. Walker, "Core Principles for an Effective Police Auditor's Office." A Report of the First National Police Auditors Conference, Omaha, NE, March 26–27. https://samuelwalker.net/wp-content/uploads/2010/06/coreprinciples.pdf.

(Holmes and Smith 2008). Indeed, oversight mechanisms, especially those focused on punishment, are in many ways responsible for the development of the more secretive elements of police culture. Inside Policing 11.7 discusses police accountability options, including new ways of thinking about accountability.

Schein (1985, 9) defined the organization culture as "the pattern of basic assumptions that a given group has invented, discovered, or developed in learning to cope with its problems of external adaptation and internal integration, [and] that have worked well enough to be considered valid." The culture is made up of values that guide the behavior of police officers. Sparrow, Moore, and Kennedy (1990) have listed what they consider some of the most influential values of police officers. These values are summarized in Inside Policing 11.8.

The values that undergird police culture are derived substantially from daily work experiences. The most important elements of police culture reflect how officers adapt to their

---

**INSIDE POLICING 11.7**   **Getting Oversight Right**

This article discusses the pros and cons of various alternatives for achieving police accountability, such as civilian review, police auditors, and special commissions. The public tends to want an independent process. However, the oversight systems don't always succeed, and they risk diluting the chief or sheriff's responsibility for discipline. Chicago is cited as one place currently trying several options at once.

**Discussion Question:** If "front-end" accountability involves citizen involvement in shaping police policy, how can departments seek this input and ensure it is representative of community viewpoints?

SOURCE: *Modern Policing* blog, January, 24, 2018, https://gcordner.wordpress.com/?s=getting+oversight+right.

---

**INSIDE POLICING 11.8**   **Building Blocks of Police Culture**

1. The public wants the police to be crime-fighters, and that is what the police think of themselves as being: the primary crime-fighting organization in government.
2. No one other than another police officer understands the "real" nature of police work and what is necessary to get the job done.
3. Police have to stick together; loyalty to one another is more important than anything else because everyone else, including the public, politicians, and police managers, seems to try to make the job of police officers more difficult. And these individuals are often unfair in their evaluations of the police.
4. Police cannot win the war on crime without violating legal, organizational, and ethical standards.
5. The public does not support or appreciate the police, and they expect too much of police officers.

SOURCE: Adapted from M. Sparrow, M. Moore, and D. Kennedy, *Beyond 911: A New Era for Policing* (New York: Basic Books, 1990), 51.

environment. Culture is the process of adaptation shared, discussed, and finally, formed into habits. Cultural values are the meanings associated with those habits.

It is the type and frequency of problems confronted by the police—not the hopes of police reformers or administrators—that determine the way police do their work and what is important to them. Externally imposed control systems, often failing to understand this simple truth, backfire by intensifying resentment and secrecy. Police will not change unless their working environment is in some way changed, but they will become more secretive. As reformers and administrators intensify their efforts to hold the police accountable for an impossible mandate—to police a democracy—the strength of the secretive elements of police culture may also increase (Manning 1998).

The next sections examine moral and ethical standards, as distinct from legal standards, that control behavior by providing officers with an internal gauge for their work. These standards are preventive, because officers are expected to anticipate outcomes of their behavior before they act. They can be divided into professional standards and ethical standards.

## Professional Standards

The concept of **professionalism** in policing is associated with the recurring attempts of reformers to ensure that police officers are honest, efficient, and effective. More specifically, to be considered a profession, an occupation must adopt certain criteria. Recognition that such adoption is a prolonged process is called a process-criterion approach. As an occupation becomes a profession, one criterion is the learning of a systematic process that uses the scientific method (Cullen 1978; Geison 1983). Inside Policing 11.9 provides a list of the criteria the authors believe indicate that an occupation has reached professional status.

### The Police Professionalization Movement

Occupations that adopt the criteria presented in Inside Policing 11.9 are professionalized and are recognized as such by the public and other professional organizations. Their members believe in these criteria and are accorded the status of professionals (Hall 1968). As professionals, they are granted wide latitude to decide how to conduct their work. Even

---

**INSIDE POLICING 11.9  Professional Criteria**

1. Professionals are represented by professional associations, which serve the purpose of transmitting knowledge of the field.
2. Professionals are provided autonomy to perform their work. Even in organizations characterized by a bureaucracy, professionals are granted the opportunity to do their work with only limited control by supervisors.
3. A profession encompasses a unique body of knowledge, associated with research, that must be constantly updated.
4. Professionals require lengthy and formal training.
5. Professionals require certification of quality and competence.
6. Professionals have a commitment to service on behalf of a clientele.

SOURCES: J. B. Cullen, *The Structure of Professionalism* (Princeton, NJ: Princeton University Press, 1978); G. L. Geison, ed. *Professions and Professional Ideology in America* (Chapel Hill: University of North Carolina Press, 1983); R. Hall, "Professionalization and Bureaucratization," *America Sociological Review* 33 (1968): 92–104.

when they work in bureaucratic organizations, they have the autonomy to define problems in their area of expertise, to respond to those problems, and to gauge the success of their work. In a word, they are largely left alone by managers. Members of professions, such as doctors and lawyers, operate on these principles.

These conditions have not been true of the police. The police professionalization movement, begun in 1893 by the International Association of Chiefs of Police and central to efforts to reform the police ever since, sought to bureaucratize the police through specialization of function and intense control of line officers (Fogelson 1977). Rather than fostering independent decision making in line officers, the movement sought centralization of command under the authority of the chief. Individual officers were not admitted to the ranks of professionals, but instead were controlled with ever-tighter accountability (Fogelson 1977). Police departments, not police officers, became professionalized (Regoli et al. 1988).

As the police professionalization movement unfolded, officers were considered the product of a management system controlled by police executives. Police executives blended bureaucratic management and chain-of-command control in an attempt to force line officers to go along with the reforms the executives wanted (Kuykendall and Roberg 1990). Consequently, police officers below the executive level were (and continue to be) rarely considered to be professional colleagues, but rather a group of individuals to be managed. These police officers were left out of the professionalization process. One consequence of this trend was the development of sharply antagonistic relationships between line personnel and management (Reuss-Ianni 1983). Such antagonisms continue to be a critical issue in the twenty-first century.

As subordinates, police officers have been told what not to do more often than what to do, and they have been laden with rules and policies seeking to control their behavior rather than to expand and sharpen their discretionary skills (Alpert and Smith 1999). Therefore, the professionalization movement itself, except for commitment to service (discussed later), did not contribute toward professionalization of policing. True professionalism did not begin until the community policing (COP) movement—with its emphasis on the decentralization of authority and empowerment of line officers—began to gain ground.

## Criteria of Police Professionalization

Characteristics of policing as a true profession are autonomy, a unique body of knowledge, education and training, certification and accreditation, and commitment to service.

**Autonomy.**  The development of professional autonomy is a central criterion in the process of professionalization. Autonomy provides professionals with the discretion to carry out their work, and its presence shows that society acknowledges their professional status.

Police departments, as previously noted, have historically sought to control the behavior of line officers. The COP movement, however, emphasizes increased autonomy, and with it the decentralization of authority and the use of creative techniques in solving problems. Each of these items expands the autonomy of police officers and thus represents movement toward professionalism.

Decentralization of authority occurs in two ways. One is the transfer of authority to make tactical decisions down the chain of command. For example, patrol officers may be given the authority to decide what kinds of crime problems to focus on; line officers are expected to make tactical decisions traditionally reserved for sergeants and lieutenants. The second is geographic decentralization, meaning that officers are assigned to specific areas and take increased responsibility in solving the problems confronted in those areas.

Increased decision making is a relaxation of traditional constraints on the use of police discretion. Wilson and Kelling (1982) argued that officers should be provided with broad latitude in controlling common public-order problems on their beat. Such problems, if unaddressed, lead to neighborhood degradation and the onset of serious crime. By allowing officers wider latitude to deal with these problems, more effective long-term solutions to crime can be developed.

"Creative, customized police work," according to Skolnick and Bayley (1986), is important in finding creative solutions to recurring public-order problems. Goldstein (1998) suggests that officers engaged in problem-solving analysis redefine problems in noncriminal terms. Tailor-made responses, he contends, are a critical ingredient in finding effective solutions.

**A Unique Body of Knowledge.** Another criterion of professionalism is that a profession has an area of unique expertise that only its practitioners are qualified to assess. Such expertise can be gained in three ways.

The first way, common especially before the 1960s, is to study the work of experts. These are well-educated, experienced practitioners, usually executives such as O. W. Wilson and August Vollmer, who lectured and wrote journal articles and books. O. W. Wilson's famous book Police Administration (1950) contains many useful ideas about how to manage police departments. Many of his ideas were the result of his extensive experience, but some were taken from writers about general management principles. Many police today continue to depend almost exclusively on the knowledge of experts as a basis for their actions.

The second way to gain expertise is by consulting and modeling. In this method, the management and practices of a police department are analyzed by experts or consultants, who then compare the results with a model of what they consider desirable—for example, an effective way to select and train officers. Models come from several sources. One source is the creativity and imagination of the expert or consultant. Another might be a police department that the consultant likes or considers progressive. If the consultant has been a police manager, the model might be the consultant's former department. Or models may come from books written by other experts in the field.

The third way to acquire expertise is by scientific research. Scientific research is empirical—that is, based on what can be observed. Two conditions apply to scientific observations. The first is that the observation has **validity**, meaning that what the observer sees is what is actually going on. The second is that it has **reliability**, meaning that if other observers conducted the research again in the same setting, they will be likely to come to similar (if not precisely the same) conclusions. Research conducted by Sherman and his colleagues (Sherman et al. 1997; Sherman 1999) and by Skogan and Frydl (2004), for example, shows how scientific research has had powerful effects on police knowledge. It has dramatically expanded knowledge about what works in policing, enabled scholars to systematically compare a wide variety of research on policing, and has provided a benchmark for thinking about the quality of police research.

**Education and Training.** A further criterion of professionalism is formal preparation. Professionals typically undergo extensive training and education, followed by certification. Chapter 6 identified the types and extent of police training. Higher education is becoming increasingly important in all aspects of policing, as discussed in Chapter 14. Over the past three decades, the numbers of educated officers and the quantity of education that they possess have increased dramatically. Nevertheless, it does not yet approach the level expected in other professions.

**Certification and Accreditation.**  Professionalism also requires **certification** as a crite-rion of its members to ensure quality and competence. Usually, state-level organizations give licenses or certifications. The legal profession, for example, has state bar associations, and all lawyers must pass the bar examinations in their state to practice law there.

State standards organizations fulfill this function for the police. They set standards for the selection, training, and certification of police officers. Currently, nearly all states have such organizations, the titles of which vary. For example, in Arizona, the state organiza-tion is called the Arizona Peace Officer Standards and Training Board; in Kentucky, it is called the Kentucky Law Enforcement Council. The central function is training, defined by Berg (1994) as learning the techniques for particular processes or procedures through example and instruction.

The first standards organization, established in California in 1959, was the Commission on Peace Officer Standards and Training. Its purpose is "to continually enhance the pro-fessionalism of California law enforcement" (Commission on Peace Officer Standards and Training 2016). In attempting to accomplish this mission, the commission develops mini-mum selection and training standards for police officers, develops and approves training programs for all levels of police officers (e.g., entry officers and supervisors), and provides recommended guidelines on various topics, among a host of other services to support its mission (Commission on Peace Officer Standards and Training 2016).

Today. Peace Officer Standards and Training commissions exist in nearly every state. They provide a wide diversity of training that focuses on skills, knowledge, cultural diver-sity, attitudes, and ethics. These state-level agencies maintain lists of individuals certified as police officers in the state, but not all keep lists of officers who have been de-certified. Moreover, some states de-certification rules result in officers who are able to maintain certification even after having resigned under investigation or even having been fired for misconduct from a police agency (Schulz 2022). A growing number of reformers have called for states to more strictly enforce de-certification and to maintain lists of de-certified officers to stop officers from simply moving to another state and getting certified again.

An important aspect of licensing is **accreditation**. Professional organizations frequently provide for means of accreditation of member associations. Universities, for example, are periodically reviewed and accredited by regional accreditation boards. The purpose of accreditation for the police is to determine whether a department meets general standards of policy and training. This determination is accomplished through self-assessment and external review in an attempt to match national standards set up by the **Commission on Accreditation for Law Enforcement Agencies** (CALEA). If a department is deemed to meet these standards, it is accredited by CALEA for a three-year period, which is renewable on reassessment if the department remains in compliance with the standards.

Proponents of accreditation believe that self-assessment helps to identify departmental strengths and weaknesses and may reduce the exposure to liability. Departments in sev-eral states have been offered reduced insurance rates for completing the process (Williams 1989). Accreditation may help departments to address administrative issues and policies and, perhaps by tightening up in these areas, to become more professional and less ex-posed to liability (McAllister 1987). Nearly all of the accreditation standards, however, require only that a formal policy or procedure be established or that records be main-tained. The process used to determine the extent that CALEA-revised policies and proce-dures are actually implemented and followed is largely an honor system.

The standards set by CALEA are extensive, and if all are applied, that department will likely become more, not less, formalized and bureaucratic. Also, most of the standards that apply to patrol work focus on law enforcement rather than order maintenance and service

(Mastrofski 1990). This situation is not entirely consistent with COP. According to Cordner and Williams (1995, 1996, 1999), an examination of these standards regarding their applicability to COP indicated that, for the most part, the standards are either silent or neutral on the subject. It is possible that such standards could constrain departments that are attempting to implement COP, especially in the areas of officer participation, encouraging risk taking in applications of discretion, and removing organizational barriers to creativity (Cordner and Williams 1996, 256). Cordner and Williams (1996, 378–379) suggested that CALEA and its sponsoring organizations (including the International Association of Chiefs of Police, the National Sheriffs Association, the National Organization of Black Law Enforcement Executives, and the Police Executive Research Forum) address the following concerns in the future:

1. Improve its research and development capacity, and establish a more proactive posture toward contemporary changes in policing.
2. Play a more active role in big-picture issues affecting policing.
3. Pay more attention to accreditation issues ,and participate more actively in CALEA's direction and focus.

Some observers have suggested that in relatively well-developed departments committed to COP, accreditation could impede managers' efforts to promote change (Oettmeier 1993; Sykes 1994). This conclusion would hold until the accreditation process places more significant emphasis on problem solving, innovation, and community input, instead of focusing on bureaucratic rules and regulations. In contrast, in less well-developed departments that have inadequate policies and procedures, accreditation may be beneficial.

**Commitment to Service.** One of the most important criteria of a professional is a commitment to service. Service means a formal obligation to act on behalf of the professional's clientele to render service as needed (Rhoades 1991). This is one area in which the police professionalism movement has contributed to the professionalism of individual officers.

One of the principal objectives of the movement was to instill a sense of calling in police officers. Early twentieth-century reformers, concerned about the lax standards many recruits brought to police work, sought to instill in officers a commitment to law enforcement. To them, this meant a commitment to a belief in the contribution of police to society. The movement was successful in instilling this sense of commitment in police recruits. Chapters 4 and 5 discussed the service activities of police officers. Indeed, in many departments today, police work is mandated as a 24-hour obligation. In a reversal of direction, some reformers today are concerned about the overcommitment of police to their work, believing that police officers are overzealous in their pursuit of "bad guys" (see Chapter 9).

## Ethical Standards

The most effective method for controlling a person's behavior is for that person to believe in the standards of conduct they are supposed to follow. Ethical standards identify right and wrong behavior in any endeavor in life. Individual ethical standards about integrity, responsible behavior, use of coercion, and compassion provide officers with internal guides for their conduct. If officers do not have an internalized standard of ethics, they are more likely to engage in some form of deviant behavior (e.g., corruption or brutality). Inside Policing 11.10 gives the code of ethics for police officers for the state of California. Part of this code was adopted from the International Association of Chiefs of Police's code of ethics, which is utilized by many states.

---

**INSIDE POLICING 11.10**    Law Enforcement Code of Ethics

**Purpose**

**Code of Ethics:** To insure that all peace officers are fully aware of their individual responsibilities to maintain their own integrity and that of their agency, every peace officer, during basic training, or at the time of appointment, shall be administered the Law Enforcement Code of Ethics.

**Code of Ethics**

**AS A LAW ENFORCEMENT OFFICER,** my fundamental duty is to serve; to safeguard lives and property; to protect the innocent against deception, the weak against oppression or intimidation, and the peaceful against violence or disorder; and to respect the Constitutional rights of all to liberty, equality, and justice.

I WILL keep my private life unsullied as an example to all; maintain courageous calm in the face of danger, scorn, or ridicule; develop self-restraint; and be constantly mindful of the welfare of others. Honest in thought and deed in both my personal and official life, I will be exemplary in obeying the laws of the land and the regulations of my department. Whatever I see or hear of a confidential nature or that is confided to me in my official capacity will be kept ever secret unless revelation is necessary in the performance of my duty.

I WILL never act officiously or permit personal feelings, prejudices, animosities or friendships to influence my decisions. With no compromise for crime and with relentless prosecution of criminals, I will enforce the law courteously and appropriately without fear or favor, malice or ill will, never employing unnecessary force or violence and never accepting gratuities.

I RECOGNIZE the badge of my office as a symbol of public faith, and I accept it as a public trust to be held so long as I am true to the ethics of the police service. I will constantly strive to achieve these objectives and ideals, dedicating myself before God[1] to my chosen profession . . . law enforcement.

[1]  Reference to religious affirmation may be omitted where objected to by the officer.

*SOURCES*: State of California Office of Administrative Law, 2020, https://post.ca.gov/peace-officer-basic-training

---

## Ethical Perspectives

Attempts to identify appropriate ethical standards for the police have proven difficult. Different schools of thought concerning what is and is not ethical show the difficulty encountered by reformers concerned with police behavior. Inside Policing 11.11, adapted from Pollock (1997), summarizes several schools of ethics.

**Ethical Formalism.** The school of **ethical formalism** places moral worth on "doing one's duty." An officer who believes that police should "go by the book" is an ethical formalist. Legalistic policing is a kind of ethical formalism. An element of legalistic policing, as noted earlier, is that officers strive for the full enforcement of the law. Police legalism does not provide for fine distinctions in police discretion. On the contrary, legalistic departments justify their presence in terms of their capacity to enforce the law fairly among all groups.

**Ethical Utilitarianism.** According to the school of **ethical utilitarianism**, it is the results of one's actions that determine what is moral or good. Behavior is judged not by the

**INSIDE POLICING 11.11** | **Schools of Ethics**

**Religion**

What is good is that which conforms to God's will.

How do we know God's will?

Bible or other religious document.

Religious authorities.

Faith.

**Ethical Formalism (Deontological Ethics)**

What is good is that which conforms to doing one's duty and the categorical imperative.

What is the categorical imperative?

Act in such a way that one would will it to be a universal law.

Treat each person as an end and not as a means.

**Utilitarianism**

What is good is that which results in the greatest benefit for the greatest number.

Act utilitarianism "weighs" the benefits of an act for just those people and just that incident.

Rule utilitarianism "weighs" the benefits after determining the consequences of making that behavior a rule for the future.

**Egoism**

What is good is that which results in the greatest benefit for me.

Enlightened egoism, however, may allow one to reciprocate favors and may be practiced by a "good" person (because it benefits the self to be nice to others).

SOURCE: Adapted from J. Pollock, "Ethics and Law Enforcement." In R. G. Dunham and G. P. Alpert (eds.), *Critical Issues in Policing*, 3rd ed. (Prospect Heights, IL: Waveland, 1997), 348.

goodness of the acts, but by the consequences that they bring. For example, if an officer thought an illegal search was necessary to arrest a serious criminal, a utilitarian argument could be used to justify that search. Officers who say that they would sooner be "judged by 12 than carried by 6" are taking a utilitarian point of view—it is wiser to use deadly force in an ambiguous although perilous encounter and take a chance of being convicted of illegal behavior by a jury than to hesitate and possibly be killed by the suspect.

**Ethical Relativism.** Perhaps the most complicated ethical position of all is **ethical relativism**. Relativism means that which is considered good varies with the particular values of groups and individuals. This perspective can be used to justify enforcing certain laws in some neighborhoods but ignoring them in others (Pollock-Byrne 1998, 12–30). Police might object strenuously that they are not relative in their ethics. Yet the idea of "full enforcement" of the law is neither realistic nor possible (Goldstein 1998). The discretionary nature of police work is widely cited. Consequently, an ethically relativistic approach to policing is probably a more realistic description of day-to-day police ethics than any other.

Elements of COP are consistent with ethical relativism. One of the tenets of COP is that community values should determine what is "good" in police work. But what a particular neighborhood considers good police work may result in the police tolerating certain types of illegal behavior or in officers engaging in illegal tactics to solve problems (e.g., conducting illegal searches of suspected drug dealers). Inside Policing 11.12 describes an incident in a California city in which ethical relativism resulted in police officers tolerating illegal behavior.

## Ethical Dilemmas

Police confront profound ethical dilemmas. To fail to recognize this fact is to fail to understand the nature of policing. An ethical dilemma central to the craft of policing is the conflict between means and ends.

In their day-to-day practice, police confront what is widely called the "Dirty Harry" problem—that is, a conflict between means and ends. The end is so obviously good that

---

**INSIDE POLICING 11.12**   **Ethical Relativism and the Law in Police Work**

In Santa Ana, California, in the early 1980s, most of the people who frequented the downtown part of the city at night were overwhelmingly Mexican. This area in effect became a *corso*, a customary part of Spanish life in which mariachi bands play and sing in cafes and bars and then come out onto the street, creating a festive atmosphere. Some of the persons participating in the *corso* were illegal aliens, but police officers made no attempt to determine the status of those individuals who frequented the area. In addition, officers did not usually provide assistance to agents of the Immigration and Naturalization Service (INS), whom many city residents called the "green gestapo" (referring to the green card that legal residents are supposed to have). In fact, the police department had a history of not cooperating with the INS, because the police chief did not agree with the methods used by INS agents to identify and arrest illegal aliens (many of whom were otherwise law-abiding).

Known prostitutes also frequented the downtown area at night. One prostitute, Sugar, was a drug addict who had four children. Sugar openly solicited young men to have sex. In one incident, Sugar met a young man on the street, engaged him in a short conversation, and then walked together with him around the corner of a building to a more private area. When the young man returned, a foot patrol officer called out in Spanish, "How was it?" The bystanders, who apparently knew what was going on, laughed at the young man's obvious embarrassment. The officer in question said: "We don't arrest these people [because] they are young men . . . who work hard [to] save up money to bring their families from Mexico. . . . They're gonna have sex. There just isn't any point in arresting people for having sex."

Note that in this example, the community—meaning those individuals who frequented the downtown area at night—openly tolerated the practice of prostitution by drug addicts; consequently, the police ignored this illegal behavior as long as prostitutes did not appear to be under the influence of drugs at the time of the sexual activity. In addition, some officers undoubtedly thought it would be pointless to enforce laws against prostitution in such circumstances. This example also illustrates how community values can be in conflict with laws enforced by other government agencies, such as the INS.

*SOURCE*: Adapted from J. H. Skolnick and D. H. Bayley, *The New Blue Line* (New York: Free Press, 1986), 40–43.

they feel compelled to pursue it, yet there are not legal means to do so. Should the officer use illegal or "dirty" means to pursue an unquestionably good end? Klockars (1991, 414) notes that police will tend to justify dirty means if "what must be known and, importantly, known before the act is committed, is that it will result in the achievement of the good end."

Klockars presented a compelling argument that the Dirty Harry problem is at the core of the police role. Police tend to think that they are dealing with people who are factually, if not legally, guilty. Consequently, an officer's belief in the certainty of guilt is not always determined by factual accuracy but by police cultural standards: "Dirty Harry problems," Klockars (1991, 414) observes, "can arise wherever restrictions are placed on police methods and are particularly likely to do so when police themselves perceive that those restrictions are undesirable, unreasonable, or unfair." In other words, Dirty Harry problems are probably more widespread, and less certain in the likelihood of factual guilt, than the police think they are.

The particular ways that means-versus-ends conflicts affect police work are expanded by Crank and Caldero (1991). The core of police work, they argue, is the "noble cause" (see Chapter 9). This is the belief in the absolute rightness of doing something about criminals. It is a compelling commitment to "get bad guys off the street." Police, they note, not only dislike lawbreakers and troublemakers but also identify intensely with victims of crime and feel a moral responsibility for their assignments. The "noble cause" is corrupted when police consider it justifiable to break the law to apprehend or punish suspected wrongdoers. Noble-cause corruption means that officers are willing to violate legal means to achieve a noble end (Delattre 1996). Officers, Crank and Caldero (1991) contend, are hired into policing already morally committed to the idea of the noble cause. They are frequently hostile to due process ideas at the time they are hired, and police culture reinforces this hostility. Only later in their career, as they move up the departmental ladder and gain a broader perspective, do some officers begin to understand how the police are part of a larger system of competing moral values.

Noble-cause corruption takes many different forms. It includes testifying wrongly or testimonial deception (Barker 1996), fluffing up evidence (Barker and Carter 1999), and in more extreme cases, drug corruption (Manning and Redlinger 1977). It encompasses all situations in which police bend the rules to sustain an arrest or obtain a conviction.

## The Limits of Professional and Ethical Standards

The idea that codes of conduct can prevent misconduct seems reasonable, yet prevention has proven to be difficult. First, although professional and ethical standards provide a good model for police work, they may have limited impact on its reality. They tend to be in written form, presented to satisfy external audiences, with little impact on day-to-day police behavior.

Second, the need for controls is driven to a certain extent by the people-based, unpredictable nature of police work. This same unpredictability, however, limits the effectiveness of those controls. And unpredictability cannot be removed from police–citizen interactions (Harmon 1995).

Third, the study of ethics can result in the development of arguments to justify deviating from established ethical or professional standards. Officers who subscribe to different ethical schools of thought may use those schools to justify their behavior. It is not hard to review the research on police ethics, for example, to find adequate justification for breaking the law to get bad guys off the street, if that is what a police officer believes in.

## W. Craig Hartley, Jr.

*Executive Director, Commission on Accreditation for Law Enforcement Agencies*

As the director of an organization with the core purpose of enhancing professionalism in the field of public safety, promoting accountability in the industry is a key objective. In fact, the entire accreditation process used by the Commission on Accreditation for Law Enforcement Agencies (CALEA) is anchored to the promulgation and administration of standards that allow participating agencies to demonstrate compliance with best practices. The process inherently creates accountability measures within the organization and with its external customers and stakeholders.

Although the process of accreditation provides compelling returns on investment, it can only be successful through sound leadership and a clear understanding on the part of public safety service providers and support personnel regarding their roles and relationships to the community. Therefore, creating an organization sensitive to these issues is critical. This can be accomplished through meaningful oaths of office, policies and procedures that reference the public as customers, review processes that take into consideration the impact of actions on victims and witnesses, and systems that adhere to guiding principles such as honesty, integrity, stewardship, and respect. These actions provide a framework for accountability, while the culture of the entity must be influenced in a positive way by those responsible for its leadership.

The leadership of accountable organizations must have open discussions about corporate expectations that are specifically related to contemporary public policy issues, including such matters as use of force and the involvement of the agency as a component of the broader criminal justice system. They should encourage personnel to ask questions to refine understanding in terms of the impact of their involvement with the community. Leaders should monitor for prevailing organization themes that do not complement the respective oaths of office and mission, and they should require training curriculums that expose examples of behaviors that are in line with core purposes. Public safety leaders should watch for benchmarking opportunities with other professional organizations and boldly accept new approaches to resolve service delivery challenges, explaining these efforts to personnel and the public.

In today's environment, it is essential for public safety organizations to accept accountability as a fundamental attribute of its service delivery model. The use of special tools like accreditation can help in shaping the desired culture; however, success will always rely on leaders and practitioners who understand why they serve and who they are obligated to protect. Armed with this information, decisions become clearer and accountability measures easier to align.

Fourth, the manner in which officers carry out their day-to-day activities is affected as much by informal group ethics—the "ethics of the street"—as by any of the ethical schools discussed. The exercise of discretion, whether or not officers follow departmental standards or the law, use force, lie, accept gratuities, or engage in other corrupt practices, may be affected as much by peer group processes as formal ethical and professional standards.

Price (1996, 87) sums up the challenge confronting the police in her essay on the quest for professionalism:

> Eradicating the excessive use of force and the scourge of police corruption are the most critical internal issues police face if they are to continue the long and arduous course toward professionalism. There have been many successes of late for law enforcement,

especially in communications technology, forensics, information systems, interagency cooperation, and the development of a commitment to their peers, if not to professional conduct. But until attitudes of the police towards those they serve can be changed, they will continue to make their own jobs more difficult and more dangerous—and professionalism for the police will not come to pass.

In "Voices from the Field," W. Craig Hartley Jr., the executive director of CALEA, presents his view on police accountability.

## Summary

Police accountability is concerned with controlling line-officer behavior. Two kinds of accountability mechanisms are oversight (internal and external) and standards (professional and ethical). Internal oversight mechanisms include bureaucratic procedure, internal investigation, and EWS or early identification systems. The primary external mechanisms of accountability are citizen review boards and police auditors. Officers are controlled primarily through administrative procedures. Internal investigations are usually associated with internal affairs units; external review is usually associated with civilian review boards.

Two primary sources of standards for police officers are professional and ethical training. The police professionalization movement has historically represented efforts to make the police occupation a profession. However, because of its preoccupation with the image of the department, it focused on controlling the behavior of line officers. Other trends in policing are consistent with ideas of professionalism at the individual level. These include COP, efforts to expand and refine police discretion, and advances in functional research. The expansion of police professional organizations, state standards organizations, and accreditation all indicate increasing levels of police professionalism.

By considering different ethical schools of thought, one can see how officers facing the same problem might come to different solutions. The Dirty Harry dilemma, for example, is commonly confronted by police officers and has no easy solution.

## Critical Thinking Questions

1. Which is more effective for controlling police behavior: an internal affairs unit or a civilian review board? Why?

2. Should internal affairs be reactive or proactive? Which would be more effective? Why?

3. Which is a more effective method of external oversight of the police: a civilian review board or a police auditor? Why?

4. How would each of the three ethical perspectives assess the Dirty Harry problem? As a citizen, how do you want the police to respond in Dirty Harry situations?

5. How would you (as an officer or a citizen) respond to witnessing an instance of police misconduct?

6. As a citizen, would you feel comfortable going to your local police precinct to file a complaint?

## References

Alpert, G., and Smith, W. 1999. "Developing Police Policy: An Evaluation of the Control Principle." In L. K. Gaines and G. W. Cordner (eds.), *Policing Perspectives: An Anthology*, pp. 353–362. Los Angeles: Roxbury.

Alpert, G., and Walker, S. 2000. "Police Accountability and Early Warning Systems: Developing Policies and Programs." *Justice Research and Policy* 2: 59–72.

Ariel, B., Farrar, W., and Sutherland, A. 2015. "The Effect of Police Body-Worn Cameras on Use of Force and Citizens' Complaints against the Police: A Randomized Controlled Trial." *Journal of Quantitative Criminology* 31: 509–535.

Ariel, B., Sutherland, A., Henstock, D., Yound, J., Drover, P., Sykes, J., Megicks, S., and Henderson, R. 2016. "Wearing Body-Cameras Increases Assaults Against Officers and Do Not Reduce Police-Use of Force: Results from a Global Multisite Experiment." *European Journal of Criminology* 136 744–755.

Ariel, B., Sutherland, A., Henstock, D., Young, J., Drover, P., Sykes, J., Megicks, S., and Henderson, R. 2017. "A Global Multisite Randomized Controlled Trial on the Effect of Body-Worn Cameras on Citizens' Complaints Against the Police." *Criminal Justice and Behavior* 44: 293–316.

Arthur, R. 2015 "How to Predict Bad Cops in Chicago." *FiveThirtyEight.com*, December 15. https://fivethirtyeight.com/features/how-to-predict-which-chicago-cops-will-commit-misconduct/.

Auten, J. 1988. "Preparing Written Guidelines." *FBI Law Enforcement Bulletin* 57: 1–7.

Barker, T. 1996. *Police Ethics: Crisis in Law Enforcement.* Springfield, IL: Thomas.

Barker, T., and Carter, D. 1999. "Fluffing Up Evidence and Covering Your Ass: Some Conceptual Notes on Police Lying." In L. K. Gaines and G. W. Cordner (eds.), *Policing Perspectives: An Anthology,* pp. 342–350. Los Angeles: Roxbury.

Berg, B. 1994. "Education v. Training." In A. Roberts (ed.), *Critical Issues in Crime and Justice,* pp. 93–109. Thousand Oaks, CA: Sage.

Bittner, E. 1970. *The Functions of Police in Modern Society.* Boston: Northeastern University Press.

Bobb, M. 2007. *Los Angeles County Sheriff's Department: 23rd Semi-Annual Report.* Los Angeles: Police Assessment Resource Center.

Braga, A. A., MacDonald, J. M., and McCabe, J. 2021 "Body-Worn Cameras, Lawful Police Stops, and NYPD Officer Compliance: A Cluster Randomized Controlled Trial." Criminology 21 124–158.

Brandl, S. G., Stroshine, M. S., and Frank, J. 2001. "Who Are the Complaint-Prone Officers? An Examination of the Relationship Between Police Officers' Attributes, Arrest Activity, Assignment, and Citizens' Complaints About Excessive Force." *Journal of Criminal Justice* 29: 521–529.

Caiden, G. E. 1977. *Police Revitalization.* Lexington, MA: Heath.

Carter, D. 1994. "Police Disciplinary Procedures: A Review of Selected Police Departments." In T. Barker and D. Carter (eds.), *Police Deviance,* 3rd ed., pp. 355–376. Cincinnati, OH: Anderson.

Carter, D., and Barker, T. 1994. "Administrative Guidance and the Control of Police Officer Behavior: Policies, Procedures, and Rules." In T. Barker and D. Carter (eds.), *Police Deviance,* 3rd ed., pp. 13–28. Cincinnati, OH: Anderson.

Commission on Peace Officer Standards and Training. 2016. https://post.ca.gov/About-Us.

Cordner, G. W. 1989. "Written Rules and Regulations: Are They Necessary?" *FBI Law Enforcement Bulletin* 58(7): 17–21.

Cordner, G. W., and Williams, G. L. 1995. "The CALEA Standards: What Is the Fit with Community Policing?" *National Institute of Justice Journal* 229: 39–40.

Cordner, G. W., and Williams, G. L 1996. "Community Policing and Accreditation: A Content Analysis of CALEA Standards." In L. T. Hoover (ed.), *Quantifying Quality in Policing,* pp. 243–261. Washington, DC: Police Executive Research Forum.

Cordner, G. W., and Williams, G. L. 1999. "Community Policing and Police Agency Accreditation." In L. Gaines and G. W. Cordner (eds.), *Policing Perspectives: An Anthology,* pp. 372–379. Los Angeles: Roxbury.

Crank, J. P., and Caldero, M. A. 1991. "The Production of Occupational Stress Among Line Officers." *Journal of Criminal Justice* 19: 339–350.

Cullen, J. B. 1978. *The Structure of Professionalism.* Princeton, NJ: Princeton University Press.

D'Arcy, S. 1990. *Internal Affairs Unit Guidelines.* San Jose, CA: San Jose Police Department.

De Angelis, J., Rosenthal, R., and Buchner, B. 2016. *Civilian Oversight of Law Enforcement: Assessing the Evidence.* Tucson: National Association for Civilian Oversight of Law Enforcement.

Delattre, E. J. 1996. *Character and Cops: Ethics in Policing,* 3rd ed. Washington, DC: American Enterprise Institute.

Dugan, J. R., and Breda, D. R. 1991. "Complaints About Police Officers: A Comparison Among Types and Agencies." *Journal of Criminal Justice* 19: 165–171.

Editorial Board. 2021. "Police Who Violate Bill of Rights don't deserve protection by local laws and unions." *USA Today*, July 15. https://www.usatoday.com/story/opinion/todaysdebate/2021/07/14/george-floyd-murder-end-police-shield-laws/7904187002/.

Fogelson, R. 1977. *Big-City Police*. Cambridge, MA: Harvard University Press.

*Garrity v. New Jersey*, 385 US 483 (1967).

Geison, G. L. (ed.). 1983. *Professions and Professional Ideologies in America*. Chapel Hill: University of North Carolina Press.

Geller, W. A. (ed.). 1985. *Police Leadership in America: Crisis and Opportunity*. New York: Praeger.

Goldstein, J. 1998. "Police Discretion Not to Invoke the Criminal Justice Process: Low Visibility Decisions in the Administration of Justice." In G. F. Cole and M. G. Gertz (eds.), *The Criminal Justice: Politics and Policies*, 7th ed., pp. 85–103. Belmont, CA: Wadsworth.

Hall, R. 1968. "Professionalization and Bureaucratization." *American Sociological Review* 33: 92–104.

Harmon, M. M. 1995. *Responsibility as Paradox: A Critique of Rational Discourse on Government*. Thousand Oaks, CA: Sage.

Helsby, J., Carton, S., Joseph, K., Mahmud, A., Park, Y., Navarrete, A., Ackermann, K., Walsh, J., Haynes, L., Cody, C., Patterson, E., and Ghani, R. 2018. "Early Intervention Systems: Predicting Adverse Interactions Between Police and the Public." *Criminal Justice Policy Review* 29(2): 190–209.

Hickman, M. J. 2006. *Citizen Complaints About Police Use of Force*. Washington, DC: US Department of Justice, Office of Justice Programs.

Holiday, B. S., and Wagstaff, J. H. 2021. "The Relationship Between Citizen Oversight and Procedural Justice Measures in Policing: An Exploratory Study." *American Journal of Criminal Justice*. https://doi.org/10.1007/s12103-021-09610-3.

Holmes, M. D., and Smith, B. W. 2008. *Race and Police Brutality: Roots of an Urban Dilemma*. Albany: State University of New York Press.

Hyland, S. S. 2018. *Body-Worn Cameras in Law Enforcement Agencies, 2018*. Washington, DC: Bureau of Justice Statistics.

Independent Commission on the Los Angeles Police Department. 1991. *Report*. Los Angeles: California Public Management Institute.

Iris, M. 2002. "Police Discipline in Houston: The Arbitration Experience." *Police Quarterly* 5: 132–151.

Jennings, W., Lynch, M. D., and Fridell, L. A. 2015. "Evaluating the Impact of Police Officer Body-Worn Cameras (BWCs) on Response-to-Resistance and Serious External Complaints: Evidence from the Orlando Police Department (OPD) Experience Utilizing a Randomized Controlled Experiment." *Journal of Criminal Justice* 43: 480–486.

Keenan, K. M., and Walker, S. 2010. "An Impediment to Police Accountability? An Analysis of Statutory Law Enforcement Officers' Bills of Rights." *Public Interest Law Journal* 14: 185–244.

Klockars, C. 1991. "The Dirty Harry Problem." In C. Klockars and S. D. Mastrofski (eds.), *Thinking About Police: Contemporary Readings*, pp. 428–438. New York: McGraw-Hill.

Kuykendall, J., and Roberg, R. R. 1990. "Police Professionalism: The Organizational Attribute." *Journal of Contemporary Criminal Justice* 6: 49–59.

Lersch, K., Bazley, T., and Mieczkowski, T. 2006. "Early Intervention Programs: An Effective Police Accountability Tool, or Punishment of the Productive?" *Policing: An International Journal of Police Strategies and Management* 29: 58–76.

Lersch, K., and Mieczkowski, T. 1996. "Who Are the Problem-Prone Officers? An Analysis of Citizen Complaints." *American Journal of Police* 15: 23–44.

Lum, C., Koper, C. S., Gill, C., Hibdon, J., Telep, C., and Robinson, L. 2016. *An Evidence-Assessment of the Recommendations of the President's Task Force on Twenty-First Century Policing—Implementation and Research Priorities*. Fairfax, VA: Center for Evidence-Based Crime Policy, George Mason University. Alexandria, VA: International Association of Chiefs of Police.

Lum, C., Stoltz, M., Koper, C. S. and Scherer, J. A. 2019 "Research on Body-Worn Cameras: What We Know, What We Need to Know." *Criminology & Public Policy* 18 93–118.

Manning, P. K. 1978. "Rules, Colleagues, and Situationally Justified Actions." In P. K. Manning and J. Van Maanen (eds.), *Policing: A View from the Street*, pp. 71–89. Santa Monica, CA: Goodyear.

Manning, P. K. 1998. *Police Work: The Social Organization of Policing*, 2nd ed. Prospect Heights, IL: Waveland.

Manning, P. K., and Redlinger, L. 1977. "Invitational Edges of Corruption: Some Consequences of Narcotic Law Enforcement." In P. Rock (ed.), *Drugs and Politics*, pp. 279–310. New Brunswick, NJ: Society/Transaction Books.

Mastrofski, S. 1990. "The Prospects of Change in Police Patrol: A Decade in Review." *American Journal of Police* 9: 1–79.

McAllister, B. 1987. "Spurred by Dramatic Rise in Lawsuits, Police Agencies Warm to Accreditation." *Washington Post*, March 17: A7.

McMullan, J. 1998. "Social Surveillance and the Rise of the Police Machine." *Theoretical Criminology* 2: 93–117.

Murphy, P. V., and Caplan, G. 1991. "Fostering Integrity." In W. A. Geller (ed.), *Local Government Police Management*, pp. 239–271. Washington, DC: International City Management Association.

National Advisory Commission on Civil Disorders. 1968. *Report*. Washington, DC: US Government Printing Office.

National Commission on the Causes and Prevention of Violence. 1969. *To Establish Justice, to Ensure Domestic Tranquility*. Washington, DC: US Government Printing Office.

Nurre, S. 2008. *Year-End Report*. San Jose, CA: Office of the Independent Police Auditor.

Oettmeier, T. N. 1993. "Can Accreditation Survive the '90s?" In J. W. Bizzack (ed.), *Issues in Policing: New Perspectives*, pp. 96–112. Lexington, KY: Autumn House.

Perez, D. 1994. *Common Sense About Police Review*. Philadelphia: Temple University Press.

Petterson, W. E. 1991. "Police Accountability and Civilian Oversight of Policing: An American Perspective." In A. J. Goldsmith (ed.), *Complaints Against the Police: The Trend to External Review*, pp. 259–289. Avon, UK: Bookcraft.

Pollock, J. M. 1997. "Ethics and Law Enforcement." In R. G. Dunham and G. P. Alpert (eds.), *Critical Issues in Policing*, 3rd ed., pp. 337–354. Prospect Heights, IL: Waveland.

Pollock-Byrne, J. M. 1998. *Ethics in Crime and Justice: Dilemmas and Decisions*, 3rd ed. Belmont, CA: West/Wadsworth.

President's Commission on Law Enforcement and Administration of Justice. 1967. *Task Force Report: The Police*. Washington, DC: US Government Printing Office.

President's Task Force on 21st Century Policing. 2015. *Final Report of the President's Task Force on Twenty-First Century Policing*. Washington, DC: Office of Community Oriented Policing Services.

Price, B. R. 1996. "Police and the Quest for Professionalism." In J. Sullivan and J. Victor (eds.), *Criminal Justice: Annual Editions 96/97*, pp. 86–87. Guilford, CT: Brown and Benchmark.

Regoli, R., Crank, J. P., Culbertson, R., and Poole, E. 1988. "Linkages Between Professionalization and Professionalism Among Police Chiefs." *Journal of Criminal Justice* 16: 89–98.

Reuss-Ianni, E. 1983. *Two Cultures of Policing: Street Cops and Management Cops*. New Brunswick, NJ: Transaction Books.

Rhoades, P. W. 1991. "Political Obligation: Connecting Police Ethics and Democratic Values." *American Journal of Police* 10: 1–22.

Schein, E. H. 1985. *Organization Culture and Leadership*. San Francisco: Jossey-Bass.

Schulz, D. M. 2022. Wandering Cops: How State Can Keep Rogue Officers from Slipping Through the Cracks. New York: Manhattan Institute.

Sherman, L. W. 1999. "Policing for Crime Prevention." In C. Eskridge (ed.), *Criminal Justice: Concepts and Issues*, 3rd ed., pp. 131–148. Los Angeles, CA: Roxbury.

Sherman, L., Gottfredson, D., MacKensie, D., Eck, J., Reuter, P., and Bushway, S. 1997. *Preventing Crime: What Works, What Doesn't, and What's Promising*. Washington, DC: US Department of Justice.

Skogan, W., and Frydl, K. (eds.). 2004. *Fairness and Effectiveness in Policing: The Evidence*. Washington, DC: National Research Council.

Skolnick, J. 1994. *Justice Without Trial: Law Enforcement in Democratic Society*, 3rd ed. New York: Wiley.

Skolnick, J., and Bayley, D. 1986. *The New Blue Line. Police Innovation in Six American Cities*. New York: Free Press.

Sparrow, M., Moore, M., and Kennedy, D. 1990. *Beyond 911: A New Era for Policing*. New York: Basic Books.

Sykes, G. W. 1994. "Accreditation and Community Policing: Passing Fads or Basic Reforms?" *Journal of Contemporary Criminal Justice* 10: 1–16.

Terrill, R. J. 1991. "Civilian Oversight of the Police Complaints Process in the United States." In A. J. Goldsmith (ed.), *Complaints Against the Police: The Trend to External Review*, pp. 291–322. Avon, UK: Bookcraft.

Terrill, T. and Ingram, J. R.. 2016. "Citizen Complaints against the Police: An Eight City Examination." *Police Quarterly* 19: 150–179.

Walker, S. 1998. *Sense and Nonsense About Crime and Drugs: A Policy Guide*, 4th ed. Pacific Grove, CA: Brooks/Cole.

Walker, S. 2001. *Police Accountability: The Role of Citizen Oversight*. Belmont, CA: Wadsworth.

Walker, S. 2003a. "Citizen Oversight, 2003: Developments and Prospects." *New York State Government, Law and Policy Journal* 5: 5–10.

Walker, S. 2003b. "Core Principles for an Effective Police Auditor's Office." A Report of the First National Police Auditors Conference, Omaha, NE, March 26–27. https://samuelwalker.net/wp-content/uploads/2010/06/coreprinciples.pdf.

Walker, S. 2003c. *Early Intervention Systems for Law Enforcement Agencies: A Planning and Management Guide*. Washington, DC: Office of Community Oriented Policing Services.

Walker, S. 2005. *The New World of Police Accountability*. Thousand Oaks, CA: Sage.

Walker, S., and Archbold, C. A. 2014. *The New World of Police Accountability*, 2nd ed. Thousand Oaks, CA: Sage.

Walker, S., and Bumphus, V. W. 1991. *Civilian Review of the Police: A National Review of the 50 Largest Cities*. Omaha: University of Nebraska.

Walker, S., and Graham, N. 1998. "Citizen Complaints in Response to Police Misconduct: The Results of a Victimization Survey." *Police Quarterly* 1: 65–89.

Walker, S., and Kreisel, B. W. 1996. "Varieties of Citizen Review: The Implications of Organizational Features of Complaint Review Procedures for Accountability of the Police." *American Journal of Police* 15: 65–88.

Wallace, B. 1990. "S. F. Watchdog Upholds Few Charges." *San Francisco Chronicle*, May 29: 1, 4–6.

West, P. 1988. "Investigation of Complaints against the Police." *American Journal of Police* 8: 101–121.

White, M. D. 2014. *Police Officer Body-Worn Cameras: Assessing the Evidence*. Washington, DC: Office of Community Oriented Policing Services.

Williams, G. L. 1989. *Making the Grade: The Benefits of Law Enforcement Accreditation*. Washington, DC: Police Executive Research Forum.

Wilson, J. Q., and Kelling, G. 1982. "Broken Windows: The Police and Neighborhood Safety." *Atlantic Monthly,* March 1: 29–38.

Wilson, O. W. 1950. *Police Administration*. New York: McGraw-Hill.

Worden, R. E., Harris, C. J., Pratte, M. A., Dorn, S. E. and Hyland, S. S. 2013. "Intervention with Problem Officers: An Outcome Evaluation of an EIS Intervention." *Criminal Justice and Behavior*, 40: 409–437.

**Part IV**

# Contemporary
# Issues

# CHAPTER 12

# Diversity and Inclusion

## CHAPTER OUTLINE

## CHAPTER OUTLINE (continued)

- Future Prospects
- Summary
- Critical Thinking Questions
- References

### KEY TERMS

- affirmative action plan
- civil service system
- de-feminization
- diversity
- double marginality
- empirical evidence

- merit system
- police culture
- police*women*
- *police*women
- quid pro quo harassment

- representative bureaucracy
- sexual harassment
- structural characteristics
- testimonial evidence

POLICING IN AMERICA REMAINS a white, male-dominated industry, even after decades of calls from reformers to diversify policing in terms of race, ethnicity, and gender. Indeed, representation of females and racial/ethnic minorities has increased during the past 30 years; however, these groups remain underrepresented in most police organizations, particularly in smaller and rural police departments, which make up the overwhelming majority of departments in the United States. As America continues to become more diverse, the **diversity** of police departments has again become important for both political and performance reasons.

This chapter presents a variety of perspectives on the benefits of diversity and inclusion within policing, including the current state of diversity in America. First, we provide a historical overview of racial minorities in policing, and then of women in policing. We next discuss legal and organizational responses to enhancing diversity, including affirmative action and equal employment opportunity. Finally, we present "where we are now" based on the best data available and discuss strategies (and challenges) associated with making racial and gender representation a reality.

## Setting the Stage

In general, more diverse police departments are considered more effective than less diverse organizations. Diversity has become so important that it is often considered a significant strategy to reform departments with performance problems, particularly as they relate to the use of force and community fear and distrust. Organizational theorists contend diversity in public agencies can enhance overall performance, and that agencies which reflect the population they serve are more likely to function properly, be responsive to the needs and desires of minority populations, and enhance the legitimacy of the public agency. This perspective is **representative bureaucracy**, which posits that "diversity within the public workforce, especially in terms of characteristics such as race and ethnicity, will help ensure that the interests of diverse groups are represented in policy formulation" (Bradbury and Kellough 2008, p. 697). Public agencies, like police departments, that are more representative of their population reinforce their commitment to equal access to power, accurately reflect group preferences, enhance group willingness to cooperate, and are a more efficient use of resources (Selden 1997; Kennedy 2012; Morabito and Shelley 2015).

There are two different dimensions to representative bureaucracy. First, passive representation is determined by a ratio of group membership within the organization to the population it serves. In other words, in a city that serves a population of 25 percent racial minorities, perfect passive representation suggests that 25 percent of the police department would be racial minorities. Second, active representation is how the composition of the department impacts outputs and policies, in that a more representative police department will produce more equitable outputs (Kennedy 2012; Morabito and Shelley 2015) or produce outputs that benefit those who are passively represented (Meier 1993). Whereas passive representation is determined in a relatively straightforward manner, active representation may be more challenging to measure. Also, it appears that passive representation is a precursor to active representation—theoretically, a less diverse police department will have a more difficult time producing equitable outputs. The President's Task Force on Twenty-First Century Policing (2015, 16) appears to echo this perspective and recommends the following:

> Law enforcement agencies should strive to create a workforce that contains a broad range of diversity including race, gender, language, life experience, and cultural background to improve understanding and effectiveness in dealing with all communities.

This recommendation suggests that enhancing diversity can benefit police departments and, as a corollary, that a lack of diversity can harm police departments. The US Department of Justice (2015) conducted an investigation of the Ferguson (MO) Police Department after the shooting of Michael Brown and subsequent civil unrest, and concluded that the department's lack of diversity undermined community trust. The Department of Justice went on to indicate the Ferguson Police Department "can and should do more to attract and hire a more diverse group of qualified police officers" (US Department of Justice 2015, 89), but also cautioned that increasing (passive) representation alone may not be enough—it is a necessary but only initial step to reform within Ferguson. The investigation went on to say that diversity of all types—including race, ethnicity, sex, national origin, religion, sexual orientation, and gender identity—can be beneficial both to police–community relationships and the culture of the law enforcement agency. Increasing gender and sexual orientation diversity in policing may be critical in re-making internal police culture and creating new assumptions about what makes policing effective (US Department of Justice 2015, 89).

An ambitious, comprehensive study of police–public interactions in Chicago (Ba et al. 2021) supports these recommendations from the President's Task Force, the Department of Justice investigation of the Ferguson Police Department, and the benefits positioned by representative bureaucracy. Researchers compiled data on millions of officer shifts involving thousands of officers over four years to assess the impact of diversity. They applied a variety of statistical controls to compare outcomes and activities across race and gender in similar neighborhoods, shifts, and contexts. They concluded that Black officers made significantly fewer arrests, used less force, made fewer stops, and engaged in significantly fewer high-discretion strops (e.g., "suspicious behavior"). Black officers were 39 percent less likely than white officers to stop Black citizens. Similar patterns were observed for Hispanic officers. Female officers made fewer arrests than male officers, particularly involving Black citizens. The researchers noted that these results are consistent with those advocating for racial and gender diversification in policing as a strategy to reduce abusive policing and mass incarceration, particularly in Black communities. Noting that violent and sometimes fatal encounters occur involving white officers and racial minorities, they

**INSIDE POLICING 12.1** | **Black Cops in Baltimore**

Reformers emphasize the importance of diversity within police ranks, but that doesn't seem to have helped the Baltimore Police Department over the last 20 years or so. This article discusses the experiences of Black officers within the department, including police commissioners, and why crime and community-relations problems have persisted.

**Discussion Question:** Is it reasonable to expect that as police departments diversify, this inclusion will translate to lower crime rates? Why or why not?

SOURCE: *Modern Policing* blog, February 19, 2016, https://www.oup.com/cordner/black-cops-in-baltimore/

conclude that the results "strongly suggest that diversification can reshape police-civilian encounters" (Ba et al. 2021, 701). Inside Policing 12.1 discusses Baltimore's challenges to diversify their police department.

The evidence regarding the impact of diversity on police effectiveness can be categorized as either testimonial or empirical. **Testimonial evidence** is based on the opinions of individuals who have strong political beliefs about the importance of diversity or whose experience (e.g., as citizens or police officers) has led them to believe that a diverse department is either more or less effective. In general, testimonial evidence about the effectiveness of diversity is usually favorable. **Empirical evidence** regarding the efficacy of diversity based on data is derived from the systematic study of one or more effectiveness criteria (e.g., crime rates, arrest rates, and citizen trust of police or fewer complaints, civil suits, and confrontations). It is not clear whether diversity makes a measurable, sustained difference in the effectiveness of the police.

There is additional evidence that diversity can make a difference in some areas of police effectiveness at least in the short term. Weitzer (2000) analyzed surveys of three Washington, DC, communities, where each community possessed different racial and class characteristics, and found that citizens in middle-class communities reported that Black and white officers act similarly in their communities; however, citizens in disadvantaged communities were more likely to report perceived variations in officer behavior. Yet when asked whether they would prefer to have mostly white or mostly Black officers working in their neighborhood, Black and white teams, or no preference, most citizens indicated that they would prefer racially mixed policing teams or indicated no preference. This was true regardless of community racial characteristics or economic characteristics. Also, citizens in New York who came into contact with female officers (when they were first put on patrol) had a higher regard for the police department than before (Sichel et al. 1978). Having a diverse police department may also improve its effectiveness and efficiency. The police rely heavily on the active participation of citizens to achieve their goals, and police departments that lack diversity may be more challenged to accomplish them.

Historically, police departments have systematically discriminated against minorities and women in employment, assignments, promotions, and social acceptance. In addition, many white men have not, and do not, consider minorities and women their equals in terms of either capabilities or competencies. Beginning in the 1960s, governmental intervention was required to eliminate discrimination in employment and promotion.

Legally, and in terms of government policy, this intervention became known as affirmative action.

During the early to mid-1960s, inner-city riots and campus demonstrations occurred that were often sparked by police actions. These events raised questions that went to the very core of the police role and operations in a democratic society: Are the police isolated from the community? How important is it to have community representation in police departments? How important to the community are the nonenforcement aspects of the police role? What type of individuals should be recruited as police officers? As discussed, several national commission reports addressing these and other fundamental questions about the police cited the need to increase especially minority but also female representation throughout the police field. The following is a brief discussion of the history of minorities and women in policing.

## Racial Minorities in Policing

Little has been written about the early development of racial minority police officers in this country. Virtually all the available literature concerns African Americans and clarifies that Blacks and other minority members, until recently, have had little access to police. For example, although there were Black police officers in Washington, DC, as early as 1861 (Johnson 1947), by 1940 they represented less than 1 percent of the police population (Kuykendall and Burns 1980). Since World War II, however, there has been a steady increase in the proportions of Black officers, as well as other minorities, in policing. In general, although the proportions of Blacks and other minorities reflect the available workforce in some communities, most departments do not have minority personnel equal to their numbers in the available workforce (see the discussion under "Increasing Diversity in Police Departments").

Minority representation of police grew in many cities only due to pressure from the Black community. In Chicago, for instance, Black citizens frequently complained of the "stupidity, prejudice and brutality" of white officers (Gosnell 1935, 245). After 1940, the use of Black police increased due to the emerging political participation of Blacks. Liberal whites (Rudwick 1962) many times supported organized movements. Often, a church or civic group would become concerned about crime rates, law enforcement in Black areas, or race relations because of either racial tension or a desire for integration. Believing that using Black officers to patrol Black areas would substantially reduce Black hostility toward the police, community leaders would usually agree to make a few experimental appointments (Johnson 1947).

### Unequal Treatment

Although African Americans were increasingly being hired into policing, they were not treated equally in powers of arrest, work assignments, evaluations, and promotions. Frequently, Black officers were allowed to patrol only in Black areas and to arrest only other Black citizens. If a white person committed a crime in a Black neighborhood, a Black officer would have to call a white officer to make the arrest. In a 1959 survey of 130 cities and counties in the South, 69 required Black officers to call white officers in arresting white suspects, and 107 cities indicated that Black officers patrolled only in Black neighborhoods (Rudwick 1962). Elysee Scott, associated with the National Organization for Black Law Enforcement Executives, grew up in a small Louisiana town in the 1950s and remembers that the Black police officers rode in cars marked "Colored Police" and were allowed to arrest only "colored" people (Sullivan 1989).

Not only were Black officers frequently restricted in type and location of assignments, but superior officers negatively manipulated performance ratings. Dismissal because of race was also a possibility. In addition, Black and white officers rarely worked together (Gosnell 1935); even as late as 1966, squad cars were not completely integrated into the Chicago Police Department (National Center on Police and Community Relations 1967). Promotions were rare for Black officers. Leinen (1984) reported that in the mid-1960s, only 22 police departments had promoted Blacks above the rank of patrol officer. Even when promotions did occur, Blacks were not congratulated by whites or given duties involving active command. In at least one instance, Black lieutenants were assigned to walk a beat as patrol officers (Gosnell 1935). However, Hickman et al. (2001) found no direct effects of officer race on outcomes of internal department disciplinary procedures in their examination of Philadelphia police officers. This may suggest that the kinds of discrimination that did exist in the past are less common today.

## Performance of African American Police

As noted previously, the riots of the mid-1960s were a major reason that increased emphasis was placed on the role of minorities in policing. Because a large number of these riots were triggered by incidents involving white officers patrolling Black areas, many people thought that community relations would be improved if there were African American officers in these areas. Several national reports came to the same conclusion. For instance, the President's Commission on Law Enforcement and Administration of Justice (1967, 162) stated:

> Police officers have testified to the special competence of Negro officers in Negro neighborhoods. The reasons given include: they get along better and receive more respect from the Negro residents; they receive less trouble . . . they can get more information; and they understand Negro citizens better.

Early evidence to support the belief that Black officers would perform more satisfactorily in Black areas was mixed. On the one hand, many Black citizens wanted Black officers, because it would provide an opportunity for more public jobs, more understanding, less white police brutality, and more effective supervision of Black criminals (Myrdal 1944; Landrum 1947). On the other hand, Rudwick (1960) argued that Blacks from lower socioeconomic classes preferred white to Black officers. He found that poorer, uneducated Blacks frequently asked for white officers when in need of help and were more likely to plead guilty to a charge made by a white officer.

Some evidence indicates that Black officers are actually more punitive on Black citizens than white officers. In a study in Philadelphia in the 1950s, Kephart (1957) found that the majority of Black officers believed it was necessary to be "stricter" with their "own" people than they were with non-Blacks. Alex (1976) found that Black officers were actually challenged more by young Blacks and may have viewed themselves as protectors of the Black community. In contrast, Black officers needed to prove to the white officers that they were not biased and therefore treated Black suspects the same as they treated white suspects—or even more harshly. Contemporary research on this issue draws similar conclusions; Brown and Frank (2006) reported that Black officers were significantly more likely than white offers to arrest Black citizens.

In his influential book *Black in Blue* (1969), Alex termed this dilemma **double marginality**. This double marginality was evident by the mid-1960s, when the apparent desire of many Black citizens for Black police began to lose appeal. Studies conducted by

Sullivan, in San Diego and Philadelphia, for example, found that some Black citizens felt that Blacks who chose to become police officers were "selling them out" (Sullivan 1989). Of course, given the tenor of the times—police officers, in general, were viewed as enemies in minority communities—such a finding is hardly surprising. It is also interesting to note that although many still believe that predominantly minority neighborhoods need minority patrol officers, others view such an approach as a form of segregation. It is ironic that many of those same people who, during the riots of the 1960s, demanded that Black officers be sent into Black areas later condemned the same practice as racist (Sullivan 1989).

There is some evidence to suggest that the racial and ethnic composition of the police organization can influence behavior, but not in the manner that may be expected. Part of the rationale for diversifying police organizations was that minority officers may "police" minority communities differently. Historically, the white, male-dominated police were viewed as treating minorities more punitively, and presumably, this disparity would be less prevalent if minorities were more adequately represented within policing. Recent research has examined this phenomenon from the perspective of race and traffic stops specifically, determining whether the racial composition of police patrol divisions impacted the proportion of minorities stopped within that area. Even after taking the racial composition of the neighborhood into account, Wilkins and Williams (2008) found that increased representation of Black officers within a patrol division resulted in higher proportions of Blacks stopped. This was true also for ethnicity: patrol divisions with higher proportions of Hispanic officers had correspondingly higher proportions of Hispanics stopped (Wilkins and Williams 2009). This may be because of the impact of officer socialization—minority officers may be more likely to identify with other officers than with minority citizens, and racial/ethnic differences in police organizations alone may have little influence on reducing disparity in behavior.

Weitzer (2000) indicated that having racially mixed policing teams could have several benefits. First, the teams can have a moderating effect on officers of each race. This means that officers could "check and balance," or compensate for, the behavior of their partners. Second, racially mixed teams can lead to socializing each officer in ways to interact with citizens of different races. Third, racially mixed teams provide a symbolic benefit for the police department, indicating unity and cohesion between officers of different races. Based on these results, little benefit appears to ensue from adhering to the old style of assigning officers to communities based on the race of the officer or the makeup of the community (e.g., Black officers in predominantly Black communities and white officers in predominantly white communities). Inside Policing 12.2 highlights a Canadian approach to engaging police executives in authentic conversations about diversity and inclusion within policing.

## Women in Policing

Women remain significantly underrepresented in policing. This might be in part because the crime-fighter image often portrayed in policing does not coincide with social perceptions of acceptable female behavior. Policing often involves male-attributed activities, such as aggression and physical competence. Common characteristics associated with women (e.g., compassion, empathy, and nurturing) are seen as less needed, if not undesired, in police work (Milton 1972; Parsons and Jesilow 2001; Garcia 2003; DeJong 2004). Regardless of the reasons why women remain underrepresented in policing, it is often indicated that healthy and effective police organizations would benefit from a more integrated force.

> **INSIDE POLICING 12.2** | **Authentic Inclusion**
>
> The Canadian Association of Chiefs of Police sponsors an annual Global Studies course for selected mid-career staff. The 2018 cohort was assigned the topic "Equity, Inclusion and Fundamental Respect in the Diverse Policing Organization." In this article and report, class members discuss their initial trepidation and what they learned from tough conversations among themselves, in their home agencies, and from visits with police in 17 other countries. They concluded that diversity is largely a reality in Canadian policing, but authentic inclusion is much more challenging and difficult to achieve.
>
> **Discussion Question:** Are diversity and inclusion more challenging to achieve in a pluralistic nation such as the United States?
>
> SOURCE: *Modern Policing* blog, January 4, 2019, gcordner.wordpress.com/2019/01/04/authentic-inclusion/

At the beginning of the twentieth century, female officers were to aid male officers by performing duties deemed to be "unmasculine" or "not true police work," such as clerical work or supervising juveniles in custody. But contemporary policing operates with male and female officers enjoying equal police powers and responsibilities (Miller 1999; Garcia 2003; Miller and Hodge 2004). The first woman to hold full police powers was Lola Baldwin in Portland, Oregon, who in 1905 was hired in a social-work capacity to protect young girls and women and, in 1908, became the first female hired as a full-time paid police officer. Such a crime-prevention role was viewed as separate from the traditional police role; as Walker (1977, 85) notes, "Once the police began to think in terms of preventing juvenile delinquency, they responded to the traditional argument that women had a special capacity for child care." Between 1905 and 1915, several police departments copied Portland's example.

The policewoman idea achieved the status of an organized movement in 1910 with the appointment of Alice Stebbins-Wells to the Los Angeles Police Department (LAPD). Like Baldwin, Stebbins-Wells had a background in social work and was assigned to care for young women in trouble with the law and to prevent delinquency among juveniles of both sexes (Walker 1977). Stebbins-Wells became the national leader for the policewomen's movement, which lasted into the 1920s. Her appointment in turn led to the appointment of women to similar positions (as police social workers) in police departments in at least 16 cities by 1916 (Walker 1977). By 1925, 210 cities had women working in police positions—417 as police social workers and 355 as jail matrons (Owings 1925).

Between 1925 and 1965, both the numbers and the functions of policewomen increased, but only minimally. For example, a 1967 survey of police departments in the nation's largest cities indicated that there were only 1,792 women with police powers (Berkeley 1969). When they were represented on the force, policewomen typically comprised less than 2 percent of the personnel (Melchionne 1967; Eisenberg, Kent, and Wall 1973) and were excluded from patrol duties. During this period, most police departments had policies that not only discouraged the hiring of women but often included quotas, usually 1 percent or less (Simpson 1977).

## Unequal Treatment

Before the 1950s, the role of women in policing was restricted primarily to social welfare assignments, including dealing with juvenile and family problems; being prison matrons; detecting purse snatchers, pickpockets, and shoplifters; investigating sexual assault; and clerical work (Eisenberg et al. 1973). During the 1950s, their role was expanded to cover narcotics and vice investigations (Garmire 1978). Ironically, advocates for women in policing during this period tended to argue that women should be allowed to join the law enforcement profession because of their "unique" contributions, including their skills with women and children, defusing domestic violence, and doing undercover work (Melchionne 1967). Of course, such an argument likely added to the prevailing view that women could handle specialist activities in "their areas" but were not suited for general police work. As Balkin (1988, 30) notes, "It is an interesting if unanswered question why there was a reluctance to demand simple equality for women in police work." Undoubtedly, a large part of the answer lies in the strong tradition placed on the law enforcement (as opposed to social service) nature of the job. In addition, in their highly influential 1963 text Police Administration, Wilson and McLaren were firmly against the equal employment of women. They argued that although women could be of some value in specialized activities and units, they were not qualified to head such units. Men, they noted, were more effective administrators and "were less likely to become irritable and overly critical under emotional stress" (Wilson and McLaren 1963, 334).

In 1968, the first women were assigned to patrol work in the Indianapolis Police Department (Milton 1972). Within five years, many of the nation's largest police forces, including those of New York, Philadelphia, Miami, Washington, DC, and St. Louis, had women working in patrol (Sherman 1973). By 1979, the percentage of policewomen assigned to patrol was approximately 87 in city departments serving populations larger than 50,000 (Sulton and Townsey 1981). A comprehensive survey for the Police Foundation (1990) of municipal departments serving populations ranging from 50,000 to more than a million found that the integration of women into all police assignments has continued to grow at a steady pace. The data indicated that by 1986, 98 percent of the responding departments assigned women to patrol, and women were being assigned to field-operations units (including patrol, special operations, and traffic assignments) in slightly greater proportion than their overall representation in policing (Martin 1989). Today, females are assigned to virtually all police functions.

## Performance of Women Officers

Early critics of gender diversity in policing argued that women could not handle the physically demanding job of patrol, thus barring them from patrol work. The influence of officer gender on behavior is inconsistent and mixed, however, making it difficult to make firm statements or broad conclusions. There is conjecture that gender diversity will change policing, because females are presumed to be less aggressive and coercive and more nurturing and supportive than males. However, there is insufficient empirical evidence to support this stereotype (Skogan and Frydl 2004), and the evidence that does exist is often conflicting or highly contingent on the nature of the behavior being examined and the context of the situation. For example, early evaluations of the first generation of women patrol officers found their performance was highly satisfactory. The first study of women on patrol was conducted in Washington, DC, in 1973 (Bloch and Anderson 1974). A matched pair of 86 newly trained policewomen and policemen were placed on patrol and evaluated for one year. The results indicated that men and women performed in a generally similar manner.

Women responded to similar calls and had similar results in handling violent citizens. Some interesting differences were also found: women made fewer arrests but appeared to be more effective than men in defusing potentially violent situations. Additionally, women had a less aggressive style of policing and were less likely to be charged with improper conduct. The unmistakable conclusion drawn from these results was that female officers can perform effectively on patrol.

Two additional major studies closely followed the Washington study, both with similar conclusions. In 1975, Sherman evaluated policewomen on patrol in the St. Louis County Police Department; the first 16 women put on patrol in the county were compared with a group of 16 men who had been trained with the women officers. The results indicated that the women were equally as effective as the men in performing patrol work. And again, interesting differences were noted: women were less aggressive, made fewer arrests, and engaged in fewer preventive activities, such as car and pedestrian stops. Citizen surveys also indicated that women were more sensitive and responsive to their needs and handled service calls, especially domestic disturbances, better than men.

The second study (Sichel et al. 1978), conducted in New York City, was comparable to the Washington study in methodological rigor and sophistication. Comparison groups of 41 women and men officers with similar background characteristics were evaluated. Based on 3,625 hours of observation on patrol and some 2,400 police–citizen encounters, the results indicated that both groups of officers performed in a similar manner. However, women officers were again judged by citizens to be more respectful, pleasant, and competent; furthermore, citizens who came into contact with women officers tended to have a higher regard for the police department. Similar findings on the effectiveness of policewomen on patrol have been reported throughout the 1970s in departments of widely divergent sizes and geographical locations (Sichel et al. 1978).

A review of these studies (Morash and Greene 1986) pointed out that despite the generally favorable evaluations, gender biases were inherent in the study designs. For example, there was an emphasis on traits stereotypically associated with "maleness" and policing. In addition, approximately two-thirds of the policing situations observed were related to direct or potential violence, although such incidents are not frequently encountered. Also important, despite the studies finding differences in men's and women's behavior, they did not consider the possibility that the women's policing style in resolving conflicts and disputes, rather than escalating incidents into unnecessary arrests, might have had a beneficial rather than a negative effect. Public policing may indeed benefit from police styles that play down the values of coercive authority, conflict, and interpersonal violence.

Contemporary research presents mixed results on the influence of gender and behavior. Specifically, much of the extant research indicates that male and female officers make similar arrest decisions during encounters with suspects (Robinson 2000; Novak, Brown, and Frank 2011). Examinations of behavior beyond law enforcement draw similar conflicting conclusions. Research by Rabe-Hemp (2008) examined whether female officers engaged in different levels of social control during encounters with citizens. She categorized this controlling behavior as either lower levels (e.g., verbal commands or advising citizens to leave the scene or cease engaging in disorderly behavior or wrongdoing) or extreme levels (e.g., threatening, searching, interrogating, restraining, or arresting citizens). Furthermore, she examined gender difference in supporting behaviors, such as telling the citizen to seek assistance from family or friends, use the legal process, or file a complaint. She found that female officers were less likely than male officers to engage in extreme controlling behaviors. However, this cannot be interpreted as a criticism of female officers or otherwise suggest they are unable, unwilling, or incapable of engaging in such behavior—it is more plausible that female officers are able to de-escalate potentially physical confrontations with citizens. Meanwhile, she also reported that lower-level controlling behavior or the propensity to provide citizens with support did not vary across officer gender. Female officers were as likely to engage in verbal social control strategies as males, and male officers were as supportive as females. Rabe-Hemp (2008, 431) concludes that "assuming female officers manifest stereotypically feminine traits in policing tasks is clearly an overly simplistic conceptualization of the meaning and impact of gender in policing." Within the context of domestic violence, there is evidence suggesting that male and female officers exercise "controlling actions" at similar rates; however, female officers are also more likely to provide support to victims during these situations (Sun 2011).

Other studies also indicate that female officers use force and coercion at parity with their male counterparts. Paoline and Terrill (2004) found little difference between genders in the use of coercion by officers. Similarly, Hoffman and Hickey (2005) found that female officers used unarmed physical force during arrests at approximately the same rate as male officers. This represents a significant departure from the stereotypical belief that female officers, because of their gender, are less capable or willing to engage in this behavior. However, they also noted that female officers exercised force with a weapon (i.e., firearms, flashlights, batons, and oleoresin capsicum [OC] spray) at a lower rate than male officers. Thus, suspects were significantly less likely to endure injuries during encounters with female officers, because female officers were less likely to use weapons during these encounters. Bazley, Lersch, and Mieczkowski (2007, 190) found that although male and female officers employ force similarly, females "applied force levels within a narrower range of justifiable options than their male counterparts," suggesting that female officers respond differently to the level of resistance they encounter.

Finally, Parsons and Jesilow (2001) argue that the attitudes and behavior of female police officers differ little from those of their male counterparts. The authors attribute these similarities to several factors, including self-selection, department screening, and socialization. They posit that many women drawn to policing possess a propensity for the stereotypically masculine characteristics outlined previously (i.e., aggression, physical competence, logic, and stable emotions). Typically, police departments continue to select and train officers according to the traditional law enforcement orientation. They further find that occupational socialization contributes to similarities in values, beliefs, and behaviors for both men and women (although women often find this process more difficult and isolating than male officers). This has separated male and female officers alike from the general population. The result is a collection of male and female officers who are more similar than many might believe.

## Affirmative Action

The *Report on Police* by the National Advisory Commission on Criminal Justice Standards and Goals (1973, 329)' stated that "when a substantial ethnic minority population resides within the jurisdiction, the police agency should take affirmative action to achieve a ratio of minority group employees in approximate proportion to the makeup of the population." The National Advisory Commission on Civil Disorders (1968, 316) suggested that police departments should not only intensify their efforts in minority recruitment but also increase the numbers of minorities in supervisory positions. Attempts to remedy past discriminatory employment and promotional practices are reflected in an **affirmative action plan**. In other words, the department tries to make an affirmative, or positive, effort to redress past practices and ensure equal employment opportunity. Such plans have been developed voluntarily, although often with political pressure, or by court order following legal action.

In one study of the nation's 50 largest cities, Walker (1989) found that affirmative action plans appeared to play an important role in police employment trends. Nearly two-thirds (64 percent) of the departments reported operating under an affirmative action plan at some point during the five-year period examined. Interestingly, 23 of the affirmative action plans were court ordered, and only 7 were voluntary. McCrary (2007) examined whether court-ordered affirmative action litigation impacted the racial composition of police departments or city crime rates. A caution of affirmative action is that police departments may hire less-qualified, less-desirable individuals to meet court-imposed quotas, and that this would compromise public safety. McCrary compared 314 cities across more than 30 years and concluded that the litigation resulted in a 14 percent increase in hiring of Black officers. He also found little support that litigation impacted crime—affirmative action did not appear to adversely impact public safety. Much of the growth of minorities in policing over the past several decades can be attributed to affirmative action plans and policies.

The impact of affirmative action plans on recruiting females is less clear. Zhao, He, and Lovrich (2006) examined the hiring practices of a representative sample of police departments serving more than 25,000 residents to determine what factors impacted female recruitment between 1993 and 2000. They found that the proportion of female officers increased from 9.03 to 10.59 percent, with significant increases in white females (6.72 to 7.39 percent) and Hispanic females (0.50 to 0.80 percent). However, the proportion of Black female officers in police departments did not change significantly. The researchers went on to examine what factors did explain these changes. They found that although informal affirmative action plans increased the proportion of females overall, and of white females in particular, informal affirmative action plans were unrelated to the proportion of Black and Hispanic females. Furthermore, police departments with court-imposed affirmative action plans were not correlated with the proportion of female officers overall or across any racial or ethnic categories. In other words, "a formal affirmative action program does not have a significant effect on the hiring of female police officers" (Zhao et al. 2006, 480). Factors that increased the proportion of Black and Hispanic females were largely external to the department—the size of the Black and Hispanic population of the city was related to increasing diversity in Black and Hispanic female officers, respectively. This research calls into question the effectiveness of court-ordered affirmative action plans in increasing gender diversity, and also notes that although informal plans may increase the proportion of female officers overall, they do not impact an increase in Black or Hispanic female representation in police departments.

## Equal Employment Opportunity

In general, the legal challenges to discrimination in employment are brought under either (1) the "equal protection of the laws" clause of the Fourteenth Amendment (which protects citizens of all states) or (2) the Equal Employment Opportunity Act of 1972 (which extended to public agencies the "anti-discrimination in employment" provisions of Title VII of the 1964 Civil Rights Act). Title VII prohibits any discrimination in the workplace based on race, color, religion, national origin, or sex. The Equal Employment Opportunity Commission was established in 1964 to investigate possible violations of the act.

Moran (1988, 274) suggests that much of the resistance to affirmative action litigation rests on the belief held by many police executives that the **civil service system**, also known as the **merit system**, is a fair and effective means of producing a professional force. This system generally involves selecting in rank order those individuals who obtained the highest combined score on an objective, multiple-choice, written exam (many of which have been shown to be culturally biased and not job-related) and an oral interview. Additionally, candidates must meet several physical, medical, and personal requirements to qualify for appointment to the department. The problem with this "fair" and "effective" system is that it has excluded women, except in some specialized positions, and many minorities from police work.

The federal courts began to recognize that many selection standards that appeared to be neutral in form and intent in fact operated to exclude minorities and women. In general, the courts have indicated (Moran 1988, 275–276) that a police department must (1) establish that a selection procedure can be scientifically linked to job performance (i.e., "job validated") or (2) restructure the selection process in a manner that does not discriminate against qualified minorities. The outcome of the affirmative action litigation has been that, from a scientific perspective, little "merit" existed in the police-selection process. In fact, such standards as height, weight, age, and gender have not been correlated to job performance.

In the landmark decision in this area, *Griggs v. Duke Power Co.* (1971), the US Supreme Court held that the use of a professionally developed examination (for intelligence) could not be used if it had a discriminatory effect. The Court pointed out that Title VII prohibited tests that are neutral in form but discriminatory in operation; that is, if a selection practice excludes minorities or women (although not intended to do so) and cannot be shown to be job validated, it is prohibited. In *Griggs*, the Court further held that once discrimination has been established, the burden of proof in establishing the validity of the practice shifts to the defendant (i.e., employer). In other words, once a police department has been judged to engage in a discriminatory practice, the department must indicate to the courts that the practice (or requirement) is job related (Moran 1988).

In contrast, if a selection standard or requirement does not have a discriminatory impact, there is no need for validation. Furthermore, if a requirement can be shown to be a valid requirement for the job, even if it may have a discriminatory impact, it may be allowed to remain as a requirement. Chapter 14, for example, discusses how higher education may be shown to be a bona fide occupational qualification for policing and thus allowed as a requirement for initial selection.

## Increasing Diversity in Police Departments

The number of women and minorities in police departments has increased consistently since the 1960s, although the increase has been uneven. Walker (1989) reported that of the nation's 50 largest cities between 1983 and 1988, nearly half (45 percent) made significant progress in the employment of Black officers; however, 17 percent reported a decline in the percentage of African American officers. Sklansky (2006) indicated that the percentage of minority officers in major police departments increased dramatically between the 1960s and 2000 and that at least two cities (Detroit and Washington, DC) were more than 50 percent minority. Three police departments (Los Angeles, San Francisco, and Washington, DC) had a higher proportion of Black officers than Black residents. Forty-two percent of the departments reported significant increases in the percentage of Hispanic officers employed, whereas approximately 11 percent indicated a decline and 17 percent reported no change. Latino representation in police departments is more likely within cities that experience rapid growth in Latino populations (Perez McClusky and McClusky 2004).

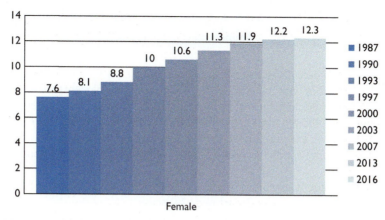

**FIGURE 12.1**  **Percentage of Female Local Police Officers, 1987–2016.**

SOURCE: S. S. Hyland and E. Davis. *Local Police Departments, 2016: Personnel* (Washington, DC: Bureau of Justice Statistics, 2019).

A survey of municipal police departments serving cities of 50,000 residents or more (Martin 1989) indicated that in 1978, women comprised 4.2 percent of sworn personnel, and by 1986, they comprised 8.8 percent. In local departments with 100 or more officers, approximately 99 percent have women officers, but fewer than 1 percent have 20 percent or more female representation. Furthermore, most of these departments are sheriffs' departments, where many women officers work in the jails (Carter, Sapp, and Stephens 1989). The Bureau of Justice Statistics conducts regular surveys on the cultural changes taking place in policing, and the percentages of women and minorities can be readily observed in Figure 12.1. Females comprised 12.3 percent of all full-time local police officers in 2016, which was roughly the same proportion from 2013 (12.2 percent) and modestly higher than that in 2007 (11.9 percent). While female representation may have stalled in recent years, it is worth noting that females comprised only 7.6 percent of sworn officers in 1987. This growth is noteworthy; however, it is still far from parity. And there is far less gender diversity in American police agencies than in police departments in many parts of the world (Brown, Prenzler, and Van Ewik 2014). Inside Policing 12.3 further illustrates diversity within large police departments, but notes too that the total proportion of minority officers has remained stable in recent years.

The uneven representation of females in supervisory positions of varying sized departments is shown in Table 12.1. Overall, females are chiefs in less than 3 percent of all police departments. Police departments serving larger jurisdictions (250,000 or more people) are significantly more likely to be led by a female executive. This pattern is repeated for immediate supervisors and sergeants/front-line supervisors. Smaller departments are significantly less likely to include female supervisors. This relationship was supported by Morabito and Shelley (2015), who report that female representation increased with increased department size. Additionally, females were more likely to occupy supervisory or leadership positions in large police departments.

As shown in Figure 12.2, Black officers accounted for 11.4 percent of the total in 2016, which is actually a lower proportion that what was observed in 2013. In fact, racial diversity appears to have plateaued in local police departments in the United States (11.9 percent in 2014, and 11.7 percent in 2003, 2000, and 1997). In contrast, much greater ethnic diversification is observed over recent years. Hispanic officers comprised 12.5 percent of

## INSIDE POLICING 12.3   Police Diversity—A Mixed Picture

Under the headline "Police Diversity Lags in Many Cities," *USA Today* presents data showing that "in at least 50 cities with more than 100,000 people, the percentage of Black police is less than half of what Blacks represent in the population." Clearly, many cities have work to do. In the same story, though, data are presented showing that nationally, the percentage of Black police in 2010 was exactly equal to the Black portion of the US population—12 percent. The story offers no comment on this positive statistic, though it is probably a surprise to many readers.

**Discussion Question:** Is it more difficult or less difficult for large police departments to diversify than mid-sized or smaller departments? Discuss.

SOURCE: *Modern Policing* blog, January 23, 2015, www.oup.com/cordner/police-diversity/.

**TABLE 12.1** Female Representation Among Selected Positions in Local Police Departments, by Size of Population Served, 2016

| POPULATION SERVED | CHIEF | INTERMEDIATE SUPERVISOR | SERGEANT OR FIRST-LINE EQUIVALENT |
|---|---|---|---|
| All sizes | 2.9 | 7.5 | 9.7 |
| 250,000 or more | 8.5 | 12.7 | 14.3 |
| 50,000–249,999 | 5.3‡ | 7.9† | 8.9† |
| 10,000–49,999 | 3.1† | 4† | 6.1† |
| 9,999 or less | 2.6† | 5† | 6.1† |

†Significant difference from comparison group at the 95 percent confidence level.
‡Significant difference from comparison group at the 90 percent confidence level.
*Source*: Bureau of Justice Statistics, Law Enforcement Management and Administrative Statistics Survey, 2016.

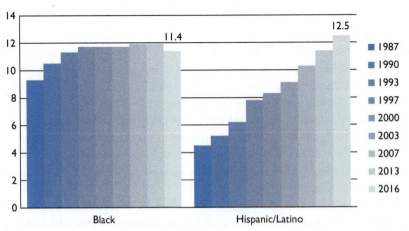

**FIGURE 12.2** Percentage of Black and Hispanic Police Officers, 1987–2016

SOURCE: S. S. Hyland and E. Davis. *Local Police Departments, 2016: Personnel.* (Washington, DC: Bureau of Justice Statistics, 2019).

full-time officers in 2016, up from 11.4 percent in 2013. Local police departments have made significant strides in ethnic diversity over the years, noting that only 4.5 percent of officers were Hispanic in 1987. Overall, approximately one in four local police officers in America are racial/ethnic minorities (23.9 percent).

African American officers, who comprised approximately 11.4 percent of all officers, also had the highest percentages in large jurisdictions. Hispanic officers were the most represented in jurisdictions with populations greater than 1 million, comprising 27 percent of officers. Morabito and Shelley (2015) also found that nonwhite and Black diversity within police departments increased with the size of the organization. Hispanic officers had the highest representation within the largest police departments, those exceeding 1 million population (see Table 12.2). In short, gender, racial, and ethnic inclusion is more likely to be observed in larger agencies that serve larger populations. While most people in the United States are served by large police departments, it is important to remember that most police departments are small.

Three surveys of women in policing further indicate their uneven development and continued gender-specific problems. The first survey of 800 police executives by the International Association of Chiefs of Police (IACP) reported that women comprise 12 percent of the police officers, but they are not represented at all in nearly 20 percent of the departments (*Law Enforcement News* 1999). Furthermore, the IACP found that 91 percent of the departments had no women in policy-making roles, and 10 percent reported that gender bias was one of the reasons women were not promoted. In addition, women had filed more than one-third of the lawsuits against departments charged with gender bias and **sexual harassment**. Based on the findings, the IACP recommended that police departments should implement fairer screening procedures, institute more rigorous policies against sexual harassment, and increase recruiting drives designed to attract and retain more women in policing.

The data indicate that many police departments are culturally diverse and becoming more so all the time. Although this trend is uneven throughout the country, within the next several decades half or more of local police officers likely will be women and minorities. Such growth, however, assumes a continued emphasis on affirmative action and equal employment opportunity programs, which may be subsiding in some departments (see Chapter 14).

## Promotional Opportunities

A comparison study of 290 police departments of female police supervisors (Martin 1989) shows that women represented 2.2 percent of all municipal supervisory levels in 1978 and 7.6 percent in 1986 (including 3.7 percent at the sergeant level, 2.5 percent at the lieutenant level, and 1.4 percent above the lieutenant level).

Another study of departments with 100 or more sworn personnel by the National Center for Women and Policing (Lonsway et al. 2002) found higher percentages of women supervisors. Evaluating the number of females in supervisory positions among large police departments as well as smaller and rural police departments, the Center found that for women, although they are underrepresented in police departments, the disparity is more pronounced at higher levels of the organizational chart. Women comprised 9.6 percent of supervisory positions (lieutenant and sergeant) in large agencies and 4.6 percent in smaller and rural agencies. Among top command positions (captain or above), women were represented at the rate of 7.3 percent in large agencies and 3.4 percent in smaller and rural agencies. In sum, although the proportion of women in American police departments continues

**TABLE 12.2** Race and Ethnicity of Full-Time Sworn Personnel in Local Police Departments by Size of Population Served, 2016

| POPULATION SERVED | WHITE (%) | BLACK (%) | HISPANIC (%) | OTHER (%) | UNKNOWN (%) |
|---|---|---|---|---|---|
| All sizes | 71.5 | 11.4 | 12.5 | 3.6 | 1.1 |
| 1 million or more | 50.4 | 16.6 | 27.0 | 5.6 | 0.4 |
| 500,000–999,999 | 59.7 | 21.5 | 10.9 | 6.8 | 1.1 |
| 250,000–499,999 | 68.0 | 14.8 | 12.6 | 4.0 | 0.6 |
| 100,000–249,999 | 72.9 | 11.7 | 10.0 | 3.4 | 2.0 |
| 50,000–99,999 | 74.7 | 7.6 | 12.9 | 2.6 | 2.2 |
| 25,000–49,999 | 86.9 | 6.0 | 5.2 | 1.3 | 0.6 |
| 10,000–24,999 | 85.2 | 6.0 | 5.9 | 1.8 | 1.1 |
| 9,999 or less | 87.1 | 4.7 | 5.5 | 1.8 | 0.9 |

*Note:* May not sum to total because of rounding.

*Source:* Bureau of Justice Statistics, Law Enforcement Management and Administrative Statistics Survey, 2016.

to experience modest increases, the proportion of females in positions of power and policy-making in these organizations remains low.

More recent research from a nationally representative sample of over 2,100 local, county, and state agencies suggests females comprise 0.03 percent of all chiefs, 0.96 percent of mid-level managers, and 1.13 percent of supervisors (Shjarback and Todak 2019). Female representation was influenced by organizational size—larger police departments (100 or more officers) had significantly more gender representation in supervisory positions; however, smaller departments (those with fewer than 50 officers) were significantly less likely to have gender representation among higher ranks. These results suggest supervisory opportunities are more prevalent among larger departments, whereas opportunities for promotion are more limited in smaller departments.

'Data on minority promotions are more limited than data on females. According to officials in African American and Hispanic national organizations, no agency routinely and systematically gathers information about the promotion of minorities. Despite the lack of data, many affirmative action specialists claim that most minority officers are not promoted equally compared with white officers and remain essentially at the entry level (Sullivan 1989). As with female officers, however, it is also true that because minority members have not been well integrated into policing, until recently they have not had a sufficient amount of time in which to be promoted.

Wide variation exists in promotion practices among police departments. In general, the departments with the best records of promoting minority officers appear to be those in cities that have large minority populations and minority leadership in the mayor's office or at the top levels in the police department. Thus, as Sullivan (1989) has noted, Black officers in Chicago, Atlanta and Detroit or Hispanic officers in Miami and Los Angeles are more likely to be promoted than their colleagues in cities with larger white populations and power bases. Walker and Turner (1993), examining the percentage of Black and Hispanic officers in eight large nationally representative police departments, reported that the percentage holding supervisory ranks is considerably lower than minority representation among officers. Sklansky (2006), highlighting the LAPD, reported that the proportion of nonwhite officers was approximately 60 percent; however, minority (particularly Hispanic) representation decreased at higher levels of the hierarchy. In 2000, nearly 70 percent of the top command in the LAPD was white.

The Supreme Court's ruling in *United States v. Paradise* (1987) also appears to set the direction in attempting to balance the need to rectify past discriminatory practices while protecting innocent third parties from discrimination. Rulings such as *Paradise*, along with continued emphasis on minority recruitment and affirmative action plans, should contribute substantially toward a higher percentage of minority personnel in supervisory positions in the near future. One interesting dilemma has developed, however, with respect to minority promotions at the local level—namely, "federal raiders," who recruit away top minority candidates (Sullivan 1989). Because federal agencies usually require some law enforcement experience prior to employment, federal agents often recruit their personnel from local police departments. Furthermore, because federal agencies tend to be viewed as more prestigious and may pay more, it is easy to understand why they are often successful in recruiting the most qualified personnel (especially minorities and women) that local departments have to offer. Such raiding results in the loss by local departments of the minority officers with the greatest potential for promotion.

Officers' motivation to seek promotion varies by race and gender, and suggesting that police organizations simply "encourage" underrepresented groups to seek promotion may be ineffective or even counterproductive. Whetstone (2001) explained that personal, professional, and organizational reasons influenced whether officers sought promotion. White officers were significantly more likely to indicate that promotion was a personal goal, whereas minorities were significantly more likely to seek promotion to achieve a leadership role. Whetstone further noted that whites were *less* likely to be encouraged to seek promotion than minorities. Similarly, Archbold and Schulz (2008) as well as Archbold and Hassell (2009) found that female officers reported being consistently encouraged by supervisors to seek promotion. However, they indicated that female officers felt they were being encouraged because of their gender, rather than because they were highly qualified or effective leaders. This belief created an unanticipated negative effect—females were actually less likely to pursue promotion, partly because they were encouraged to do so under what they interpreted as illegitimate reasons.

Whetstone (2001) indicated that male officers were much more likely not to seek promotion because doing so would result in a loss of pay. Although promotion almost universally includes an increase in base salary, the earning potential of sergeants can decrease because they may not be able to engage in lucrative off-duty assignments (or "side jobs"). Female officers, in contrast, were significantly more likely to cite child-care concerns for opting out of the promotional process (Archbold and Hassell 2009; Todak, Leban and Hixon 2021). Shifts are often assigned based on seniority, with new sergeants given the least desirable shifts (e.g., midnights). Because overnight child-care options are scarce, a promotion to sergeant is viewed as an unnecessary hardship for officers, particularly for females.

Police organizations must encourage and promote diversity at all levels of the hierarchy, and minorities and females appear particularly underrepresented in supervisory positions. But addressing the issue of disparity at supervisory levels appears complicated and should be approached delicately. Simply encouraging minorities and females seek promotion can cause some to feel slighted and marginalized, resulting in otherwise qualified individuals choosing not to seek promotion. Additionally, various factors appear to influence the decision to pursue (or not pursue) promotion, some of which vary across race and gender. Responsible organizations must consider these while creating a culture that provides qualified officers with the opportunity to seek promotion.

## Making Policing Inclusive

The preceding discussion indicates that an increasing percentage and number of both minorities and women are entering the law enforcement field. Much of this increase, however, is caused by the passage of the 1972 amendments to the Civil Rights Act of 1964. These amendments, as well as subsequent court decisions based on them, forced police departments to alter, radically in some instances, their selection and promotional practices. Hence, the question remains: How well are these "nontraditional" officers being treated once they are inside the department? This section examines how well women and minorities appear to be integrating into the police work environment, as well as prospects for the future.

Because many male officers have been opposed to women in policing in general and women on patrol in particular (see, e.g., Bloch and Anderson 1974; Martin 1980; Charles 1981; Linden 1983), it is not surprising that women have had a particularly difficult time breaking into policing. Although many departments are moving toward community policing, for the most part, they remain tradition-bound and masculine. Linden (1983) contends that men tend to object to women on patrol because they fear that women will not be able to cope with physical violence and that the image of the police will suffer. For example, a survey of police departments in the Northwest (Brown 1994) indicated that only one-third of male patrol officers actually accepted a woman on patrol and that more than half did not think women could handle the physical requirements of the job as well as men can. Martin (1980) further notes that women threaten to disrupt the division of labor, the work norms, the work group's solidarity, the insecure occupational image, and the sexist ideology that is contrary to the men's definition of police work as "men's work" and their identity as masculine men.

## Police Culture

The major underlying dilemma confronting women in policing is the **police culture**, which has as its foundation a sexist and macho perception of the role of police. As Martin (1989, 11) has noted,

> The use of women on patrol implies either that the men's unique asset, their physical superiority, is irrelevant (as it is, on most assignments) or that the man with a female partner will be at a disadvantage in a physical confrontation that he would not face with a male partner.

The nature of police work creates a peer culture between officers that makes it difficult for women to assimilate. Franklin (2005) summarizes elements of police culture to include machismo and adventure, coercive power and control, heterosexism, solidarity and group loyalty, sexism, physical conflict resolution, glorification of violence, desire for action, and excitement and danger. She concludes that these elements "form the social systems that serve to keep women from fully participating in policing" (Franklin 2005, 7). According to this research, many individuals within the policing industry continue to view women as outsiders and as inappropriate for policing.

As emphasized previously, the police role in general is not physically demanding and requires a much stronger mental than physical capacity. In addition, no research indicates that strength is related to police functioning, nor does any research suggest that physical strength is related to an individual's ability to successfully manage a dangerous situation (Charles 1981).

As the earlier review of the research on the performance of policewomen indicated, women not only perform satisfactorily on patrol but also tend to be exemplary in the less aggressive, nontraditional aspects of the role (e.g., interacting with citizens and handling domestic disturbances). This finding suggests that in many respects, women may actually be better suited for police work than men. McDowell (1992) reports that the Christopher Commission (investigating the LAPD after the Rodney King beating) found that the 120 officers with the most use-of-force reports were all men and that civilian complaints against women were consistently lower. Policewomen, by contrast, tended to perform better in meeting the public, handling domestic violence, and dealing with rape victims.

Women face other hurdles in attempting to be accepted into the policing profession. For instance, the use of sexist language, sexual harassment, sexual jokes, tokenism, and sex-role stereotyping all contribute to severe adjustment problems for women (Martin 1989; Martin and Jurik 1996). Men frequently use language to keep women officers in their "place" by referring to them as "ladies" or "girls," suggesting that they need to be protected. Women who do not conform to sex-role stereotypes and are "tough" enough to gain respect as officers may be labeled "bitches" or "lesbians" in an attempt to neutralize their threat to male dominance (Berg and Budnick 1986; Prokos and Padavic 2002), a process referred to as **de-feminization**.

Possibly because of the hurdles women face on entering policing, some research (Martin 1979) has suggested that two separate identities may develop: *police*women and police*women*. The former attempts to gain her male colleagues' approval by adhering to traditional police values and norms, with law enforcement her primary orientation; the latter attempts to perform her duties in a "traditionally feminine manner" by making few arrests, infrequently using physical activity, and placing strong emphasis on "being a lady." Although Martin's (1979) research included only 32 female officers, 7 of whom were classified as police*women* and 8 as *police*women (with the rest in between), it is important that police departments promote policies and practices that allow female officers to be "themselves" and to utilize the particular strengths that many women bring to the job. In fact, Rabe-Hemp (2009) suggests this may actually be the case. Through interviews with officers, she found that females tend to negotiate between the *police*women and police*women* ends of the spectrum. Female officers she interviewed rated themselves higher than their male counterparts across "feminized forms of police work" (Rabe-Hemp 2009, 124), including dealing with victims, children, and juveniles as well as community policing. However, female officers were critical of female peers who appeared to proscribe to a dominant end of the *police*women and police*women* continuum.

In general, research on policewomen suggests that they are still struggling for acceptance, believe that they do not receive equal credit for their work, and are often sexually harassed by their coworkers (Daum and Johns 1994). One study of more than 500 women officers from nine western states revealed that open sexual discrimination and sexual harassment (discussed in more detail later) were far more common today than expected, especially by supervisors and commanders, who not only tolerate such practices by others but also frequently engage in such practices themselves (Timmins and Hainsworth 1989). The survey also indicated that duty assignments were often based on gender. Martin (1989) further notes that frequent sexual jokes and informal harassment cause many women to avoid interaction with men that might be viewed as having a sexual connotation. To maintain their moral reputation, they may sacrifice the opportunity to build close interpersonal relationships that are necessary for gaining sponsors and mentors (i.e., an influential person who provides guidance and assistance). Without backing from the informal political network within the department, women will likely have a more difficult time being promoted or gaining specialized job assignments.

This lack of access to the informal political network within a department also applies to minority officers. Although there are many reasons why minorities may not be assigned to specialized jobs or promoted equally compared with whites, some of which were discussed earlier, Sullivan (1989) believes the major reason is that minority networks usually do not reach the upper echelons of power and the existing white network. He suggests that this is a catch-22 situation—that is, minority promotions will increase only when more minority officers are promoted. Once again, it is important to recognize how necessary equal promotional opportunities are for both minority and female officers.

## Structural Characteristics

Women also face problems relating to the **structural characteristics** or features of police departments (Martin 1989). For example, most training academies place a strong emphasis on physical fitness. Once a certain level of fitness and performance has been achieved, however, it generally need not be maintained; that is, few departments require any testing of physical performance beyond that of the academy. Such an emphasis tends to magnify the importance of physical differences between the sexes, which tends to perpetuate the sex-role stereotype. This is not to suggest that officers should not be physically fit, but that fitness should be within the parameters of job-related standards. Furthermore, if physical standards are job-related, then they should be maintained throughout an officer's career, at least in those jobs where such a requirement is necessary.

Training academies also often fail to place the proper amount of importance on the development of the *interpersonal skills* that are essential to effective police work. Such skills are usually more highly developed in women than in men, and their absence from the training curriculum deprives women of excelling in an important job-relevant area. Consequently, as Martin (1989, 12) observed, "New women recruits enter male turf on male terms with little recognition of their own problems or strengths." Associated with the problem of not recognizing the importance of interpersonal skills is the performance-evaluation process itself. Despite the favorable response to the effectiveness of women on patrol, internal performance-evaluation criteria tend to have a gender bias that is favorable toward males. Some research (Morash and Greene 1986) has discovered that such criteria tend to emphasize traits that are primarily associated with a male stereotype (e.g., forcefulness and dominance). Additionally, Lonsway (2003) reviewed research related to women's lack of physical prowess making them unsuitable for police work. She noted that although there are times when physical strength is advantageous for officers, such situations are relatively rare in everyday policing. Furthermore, she notes that police departments have been unable to create valid tests that can predict the successful performance of physical activities.

## Sexual Harassment

Maintaining a healthy working environment free from sexual harassment is a priority for all employers. However, the environment for policing may be particularly susceptible to sexual harassment, because it is male dominated: policing generally encourages a culture of machismo. The previous discussion on police culture established that policewomen still face sexual harassment by their coworkers—and if women officers are to gain equal treatment and status in police departments, sexual harassment must be taken seriously by the department and be eliminated. Title VII of the Civil Rights Act prohibits sex discrimination. Sexual harassment is simply another form of sex discrimination.

Sexual harassment in the workplace has been defined across three different dimensions, discussed here. *Unwanted sexual attention* includes sexually suggestive comments that are made to or about a person as well as inappropriate touching. *Gender harassment* includes behaviors such as dirty jokes or stories told in the workplace or comments that put women down. *Quid pro quo* literally translates to "this for that"; the term is used to describe situations where an employee is forced to submit to unwanted sexual advances as a condition of employment, with either a tangible job reward for complying or a punishment for refusing (Lonsway, Paynich, and Hall 2013).

Research confirms that sexual harassment continues to exist in American police organizations. Somvadee and Morash (2008) utilized a sexual experience questionnaire (SEQ; developed by Fitzgerald et al. 1988) to categorize harassment in policing across several dimensions: gender harassment (suggestive, crude, sexist remarks), unwanted sexual attention, and sexual coercion. In interviews with 117 female officers across a number of different agencies, they found gender harassment was common. The most common form of harassment was suggestive stories or offensive jokes—83.7 percent of officers indicated experiencing this behavior at least once over the previous two-year period. Other common forms of harassment included being treated differently because of their sex (69.2 percent), crude sexual remarks (68.3 percent), putdowns because of their sex (53.8 percent), and sexist remarks (51.2 percent). Unwanted sexual attention was less common; however, 45.2 percent of officers reported discussion of sexual or personal matters at work. Other unwanted sexual attention included unwelcome touching (36.7 percent). Other more perverse harassment was relatively rare, although alarming. A total of 5.1 percent of female officers experienced subtle sexual bribery over the previous two-year period, and 5.9 percent reported being treated badly for sexual noncooperation.

Subsequent research also utilizing the SEQ reports similar experiences with sexual harassment. Lonsway et al. (2013) reported that 82.6 percent of male officers and 92.5 percent of female officers experienced sexual harassment in the previous year. It's noteworthy to mention that the survey questions were asked in a manner that made it possible for males and females to experience sexual harassment without necessarily being the target of it. For example, being in proximity to sexually suggestive comments would be considered *experience*. The high percentage of males may also suggest that a large proportion are aware of behaviors considered sexual harassment, and that this is a part of police culture. Of female officers, 48.5 percent reported unwanted sexual attention (e.g., sexually suggestive remarks and sexual or romantic advances), 4.3 percent reported **quid pro quo harassment**, and 91.2 percent reported gender harassment (e.g., dirty jokes or saying things that put women down). The perpetrator of sexual harassment typically was a coworker (not a supervisor). Consequences associated with sexual harassment included work withdrawal, decreased work, supervisor and coworker satisfaction, job and life stress, as well as depression and anxiety. The vast majority of officers never reported sexual harassment to supervisors—85.5 percent of female officers never reported. The most common reason for nonreporting was that the incident was not perceived as serious enough to file a report; however, it is worth noting that 27.5 percent of female officers cited concern about the reaction of a supervisor or coworker as influencing their decision to not report. Notably, 23.2 percent of female officers indicated concern about how reporting could impact their career, whereas only 15.7 percent of male officers noted this concern.

This harassment has negative impacts on female officers. Haarr (1997) conducted interviews with and observations of officers in a Midwestern police department. Every female participant in her study reported experiencing some degree of sexual harassment. This harassment was often intended to marginalize women in the police department, indicating that policing is not a legitimate occupation for women. In addition, Morash and Haarr (1995) indicated that sexual harassment was a significant contributor to female officer workplace stress. Any sexual harassment, no matter how seemingly benign or harmless to the perpetrator, can significantly impact women with regard to stress, socialization, and patterns of interaction within the organization.

Collins (2004) examined sexual harassment cases filed with the Florida Criminal Justice Standards and Training Commission between 1993 and 1997. Female officers alleged that male officers exposed them to crude or offensive remarks in 73 percent of the cases, and 33 percent of the cases alleged "frequent sexist remarks." Twenty-four percent of the cases alleged sexual coercion—namely, job-related considerations that would be traded for sexual favors. Thirty-six percent of these cases ended in punitive discipline for the harasser, such as probation, remedial training, suspension, or some combination thereof. Termination resulted in only 16.7 percent of the cases. Although this research provides a good overview of the nature and outcome of sexual harassment cases, it is unclear whether it is descriptive of sexual harassment in general, because so few cases are officially reported.

Police departments must have a policy that defines and prohibits sexual harassment, because failure to have such a policy may be construed as *deliberate indifference*, exposing the department to claims of liability. Employees who claim sexual harassment will not have to prove economic or psychological injury to win a claim. Even when such a policy exists, the department may still be held liable. Even if they did not know of the offending behavior, departments can also be held liable if a court determines that they should have known about it. Departments are also generally liable for the acts of their supervisory personnel (Rubin 1995). Accordingly, every complaint of sexual harassment should be taken seriously and acted on immediately, with a follow-up investigation. Confidentiality should be maintained, and every step of the investigation should be documented. Whenever harassment is found, swift remedial action—including warnings, reprimands, suspension, or dismissal—should be taken (Rubin 1995). This action sends a message that sexual harassment will not be tolerated and indicates (to the courts) that the department is seriously attempting to control harassment.

Inside Policing 12.4 summarizes recommendations from the National Institute of Justice's Research Summit on Women in Policing and outlines various action steps to enhance gender representation within policing. Many of these are contained in a podcast episode in *Reducing Crime*, highlighted in Inside Policing 12.5.

## Lesbian, Gay, Bisexual, Transgender, Queer + Officers

So far, this chapter has focused on diversity issues related to race/ethnicity and gender; however, the introduction of diversity related to sexual orientation deserves highlighting. Lesbian and gay officers may share many of the experiences of other minorities within policing. Early hypothesized benefits of diversity within policing included providing the police with a different, more representative lens through which they view the community and the unique crimes, problems, and need for services across communities; parallel barriers for integration of lesbian, gay, bisexual, and transgender (LGBTQ+) officers in policing may also exist.

This chapter previously noted that elements of police culture include machismo, heterosexism, and sexism (Franklin 2005). Policing is a hypermasculine occupation and adheres to strong in-group norms, making integration of lesbian and gay officers difficult. Unlike racial/ethnic minorities and females, LGBTQ+ officers are not outwardly or immediately identifiable as minorities. Therefore, officers may choose to hide their sexual orientation and "serve in silence" to avoid alienation and avoid harassment (Colvin 2014), and may experience double marginality in ways discussed earlier in this chapter related to African American police officers. The extent of diversity in police departments with regard to sexual orientation is unclear, because unlike racial/ethnicity and gender, police departments do not (cannot) track or report the sexual orientation of their workforce. Policing LGBTQ+ communities is discussed further in Chapter 15, and this chapter discusses experiences and diversity of lesbian and gay officers.

Full understanding of LGBTQ+ diversity within police departments remains understudied, but surveys of LGBTQ+ officers indicate integration issues similar to those experienced by racial/ethnic minorities and female policing pioneers. On the one hand, LGBTQ+ officers report good relationships with nongay supervisors and peers, and LGBTQ+ officers overwhelmingly report positive relationships with gay and nongay communities. On the other hand, however, LGBTQ+ officers reported their sexual orientation was a barrier to professional development. In fact, only 48 percent of LGBTQ+ officers agreed with the statement "My job advancement opportunities are the same as nongay

| INSIDE POLICING 12.4 | **Steps to Enhance Gender Inclusivity in American Policing** |
|---|---|
| Prioritize the issue | Police agencies should consider creating a unit on equity and inclusion, |
| Support mentoring and sponsorship | Strong role models, advocates, and mentors are important in female officer's career track and success, |
| Flexible, family-friendly policies | Police agencies should adopt standards that promote equality and equity for all employees, which include family-friendly policies like parental leave, postnatal nursing, and nonrotating shifts, |
| Improve and enforce harassment policies | Barriers for reporting harassment, like weak anti-retaliation policies, unnecessarily lengthy processes, and failure to keep complains confidential and anonymous, should be removed. |
| Find advocates for change | Allies include male officers, chiefs, majors, trade organizations, and politicians. |
| Re-examine physical fitness standards | Physical fitness standards represent a barrier for recruiting females into policing, yet these standards often do not accurately reflect the physical demands of the job. |
| Support women | Support groups within policing can help female recruits prepare for physical fitness tests, create a network of female officers, advocate for these officers, and increase the promotion of females within policing. |
| Reframe the profession | Shifting the profession toward an emphasis on community policing, valuing relationships, and increasing trust will aid in the recruitment and retention of female officers. |
| Look for success stories, and learn from efforts abroad | It is wise to learn from police agencies (in the United States and internationally) that have been able to increase gender representation. |
| Research the issue | Creating space for relevant research on gender in policing, communicating implications clearly to policymakers, and learning from other fields can provide an impetus for change. |
| Reframe the conversation | Often, conversations focus on how to accommodate female employees better. Instead, consider how agencies can optimally use their talent pool and optimize human resources. |
| Commit to long-term work | Short-term solutions are unlikely to be successful in the long run without a genuine commitment to address the negative aspects of organizational culture, policies, and practices that discourage inclusivity. |

*SOURCE*: Adapted from National Institute of Justice, *Women in Policing: Breaking Barriers and Blazing a Path* (Washington, DC: US Department of Justice, 2019).

> **INSIDE POLICING 12.5** | **Increasing Gender Representation in Policing**
>
> In this podcast, Jerry Ratcliffe interviews Maureen McGough on the role of females within policing, the benefits of increasing gender representation within American policing (noting that many other countries have far surpassed the United States in gender representation; see Brown et al. 2014), and how organizational culture, recruitment strategies, and performance evaluations can impede representativeness.
>
> **Discussion Question:** McGough discusses the 30x30 Initiative, which seeks to increase female representation in policing to 30% by 2030. How likely is it that this will succeed? What are the biggest challenges to achieving 30% representation?
>
> *SOURCE: Reducing Crime.* Podcast audio. May 26, 2020, https://soundcloud.com/reducingcrime/23-mo-mcgough.

officers" (Colvin 2014, p. 197). Officers indicated this was in part because of assignments tending to be people-focused (e.g., recruiting, public relations, training, and liaison) rather than specialized crime-focused assignments (e.g., homicide or narcotics unit). This suggests that sexual orientation may indirectly impede promotional opportunities. Other barriers for equal employment opportunities include performance evaluations, work schedules, and assignment of partners (Colvin 2009).

Differential treatment within the workplace is also common, regardless of whether peers and supervisors are aware of officers' sexual orientation. Most LGBTQ+ officers reported exposure to homophobic talk in the workplace (67 percent) and feeling like an outsider within their police department (51 percent). LGBTQ+ officers also reported a high rate of social isolation (48 percent), tokenism (43 percent), and repeated harassment (34 percent; Colvin 2014). Perceptions of fairness and equity are important aspects of diversity within healthy police departments, and although the extent of LGBTQ+ diversity or experiences of LGBTQ+ officers is limited and anecdotal, it appears that the experiences of this minority population may be similar to those of racial minorities and females.

## Future Prospects

Over the past three decades, substantial progress has been made in the recruitment and hiring of minorities and women in policing. However, although some departments have accomplished this voluntarily, others have been reluctant and forced by the courts. This situation, combined with the traditional police culture, has created serious problems for minorities and women with respect to integration and equal treatment within the field. In "Voices from the Field," Chief (ret.) Carmen Best discusses the necessity of diversity and inclusion within policing and the anticipated benefits.

Police departments will continue to struggle with the complex problems associated with minority hiring and promotion. If they are to increase—or, in some instances, maintain—their minority representation, they should pay particular attention to several areas (Sullivan 1989). First, agencies must continue to actively recruit among minorities while attempting to improve community relations and eliminate the reasons many minorities have had to distrust the police. Second, because studies have indicated that many of the entry-level, paper-and-pencil tests are not job-validated, it may be necessary to

## VOICES FROM THE FIELD

### Carmen Y. Best
*Chief (ret.), Seattle Police Department*

With recent, high-profile deaths of young Black men and women during officer-involved shootings nationwide, the divide between communities of color and the police appears to be especially pronounced. Now more than ever, diversity in law enforcement is essential to building community trust and legitimacy.

Diversity and inclusion must work in tandem: diversity on its own cannot be successful without inclusion. Diversity is more than a buzzword, a box checked. This starts at the top. At the Seattle Police Department, our command staff reflects the community we serve, being one of the most diverse in the department's history. Members from the African American, Asian Pacific Islander, Hispanic, and LGBTQ+ communities having a seat at the table provides valuable contributions to the department every day. Diversity and inclusion must be engrained into the fabric of organizations to be truly successful.

Throughout our sworn ranks, the Seattle Police Department has significantly increased the diversity of new hires, with 36 percent in 2018 being nonwhite, including 10 percent identifying as Hispanic, and an additional 14 percent identifying as two or more races. A study by the Community Police Commission and the Associated Press found that the Seattle Police Department is more diverse in its racial and ethnic composition compared to law enforcement agencies in other cities.

While we have made progress, there is still so much work to do to achieve a department that is truly

a microcosm of the community. We must continue to work to foster a culture of continuous improvement and innovation. Police departments nationwide are struggling to recruit new officers in general; this includes recruits from all races. Regardless of their background, applicants must first be qualified and able to perform the job of policing. To lower our standards is not an option.

We must continue to strive for diversity because it conveys a sense of equity to the public, increasing the likelihood that officers will understand the perspectives of diverse communities. This works both ways: when the community sees officers that look like them, they are more likely to cultivate better relationships and collaboration.

Moreover, diversity is not just about recruiting diverse pool officers. It is also about including people from diverse backgrounds throughout your organization who can offer unique perspectives to issues facing your department. It is also about creating meaningful policy and training to foster an open environment that addresses how people are treated.

Ultimately, diversity and inclusion will lead to closer ties with the community. Often when our officers are out talking with the public, we have come to find out we have more in common than we realize. We agree that we want safe neighborhoods, we all want to be treated fairly, and we can all work together, moving the police forward for safer communities, with equitable police services for everyone.

design a new series of tests that can more accurately measure potential police performance while ensuring that they do not discriminate against racial or ethnic groups. Finally, because minority members may have been at a disadvantage before their police service, departments may need to initiate special programs to help these officers develop the required skills and knowledge to perform effectively on the job. This final suggestion applies equally to female candidates, especially with respect to the physical requirements of the hiring

## INSIDE POLICING 12.6 Recruiting Females into Policing

Recognizing the fact that females remain underrepresented in policing and citing research identifying the advantages of having gender diversity in the workforce, staff at the Vermont Works for Women (a nonprofit organization that has a track record of recruiting and preparing women to work in nontraditional occupations) created Step Up to Law Enforcement. This program, established in 2004, is a six-week, pre-academy, gender-specific course designed to provide training and a real-world introduction to working in policing and corrections.

The program emphasizes key components, including preparation for physical tests required for academy entry, introduction to critical issues in policing and corrections, introduction to firearms, employment skills for policing, preparing for oral board interviews, interviews with local police departments and corrections agencies, employment support from Vermont Works for Women staff after graduation, and access to Vermont Works for Women job banks.

*SOURCE*: https://vtworksforwomen.org/sule/.

process. Inside Policing 12.6 highlights Vermont's efforts to recruit and prepare females for policing.

To improve the recruitment and retention of women in policing, departments must attempt to accelerate change in the traditional, militaristic, male-dominated, sexist police culture. Although important strides have been made with respect to de-emphasizing the highly militaristic and masculine approach to police organization and management, especially by those departments moving toward community policing, such traditions are firmly entrenched and difficult to overcome. As more women enter the field and move into supervisory positions where they can impact policy, change is likely to occur more quickly. As with minority personnel, police departments must continue to eliminate those aspects of the selection process that are discriminatory toward women and that cannot be job-validated.

Departments must implement policies and practices that are not discriminatory. Minority and female personnel must become fully integrated into police work. Only then can these officers become true role models and not merely tokens within their departments. Possibly the best recruitment device at a police department's disposal is its own personnel, who can act as sponsors and mentors for others who wish to enter the field. Additionally, real and perceived barriers to reporting sexual harassment should be removed. It is inadequate to merely have an organizational policy forbidding sexual harassment; it is also necessary to ensure that reporting processes are easily available, that complaints are taken seriously, and that perceptions of retaliation are mitigated.

Over the next decade, one important influence on minority and women recruitment is making police work attractive to them. Since these groups are recruited vigorously by other public-sector (including federal police departments) and private-sector agencies, the pool of qualified applicants may be shrinking. Accordingly, it may be even more difficult in the future to recruit qualified candidates. At least one study (Hochstedler and Conley 1986) has indicated that a major reason Blacks tend to be underrepresented in municipal police departments is that they simply choose not to pursue a career in policing. One thing is clear: if departments are to remain competitive for minorities and women in the future, they must have an active and innovative recruitment strategy, promote a police culture that treats all employees equally and with respect, and if necessary, have an equitable plan regarding selection, duty assignment, and promotional opportunity.

## Summary

Given all the possible factors that can influence the relationship between police and citizens, a police department that is a perfect cultural match for a community will not necessarily be more effective for that reason alone. In the long term, the integrity, competence, and style of the officer as well as the philosophy, strategies, and methods of the department have the greatest impact on effectiveness. However, diversity and inclusion continue to have substantial political support, because many people assert that it is equitable to employ minorities and women, given the discrimination they have experienced in the past.

The development of diversity in policing was traced in this chapter. Included in this analysis was an examination of how minorities and women, once they enter the profession, are treated unequally, although their performance is generally satisfactory. There has been litigation regarding the impact of equal employment opportunity legislation and the use of the civil service, or merit, system. Reliance on using a non-job-validated merit system for both selection and promotion in policing has led many police traditionalists to believe that reverse discrimination and lowering of standards is occurring. Although the implementation of affirmative action plans in policing is complex, such plans have played an important role in police employment trends, in some cases significantly increasing the number and percentage of minorities and women. Once inside the department, however, these nontraditional officers have not always been well received—in large part because of the traditional police culture. As more minority and women officers enter policing and are promoted to higher ranks, their integration and acceptance into the field should become easier. Whether police departments can continue to attract qualified minority and women personnel depends on the public's interest in the police occupation, an active recruitment strategy, a departmental culture that treats members equally and with respect, and perhaps, a well-developed affirmative action plan.

## Critical Thinking Questions

1. Is gender, racial, and ethnic diversity important in policing? Explain why or why not.
2. Briefly discuss the types of unequal treatment received by minority and female officers when they first entered policing. Were their experiences essentially the same, or did they differ in significant ways?
3. What is the civil service system? Is it discriminatory? Why or why not?
4. Discuss the importance of the *Griggs* and *Paradise* decisions by the US Supreme Court regarding affirmative action plans.

5. Briefly discuss the growth of diversity in police departments over the past several decades. What is the significance of this growth?

6. Briefly describe several problems confronting women and minorities in attempting to integrate into the police work environment. What are the prospects for the future?

# References

Alex, N. 1969. *Black in Blue*. Englewood Cliffs, NJ: Prentice Hall.

Alex, N. 1976. *New York Cops Talk Back*. New York: Wiley.

Archbold, C. A., and Hassell, K. D. 2009. "Paying the Marriage Tax: An Examination of the Barriers to the Promotion of Female Officers." *Policing: An International Journal of Police Strategies and Management* 32: 56–74.

Archbold, C. A., and Schulz, D. M. 2008. "Making Rank: The Lingering Effects of Tokenism on Female Police Officers' Promotion Aspirations." *Police Quarterly* 11: 50–73.

Ba, B., Knox, D., Mummolo, J., and Rivera, R. 2021. "The Role of Officer Race and Gender in Police-Civilian Interactions in Chicago." *Science*, 371: 696–702.

Balkin, J. 1988. "Why Policemen Don't Like Policewomen." *Journal of Police Science and Administration* 16: 29–38.

Bazley, T. D., Lersch, K. M., and Mieczkowski, T. 2007. "Officer Force Versus Suspect Resistance: A Gendered Analysis of Patrol Officers in an Urban Police Department." *Journal of Criminal Justice* 35: 183–192.

Berg, B., and Budnick, K. 1986. "Defeminization of Women in Law Enforcement: A New Twist in the Traditional Police Personality." *Journal of Police Science and Administration* 14: 314–319.

Berkeley, G. E. 1969. *The Democratic Policeman*. Boston: Beacon.

Bloch, P., and Anderson, D. 1974. *Policewomen on Patrol: Final Report*. Washington, DC: Police Foundation.

Bradbury, M. D., and Kellough, J. E. 2008. "Representative Bureaucracy: Exploring the Potential for Active Representation in Local Government." *Journal of Public Administration Research and Theory* 18: 697–714.

Brown, J., Prenzler, T., and van Ewik, A. R. 2014. "Women in Policing." In Bruinsma, G. and D. Weisburd (eds.) *Encyclopedia of Criminology and Criminal Justice*, pp. 5548–5560. Springer: New York.

Brown, M. 1994. "The Plight of Female Police: A Survey of NW Patrolmen." *The Police Chief* 61: 50–53.

Brown, R. A., and Frank, J. 2006. "Race and Officer Decision Making: Examining Difference in Arrest Outcomes Between Black and White Officers." *Justice Quarterly* 23: 96–126.

Carter, D. L., Sapp, A. D., and Stephens, D. W. 1989. *The State of Police Education: Policy Direction for the Twenty-First Century*. Washington, DC: Police Executive Research Forum.

Charles, M. T. 1981. "Performance and Socialization of Female Recruits in the Michigan State Police Training Academy." *Journal of Police Science and Administration* 9: 209–223.

Collins, S. C. 2004. "Sexual Harassment and Police Discipline: Who's Policing the Police?" *Policing: An International Journal of Police Strategies and Management* 27: 512–538.

Colvin, R. 2009. "Shared Perceptions Among Lesbian and Gay Police Officers: Barriers and Opportunities in the Law Enforcement Work Environment." *Police Quarterly* 12(1): 86–101.

Colvin, R. 2014. "Policing the Lesbian and Gay Community: The Perceptions of Lesbian and Gay Police Officers." In D. Peterson and V. R. Panfil (eds.), *Handbook of LGBT Communities, Crime, and Justice*, pp. 183–205. New York: Springer.

Daum, J., and Johns, C. 1994. "Police Work from a Woman's Perspective." *The Police Chief* 61: 46–69.

DeJong, C. 2004. "Gender Differences in Officer Attitude and Behavior: Providing Comfort and Support." *Women and Criminal Justice* 15: 1–32.

Eisenberg, T., Kent, D. A., and Wall, C. R. 1973. *Police Personnel Practices in State and Local Government*. Washington, DC: Police Foundation.

Fitzgerald, L., Shullman, S. L., Bailey, N., Richards, M., Swecker, J., Gold, Y., Ormerod, M., and Weitzman, L. 1988. "The Incidence and Dimensions of Sexual Harassment in Academia and the Workplace." *Journal of Vocational Behavior* 32: 152–175.

Franklin, C. A. 2005. "Male Peer Support and the Police Culture: Understanding the Resistance and Opposition of Women in Policing." *Women and Criminal Justice* 16(3): 1–25.

Garcia, V. 2003. "Difference in the Police Department." *Journal of Contemporary Criminal Justice* 19: 330–344.

Garmire, B. L. (ed.). 1978. *Local Government, Police Management*. Washington, DC: International City Management Association.

Gosnell, H. F. 1935. *Negro Politicians: The Rise of Negro Politics in Chicago*. Chicago: University of Chicago Press.

*Griggs v. Duke Power Co.*, 401 US 432 (1971).

Haarr, R. N. 1997. "Patterns of Interaction in a Police Patrol Bureau: Race and Gender Barriers to Integration." *Justice Quarterly* 14: 53–85.

Hickman, M. J., Lawton, B. A., Piquero, A. R., and Greene, J. R. 2001. "Does Race Influence Police Disciplinary Process?" *Justice Research and Policy* 3: 97–113.

Hochstedler, E., and Conley, J. A. 1986. "Explaining Underrepresentation of Black Officers in City Police Agencies." *Journal of Criminal Justice* 14: 319–328.

Hoffman, P. B., and Hickey, E. R. 2005. "Use of Force by Female Police Officers." *Journal of Criminal Justice* 33: 145–151.

Johnson, C. S. 1947. *Into the Mainstream: A Survey of Best Practices in Race Relations in the South*. Chapel Hill: University of North Carolina Press.

Kennedy, B. 2012. "Unraveling Representative Bureaucracy: A Systematic Analysis of the Literature." *Administration and Society* 46: 395–421.

Kephart, W. M. 1957. *Racial Factors and Urban Law Enforcement*. Philadelphia: University of Pennsylvania Press.

Kuykendall, J. L., and Burns, D. E. 1980. "The Black Police Officer: An Historical Perspective." *Journal of Contemporary Criminal Justice* 4: 4–12.

Landrum, L. W. 1947. "The Case of Negro Police." *New South* 11: 5–6.

*Law Enforcement News*. 1999. "Plenty of Talk, Not Much Action: IACP Survey Says PDs Fall Short on Recruiting, Retaining Women." January 15/31: 1, 14.

Leinen, S. 1984. *Black Police, White Society*. New York: New York University Press.

Linden, R. 1983. "Women in Policing—A Study of Lower Mainland Royal Canadian Mounted Police Detachments." *Canadian Police College Journal* 7: 217–229.

Lonsway, K. A. 2003. "Tearing Down the Wall: Problems with Consistency, Validity, and Adverse Impact of Physical Agility Testing in Police Selection." *Police Quarterly* 6: 237–277.

Lonsway, K., Carrington, S., Aguire, P., Wood, M., Moore, M., Harrington, P., Smeal, E., and Spillar, K. 2002. *Equality Denied: The Status of Women in Policing, 2001*. Beverly Hills, CA: National Center for Women and Policing.

Lonsway, K. A., Paynich, R., and Hall, J. N. 2013. "Sexual Harassment in Law Enforcement: Incidence, Impact, and Perception." *Police Quarterly* 16(2): 177–210.

Martin, S. E. 1979. "*Police*women and Police*women*: Occupational Role Dilemmas and Choices of Female Officers." *Journal of Police Science and Administration* 7: 314–323.

Martin, S. E. 1980. *Breaking and Entering: Policewomen on Patrol*. Berkeley: University of California Press.

Martin, S. E. 1989. "Women in Policing: The Eighties and Beyond." In D. J. Kenney (ed.), *Police and Policing: Contemporary Issues*, pp. 3–16. New York: Praeger.

Martin, S. E., and Jurik, N. C. 1996. *Doing Justice, Doing Gender: Women in Law and Criminal Justice Occupations*. Thousand Oaks, CA: Sage.

McCrary, J. 2007. "The Effect of Court-Ordered Hiring Quotas on the Composition and Quality of Police." *American Economic Review* 97: 318–353.

McDowell, J. 1992. "Are Women Better Cops?" *Time* 132: 70–72.

Meier, K. 1993. "Representative Bureaucracy: A Theoretical and Empirical Exposition." *Research in Public Administration* 2: 1–34.

Melchionne, T. M. 1967. "Current Status and Problems of Women Police." *Journal of Criminal Law, Criminology and Police Science* 58: 257–260.

Miller, S. L. 1999. *Gender and Community Policing: Walking the Talk*. Boston: Northeastern University Press.

Miller, S. L., and Hodge, J. P. 2004. "Rethinking Gender and Community Policing: Cultural Obstacles and Policy Issues." *Law Enforcement Executive Forum* 4: 39–49.

Milton, C. 1972. *Women in Policing*. Washington, DC: Police Foundation.

Morabito, M., and Shelley, T. O. 2015. "Representative Bureaucracy: Understanding the Correlates of the Lagging Progress of Diversity in Policing." *Race and Justice* 5: 330–355.

Moran, T. K. 1988. "Pathways Toward a Nondiscriminatory Recruitment Policy." *Journal of Police Science and Administration* 16: 274–287.

Morash, M., and Greene, J. R. 1986. "Evaluating Women on Patrol: A Critique of Contemporary Wisdom." *Evaluation Review* 10: 231–255.

Morash, M., and Haarr, R. N. 1995. "Gender, Workplace Problems and Stress in Policing." *Justice Quarterly* 12: 113–140.

Myrdal, G. 1944. *An American Dilemma: The Negro Problem and Modern Democracy*. New York: Harper & Brothers.

National Advisory Commission on Civil Disorders. 1968. *Report of the National Advisory Commission on Civil Disorders*. Washington, DC: US Government Printing Office.

National Advisory Commission on Criminal Justice Standards and Goals. 1973. *Report on Police*. Washington, DC: US Government Printing Office.

National Center on Police and Community Relations. 1967. *A National Survey of Police and Community Relations, Field Survey V*. Washington, DC: US Government Printing Office.

Novak, K. J., Brown, R. A., and Frank, J. 2011. "Women on Patrol: An Analysis of Difference in Officer Arrest Behavior." *Policing: An International Journal of Police Strategies and Management* 34(4): 566–587.

Owings, C. 1925. *Women Police*. New York: Hitchcock.

Paoline, E. A., and Terrill, W. 2004. "Women Police Officers and the Use of Coercion." *Women and Criminal Justice* 15(3/4): 97–119.

Parsons, D., and Jesilow, P. 2001. *In the Same Voice: Women and Men in Law Enforcement*. Santa Ana, CA: Seven Locks Press.

Perez McClusky, C., and McClusky, J. 2004. "Diversity in Policing: Latino Representation in Law Enforcement." *Journal of Ethnicity in Criminal Justice* 2: 67–81.

Police Foundation. 1990. *Community Policing: A Binding Thread through the Fabric of Our Society*. Washington, DC: Police Foundation.

Prokos, A., and Padavic, I. 2002. "'There Oughta Be a Law Against Bitches': Masculinity Lessons in Police Academy Training." *Gender, Work and Organization* 9: 439–459.

President's Commission on Law Enforcement and Administration of Justice. 1967. *Task Force Report: The Police*. Washington, DC: US Government Printing Office.

President's Task Force on Twenty-First Century Policing. 2015. *Final Report of the President's Task Force on 21st Century Policing*. Washington, DC: Office of Community Oriented Policing Services.

Rabe-Hemp, C. E. 2008. "Female Officers and the Ethic of Care: Does Officer Gender Impact Police Behaviors?" *Journal of Criminal Justice* 36: 426–434.

Rabe-Hemp, C. E. 2009. "POLICEwomen or PoliceWOMEN? Doing Gender in Police Work." *Feminist Criminology* 4: 114–129.

Robinson, A. L. 2000. "Effect of a Domestic Violence Policy Change on Police Officers' Schemata." *Criminal Justice and Behavior* 27: 600–624.

Rubin, P. N. 1995. "Civil Rights and Criminal Justice: Employment Discrimination Overview." *Research in Action*. Washington, DC: National Institute of Justice.

Rudwick, E. 1960. "The Negro Policeman in the South." *Journal of Criminal Law, Criminology and Police Science* 11: 273–276.

Rudwick, E. 1962. *The Unequal Badge: Negro Policemen in the South, Report of the Southern Regional Council*. Atlanta: Southern Regional Council.

Selden, S. C. 1997. "Representative Bureaucracy: Examining the Linkage Between Passive and Active Representation in the Farmers Home Administration." *The American Review of Public Administration* 27(1): 22–42.

Shjarback, J. A., and Todak, N. 2019. "The Prevalence of Female Representation in Supervisory and Management Positions in American Law Enforcement: An Examination of Organizational Correlates." *Women and Criminal Justice*, 29, 129–147.

Sherman, L. J. 1973. "A Psychological View of Women in Policing." *Journal of Police Science and Administration* 1: 383–394.

Sherman, L. J. 1975. "Evaluation of Policewomen on Patrol in a Suburban Police Department." *Journal of Police Science and Administration* 3: 434–438.

Sichel, J. L., Friedman, L. N., Quint, J. C., and Smith, M. E. 1978. *Women on Patrol—A Pilot Study of Police Performance in New York City*. New York: Vera Institute of Justice.

Simpson, A. E. 1977. "The Changing Role of Women in Policing." In D. E. J. MacNamara (ed.), *Readings in Criminal Justice*, pp. 71–74. Guilford, CT: Dushkin.

Sklansky, D. A. 2006. "Not Your Father's Police Department: Making Sense of the New Demographics of Law Enforcement." *Journal of Criminal Law & Criminology* 96: 1209–1244.

Skogan, W., and Frydl, K. 2004. *Fairness and Effectiveness in Policing; The Evidence*. Washington, DC: National Academies Press, National Research Council of the National Academies.

Somvadee, C., and Morash, M. 2008. "Dynamics of Sexual Harassment for Policewomen Working alongside Men." *Policing: An International Journal of Police Strategies and Management* 31: 485–498.

Sullivan, P. S. 1989. "Minority Officers: Current Issues." In R. G. Dunham and G. P. Alpert (eds.), *Critical Issues in Policing: Contemporary Readings*, pp. 331–345. Prospect Heights, IL: Waveland.

Sulton, C., and Townsey, R. A. 1981. *Progress Report on Women in Policing*. Washington, DC: Police Foundation.

Sun, I. Y. 2011. "Policing Domestic Violence: Does Officer Gender Matter?" *Journal of Criminal Justice* 35(6): 581–595.

Timmins, W. M., and Hainsworth, B. E. 1989. "Attracting and Retaining Females in Law Enforcement." *International Journal of Offender Therapy and Comparative Criminology* 33: 197–205.

Todak, N., Leban, L, and Hixon, B. 2021. "Are Women Opting Out? A Mixed Methods Study of Women Patrol Officers' Promotional Aspirations." *Feminist Criminology*, 15, 658–679.

*United States v. Paradise*, 107 US 1053 (1987).

US Department of Justice. 2015. *Investigation of the Ferguson Police Department*. Washington, DC: US Department of Justice, Civil Rights Division.

Walker, S. 1977. *A Critical History of Police Reform*. Lexington, MA: Lexington Books.

Walker, S. 1989. *Employment of Black and Hispanic Police Officers, 1983–1988: A Follow-Up Study*. Omaha: Center for Applied Urban Research, University of Nebraska at Omaha.

Walker, S., and Turner, K. B. 1993. *A Decade of Modest Progress: Employment of Black and Hispanic Police Officers, 1983–1992*. Mimeo. Omaha: University of Nebraska at Omaha.

Weitzer, R. 2000. "White, Black, or Blue Cops? Race and Citizen Assessments of Police Officers," *Journal of Criminal Justice* 28: 313–324.

Whetstone, T. S. 2001. "Copping Out: Why Police Officers Decline to Participate in the Sergeant's Promotional Process." *American Journal of Criminal Justice* 25: 147–159.

Wilkins, V. M., and Williams, B. N. 2008. "Black or Blue: Racial Profiling and Representative Bureaucracy." *Public Administration Review* 68: 652–662.

Wilkins, V. M., and Williams, B. N. 2009. "Representing Blue: Representative Bureaucracy and Racial Profiling in the Latino Community." *Administration and Society* 40: 775–798.

Wilson, O. W., and McLaren, R. C. 1963. *Police Administration*, 3rd ed. New York: McGraw-Hill.

Zhao, J., He, N., and Lovrich, N. P. 2006. "Pursuing Gender Diversity in Police Organizations in the 1990s: A Longitudinal Analysis of Factors Associated with the Hiring of Female Officers." *Police Quarterly* 9: 463–485.

## CHAPTER 13

# Stress and Officer Safety

### CHAPTER OUTLINE

## CHAPTER OUTLINE  (continued)

### KEY TERMS

- actual danger
- acute stress
- chronic stress
- critical-incident debriefing
- distress
- eustress
- peer-counselling program
- perceived danger
- person-initiated danger
- physiological stress
- police stressors
- posttraumatic stress disorder
- potential danger
- psychological stress
- sensitization training
- situational danger
- social-supports model
- stressor-outcome model
- suicide prevention training

**T**HE NEGATIVE EFFECTS of stress on humans are well documented, and job-related stress is not unique to police. However, understanding the role of stress in policing is critically important, given the unique responsibilities of the police. In addition, policing entails unique sources of stress that are less prevalent, or even nonexistent, in many other occupations. These include departmental practices, shift work, danger, public apathy, boredom, and exposure to human misery. In addition, officers are expected to be in control at all times, yet they frequently encounter people at their very worst. This demand for ongoing restraint, coupled with a set of unique job stressors, may lead to high stress levels and, concomitantly, poor performance, dysfunctional behavior, burnout, and attrition.

Police officers routinely find themselves in risky and unsafe situations. Hundreds of officers die or are injured on duty each year, often at the hands of citizens they encounter, but more commonly while engaged in routine activities associated with the job. Reflecting upon the realities of officer safety is a critical part of any comprehensive examination of the police. The President's Task Force on Twenty-First Century Policing (2015, 61) identified officer wellness and safety in this way:

> The wellness and safety of law enforcement officers is critical not only to themselves, their colleagues, and their agencies but also to public safety. An officer whose capabilities, judgment, and behavior are adversely affected by poor physical or psychological health not only may be of little use to the community he or she serves but also may be a danger to the community and to other officers.

This chapter examines the concept of stress and stressors unique to police work, stress and emotional problems, policies and programs to help cope with stress, and officer safety.

## The Concept of Stress

Stress is a highly complex concept because of the overlap of both physiological and psychological processes. **Physiological stress** deals with the biological effects on the individual, including such factors as increased heart disease and high blood pressure (Violanti 2005).

**Psychological stress** is much less clear and more difficult to evaluate. According to Farmer (1990), most psychologists prefer to use the term *stress* to refer to the physiological changes that can be determined and the term *anxiety* to capture the psychological effects. This book will use the more popular conception of stress, which includes anxiety within its scope.

Although stress is difficult to define, one of the more accepted interpretations comes from the pioneering work of Selye (1974, 60), who suggests that "the body's nonspecific response to any demand placed on it" can cause stress. A person can be considered under stress when required to adapt to a particular situation. Selye further identifies two main types of stress: **eustress**, which is positive, and **distress**, which is negative. Some stress, then, is considered positive or pleasurable—for example, the stress produced by a challenging sporting activity. Police stress, by contrast, relates to those aspects of police work that lead to negative psychological and physiological consequences.

Two forms of distress may affect police behavior (Farmer 1990). The first is **acute stress**, which represents high-order emergency or sudden stress, such as shootings or high-speed chases. The second type is **chronic stress**, or low-level, gradual stress that includes the day-to-day routine of the job. Each type of stress is important to police work. Acute stressors, however, require large amounts of physical and psychological adaptation, while chronic stressors do not.

In studying the possible effects of stress, there are several key concerns:

1. **Stress, like beauty, is in the eye of the beholder.** One person's experience of stress may have little or nothing in common with another person's experience.

2. **Stress is cumulative.** Minor stresses may pile up to produce major stress that leads to a heart attack or actual physical or mental breakdown.

3. **Prolonged emotional stress.** Stress that is a part of the everyday work environment can produce wear and tear on the body, with effects that may prove irreversible if not treated in time.

4. **When it comes to stress, there are no supermen or superwomen.** Stress tolerance levels may vary from person to person, but everyone is susceptible to the ravages of stress. (Territo and Vetter 1981, 7)

## Occupational Stress

How stressful is police work? In general, there has been a tendency to give an alarmist answer, which is interesting in that existing research does not unanimously support this conclusion (Terry 1981, 1985). In a review of research on police stress, Brown and Campbell (1994) concluded that police do not experience more stress than people in other occupations.

Pendleton et al. (1989), for example, compared the stress and strain levels of police officers, firefighters, and government employees and found that government workers experienced the greatest stress and firefighters the least, with police falling in the middle. Thus, these authors concluded that contrary to popular belief, the police as a work group do not experience more health and social problems than all other occupations. The study urged caution, however, in that the research could not control for the possibility that police work could actually be more stressful but that those selected to be police officers might be better able to manage stress. As noted in Chapter 6, officers undergo a thorough screening process, including psychological screening. In a study of more than 500 officers in an Australian police department, Hart, Wearing, and Headey (1995) discovered that compared with other groups, police display relatively high levels of psychological well-being and concluded that collectively, their findings indicate that policing is not highly stressful. Furthermore, Terry (1985, 509) has suggested that the push to support policing as a high-stress occupation may lie in an attempt to develop professional recognition and create a professional self-image:

> The concept of stress . . . provides a tidy symbolic representation of the crime control and order maintenance functions of police work as well as providing a ready link to other professional occupations that bear responsibility for other people's lives.

Some research suggests that levels of stress vary by job assignments. Specifically, Wallace, Roberg, and Allen (1985), in a study of five police departments, found that narcotics investigators had significantly higher job burnout rates than either former narcotics investigators or patrol officers. In another comparative study of job burnout and officer assignment, Roberg, Hayhurst, and Allen (1988) discovered that although narcotics investigators had the highest levels of burnout, civilian dispatch personnel exhibited significantly higher levels of occupational stress than did either former narcotics investigators or patrol officers. The authors concluded that although patrol work may be stressful, other job assignments (including civilian dispatchers) may be more stressful. Accordingly, although appropriate actions to prevent or reduce stress for patrol officers are warranted, it should be recognized that all police personnel should be afforded appropriate stress-reduction programs.

## Overview of Stressors

Loo (2005) summarizes **police stressors** into five distinct categories: stressors related to (1) police work itself, (2) the police organization, (3) the criminal justice system, (4) the public or community, and (5) personal life and family. Loo (2005, 103–104) elaborates as follows:

> Police work itself is the source of many stressors due to work overload, shift work, exposure to violent and life-threatening situations, and frustrations in trying to solve cases. The police organization is another source of stressors because of departmental politics, inadequate resources to do the job, lack of support and recognition from management, and autocratic leadership styles, among other factors. The criminal justice system is a common source of stress because of the demands of court appearances, being challenged in court, and the perception that the justice system is slow and too lenient on criminals. Relations with the public and community can be major sources of stress when police believe that their efforts are not appreciated by the community they serve and that the public is apathetic about supporting the police. Complaints and assaults against police only reinforce the belief that they stand alone. Finally, but importantly, policing affects the family in substantial ways. Shift work, temporary assignments, and postings disrupt family life as well as the officers' social life and, likely, physical and mental health. Because police want to protect their families from violence, crimes, and nastiness that they experience on the job, spouses and children may view police as uncommunicative and distant, thus leading to marital problems and marital breakdown.

### Sources of Stress in Policing

Violanti and Aron (1995) ranked 60 police work stressors for 103 officers in a large police department in New York State. The top 15 stressors are ranked by their mean scores in Table 13.1. The top two stressors were "killing someone in the line of duty" and "fellow

**TABLE 13.1** Police Stressors Ranked by Mean Scores

| STRESSOR | MEAN SCORE |
| --- | --- |
| Killing someone in the line of duty | 79.4 |
| Fellow officer killed | 76.7 |
| Physical attack | 71.0 |
| Battered child | 69.2 |
| High-speed chase | 63.7 |
| Shift work | 61.2 |
| Use of force | 61.0 |
| Inadequate department support | 61.0 |
| Incompatible partner | 60.4 |
| Accident in patrol car | 59.9 |
| Insufficient personnel | 58.9 |
| Aggressive crowds | 56.7 |
| Felony in progress | 55.3 |
| Excessive discipline | 53.3 |
| Plea bargaining | 52.8 |
| Overall mean score of 60 ranked stressors | 44.8 |

*Source*: Adapted from J. M. Violanti and F. Aron, "Police Stressors: Variations in Percent among Police Personnel." *Journal of Criminal Justice* 23 (1995): 290.

officer killed." Although these incidents occur infrequently, they have a significant psychological impact on the individuals involved. It is further interesting to note that 8 of the top 15 stressors (i.e., killing someone, officer killed, physical attack, high-speed chase, use of force, auto accidents, aggressive crowds, and a felony in progress) are related to potentially dangerous aspects of the work. Shift work was also reported as a major stressor because sleep patterns, as well as eating habits and family relationships, may be affected by rotating shifts. "Inadequate department support" (by supervisors) was another high-ranking stressor because of the paramilitary structure of the department that minimizes interpersonal relationships between supervisors and subordinates. Other findings indicated that officers with work experience of 6 to 10 years had higher mean stressor scores than those with work experience of 1 to 5 years. This may be because newer officers with less work experience may remain challenged and still cling to idealism, whereas the more experienced officers may be less enchanted with police work and thereby find it more stressful and frustrating.

The most significant early study attempting to identify police stressors was that of Kroes, Margolis, and Hurrell (1974), whose research design was similar to that of Violanti and Aron's (1995) study. These researchers interviewed 100 male officers and asked them what they considered the most "bothersome" aspects about their job (it was assumed that "bothersome" and "stressful" were synonymous terms). Table 13.2 indicates the 12 categories into which the responses fell and the frequency of the responses.

Court leniency with criminals and the scheduling of court appearances on "off days" were the highest stressors. The second-highest stressors were administrative policies

**TABLE 13.2 Bothersome Aspects of Police Work**

| CATEGORY | DEFINITION | NUMBER OF RESPONSES |
|---|---|---|
| Courts | Court rulings and procedures | 56 |
| Administration | Administrative policies/procedures; administrative support of officers | 51 |
| Equipment | Adequacy/state of repair of equipment | 39 |
| Community relations | Public apathy/negative reaction to and lack of support of policemen | 38 |
| Changing work shifts | 28-day rotating shift schedule | 18 |
| Relations with supervisor | Difficulties in getting along with supervisor | 16 |
| Nonpolice work | Tasks required of the officer that are not considered police responsibility | 14 |
| Other policemen | Fellow officers not performing their job | 8 |
| Bad assignment | Work assignment that the officer disliked | 6 |
| Other | Stresses that did not readily fit into the above categories | 5 |
| Isolation/boredom | Periods of inactivity and separation from social contacts | 3 |
| Pay | Adequacy or equity of salary | 2 |

*Note*: Because officers may mention more than one stressor, the overall total can exceed 100.

*Source*: Adapted from W. H. Kroes, B. L. Margolis, and J. L. Hurrell, Jr., "Job Stress in Policemen," *Journal of Police Science and Administration* 2 (1974): 145. Reprinted by permission.

regarding work assignments, procedures, personal conduct, and lack of administrative support. The third most significant stressor was the inadequacy and poor state of repair of equipment. The fourth stressor was poor community relations, including apathy and negative responses exhibited by the public toward officers. Crisis situations that might affect officer health and safety were categorized under "other," because few officers mentioned them.

The most striking difference between these two studies is that the dangerous stressors listed in Violanti and Aron's (1995) study do not appear in the Kroes et al. (1974) study. One of the reasons for these differences may be the ways the surveys were conducted. The 1995 study used a 60-item check-off list (listing potentially dangerous stressors); the 1974 study, as mentioned, asked officers to list those aspects of policing that were "bothersome" to them.

A similar finding was reported in a study by Crank and Caldero (1991), where concerns over occupational danger were among the least frequently cited stressors. As one officer commented, "the stress caused by work on the street is nothing compared to the stress caused by the administration in this department" (Crank and Caldero 1991, 336).

Specifically, the survey conducted by Crank and Caldero (1991) studied 167 line officers in eight medium-size municipal departments in Illinois. Responses were categorized into five areas: (1) organization, (2) task environment, (3) judiciary, (4) personal or family concerns, and (5) city government. More than two-thirds of respondents (68 percent) identified the department as their principal source of stress, especially problems relating to management and supervisors (42 percent), followed by shift changes (17 percent). The second most frequently cited source of stress (16 percent) was the task environment, with citizen contact as the primary source in this category (29 percent) and concerns regarding potential danger as the second source (21 percent). The judiciary was the third-ranked source (7 percent); the primary concern here was related to the court's failure to prosecute criminals adequately. Personal or family concerns were ranked fourth (4 percent), and city government was ranked fifth (3 percent).

The findings of this 1991 study are similar to those of the 1974 and 1995 studies regarding stress relating to inadequate departmental support and shift work. One conclusion from the many studies on police stressors is that organizational stressors (e.g., supervisors or shift work) produce more stress than the dangerous elements of police work typically assumed to be the most stressful aspects of the job (Violanti 2005). The reason for differences in studies is likely the result of different survey methodologies. When officers are simply asked what is most stressful, they are more likely to note organizational features of the job. And when surveys list job aspects and include the dangerous elements, officers are more likely to rank these dangerous elements as more stressful (Abdollahi 2002). However, as Kroes et al. (1974) suggest, officers may not consciously think about physical dangers at work so as to maintain their psychological well-being.

Interestingly, with respect to the courts or judiciary, the two studies from the 1990s found relatively low rankings (3 of 5 in 1991 and 30 of 60 in 1995) compared with the 1974 findings (first). In the years since the study by Kroes et al. (1974), officers likely have learned more about and adapted to court decisions with which they may not agree. In addition, departments likely have improved courtroom training to ensure that officers meet certain requisites when testifying in court.

## Emerging Sources of Stress

In their interviews with approximately 100 people, including law enforcement administrators, union and association officials, mental health practitioners, and 50 line officers and family members from large and small departments, Finn and Tomz (1997) discovered that today's police encounter new sources of stress. For example, although community policing (COP) has produced increased job satisfaction among many officers, others have found the transition stressful. Lord (1996, 2005), in her studies of the Charlotte–Mecklenburg Police Department, which was attempting to move to COP, found increased levels of stress among officers and sergeants, particularly for role conflict and role ambiguity. Some officers reported that the higher expectations of solving community crime problems enhanced job pressure and burnout. Furthermore, some officers experienced disapproval from those not involved in COP, which requires attributes that some officers may not possess and not be screened for, such as interpersonal, verbal, and problem-solving skills. Therefore, the transition to COP may be difficult and require training and communication to circumvent this new form of stress.

A newer source of stress noted by Finn and Tomz (1997) involves what officers perceive as negative media coverage, public scrutiny, and prospective litigation. Many officers felt stressed by negative publicity such as that surrounding the Rodney King incident, the

Abner Louima incident, the Amadou Diallo shooting in New York, police corruption scandals, allegations of police abuse in post-Katrina New Orleans, and other dubious police incidents. These perceptions likely are even more intense after high profile use-of-force incidents following video footage from the events in Ferguson, Missouri, and elsewhere across the country. Generally, officers perceived that the media focused attention on offenders' rights instead of victims' rights or officers' rights, which officers resented. More important, respondents demonstrated an increased fear of lawsuits, both civil and criminal, and consistently worried about the use of force endangering their lives.

Finally, it has been recognized that stress may vary across gender and racial lines. As discussed in Chapter 12, women and racial/ethnic minorities often experience harassment, discrimination, and bias within the policing occupation. It follows that these experiences (coupled with the typical sources of stress) can result in higher levels of stress among women and people of color. He, Zhao, and Archbold (2002) reported that female officers had significantly higher levels of depression and somatization (e.g., physical reactions to stress like headaches, nausea, and stomach pains) than their male counterparts. Morash and Haarr (1995) reported similar results for levels of stress between male and female officers. This difference was even greater for Black female officers, possibly as a reaction to double stigmatization. The authors went on to note that women also reported different sources of stress, specifically difficulties related to their outsider status in policing. Women reported stressors that included bias, language and sexual harassment, and stigma resulting from appearance. Minorities reported feeling invisible within the organization as a source of stress and significantly higher levels of stress from lack of advancement opportunities as well as stigma resulting from appearance (see also Morash, Kwak, and Haarr 2006). Piquero (2005) examined strain and stress among police officers in Baltimore and found that female officers reported higher levels of depression. The sources of stress also appeared to vary across gender—male officers reported elevated levels of stress from job-related tasks and the media, whereas female officers identified gender-specific stressors such as discrimination.

Research by He, Zhao, and Ren (2005), however, complicates this area of study. Consistent with earlier research, the authors found that female officers had higher levels of stress than male officers. But their research also indicated that white males experienced higher levels of stress than Black male officers, whereas stress levels did not vary between white and Black female officers.

The COVID-19 pandemic and the death of George Floyd in 2020 were new sources of stress in policing. First responders like the police routinely operated in harm's way during the pandemic, and as we will discuss later in this chapter, many officers died from COVID-related complications. After Floyd's murder, many cities experienced protests and anti-police demonstrations, and there were calls for defunding or even abolishing the police. There is evidence that the fallout from the Floyd murder correlated with officers leaving policing. Specifically, Mourtgos, Adams, and Nix (2022) found a 279 percent increase in officer resignations after the protests in May 2020 began, yet they also reported no change in retirements or involuntary separations. In other words, the stress associated with policing immediately after the Floyd murder did not motivate officers to retire or increase departments firing officers; rather, officers were quitting. They noted this can have serious consequences for policing, including a loss of institutional memory, reduced organizational performance, and increased workload for remaining officers.

Eisenberg (1975) pointed out that minority officers face the additional stresses of rejection and skepticism by members of their own race and may not be accepted into the "police family," a source of support, camaraderie, and occupational identity. In support of Eisenberg, Haarr and Morash (1999) found in their national survey of more than 1,000 officers in 24 departments that African American officers were significantly more likely than whites to use bonding with officers with whom they shared a racial bond as a strategy for coping with stress.

In "Voices from the Field," Chief (ret.) Joseph McHale from the Marion (IA) Police Department discusses his perspective on stress in police patrol work.

## Line-of-Duty and Crisis Situations

The continual potential for crisis situations in the line of duty is what tends to differentiate police work from most other occupations. On the one hand, routine patrol can be extremely busy, emotionally draining, and potentially dangerous. On the other hand, the routine can become boring and uneventful. The amount and type of activity on any particular patrol depends on many factors, including the type of city, beat, and shift. In some patrol areas, there can be little doubt that the high workload, combined with intense emotional demands and potential physical harm, is conducive to high levels of stress and strain. Understanding the level of stress induced by these, and other, circumstances is crucial.

Research involving physiological measures (e.g., heart rate and salivary cortisol) has attempted to identify the specific situations police officers confront on the street that elicit high levels of stress. Anderson, Litzenberger, and Plecas (2002) monitored the heart rates of individuals while they were on patrol. The authors noted that an elevated heart rate is a particular indicator of physical stress. Thus, their research attempted to monitor and categorize activities that produced the highest elevation in heart rates among police officers. They learned that heart rates begin to elevate prior to the commencement of the shift. Once in uniform, officers experienced anticipatory stress, resulting in a 23 percent increase in heart rates. In fact, the authors found that an officer's heart rate was 17 percent higher during the entire shift than when at rest. This finding indicates that officers experience physical reactions to policing, even absent critical incidents.

### Posttraumatic Stress Disorder

The psychological stress caused by exposure to crises or traumatic events can lead to a condition known as **posttraumatic stress disorder** (PTSD). Although officers may not suffer physical injury, emotional trauma may be catastrophic and could result in PTSD. Although some officers recover within a few weeks, others may experience protracted trauma, which could adversely affect both the department and the personal lives of the officers. This disorder has been found in veterans who have been exposed to the stresses and violence of a war experience.

Officers reporting higher levels of work-related stress is positively related to symptoms of PTSD (Liberman et al. 2002; Violanti et al. 2018), though understanding how work-related stress evolves to PTSD, or what coping mechanisms may be used to reduce PTSD, remains inconsistent. Martin, McKean, and Veltkamp (1986) conducted a study of a group of 53 officers and discovered that 26 percent suffered from PTSD. Stressors leading to PTSD included shooting someone; being shot; working with child abuse, spouse abuse, and rape cases; being threatened or having family threatened; and observing death through homicide (including colleagues being killed), suicide, or natural disaster. There is a cumulative effect in which officers are exposed to more traumatic events over time, which in turn are related to experiencing PTSD symptoms. In other words, officers are exposed to more traumatic events over time (e.g., being involved in a shooting, having a coworker shot

# Joseph McHale

*Senior Manager, Institute for Intergovernmental Research and Chief (ret.), Marion (IA) Police Department*

When I began my career with the Kansas City (MO) Police Department in 1991, I remember watching the events unfold in Los Angeles with the LAPD and Rodney King. I was 21 years old and attempting to assimilate into my role as a police officer. The mystique of "protect and serve" quickly evaporated into "distrust and animosity" from a society that had been given an unprecedented glimpse of the stark reality of police misconduct.

During my FTO [field training officer] phase, I realized the stress to perform was immense, and the lessons of the rigorous academy curriculum made it evident in my mind that there was a threat to my personal safety at every turn of my day. In April 1992, the officers involved in the Rodney King incident were acquitted, and I was thrust into riot gear and placed in tactical positions across the city as Los Angeles erupted into chaos. Fortunately, Kansas City experienced very little disorder, and my role quickly returned to normal.

That part of my career is one of the most vivid memories I have and is very similar to what we have seen in the United States over the past few years. As the Division Commander, I am now responsible for the management and deployment of my personnel that resemble that 21-year-old kid who endured the Rodney King era. I wonder how I would have done as a new officer in 2016 with the stressors placed on current officers.

The internal stressors are abundant in policing in ways they never had been before. The typical field officer is under constant scrutiny via video recording systems and the tracking of every keystroke that is made via computer systems. The age of roll call as captured in pop culture is long gone—today, roll call is an arduous process of ensuring body-worn cameras are working, computers are logged on, Tasers are tested, emails are checked, and so on and so on. My greatest stressor in 1992 was to ensure my clipboard had all the necessary reports ready to go for my shift. I would grab my baton, helmet, and car keys and walk out the door to my patrol car. All of the 2016 roll-call processes are critical and "not to be missed" or disciplinary action results, and you haven't even left the station yet. Officers are now scrutinized

internally more than ever before. Reviews of driving habits, car chases, and use of force are mandated and routinely conducted by command staff. While these reviews are well intended and certainly necessary, the stress that is placed internally on officers has never been this high. Police managers must be cognizant of these stressors and understand how they can be perceived by line personnel.

The external stressors of social media, the 24-hour news cycle, and video cameras in every pocket present a unique challenge to the future of law enforcement. A 10-second clip from an incident that unfolded over several hours is now flashed across media outlets, judgments are made, and public perceptions are changed in an instant. The public never receives the "after action" files to review, and the media certainly draw conclusions that vary widely based on political and moral views. Errors or misconduct by officers captured on video and looped across the media impact community relations across the country and contribute to officers' stress.

Stress affects our bodies in many different ways and is processed differently by human beings. Mental and physical breakdowns of law enforcement officers are commonplace and often accompanied by alcoholism, divorce, and contribute to misconduct. For officers to admit that they are having a problem dealing with stress continues to be an issue for police managers because in the past officers risked being labeled as weak, or incompetent, which still hampers efforts to deal with issues in a productive manner. As the President's Task Force on Twenty-First Century Policing noted, programs to assist our personnel in their personal lives and to deal with the stressors this law enforcement profession places upon them must continue to be enhanced.

The future of law enforcement is upon us, and our new generations of employees are more capable and competent than ever before. The use of intelligence and technology will enable us to make arrests that matter and not just "make arrests." Additionally, it is important for police managers to keep a vigilant eye on officers' well-being in an effort to identify officers and situations that may be contributing to distress and vulnerability.

on-duty, responding to an incident involving the death of a child), and these are related to stress symptoms (e.g., nightmares, recurring memories, re-experiencing physical reactions related to the trauma; Craddock and Telesco 2022).

Another study of 100 suburban officers found a correlation between duty-related stress and symptoms of PTSD (Robinson, Sigman, and Wilson 1997). Thirteen percent of the sample met the criteria for PTSD; the best predictors for the diagnosis were associated with a critical event related to the job and exposure to a life-and-death threat. Sixty-three percent of the respondents stated that a **critical-incident debriefing** (i.e., counseling) would be beneficial following an extremely stressful crisis event.

There is reason to question the short- and long-term impact of critical-incident debriefing, however. Rose and colleagues (2002) conducted a large, systematic examination of studies performed in a number of different countries and reported the impact is far from what would be expected. They found that single-session debriefings of officers experiencing a traumatic event did not reduce the likelihood of experiencing PTSD. Null results were observed at different periods, including 1 to 4 months, 6 to 13 months, and 3 years. In other words, a single psychological debriefing was no better than no briefing at all. One study, in fact, found single-session debriefings were correlated to *increased* PTSD after one year. Additionally, no benefit was observed for less serious consequences of trauma, such as depression or anxiety. While single-session debriefings may be common sense and humane responses to traumatic events, the research evidence suggests they are at ineffective and at worst make a bad situation worse.

Loo (1986) found that officers experienced the most stress reactions within three days after a critical incident. The symptoms most commonly reported were preoccupation with the traumatic incident (39 percent) and anger (25 percent). Other reported symptoms of PTSD were sleep disturbances, flashbacks, feelings of guilt, wishing it had not happened, and depression (see Table 13.3). Many of the officers continued to report increased anger and lowered work interest one month after the incident. The course of recovery varied, but the average time for a return to "feeling normal" was 20 weeks after the critical incident.

Martin et al. (1986) concluded from their study that **sensitization training** regarding officers' work with victims, as well as their own victimization, should be conducted early in their careers. Such training may help to increase officers' empathy for crime victims and ability cope with their own reactions to the stress caused by dealing with such situations. Kureczka (1996) believes that officers will not ask for help for fear of being stigmatized. In other words, in an effort to preserve their "macho" image, officers remain reluctant to discuss their emotional responses to critical incidents.

As a routine practice, department policy should mandate that officers visit a mental health professional for screening and further psychological treatment, as needed, subsequent to any critical incident. However, single-session debriefings as a sole response to trauma should be avoided. Stress-management programs should be provided to all recruits, and ongoing stress-education programs should be provided for all officers. As an added precaution, Kureczka (1996) advocates the use of officers who are specially trained to recognize problems and make referrals as deemed necessary. Such a **peer-counseling program** has been established in the Fort Worth Police Department, under the supervision of the Psychological Services Unit (Greenstone, Dunn, and Leviton 1995). Peer counselors are available 24 hours a day, seven days a week, and serve voluntarily and without compensation in addition to their regular police duties. The counselors receive basic training in crisis intervention and critical-incident debriefing. Inside Policing 13.1 describes a wellness program developed in Stockton,

**TABLE 13.3** Common Reactions to Stress in Policing

| PHYSICAL REACTIONS | EMOTIONAL REACTIONS | COGNITIVE REACTIONS | BEHAVIOR/COPING REACTIONS |
|---|---|---|---|
| • Headaches | • Anxiety | • Flashbacks | • Reduced motivation |
| • Muscle aches | • Fear | • Nightmares | • Reduced job satisfaction |
| • Sleep disturbances | • Guilt | • Slowed thinking | • Lack of job involvement |
| • Changes in appetite | • Sadness | • Difficulty making decisions and problem solving | • Lack of job involvement |
| • Decreased interest in sexual activity | • Anger | • Disorientation | • Absenteeism |
| • Heart disease | • Irritability | • Lack of concentration | • Premature retirement |
| • Ulcers | • Feeling lost or unappreciated | • Memory lapses | • Poor relationships with nonpolice friends |
| • High blood pressure | • Withdrawal | • Posttraumatic stress disorder | • Divorce |
| | | | • Substance abuse |
| | | | • Suicide |

*Sources:* Adapted from A. W. Kureczka, "Critical Incident Stress in Law Enforcement." *FBI Law Enforcement Bulletin* 62 (1996): 15; V. B. Lord, "An Impact of Community Policing: Reported Stressors, Social Support, and Strain among Police Officers in a Changing Police Department." *Journal of Criminal Justice* 24, no. 6 (1996): 503–522; V. B. Lord, D. O. Gray, and S. B. Pond, "The Police Stress Inventory: Does It Measure Stress?" *Journal of Criminal Justice* 19 (1991): 139–150; J. M. Violanti, "Dying for the Job: Psychological Stress, Disease, and Mortality in Police Work." In H. Copes (ed), *Policing and Stress* (Upper Saddle River, NJ: Pearson Prentice Hall, 2005), 87–102.

---

**INSIDE POLICING 13.1**  **Improving Mental Health in Policing**

This article describes the Stockton, California, Police Department's wellness network aimed at helping officers deal with stress and trauma. The award-winning initiative includes a significant orientation for new recruits and proactive measures when officers encounter difficult situations in the field. The department endured layoffs earlier in the decade while the city went through bankruptcy, adding to the burdens facing officers in a violent, high-crime environment. So far, worker's compensation claims are down, as are citizen complaints.

**Discussion Question:** How would comprehensive wellness programs differ throughout officers' life course? Would new officers benefit from a different wellness curriculum than veteran officers? Why, and how might it be different?

SOURCE: *Modern Policing* blog, February 23, 2019, gcordner.wordpress.com/2019/02/23/focus-on-wellness-in-stockton/.

---

California, that is implemented during officers' orientation and has been hailed as a model for other departments to emulate.

Finally, counseling services or some type of stress-management program should also be made available to family members. In turn, family members might be able to understand and provide further nurturing and support to the officer involved (see the discussion under "Social Supports and Police Stress"). More important, intervention and treatment may prevent suicide, the worst possible outcome of work-related stress.

Although little is known about how PTSD influences officers at work, it has been suggested that such a disorder might lead to increased brutality by the police. Kellogg and Harrison (1991), for instance, contend that much police brutality can be attributed to PTSD. Although they present no empirical evidence to support their claims, it seems likely that some officers suffering from PTSD could vent their anger and frustration on citizens through violence. Consequently, this is an important area for future study. It is important that scholars attempt to determine how widespread PTSD may be among the nation's police, as well as its potential impact on police behavior.

### Shift Work

Shift work not only adversely affects an officer's performance but also puts an added burden on family and friends. Although much of the rest of society orchestrates their leisure activities around a day schedule, officers reserve their activities for days off, because on workdays, many find it difficult to do anything other than eat, sleep, and go to work. According to O'Neill and Cushing (1991), relationships with family and friends are disrupted, and many officers experience sleep alterations (consisting of subjective self-ratings of poor sleep quality, difficulty in falling asleep, frequent awakenings, and insomnia); persistent fatigue (which does not disappear after sleep, weekends, or vacations, thus differing from physiological fatigue caused by physical or mental effort); behavioral changes (e.g., irritability, tantrums, malaise, and inadequate performance); and digestive troubles (including dyspepsia to epigastric pain and peptic ulcers). Charles et al. (2007) reported that working night shifts was correlated with sleep-related problems. In their sample of Buffalo police officers, those assigned to night shifts slept in shorter durations and were more likely to snore, which is often associated with fatigue and other sleep-related issues. To combat the fatigue that appears inherent to working this shift, the authors advocate for worksite exercise programs to improve officers' sleep quality and avoid work-related problems and safety issues.

Some evidence indicates that many of the problems associated with shift changes, including sleep problems and fatigue, use of alcohol and sleeping pills, increased sick time, and accidents, can be substantially reduced if schedules are designed to accommodate the body's natural circadian rhythm, which controls sleep–wake cycles. In recent years, police departments have been moving away from rotating shifts, instead implementing fixed shifts. Amendola et al. (2011a) report that nearly half (46 percent) of police departments implemented rotating shifts in 2005; however, by 2009, only 24.7 percent of police departments were still using rotating shifts.

Compressed workweek shifts have become increasingly popular within American policing, and there is scientific support for implementing 10-hour or 12-hour shifts rather than the traditional 8-hour workday. Amendola et al. (2011b) report that officers working 10-hour shifts benefit from approximately half an hour of additional sleep per night, which over the course of a year can significantly contribute to reduced fatigue and increased officer safety (i.e., fewer job-related accidents). Officers on compressed workweek shifts reported working less overtime, whereas officers on 8-hour shifts had five times as much overtime as those on 10-hour shifts. Furthermore, officers on 10-hour shifts reported a higher quality of life off the job. Overall, there appear to be important benefits to officers of working 10-hour shifts, which can translate into organizational benefits as well. Specifically, reduction in overtime can represent a fiscal benefit for police departments in an era of shrinking budgets, and if fatigue and safety are indeed impacted, then this reduction in overtime will also translate into reduced costs associated with absenteeism, sick leave, and medical concerns.

## Social Supports and Police Stress

Almost all research on police stress has been based on a **stressor-outcome model**, meaning that a stressful circumstance or stressor leads directly to a negative outcome, such as psychological stress or a physical ailment. Another perspective to the study of stress, however, the **social-supports model**, suggests that an individual may be more or less insulated against the effects of stressors depending on whether that person has a social-support network—friends, coworkers, and family members—in place. In other words, social supports may help people cope with stressful circumstances and thus lessen the potential negative effects.

From this perspective, Cullen et al. (1985) studied police stress in five suburban police departments in a large Midwestern city. The authors classified police stress along two different dimensions: that involving work and that affecting the officer's personal life. Work-related stressors that were not infrequent situations but rather ongoing parts of the police officer's job were chosen, such as role problems, court problems, potential danger, and shift changes. Social support measures included two work-related sources (peer support and supervisory support) and two nonwork sources (family support and community support). The authors discovered that work stress was most significantly influenced by perceived danger, which could be counteracted by supervisory support. Life stress was influenced not only by perceived danger but also by court problems and shift changes. It was further found that family support counteracted stress in personal life.

Danger was the only stressor significantly related to both dimensions of stress. Although the respondents worked in communities with relatively low rates of serious crime and 86 percent disagreed with the statement that "A lot of people I work with get physically injured in the line of duty," the vast majority of the sample also believed that they had a "chance of getting hurt in my job." In other words, they perceived the *potential* for physical injury as ever-present and inherent in their work. Thus, although policing may not be particularly dangerous in low-crime communities, the threat of injury is constant and may have stress-related consequences. Another interesting finding was that both court problems and shift changes were significantly related to stress in an officer's personal life, but not to work stress. This finding is important in that it "sensitizes us to the possibility that officers may adjust to the more strenuous features of their occupation while at work but nevertheless suffer deleterious effects on their general psychological health" (Cullen et al. 1985, 514).

Research has reported that seeking social support reduces the impact of work stressors and emotional distress. However, stress-management programs should be expanded to consider a range of stressful life events, including off-duty stressors (Patterson 2003).

Supervisory support clearly mitigated work stress, whereas family support was helpful in lessening personal-life stress. These findings suggest that departments should establish programs and provide training adequate to deal with stress in both work and personal life while taking into account various social supports.

## Consequences of Stress

Chronic and persistent stress can contribute to premature death, and additional research on stress and emotional problems experienced by officers has focused on a variety of issues, including alcohol and drug abuse, suicide, and marital and family-related problems (e.g., divorce). This section highlights negative or passive coping strategies related to work-related stress.

### Alcohol Abuse

Hurrell and Kroes (1975) have suggested that police work may be especially conducive to excessive drinking, because officers frequently work in an environment in which social drinking is common. Stress, peer pressure, social isolation, young males, and a subculture that condones alcohol use all contribute to acceptance of excessive alcohol use (Violanti et al. 2011). This pattern of alcohol consumption can have negative effects on officers as well as police departments. Stinson et al. (2013) documented 782 separate incidents where officers were arrested for driving under the influence between 2005 and 2010. More than half of these arrests involved traffic accidents, and more than 24 percent involved injuries. The authors further reported that more than 30 percent of officers involved with arrests for driving under the influence lost their job as a result. These incidents certainly create questions of police legitimacy in the mind of the public, similar to corruption and misconduct.

In their survey of 852 police officers in metropolitan Sydney (Australia), Richmond et al. (1998) reported relatively high rates of unhealthy lifestyles. They found that almost half of the respondents reported excessive alcohol consumption and that younger officers were particularly likely to consume alcohol. In fact, they reported that approximately two-fifths of male officers and one-third of female officers reported binge drinking. The authors warned that excessive consumption of alcohol could have detrimental effects on officer performance, including slower reaction time, impaired performance, absenteeism, and liver problems. The authors cited other research that found deaths from alcoholic liver disease among officers (1.2 percent) to be twice as high as in the general public (0.6 percent). They also noted a high level of other unhealthy behaviors, including smoking, being overweight, and absence of exercise.

Davey, Obst, and Sheehan (2000) found the frequency at which officers consumed alcohol was similar to the national averages; however, they also reported that officers were more likely to engage in binge drinking. In their sample of 4,193 officers, 30 percent were classified as at risk for harmful levels of consumption, whereas 3 percent were classified as alcohol dependent. Consumption and substance abuse may not be limited to off-duty behavior. Perhaps most startling was the fact that 25 percent of the sample reported drinking alcohol while on duty.

The policing occupation may be particularly susceptible to alcohol use, in part because it is a male-dominated profession. However, evidence also exists that female officers use alcohol at rates similar to those of their male counterparts. Research by Ballenger et al. (2010) classified 11 percent of male officers and almost 16 percent of female officers as at risk for alcohol abuse, and more than 36 percent of officers reported binge drinking in the past 30 days. Ballenger et al. (2010, 27) also noted that 18 percent of male officers and 16 percent of female officers had "significant lifetime histories of adverse social and interpersonal consequences related to alcohol use, with 7.5 percent reporting MAST (Michigan Alcoholism Screening Test) scores consistent with . . . alcohol abuse or dependence." They go on to note that 3.4 percent of males and 3.7 percent of females reported having more than 28 drinks in the previous week.

Evidence suggests a relationship between strain and alcohol use among officers. Swatt, Gibson, and Piquero (2007) found officer with higher levels of stress reported increased alcohol consumption. Specifically, officers with higher levels of strain (stress) reported correspondingly higher levels of anxiety, depression, and anger. In addition, they reported that anxiety and depression were positively related to problematic alcohol intake, although no relationship was observed for anger and alcohol. This finding provides partial support for the assertion that officers use alcohol as a mechanism to cope with anxiety and depression brought on by job-related stress. Negative, or passive, coping strategies (including alcohol use but also denial, self-blame, or behavioral disengagement) were also strongly associated with work-related stress overall, as well as with symptoms of PTSD (Violanti et al. 2018).

Police departments have traditionally used the "character flaw" theory to deal with alcohol abuse. This theory calls for the denunciation and dismissal of officers with an alcohol problem, because they reflect badly on the department's reputation and legitimacy. What is not recognized is that "alcoholism may result from the extraordinary stresses of the job and that eliminating the officer does not do away with the sources of stress" (Hurrell and Kroes 1975, 241). Today, however, many departments are attempting to deal with alcoholic employees through in-house educational programs and admittance to outpatient programs designed to deal with such problems.

The following benefits are expected to accrue to those departments that develop procedures to help problem drinkers or alcoholics recover from their illness:

1. Retention of the majority of officers who had suffered from alcoholism.
2. Solution of a set of complex and difficult personnel problems.
3. Realistic and practical extension of the department's program into the entire city government structure.
4. Improved public and community attitudes caused by the degree of concern for the officer and the officer's family and by eliminating the dangerous anti-social behavior of officers.

5. Full cooperation with rehabilitation efforts from the police associations and unions that may represent officers.

6. The preventive influence on moderate drinkers against the development of dangerous drinking habits that may lead to alcoholism. In addition, an in-house program will motivate some officers to undertake remedial action on their own, outside the scope of the department program (Dishlacoff 1976).

## Drug Abuse

Although little direct evidence exists regarding the prevalence of drug abuse among police officers, there is little doubt the problem is increasing in the police population, as well as in the general population. The principal category of illegal drugs is narcotics. In an attempt to reduce the problem of illegal drug use, departments utilize drug testing to screen out police applicants who may have a drug-abuse problem (see Policies and Programs later in this chapter). In addition, police administrators are increasingly testing officers on the job for illegal drug use. Because drug use is illegal and officers are required to enforce laws against it, the usual result of a positive testing is dismissal from the force.

Kraska and Kappeler (1988) examined on- and off-duty drug use by police officers in one police department. They reported that 20 percent of officers had used marijuana while on duty. Use was higher among middle management (27.3 percent) than among line officers (21.9 percent). Furthermore, the overall performance ratings of officers who used drugs on duty were higher than that of officers who did not report on-duty drug use. Although this study was largely exploratory and consisted of a relatively small sample of 49 officers from one jurisdiction, the results are reason for serious concern regarding the extent of illegal drug use by police officers.

## Suicide

Suicide has become the most dreaded consequence of a police officer under stress. Although it is difficult to obtain accurate data regarding whether the number of police suicides is in fact higher than that in the general population, the perception appears to be true, at least in some departments. Most of the early research suggests that suicide among police officers is higher than in the general population.

Violanti and Steege (2021) examined death certificate data and information from the National Occupational Mortality Surveillance database (maintained by the Centers for Disease Control and Prevention) to understand whether police officers commit suicide at higher rates than other occupations. Overall, they reported that officers were 54 percent more likely to commit suicides than people in other occupations. They discovered that officers' characteristics and assignments were also related to suicides Specifically, detectives were 64 percent more likely to commit suicide than all workers, and Black officers had an 88 percent higher likelihood of suicide. Thinking of assignment and race as suicide risk factors, Violati and Steege noted that Black male detectives were 137 percent more likely to commit suicide than other workers.

According to a report in *Law Enforcement News* (1996), police are at a higher risk for committing suicide for a variety of reasons, including access to and familiarity with firearms (95 percent of the suicides were by firearm), continuous exposure to human misery, shift work, social strain and marital difficulties, drinking problems, physical illness, impending retirement (i.e., separation from police peers and subculture), and lack of control over their jobs and personal lives. Other research supports the general tenor of these findings. For example, Ivanoff (1994) found that 94 percent of police suicides in New York involved a firearm and that 57 percent were believed to be precipitated by relationship difficulties; Wagner and Brzeczek (1983) found that the majority of police officers who committed suicide abused alcohol; Loo (1986) found that 15 percent of police suicides in the Royal Canadian Mounted Police involved officers who had been exposed to a traumatic work incident; and Gaska (1982) found a 10-fold higher risk of suicide among police retirees. Interestingly, Ivanoff (1994) also found that in New York, officer suicide tends to result from personal problems, substance abuse, and depression instead of job-related stress—that is, continuing life problems that people do not know how to solve. Ivanoff's study based its findings on surveys of 18,000 patrol officers between 1990 and 1993 and on studies of 57 suicides of officers from 1985 to 1994. These findings are noteworthy because they suggest that police suicides may not result from job stress, which in turn may suggest that different intervention strategies are necessary. More research is needed to better understand the causes and effects of police suicides and prevention programs. Inside Policing 13.2 provides a detailed description of one family's experience with suicide.

The relationship between suicide and policing is inconsistent. For example, Stack and Kelley (1999) observed inconsistencies in empirical research and noted that most research on police suicide was limited to samples drawn from a few local police departments. To combat this apparent shortcoming, their analysis used the 1985 National Mortality Detail File and included data from 12,000 local police departments, 3,000 sheriff's offices, 49 state police agencies, and various federal law enforcement agencies. Suicide rates for police officers were compared with those for other males in the population. The analysis indicated that suicide rates for police officers (25.6 per 100,000) were only slightly higher than the suicide rate for nonpolice (23.8 per 100,000). Furthermore, after controlling for socioeconomic status and other variables, *being a police officer was not significantly related to the odds of death by suicide.* This finding indicates that although the policing occupation may be inherently stressful, occupational stress may not truly be related to suicide.

One of the primary problems of attempting to prevent police suicide is that traditionally, officers refrain from asking for help. Often, they do not want to appear weak in front of their peers, and they see themselves as problem solvers, not persons with problems. In addition, officers fear a possible negative effect on their career if they acknowledge a

---

### INSIDE POLICING 13.2 | Police Suicide

This article recounts the heartbreaking circumstances surrounding an officer's suicide in Wisconsin. His mother put some of the blame on "years and years of this drip, drip, drip of evil and unappreciation." Nationally, police suicides outnumber felonious deaths by at least 3 to 1, with many unreported. One expert notes that police face "elevated risk of depression, substance abuse and posttraumatic stress disorder" while "shootings are the biggest stressors." The work can affect officers' mental health, but experts say police "are often particularly adept at hiding the warning signs. They are practiced at burying their emotions on the job."

**Discussion Question:** What can police organizations do to systematically identify warning signs of suicide?

SOURCE: *Modern Policing* blog, December 21, 2018, https://gcordner.wordpress.com/2018/12/21/police-suicide/

problem. Officers should receive training to help them recognize and avoid psychological factors leading to suicide. It is important to understand that suicide generally results not from a single crisis, but from the accumulation of apparently minor life events. Training should begin at the academy, before new officers are exposed to the police socialization process. Ivanoff (1994) suggests that **suicide prevention training** should include recognizing psychological depression, communication skills, conflict resolution, and maintenance of intimate relationships. Loo (2005) outlines a variety of suicide prevention measures that police departments should consider:

1. Recruitment selection criteria: Police departments conduct thorough screenings of officer applicants, and factors related to suicide predisposition or precipitating factors often can be identified. Although screening out applicants demonstrating these factors may be challenging, departments should closely monitor these officers to determine whether indicators of suicide risk develop.

2. Stress management and inoculation training: Police departments should provide ongoing training on how officers can self-manage chronic stress and stress associated with critical incidents.

3. Supervisor training: Police administrators and those responsible for supervising officers should be trained to identify early warning signs for suicide. This appears particularly important for sergeants who interact with street-level officers on a regular basis and can best identify changes in behavior.

4. Psychological assessments for special duties: Special attention should be focused on officers in particularly high-stress assignments, such as Special Weapons and Tactics (SWAT) or undercover officers.

5. Critical incidents: Crisis intervention teams should be in place to conduct debriefings and assessments after traumatic incidents. The team could consist of specially trained police personnel as well as nonpolice, like clergy and health-care professionals.

6. Psychological services: Contracting with external health-care providers to provide ongoing psychological services for officers.

7. Programs to promote healthy lifestyles.

8. Suicide hotlines.

9. Peer and spousal support programs.

10. Preretirement counseling and postretirement networks: Retirement can often be particularly challenging for officers for various reasons. New retirees experience a loss of camaraderie that they have grown accustomed to, and many police departments have mandatory retirement after a specific number of years of service (Barker 1999). Relatively young retirees may need additional assistance managing finances in retirement. Retirement networks can provide opportunities for retirees to serve as peer counselors within departments or mentor young officers.

The research highlighted here provides a better understanding of the extent and nature of police suicide; however, right now, there are no national estimates of police suicide. This may change. In 2020, the President of the United States signed the Law Enforcement Suicide Data Collection Act, whose purpose is to collect information on police suicides and therefore develop better strategies to prevent police officer suicide. In 2022, the FBI launched the Law Enforcement Suicide Data Collection (LESDC) initiative as part of its Uniform Crime Reporting program. Information will be collected on current and former officer suicides (and attempted suicides), including the circumstances and events that occurred before each suicide, location, demographic information, occupational category, and method used (see https://www.fbi.gov/services/cjis/ucr/law-enforcement-suicide-data-collection). The FBI has not released any reports from the LESDC initiative as of this writing; however, this appears to be an encouraging initiative to more fully understand the extent, nature, and dynamics of suicide amongst police officers.

## Stress and the Impact on Families

Maintaining healthy social support networks can insulate officers from the negative consequences associated with police-related stress. However, certain job characteristics appear to contribute to marital breakup and family problems. Officers are required to work rotating or odd shifts, including weekends and holidays, which make it more challenging to maintain a healthy family routine. Quality time with spouses, children, and nonpolice friends is less predictable, creating stress and often resentment. Police officers routinely view trauma and human suffering, resulting in a hardening of emotions, which officers may bring home with them. Police work can also create opportunities for infidelity that may not be present in other occupations (Kroes et al. 1974; Kappeler and Potter 2005; Miller 2007). The occupation appears to provide an environment that would be risky for marriages.

Alexander and Walker (1996) found that police work adversely impacted officers' social lives. The major problems included long hours, shift work, and canceled leave. Surprisingly, , dangerous duties and working with the opposite sex usually did not adversely affect officer spouses. Roberts and Levenson (2001), however, reported that male officers are prone to take job-acquired stress home to their spouses. Both officers and spouses reported adverse reactions to the officers' on-the-job stress, and they concluded that stress and exhaustion likely have a negative impact on the family unit.

In view of these types of family problems, it was assumed, as with alcoholism and suicide rates, that divorce rates for police officers are far higher than those for the rest of the population. Some research has supported this view, but the preponderance of the empirical research has indicated that divorce rates for police are no higher than for many other occupations (the divorce rate for the general population is approximately 50 percent). Davidson and Veno (1978), in their review of the literature, cite several weaknesses in the studies that support high divorce rates for police, including the failure to consider a number of factors that strongly influence divorce rates, such as age at marriage and number of children. McCoy and Aamodt (2010) examined 449 different occupations and reported divorce and separation rates for police officers to be lower than the national average.

Whether police divorce rates are higher than those of the rest of the population is not at issue: healthy organizations should be mindful of the well-being of their members and ideally provide mechanisms or services to counteract job-related issues that could lead to family problems. Because marital and family problems can have a devastating impact on job performance, many police departments are developing programs aimed at helping family members understand and cope with the stressors inherent in police work. Such programs should, in the long run, lead to improved job performance.

## Policies and Programs

Based on the literature reviewed in this chapter, a number of policies and programs could be implemented by police management to help control the stressors encountered by police personnel. Of course, not every department can—or should—attempt to implement all of the recommendations. Each department has different needs and budgetary constraints and therefore must decide what type of policies and programs best fit its particular needs. The following recommendations, however, which are adapted from Farmer (1990, 214–215), provide a proper foundation for controlling police stress in both working and nonworking environments:

1. Establish quality-of-work life activities designed to improve communication and increase participation in decision making throughout the department.

2. Address workplace environmental issues, including quality of equipment, work space, compensation packages, and related aspects.

3. Develop training programs in stress awareness. Police should consider stress management simply another skill to be learned, like criminal law or police procedure.

4. Establish specific stress programs. These can be part of larger departmental psychological services, a health program, or a general employee-assistance program.

5. Establish operational policies that reduce stress. Consider the effects of shift assignments and scheduling, report writing, and so forth.

6. Improve management skills overall, especially in people-oriented aspects of supervision and management. Include stress management skills in supervisory practice.

7. Utilize peer-counseling programs. Because peers may have already experienced many of the same problems, they can be of invaluable help to fellow officers.

8. Develop support groups by taking advantage of the natural groups that already exist informally and formally within the department.

9. Establish physical fitness programs that can strengthen the individual to withstand occupational stress. Such programs should also address stress-related dietary issues.

10. Encourage family activities as an important source of assistance to the officer. In particular, as spouses know more about police work and its stresses, they are in a better position to provide support.

Research by Dowler (2005) offers empirical support for several of the aforementioned policy recommendations and found that officers reported lower levels of occupational burnout and lower levels of depression related to their jobs when stress debriefing programs were available. Social support from family and friends also decreased feelings of burnout and depression, and officers felt less depressed if there was support from police administration. Individual officers can also engage in positive coping strategies to reduce stress.

## Officer Safety

Each year, the FBI compiles information on officer safety across several broad categories: officers feloniously killed, officers accidentally killed, and officers assaulted. These reports provide useful descriptive information on officer safety and permit observation of longitudinal trends. Before proceeding, however, it is necessary to provide a few words of caution when interpreting these data.

Estimating officer safety is challenging, because the FBI is reliant on local police agencies to voluntarily provide them with accurate information. Some have questioned the validity of data on officers assaulted contained in the FBI reports. Uchida and King (2002, 7) observed what appeared to be alarming and counterintuitive discrepancies among the number of assaults, number of officers, and population served. They concluded these data "should be viewed carefully" and called for external benchmarks to assess their validity. These data may be prone to underreporting, as is inherent with other data collected by the FBI (e.g., the Uniform Crime Reports). As such, we only present data on officers feloniously killed and officers accidentally killed. Unfortunately, no trustworthy national data exist on nonlethal assaults on officers.

The data in Figure 13.1 cover almost 50 years of felonious police killings, and were gathered from various reports and dashboards appearing on the FBI's Law Enforcement Officers Killed and Assaulted (LEOKA) website (https://www.fbi.gov/services/cjis/ucr/leoka). On average, 71 officers are feloniously killed annually in the United States; however, this figure also displays a measurable drop between 1976 and 1986. In fact, the average number of felonious deaths per decade are as follows:

- 1970s = 114 per year
- 1980s = 80 per year
- 1990s = 66 per year
- 2000s = 54 per year
- 2010s = 51 per year
- 2020–2021 = 60 per year

In 2013, a total of 27 officers were feloniously killed in the line of duty, representing the fewest fatalities over the past four decades. Since that time, the number of officers feloniously killed in the line of duty has crept up. Firearms overwhelmingly account for the majority of officer fatalities, particularly handguns. Roughly 70 percent of officer firearm deaths occurred with a handgun. Figure 13.1 also demonstrates that felonious fatalities

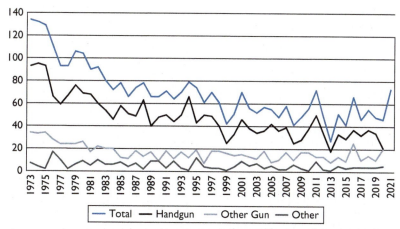

**FIGURE 13.1** Police Officers Feloniously Killed in the Line of Duty, 1973-2021.*

*2001 excludes 72 officers killed on September 11; Type of weapon for 2021 unavailable at time of writing.

SOURCE: Federal Bureau of Investigation, *Law Enforcement Officers Killed and Assaulted, 1973–2021.*

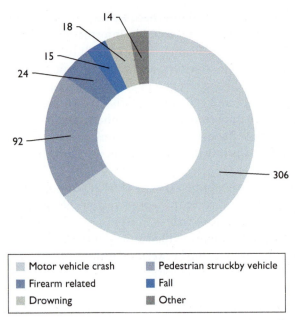

**FIGURE 13.2** Number of Law Enforcement Officers Accidentally Killed (n= 477): Circumstances at Scene, 2011–2020.

SOURCE: Federal Bureau of Investigation, *Law Enforcement Officers Killed and Assaulted, 2017.* Retrieved April 5, 2022, at https://crime-data-explorer.app.cloud.gov/pages/home.

increased dramatically in 2021 to 73, which was roughly a 58 percent increase from the previous year. The information from 2021 was preliminary at this writing, meaning the actual number may fluctuate, and the type of weapon used was unknown.

Another set of data reviewed involves police officers who are accidentally killed and the circumstances at the scene of the incident. As Figure 13.2 shows, 477 officers were accidentally killed while on duty between 2011 and 2020. The leading circumstance of accidental death was automobile accidents, which accounted for slightly more than 64 percent. A total of 92 officers (20 percent) officers were killed when struck by a vehicle directing traffic or assisting motorists. A small but noteworthy proportion of accidental deaths were attributed to accidental shootings. All other types of on-duty accidental deaths comprised 6.7 percent of the total. These data reinforce the fact that officers are most likely to be accidentally killed in events related to operating a police vehicle and engaging in traffic enforcement.

Comprehensive research on line-of-duty deaths provides additional context to these observations. White, Dario, and Shjarback (2019) examined trends in officer safety between 1970 and 2016, and also noted the steady decline of both felonious and nonfelonious line-of-duty deaths over time. Over this era, felonious deaths dropped nearly 80 percent, while nonfelonious deaths declined about 69 percent per capita. The declining trend in nonfelonious deaths was not quite as dramatic, and they noted that the gap between the rates of felonious and nonfelonious deaths (about 2:1 in 1970) had all but disappeared by 2016. Policing, as measured by line-of-duty deaths, is far safer today than in past decades. They go on to state, "policing in the second decade of the twenty-first century is much safer than it was 50 years ago" (White et al. 2019, 18).

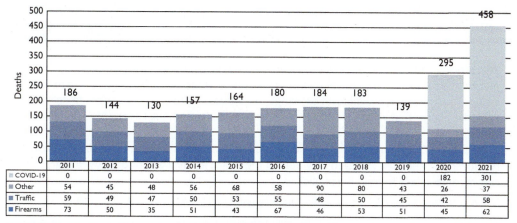

**FIGURE 13.3** Officer Line-of-Duty Deaths, 2011–2021.

*SOURCE:* Data from https://nleomf.org/wp-content/uploads/2021/07/causes-le-deaths-updated-July-19-2021.pdf and https://nleomf.org/wp-content/uploads/2022/01/2021-EOY-Fatality-Report-Final-web.pdf Accessed March 6, 2022.

Figure 13.3 provides additional descriptions of officer line-of-duty deaths between 2011 and 2021. These estimates, compiled by the National Law Enforcement Officers Memorial Fund (NLEOMF) uses information from the FBI's LEOKA website. Some small inconsistencies may be present, however, because NLEOMF is continuously updating and reconciling their estimates and may not gather data from the same sources as reported by the FBI. Comparisons between these different sources may be hazardous. Figure 13.3 shows the number of line-of-duty deaths was relatively stable between 2011 and 2019. The total number of deaths more than doubled in 2020, and then increased by about 55 percent in 2021. This increase was directly related to COVID-19. The number of non-COVID deaths in 2020 and 2021 were pretty similar to those in previous years. COVID-19-related deaths in 2020 and 2021 were the single highest cause of officer deaths in their respective years (NLEOMF 2021, 2022). This is likely because police officers are front-line, essential workers who can hardly work from home or maintain social distancing while on duty, but also may be in part related to vaccine hesitancy amongst large portions of officers (Bates 2021; Medina 2021).

Mandatory seat belt policies for police officers may be one relatively easy way to enhance officer safety. The information presented earlier indicates that a large proportion of officers are killed annually in traffic accidents. However, it is unknown how many officers are injured in traffic accidents or in what proportion of accidents officers were not using seat belts. Seat belt use in America has increased dramatically over the past several decades, from 60 percent in 1995 to 87 percent in 2013 (National Highway Traffic Safety Administration 2014), but there is a reason to believe officers do not buckle up as frequently as the public. Officers note that seat belts are difficult or uncomfortable to wear while also wearing bulletproof vests and gun belts, and they indicate seat belts may keep them from exiting the car quickly in an emergency (Cowan, Jones, and Ho 2006; Ashton 2009). Nevertheless, the President's Task Force on Twenty-First Century Policing (2015) recommended police departments require officers to wear seat belts in an effort to reduce officer injuries. This may be easier said than done, however, and officers may resist such policies if they conflict with officer culture, norms, or habit.

Inside Policing 13.3 provides details of a high-profile felonious killing of officers that occurred July 7, 2016. The ambush that killed five Dallas Police Department officers was

---

**INSIDE POLICING 13.3** | **Station In Dallas**

This article offers a detailed account of the Dallas SWAT response in July 2016 after a lone gunman had killed five police officers and taken refuge inside El Centro College. The response included negotiations, a significant exchange of gunfire, and then use of a robot to deliver an explosive charge that killed the shooter, who had vowed to continue killing police until he was killed.

**Discussion Question:** What impact do events like those in Dallas have on police-community relationships? The public tend to rally behind the police in the wake of tragedy, but are officers more reluctant to trust the public?

SOURCE: *Modern Policing* blog. February 5, 2018, https://gcordner.wordpress.com/2018/02/05/standoff-in-dallas/.

---

the deadliest event for police officers since the 9/11 attacks. Ten days later, three officers were shot and killed (and three more injured) in Baton Rouge, Louisiana. In 2021, the NLEOMF reported increases in firearms-related fatalities, including an increase in ambush-style fatalities from 6 (in 2020) to 19 (in 2021).

### Danger and Police Work

How dangerous is police work? Danger can be considered from three perspectives: perceived, potential, and actual. **Perceived danger** relates to the individual's or public's belief about the danger in police work. It is influenced by various factors, including media coverage, television, movies, books, and the actual experiences of officers. In general, many people, including police officers, believe that police work is a perilous job. **Potential danger** relates to those situations that could become dangerous for an officer (e.g., a felony car stop or investigating a suspicious circumstance). Potentially dangerous encounters are often characterized by a suspect's behavior that adds to the officer's concern (e.g., threats, shouting, challenges to police authority, and name-calling). **Actual danger** involves the specific number and rates of injuries and deaths that result from accidents and attacks from citizens.

Another useful way to analyze danger in police work is to categorize it in terms of how it is precipitated: Does a person initiate it, or is it a function of the situation? Few occupations include both the possibility and the reality of **person-initiated danger**—that is, an attack by another person (as discussed in Figure 13.1). **Situational danger** is a function of a particular problem, such as a high-speed chase in policing, a taxi driver's risk of a traffic accident, the use of certain equipment, or the height at which a person must work.

One of the more telling aspects of danger to police is that officers initiate a substantial number of encounters in which they are injured or killed. They often know that these situations are potentially dangerous. In one study on officer fatalities, Konstantin (1984) discovered that contrary to popular belief, most police are not killed in citizen-initiated contacts; rather, approximately 75 percent of incidents resulting in officer deaths were initiated by the officers themselves. In addition, most officers are killed in the types of situations that they know are the most dangerous; the top three incidents were attempting arrests, situations involving robbery, and car stops. In order of occurrence, other situations were assaults on officers, investigating suspicious persons, car stops of known offenders, responding to domestic disturbances, handling mentally deranged persons, and handling prisoners. Even with this knowledge, officers may fail to follow the training and procedures that would reduce the likelihood of injury or death.

The general conclusions that can be reached from this study are important if officer fatalities are to be reduced. First, most fatalities occur in situations that the police know are dangerous; second, most of the incidents (approximately three-quarters) that lead to killings are *officer initiated*. Such conclusions suggest that the police are often not prepared to handle these potentially dangerous situations. More thorough preparation and training in these areas could help officers to make better decisions about whether to intervene and, once the decision is made, how to handle the situation from the safest perspective. As Konstantin (1984, 42) points out,

> Police training emphasis on the great majority of routine encounters that are citizen-initiated is well-meaning but insufficient. Such emphasis should not come at the expense of training officers to approach carefully situations where they themselves make decisions to intervene

The issue of proactive police behavior and dangerousness is a matter of debate, however. Police culture has supported the notion that traffic enforcement is extremely dangerous because of the fear of the unknown. As such, the US Supreme Court has, over time, relaxed civil liberties during traffic stops, in part based on considerations of officer safety (see Chapter 3). But how dangerous, really, is traffic enforcement? Lichtenberg and Smith (2001) used the aforementioned FBI data to determine the "danger ratio" associated with traffic enforcement. They defined the danger ratio as the number of harmful encounters (i.e., death or assault) divided by the total number of activities (i.e., traffic stops). They conclude that in fact, traffic encounters are not particularly dangerous. Examining data over a 10-year period, they found that officers are killed in approximately 1 in every 9.2 million traffic stops. Furthermore, officers are assaulted at the rate of about 1 in every 20,512 traffic stops. Whether these estimates are alarmingly high or very low might be in part interpreted through the lens of the consumer, but the authors suggested that the Supreme Court overestimated the dangerousness of these encounters when determining legal precedent.

Under what circumstances suspects are most likely to resist or be combative during arrest encounters? Kavanagh (1997) examined arrests made over a one-year period in New York. He found that circumstances increasing the likelihood of force being used by either police or citizens included the seriousness of the crime, suspect intoxication, whether other arrestees were present, and suspect disrespect. Like Konstantin, Kavanagh found that officer-initiated arrests increased the likelihood of violence. Interestingly, he also found that arrests occurring in the daytime had an increased likelihood of violence. Factors unrelated to violence included officer race, officer education, citizen race, and citizen gender. Hence, it appears to be possible to determine situational factors in advance that increase the chances of violence during arrest encounters. Understanding these factors, with focused training on how to recognize and diffuse such encounters, can assist the police in reducing the number of assaults that occur during arrest situations.

Under what circumstances are officers injured during assaults? Kaminski and Sorensen (1995) examined 1,550 nonlethal police assaults in Baltimore County over two years. They found that the odds of officer injury during an assault increased when certain situational characteristics were present. Officers were more likely to be injured during an assault when (1) more than one officer was assaulted; (2) suspects used bodily force rather than a weapon; (3) there was a single assailant; (4) suspects were under arrest, attempting to escape, or fighting on arrival (rather than approaching or conversing with the officer); (5) the assailant was not intoxicated; and (6) officers were responding to disturbances or other legal situations (rather than domestic disputes).

The authors suggested that these final two findings may be because officers perceive encounters with intoxicated citizens and domestic disputes to be dangerous and thus exercise greater caution when encountering these citizens. They found that officers were more likely to be injured during encounters with nonwhite suspects, indicating that these encounters were characterized by greater hostility. They also reported that the officers' characteristics were related to the injury. For example, short and tall officers were more likely to sustain injury when compared with medium-size officers, and younger officers and officers without a college education were more likely to be injured than seasoned veterans or officers with a college education. Finally, they found that some individual officers sustained injuries on multiple occasions.

Research conducted in Orlando, Florida, came to slightly different conclusions. Covington, Huff-Corzine, and Corzine (2014) examined three years of incident reports on officer battery (or actual physical contact) and injury. They report officer battery is more likely when multiple officers are present. Although this may appear counterintuitive, it may partly be the result of multiple officers being assigned to calls when there is an elevated risk of violence. Hence, it is unclear whether citizens are more likely to batter officers because they are interacting with more officers during the encounter or whether multiple officers are present because there is more likely to be a physical altercation. Officers are more likely to be battered when the assailant is under the influence of alcohol, which seems to conflict with Kaminski and Sorensen's (1995) observation on officer injuries. Interestingly, Covington et al. (2014) also report that female citizens are significantly more likely to be involved in officer batteries than male citizens. This may also be counterintuitive, because traditional societal stereotypes suggest males are more physically aggressive than females. However, it is unclear from this study whether female aggressors are more likely to cause injury or simply engage in physical battery.

Finally, a complicated interaction effect seems to exist between intoxication and mental illness that may impact officer safety. Morabito and Socia (2015) examined risk factors associated with officers' injuries using three years of police reports from Portland. The results indicate that subjects' mental illness was unrelated to whether officers sustain injuries, and substance abuse decreased the likelihood of injury. However, officers were 19 percent more likely to be injured during encounters with mentally ill and intoxicated citizens. Likewise, mentally ill subjects who were intoxicated were 65 percent more likely to sustain injuries themselves. The pattern of risk factors associated with officer injuries varies considerably, and the research on this phenomenon continues to be mixed and inconsistent.

Are officers more likely to experience assaults in specific communities? Kaminski, Jefferis, and Gu (2003) researched the spatial distribution of aggravated assaults on Boston police officers over seven years. They noted that officers are more likely to be assaulted in areas characterized by economic distress and family disruption. They also reported that areas with high arrest rates had correspondingly higher rates of officer assaults. They remarked that high-arrest areas present a greater risk level for officer-focused violence. This factor was the most important variable in their analysis of officer assaults.

How dangerous is policing compared with other occupations? McLeod (1990) examined the mortality rate of 56 occupations for males between the ages of 16 and 64 and compared it with the normal death rate for all working men. This database considers the causes of death regardless of whether the deaths occurred on or off the job; thus, people in high-mortality occupations tend to die not only more often on the job but also from physical or mental ailments (e.g., hypertension, stroke, cirrhosis, or suicide) that may cause death off the job. Of the 56 occupations listed, deckhands and tankermen (on ships) had the highest mortality rating, at 3.93 (i.e., a deckhand's death rate is 3.93 times the average rate for all working males). The next highest mortality rates (in rank order) were as follows: (2) structural metal workers (3.17); (3) roofers (2.29); (4) industrial helpers (2.22); (5) foresters (2.19); (6) miners and drillers (2.17); (7) operating engineers (2.17); and (8) construction workers (2.13). Police officers and firefighters were ranked thirty-first, with a 1.07 mortality rating. In a separate study of police mortality, Hill and Clawson (1988) found that police officers' average age at death appears to be only slightly lower (by seven months) than that of individuals employed in 194 other occupations. Thus, it appears that police work is only moderately dangerous compared with other occupations.

Much of the current discussion has focused on safety issues related to assaults and officer deaths. Data on officer injuries are less available than information on deaths and injuries related to assaults, but no conversation on police safety would be complete without a discussion of the propensity for officers to be injured in accidents unrelated to the act of controlling or arresting a criminal suspect. Brandl and Stroshine (2003) examined accident reports completed by city employees within a large urban city. They found that of all the injuries sustained by officers, more than half (50.4 percent) were the result of on-the-job accidents. The remaining injuries were related to subjects who were resisting (39.2 percent) or assaultive (10.4 percent). This finding implies that if discussions of officer safety only included those injuries sustained during law enforcement–related incidents with suspects, then more than half of the true injuries would be counted. Of officers who were injured as a result of an accident, 24.7 percent reported having contact with infectious diseases. Brandl and Stroshine's research indicated that officers were somewhat less likely to seek medical attention for injuries resulting from accidents than for injuries sustained in dealing with assaults or resistant suspects. Yet 13.8 percent of injuries resulting from accidents involved time off from work, whereas officers injured during assaults (7.5 percent) and resisting arrest encounters (11.8 percent) experienced less time off from work. Thus, the outcomes of accident-related injuries were at least as serious as those sustained during interactions with resistant/combative suspects.

## Improving Safety and Reducing Fatalities

The research presented here indicates that more training and newer or clearer policies are needed in several key areas of police officer safety. There appears to be a need for continual retraining in safety procedures as well. For instance, arrest situations, traffic stops, investigation of suspicious persons or situations, and disturbance calls all require more attention. Since approximately half of all police killings are accidental, departments should review the circumstances in which they occur as well as the level of training and policies provided in these areas. One study of police killings in drug situations (Sherman et al. 1989), for instance, advised that rehearsing each drug raid could substantially reduce the danger to police.

The FBI, in its in-depth studies of officers killed in the line of duty (FBI 1992) and officers who survived a serious assault (FBI 1997), has also made a number of training and policy recommendations. The researchers found that in a significant number of incidents, officers made tactical errors, such as improperly approaching a vehicle or suspect, or failed to conduct a thorough search of a suspect. Increased training was recommended in those areas as well as in the handling of traffic stops, weapons retention, handcuff use, and waiting for backup. With respect to traffic stops, department regulations should include sections on officer safety, including the proper selection of a safe stop location, dispatcher notification, and wearing of soft body armor. Body armor, or bulletproof vests, has been credited with saving more than 2,000 officer lives since 1980; FBI statistics indicate that approximately 42 percent of police officers killed with guns since 1980 could have been saved if they had been wearing vests (*Law Enforcement Journal* 1998). In addition, the FBI recommends that citizens be advised of the proper response when stopped by a marked police unit (i.e., they should remain in the vehicle, keep hands in plain view, and wait for further directions from the officer). Finally, since a large number of officers are killed while off duty (approximately one of every seven), departments should provide a well-defined policy for off-duty performance (e.g., carrying or not carrying firearms and how to act when observing an offense).

Another strategy that deserves continued evaluation is the adoption and use of less-lethal weapons. Although the use of force is described in greater detail in Chapter 10, commentary on officer safety is deserved here. For decades, the police had few options when facing aggressive and hostile suspects, and officers often relied on open-hand techniques, impact weapons (e.g., batons or PR-24s), and firearms. However, technological developments have provided officers with additional midlevel options, including oleoresin capsicum (OC) spray or conducted energy devices (CEDs; e.g., Tasers). These options have been met with welcome arms in the policing community, because they can be deployed when officers and suspects are at a distance. The General Accountability Office (2005) indicated that Tasers can be discharged from 25 feet. These devices provide officers an intermediate use-of-force option that can reduce the likelihood of officer (and suspect) injury. The same report estimates that more than 7,000 police departments use Tasers. However, there is also controversy surrounding CEDs. Amnesty International (2008) noted an unacceptable frequency of in-custody deaths during CED applications and called for police departments to discontinue or significantly limit their use. Although Smith et al. (2007) indicate a lack of consensus in the research community regarding the causal relationship between CEDs and unintended fatalities, they also point out that relatively little is known regarding officer and suspect injuries.

Both CED and OC spray adoption by police departments can reduce officer injury. In their research of Richland County and Miami-Dade County, Smith et al. (2007) conclude that overall, use of these devices reduces the incidence of injury as well as the intensity of injuries. MacDonald, Kaminski, and Smith (2009), in analyzing data from 12 separate agencies, found that CED or OC use was associated with decreased risk of suspect injury.

When examining the introduction of CEDs in Orlando, they found that the incidence of suspect injury decreased 53 percent, and that of officer injury decreased 62 percent. In Austin, Texas, suspect injury decreased 30 percent and officer injury declined 25 percent after police departments introduced CEDs into their use-of-force repertoire. MacDonald et al. (2009, 2273) concluded that "law enforcement agencies should encourage the use of OC spray or CEDs in place of impact weapons and should consider authorizing their use as a replacement for hands-on force tactics against physically resistant suspects." An examination of more than 12,000 use-of-force incidents across six jurisdictions revealed that officers were significantly less likely to be injured during encounters when employing CED compared with not using a CED (Paoline, Terrill, and Ingram 2012). Defining the appropriate use of these less-lethal weapons should continue to engender public debate; it is encouraging to note that these devices can be associated with improved officer safety.

Police managers, especially first-line supervisors and midlevel managers (i.e., sergeants and lieutenants), can also contribute to reducing the number of injuries and deaths (Roberg, Kuykendall, and Novak 2002). Managers must be ever vigilant to ensure that officers follow departmental safety and response guidelines. In addition, all incidents involving the use of force and citizen resistance should be reported and used by a department both to assess the officer's style and discretion and as a basis for improving future police responses. Whenever a police officer or citizen is injured or killed, the department should undertake an immediate and comprehensive reassessment of all related programs, policies, and personnel. This type of response is necessary, because police managers must reduce the fear level of officers if they hope to modify behavior resulting from irrational fear, including verbal abuse of citizens, overreliance on the use of force, unnecessary and excessive force, and brutality. Police managers must convince officers that officer safety is the most important priority in the department, next to integrity (Roberg et al. 2002).

Roberg et al. (2002) further suggest that departments undertake an extensive community education program to instruct citizens how to behave when interacting with officers; this goes beyond the FBI's recommendation about citizens' behavior during traffic stops. Essentially, citizens must understand that they must cooperate with the police and follow police orders, and that citizens' grievances should not, and cannot, be resolved in the streets but rather, if necessary, in the courts or through some other formal mechanism. Unfortunately, some people believe that it is their right to challenge police authority at the very moment that authority is being exercised. The police will have problems with such individuals until there is a change in citizen attitudes. Just as the police must modify their behavior in some situations to secure public respect and cooperation, citizens must also modify their behavior to reduce officers' fear.

## Summary

Stress and danger confront the police, but methods are available to reduce both. There are two major categories of police stressors: departmental practices and the inherent nature of police work. The first may include authoritarian structure, lack of administrative support, or minimal participation in decision making; the second may include rotating shift work, boredom, danger, public apathy, and exposure to human misery, including death or injury to fellow officers. In addition, some new forms of stress include efforts toward COP, especially role conflict and role ambiguity, and perceived negative news media coverage. In addition, the psychological stress caused by frequent or prolonged exposure to crises or trauma can lead to PTSD. Police stress can also lead to alcohol and drug abuse, suicide, and various family problems. Social support systems (e.g., supervisory and family support) can mitigate work stress and general life stress. Numerous policies and programs have been designed to reduce police stress.

Finally, although police fatalities have lessened over the past two decades, policing is a potentially dangerous occupation. Most officer fatalities occur in situations that the police know to be dangerous, and they are typically initiated by the officer. Research has demonstrated that situational and community-level factors are significantly related to the likelihood that an officer will sustain injury from an assault. More and better training is needed with regard to managing dangerous situations, particularly related to the use of OC spray and CEDs. Policy review, management's insistence on adhering to departmental safety and response guidelines, and community education can all play roles in reducing danger in policing.

## Critical Thinking Questions

1. Briefly define the concept of stress, and differentiate between the two forms of stress that may affect police behavior.

2. Describe the two major categories of police occupational stressors, and provide several examples of each.

3. Discuss at least three types of new sources of stress for today's police. Will police work become more or less stressful in the future? Discuss.

4. What is posttraumatic stress disorder, and how does it apply to the police?

5. Describe the social supports for the study of stress and their implications for policing.

6. Discuss the common methods officers use to cope with occupational stress (e.g., alcohol abuse, drug abuse, and suicide). Are officers more prone to these coping mechanisms than those in other occupations? What can police organizations do about this?

7. Discuss at least three aspects of police stress that influence the quality of family life. What are some programs that attempt to deal with such problems?

8. Is policing a dangerous occupation? What factors are commonly associated with officer assaults and injuries? Discuss strategies police departments can adopt to enhance the safety of officers.

## References

Abdollahi, M. K. 2002. "Understanding Police Stress Research." *Journal of Forensic Psychology Practice* 2: 1–24.

Alexander, D. A., and Walker, L. G. 1996. "The Perceived Impact of Police Work on Police Officers' Spouses and Families." *Stress Medicine* 12: 239–246.

Amendola, K. L., Slipka, M. G., Hamilton, E. E., Soelberg, M., and Koval, K. 2011a. *Trends in Shift Length: Results from a Random National Survey of Police Agencies*. Washington, DC: Police Foundation.

Amendola, K. L., Weisburd, D., Hamilton, E. E., Jones, G., and Slipka, M. 2011b. *The Shift Length Experiment: What We Know about 8-, 10-, and 12-Hour Shifts in Policing*. Washington, DC: Police Foundation.

Amnesty International. 2008. *"Less Than Lethal"? The Use of Stun Weapons in US Law Enforcement*. London: Amnesty International.

Anderson, G. S., Litzenberger, R., and Plecas, D. 2002. "Physical Evidence of Police Officer Stress." *Policing: An International Journal of Police Strategies and Management* 25: 399–420.

Ashton, R. J. 2009. "Buckling Up: A Matter of Officer Survival." *Police Chief*. https://www.policechief-magazine.org/buckling-up-a-matter-of-officer-survival/

Ballenger, J. F., Best, S. R., Metzler, T. J., Wasserman, D. A., Mohr, D. C., Liberman, A., Delucchi, K., Weiss, D. S., Fagan, J. A., Waldrop, A. E., and Marmar, C. R. 2010. "Patterns and Predictors of Alcohol Use in Male and Female Urban Police Officers." *American Journal on Addictions* 20(1): 21–29.

Barker, J. C. 1999. *Danger, Duty and Disillusion: The Worldview of Los Angeles Police Officers*. Prospect Heights, IL: Waveland.

Bates, J. 2021. "'I Just Don't Feel Like I need it Yet.' Why the NYPD is Grappling with COVID-19 Vaccine Hesitancy." *Time*, August 27. https://time.com/6092508/nypd-low-covid-19-vaccination-rate/.

Brandl, S. G., and Stroshine, M. S. 2003. "Toward an Understanding of the Physical Hazards of Police Work." *Police Quarterly* 6: 172–191.

Brown, J. M., and Campbell, E. 1994. *Stress and Policing: Sources and Strategies*. Chichester, UK: Wiley.

Charles, L. E., Burchfeil, C. M., Fekedulegn, D., Vila, B., Hartleyu, R. A., Slaven, J., Mnatsakanova, A., and Violanti, J. M. 2007. "Shift Work and Sleep: The Buffalo Police Health Study." *Policing: An International Journal of Police Strategies and Management* 30: 215–227.

Covington, M. W., Huff-Corzine, L., and Corzine, J. 2014. "Battered Police: Risk Factors for Violence Against Law Enforcement Officers." *Violence and Victims* 29(1): 34–52.

Cowan, J. A., Jones, B., and Ho, H. 2006. "Safety Belt Use by Law Enforcement Officers on Reality Television: A Missed Opportunity for Injury Prevention?" *Journal of Trauma-Injury Infection and Critical Care* 61(4): 1001–1004.

Craddock, T. B., and Telesco, G. 2022. "Police Stress and Deleterious Outcomes: Efforts Towards Improving Police Mental Health." *Journal of Police and Criminal Psychology*, 37: 173–182.

Crank, J. P., and Caldero, M. 1991. "The Production of Occupational Stress in Medium-Sized Police Agencies: A Survey of Line Officers in Eight Municipal Departments." *Journal of Criminal Justice* 19: 339–349.

Cullen, F. T., Lemming, T., Link, B. G., and Wozniak, J. F. 1985. "The Impact of Social Supports on Police Stress." *Criminology* 23: 503–522.

Davey, J. D., Obst, P. L., and Sheehan, M. C. 2000. "Developing a Profile of Alcohol Consumption Patterns of Police Officers in a Large-Scale Sample of an Australian Police Service." *European Addiction Studies* 6: 205–212.

Davidson, M. J., and Veno, A. 1978. "Police Stress: A Multicultural, Interdisciplinary Review and Perspective, Part I." *Abstracts on Police Science* 6 (4): 187–199.

Dishlacoff, L. 1976. "The Drinking Cop." *Police Chief* 43: 34–36, 39.

Dowler, K. 2005. "Job Satisfaction, Burnout, and Perception of Unfair Treatment: The Relationship Between Race and Police Work." *Police Quarterly* 8(4): 476–489.

Eisenberg, T. 1975. "Job Stress and the Police Officer: Identifying Stress Reduction Techniques." In W. H. Kroes and J. J. Hurrell Jr. (eds.), *Job Stress and the Police Officer: Identifying Stress Reduction Techniques*, pp. 26–34. Washington, DC: US Department of Health, Education, and Welfare.

Farmer, R. E. 1990. "Clinical and Managerial Implications of Stress Research on the Police." *Journal of Police Science and Administration* 17: 205–218.

Federal Bureau of Investigation (FBI). 1992. *Killed in the Line of Duty: A Study of Selected Felonious Killings of Law Enforcement Officers*. Washington, DC: US Department of Justice.

Federal Bureau of Investigation (FBI). 1997. *Law Enforcement Officers Killed and Assaulted, 1996*. Washington, DC: US Department of Justice.

Finn, P., and Tomz, J. E. 1997. *Developing a Law Enforcement Stress Program for Officers and Their Families*. Washington, DC: National Institute of Justice.

Gaska, C. W. 1982. *The Rate of Suicide, Potential for Suicide, and Recommendations for Prevention among Retired Police Officers*. PhD dissertation, Wayne State University.

General Accountability Office. 2005. *Taser Weapons: Use of Tasers by Selected Law Enforcement Agencies*. Washington, DC: Author.

Greenstone, J. L., Dunn, J. M., and Leviton, S. C. 1995. "Police Peer Counseling and Crisis Intervention Services into the Twenty-First Century." *Crisis Intervention and Time-Limited Treatment* 2: 167–187.

Haarr, R. N., and Morash, M. 1999. "Gender, Race, and Strategies of Coping with Occupational Stress in Policing." *Justice Quarterly* 16: 303–336.

Hart, P. M., Wearing, A. J., and Headey, B. 1995. "Police Stress and Well-Being: Integrating Personality, Coping and Daily Work Experience." *Journal of Occupational and Organizational Psychology* 68: 133–156.

He, N., Zhao, J., and Archbold, C. A. 2002. "Gender and Police Stress: The Convergent and Divergent Impact of Work Environment, Work–Family Conflict, and Stress Coping Mechanisms of Female and Male Police Officers." *Policing: An International Journal of Police Strategies and Management* 25: 687–708.

He, N., Zhao, J., and Ren, L. 2005. "Do Race and Gender Matter in Police Stress? A Preliminary Assessment of the Interactive Effects." *Journal of Criminal Justice* 33: 535–547.

Hill, K. Q., and Clawson, M. 1988. "The Health Hazards of 'Street Level' Bureaucracy: Morality Among the Police." *Journal of Police Science and Administration* 16: 243–248.

Hurrell, J. J., Jr., and Kroes W. H. 1975. "Stress Awareness." In W. H. Kroes and J. J. Hurrell Jr. (eds.), *Job Stress and the Police Officer: Identifying Stress Reduction Techniques*, pp. 234–246. Washington, DC: US Department of Health, Education, and Welfare.

Ivanoff, A. 1994. *The New York City Police Suicide Training Project*. New York: Police Foundation.

Kaminski, R. J., Jefferis, E., and Gu, J. 2003. "Community Correlates of Serious Assaults on Police" *Police Quarterly* 6: 119–149.

Kaminski, R. J., and Sorensen, D. W. M. 1995. "A Multivariate Analysis of Individual, Situational and Environmental Factors Associated with Police Assault Injuries." *American Journal of Police* 14: 3–48.

Kappeler, V. E., and Potter, G. W. 2005. *The Mythology of Crime and Criminal Justice*, 4th ed. Long Grove, IL: Waveland.

Kavanagh, J. 1997. "The Occurrence of Resisting Arrest in Arrest Encounters: A Study of Police–Citizen Violence." *Criminal Justice Review* 22: 16–33.

Kellogg, T., and Harrison, M. 1991. "Post-Traumatic Stress Plays a Part in Police Brutality." *Law Enforcement News* April 30: 12, 16.

Konstantin, D. N. 1984. "Homicides of American Law Enforcement Officers, 1978–1980." *Justice Quarterly* 1: 29–45.

Kraska, P. B., and Kappeler, V. W. 1988. "Police On-Duty Drug Use: A Theoretical and Descriptive Examination." *American Journal of Police* 7: 1–28.

Kroes, W. H., Margolis, B. L., and Hurrell, J. J., Jr. 1974. "Job Stress in Policemen." *Journal of Police Science and Administration* 2: 145–155.

Kureczka, A. W. 1996. "Critical Incident Stress in Law Enforcement." *FBI Law Enforcement Bulletin* 65: 10–16.

*Law Enforcement Journal*. 1998. "Congress OK's $75M Body-Armor Fund." May 15: 1.

*Law Enforcement News*. 1996. "What's Killing America's Cops? Mostly Themselves, According to New Study." November 15: 1.

Liberman, A. M., Best, S., Metzler, T. J., Fagan J. A., Weiss, D.S., and Marmar, C. R. 2002. "Routine Occupational Stress and Psychological Distress in Police." *Policing: An International Journal of Police Strategies and Management* 25: 421–441.

Lichtenberg, I. D., and Smith, A. 2001. "How Dangerous Are Routine Police-Citizen Traffic Stops? A Research Note." *Journal of Criminal Justice* 29: 419–428.

Loo, R. 1986. "Suicide Among Police in a Federal Force." *Suicide and Life-Threatening Behavior* 16: 379–388.

Loo, R. 2005. "A Psychosocial Process Model of Police Suicide." In H. Copes (ed.), *Policing and Stress*, pp. 103–125. Upper Saddle River, NJ: Pearson Prentice Hall.

Lord, V. B. 1996. "An Impact of Community Policing: Reported Stressors, Social Support, and Strain among Police Officers in a Changing Police Department." *Journal of Criminal Justice* 24: 503–522.

Lord, V. B. 2005. "The Stress of Change: The Impact of Changing a Traditional Police Department to a Community-Oriented, Problem-Solving Department." In H. Copes (ed.), *Policing and Stress*, pp. 55–72. Upper Saddle River, NJ: Pearson Prentice Hall.

MacDonald, J. M., Kaminski, R. J., and Smith, M. R. 2009. "The Effect of Less-Lethal Weapons on Injuries in Police Use-of-Force Events." *American Journal of Public Health* 99: 2268–2274.

Martin, C. A., McKean, H. E., and Veltkamp, L. J. 1986. "Post-Traumatic Stress Disorder in Police and Working with Victims: A Pilot Study." *Journal of Police Science and Administration* 14: 98–101.

McCoy, S. P., and Aamodt, M. G. 2010. "A Comparison of Law Enforcement Divorce Rates with Those of Other Occupations." *Journal of Police and Criminal Psychology* 25: 1–16.

McLeod, R. G. 1990. "Who Has California's Deadliest Jobs?" *San Francisco Chronicle*, January 22.

Medina, E. 2021. "Vaccine Hesitancy, an Issue Among Police Officers, is Also Evident Among Firefighters." *New York Times,* October 9. https://www.nytimes.com/2021/10/09/us/la-firefighters-vaccine-mandate-lawsuit.html.

Miller, L. 2007. "Police Families: Stresses, Syndromes, and Solutions." *American Journal of Family Therapy* 35: 21–40.

Morabito, M. S., and Socia, K. M. 2015. "Is Dangerousness a Myth? Injuries and Police Encounters with People with Mental Illness." *Criminology and Public Policy* 14(2): 253–276.

Morash, M., and Haarr, R. 1995. "Gender, Workplace Problems, and Stress in Policing." *Justice Quarterly* 12: 113–140.

Morash, M., Kwak, D.-H., and Haarr, R. 2006. "Gender Differences in the Predictors of Police Stress." *Policing: An International Journal of Police Strategies and Management* 29: 541–563.

Mourtgos, S. M., Adams, I. T. and Nix, J. 2022. "Elevated Police Turnover Following the Summer of George Floy Protests: A Synthetic Control Study." *Criminology and Public Policy*, 22: 9–33.

National Highway Traffic Safety Administration. 2014. *Traffic Safety Facts: A Research Note.* DOT HS 811 875. Washington, DC: US Department of Transportation.

National Law Enforcement Officers Memorial Fund (NLEOMF). *2021 End-Of-Year Preliminary Law Enforcement Officers Fatalities Report.* (Washington DC: NLEOMF, 2021), https://nleomf.org/wp-content/uploads/2022/01/2021-EOY-Fatality-Report-Final-web.pdf

National Law Enforcement Officers Memorial Fund (NLEOMF). 2021. *Law Enforcement Officers Fatalities Report: 2020.* Washington, DC: National Law Enforcement Officers Memorial Fund.

National Law Enforcement Officers Memorial Fund (NLEOMF). 2022. *Law Enforcement Officers Fatalities Report: 2021 End-of-Year Preliminary.* Washington, DC: National Law Enforcement Officers Memorial Fund.

O'Neill, J. L., and Cushing, M. A. 1991. *The Impact of Shift Work on Police Officers.* Washington, DC: Police Executive Research Forum.

Paoline, E. A., Terrill, W., and Ingram, J. R. 2012. "Police Use of Force and Officer Injuries: Comparing Conducted Energy Devices (CEDs) to Hands- and Weapon-Based Tactics." *Police Quarterly* 15(2): 115–136.

Patterson, G. T. 2003. "Examining the Effects of Coping and Social Support on Work and Life Stress Among Police Officers." *Journal of Criminal Justice* 31: 215–226.

Pendleton, M., Stotland, E., Spiers, P., and Kirsch, E. 1989. "Stress and Strain Among Police, Firefighters, and Government Workers: A Comparative Analysis." *Criminal Justice and Behavior* 16: 196–210.

Piquero, N. L. 2005. "Understanding Police Stress and Coping Resources across Gender: A Look toward General Strain Theory." In H. Copes (ed.), *Policing and Stress*, pp. 126–139. Upper Saddle River, NJ: Pearson Prentice Hall.

President's Task Force on Twenty-First Century Policing. 2015. *Final Report of the President's Task Force on Twenty-First Century Policing.* Washington, DC: Office of Community Oriented Policing Services.

Richmond, R. L., Wodak, A., Kehoe, L., and Heather, N. 1998. "How Healthy Are the Police? A Survey of Life-Style Factors." *Addiction* 93: 1729–1737.

Roberg, R. R., Hayhurst, D. L., and Allen, H. E. 1988. "Job Burnout in Law Enforcement Dispatchers: A Comparative Analysis." *Journal of Criminal Justice* 16: 385–393.

Roberg, R. R., Kuykendall, J., and Novak, K. 2002. *Police Management*, 3rd ed. Los Angeles: Roxbury.

Roberts, N. A., and Levenson, R. W. 2001. "The Remains of the Workday: Impact of Job Stress and Exhaustion on Marital Interaction in Police Couples." *Journal of Marriage and Family* 63: 1052–1067.

Robinson, H. M., Sigman, M. R., and Wilson, J. R. 1997. "Duty-Related Stressors and PTSD Symptoms in Suburban Police Officers." *Psychological Reports* 81: 835–845.

Rose, S., Bisson, J., Churchill, R., and Wessely, S. 2002. "Psychological Debriefing for Preventing Post Traumatic Stress Disorder (PTSD) (Review)." *Cochrane Database of Systematic Reviews*, Issue 2. Article Number CD000560. doi:10.1002/14651858.CD000560.

Selye, H. 1974. *Stress Without Distress*. Philadelphia: Lippincott.

Sherman, L. W., DeRiso, D., Gaines, D., Rogan, D., and Cohn, E. 1989. *Police Murdered in Drug-Related Situations, 1972–1988*. Washington, DC: Crime Control Institute.

Smith, M. R., Kaminski, R. J., Rojek, J., Alpert, G. P., and Mathis, J. 2007. "The Impact of Conducted Energy Devices and Other Types of Force and Resistance on Officer and Suspect Injuries." *Policing: An International Journal of Police Strategies and Management* 30: 423–446.

Stack, S., and Kelley, T. 1999. "Police Suicide." In D. J. Kenney and R. P. McNamara (eds.), *Police and Policing: Contemporary Issues*, 2nd ed., pp. 94–107. Westport, CT: Praeger.

Stinson, P. M., Liederbach, J., Brewer, S. L., and Todak, N. E. 2013. "Drink, Drive, Go to Jail? A Study of Police Officers Arrested for Drunk Driving." *Journal of Crime and Justice* 37(3): 356–326. doi:10.1080/0735648X.2013.805158.

Swatt, M. L., Gibson, C. L., and Piquero, N. L. 2007. "Exploring the Utility of General Strain Theory in Explaining Problematic Alcohol Consumption by Police Officers." *Journal of Criminal Justice* 35: 596–611.

Territo, L., and Vetter, H. J. (eds.). 1981. *Stress and Police Personnel*. Boston: Allyn & Bacon.

Terry, W. C. 1981. "Police Stress: The Empirical Evidence." *Police Science and Administration* 9: 61–75.

Terry, W. C. 1985. "Police Stress as a Professional Self-Image." *Journal of Criminal Justice* 13: 501–512.

Uchida, C. D., and King, W. R. 2002. "Police Employee Data: Elements and Validity." *Justice Research and Policy* 4: 1–9.

Violanti, J. M. 2005. "Dying for the Job: Psychological Stress, Disease, and Mortality in Police Work." In H. Copes (ed.), *Policing and Stress*, pp. 87–102. Upper Saddle River, NJ: Pearson Prentice Hall.

Violanti, J. M., and Aron, F. 1995. "Police Stressors: Variations in Perception among Police Personnel." *Journal of Criminal Justice* 23: 287–294.

Violanti, J. M., Ma, C. C., Mnatsakanov, A., Fekedulegn, D., Hartley, R. A., Gu, J. K., and Andrew, M. E. 2018. "Associations Between Police Work Stressors and Posttraumatic Stress Disorder Symptoms: Examining the Moderating Effects of Coping." *Journal of Police and Criminal Psychology* 33: 271–282.

Violanti, J. M., Slaven, J. E., Charles, L. E., Curchfiel, C. M. Andrew, M. E., and Homish, G. G. 2011. "Police and Alcohol Use: A Descriptive Analysis and Associations with Stress Outcomes." *American Journal of Criminal Justice* 36: 344–356.

Violanti, J. M., and Steege, A. 2021. "Law Enforcement Worker Suicide: An Updated National Assessment." Policing: An International Journal 44: 18–31.

Violanti, J. M., Vena, J. E., and Marshall, J. R. 1986. "Disease Risk and Mortality Among Police Officers." *Journal of Police Science and Administration* 14: 17–23.

Wagner, M., and Brzeczek, R. J. 1983. "Alcoholism and Suicide: A Fatal Connection." *FBI Law Enforcement Bulletin* 52: 8–15.

Wallace, P. A., Roberg, R. R., and Allen, H. E. 1985. "Job Burnout Among Narcotics Investigators: An Exploratory Study." *Journal of Criminal Justice* 13: 549–559.

White, M. D., Dario, L. M., and Shjarback, J. A. 2019. "Assessing the Dangerousness in Policing: An Analysis of Officer Deaths in the United States, 1970–2016." *Criminology and Public Policy*, 18: 11–35.

# CHAPTER 14

# Higher Education

## CHAPTER OUTLINE

# CHAPTER OUTLINE (continued)

- Validating Higher Education for Police
    - Higher Education as a Bona Fide Occupational Qualification
    - Higher Education and Access
- Higher-Education Incentive Programs
- Higher-Education Requirements and Policy Implications
- Moving Forward
    - What Kind of Education and How Much?
    - Beyond Traditional University-Based Education?
- Summary
- Critical Thinking Questions
- References

## KEY TERMS

- *Arnold v. Ballard* (1975)
- bona fide occupational qualification
- *Castro v. Beecher* (1972)
- *Davis v. City of Dallas* (1985)
- *Griggs v. Duke Power Co.* (1971)
- Law Enforcement Assistance Administration

- Law Enforcement Education Program
- National Advisory Commission on Criminal Justice Standards and Goals
- National Advisory Commission on Higher Education for Policed Officers

- Omnibus Crime Control and Safe Streets Act
- Police Executive Research Forum
- President's Commission on Law Enforcement and Administration of Justice

THERE HAS BEEN A long-standing debate over whether a college education for police officers is necessary, or even desirable. In present-day society, with the ever-expanding complexity of the police role and the transition toward community policing (COP), this question is more significant than ever. Interestingly, the initial requirement of a high school diploma to enter the field of policing occurred when most of the nation's population did not finish high school. Thus, a high school education requirement actually identified individuals with an above-average level of education. Statistics from the US Department of Health, Education, and Welfare, for instance, indicate that immediately after World War II, less than half of the 17-year-old population had earned a high school diploma in 1946 (National Advisory Commission on Criminal Justice Standards and Goals 1973). Although it is difficult to determine precisely when the high school diploma (or its equivalent, the general education diploma) became a standard requirement for most of the country's police departments, it was a well-established trend after World War II.

Today, the high school diploma has essentially been replaced by a college degree as the above-average level of educational attainment in the United States. In fact, 37.5 percent of Americans age 25 and older have a four-year college degree or higher (US Census Bureau 2020). Consequently, the police departments that have not raised their educational requirements for entry have failed to keep pace with their tradition of employing people with an above-average education. Additionally, police forces at different governmental levels have traditionally required different levels of education for employment. For example, most federal agencies have long required at least a four-year college degree, but only a minimal number of city and state police and sheriff's departments require one. Many others require a minimum two-year degree or its equivalent in college units. Baro and Burlingame (1999) noted that an increasing number of officers are completing college units even without a formal degree requirement. However, they argue that this practice could represent degree inflation, because an associate's (two-year) degree today may be the equivalent of a high school diploma in the 1960s (Baro and Burlingame 1999).

The President's Task Force on Twenty-First Century Policing (2015) advocated increased education among police officers. They specifically called for federal, state, and local governments to identify ways to encourage and incentivize higher education, noting that more education raises the quality of officer performance. Enhanced training and education should be incorporated throughout an officer's career, and incentives should also be in place to permit officers to continue their education after hiring. The Task Force also recommended that the federal government establish training and innovation hubs involving universities and academies, along with a national postgraduate institute for police leaders.

There are many anticipated or actual benefits from a more educated police force. Advocates argue that college-educated officers possess superior communication skills (written and oral) and a better understanding of the criminal justice system, display clearer thinking, are more understanding of diverse populations, adapt better to organizational change, receive fewer complaints or disciplinary actions, are more open-minded and less rigid in their belief systems, and make better discretionary decisions (Paynich 2009). Paterson (2011) argues that higher education could enhance professionalism, accountability, and legitimacy, and Brown (2020, 12) has built upon this framework, indicating that higher education could contribute to:

- Reforming the police culture implicated in corruption and malpractice (accountability).
- Responding to changes in the complexities and types of police tasks (efficiency and effectiveness of performance).
- Offsetting crises of public confidence (legitimacy).
- Improving the standing and status of policing (professionalism).
- Dealing with economic downturns and austerity measures (economy).

The research literature is mixed, however, and at times even contradictory. In reviewing the existing research on the effects of education within policing, the National Research Council (2004, 139) concluded the evidence "does not permit conclusions regarding the impact of education on decision making." Yet the debate over higher education is much more complicated than determining whether police requirements are above or below national population norms. The development of higher-education programs and evaluation of the ensuing debate are the focus of this chapter.

## The Development of Higher-Education Programs for Police

The debate over higher-educational requirements for police officers is not new. Starting in the early 1900s, August Vollmer, a police chief in Berkeley, California, called for the recruitment of officers who were not only trained in the "technology of policing" but also understood "the prevention of crime or confrontation through [their] appreciation of the psychology and sociology of crime" (Carte 1973, 275). Contrary to traditional practices of the time, Vollmer felt officers learn such skills both on the street and in the classroom.

Calling for the "very best manhood in the nation" to join the police profession (Carte 1973, 277), Vollmer campaigned strongly for police courses in higher education and about the need for college-educated personnel throughout the police ranks. He was primarily responsible, along with the faculty, for establishing the first police school in higher education at the University of California, Berkeley, which he joined part-time in 1916 and full-time in 1932 after his retirement from the Berkeley Police Department (Caiden 1977). For his efforts to reform and professionalize the police, Vollmer eventually gained a reputation as the father of modern US policing.

These early programs laid the foundation for higher education in criminal justice, which was typically labeled police science, police administration, or law enforcement. Such curricula were developed in selected four-year institutions and many community colleges through the mid-1960s. The focus of these programs was usually on administration and supervision issues in policing and the practical applications of the "science" of policing, including such topics as patrol procedures, traffic enforcement, criminalistics, criminal investigation, and report writing. It is interesting to note that during these years, most police departments had no formalized training programs; many of these programs were designed to fill this training gap.

Two significant and interrelated events took place in the mid to late 1960s that required the country to take a hard look at the level of professionalism and the quality of US police forces, along with the rest of the criminal justice system. These two events played a major role in ushering in the golden age of higher education for the police (Pope 1987). First, there was the enormous increase in the crime rate that began in the early 1960s, leveled off in the early 1980s, and began to increase again in the mid-1980s. In 1968, for the first time in three decades of opinion sampling, the Gallup poll found crime ranked as the most serious national issue (ahead of civil rights, the cost of living, and poverty) as well as the most important local issue (ahead of schools, transportation, and taxes). Furthermore, Gallup found that 3 persons in 10, and 4 in 10 for both women and residents of larger cities, admitted they were afraid to go out alone at night in their own neighborhoods (Saunders 1970). Second, there was urban rioting. The burning, looting, and general turmoil in many of the nation's major cities was the catalyst that spurred the public and the government into action. At this juncture, the "war on crime" began (Pope 1987).

"Crime in the streets" thus became a national issue in the 1964 presidential campaign. The following year, Congress passed the Law Enforcement Assistance Act of 1965, a modest grant program that expressed a national concern about the adequacy of local police departments. Two years later, the **President's Commission on Law Enforcement and Administration of Justice** (1967) documented the serious impact of crime on US society. Although the report issued more than 200 specific proposals for action involving all levels of government and society, a majority of the recommendations dealt—either directly or indirectly—with the police as the front line of the criminal justice system.

Serious and continuing problems between the police and the community, especially minority group members, were a major concern of the commission. It was thought that without respect for the police or community participation in crime prevention (both major foundations of COP), there could be little impact on the crime rate. Because much of this problem was associated with the low quality of police personnel, many of the commission's recommendations dealt with the need for "widespread improvement in the strength and caliber of police manpower . . . for achieving more effective and fairer law enforcement"

(President's Commission 1967, 294). The commission thought that one of the most important ways to upgrade the quality of police personnel would be through higher education. Consequently, one of their most significant—and controversial—recommendations was that the "ultimate aim of *all* police departments should be that *all* personnel with general enforcement powers have baccalaureate degrees" (President's Commission 1967, 109, emphasis added). Perhaps just as important, the commission further recommended that police departments should "take *immediate* steps to establish a minimum requirement of a baccalaureate degree for all supervisory and executive level positions" (President's Commission 1967, 110, emphasis added).

## Federal Programs and Support for Higher Education

Shortly after that, Congress passed the **Omnibus Crime Control and Safe Streets Act** of 1968, which created the **Law Enforcement Assistance Administration (LEAA)**. Through the LEAA, the federal government poured billions of dollars into the criminal justice system—focusing on the police—to improve their effectiveness and reduce crime. This money was initially earmarked for the research and development of innovative programs in policing, but it was instead used primarily to purchase additional hardware (e.g., cars, communications equipment, and weapons) that departments could not afford on their own and secondarily for training. The result was that most police departments operated from a perspective of more of the same, rather than introducing new programs.

Under LEAA, an educational-incentive program, known as the **Law Enforcement Education Program (LEEP)**, was established in the late 1960s. It provided financial assistance to police personnel, as well as to others who wished to enter police service, to pursue a college education. The impact of LEEP on the growth of law enforcement programs in both two-year and four-year schools was nothing short of phenomenal. For example, it has been reported that in 1954, there were a total of 22 such programs in the country (Deutsch 1955). By 1975, the numbers had increased to more than 700 in community colleges and nearly 400 in four-year schools (Korbetz 1975), and 100,000 students has been funded (Sherman 1978).

In the highly influential *Report on Police*, the **National Advisory Commission on Criminal Justice Standards and Goals** (1973) further advanced the higher-education recommendations made by the President's Commission on Law Enforcement and Administration of Justice. The report included a *graduated timetable* that would require all police officers, at the time of initial employment, to have completed at least two years of education (60 semester units) at an accredited college or university by 1975, three years (90 semester units) by 1978, and a baccalaureate degree by 1982. In the same year, the American Bar Association (1973) issued another influential report, *Standards Relating to the Urban Police Function*, which recognized the demanding and complex nature of the police role in a democracy. That report further elaborated on the need for advanced education to meet the professional skills required by such a role:

> Police agencies need personnel in their ranks who have the characteristics which a college education seeks to foster: intellectual curiosity, analytical ability, articulateness, and a capacity to relate the events of the day to the social, political, and historical context in which they occur. (American Bar Association 1973, 212)

## Evolving Quality of Higher-Education Programs

The meteoric, unregulated rise of programs in police science or law enforcement led to serious questions about their academic rigor and viability. The increase coincided with the infusion of federal money distributed through LEEP. Many schools hurriedly spliced together programs to study the police in order to capture their fair share of the federal funds. Because of a lack of faculty with an expertise in criminal justice in general and policing in particular, many part-time instructors, frequently selected from the local police or sheriff's departments, were employed to teach classes. Little attempt was made to introduce current research or critical analysis of contemporary issues and practices, and too often, instructors focused on training, using readily available models from their own experience. They concentrated on their department's operating policies and procedures and offered "war stories" from their street experiences as examples of the "way things are." The students taking these courses were overwhelmingly in-service—that is, full-time police or criminal justice employees returning to school through the provision of LEEP funds. Because such narrowly focused training-oriented programs were not traditionally found in a university setting, it is not surprising that they encountered stiff opposition from the established academic disciplines.

In the late 1960s and early 1970s, many programs began to broaden their focus, emphasizing criminal justice–related topics rather than technical police training. The titles of the programs began to change to reflect this broader approach; common new titles for these departments were Criminal Justice, Criminology, or Administration of Justice. Reflecting on these changes, Pope (1987, 475) comments:

> Curriculums became much less practice-oriented (at least in the four-year institutions) and more academically based. Some criminal justice programs even took a more critical stance toward the criminal justice system, adding courses based on a radical perspective. Many programs eliminated courses on patrol, traffic and the like, or at least expanded offerings to include race, gender, victims and related issues. It was a period when criminal justice attempted to gain academic respectability and institutional support.

Following a decade of tremendous growth, accompanied by severe criticism of police programs in higher education, the Police Foundation convened noted educators, police administrators, and public officials to evaluate the quality of these programs. Known as the **National Advisory Commission on Higher Education for Police Officers**, the commission spent two years conducting a national survey and documenting the problems of police education (Sherman and the National Advisory Commission on Higher Education for Police Officers 1978). The report was extremely critical of the state of the art of police education at the time, and it recommended significant changes in virtually all phases of police higher education, including institutional, curriculum, and faculty. Among the more crucial recommendations were the following:

1. The majority of federal funds for police higher education should go to programs with broad curriculums and well-educated faculty rather than to narrow technical programs.

2. No college credit should be granted for attending police department training programs.

3. Community colleges should phase out their terminal two-year degree programs in police education.

4. Colleges should employ primarily full-time police-education teaching staffs, seeking faculty members with PhD degrees in arts and sciences.

5. Prior employment in criminal justice should be neither a requirement nor a handicap in faculty selection.

6. Government policies should encourage educating police officers before they begin their careers.

These recommendations struck at the heart of many police programs throughout the country and consequently were not well received by many. As discussed earlier, however, improvements had already begun.

As the LEEP program was eventually phased out, so too were many of the weaker police programs in higher education. The stronger programs continued to recruit PhDs trained in criminal justice and other social sciences for their faculties, thus establishing a more scholarly approach toward teaching and research. The emphasis on a broader-based curriculum became firmly established, and the students became less vocationally and in-service oriented.

These changes in higher education in criminal justice, including faculty quality, student body makeup, and curricular content, have allowed the field to mature rapidly. However, there continue to be widespread differences with respect to academic rigor and course content across criminal justice programs. As such, many of these programs are still not widely accepted by traditional academic disciplines. To address this, some programs are attempting to become broader based and more theoretically oriented by expanding their curriculums beyond traditional criminal justice system issues. These departments may also change their titles to reflect this broader perspective—for example, to Law, Society, and Justice or Justice Studies. In general, on college campuses where degree programs have become firmly established, program quality and student interest continue to increase.

## Higher-Education Requirements for Police

Advances in raising educational requirements for police have been slow and sporadic. Until the 1980s, in many police departments an officer with a college degree was often viewed with contempt or resentment; it was not understood why someone with a degree would want to enter policing. Indeed, a college degree requirement today for initial selection purposes is still the rare exception.

No state standards and training require a four-year degree for police officers, and only Minnesota requires a two-year degree (Hilal and Erickson 2009; Hilal, Densley, and Zhao 2013). A national survey in 2007 by the Bureau of Justice Statistics of approximately 3,100 state and local law enforcement agencies, serving communities of all sizes, indicates that only 1 percent of officers worked in departments that required a college degree for employment.

Table 14.1 reveals an interesting trend (or lack thereof) in college education requirements over a 25-year period. Preemployment educational requirements have remained remarkably static over time. The proportion of police departments requiring a four-year degree has remained around 1 percent, and when coupled with two-year degrees, the proportion of departments increased only modestly, from 8 percent in 1993 to 11 percent in 2016. During this period, the proportion of adults with a college degree increased from 22 percent (in 1993) to 33 percent (in 2016). One interpretation of these data is that despite a higher proportion of the American public achieving a baccalaureate degree, the minimal requirements in policing have by and large remained unchanged, and policing has not kept up with educational trends in the United States. However, these data from the Bureau of Justice Statistics must be interrupted cautiously, as they represent the proportion of officers who work in departments with these education requirements. This does not mean that all officers in these departments have attained these degrees, because as policies change, departments commonly exempt officers who did not meet the requirement at the time they were hired. In reality, 84 percent of all police departments in the United States require a high school diploma, 4 percent some college, 10 percent a two-year degree, and 1 percent a four-year degree. The largest police departments (those serving more than

**TABLE 14.1** Minimum educational requirement for new officer recruits in local police departments

|  | 1993 | 2003 | 2013 | 2016 |
|---|---|---|---|---|
| Total with requirement | 97% | 98% | 98% | 99% |
| High school diploma | 86% | 81% | 84% | 82% |
| Some college (non degree) | 4% | 8% | 4% | 6% |
| Two-year college degree | 7% | 9% | 10% | 10% |
| Four-year college degree | 1% | 1% | 1% | 1% |

*Sources*: B. A. Reaves, Local Police Departments, 1993: Personnel, Policies and Practice (Washington, DC: Bureau of Justice Statistics, 1996), B. A. Reaves, Local Police Departments, 2013: Personnel, Policies and Practice (Washington, DC: Bureau of Justice Statistics, 2015), M.J. Hickman and B. A. Reaves, Local Police Departments, 2003: Personnel, Policies and Practice (Washington, DC: Bureau of Justice Statistics, 2006), and S. S. Hyland and E. Davis, Local Police Departments, 2016: Personnel, (Washington, DC: Bureau of Justice Statistics, 2019).

1 million people) were most likely to require a two-year degree. More than half of all police departments with a degree requirement considered military services as an alternative (Hyland and Davis 2019).

Although the development of formal educational requirements has been slow, some research suggests that up to one-third of officers in the field have post–high school education and degrees, most likely because of the increased number of colleges and universities offering criminal justice–related or criminology degrees. For instance, a national survey indicated that more than 50 percent of officers have a two-year degree, about 30 percent have a four-year degree, and over 5 percent have a graduate degree (Gardiner 2017). This report goes on to indicate that unionized police departments are more likely to have officers with two- or four-year degrees. There is also some evidence of "leading by example"— agencies headed by a chief or sheriff with a graduate degree employ significantly higher proportions of officers with at least a four-year degree. In addition, as noted in Chapter 6, some agencies are not only reducing minimum educational requirements to increase applicant pools but also substituting military experience for college credit. These findings suggest that although a modest trend of college graduates entering the field is developing, agencies themselves are doing little to increase the rate of college graduates in their ranks and, in some cases, are implementing policies that lessen the importance of a college degree. Such findings do not bode well for the development of COP approaches or increased levels of professionalism for the field.

## The Impact of Higher Education on Policing

For college to be a requirement for policing, as proponents suggest, it will be necessary to indicate to the courts the relevance of such a requirement to on-the-job performance. In other words, where is the evidence of impact? Over the past four decades, research on higher education and police officer behavior has focused on two major areas: the relationship between education and police attitudes and the relationship between education and police performance. Brown (2020, 19) summarizes the current state of evidence as follows:

> Whilst a case could be made on value grounds that university educated police officers are a "good thing" to manage complexity in the modern world, the empirical evidence base is not strong enough to draw definitive conclusions about the improvements that more specific graduate attributes bring to policing.

### Does Higher Education Impact Attitudes?

Much of the early research on higher education and the police centered on exploring the relationship between higher education and police attitudes, generally by comparing levels of authoritarianism (i.e., open/closed belief system) in college-educated police versus police with little or no college. Although much of this early research was less sophisticated in design than contemporary research (especially with respect to small sample sizes and lack of relevant control variables), the findings were virtually unanimous in their support for higher education and police who were more open-minded. For instance, police with some college (Smith, Locke, and Walker 1968) and those with college degrees (Smith, Locke, and Fenster 1970) were significantly less authoritarian than their non-college-educated colleagues. Guller (1972) and Roberg (1978) found that police officers who were college seniors showed lower levels of authoritarianism than officers who were college freshmen and of similar age and work experience; this indicated that the higher the level of education, the more flexible or open one's belief system might be. Dalley (1975) further discovered that authoritarian attitudes correspond with a lack of a college education and increased work experience; he suggested that a more liberal attitude is more conducive to the discretionary nature of law enforcement.

In addition, early research indicated that college-educated officers were thought to be more understanding of human behavior, to be more sensitive to community relations, and to hold a higher, more professional service standard (Miller and Fry 1976; Regoli 1976). Furthermore, some evidence indicated that college-educated officers not only were more aware of social and ethnic problems in their community but also had a greater acceptance of minorities (Weiner 1976). More recently, a study of an urban, municipal department in Southern California (Gau and Gaines 2012) surveyed 268 sworn personnel in an attempt to determine what influenced the officers' perceptions of the importance of public order maintenance strategies, which the department was attempting to emphasize, compared with more traditional methods of random patrol and rapid response to calls for service. Results indicated that better-educated officers were significantly more likely to support public order maintenance than less-educated officers; these findings indicate that higher education may lead to increased acceptance of nontraditional methods of policing.

There is evidence that education influences officers' attitudes on abuse of authority. Telep (2011) measured officers' support for several aspects of abuse of authority, including unreasonable extensions of police authority, the code of silence, breaking rules to get the job done (similar to noble-cause corruption, outlined in Chapter 9), and outsiders being too concerned with police brutality. Officers with higher levels of education expressed less support for abuse of authority, regardless of their level of education. This was true for officers who obtained their degree preemployment and those who pursued higher education postemployment. This observation supports the value of higher education among police officers, and it may be particularly important given the centrality of national conversations on abuse of authority, use of force, and police legitimacy.

Concerning the study by Roberg (1978), the relationships among higher education, belief systems (attitudes), and on-the-job performance (supervisory ratings) of 118 patrol officers of the Lincoln, Nebraska, Police Department were analyzed. It should be noted that this was a highly educated department for the time, at least partially attributable to their 2.5 percent pay increase for every 30 semester hours of college credit earned, culminating in a 10 percent increase for completing a college degree. Of the patrol officer study participants, 27 percent had a college degree, 24 percent were upper class (junior or senior standing), 43 percent were lower class (freshman or sophomore standing), and 13 percent had completed high school, but with no college credits.

The findings were consistent across all educational levels in that "officers with higher levels of education had more open belief systems (were less authoritarian) and performed in a more satisfactory manner on the job than those patrol officers with less education"; in addition, patrol officers with "college degrees had the most open belief systems and the highest levels of job performance, indicating that college-educated officers were better able to adapt to the complex nature of the police role" (Roberg 1978, 344). Control variables included age, seniority, student status (preservice, in-service, and continuing), and college major (by highest percentage of participants: criminal justice, education, business, sociology, and psychology), and no control variable impacted the results. The overall findings suggested that the university experience led to more open belief systems, which in turn led to improved performance.

The preponderance of available research supports, in general, the belief that a *college degree* (not some college or a two-year degree) significantly impacts police attitudes and behavior. The research indicates that a college education is related to less authoritarian beliefs, greater tolerance toward others, a greater acceptance of minority groups and understanding of civil rights issues, and more professional attitudes. Additionally, the research suggests that college-educated officers tend to make better decisions than their non-college-educated colleagues, are less likely to use force or be involved in civil liability complaints, and are more likely to take leadership roles and be promoted.

## Does Higher Education Impact Performance?

Because police departments are so diverse, it is difficult to define performance measures; that is, what is considered "good" or "poor" performance may vary from department to department. The criteria used to measure police performance, then, are not clear-cut and are often controversial. Accordingly, research findings on police performance will usually be more useful if they are based on a wide variety of performance indicators.

The research described next, on the relationship between higher education and police performance, is based on a number of different indicators, or measures, of performance. Another issue today, as noted in Chapters 5 and 6, is that although many departments state they are "doing" COP, they have not changed their performance evaluation criteria to reflect "nontraditional" activities required of COP approaches, such as citizen interactions and communication, organizing and running community meetings, problem solving, and the de-escalation of force in solving conflicts, to name but a few. Thus, the type of activities in which college-educated officers may excel frequently are not even measured, let alone rewarded.

Researchers over nearly four decades have found college to have a positive effect on numerous individual performance indicators. For example, several researchers have found college-educated officers to have fewer citizen complaints filed against them (Cohen and Chaiken 1972; Wilson 1999; Lersch and Kunzman 2001; Johnston and Cheurprakobkit 2002). Additional research has indicated that college-educated officers tend to have fewer disciplinary actions taken against them by the department, have lower rates of absenteeism, receive fewer injuries on the job, are involved in fewer traffic accidents (Cohen and Chaiken 1972), and are better decision makers (Worden 1990; Johnston and Cheurprakobkit 2002).

In a study on decision making, LaGrange (2003) found that college education played a significant role in handling difficult situations involving mentally ill persons. Officers with college degrees reported making psychiatric referrals much more frequently (over 80 percent) compared with those having some college or a high school education (about 50 percent), while making far fewer arrests (2 percent) compared with officers having some college (12 percent) or high school only (19 percent). The author concluded that college-educated officers are more likely to use a set of "interpretive tools" to deal more appropriately with complex situations.

The influence of higher education on performance is inconsistent, however. In a comprehensive study of traffic stop behaviors in St. Louis, Rosenfeld, Johnson, and Wright (2018) reported college-educated officers tended toward more vigorous discretionary decisions during encounters with the public. College-educated officers were significantly more likely to stop motorists for nonmoving and nonspeeding violations (20 percent and 50 percent, respectively) and were significantly more likely to engage in discretionary consent searches (this was particularly true for male college-educated officers). Despite this, college-educated officers were no more likely to discover contraband during searches of motor vehicles; in other words, assuming contraband discovery is an indicator of a productive or successful search, college-educated officers were no more productive or successful than their counterparts. The authors posited that college-educated officers may be more motivated by organizational advancement, be achievement-oriented and sensitive to organizational performance measures (e.g., law enforcement–oriented outcomes), and therefore be more likely to engage in activities consistent with these views. This may be contrary to the presumed impact of college education on performance—namely, that college- educated officers would more selectively enforce the law or use a variety of tactics beyond law enforcement to support their objectives. The St. Louis study calls into question this commonly held belief; in fact, education may encourage *more* enforcement activities.

## Does Higher Education Impact the Use of Force and Coercion?

Several contemporary studies on the use of force indicate that citizen encounters involving inexperienced and less-educated officers resulted in increased levels of police force (Terrill and Mastrofski 2002). A study on deadly force by McElvain and Kposowa (2008), using data from 186 officer-involved shootings in Southern California, found that college-educated officers were 41 percent less likely to discharge their firearms than were officers with a high school diploma or some college only.

A large observational study by Paoline and Terrill (2007) of more than 3,300 police–citizen encounters in the Indianapolis and St. Petersburg police departments analyzed the influence of an officer's level of education and years of experience on use of force on suspects, as measured by both verbal and physical coercion. The data were collected as part of the Project on Policing Neighborhoods using both observations and interviews. Findings indicated that officers with some college education or a four-year degree were significantly less likely to use verbal (coercive) force during encounters with suspects. However, only encounters involving officers with a four-year degree resulted in significantly less use of physical force (see also Police Executive Research Forum [PERF] 2021).

Another study by Rydberg and Terrill (2010), utilizing the same two Project on Policing Neighborhoods data sets of more than 3,300 officers described earlier (Paoline and Terrill 2007), analyzed the effect of higher education on arrests, searches, and use of force, which was defined as acts that threaten or inflict physical harm on citizens. Findings indicated no relation between higher education and the probability of an arrest or search occurring in a police–suspect encounter. However, officers with some college or a college degree were significantly less likely to use force in an encounter. With respect to explicating these findings, the authors suggest that unlike arrests and searches, the use of force is not inherently an end product to a police–citizen encounter but may be used throughout an encounter to control the behavior of a suspect. Thus, there is great discretion in the application of force, so it is likely that "as opposed to the decision to arrest or search, there is more room for officer education to have an impact on discretion with respect to force" (Rydberg and Terrill 2010, 111). This finding is critical in that it suggests officers are performing their enforcement roles without resorting to the use of force; this approach can go a long way toward improving citizen perceptions of procedural justice and police legitimacy.

Another study further supports the aforementioned findings. Chapman (2012) surveyed 522 officers with respect to their use of force in three police departments in low-income minority communities in New Jersey. The researcher found a strong relationship between the educational level of patrol officers and use of force: the more educated officers not only used less force overall but also used lower levels of force in making arrests. There is also evidence that college-educated officers become involved in cases of "individual liability significantly less frequently than noncollege officers" (Carter and Sapp 1989, 163) and that college-educated officers tend to have a broader understanding of civil rights issues from legal, social, historical, and political perspectives (Carter and Sapp 1990). This appears to complement the research cited earlier, indicating that college-educated officers use lower levels of force during encounters with the public because high proportions of civil suits are based on excessive use of force. Because lawsuits claiming negligence on behalf of police departments are on the increase, as are the amount of damages being awarded (often between $1 million and $2 million per case), this is another important area for future research. If a correlation between higher education and reduced liability of risk can be established, the availability and cost of risk insurance to police departments could be substantially affected.

### Does Higher Education Lead to Promotion?

Interesting findings with respect to the future development of police departments indicate that college-educated officers are more likely to attain promotions (Cohen and Chaiken 1972; Roberg and Laramy 1980; Whetstone 2000; Polk and Armstrong 2001; Gau, Terrill, and Paoline 2013; Rosenfeld et al. 2018) and are more likely to take leadership roles in the department and to rate themselves higher on performance measures (Cohen and Chaiken 1972; Krimmel 1996). Truxillo, Bennett, and Collins (1998) studied a cohort of 84 officers in a southern metropolitan police department over 10 years and found that college education was significantly correlated with promotions as well as with supervisory ratings of job knowledge. Kakar (1998) indicates that those officers with higher education rated themselves higher in leadership, responsibility, problem-solving, and initiative-taking skills than less-educated officers. A recent large, multicity examination revealed that officers with more education were significantly more committed to being promoted and had higher aspirations for their career trajectories. Gau et al. 2013) found that, controlling for other relevant factors such as gender, race, and experience, officers with some college or a four-year degree aspired for promotion and were significantly more likely to expect to retire at a higher rank. Officers with a college education were more likely to anticipate retiring as a first-line supervisor (e.g., sergeant) or middle manager (e.g., lieutenant or captain). In the Voices from the Field, Dan Haley discusses the importance of higher education in preparing future policing leaders.

### Does Higher Education Enhance Job Satisfaction?

Does higher education lead to increased job satisfaction or dissatisfaction for officers? The number of job-satisfaction studies related to policing is surprisingly small, but overall, the results suggest that education has no effect on job satisfaction or that officers with more education are less satisfied with their jobs. Early research in this area suggested that officers with a college education would be more frustrated and less satisfied because of unmet

## VOICES FROM THE FIELD

### Dan B. Haley
*Major, Kansas City (MO) Police Department*

The role of higher education in twenty-first century policing is to prepare officers for leadership positions in their organizations. Formal education stimulates intellectual, emotional, and social growth. This is particularly important for people pursuing the policing profession, because higher education is an opportunity to engage in in-depth thought, have those thoughts challenged in an academic setting, and reformulate those thoughts into a progressive and defensible position. Intellectually, this growth develops the officer to address complex issues with multifaceted approaches. Emotionally, this growth develops an officer's emotional intelligence through constructive criticism causing an officer to regulate their conflict management skills when presenting ideas. Socially, higher education exposes officers to other future leaders developing their social network. This combination of intellectual, emotional, and social growth prepares officers for twenty-first century policing, but is particularly important for people in leadership roles in their organizations.

It is important that twenty-first century police organizations invest in officers' higher education to build the organization's leadership pipeline. From an organizational standpoint, officers learn how to perform their jobs through academy training, field training, roll-call training, in-service training, and general police cultural cues. When twenty-first century police organizations encourage officers to pursue higher education (e.g., providing tuition reimbursement), newfound skills (e.g., problem solving, public speaking, communication, and leadership) are developed, making the organization and the officer better. Police organizations that invest in officers' higher education demonstrate a commitment to succession planning, leadership development, and officer retention.

Regardless of the reason officers start down the path of higher education, the benefits build a foundation for twenty-first century leadership. Common reasons police officers pursue higher education are to add tools to their toolbox, meet educational requirements for promotion, and retool for another career after retirement. These common reasons lead to the enhancement of officers' problem-solving, cultural competency, public speaking, communication, and leadership skills, further building the foundation for leadership. For me, higher education has built a foundation for twenty-first century leadership in my community, organization, and life.

expectations for promotion (Niederhoffer 1967). There is some evidence that highly educated officers are more likely to terminate their careers in policing (Levy 1967; Cohen and Chaiken 1972; Stoddard 1973; Weirman 1978) and to hold differing and more negative views of job satisfaction (Griffin, Dunbar, and McGill 1978). It is possible, and even likely, however, that such results may be related to the traditional bureaucratic nature and macho culture of police departments. Since higher education affects authoritarian attitudes, it would follow that college-educated police would be less willing to work in, and would be less satisfied with, authoritarian departments and managerial practices. For example, Kakar (1998) indicates that with respect to job satisfaction, college-educated officers self-reported lower scores, coupled with higher levels of frustration due to not feeling rewarded or feeling understimulated by the duties of traditional patrol work. In addition, officers with higher levels of education felt unrewarded and expressed frustration because of their inability to use their professional knowledge. Dantzker (1998) as well as Paoline, Terrill, and Rossler (2015) also reported lower levels of job satisfaction among officers with higher education.

## Validating Higher Education for Police

Given the increasing number of college-educated officers in the field, such slow progress in developing higher-education standards is perplexing, especially considering the evidence that college education generally positively affects officer attitudes, performance, and behavior. With such support for higher education, why have most police departments not significantly raised their standards? Carter, Sapp, and Stephens (1989) identified two common reasons: (1) fear of being sued because a college requirement could not be quantitatively validated to show job-relatedness and (2) fear that college requirements adversely impact racial minorities. Each of these important issues warrants discussion.

### Higher Education as a Bona Fide Occupational Qualification

As the PERF study of police executives reported (Carter et al. 1989), one of the primary reasons departments had not embraced higher-education requirements more vigorously was the dilemma of not being able to validate such a requirement for the job, thus opening the department to a court challenge. Establishing higher-education requirements as a **bona fide occupational qualification** (BFOQ) for police work could be an important step in facilitating the use of advanced education as a minimum entry-level selection criterion. A brief discussion of higher education as a BFOQ for police work follows.

Interestingly, the courts in this country have continuously upheld higher-education requirements in policing as *job-related*. In **Castro v. Beecher (1972)**, the requirement of a high school education by the Boston Police Department was affirmed, citing the recommendations of the President's Commission on Law Enforcement and Administration of Justice (1967) and the National Advisory Commission on Civil Disorders (1968). **Arnold v. Ballard (1975**, 738) supported the notion that an educational requirement can be quantitatively job validated in stating that such requirements "indicate a measure of accomplishment and ability which . . . is essential for . . . performance as a police officer." Furthermore, in **Davis v. City of Dallas (1985)**, the Court upheld a challenge to the Dallas Police Department's requirement of 45-semester units (equivalent to one-and-a-half years of college) with a minimum of a C average from an accredited university.

In *Davis*, the Court's decision was based partially on the complex nature of the police role and the public risk and responsibility that are unique to that role. Such a decision indicates that higher qualification standards can be applied to the job, because police decision making requires an added dimension of judgment. This logic has been applied by the courts to other occupations, such as airline pilots and health-related professions. Thus, the *Davis* decision can be viewed as the next logical step in increasing police professionalism and may provide further support for police executives to require higher education (Carter, Sapp, and Stephens 1988).

To validate the need for higher-education requirements, possibly the best approach, and one that has withstood the scrutiny of the courts, is to use national studies and commission reports (see, e.g., President's Commission 1967, National Advisory Commission on Criminal Justice 1973, and others cited in this chapter) and the opinion of experts (including both police scholars and police executives). The PERF study recommended a preventive approach for a department that is going to require higher education for employment. This can be accomplished by having an expert prepare a *policy support paper* citing the "benefits and need of college-educated officers" (Carter et al. 1988, 16). The study further suggested that although general studies and reports should be used, the policy support document should be specific to the individual department. The probability of litigation should be substantially lessened with such a document, and the educational program can also be based on the policies developed in the document. Inside Policing 14.1 provides an example for the framework of such a policy.

### Higher Education and Access

A second area of concern reported to PERF by police executives was the potential impact the higher-education requirement might have on the employment of minorities. If minority group members do not have equal access to higher education, such a requirement could be held to be discriminatory by the courts. In addition, there are obvious ethical and social issues. Any educational requirements for policing, then, must not only be job related but also nondiscriminatory.

In the *Davis* case, the suit contended that higher-education requirements were discriminatory in the selection of police officers. According to Title VII of the Civil Rights Act, there cannot be employment barriers (or practices) that discriminate against minorities, even if they are not intended to do so. However, in ***Griggs v. Duke Power Co. (1971)***, the Supreme Court held that if an employment practice is job-related (or a "business necessity"), it may be allowed as a requirement even if it has discriminatory overtones. Thus, courts must base decisions on the balance between requirements necessary for job performance and avoiding discriminatory practices. The City of Dallas conceded that the college requirements had a "significant disparate impact on Blacks" (*Davis v. City of Dallas* 1985, 207). As noted previously, the Court held that the complex requirements of police work (e.g., public risk, responsibility, and amount of discretion) mitigated against the discriminatory effects of a higher-education requirement.

In other words, if certain requirements for the job can be justified even though they may discriminate against certain groups, the benefits of such requirements may be judged to outweigh the discriminatory effects. Following this line of reasoning, if higher-education requirements can be shown to be a BFOQ, such a requirement would be considered a business necessity and thus a legitimate requirement for successful job performance. Inside Policing 14.2 outlines considerations for police executives to consider when implementing educational standards within departments.

---

**INSIDE POLICING 14.1** | **Higher Standards for Police Employment**

This article describes higher education and experience standards being applied by several agencies in the Minneapolis region. Police chiefs cite increased complexity, diversity, and also deep applicant pools as reasons behind the trend.

**Discussion Question:** If many police chiefs indicate a desire to recruit college-educated officers, what changes might they consider within their department to attract the most desired candidates?

*SOURCE: Modern Policing* blog, January 6, 2014, www.oup.com/cordner/higher-standards-for-police-employment/.

## INSIDE POLICING 14.2    Developing a Higher-Education Policy for Police Departments

Each department should have a written policy defining college education as a BFOQ as it uniquely relates to the department, regardless of the requirements adopted. The department can then be fully prepared for any questions concerning the validity of any new educational requirements.

Policy development should include input from all levels of the department, particularly the local collective-bargaining organizations. This provision will lead to a common understanding of the rationale for the policy, enhance its acceptance, and expedite its implementation.

### Promotional Requirements

If the entry-level educational requirements are raised, then the educational requirements for promotion should also be reviewed. As more highly educated officers enter policing, more highly educated supervisors, managers, and police executives will be needed.

### Policy Standards

Educational policies should specify standards, especially that college credit and degrees be awarded from an accredited college or university. Acceptable credit should be based on a minimum grade average of C, or 2.0 on a 4.0 scale. Other standards could include the requirement that college credits earned be directly in pursuit of a degree. This rule ensures that the student has a liberal arts background in addition to courses in a major area.

### Women and Minority Candidates

Attracting qualified women and minority candidates continues to be a concern for police departments. It is increasingly evident, however, that there is no need to limit entry or promotional educational requirements for these groups so long as innovative and aggressive recruiting programs are in place.

SOURCE: Adapted from D. L. Carter and A. D. Sapp, "College Education and Policing: Coming of Age," *FBI Law Enforcement Bulletin*, January 1992: 12.

Some data suggest, however, that requiring a bachelor's degree may impact race. For example, Decker and Huckabee (2002) explored the effect of raising educational requirements to a bachelor's degree by analyzing recruit information from the Indianapolis Police Department over four years. They concluded that almost two-thirds (65 percent) of successful candidates overall would have been ineligible, and that 77 percent (30 of 39) of African American applicants did not have degrees. Although the research did not discuss whether any recruitment efforts were made to increase the pool of college-educated minority applicants, it is worth noting that 9 of the 39 African American applicants did possess baccalaureate degrees. Because a college degree was not a requirement for the job, it is unclear how such a requirement would have impacted the applicant pool in this case. However, an impact on race and the overall applicant pool is likely to occur when departments attempt to improve the quality of their personnel by raising standards. Departments that raise their educational requirements also must likely enhance their recruitment efforts, as other professional organizations have done. As discussed in Chapter 7, if strong recruitment efforts are made to attract college-educated minorities, a college degree requirement should not seriously impact minority hiring and may even increase the total number of both minority and female applicants.

## Higher-Education Incentive Programs

Forty-two percent of law enforcement agencies in the United States have an educational incentive plan (US Department of Justice 2015). Supporting programs and policies must be established for those departments recruiting college-educated officers. One of the most important strategies for college recruitment is the use of incentives relating to higher-education levels. For example, the national PERF study (2021) found that most of the departments had developed one or more educational incentive programs to encourage officers to continue their education beyond that required for initial employment. As Table 14.2 indicates, these incentive programs include tuition assistance or reimbursement, educational pay, flexible hours to attend class, and permission to attend classes during work hours

In 1970 the Massachusetts Legislature passed the Quinn Bill (MGL, Chapter 41, Section 108L) as an educational incentive program for full-time employees. Also known as the Police Career Incentive Pay Program, it was to encourage college-educated individuals to pursue positions in policing and existing officers to continue their higher education within criminal justice and law enforcement degree programs. The Commonwealth would infuse funding within local police departments to assist with this program, which included increases in base rate pay by 10 percent for an associate's degree, 20 percent for a bachelor's degree, and 25 percent for a master's degree (Gavin 2015). This incentive often resulted in college-educated officers making thousands of dollars more than their non-college-educated peers, and these incentives cost taxpayers millions annually. The Commonwealth scaled back their contributions to local police departments pursuant to the Quinn Bill. And in 2012, the Massachusetts Supreme Judicial Court indicated that cities were only required to pay 50 percent of whatever the Commonwealth provided, but most cities still find money in their local budgets to continue this incentive program.

A study by Stewart (2006) of 47 Texas police departments, diverse in size (e.g., the Houston Police Department with 5,732 sworn officers and the Greenville Police Department with 46 sworn officers) and organizational structure, found that approximately 90 percent offer at least one type of educational policy. The most common type of policy was for pay incentive ($n = 30$; 64 percent), followed by full tuition reimbursement ($n = 19$;

**TABLE 14.2**  Higher-Education Incentive Policies for Sworn Officers

| INCENTIVE POLICY | PERCENTAGE |
|---|---|
| Tuition assistance | 38.6% |
| Education pay | 33.7% |
| Flexible shifts to attend class | 9.2% |
| Use of department vehicle to attend class | 7.9% |
| Attend class on duty | 7.1% |
| Schedule preferences to accommodate college semester | 5.0% |
| Accelerate career ladder | 4.9% |

ADAPTED FROM: C. Gardiner. "Policing Around the Nation: Education, Philosophy, and Practice." *Police Foundation*, 2017.

40 percent), partial tuition reimbursement ($n = 15$; 32 percent), and adjustments to shift/days-off schedule ($n = 5$; 11 percent).

## Higher-Education Requirements and Policy Implications

As discussed previously, if college education is ever to become an entry-level requirement for policing, supporting policies must also be established. Additionally, it is helpful to have a competitive salary scale, good employment benefits, and high-quality working conditions. It is important to point out that many medium-size and large police departments have implemented highly competitive salary structures over the past two decades, in line with (and often substantially above) the starting salaries for college graduates in most public- and many private-sector jobs. At the same time, small and rural agencies face more obstacles to enhancing education requirements because of less-competitive pay and a smaller overall college-educated population. Health benefits and retirement packages are generally very good. In the long term, however, adopting a less-bureaucratic, paramilitary structure and command style will likely be necessary to significantly enhance police working environments, creating a professional atmosphere where college graduates will feel comfortable and flourish. As one former Baltimore City police officer has observed (Moskos 2003, 8):

> [T]too many potentially good police won't join an organization filled with Marine haircuts, snappy salutes and a six-month boot camp. Too few people with four-year degrees and liberal upbringing want a job in a conservative organization with archaic grooming codes. What other civilian profession hides behind a conservative faux military facade? What other occupation demands that you stand at attention every time a boss enters the room? If police departments treated their employees more like professionals, more professionals would join the police.

In the final analysis, it appears that evidence (both empirical and experiential) has been established to support a strong argument for a college-degree requirement for entry-level police officers:

1. The benefits provided by a higher education, combined with social and technological changes, the threat of terrorism (along with civil rights issues), and the increasing complexity of police work, suggest that a college degree should be a requirement for initial police employment.

2. The types of significant changes described earlier further call for the development of the police field to move away from the status of a vocational craft toward a bona fide profession, which not only understands the importance of research but also relies on valid and reliable research to guide their policy decisions.

3. If educational and recruitment policies are appropriately developed, a higher-education requirement should not adversely affect minority recruitment or retention.

Recognizing that there are diverse types of police departments throughout the country with differing styles of operation, levels of performance, and community needs, it is apparent that some can adapt to a college-degree requirement more readily than others. Consequently, perhaps some type of *graduated timetable* for college requirements—similar to those found in the National Advisory Commission on Criminal Justice's (1973) *Report on Police*—would be appropriate (the commission recommended that all officers be required to have a baccalaureate degree by 1982). A graduated timetable could again be set up for phasing in, first, a two-year degree requirement and, second, a baccalaureate degree for initial selection purposes. At the same time, requirements could be established for supervisory and executive personnel, first at the baccalaureate level and then, at least for executives, at the master's level. Inside Policing 14.3 provides additional rationales for enhancing officers' education levels.

These requirements may be adjusted to account for different types of agencies; for example, larger agencies serving larger and more diverse populations could have the requirements phased in earlier. The bottom line, however, would ultimately require any officer with general enforcement powers to have a degree, regardless of location or type of agency. Those departments or cities that feel they cannot comply with such a requirement could contract with a nearby agency that is able to meet the requirements. Such an arrangement is not without precedent, because many small and rural cities that feel they cannot afford to support their own police department contract for local police services through larger municipal or county agencies.

For higher education to become entrenched throughout the field, however, a serious push will likely be needed from the federal government, perhaps along the lines of the Justice Department's COPS program, which provided funds nationally to promote COP (but with stronger requirements and oversight attached). Initially, federal funding could be provided to departments for achieving measurable standards, including broad-based recruiting efforts (including universities), developing educational incentive programs, elimination of policies that restrict applicant searches (including residency requirements), and the development of a written policy defining college education as a BFOQ as it relates to departmental needs (Roberg and Bonn 2004). In time, we may see further federal incentives for educating law enforcement in the United States, as evidenced by the recommendations outlined in the President's Task Force on Twenty-First Century Policing (2015). This could include student loan repayment and forgiveness incentive programs similar to those that currently exist for other governmental service and similar to programs previously implemented under LEEP.

At the same time, it is important to recognize the fiscal realities that many police departments face regarding higher-education incentives and requirements. During fiscal downturns, programs like higher-education incentives are often among the first line items to be cut from police budgets. When recessions occur, like in 2008 and 2020, police departments will often reconsider minimum education requirements for preemployment. Inside Policing 14.4 highlights how several large police departments—Chicago, Philadelphia, and New Orleans—relaxed their preemployment education requirements to encourage more people to apply for sworn positions. Inside Policing 14.5 discusses the United Kingdom's debate over university education for police.

## Moving Forward

The role of higher education in policing remains unclear. On one hand, over time the number of police officers with advanced degrees has increased, and many have noted various benefits from a highly educated work force. Higher education has become more attainable for people than when Vollmer advocated more education in policing. But on the other hand, empirical evidence of the benefits of higher education is a mixed bag, and some police departments who raised pre-entry educational standards have since relaxed the requirements. Recognizing this, it seems reasonable to focus future conversations on what kind of education demonstrates the greatest value in policing, how much education

## INSIDE POLICING 14.3   Support for College Education Requirement for Entry-Level Police Officers

At least three significant changes support a college degree requirement for initial selection of police.

### Organizational Changes

Today's police departments are very different from those that existed when LEAA and LEEP were begun in the 1970s. Many more police officers and managers have college degrees (and advanced degrees), and the police cultural bias against "college cops" has significantly declined. The challenges of COP require officers to use more discretion in problem solving and decision making. At the same time, officers must be aware of cultural differences in, and have sensitivity to the needs of, the community.

### Societal Changes

In general, the proportion of people in the United States who have earned a degree in higher education has increased over time. In 1940, only about 5 percent of the adult population in the United States had completed a postbaccalaureate degree—by 2020, about 35 percent had earned a baccalaureate degree or higher. This is particularly true for the younger population. In 1976, approximately 24 percent of people aged 25 to 29 had completed a bachelor's degree. This proportion remained pretty stable through 1995, when the proportion began to increase. By 2015, approximately 36 percent of people aged 25 to 29 had earned a degree (Ryan and Bauman 2016). In other words, in the United States, the proportion of people who have completed a degree has increased over time, and overall, people have become more educated. The call for higher education within policing is consistent with this trend of higher education overall.

Today's police officers must be culturally competent and able to value ethnic differences. Most college-degree programs offer courses in such areas as cultural diversity, ethics, and cross-cultural comparisons, and some even require a foreign language. In addition, courses in sociology, psychology, and other human-behavior courses (including criminal justice and criminology) all contribute to a better understanding of the complex society in which we live. Research has demonstrated that officers who are exposed to such an educational experience deal better with diverse community groups.

Police departments must also recognize that as members of the community are becoming more educated, their expectations of police service will also increase. Thus, police departments must raise their educational requirements to represent the populations they serve.

### Technological Changes

Today's police officer utilizes more modern technology than ever before. The laptop computer has replaced the field notebook. The Internet, World Wide Web, and e-mail have greatly expanded resources and data-collection and analytical techniques, and the emphasis on solution-oriented policing has placed greater demands on crime analysis, problem solving, and computer sophistication.

As innovative programs are developed to address crime and disorder, departments must have officers who can evaluate their impact with methodologically sound techniques. Most college-degree programs require coursework (e.g., computer science, research methods, and math and statistics) that is beneficial in today's technologically sophisticated environment.

*SOURCE*: Adapted from R. Garner, "Community Policing and Education: The College Connection," *Texas Law Enforcement Management and Administrative Statistics Program*, January 1998: 7–9.

---

**INSIDE POLICING 14.4**   Relaxing Education Requirements

Several police departments have stopped requiring some college as a minimum standard in the hiring process. This article focuses on Chicago, which had required 60 college credits. Officials there and elsewhere point to the downturn in applicants as the main justification. Chicago will now "waive a college credit requirement for recruits who have two years of military or peace officer experience, or three years in corrections, social services, health care, trades, or education." Applications reportedly spiked as soon as the 60-credit mandate was relaxed. The article cites Philadelphia and New Orleans as two other police departments that have lowered their educational requirements, as well as New York's mayor expressing interest in following suit.

   **Discussion Question:** Even if these decisions in Chicago, Philadelphia, and New Orleans are temporary, how might these decisions impact policing in these departments in the future?

SOURCE: *Modern Policing blog*, March 25, 2022, https://gcordner.wordpress.com/2022/03/25/police-departments-lowering-education-requirements/

---

**INSIDE POLICING 14.5**   Policing and Higher Education

The United Kingdom is engaged in a vigorous debate over whether to begin requiring university education for police. Some members of the police force think the country's College of Policing has been pushing the academic agenda too hard, at the expense of recognizing the skills and experience obtained within the profession. This brief essay reviews the arguments, urging both sides to focus on "the value and worth that external formal recognition can add onto the complex work that police officers and staff do on a daily basis" while also giving "policing professionals . . . a greater say in shaping their own policing context."

   **Discussion Question:** Discuss what a model higher-education curriculum focused on policing would include, and why.

SOURCE: *Modern Policing* blog, December 3, 2018, gcordner.wordpress.com/2018/12/03/policing-higher-education/

---

officers should have, and whether there are approaches beyond the traditional university-based structure.

## What Kind of Education and How Much?

It is unclear whether the academic discipline officers study significant influences many of the outcomes described throughout this chapter. Since the 1970s, the default assumption is that a degree in criminal justice or criminology is directly relevant to policing. This makes intuitive sense. But it is important to note that students with a criminal justice academic major complete a significant amount of coursework not directly focusing on policing. Cordner (2019) described how policing-focused coursework comprises a minute portion of typical criminal justice curricula—his examination of 10 academic programs revealed that only three *required* students to complete a course on policing during their academic studies. And while all programs offered one or more policing classes (perhaps like the one you are completing right now) that could be completed as electives, these courses comprised a relatively small proportion of all criminal justice classes. While recognizing the need for enhancing education among police officers may have been a catalyst for universities to create criminal justice programs, over time other subareas of study in criminal justice (e.g., corrections, courts, law, ethics, theory, research methods, and statistics) appear to have taken over the focus of the curricula. This is not necessarily a bad thing, and this may be consistent with the liberal arts focus of criminal justice programs. Moreover, there is value in officers being well-rounded and interdisciplinary, because they confront a wide range of human and community problems that are beyond the scope of the legal system.

It is also unclear how much education is ideal. Cordner (2019) noted that some countries require some college completion or degrees to become a police officer, but earlier in this chapter, we described how there is great variation in this across US police departments. Furthermore, there is little scientific consensus as to what is the ideal amount of education, and why. Some universities and police departments have articulation agreements where students can "double dip" and receive academic credit for police academy participation, which blurs the line between education and training. Clearer evidence on the "how much" question is needed before a definitive conclusion can be drawn.

### Beyond Traditional University-Based Education?

Over time, the presence of higher-educated police officers in the United States has increased, although the benefits envisioned by early reformers remain unfulfilled. In addition, research on the direct impact of higher education within policing remains mixed or inconclusive. Yet the anticipated benefits of a more highly educated policing industry remain a goal worth pursuing, and as noted, the President's Task Force on Twenty-First Century Policing (2015) highlights and recommends mechanisms to encourage officers to pursue formal education. The President's Task Force (2015, 55) also notes, "The US Department of Justice should develop, in partnership with institutions of higher education, a national postgraduate institute of policing for senior executives with a standardized curriculum preparing them to lead agencies in the twenty-first century." They indicated that a similar model in place at the Naval Postgraduate School could be implemented for police executives to develop critical leadership within policing. Cordner (2016) noted that graduate-level programs exist in the United Kingdom (https://www.college.police.uk/Pages/Home.aspx/) and posits that a similar focused policing curriculum may be more consistent with the Task Force recommendations than what is currently available within university graduate programs in criminal justice. This development could complement (rather than replace) university education within policing and would specifically focus on senior-level executives. This would fill a void within US policing and promote Vollmer's vision of a highly educated police force.

## Summary

August Vollmer, the Berkeley police chief, began a campaign for higher education for police that has continued today. Major universities developed programs for police education, despite the resistance of many street officers. Research has indicated that higher education can be job validated for police entry and that such a requirement should not adversely impact minority recruitment or retention if appropriate recruitment policies and efforts are developed. While there are indications across a variety of dimensions that benefits are associated with having a more highly educated workforce, the evidence of impact remains frustratingly scant (and at times inconsistent). It is unclear, based on the research, that the rhetoric meets reality.

This topic is fraught with contradictions. The proportion of people in the United States with a college degree has increased over time, and many see the value of higher education within policing. A considerable proportion of police departments have adopted one or more incentives for officers to obtain a degree, and this indirectly suggests that policy makers see the value in a highly educated force. Yet, a relatively small proportion of police departments have a degree as a pre-employment requirement.

Generally, college education for entry-level police officers can be supported based on ongoing changes, including organizational, societal, and technological changes. In the final analysis, enough evidence has been established to support the requirement of a college degree for policing. Yet direct, consistent, measurable impacts of higher education on policing remain elusive. A graduated timetable for development and federal funding for support will likely be necessary for national recognition and implementation.

## Critical Thinking Questions

1. Should college education be required for those applying to become police officers? Defend your argument.

2. Why were the President's Commission on Law Enforcement and Administration of Justice and the National Advisory Commission on Criminal Justice Standards and Goals important to higher education for police?

3. In your opinion, was LEAA successful? Why or why not?

4. Briefly describe what you believe to be the important empirical research on the impact of higher education on policing. What areas are in need of further research?

5. In your opinion, can higher education be supported as a BFOQ in policing if a COP approach is not adopted? Why or why not?

6. Do you think that the field of policing is a profession if higher-education requirements are not ultimately adopted? Give several specific reasons why or why not.

7. How steps must police departments take to attract and retain highly educated officers?

8. If you were a police chief, would you attempt to require higher-education requirements first for entry-level positions or for promotions? Defend your answer.

## References

American Bar Association. 1973. *Standards Relating to the Urban Police Function*. New York: American Bar Association.

*Arnold v. Ballard*, 390 F. Supp., N.D. Ohio (1975).

Baro, A. L., and Burlingame, D. 1999. "Law Enforcement and Higher Education: Is There an Impasse?" *Journal of Criminal Justice Education* 10(1): 57–73.

Brown, J. 2020. "Do Graduate Police Officers Make a Difference to Policing? Results of an Integrative Literature Review." *Policing: A Journal of Policy and Practice*, 14(1): 9–30.

Caiden, G. E. 1977. *Police Revitalization*. Lexington, MA: Heath.

Carte, G. E. 1973. "August Vollmer and the Origins of Police Professionalism." *Journal of Police Science and Administration* 1: 274–281.

Carter, D. L., and Sapp, A. D. 1989. "The Effect of Higher Education on Police Liability: Implications for Police Personnel Policy." *American Journal of Police* 8: 153–166.

Carter, D. L., and Sapp, A. D. 1990. "Higher Education as a Policy Alternative to Reduce Police Liability." *Police Liability Review* 2: 1–3.

Carter, D. L., Sapp, A. D., and Stephens, D. W. 1988. "Higher Education as a Bona Fide Occupational Qualification (BFOQ) for Police: A Blueprint." *American Journal of Police* 7: 1–27.

Carter, D. L., Sapp, A. D., and Stephens, D. W. 1989. *The State of Police Education: Policy Direction for the Twenty-First Century*. Washington, DC: Police Executive Research Forum.

*Castro v. Beecher*, 459 F.2d 725, 1st Cir. (1972).

Chapman, C. 2012. "Use of Force in Minority Communities Is Related to Police Education, Age, Experience, and Ethnicity." *Police Practice and Research* 13: 421–436.

Cohen, B., and Chaiken, J. M. 1972. *Police Background Characteristics and Performance*. New York: Rand Institute.

Cordner, G. 2016. "The Unfortunate Demise of Police Education." *Journal of Criminal Justice Education* 27(4): 485–496. doi:10.1080/10511253.2016.1190134.

Cordner, G. 2019. "Rethinking Police Education in the United States." *Police Practice and Research* 19, 225–239.

Dalley, A. F. 1975. "University and Nonuniversity Graduated Policemen: A Study of Police Attitudes." *Journal of Police Science and Administration* 3: 458–468.

Dantzker, M. L. 1998. "Police Education and Job Satisfaction: Educational Incentives and Recruit Educational Requirements." *Police Forum* 8(3): 1–4.

*Davis v. City of Dallas*, 777 F.2d 205, 5th Cir. (1985).

Decker, L. K., and Huckabee, R. G. 2002. "Raising the Age and Education Requirements for Police Officers: Will Too Many Women and Minority Candidates Be Excluded?" *Policing* 25: 789–801.

Deutsch, A. 1955. *The Trouble with Cops*. New York: Crown.

Feldman, K. A., and Newcomb, T. M. 1969. *The Impact of College on Students*. San Francisco: Jossey-Bass.

Gardiner, C. 2017. "Policing Around the Nation: Education, Philosophy, and Practice. Washington, DC: Police Foundation.

Gau, J. M., and Gaines, D. C. 2012. "Top-Down Management and Patrol Officers' Attitudes About the Importance of Public Order Maintenance: A Research Note." *Police Quarterly* 15: 45–61.

Gau, J. M., Terrill, W., and Paoline, E. A. 2013. "Looking Up: Explaining Police Promotional Aspirations." *Criminal Justice and Behavior* 40: 247–269.

Gavin, P. W. 2015. *The Massachusetts Quinn Bill: A Case Study in the Quest for Quality*. PhD dissertation, Rutgers-State University of New Jersey.

Griffin, G. R., Dunbar, R. L. M., and McGill, M. E. 1978. "Factors Associated with Job Satisfaction among Police Personnel." *Journal of Police Science and Administration* 6: 77–85.

*Griggs v. Duke Power Co.*, 401 US 432 (1971).

Guller, I. B. 1972. "Higher Education and Policemen: Attitudinal Differences between Freshman and Senior Police College Students." *Journal of Criminal Law, Criminology, and Police Science* 63: 396–401.

Hilal, S., Densley, J., and Zhao, R. 2013. "Cops in College: Police Officers' Perceptions on Formal Education." *Journal of Criminal Justice Education* 24(4): 461–477.

Hilal, S. M., and Erickson, T. E. 2009. "College Education as a State-Wide Licensing Requirement: An Analysis of the Minnesota Model 30 Years Later." *Critical Issues in Justice and Politics* 2(2): 1–19.

Hyland, S. H., and Davis, E. 2019. *Local Police Departments, 2016: Personnel*. Washington, DC: Bureau of Justice Statistics.

Johnston, W., and Cheurprakobkit, S. 2002. "Educating Our Police: Perceptions of Police Administrators Regarding the Utility of a College Education, Police Academy Training and Preferences in Courses for Officers." *International Journal of Police Science and Management* 4: 182–197.

Kakar, S. 1998. "Self-Evaluation of Police Performance: An Analysis of the Relationship between Police Officers' Education Level and Job Performance." *Policing: An International Journal of Police Strategies and Management* 21: 632–647.

Korbetz, R. W. 1975. *Law Enforcement and Criminal Justice Education Directory, 1975–1976*. Gaithersburg, MD: International Association of Chiefs of Police.

Krimmel, J. T. 1996. "The Performance of College-Educated Police: A Study of Self-Rated Police Performance Measures." *American Journal of Police* 15: 85–96.

LaGrange, T. C. 2003. "The Role of Police Education in Handling Cases of Mental Disorder." *Criminal Justice Review* 28: 88–113.

Lersch, K. M., and Kunzman, L. L. 2001. "Misconduct Allegations and Higher Education in a Southern Sheriff's Department." *American Journal of Criminal Justice* 25: 161–172.

Levy, R. J. 1967. "Predicting Police Failures." *Journal of Criminal Law, Criminology, and Police Science* 58: 265–276.

McElvain, J. P., and Kposowa, A. J. 2008. "Police Officer Characteristics and the Likelihood of Using Deadly Force." *Criminal Justice and Behavior* 35: 505–525.

Miller, J., and Fry, L. 1976. "Reexamining Assumptions about Education and Professionalism in Law Enforcement." *Journal of Police Science and Administration* 4: 187–196.

Moskos, P. 2003. "Old-School Cops in a New-School World." *Law Enforcement News* October 15/31: 8.

National Advisory Commission on Civil Disorders. 1968. *Report*. Washington, DC: US Government Printing Office.

National Advisory Commission on Criminal Justice Standards and Goals. 1973. *Report on Police*. Washington, DC: US Government Printing Office.

National Research Council. 2004. *Fairness and Effectiveness in Policing: The Evidence*. Washington, DC: National Academies Press.

Niederhoffer, A. 1967. *Behind the Shield: The Police in Urban Society*. Garden City, NY: Doubleday.

Paoline, E. A., and Terrill, W. 2007. "Police Education, Experience, and the Use of Force." *Criminal Justice and Behavior* 34: 179–196.

Paoline, E. A., Terrill, W., and Rossler, M. T. 2015. "Higher Education, College Degree Major, and Occupational Attitudes." *Journal of Criminal Justice Education* 26: 49–73.

Pascarella, E. T., and Terenzini, P. T. 2005. *How College Affects Students (Vol. II): A Third Decade of Research*. San Francisco: Jossey-Bass.

Paterson, C. 2011. "Adding Value? A Review of the International Literature on the Role of Higher Education and Police Training and Education." *Police Practice and Research*. 12: 286-297.

Paynich, R. L. 2009. "The Impact of a College-Educated Police Force: A Review of the Literature." Working paper, Curry College.

Police Executive Research Forum (PERF). 2021. *What Police Chiefs and Sheriffs Need to Know about Collecting and Analyzing Use-of-Force Data*. Police Executive Research Forum, Washington DC.

Polk, E., and Armstrong, D. A. 2001. "Higher Education and Law Enforcement Career Paths: Is the Road to Success Paved by Degree?" *Journal of Criminal Justice Education* 12: 77–99.

Pope, C. E. 1987. "Criminal Justice Education: Academic and Professional Orientations." In R. Muraskin (ed.), *The Future of Criminal Justice Education*. Brookeville, NY: Long Island University.

President's Commission on Law Enforcement and Administration of Justice. 1967. *The Challenge of Crime in a Free Society*. Washington, DC: US Government Printing Office.

President's Task Force on Twenty-First Century Policing. 2015. *Final Report of the President's Task Force on Twenty-First Century Policing*. Washington, DC: Office of Community Oriented Policing Services.

Regoli, R. M. 1976. "The Effects of College Education on the Maintenance of Police Cynicism." *Journal of Police Science and Administration* 4: 340–345.

Roberg, R. R. 1978. "An Analysis of the Relationships among Higher Education, Belief Systems, and Job Performance of Patrol Officers." *Journal of Police Science and Administration* 6: 336–344.

Roberg, R., and Bonn, S. 2004. "Higher Education and Policing: Where Are We Now?" *Policing: An International Journal of Police Strategies & Management* 27: 469–486.

Roberg, R. R., and Laramy, J. E. 1980. "An Empirical Assessment of the Criteria Utilized for Promoting Police Personnel: A Secondary Analysis." *Journal of Police Science and Administration* 8: 183–187.

Rosenfeld, R., Johnson, T. L, and Wright, R. 2018. "Are College-Educated Police Officers Different? A Study of Stops, Searches, and Arrests." *Criminal Justice Policy Review* 31(2): 206–236. doi:10.1177/0887403418817808.

Ryan, C. L., and Bauman, K. 2016. *Educational Attainment in the United States: 2015.* Washington, DC: US Department of Commerce, US Census Bureau.

Rydberg, J., and Terrill, W. 2010. "The Effect of Higher Education on Police Behavior." *Police Quarterly* 13: 92–120.

Saunders, C. B. 1970. *Upgrading the American Police.* Washington, DC: Brookings Institution.

Sherman, L. W., and the National Advisory Commission on Higher Education for Police Officers. 1978. *The Quality of Police Education.* San Francisco: Jossey-Bass.

Smith, A. B., Locke, B., and Fenster, A. 1970. "Authoritarianism in Policemen Who Are College Graduates and Noncollege Graduates." *Journal of Criminal Law, Criminology, and Police Science* 61: 313–315.

Smith, A. B., Locke, B., and Walker, W. F. 1968. "Authoritarianism in Police College Students and Nonpolice College Students." *Journal of Criminal Law, Criminology, and Police Science* 59: 440–443.

Stewart, D. M. 2006. *Collegiate Educational Standards.* Huntsville, TX: Texas Law Enforcement Management and Administrative Statistics Program, May/June.

Stoddard, K. B. 1973. "Characteristics of Policemen of a County Sheriff's Office." In J. R. Snibbe and H. M. Snibbe (eds.), *The Urban Policemen in Transition*, pp. 281–297. Springfield, IL: Thomas.

Telep, C. W. 2011. "The Impact of Higher Education on Police Officer Attitudes Toward Abuse of Authority." *Journal of Criminal Justice Education* 22(3): 392–419.

Terrill, W., and Mastrofski, S. D. 2002. "Situational and Officer-Based Determinants of Police Coercion." *Justice Quarterly* 19(2): 215–248.

Truxillo, D. M., Bennett, S. R., and Collins, M. L. 1998. "College Education and Police Job Performance: A Ten-Year Study." *Public Personnel Management* 27(2): 269–280.

US Census Bureau. 2020. "Educational Attainment in the United States: 2014." https://www.census.gov/data/tables/2020/demo/educational-attainment/cps-detailed-tables.html.

US Department of Justice. 2015. *Office of Justice Programs. Bureau of Justice Statistics. Law Enforcement Management and Administrative Statistics (LEMAS), 2013.* ICPSR36164-v2. Ann Arbor, MI: Interuniversity Consortium for Political and Social Research. doi.org/10.3886/ICPSR36164.v2.

Weiner, N. L. 1976. "The Educated Policeman." *Journal of Police Science and Administration* 4: 450–457.

Weirman, C. L. 1978. "Variances of Ability Measurement Scores Obtained by College and Non-College Educated Troopers." *Police Chief* 45: 34–36.

Whetstone, T. S. 2000. "Getting Stripes: Educational Achievement and Study Strategy Used by Sergeant Promotional Candidates." *American Journal of Criminal Justice* 24: 247–257.

Wilson, H. 1999. "Post-Secondary Education of the Police Officer and Its Effect on the Frequency of Citizen Complaints." *Journal of California Law Enforcement* 33: 3–10.

Worden, R. E. 1990. "A Badge and a Baccalaureate: Policies, Hypotheses, and Further Evidence." *Justice Quarterly* 7: 565–592.

# Emerging Issues

## CHAPTER OUTLINE

# CHAPTER OUTLINE (continued)

## KEY TERMS

- active shooter response
- crime-detection technology
- crime-solving technology
- cybercrime
- de-institutionalization

- domestic terrorism
- federalization
- Global Positioning System
- international terrorism
- militarization

- privatization
- professionalization
- rapid-response technology
- unmanned aerial vehicles

PREDICTING THE FUTURE IS tricky. One might think it would be sufficient to extrapolate current trends in policing, but the importance of often-uncontrollable external influences, such as the COVID-19 pandemic, cannot be overestimated. Unexpected events can undermine even the most reasonable forecasts, reminding us that the future will be predictable in the same way as the past—in retrospect.

Thoughtful observers have noted that police in the United States are in the midst of profound change. Within police departments, shifts in roles, function, technology, and philosophy are important trends. Outside the police system itself, changes in the character of those being policed, along with changes in government, the academic world, the criminal world, and technology, may lead to even more fundamental and far-reaching changes than those seen in the past 25 years. Given the number of issues currently affecting the American police, trying to make sense of its present is already difficult; delineating the future is nearly impossible. Nevertheless, this chapter will try to identify trends in present-day society and policing that indicate potential future directions.

Police departments are *institutionalized organizations*—that is, they are responsible for acting on behalf of the values a society holds dear. Unlike economic organizations (businesses), which prosper through their own technical efficiency, police organizations prosper by successfully supporting and reproducing society's sense of right and wrong. To do this, they must look beyond themselves to the larger society.

What does this mean? Police departments must deal with criminals and provide assistance to victims, witnesses, complainants, and people with vulnerabilities. They also must address the concerns of mayors, city councils, organizations such as Mothers Against Drunk Driving, business groups, and police unions. They must deal with prosecutors and the courts, and they must always be sensitive to changes in the law. They must deal with hostile relations between different ethnic groups. They must contend with rebellious youth and youth gangs. And they always must keep an eye on the media, which can support or embarrass the police with printed, televised, or online news. In short, the police must function in an environment of great complexity.

In addition, the police must respond to technological changes. Consider the ways in which technology has changed the police over the past century. Installing a two-way radio in a police car in the first third of the twentieth century profoundly changed the delivery of police service. The linkage of these two technologies (cars and radios) with the telephone made it possible for citizens to call the police station and for the station to dispatch a police car to respond to the citizen's needs. This style of policing, based on motorized preventive patrol and rapid response, still constitutes the dominant style of policing in many communities. It would have been an unlikely prediction 100 years ago, and Facebook, drones, smartphones, and body-worn cameras would have been even more unimaginable at that time.

## Changes in American Society

Changes in society are likely to influence the future of policing. This section reviews ongoing demographic, economic, and geographic changes in US society that will likely affect policing in the coming decades (see Table 15.1 for a summary of demographic changes that occurred in the United States during the twentieth century).

---

**TABLE 15.1** Demographic Changes in the United States During the Twentieth Century

- The US population more than tripled, from 76 million people in 1900 to 281 million people in 2000. The increase of 32.7 million people in the 1990s represented the largest numerical increase of any decade in US history.

- The US population grew increasingly metropolitan each decade, from 28 percent in 1910 to 80 percent in 2000. Suburbs rather than centralized cities accounted for most of the metropolitan growth. By 2000, half of the US population lived in suburban areas.

- The population of the West grew faster than the population in each of the other three regions of the country in every decade of the twentieth century.

- The Northeast was the most densely populated region and had the highest percentage of its population living in metropolitan areas.

- At the beginning of the century, half of the US population was less than 22.9 years old. At the century's end, half of the population was more than 35.3 years old, the country's highest median age ever.

- Children under age 5 represented the largest five-year age group in 1900 and again in 1950. By 2000, the largest five-year age groups were people ages to 39 and 40 to 44, large segments of the baby-boom generation.

- The United States' gender composition shifted from a majority-male population to a majority-female population around midcentury.

- From 1980 to 2000, the Hispanic population more than doubled.

- By the end of the century, three states (California, Hawaii, and New Mexico) and the District of Columbia had majority "minority populations" (including Hispanics).

- Prior to 1950, more than half of all occupied housing units were rented. By 1950, home ownership became more prevalent than renting.

- In 1900, the most common household contained seven or more people; from 1940 to 2000, it contained two people.

- In 1900, nearly half of the US population lived in households of six or more people; by 2000, more than half lived in households of one, two, or three people.

- Between 1950 and 2000, married-couple households declined from more than three-fourths of all households (78%) to just more than one-half (52%).

*Source*: US Census Bureau, *Demographic Trends in the 20th Century* (Washington, DC: US Government Printing Office, 2002), Special Reports, Series CENSR-4.

## Demographic Trends

The United States has a growing and aging population. As of mid-2021, the population was almost 332 million (US Census Bureau 2022). The country saw a significant increase in the average life span, from less than 50 years in 1900 to almost 79 years as of 2017 (Centers for Disease Control and Prevention [CDC] 2016), but it has dropped to 77 years since then, mainly due to suicides, drug overdoses, and the pandemic (Solly 2018; CDC 2021b, 2021c). In 1900, those age 65 years or older—considered elderly—constituted 4 percent of the population (Administration on Aging 2021); today, this group accounts for 16.5 percent of the population (US Census Bureau 2022). The 65-or-order group numbered less than 5 million in 1900 but will grow to almost 100 million in 2060 (Colby and Ortman 2015).

The elderly pose specific dilemmas for criminal justice. First, among those over 85 years old, 56 percent of men, but only 19 percent of women, are still married (Kreider and Simmons 2003). On average, women live five years longer than men (CDC 2021c). Men generally die younger, leaving many widows. This longevity does not mean that the quality of life for surviving women is high. On the contrary, both women and elders comprise one of the populations that is most vulnerable to victimization (see Inside Policing 15.1). Also, one in five individuals older than 85 lives in a nursing home or similar facility. As this institutionalized population dramatically increases over the coming decades, there are likely to be sharp increases in white-collar crime in the health-care industry against the elderly.

Second, the elderly, usually dependent on fixed budgets, tend to mobilize to vote against tax increases to support social infrastructure. They particularly tend to oppose property tax increases needed to support school budgets. The growing elderly population will likely strain the Social Security system and Medicaid, as well as the resources of their adult-age children. The grandchildren of these elderly, then, may encounter poorer schools and recreational opportunities, as well as overburdened parents.

The most crime-prone population is widely regarded by criminologists to be people between the ages of 18 and 24. Judging by population forecasts, this population will not increase at high rates for many years. The number of Americans in the 18- to 24-year age group is not expected to exceed the 1980 level until at least 2030 (Roberts 1994).

---

### INSIDE POLICING 15.1 | Elder Fraud

US authorities announced a year-long, "largest-ever," elder fraud crackdown, resulting in criminal and civil charges against 260 defendants for defrauding more than 2 million victims out of $750 million, as reported here. The total annual loss to elderly Americans is estimated at $3 billion. The investigation was aided by Europol and police in several individual countries, with "alleged fraudsters charged criminally and extradited from Canada, the Cayman Islands, Costa Rica, Jamaica and Poland." An additional 600 US-based "money mules" who helped transfer funds were identified, most receiving warning letters rather than charges because they didn't realize they were facilitating scams.

**Discussion Question:** With the number of senior citizens multiplying, scams like these are bound to increase. Realistically, federal law enforcement can only investigate the biggest and most organized ones. What can state and local police do to reduce the harm caused by these scams to such a vulnerable population?

SOURCE: *Modern Policing* blog, March 8, 2019, https://gcordner.wordpress.com/2019/03/08/elder-fraud/.

Another consequence of this imbalance between older and younger Americans may be police recruiting challenges, since police departments traditionally focus on 21- to 25-year-olds when looking for new employees.

In 2019, so-called millennials (those born between 1981 and 1997) surpassed baby-boomers (those born between 1946 and 1964) as the most populous generation in the United States (Fry 2020). Although characteristics of generational groups are sometimes exaggerated, it can be noted that millennials, compared with the three previous generations at the same age, are less likely to be married, less likely to be military veterans, more likely to be college graduates, and more likely to be living in a metropolitan area (Fry, Igielnik, and Patten 2018). In addition, millennials have fewer attachments to traditional political and religious institutions than previous generations, are less trusting of other people, and have more financial burdens, including debt and unemployment (Drake 2014). Although some of these conditions sound troublesome, the overall picture is positive. According to Howe (2010),

> it's useful remembering that when Boomers were coming of age, we had 17 uninterrupted years of declining SAT scores, rising drug use, rising teen pregnancy, rising suicide, rising rates of self-inflicted accidents, rising crime—of that crime, the share that was violent was rising. Millennials have been moving most of these indicators in the opposite direction. And that's truly remarkable . . . when they came along was precisely a time at which childhood was revalued again in America. This was a period—the early 80s—when suddenly things began improving for children. Alcohol consumption per capita among all Americans has been gradually declining since about 1981. Drug use has been gradually declining. The abortion rate, the divorce rate have all been gradually declining.

In addition to having a growing and aging population, the United States continues to become more ethnically and racially diverse. Estimates in 2021 identified Americans as 60 percent white (non-Hispanic), 18 percent Hispanic or Latino, 13 percent Black or African American, and 6 percent Asian (US Census Bureau 2022). The long-term projection is that by about 2044, no racial or ethnic group will constitute a majority in the United States (Colby and Ortman 2015); in other words, the white (non-Hispanic) category will drop below 50 percent.

Religious differences are another aspect of cultural diversity. Religion has the capacity to become the basis of cultural friction across the United States, as discovered in the aftermath of September 11, 2001, when some Americans turned their anger toward followers of Islam, as well as toward people of Middle Eastern descent. Some of this friction has lingered since 9/11 and has been rekindled with the spread of ISIS-inspired violence around the world. In this situation, police increasingly have the responsibility of managing conflicts among religious groups, seeking to find common ground among them, and facilitating their coexistence.

Joining race, ethnicity, and religion as significant bases of cultural diversity are gender identity and sexual orientation. About 7 percent of the US population identifies as lesbian, gay, bisexual, or transgender (Jones 2022), but in surveys, the public tends to dramatically overestimate the proportion. This misperception probably reflects a degree of moral hysteria, especially among older Americans, yet it is important to recognize that public approval of same-sex relations has increased substantially in recent years, from 35 percent in 2001 to 61 percent in 2019 (Pew Research Center 2019).

The importance of diversity within police departments was discussed thoroughly in Chapter 12. A main reason for a diverse police organization is to reinforce and demonstrate the American value of equal opportunity, but another reason is to improve the quality of policing within a diverse community. Because of the nature of the police function, including authority and discretion, a major challenge is to avoid discriminating against people and groups because their origin, skin color, beliefs, or orientations differ from those of the majority of society. Moreover, police must go beyond simply not discriminating—they are required, and expected, to provide equal protection under the law. Because minority groups of all kinds can be unpopular, they often need protection. Police have a special duty to protect those who are vulnerable or marginalized, and doing so helps demonstrate fairness and rule of law to the rest of society. When police embrace diversity, avoid discrimination, and provide equal protection, they can play a leadership role in building a society in which people are judged not by their color or any other group characteristic, but solely on the content of their character.

## Immigration and Migration

Immigration has become a tremendously controversial political issue in recent years, particularly in regard to the porous US-Mexican border and the large number of illegal and undocumented immigrants who cross that border in search of work, asylum, or just a better life for their family. In difficult economic times, it is not unusual for public opinion to turn against immigrants, especially illegal immigrants, since they compete with US citizens for scarce jobs. People commonly believe that immigrants cause crime to increase, although the evidence indicates the opposite (Wadsworth 2010).

Immigration is not a new phenomenon in American society. As a nation, the United States was established by immigrants and has long been known as a beacon and destination for people from around the world looking for freedom and economic opportunity. Native Americans represent only about 2 percent of the entire population (Colby and Ortman 2015), so the remaining 98 percent of Americans are immigrants or the descendants of immigrants.

Traditionally, the federal government has shouldered the responsibility for enforcing immigration laws. Over the past decade or two, however, pressure has grown to use local police to enhance immigration enforcement. Initially, this was most often in response to local concerns about immigration, but at times, the federal government has applied pressure to get state and local authorities to assist (Egelko 2018). Frequently, local police have argued against this trend, mainly because it creates a significant barrier between the police and the immigrant community, making it less likely that crime victims and witnesses will freely cooperate with police (Dickey 2010). Local police usually prefer to focus directly on crime and disorder, leaving the enforcement of federal immigration laws to the federal government.

Migration *within* the United States has had at least as much impact on communities as immigration from outside the country. In the nineteenth and twentieth centuries, the main migration patterns were westward, as the American frontier expanded to California (from 1900 to 2000, the West region grew from 5 percent of the nation's population to 23 percent) and then northward, as rural residents moved to cities in search of better-paying industrial jobs. Those patterns were followed by movement to suburbs that sprang up within commuting distance of cities, and then by substantial population shifting from the "Rust Belt" to the "Sun Belt" when older industrial cities started losing jobs and people sought better employment opportunities (and sometimes better weather) in the South and Southwest. From 1900 to 2000, Florida went from thirty-third in population to fourth, and California went from twenty-first to first (Hobbs and Stoops 2002).

Future migration patterns may become more mixed. Modern technology enables many workers to telecommute from home or other remote sites, which may encourage more people to move to exurbs (beyond original suburbs) or even rural areas. Of course, this trend increased even more during the COVID-19 pandemic. However, there is also renewed interest in urban living and walkable neighborhoods, especially among young professionals. How these shifting patterns will affect crime and policing is hard to predict at the national level but necessary to monitor at the local level, since significant increases or decreases in the resident population and tax base generally impact police workload and police budgets.

### Shifting Economics

Economic conditions affect crime, disorder, and the demand for police services. Economics change over time, and it is risky to predict them—as stock market investors know well. The US economy was slow to recover from the 2008 meltdown in the financial system (the Great Recession) but was back to "normal" when the COVID-19 pandemic struck in early 2020. Then, suddenly, many businesses were forced to cut back or close, and unemployment soared. As of early 2022, employment was almost back to its 2020 level, with some increase in average wages, but supply chain disruptions and international conflicts have contributed to inflation and other economic concerns.

One long-term trend in the nature of employment has been from hunting and gathering to farming to manufacturing jobs to service jobs to today's information-based economy. In 2021, approximately 78 percent of American workers were in management, professional, service, sales, or related jobs, whereas only about 22 percent were in construction, transportation, manufacturing, farming, and related jobs (Bureau of Labor Statistics [BLS] 2022b). Employment today is more likely to be white collar, indoors, and in an office (or teleworking from home) than in the past.

As textile workers, steel workers, and others have learned the hard way, employment markets are much more global today. The promotion of free trade over the past two to three decades has created more opportunities for companies to move part—or all—of their operations to countries with lower labor costs, weaker environmental protections, and less concern for workplace safety. Until recently, this trend has mostly affected blue-collar employment and has helped account for the decline in manufacturing jobs in the United States, a factor that has caused the federal government to impose or threaten trade tariffs. The same long-term forces have begun to affect white-collar and creative employment as well (Florida 2004). If these types of jobs, the very ones expected to take up the slack from declining manufacturing, also go offshore, the United States may face serious unemployment challenges in the future.

Another substantial economic change has occurred in the participation of women in employment. In 2020, 56 percent of women aged 16 years and older were in the labor force, which was up from 33 percent in 1948, although down from the peak of 60 percent in 1999 (BLS 2022c). This shift has changed the characteristics of the workforce that the police encounter and helped empower women economically, but it has also affected whether parents are present or absent from the home with their children after school and at other times.

The *unemployment rate*, which is measured as the percentage of adults seeking work who are not successful in gaining employment, is one of the most important measures of economic well-being. Since 1948, the monthly unemployment rate in the United States has varied between 2.5 percent (in May and June 1953) and 14.7 percent (in April 2020). During good economic times, the US unemployment rate has generally ranged between

4 and 6 percent, which is considered a low rate of unemployment, since some degree of joblessness is inevitable in a dynamic economy. After spiking in the early stages of the COVID-19 pandemic, the unemployment rate has dropped substantially, reaching 3.6 percent as of March 2022 (BLS 2022a).

The official unemployment rate can be deceiving, however. Marginally attached workers (those who are not working and not actively looking for a job, but say they want one and have had one within the past year) are not included, nor are workers who had only part-time employment yet wanted full-time jobs. Including those workers roughly doubles the official unemployment rate.

Another important economic measure is the *poverty rate*. This statistic is even less precise than the unemployment rate, since defining an income level that puts one in or above poverty is subjective. Nevertheless, it is a closely watched economic indicator. In 2020, 11.4 percent of individuals fell below the poverty line (US Census Bureau 2021). Looking historically, the poverty rate fell from 22.4 percent to 15 percent between 1959 and 1966, and has varied since then between 10 and 15 percent (US Census Bureau 2018).

Yet another key economic measure is *income inequality,* which indicates how much range exists between low-income and high-income individuals or families. In the United States, income inequality decreased from 1947 to 1968, but it has been increasing ever since (Weinberg 1996; Lowry 2012). In other words, since 1968 the rich have been getting richer.

How much of a problem this represents is a matter of opinion. Democrats and liberals, on the one hand, tend to see income inequality as a serious social and economic problem and generally push for income redistribution remedies, such as progressive income, estate, and inheritance taxes as well as higher unemployment and welfare payments. Republicans and conservatives, on the other hand, do not necessarily regard income inequality as a problem, seeing it instead as a natural consequence of capitalism (market forces) and differences in peoples' abilities and willingness to work hard. Both sides tend to agree, however, that a strong middle class is good for the country. Unfortunately, the percentage of adults living in middle-class households has steadily declined since 1971, and the average income and wealth of middle-class families has grown more slowly than for upper-income families (Pew Research Center 2015).

In sum, the US economy has thrived for several decades, despite some ups and downs, and Americans are better off economically than most other people in the world. However, some trends in income inequality, full-time unemployment, and the poverty rate are worrisome. Also, globalization, the changing nature of jobs, and the much greater participation of women in the workforce all have ripple effects for social relations, families, and other aspects of modern society. Collectively, these changes are likely to affect the nature of crime, disorder, and the demand for police services in the future, albeit in unpredictable ways.

## Climate Change

It is difficult to imagine anything more likely to cause fundamental changes in our society than global warming. According to the Intergovernmental Panel on Climate Change (Intergovernmental Panel on Climate Change 2021), "Many of the changes observed in the climate are unprecedented in thousands, if not hundreds of thousands of years, and some of the changes already set in motion—such as continued sea level rise—are irreversible over hundreds to thousands of years." While public opinion about climate change is not unanimous, 72 percent of Americans believe global warming is happening, 64 percent believe it is affecting the weather, and 57 percent believe it is caused mostly by human activities (Marlon et al. 2022).

Climate change is likely to impact policing in two major ways. One has to do with disasters. Because weather-related events such as hurricanes, tornados, wildfires, floods, droughts, and severe heat waves are becoming more common and more destructive, police responsibilities associated with disaster management and recovery will become more demanding. This includes such tasks as evacuation, search and rescue, and curfew enforcement. Carrying out these duties will entail close cooperation with other public safety and emergency management agencies, as well as with nongovernmental groups like the American Red Cross. A personally challenging feature of disaster policing is that officers typically have to work long hours in dangerous conditions, while at the same time worrying about the safety of their own families. With more disasters, those kinds of stressful situations will increase.

Another type of impact will follow from whatever ways climate change affects social and economic conditions. For example, the need to reduce greenhouse gas emissions might lead to more people teleworking. That might result in less traffic congestion and fewer people in center cities during the day, which could affect how police resources are allocated. Rising sea levels might lead to significant population shifts from coastal to inland areas, while rising temperatures could reverse the decades-long population migration from the North and the Rust Belt toward the Sun Belt. Some places might need more police, others less. Increases in the cost of gasoline, electricity, and water could make those commodities more attractive as crime targets, while extreme shortages could lead to civil unrest. These specific possibilities are not certain, but what does seem certain is that the changing environment will have consequences for the ways people live and work, which in turn will have consequences for policing.

## Modern Problems

In addition to the kinds of social, demographic, and environmental changes already described, the specific problems facing the police will likely change over time. These problems are difficult to forecast, so this section discusses four issues that are identifiable today and are not likely to soon disappear—crime and drugs, mass shootings, mental health, and police legitimacy. See Inside Policing 15.2 for an engaging discussion of many of these issues.

---

**INSIDE POLICING 15.2**   **Issues and Challenges Facing Policing**

In this *Reducing Crime* podcast, Jerry Ratcliffe interviews Chuck Ramsey, who came up through the ranks to Deputy Superintendent in Chicago, then served as Police Chief in Washington, DC, and Police Commissioner in Philadelphia. He was also a member of President Obama's Task Force on Twenty-First Century Policing. They discuss a wide range of issues facing policing today, with the benefit of Chief Ramsey's long career and varied experience.

**Discussion Question:** Chief Ramsey had a distinguished career in three big cities: Chicago, Washington, DC, and Philadelphia. In what ways were the challenges in those cities similar or different?

*SOURCE: Reducing Crime* podcast, November 29, 2021, https://soundcloud.com/reducingcrime/41-charles-ramsey.

## Crime Trends

An ongoing challenge for police is reacting and adapting to changing trends and patterns in crime. In some ways, crime does not change much. People steal because they want something but cannot obtain it legally; people become intoxicated or angry and do harm to others—the basic forms of crime and the motivations behind them are timeless. But the details do change. Horse stealing is less common than it used to be, and few eight-track tape players have been stolen lately, whereas far more smartphone thefts occur today than 15 or 20 years ago and ghost guns are a brand-new phenomenon.

An important consideration for police is the amount of crime. Nationally, taking a long-term view, serious crime peaked in the early 1990s and is much lower now. Violent crime victimization fell 74 percent between 1993 and 2019, and property crime fell 71 percent (Gramlich 2020). The trend has become troubling more recently, however. The murder rate increased 30 percent from 2019 to 2020 (Gramlich 2021) and did not come back down in 2021. Of course, crime rates and crime trends vary across jurisdictions. For example, overall, major cities saw a 5 percent increase in homicide in 2021 (Rosenfeld and Lopez 2022), but Boston, Seattle, and San Jose all saw greater than 20 percent decreases (Robertson and Turcotte 2022).

One particularly serious problem that also seems to be increasing in many cities is shootings, a type of crime that has not been consistently measured in the past. In traditional crime reporting, people shot and killed have been counted as murders, with people shot and wounded normally counted as aggravated assaults (if the police were notified). But the number of people who are simply *shot or shot at* may not be included in the Uniform Crime Report, especially if gang members, drug dealers, or others shoot at each other and do not wait for the police to arrive. In some cities today, chiefs believe that the number of shootings has increased significantly, reflecting easy gun availability and brazen criminal behavior.

As mentioned, trends in the nature and types of crime, both national and local, are significant for police. For example, old-fashioned bank robberies occur much less frequently these days (Ross 2014)—to be sure, people still steal money from banks, but now they do it electronically (Lobosco 2013). Similarly, auto thefts had been decreasing substantially for 25 years, due in large part to improved security measures built into vehicles (National Insurance Crime Bureau 2014). But there was a 30 percent increase in car thefts between 2017 and 2021, including a big jump in carjacking in some cities. From 2019 to 2021, the carjacking increase was 286 percent in New York, 238 percent in Philadelphia, and 207 percent in Chicago (Festa 2022).

**Cybercrime** (computer crime) did not exist a few decades ago but is now one of the most common types of property crime, often used to commit theft (including identity theft), fraud, extortion, and malicious tampering. Three categories of cybercrime involve (1) the computer as a target, (2) the computer as a tool for the commission of a crime, and (3) the computer as incidental to the crime itself or, simply put, as evidence. Crimes in which the computer is the target involve individuals breaking into or attacking a victim's system and may include activities such as hacking, cracking, sabotage, or so-called denial of service (overwhelming a website, server, or network; see Inside Policing 15.3). Crimes in which the computer is used as a tool are typically traditional crimes, such as fraud, theft, forgery, embezzlement, and even stalking committed in new ways. Crimes in which the computer is incidental to the criminal activity could include using a computer to keep financial records of illegal business activities or having incriminating pictures on social media or one's smartphone (Brenner 2001).

**INSIDE POLICING 15.3**    **The NotPetya Cyberattack**

This article provides details about the 2017 NotPetya cyberattack estimated to have cost $10 billion. Originating as a Russian military hack of a Ukrainian accounting firm, it quickly spread around the world, immobilizing numerous corporations. Maersk, a global shipping company operating 800 vessels out of 76 ports, was likely the single hardest hit victim. All of its computers were down for days, interrupting thousands of "just-in-time" deliveries that wreaked further havoc on suppliers and customers—but for the hard drive in a computer server in Ghana that happened to be off-line due to a power outage, losses would have been even greater.

  **Discussion Question:** Experts always report that the most effective step in cybersecurity is for individual computer system users to be more careful—don't click on unknown links and don't use obvious passwords. How careful are you? What is the police role in cybersecurity and cybercrime investigation?

SOURCE: *Modern Policing* blog, August 27, 2018, https://worldpolicing.wordpress.com/2018/08/27/the-notpetya-cyberattack/.

The FBI's Internet Crime Complaint Center received almost 800,000 reports of phishing, identity theft, and other cybercrimes in 2020, resulting in $4.2 billion in losses (FBI 2020). These numbers undoubtedly represent just the tip of the iceberg. Looking ahead, Internet- and computer-related crime is likely to become an ever-bigger portion of all crime and therefore a growing priority for both prevention and investigation by police.

## Drugs

Drug abuse is a particularly frustrating crime and social problem thrust into the lap of the police. It is far beyond the scope of this chapter to delve into all the debates around drugs, liquor, prohibition, the "War on Drugs," de-criminalization, legalization, informants, undercover work, or the causal relationships among drugs, gangs, guns, and crime. The reality is that even in those states that have relaxed or eliminated their laws pertaining to marijuana possession, numerous substances remain illegal; thus, drug-related investigation, enforcement, and problem solving are still part of the police mission.

Prior to COVID-19, the good news about substance abuse was that the use of tobacco and underage consumption of alcohol had declined steadily from 2002 to 2017 (Substance Abuse and Mental Health Services Administration 2018). However, use of marijuana had increased about 50 percent, use of cocaine had been increasing since 2011, and there had been a resurgence in availability of heroin, together with a variety of other opioids and related synthetic substances. The number of heroin overdose deaths increased sevenfold between 1999 and 2016, while those caused by synthetic opioids such as fentanyl increased 20-fold over that period (CDC 2018). These numbers have continued to climb during the pandemic; there were almost 92,000 drug overdose deaths in 2020, a 31 percent increase from the year before (CDC 2021a)—with an equally large increase projected for 2021 (McPhillips 2022).

Two police-related responses to the current drug abuse crisis are noteworthy. First, many police departments have adopted a harm-reduction, public health approach to drug possession and consumption. Patrol officers often carry Narcan (naloxone) nasal spray, a quick-acting, life-saving antidote to opioid overdose with few, if any, side effects. Thousands of overdose victims have been saved as a result. The police chief in Gloucester, Massachusetts, attracted national attention when he announced (via Facebook) that "addicts who seek help from police will not face charges for possession of drugs or paraphernalia" but rather would be connected with treatment and recovery programs, "not in hours or days, but on the spot" (Kardish 2015). Seattle, Philadelphia, and other cities have proposed establishing "safe use" sites where hard drug users could inject and smoke under medical supervision.

A second drug-related challenge of growing concern is driving under the influence of drugs, especially marijuana, since it relates to traffic crashes, injuries, and fatalities. User-friendly technology similar to the breathalyzer and preliminary breath test device, which detect and measure alcohol, has not yet been perfected for marijuana or other drugs. There are also debates about how significantly marijuana affects driving ability—that is, even if it can be detected in a driver's breath or blood, does it demonstrate driving impairment? These questions have existed for decades, but they have assumed new importance now that 37 states have legalized medical marijuana (National Conference of State Legislatures 2022), 18 states have made marijuana possession fully legal, and in only 6 states is it fully illegal (DISA 2022).

## Mass Shootings

The number of people killed in mass shootings (defined as four or more fatalities) accounts for only about 1 percent of all murders each year, but for understandable reasons, these gruesome and tragic events have a significant impact on the public and get considerable media attention. Records show that mass killings are not a new phenomenon. There were 271 mass shootings in the United States between 2009 and 2021, resulting in 1,518 shooting deaths and another 980 people wounded by gunfire (Everytown 2022). Mass shootings with 10 or more deaths since 2012 are listed in Table 15.2.

One important point about mass shootings is that most are not related to terrorism. Hate crime, mental health issues, bullying, and disgruntled employees account for the vast majority of high-casualty mass murders (Lemieux 2018). It should also be noted that if *mass murder* is defined as involving as few as two or three victims, then intrafamily, domestic-related cases, including murder-suicides involving spouses/couples, are actually the most frequent, and the most common location is in the home.

Mass shooting incidents are obviously very challenging for police. Tactically, police have been trained in the **active shooter response** since the Columbine school shooting in 1999. Instead of waiting for a Special Weapons and Tactics (SWAT) unit, negotiator, or reinforcements, the first arriving officers are now expected to engage the shooter as soon as possible. As evidenced by the school shootings in Parkland, Florida in 2018 and in Uvalde, Texas in 2022, however, it takes courage and commitment to immediately run toward danger, even for police, and sometimes they fail to follow their training, with tragic consequences.

In active shooter situations, finding the assailant in the midst of a large building with hundreds of fleeing or hiding victims and potential victims can be extremely difficult, plus there is the need to provide first aid to those who have been shot. Coordination of officers searching for the suspect can be a further challenge, especially if officers respond from different police departments. Then, once the shooter is captured, killed, or has fled, tending to mass casualties and a dispersed crime scene can be a huge, stressful, and time-consuming undertaking, likely to overwhelm all but the largest law enforcement agencies. In addition,

**TABLE 15.2** Recent High-Casualty Mass Shootings in the United States

| WHEN | WHERE | DEATHS | SITUATION |
|------|-------|--------|-----------|
| October 2017 | Las Vegas, NV | 59 | Music festival |
| June 2016 | Orlando, FL | 50 | Nightclub |
| December 2012 | Sandy Hook, CT | 28 | School |
| November 2017 | Sutherland Springs, TX | 27 | Church |
| August 2019 | El Paso, TX | 23 | Retail Store |
| May 2022 | Uvalde, TX | 21 | School |
| February 2018 | Parkland, FL | 17 | School |
| December 2015 | San Bernardino, CA | 16 | Workplace |
| May 2019 | Virginia Beach, VA | 13 | Workplace |
| November 2018 | Thousand Oaks, CA | 13 | Nightclub |
| September 2013 | Washington, DC | 13 | Workplace |
| October 2018 | Pittsburgh, PA | 11 | Synagogue |
| May 2022 | Buffalo, NY | 10 | Grocery Store |
| May 2021 | San Jose, CA | 10 | Workplace |
| March 2021 | Boulder, CO | 10 | Retail Store |
| August 2019 | Dayton, OH | 10 | Bar |
| May 2018 | Santa Fe, TX | 10 | School |
| October 2015 | Roseburg, OR | 10 | College |

*Source*: Information derived from https://www.gunviolencearchive.org/reports/mass-shooting.

parents, family members, and friends of people who may have been victims in the incident are likely to respond to the area and will have to be contained, kept informed, and offered as much support as possible.

In the aftermath of this kind of event, officers who were involved will also need support. Regardless of how well it was handled, officers will have experienced fear, seen innocent suffering, and may blame themselves for not having saved more lives. Police agencies today are generally conscious of the need to provide appropriate support for their staff following traumatic incidents of all kinds, including cases involving mass casualties.

## Mental Health

In the United States, 21 percent of adults suffer from a mental illness affecting mood, anxiety, eating, impulse control, substance use, adjustment disorders, and psychotic symptoms, and 5.6 percent have *serious* mental illness defined as "functional impairment, which substantially interferes with or limits one or more major life activities" (National Institute of Mental Health 2022). The prevalence rates for adolescents (ages 13 to 18) are even higher, estimated at nearly 50 percent for any mental disorder and 22 percent for serious mental illness.

The reason that this medical issue has become a significant police problem is referred to as **de-institutionalization**. Starting 50 years ago, the practice of committing people with serious psychiatric illness to mental hospitals ("locking them away") was deemed unfair and inhumane, and the use of such hospitals was significantly reduced (Cordner 2006).

Community-based and outpatient services were supposed to be increased at the same time, but the response has been inadequate and woefully underfunded. Consequently, more people with serious mental health issues are "on the street" or in substandard housing arrangements, and when they experience a crisis, the police are usually called. Although police are not psychiatrists or psychologists, they end up being responsible for dealing with the problem.

Police often handle cases involving people with mental illness in creative and sensitive ways, but two outcomes are both common and problematic. In one outcome, people in mental health crises are arrested and taken to jail. This option is not desirable unless the person has committed a serious crime, which is not typical. Most often, the crime is minor or the individual is a public nuisance, but if no other options exist, arrest and jail may seem to be the only choice. Police generally prefer to pass the person on to a treatment provider, but the "safety net" in many communities is not sufficient to meet the need.

The other problematic outcome involves police use of deadly force. People in mental health crisis often fail to follow police commands and sometimes feel so threatened that they brandish a weapon or physically resist police efforts to control them. Police officers may then interpret the behavior as threatening, leading to an escalation of the conflict. As a result, the police have shot and killed many people over the years who were armed with knives or bats and refused to drop their weapons, but were later determined to have been suffering such a serious mental health crisis that they likely misinterpreted what was going on. Sadly, the catalyst for these tragic endings is often a phone call from a family member trying to get help for a relative.

Major efforts have been implemented to improve police response to people with mental illness. The most common is the crisis intervention team (CIT) approach, which involves giving a subset of patrol officers additional training and facilitating closer collaboration with hospitals, treatment centers, and mental health professionals (CIT International 2022). Under this model, specially trained officers are dispatched to crisis situations, take over once they arrive, emphasize de-escalation and conflict management techniques, and try to deliver the person to a medical facility or treatment provider, rather than jail, whenever possible. In addition, mental health service providers become familiar with these officers and are more likely to accept their observations and suggestions as valid and credible.

The same issues and concerns apply to police handling of people with intellectual and developmental disabilities, those who are homeless, and others who have vulnerabilities (Bartkowiak-Theron et al. 2022). Police may encounter these people as crime victims or suspects, or simply as persons behaving suspiciously or oddly. Often, someone will have called the police to report behavior they regard as disorderly or simply inappropriate. If police end up using force or making an arrest, or just requiring the person to "move along," it becomes another example of exercising police authority and the criminal justice system to deal with what is better understood as a medical or social issue.

Over the last few years, more and more jurisdictions have begun to experiment with behavioral health responses that either pair police with clinicians or avoid police response altogether. One non-police response alternative has been in operation in Eugene, Oregon, since 1989 and now handles nearly 20,000 calls a year (Eugene Police Department 2022). As other jurisdictions implement similar models, it will be important to learn what proportion of behavioral health calls and incidents can safely be handled without police presence, and how well emergency call-takers and dispatchers can tell, in advance, whether police will be needed or not (Graham 2022). Ideally, a continuum of response options will

| INSIDE POLICING 15.4 | Non-Police and Co-Response Models |
|---|---|

Interest in non-police and co-response models to calls involving behavioral health and behavioral crisis continues to be strong. Eugene, Oregon, and Denver, Colorado, are among cities that have adopted non-police response options. Dallas, Texas, is one example of a city that employs co-responders (police, clinician, and paramedic). Here's a nice 7-minute video highlighting some of the options currently being used in several jurisdictions.

**Discussion Question:** Everyone agrees that many situations involving behavioral health and other vulnerabilities like homelessness shouldn't require police involvement. Historically, however, taxpayers haven't been willing to fund social services at the level that would be needed to turn these problems over to professional clinicians. What will it take to fund and implement a more well-rounded response to these kinds of issues?

SOURCE: *Modern Policing* blog, October 10, 2020, gcordner.wordpress.com/2020/10/10/non-police-and-co-response-models/.

be available that includes non-police response, co-responders (police teamed with clinicians), and police only (see Inside Policing 15.4). A big question yet to be answered is whether taxpayers and political leaders will make the financial commitments necessary to implement a full range of responses to behavioral health problems and crises.

### Police Legitimacy

Police legitimacy matters. In a democratic and free society, police operate with the consent of the people. If people do not have trust and confidence in their police, they withdraw that consent, which leads to less cooperation, less support, and more resistance. Peoples' willingness to assist police and serve as witnesses decreases. Police recruiting and retention can suffer. Defunding the police can sound like a good idea, but policing becomes more difficult and less effective when legitimacy is disputed or denied.

Since 2015, it has been very common for observers, activists, academics, politicians, and the police themselves to refer to the "legitimacy crisis" in policing. Thanks to more thorough data collection, one factor has been the recognition that about 1,000 people die in police custody every year. Another factor has been racial disproportionality in police stops, searches, and use of force, which can result in more people of color coming into contact with "downstream" components of the criminal justice system, like courts and corrections. High-profile incidents, especially the murder of George Floyd in 2020, have added to the sense of crisis. The fact that so many police actions are now captured on cell phone video and police body-worn cameras, to be viewed live or later on social media, further contributes to public awareness of the good, the bad, and the ugly of police work.

Many of the aspects of policing that influence legitimacy, positively or negatively, have been discussed throughout this text, including community policing, police discretion, procedural justice, use of force, police misconduct, transparency, accountability, and diversity. Here, in this final chapter, we want to focus on three related issues.

First, one can question whether there is a police legitimacy crisis. According to Gallup polls that track public opinion toward 14 major institutions, 52 percent of Americans had a lot of confidence in police in 1993; the figure was nearly identical in 2021, at 51 percent

(Brenan 2021). In the years between, confidence reached 64 percent after 9/11 (2011), but later dropped to 48 percent after George Floyd in 2020. So confidence has gone up and down, yet as of 2021, it was back where it started. Interestingly, from 2020 to 2021, only one American institution showed an increase in public confidence—police. Also of note, police ranked third highest among the 14 institutions, below only small business and the military. Confidence in police was more than twice as high as confidence in Congress, television news, big business, the criminal justice system, and newspapers.

Second, there is a big racial gap in police legitimacy. In the same 2021 Gallup polling noted earlier, only 27 percent of Black adults reported having a lot of confidence in police, compared to 49 percent of Hispanic adults and 56 percent of white adults (Jones 2021). The gap between the confidence levels of Black and white respondents was consistently in the 25 percent range from 1993 to 2015, but then grew to 37 percent in 2020 before narrowing somewhat in 2021. Looking at all 14 institutions included in the polling, the gap in confidence between Black and white adults in 2021 was greater for police than for any of the other institutions. This provides rather stark evidence that police do have a legitimacy crisis in the eyes of Black Americans, albeit not a new one.

Third, there has been a tendency to regard procedural justice as the key to police legitimacy. In a nutshell, if police treat people fairly, legitimacy increases. This widely accepted perspective has two main limitations: (1) the presumed connection may not operate as expected, and (2) legitimacy may depend on more than just fairness. On the first point, a recent randomized experiment in three cities showed that officers could successfully implement procedural justice, and residents did perceive getting better treatment, but measures of legitimacy were unaffected (Weisburd et al. 2022). On the second point, recall the discussion in Chapter 1 about the multiple dimensions of police performance. People assess the police on several criteria, not just fairness. Studies have shown that peoples' trust and confidence in police is also affected by whether they are corrupt, provide good service, prevent serious crime, solve crimes, and so on (Tankebe 2013).

The bottom line is that policing in a free society is a complicated business. To achieve and retain legitimacy in the eyes of the public, police need to be seen as both effective and fair by a multiplicity of diverse groups that, historically, have had widely different experiences with the police and that, today, may have differing needs and interests. The recent polarization in American society has not made this any easier to accomplish. However, it is also true that almost everyone wants to live in a community that is safe for them and their families. Today, most people continue to see the police as critical guardians of their safety (Parker and Hurst 2021), which helps explain why overall trust in the police remains relatively high.

## Modern Technology

Technology has clearly changed policing in the past. Patrol cars, two-way radios, 911 telephone systems, and in-car computers have changed the way police do their work and interact with the public. Similarly, automobiles, televisions, air conditioning, computers, the Internet, and a host of other technologies have changed American society, patterns of social behavior, and consequently, the police–community relationship. As technological change accelerates in the twenty-first century, changes in society and policing are likely to occur even faster.

New technologies are not always as beneficial as expected, however, and may have unanticipated consequences. Putting police in cars, for example, improved their response time to calls from the public and allowed them to patrol wider areas, but it also made patrolling less personal and less interactive. More recently, license-plate readers have typically been deployed for the stated purpose of locating cars either stolen or associated with people on terrorism watch lists, but they are most likely to identify vehicles with expired registration. One study concluded "the evidence that is available on technology and police performance suggests that technology's impacts may be limited or offset by many factors ranging from technical problems to officer resistance" (Koper et al. 2015, 3). In "Voices from the Field," Chief Richard Myers reminds us that although technology is important in policing, ultimately the effectiveness of police organizations is most dependent on leadership and the talents of the people attracted to the policing mission.

## VOICES FROM THE FIELD

### Richard W. Myers

*Chief of Police (ret.), Newport News, Virginia Police Department; Executive Director, Major Cities Chiefs Association (ret.)*

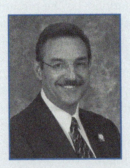

While technology and innovation have stimulated ideas and programs to nudge policing to a more progressive future, the remaining icon of policing that desperately needs to be moving toward the future is *leadership*. Leading police organizations in the future is likely to be significantly different than traditional police leadership, and it's not too soon to develop future models.

Some elements of leadership are *not* likely to change: strong interpersonal skills, the ability to communicate effectively, and the importance of inspiring employees will always be necessary components of a great leader. Leadership styles are quite varied, with some leaders practicing hands-on direction at the ground level while others focus more on the big-picture view. Regardless of present leadership styles, future models will surely draw some from the present, mixed with previously untested methods.

The classic leadership model that has always dominated in policing is the pyramidal hierarchy. Many progressive organizations have already begun the shift to more net-centric structures. In a networked model, the leader's job is to define the boundaries within which empowered employees can work with greater autonomy, persistently clarify the organizational mission, and provide the networked employees the resources they need to do their work.

Providing the context of the mission and keeping the network intensely focused on its achievement will dominate the future leader's role.

Leadership will also have to change to reflect the profile of future employees: techno-savvy, diverse in thought and backgrounds, less responsive to autocratic direction, more mission-focused than task-driven. Applying traditional leadership with such a future workforce will likely lead to a dysfunctional outcome.

Just as leadership in the future will be different, the selection of police officers also will be different. Selecting candidates with high character indicators and effective communication skills will continue, but there will be far less importance on knowledge of law, police procedures, and even physical prowess. A team of blended skill sets, many previously undervalued in policing, is most likely to yield a creative and outcome-focused work unit that can work equally well within the high-tech environment and the high-touch human community. Relying on the old "tried and true" selection tests will not identify the blend of skills needed for the officer of the future.

There's an old saying that the best day to plant a tree was 50 years ago; the second best day is today. The same could be said for planning and developing future police leadership models.

### Crime Control

One category of technological change pertains to crime control. **Crime-detection technology** includes devices to detect weapons and drugs, cameras that can record illegal behavior (including traffic violations), listening devices that can intercept illicit conversations, and biometric techniques (e.g., retinal scanning and facial recognition) that can identify wanted persons. Each of these technologies raises concerns about privacy and civil liberties, a topic discussed in the next subsection.

Technology for finding latent fingerprints, human tissue (for DNA), and ballistic evidence (bullets and shell casings) at crime scenes and linking them to suspects has helped solve many crimes over the years. To be sure, the use of **crime-solving technology** to solve crimes in the real world is not nearly as systematic or effective as portrayed on television, mainly because most police departments cannot afford the latest equipment and most crime labs do not have sufficient staff to analyze all the evidence submitted to them. Nevertheless, science and technology have improved police crime-solving effectiveness, and are likely to improve it even more in the future (Cordner 2013).

Another important category is **rapid-response technology**. One example is acoustic gunshot detection, intended to help police get to the scenes of shootings more quickly, potentially to apprehend shooters and provide first aid to victims. Although the logic of these systems seems obvious, so far they have not been shown to be effective in reducing shootings or arresting shooters, and they have been criticized for adding to overpolicing of poor neighborhoods (Daley 2021). A different rapid-response technology involves using drones to quickly reach the scenes of crimes in progress, vehicle crashes, and other critical incidents in order to provide responding officers and their commanders an "eye in the sky" for situational awareness and tactical guidance. The police department in Chula Vista, California, credited this technology with 57 arrests in the first six months of operation, 50 calls that the agency was able to cancel, and an average drone response time of one minute and 45 seconds (Lardieri 2019).

A number of other technological breakthroughs might be game changers in the near or medium-term future if they in fact are scientifically feasible and practical to use. The following are a few examples:

- **Weapon detection:** Technology that would alert police to the presence of a weapon on a person or in a car would have obvious officer-safety benefits and might reduce the need for frisks and searches.

- **Drug detection:** Technology that would alert the police to the presence of illegal drugs might also reduce the need for frisks and searches. To be most useful, this technology would need to be cheaper and more effective than the current "technology," police dogs.

- **Drug identification:** A "crime lab in a box" that would quickly and reliably identify suspicious substances would have advantages over current field-testing methods.

- **Intoxication detection and measurement:** Technology that would reliably detect and measure the amount of drugs and alcohol in a person's system would have obvious benefit for the enforcement of driving under the influence. The existing breath-testing equipment only works for alcohol, and its reliability has been questioned in court.

- **Rapid DNA testing:** This technology is available now but is not yet in wide use. It will allow police in the field to more quickly identify suspects and associations between suspects and crime scenes.

■ **Lie detection:** Current technologies, including the polygraph and voice-stress analysis, are not generally accepted in court, and their reliability is widely questioned. A future technology that can accurately detect lies would have tremendous value, especially in criminal investigation.

## Surveillance and Privacy

Crime-control technologies raise many privacy and civil liberty issues. The debate over the federal government's massive eavesdropping on telephone and Internet communication for the purpose of detecting terrorist acts is a case in point. On a more mundane level, fingerprints and DNA evidence are most productive for crime solving when they can be compared against large databases, but most Americans do not favor the creation of universal fingerprint or DNA registries. Therefore, available government databases tend to be limited to previously convicted offenders and military personnel. In an interesting recent twist, however, police have begun using genealogical DNA repositories to look for exact or "familial" matches to crime scene DNA evidence, resulting in a number of cold case clearances. This approach is ingenious, but it has sparked a new debate about privacy and police access to personal identification data without people's explicit permission.

Another potentially invasive technology would be some kind of X-ray or sensor for weapon detection. As mentioned previously, an effective technology of this type would be a boon for officer safety and would undoubtedly help police identify and arrest serious criminals. However, many citizens have the legal right to carry a concealed weapon, including a firearm. These citizens might object to the proposed technology and would likely be upset if its use caused them to be stopped and searched by the police at gunpoint. In other words, the technology might be able to detect a concealed weapon, but not whether the concealment was legal or illegal.

Other police technologies are already extending the degree of surveillance in society. Surveillance cameras have proliferated dramatically in both the public and private sectors. In addition, the use of fixed automated license-plate readers is quickly spreading, providing a database of which vehicles pass by which spots at what times. Cell phone service providers also have databases that show the location of cell phones every few minutes, information that is generally provided to law enforcement when requested. In combination, these and other surveillance systems undeniably reduce privacy, although they are also very helpful for detecting and solving crimes. Striking the right balance will be a never-ending challenge.

Public concern over surveillance and privacy also arises in debates over whether police departments should be allowed to use **unmanned aerial vehicles** (UAVs), often called drones. The Federal Aviation Administration was slow to begin authorizing police use of UAVs, out of concern for airplane safety, and public opinion was initially quite guarded, with several states imposing moratoriums (Sengupta 2013). Early adopter agencies typically received permission for limited use of UAVs for such situations as search and rescue and disaster assessment (McCullough 2014). Several years later, public wariness still exists, but over 1,500 law enforcement agencies were operating UAVs as of March 2020, a dramatic increase in a short period of time (Gettinger 2020).

## Officer Safety and Accountability

A police technology item that is largely taken for granted today is body armor (the bulletproof vest), which has been widely available since the 1970s and is now mandatory equipment in most police departments. Officer safety has been further enhanced over the years by improved communications equipment, evolving from the police radio in the patrol car to portable radios (walkie-talkies) and now enhanced by earphones and shoulder microphones, with cell phone backup and much more interoperability across agencies than in the past. In addition, development of the **Global Positioning System** (GPS) has made it possible for police departments to identify the locations of officers and patrol cars. When automated vehicle locator systems based on earlier technology were first introduced about 30 years ago, they were resisted by police officers who did not want management keeping such close track of them, but in the current era, these systems have become more acceptable because of their role in promoting officer safety (Farrell 2009).

The most popular police technology item today is certainly the body-worn camera (BWC). The primary impetus behind BWCs has been police officer accountability, especially in use-of-force incidents. Interestingly, however, many police have themselves sought the technology, believing that its main contribution will be to exonerate them if they are accused of misconduct. Also, some officers point to the value of the cameras for recording witness statements and other evidence in the field. Studies of the impact of BWCs have shown inconsistent results from department to department. Though the technology is not a panacea, improved officer and citizen behavior have often been observed, and officers and citizens have usually supported the use of BWCs (Lum et al. 2019; White and Malm 2020).

Privacy considerations associated with BWCs are more complex than originally expected. For example, some states have very restrictive legislation about recording conversations, and as a result, officers may have to ask each person they encounter for permission to use the audio feature of the BWC, turning it off if permission is denied. Similarly, recording video inside private homes, without permission, may be prohibited by law in some circumstances. Beyond these kinds of legal limitations are additional privacy concerns that may apply to crime victims, suspects, and juveniles. Further complicating the situation are right-to-know and public-records laws that, in some states, classify police BWC video as open records. It is one thing for crime victims to wonder whether they want the police to have audio and video of them and the inside of their homes; it is another thing to anticipate that any citizen might have access to it, or that it might be posted on YouTube.

These significant privacy and public-records considerations also contribute to the financial cost of a BWC program in a police department (Police Executive Research Forum [PERF] 2018). The purchase price for each camera is typically $500 or less, depending on quality and features. Storing hundreds and thousands of hours of digital video can be a great expense, however, requiring additional servers and software or cloud-based storage fees. Some vendors offer to manage the entire digital storage process, but usually at a high price. In addition, staff time may be consumed managing the data so that it can be found, retrieved, and authenticated when needed—resulting in one or more full-time positions in some agencies. Finally, returning to the public-records discussion, responding to right-to-know requests can tie up additional staff time, especially if certain information on requested videos must be redacted before release. Larger departments are now spending hundreds of thousands of dollars annually, over and above the base purchase price of the cameras, to staff and manage their BWC programs. These high costs are leading some agencies to drop their BWC programs, and dissuading others from adopting them (Lockhart 2019).

A final set of BWC considerations relates to policies and procedures. Because of the legal and privacy restrictions noted previously, it is not as easy as instructing officers to activate their BWC at the beginning of each shift. Providing thorough and sensible written guidelines that explain when the BWC should be turned on and off, and which features should be used in which situations, has proved challenging. The guidelines typically include some discretion, which guarantees that the wisdom of decisions can later be debated. Additionally, when officers fail to activate their BWC when they should, determining whether the action was human error or intentional obstruction is difficult, especially since these may be tense incidents during which officers have much to think about and pay attention to. In sum, BWC technology is replete with technical, privacy, financial, and practical considerations that police departments will likely wrestle with for years to come.

### Social Media

Facebook, Twitter, Instagram, WhatsApp, YouTube, TikTok, texting, and other aspects of social networking and social media have become routine ingredients of modern life, and most police agencies have now adopted at least some of these technologies (Tiry, Oglesby-Neal, and Kim 2019; Hu and Lovrich 2020). One key purpose is for enhanced communication with the public. Police departments can quickly and widely disseminate press releases, publicize their programs, and send out emergency notices, which was dramatically illustrated by the Boston Police Department immediately following the Boston Marathon bombings (Bar-Tur 2013). Of equal importance, police can solicit information from the public in the form of tips, complaints, and suggestions. Used properly, these social media and social networking technologies can help the police engage the public and create a sense of community and togetherness.

Police also use social media technologies in criminal investigation. Police have discovered that people send texts and tweets to their friends and associates and make posts on their Facebook pages that can be used as evidence (Hewlett 2010). Checking these digital places for evidence has become a standard step in the investigative process. Police investigators may also utilize social media more proactively to search out offenders and set up sting operations (Hamilton and Schram 2013). As well, it is increasingly common for police intelligence analysts to monitor social media posts to detect crime problems that are brewing in a certain area, such as around a school, or to learn more about the social networks among gang members and other organized crime groups. As more and more human interaction occurs on the Internet and in virtual digital worlds, some of that interaction is related to real crime and disorder, making overt police presence and covert police surveillance an inevitable feature of virtual reality, just like in the real world.

## Long-Term Trends

An important part of forecasting is to identify significant trends that will likely have future consequences. Some demographic and economic trends were identified earlier in the chapter, such as generational differences and diversity in the population, increased participation of women in the labor force, and the changing nature of jobs. Also noted was the trend toward more high-tech crime and police adoption of various modern technologies. In this section, we briefly discuss five additional long-term trends directly connected to modern policing: professionalization, privatization, federalization, militarization, and homeland security.

### Professionalization

It is fair to say that the police have been professionalizing for about 100 years. The evolution of American policing from the political era into the reform or professional era was discussed at length in Chapter 2. You may recall that the community policing era came along next (Kelling and Moore 1988), but it is not accurate or logical to think that it replaced the professional era. Rather, it primarily built on the foundation of the professional era—a foundation consisting of training, education, high standards, and modern technology.

Despite 100 years of professionalizing, the effort continues and is not complete. Stone and Travis (2011, 3) argued for a new conception of police professionalism: "for any profession to be worthy of that name, its members must not only develop transportable skills but also commit themselves both to a set of ethical precepts and to a discipline of continuous learning." They propose four elements of new police professionalism: (1) accountability, (2) legitimacy, (3) continuous innovation, and (4) national coherence. Accountability and legitimacy were previously discussed in this chapter and elsewhere in the text. Continuous innovation corresponds to some of the management topics in Chapter 5, such as continuous improvement, developing police departments as learning organizations, and making a commitment to identify and implement evidence-based practices. National coherence sounds more radical, but it is not an extreme call for police consolidation. Rather, it is a call for clearer national standards and protocols so that the quality of policing is more consistent across the country, while still allowing local customs and practices. In truth, as a result of national police associations, the influence of the federal government, national and state accreditation programs, state-level minimum training standards, and the homogenizing effect of the Internet, more national coherence likely exists in our policing system today than most people realize.

Although many police departments may already have a basis for claiming to meet these elements of **professionalization**, the more difficult remaining task might be to convince street cops that this new professionalism is in their best interests. To the extent that police officers continue to see themselves more as workers and employees—that is, as laborers in constant conflict with management—the mantel of professionalism is an awkward fit, and elements such as accountability may seem particularly threatening. Over the past century, American police have tended to treat professionalism more as an image and status than as a responsibility to transform their performance and their relationship with the public. As long as this approach continues, achieving real professionalism may take another 100 years.

## Privatization

Private policing is not new. In fact, private police preceded the formation of public police in London in 1829, and private detectives like the Pinkertons conducted most criminal investigations in the United States throughout much of the 1800s. Nevertheless, Americans today are accustomed to thinking about the police as a public agency. Their public responsibilities, to represent the government and enforce the law, are central to the way most citizens believe the police should behave in a democratic setting. However, the public role played by the police may now be shrinking in the face of **privatization**. Over the past 30-plus years, the traditional monopoly of the government over police services has diminished. In the United States today, there are many more private security agents than public police officers (BLS 2021).

The trend toward private security is likely to continue for several reasons. First, the police, by themselves, can only do so much about crime. Their behavior is constrained by due process of law as well as by social and economic variables outside their control. Yet the public's fear of crime is not likely to decline and may increase. Private security has already begun to fill the gap for those who can afford to pay the price for extra protection.

Second, there is a change in the way we use physical space. The latter half of the twentieth century witnessed the rise of what Bayley and Shearing (1998) call *mass private property*—facilities that are privately owned but used by the public. These include shopping malls, college and school campuses, residential communities, high-rise condominiums, banks, commercial facilities, and recreational complexes. To that list could be added the increasing popularity of gated communities separated from their surrounding areas by walls and gates staffed by security guards. Private security specialists are the most likely form of policing for these kinds of facilities. Market-based private security will follow the incentives offered by the private economy, likely resulting in policing stratified by class and race.

Some fear that Western democratic societies are moving inexorably into a "Clockwork Orange" world where both the market and the government protect the affluent from the poor—one by barricading and excluding and the other by repressing and imprisoning—and where civil society for the poor disappears in the face of criminal victimization and governmental repression (Bayley and Shearing 1998). This vision of the future raises a key question: Can we avoid a system where public crime control is carried out primarily against the poor?

Bayley and Shearing (1998) contend that we can, but only if we make two conscious policy choices. First, empower poor people to participate in the market for security through financial assistance. Second, reinforce community policing as the organizing principle of public policing. Since safety is fundamental to the quality of life, coproduction between the police and the public legitimates government, lessening the corrosive alienation that disorganizes communities and triggers collective violence. Community policing is the only police strategy that incorporates the problems encountered by the poor into decision making by the police.

### Federalization

A strong trend since the second half of the twentieth century has been the **federalization** of crime control and law enforcement. Over the years, the US Congress has passed more and more federal criminal laws, giving wider jurisdiction to federal prosecutors and federal police. Many crimes today, especially those involving guns or drugs, can be investigated and prosecuted federally as well as by state and local law enforcement. One might think that this would be an unmitigated positive trend, but an American Bar Association study (Task Force on the Federalization of Criminal Law 1998, 50) concluded differently:

- It generally undermines the state–federal fabric and disrupts the important constitutional balance of federal and state systems.
- It can have a detrimental impact on the state courts, state prosecutors, attorneys, and state investigating agents who bear the overwhelming share of responsibility for criminal law enforcement.
- It has the potential to relegate the less glamorous prosecutions to the state system, undermine citizen perception, dissipate citizen power, and diminish citizen confidence in both state and local law enforcement mechanisms.
- It creates an unhealthy concentration of policing power at the federal level.
- It can cause an adverse impact on the federal judicial system.
- It creates inappropriately disparate results for similarly situated defendants, depending on whether their essentially similar conduct is selected for federal or state prosecution.
- It increases unreviewable federal prosecutorial discretion.
- It contributes, to some degree, to costly and unneeded consequences for the federal prison system.

- It accumulates a large body of law that requires continually increasing an unprofitable congressional attention in monitoring federal criminal statutes and agencies.

- It diverts congressional attention from a needed focus on that criminal activity that, in practice, only federal prosecutions can address.

- Overall, it represents an unwise allocation of scarce resources needed to meet the genuine issues of crime.

It is particularly significant that the American Bar Association Task Force reached these conclusions well before September 11, 2001. Since then, the nation's heightened concern about international terrorism and weapons of mass destruction has led to an even greater tendency to rely on federal laws and federal law enforcement. The American Bar Association has continued to lobby against the trend toward over-federalization, and Congress has continued to hold hearings on it (US House of Representatives 2013).

The federal government has sought to influence local and state policing in other ways as well. Since the late 1960s, federal grants have been available to agencies interested in training, education, new technology, and innovative programs. In the 1990s, these grants strongly supported community policing, while after 9/11, they helped agencies develop homeland security capacity. After the murder of George Floyd in 2020, proposals were advanced in Congress to mandate certain training programs, incentivize police agency accreditation, eliminate qualified immunity for police, and address other "hot button" issues on a national scale. As of this writing, those proposals have not become law (Summers 2021), but they do show a greater willingness to consider imposing national standards on America's traditionally localized policing system.

## Militarization

The **militarization** trend is similar to the federalization trend. Traditionally, the regular military has been very restricted in its role in crime control and policing within the US borders. Military police have had jurisdiction on military bases and with respect to military personnel, of course, but otherwise, the military has only been used for law enforcement or order-maintenance duties in serious emergencies, such as natural disasters or mass civil disorder, when martial law is declared. These limitations on the domestic police role of the military were enacted in the Posse Comitatus Act of 1878, which generally "prohibits US military personnel from interdicting vehicles, vessels and aircraft; conducting surveillance, searches, pursuit and seizures; or making arrests on behalf of civilian law enforcement authorities" (Nunn 2021).

Military involvement in domestic law enforcement had been most common in conjunction with the so-called war on drugs until the terrorist attacks of September 11, 2001. Immediately after 9/11, it was common to see military personnel guarding airports and other critical facilities, and there have been calls for military participation in other types of counterterrorism efforts, such as controlling the US–Mexican border. Similarly, after Hurricane Katrina hit New Orleans and other parts of the Gulf Coast in 2005, military assistance was instrumental in restoring order as well as providing humanitarian relief.

Although Americans have historically viewed the separation of the police and the military as an essential characteristic of their democratic heritage, this view may be changing. Kraska (1994, 1) observed a heightened level of activity linking the military to the police in the United States and argued that the traditional separation of the police and the military is eroding, "resulting in a military involved in law enforcement, and the police at times operating 'militarily,' all under the guise of ameliorating 'social problems'." In regard to the police operating more "militarily," studies have suggested that police SWAT units, originally developed in the 1970s and 1980s to improve response to emergency situations, have engaged in "mission creep," gradually becoming more involved in drug raids, tactical patrol, and similar duties (Kraska and Paulsen 1997).

More recently, concern about police militarization peaked during the civil unrest in Ferguson, Missouri, when images of police atop armored personnel carriers grabbed national attention. Subsequent clashes with protesters in Ferguson, in other cities, and then around the nation following the murder of George Floyd in 2020 sparked a debate over whether the best police response was an immediate overwhelming show of force or a softer initial deployment, with riot police ready but out of sight. Some activists and political leaders questioned whether police really needed armored vehicles and heavy weapons, causing the federal government to place more restrictions on the 1033 Program through which surplus military equipment is donated to local police departments (Executive Office of the President 2014).

Public discussion and debate over police militarization will likely continue. Considering the lethal threats that police are expected to control, including active shooters and terrorism, effective modern equipment is necessary. By the same token, Americans want their police to look and act differently from soldiers. Striking the right balance between these two realities will be a long-term challenge.

### Homeland Security

Several years ago, Ed Flynn, then Massachusetts public safety secretary and later police chief in Milwaukee, called terrorism "the monster that ate criminal justice" (Rosen 2003, 1). After the events of 9/11, terrorism and homeland security led to new legislation, a significant reorganization of the federal government, and dramatically changed national funding priorities. Over two decades later, in the public's mind, defending against terrorism remains a higher national priority than reducing crime (Pew Research Center 2022). Despite these shifts, however, it is important to remember that policing, especially local and state policing, has many other responsibilities and concerns, as illustrated by the numbers—the United States has over 50,000 murders and traffic fatalities per year, compared to the 29 extremism-related deaths that occurred in 2021 (Anti-Defamation League [ADL] 2022).

The attack of September 11, 2001, demonstrated that a weapon of mass destruction could be delivered in the United States with catastrophic results. It also demonstrated that a small group of individuals from halfway around the world could have both the hatred and the determination to plan and carry out such an attack on American soil. As so many subsequently noted, nothing will ever be the same again. For police, the fact that these individuals lived in American cities and towns for an extended period before the attack, taking flying lessons and making other preparations, raised the possibility that they might have been identified in advance if neighbors, patrol officers, and intelligence analysts had only been a bit more observant. Whether local police could possibly have anticipated the intentions of these terrorists has never been established, but police now look carefully for any individuals or groups who might have similar intentions (Hays 2010).

One of the clearest lessons from the 9/11 attack is the need for local, state, and federal authorities to improve intelligence analysis and sharing (Hoover 2002). At the local level, few police departments had sophisticated intelligence operations of any type, much less ones focused on **international terrorism**. At the national level, in the aftermath of the attack, it became evident that the FBI, in particular, had a weak intelligence analysis capacity (Marshall 2003). For many reasons, but mainly its historic focus on criminal investigation, the FBI never developed a strong intelligence capability in the counterterrorism arena, especially after the end of the Cold War. This shortcoming might not have been as serious if there was a strong tradition of information sharing among the federal agencies with intelligence responsibilities, such as the FBI, the Central Intelligence Agency (CIA), and the National Security Agency (NSA), but unfortunately, these agencies have often behaved more like competitors than partners.

The federal government reorganization that created the US Department of Homeland Security was designed to improve information sharing and coordination among the various federal agencies with counterterrorism and law enforcement responsibilities. None of the major intelligence-gathering agencies, including the FBI, CIA, and NSA, was moved to the Department of Homeland Security, though, clearly indicating that interagency relations are still key, even at the federal level. At the state and local levels, fusion centers have been established, with federal participation as well, in an effort to improve information sharing and intelligence analysis. In addition, Joint Terrorism Task Forces have been expanded all around the country to provide more vigorous and coordinated federal, state, and local terrorism investigations (Cordner and Scarborough 2010).

Terrorism is such a serious threat that some have contemplated whether existing police strategies are up to the job. Because terrorists are so violent and so determined to commit dreadful acts on behalf of their causes, it has been suggested that policing strategies based on openness, consent, and cooperation must be reconsidered (de Guzman 2002). Although understandable, this point of view seems shortsighted and, ultimately, a concession to those who use terror to achieve their ends. Many others in the police field are more inclined to argue that community policing and problem-oriented policing represent the most promising approaches to homeland (and hometown) security (Burack 2003; Newman and Clarke 2008). Neither of these approaches, of course, precludes the use of intelligence-led policing, along with supplementary and specialized responses to terrorism. But community policing and problem-oriented policing, when used in tandem, are the most effective police strategies for controlling crime and disorder and reducing fear while still protecting the legitimacy of the police institution in a free and open society. This view was echoed by Charles Ramsey (2002, 6–7), former police commissioner in Philadelphia and chief of police in Washington, DC:

> While many US law enforcement agencies have adopted community-policing strategies in recent years, traumatic events like the 9/11 attacks can cause organizations to fall back on more traditional methods of doing business. Some police departments may abandon community policing for seemingly more immediate security concerns. Community policing, however, should play a central role in addressing these issues.

Two aspects of the current terrorism problem demonstrate the need for clear thinking and rational responses. One is that the situation has been getting better and Americans are far safer than most. Worldwide, the number of terror attacks and terrorism-related fatalities has been decreasing since 2014 (Global Terrorism Database 2020). Typically, less than 1 percent of the world's terror attacks occurred in the United States (LaFree 2019). Second, in most years, **domestic terrorism** and right-wing extremist violence account for more deaths in the United States than international terrorism (see Inside Policing 15.5). Most recently, 26 of 29 deaths in 2021 were attributed to domestic right-wing extremists (ADL 2022). Intelligence and law enforcement agencies have identified homegrown terrorism as a greater threat than international terrorism, but their assessments have not always been accepted by political leaders (German and Robinson 2018; Wray 2018).

**INSIDE POLICING 15.5**  Growing Threat of Right-Wing Extremist Violence

The mosque massacre in New Zealand has focused attention on right-wing and white nationalist violence, as reported here. Last year [2018] in the United States, 49 of 50 extremist-related killings were tied to far-right perpetrators, and the European Union saw a doubling in 2017 of arrests for right-wing extremist offenses. Hate crimes in US cities have increased in each of the last five years. One expert observes that "white nationalism has emerged into a coalesced and growing socio-political force, with tentacles that extend into the mainstream. That's something many other extremist movements do not have."

**Discussion Question:** The world can be a dangerous place. As you look at international developments as well as those in the United States, what threats to the safety of Americans do you think are most serious? What steps should local and state police take, if any, to counter those threats?

SOURCE: *Modern Policing* blog, March 20, 2019, https://gcordner.wordpress.com/2019/03/20/growing-threat-of-right-wing-extremist-violence/.

The American people want to be safe and free. Over time, and especially in response to crime waves, drug epidemics, and most recently, terrorism, the immediate concern for safety often gets stronger, leading to new laws and more funding for police and public safety. Usually, however, the countervailing desire for freedom helps check increases in government power and authority. Also, new laws and practices are subject to constitutionality questions, and sometimes the courts tell the executive or legislative branches that they have gone too far. Balancing the public's twin desires for safety and freedom is something that local and state police have a great deal of experience with, and we must hope that they draw on that experience in the era of terrorism and homeland security.

## Summary

American society has always been dynamic, and the current situation is no different. Consideration of police *and society,* then, must account for the changing nature of that society. Important facets of ongoing societal change include generational differences among the population, the increasing diversity of the American people, immigration from other countries, internal migration patterns, shifts in jobs and other economic conditions, and climate change. Among the most obvious factors affecting policing are the different cultures and languages they now encounter, increasing income inequality, and a vast increase in the number of families with both parents working outside the home, leaving more children unsupervised after school and at other times.

Changing times create new challenges and issues. Among the most contentious contemporary issues facing policing are crime trends, mass shootings, mental health issues, and police legitimacy. Police practices need continuous refinement to ensure that policing is done in an efficient, effective, and equitable manner. Crime and disorder problems in the community need careful analysis and attention, whether they are of a long-standing nature, such as dealing with violence and theft, or newer problems, such as computer crime. Another crime-related challenge is dealing with drug crimes and drug abuse, which is not a new police mission, but drug use patterns continue to shift, with marijuana being legalized or decriminalized in many states while the opioid/fentanyl crisis demonstrates the ongoing ravage of addiction. A particular crime-related issue in recent years has been mass shootings, some of which have a nexus to terrorism, some to hate crime, others to mental health, and some in which the motivation cannot be determined. Handling people experiencing behavioral health crises is not a new challenge either, but it is receiving increased attention as society becomes more aware that police and jail are not the best answers to what are really health problems. Dealing with these and similar issues fairly and effectively are crucial to building and maintaining the public's trust and confidence in the police.

There is probably no surer forecast than that technology will continue to change, and change ever faster, affecting society and policing. Improvements in technology associated with crime detection, crime solving, surveillance, officer safety, accountability, and exploitation of social media are likely to make tremendous contributions toward more effective and efficient policing. The technology du jour is BWCs, which are not a panacea but can make important contributions to transparency and accountability. It is hard to predict all the unintended consequences that will follow from these and other new technologies, especially as they relate to issues of privacy and civil liberties, except to say that there will be some.

Significant long-term trends that seem likely to continue to affect policing in the future include professionalization, privatization, federalization, militarization, and homeland security. Together, these trends have the potential to radically change the distinctive nature of American policing—public, local, fragmented, and civilian. Whether the momentum behind these trends is inexorable or more temporary is open to debate. The increasingly complex and transnational nature of crime and the emergence of international terrorism suggest that these trends can only increase in momentum. Everyday crime and disorder are still much more common than sophisticated international crime, however, and more of a threat to the average American, suggesting that local police may not become an endangered species anytime soon.

## Critical Thinking Questions

1. The American population, on average, is aging. How will this make your life different from what your parents experienced? What impact will it have on policing in the future?

2. The US economy was once based heavily on farming and later on manufacturing. Now, most jobs are in the service, information, technology, and creative sectors. What are the implications of these fundamental economic changes for social relations, crime, and policing?

3. Cybercrime and other types of electronic and white-collar crime are complicated and technical. Do you think the average small police department will ever have personnel competent to investigate them? If not, who will investigate these types of crime in the future?

4. Which of the significant trends discussed in the chapter (professionalization, privatization, federalization, militarization, and homeland security) do you think will have the biggest impact on future policing? Why? Which of the trends concerns you the most and why?

5. Police commanders will soon have the technical capability to sit in the police station, monitor what all of their officers are doing in the field in real time, and then tell

them what to do, thanks to body-worn video cameras broadcasting across generous bandwidth. What effect do you think this will have on police work? As a police officer, would you welcome this new technology? Would you welcome it as a member of the public?

# References

Administration on Aging. 2021. *A Profile of Older Americans: 2020*. https://acl.gov/sites/default/files/Aging%20and%20Disability%20in%20America/2020ProfileOlderAmericans.Final_.pdf.

Anti-Defamation League (ADL). 2022. "Murder and Extremism in the United States in 2021." June 14. https://www.adl.org/murder-and-extremism-2021.

Bar-Tur, Y. 2013. "Boston Police Schooled Us All on Social Media." *Mashable*, April 22. https://mashable.com/2013/04/22/boston-police-social-media/.

Bartkowiak-Theron, I., Clover, J., Martin, D., Southby, R., and Crofts, N. (eds.). 2022. *Law Enforcement and Public Health: Partners for Community Safety and Wellbeing*. Switzerland: Springer.

Bayley, D., and Shearing, C. 1998. "The Future of Policing." In G. Cole and M. Gertz (eds.), *The Criminal Justice System: Politics and Policies*, 7th ed., pp. 150–167. Belmont, CA: West/Wadsworth.

Beekman, D. 2016. "Heroin, Cocaine Users in Seattle May Get Country's First Safe-Use Site." *The Seattle Times*, April 4. https://www.seattletimes.com/seattle-news/politics/heroin-other-drug-users-may-get-a-safe-use-site-in-seattle/.

Brenan, M. 2021. "America's Confidence in Major US Institutions Dips." *Gallup*, July 14. https://news.gallup.com/poll/352316/americans-confidence-major-institutions-dips.aspx.

Brenner, S. W. 2001. "Defining Cybercrime: A Review of State and Federal Law." In R. D. Clifford (ed.), *Cybercrime: The Investigation, Prosecution and Defense of a Computer-Related Crime*, pp. 11–69. Durham, NC: Carolina Academic Press.

Burack, J. 2003. "Community Policing in a Security-Conscious World: Working to Prevent Terrorism in Rural America." *Subject to Debate* 17(8): 1, 3, 7.

Bureau of Labor Statistics (BLS). 2021. "Protective Service Occupations." https://www.bls.gov/ooh/protective-service/home.htm.

Bureau of Labor Statistics (BLS). 2022a. "Databases, Tables & Calculators by Subject: Unemployment Rate." https://data.bls.gov/pdq/SurveyOutputServlet.

Bureau of Labor Statistics (BLS). 2022b. "Employed Persons by Occupation, Sex, and Age." https://www.bls.gov/cps/cpsaat09.htm.

Bureau of Labor Statistics (BLS). 2022c. "Women in the Labor Force: A Databook." *BLS Reports*, March. https://www.bls.gov/opub/reports/womens-databook/2021/home.htm.

Centers for Disease Control and Prevention (CDC). 2016. "Deaths: Final Data for 2013." *National Vital Statistics Reports* 64, February 16. https://www.cdc.gov/nchs/data/nvsr/nvsr64/nvsr64_02.pdf.

Centers for Disease Control and Prevention (CDC). 2018. *2018 Annual Surveillance Report of Drug-Related Risks and Outcomes*. Washington, DC: Author. https://www.cdc.gov/drugoverdose/pdf/pubs/2018-cdc-drug-surveillance-report.pdf.

Centers for Disease Control and Prevention (CDC). 2021a. *Drug Overdose Deaths in the United States, 1999–2020*. Washington, DC: Author. https://www.cdc.gov/nchs/data/databriefs/db428.pdf.

Centers for Disease Control and Prevention (CDC). 2021b. *Life Expectancy in the US Declined a Year and Half in 2020*. Washington, DC: Author. https://www.cdc.gov/nchs/pressroom/nchs_press_releases/2021/202107.htm.

Centers for Disease Control and Prevention (CDC). 2021c. *Mortality in the United States, 2020*. Washington, DC: Author. https://www.cdc.gov/nchs/products/databriefs/db427.htm.

CIT International. 2022. "CIT is More Than Just Training." https://www.citinternational.org/What-is-CIT.

Colby, S. L., and Ortman, J. M. 2015. "Projections of the Size and Composition of the US Population: 2014 to 2060." *Current Population Reports*. Washington, DC: US Census Bureau. https://census.gov/content/dam/Census/library/publications/2015/demo/p25-1143.pdf.

Cordner, G. 2006. *People with Mental Illness*. POP Guide No. 40. Washington, DC: Office of Community Oriented Policing Services.

Cordner, G. 2013. "Science Solves Crime: Myth or Reality." In R. M. Bohm and J. T. Walker (eds.), *Demystifying Crime and Criminal Justice*, 2nd ed., pp. 157–165. New York: Oxford.

Cordner, G., and Scarborough, K. 2010. "Information Sharing: Exploring the Intersection of Policing with National and Military Intelligence." *Homeland Security Affairs Journal* 6. https://www.hsaj.org/?article=6.1.5/.

Daley, J. 2021. "In Chicago, Controversy Mounts Over the Use of Gunshot Detection Sensors." *The Trace*, August 27. https://www.thetrace.org/2021/08/chicago-police-shotspotter-gunshot-detection-shooting-contract/.

de Guzman, M. C. 2002. "The Changing Roles and Strategies of the Police in Time of Terror." *ACJS Today* 22(3): 8–13.

Dickey, C. 2010. "How Immigrants Actually Reduce Crime." *Newsweek*, May 26. https://www.newsweek.com/how-immigrants-actually-reduce-crime-72555.

DISA. 2022. "Map of Marijuana Legality by State." https://disa.com/map-of-marijuana-legality-by-state.

Drake, B. 2014. "6 New Findings about Millennials." *Pew Research Center*, March 7. https://www.pewresearch.org/fact-tank/2014/03/07/6-new-findings-about-millennials/.

Egelko, B. 2018. "Law Enforcement Objects to Trump Administration Order to Target Immigrants." *San Francisco Chronicle*, January 30. https://www.sfgate.com/nation/article/Police-prosecutors-condemn-Trump-administration-12537639.php.

Eugene Police Department. 2022. "CAHOOTS." https://www.eugene-or.gov/4508/CAHOOTS.

Everytown. 2022. "Mass Shootings in America." https://everytownresearch.org/maps/mass-shootings-in-america/.

Executive Office of the President. 2014. *Review: Federal Support for Local Law Enforcement Equipment Acquisition*. Washington, DC: The White House. https://obamawhitehouse.archives.gov/sites/default/files/docs/federal_support_for_local_law_enforcement_equipment_acquisition.pdf.

Farrell, M. B. 2009. "San Jose Police Get Ear-Mounted Video Cameras in Battle for Image." *Christian Science Monitor*, December 22. https://www.csmonitor.com/USA/2009/1222/San-Jose-police-get-ear-mounted-video-cameras-in-battle-for-image/.

Federal Bureau of Investigation (FBI). 2018. *Uniform Crime Reports, 2017*. Washington, DC: Author. https://ucr.fbi.gov/crime-in-the-u.s/2017/crime-in-the-u.s.-2017/home.

Federal Bureau of Investigation (FBI). 2020. *Internet Crime Report: 2020*. Washington, DC: Author. https://www.ic3.gov/Media/PDF/AnnualReport/2020_IC3Report.pdf.

Festa, E. 2022. "Carjacking Spikes Worry Insurance Industry; Could Lead to Higher Premiums." *Investopedia*, March 10. https://www.investopedia.com/carjacking-spikes-worry-insurance-industry-5221572.

Florida, R. 2004. "Creative Class War." *The Washington Monthly* 36(2): 31–37.

Fry, R. 2020. "Millennials Overtake Baby Boomers as America's Largest Generation." *Pew Research Center*, April 28. https://www.pewresearch.org/fact-tank/2020/04/28/millennials-overtake-baby-boomers-as-americas-largest-generation/.

Fry, R., Igielnik, R., and Patten, E. 2018. "How Millennials Today Compare with Their Grandparents 50 Years Ago." *Pew Research Center*, March 16. https://www.pewresearch.org/fact-tank/2018/03/16/how-millennials-compare-with-their-grandparents/.

German, M. and Robinson, S. 2018. "Wrong Priorities on Fighting Terrorism." Brennan Center for Justice, New York University. https://www.brennancenter.org/sites/default/files/publications/2018_10_DomesticTerrorism_V2%20%281%29.pdf.

Gettinger, D. 2020. "Public Safety Drones, 3rd Edition." Center for the Study of the Drone at Bard College. https://dronecenter.bard.edu/projects/public-safety-drones-project/public-safety-drones-3rd-edition/.

Global Terrorism Database. 2020. *Global Terrorism Overview*. https://www.start.umd.edu/pubs/START_GTD_GlobalTerrorismOverview2019_July2020.pdf

Graham, D. 2022. "The Stumbling Block to One of the Most Promising Police Reforms." *The Atlantic*, February 22. https://www.theatlantic.com/ideas/archive/2022/02/mental-health-crisis-police-intervention/622842/.

Gramlich, J. 2020. "What the Data Says (and Doesn't Say) About Crime in the United States." *Pew Research Center*, November 20. https://www.pewresearch.org/fact-tank/2020/11/20/facts-about-crime-in-the-u-s/.

Gramlich, J. 2021. "What We Know About the Increase in US Murders in 2020." *Pew Research Center*, October 27. https://www.pewresearch.org/fact-tank/2021/10/27/what-we-know-about-the-increase-in-u-s-murders-in-2020/.

Hamilton, B., and Schram, J. 2013. "New NYPD Tactics Slash Murder Rate." *New York Post*, February 24. https://nypost.com/2013/02/24/new-nypd-tactics-slash-murder-rate/.

Hays, T. 2010. "NYPD Undercover Unit Key in NJ Terror Arrests." *NBC New York*, June 8. https://www.nbcnewyork.com/news/local/NYPD-Undercover-Unit-Key-in-NJ-Terror-Arrests-95844414.html.

Hewlett, J. 2010. "Lexington Woman Indicted on Manslaughter Charge for Fiery Crash," *Lexington Herald-Leader*, May 27. https://www.kentucky.com/latest-news/article44033847.html.

Hobbs, F., and Stoops, N. 2002. *Demographic Trends in the 20th Century*. Washington, DC: US Census Bureau.

Hoover, L. T. 2002. "The Challenges to Local Police Participation in the Homeland Security Effort." *Subject to Debate* 16(10): 1, 3–4, 8–10.

Howe, N. 2010. "Portrait of the Millennials." *Pew Research Center*, March 11. https://www.pewresearch.org/2010/03/11/portrait-of-the-millennials/.

Hu, X., and Lovrich, N. 2020. *Electronic Community-Oriented Policing: Theories, Contemporary Efforts, and Future Directions*. Lanham, MD: Lexington Books.

Intergovernmental Panel on Climate Change. 2021. "Climate Change Widespread, Rapid, and Intensifying. Intergovernmental Panel on Climate Change," August 9. https://www.ipcc.ch/2021/08/09/ar6-wg1-20210809-pr/.

Jones, J. 2021. "In US, Black Confidence in Police Recovers From 2020 Low." *Gallup*, July 14. https://news.gallup.com/poll/352304/black-confidence-police-recovers-2020-low.aspx.

Jones, J. 2022. "LGBT Identification in US Ticks Up to 7.1%." *Gallup*, February 17. https://news.gallup.com/poll/389792/lgbt-identification-ticks-up.aspx.

Kardish, C. 2015. "Police in This City Vow to Stop Arresting Drug Addicts." *Governing*, May 8. https://www.governing.com/topics/public-justice-safety/gov-gloucester-drug-addicts-heroin.html.

Kelling, G. L., and M. H. Moore. 1988. "The Evolving Strategy of Policing." *Perspectives on Policing*. Washington, DC: National Institute of Justice.

Koper, C. S., Lum, C., Willis, J. J., Woods, D. J., and Hibdon, J. 2015. *Realizing the Potential of Technology in Policing*. Fairfax, VA: Center for Evidence-Based Crime Policy, George Mason University. https://cebcp.org/wp-content/technology/ImpactTechnologyFinalReport.pdf.

Kraska, P. 1994. "The Police and the Military in the Cold-War Era: Streamlining the State's Use of Force Entities in the Drug War." *Police Forum* 4(1): 1–7.

Kraska, P. B., and Paulsen, D. J. 1997. "Grounded Research into US Paramilitary Policing: Forging the Iron Fist inside the Velvet Glove." *Policing and Society* 7: 253–270.

Kreider, R. M., and Simmons, T. 2003. "Marital Status: 2000." Washington, DC: US Census Bureau. https://www2.census.gov/library/publications/decennial/2000/briefs/c2kbr-30.pdf.

LaFree, G. 2019. "Will Terrorism Continue to Decline in 2019?" *Homeland Security News Wire*, February 27. https://www.homelandsecuritynewswire.com/dr20190227-will-terrorism-continue-to-decline-in-2019.

Lardieri, A. 2019. "California Police Department Uses Drones as First Responders." *US News & World Report*, April 12. https://www.usnews.com/news/national-news/articles/2019-04-12/california-police-department-uses-drones-as-first-responders.

Lemieux, F. 2018. "Five Things to Know About Mass Shootings in America." *Homeland Security News Wire*, May 21. https://www.homelandsecuritynewswire.com/dr20180521-five-things-to-know-about-mass-shootings-in-america.

Lobosco, K. 2013. "Cyber Attacks Are the Bank Robberies of the Future." *CNN Money*, July 9. https://money.cnn.com/2013/07/09/technology/security/cybercrime-bank-robberies/.

Lockhart, P. R. 2019. "Why Some Police Departments are Dropping Their Body Camera Programs." *Vox*, January 15. https://www.vox.com/2019/U24/18196097/police-body-cameras-storage-cost-washington-post.

Lowry, A. 2012. "Income Inequality May Take Toll on Growth." *New York Times*, October 16. https://www.nytimes.com/2012/10/17/business/economy/income-inequality-may-take-toll-on-growth.html.

Lum, C., Stoltz, M., Koper, C., and Scherer, J. 2019. "Research on Body-Worn Cameras: What We Know, What We Need to Know." *Criminology & Public Policy* 18(1): 93–118.

Marlon, J., Neyens, L., Jefferson, M., Howe, P., Mildenberger, M., and Leiserowitz, A. 2022. "Yale Climate Opinion Maps 2021." *Yale Program on Climate Change Communication*, February 23. https://climatecommunication.yale.edu/visualizations-data/ycom-us/.

Marshall, J. M. 2003. "The FBI: The Nineties and 9/11." *Understanding Government*. Washington, DC: American University.

McCullough, D. R. C. 2014. "Unmanned Aircraft Systems (UAS) Guidebook in Development." *Community Policing Dispatch* 7, August. https://cops.usdoj.gov/html/dispatch/08-2014/UAS_Guidebook_in_Development.asp.

McPhillips, D. 2022. "US Drug Overdose Deaths Reach Another Record High as Deaths from Fentanyl Surge." *CNN*, March 16. https://www.cnn.com/2022/03/16/health/overdose-deaths-record-high-fentanyl/index.html.

National Conference of State Legislatures. 2022. "State Medical Cannabis Laws." https://www.ncsl.org/research/health/state-medical-marijuana-laws.aspx.

National Highway Traffic Safety Administration. 2018. "US DOT Announces 2017 Roadway Fatalities Down." https://www.nhtsa.gov/press-releases/us-dot-announces-2017-roadway-fatalities-down.

National Insurance Crime Bureau. 2014. *A Historical Look at Vehicle Theft in the United States*. Des Plaines, IL: Author.

National Institute of Mental Health. 2022. Mental Illness. Bethesda, MD: Author. https://www.nimh.nih.gov/health/statistics/mental-illness.

Newman, G., and Clarke, R. V. 2008. *Policing Terrorism: An Executive's Guide*. Washington, DC: Office of Community Oriented Policing Services. https://popcenter.asu.edu/sites/default/files/library/reading/PDFs/PolicingTerrorism.pdf.

Nunn, J. 2021. "The Posse Comitatus Act Explained." Brennan Center for Justice, October 14. https://www.brennancenter.org/our-work/research-reports/posse-comitatus-act-explained.

Parker, K., and Hurst, K. 2021. "Growing Share of Americans Say They Want More Spending on Police in Their Area." *Pew Research Center*, October 26. https://www.pewresearch.org/fact-tank/2021/10/26/growing-share-of-americans-say-they-want-more-spending-on-police-in-their-area/.

Pew Research Center. 2015. "The American Middle Class Is Losing Ground." December 9. https://www.pewsocialtrends.org/2015/12/09/the-american-middle-class-is-losing-ground/.

Pew Research Center. 2019. "Attitudes on Same-Sex Marriage." May 14.

Pew Research Center. 2022. "Public's Top Priority for 2022: Strengthening the Nation's Economy." February 16. https://www.pewresearch.org/politics/2022/02/16/publics-top-priority-for-2022-strengthening-the-nations-economy/.

Police Executive Research Forum (PERF). 2018. *Costs and Benefits of Body-Worn Camera Deployments*. Washington, DC: Author. https://www.policeforum.org/assets/BWCCostBenefit.pdf.

Ramsey, C. 2002. "Community Policing: Now More Than Ever." *On the Beat* 19: 6–7. Washington, DC: Office of Community Oriented Policing Services.

Roberts, S. 1994. *Who We Are: A Portrait of America Based on the Latest US Census*. New York: Random House/Times Books.

Robertson, N., and Turcotte, J. 2022. "Is Murder Upswing Starting to Abate? Some Cities See Declines." *Christian Science Monitor*, January 11. https://www.csmonitor.com/USA/Justice/2022/0111/Is-murder-upswing-starting-to-abate-Some-US-cities-see-declines.

Rosen, M. R. 2003. "2003: A Year in Retrospect." *Law Enforcement News* December: 1, 4.

Rosenfeld, R., and Lopez, E. 2022. *Pandemic, Social Unrest, and Crime in US Cities: 2021 Year-End Update*. New York: Council on Criminal Justice. https://counciloncj.org/crime-trends-yearend-2021-update/.

Ross, A. 2014. "Bank Robberies Down in Most Regions." *Banking Blog*, September 10. https://www.bankrate.com/financing/banking/bank-robberies-down-in-most-regions/.

Sengupta, S. 2013. "Rise of Drones in US Drives Efforts to Limit Police Use." *New York Times*, February 15. https://www.nytimes.com/2013/02/16/technology/rise-of-drones-in-us-spurs-efforts-to-limit-uses.html/.

Solly, M. 2018. "US Life Expectancy Drops for Third Year in a Row, Reflecting Rising Drug Overdoses, Suicides." *Smithsonian Magazine*, December 3. https://www.smithsonianmag.com/smart-news/us-life-expectancy-drops-third-year-row-reflecting-rising-drug-overdose-suicide-rates-180970942/.

Stone, C., and Travis, J. 2011. "Toward a New Professionalism in Policing." *New Perspectives in Policing*. Washington, DC: National Institute of Justice. https://www.ncjrs.gov/pdffiles1/nij/232359.pdf/.

Substance Abuse and Mental Health Services Administration. 2018. *Key Substance Use and Mental Health Indicators in the United States: Results from the 2017National Survey on Drug Use and Health*. Rockville, MD: Center for Behavioral Health Statistics and Quality, Substance Abuse and Mental Health Services Administration. https://www.samhsa.gov/data/sites/default/files/cbhsq-reports/NSDUHFFR2017/NSDUHFFR2017.pdf.

Summers, J. 2021. "Congressional Negotiators Have Failed to Reach a Deal on Police Reform." *National Public Radio,* September 22. https://www.npr.org/2021/09/22/1039718450/congressional-negotiators-have-failed-to-reach-a-deal-on-police-reform.

Tankebe, J. 2013. "Viewing Things Differently: The Dimensions of Public Perceptions of Police Legitimacy." *Criminology* 51(1): 103–135.

Task Force on the Federalization of Criminal Law. 1998. *The Federalization of Criminal Law*. Washington, DC: American Bar Association.

Tiry, E., Oglesby-Neal, A., and Kim, K. 2019. *Social Media Guidebook for Law Enforcement Agencies: Strategies for Effective Community Engagement*. Washington, DC: Urban Institute.

US Census Bureau. 2018. "Income and Poverty in the United States: 2017." https://www.census.gov/content/dam/Census/library/publications/2018/demo/p60-263.pdf.

US Census Bureau. 2021. "Income and Poverty in the United States: 2020." https://www.census.gov/library/publications/2021/demo/p60-273.html.

US Census Bureau. 2022. "Quick Facts: United States." https://www.census.gov/quickfacts/US.

US House of Representatives. 2013. *Defining the Problem and Scope of Over-Criminalization and Over-Federalization*. Washington, DC: Committee on the Judiciary. https://www.govinfo.gov/content/pkg/CHRG-113hhrg81464/html/CHRG-113hhrg81464.htm.

Wadsworth, T. 2010. "Is Immigration Responsible for the Crime Drop? An Assessment of the Influence of Immigration on Changes in Violent Crime Between 1990 and 2000." *Social Science Quarterly* 91: 531–553.

Weinberg, D. H. 1996. "A Brief Look at Postwar US Income Inequality." Washington, DC: US Census Bureau. https://www2.census.gov/library/publications/1996/demographics/p60-191/p60-191.pdf.

Weisburd, D., Telep, C., Vovak, H., Zastrow, T., Braga, A., and Turchan, B. 2022. "Reforming the Police Through Procedural Justice Training: A Multicity Randomized Trial at Crime Hot Spots." *Proceedings of the National Academy of Sciences (PNAS)* 119(14): e2118780119. https://www.pnas.org/doi/full/10.1073/pnas.2118780119.

White, M., and Malm, A. 2020. *Cops, Cameras, and Crisis: The Potential and the Perils of Police Body-Worn Cameras*. New York: New York University Press.

Wray, C. 2018. "Threats to the Homeland." Federal Bureau of Investigation, Statement Before the Senate Homeland Security and Governmental Affairs Committee, October 10. https://www.fbi.gov/news/testimony/threats-to-the-homeland-101018.

# "VOICES FROM THE FIELD": BIOGRAPHICAL SKETCHES

**Jean Peters Baker** has spent more than 20 years in the Jackson County (MO) Prosecutor's Office, serving in nearly every office unit before she was appointed prosecutor in May 2011 and elected to the position in November 2012. She is only the second woman elected to lead the office. In 2012, Jean initiated a new violence reduction effort that is now known as the Kansas City No Violence Alliance. The effort is an evidence-based or proven approach known as focused deterrence. In 2014, homicides in Kansas City fell to the lowest level in four decades. Jean's office attracted national attention in 2011 after a grand jury indicted the bishop of the Diocese of Kansas City–St. Joseph, making him the highest-ranking cleric in the United States to face a criminal charge related to the Catholic Church's child sex abuse scandal. In October 2013, Baker served as special prosecutor to investigate the filing of charges in a high-profile sexual assault involving high school football players, once again attracting national attention. She holds a Bachelor's degree from Columbia College, a Master's degree from the University of Missouri, and a JD from the University of Missouri–Kansas City.

**Shon F. Barnes,** joined the Madison (WI) Police Department as Chief of Police in 2021. He previously worked a deputy chief at the Salisbury (NC) Police Department and as captain at the Greensboro (NC) Police Department, where he began his career as a patrol officer in November 2000. He has vast experience in police leadership, serving as the commander of the Central Patrol Division, Southern Patrol Division, Operational Support Division, and the Training Division. He received a BA in History / Prelaw from Elizabeth City State University, an MA in Criminal Justice from the University of Cincinnati, and a PhD in Leadership Studies from North Carolina Agricultural and Technical State University. His dissertation focus was racial disparities in traffic stops and the role of police leadership in community engagement efforts. He has completed the Senior Management Institute for Police and is an alumnus of the Southern Police Institute at the University of Louisville. Barnes was a 2015 National Institute of Justice LEADS Scholar for conducting research using a meta-analysis predictive-policing algorithm based on five years of reported crime data. Chief Barnes's areas of expertise include procedural justice, community–police relations, stratified-policing model, biased-based policing, and racial disparity in police self-initiated activity.

**Carmen Y. Best,** chief (ret.), served the Seattle Police Department for nearly 30 years. Prior to being named chief in 2018, she served as deputy chief, overseeing the Patrol Operations, Investigations, and Special Operations Bureaus, as well as the Community Outreach section. Chief Best completed the Senior Management Institute for Police, the FBI

National Academy, and the Criminal Justice Executive Leadership Academy. In 2015, she received the Newsmaker of the Year award from the Seattle Black Press. In 2016, Chief Best completed the Major Cities Chiefs Association Police Executive Leadership Institute. Chief Best is a member of the National Organization of Black Law Enforcement Executives (NOBLE), the National Latino Police Officers Association (NLPOA), and the Law Enforcement Immigration Task Force (LEITF), and she serves as the Chair of the Human and Civil Rights Committee (HCRC) for the International Association of Chiefs of Police (IACP). She is also on the Trustee Board for Lakeside School, the Visit Seattle Advisory Board, and the National Law Enforcement Exploring Committee. Additionally, Chief Best serves on the IACP Board of Directors, as well as the Leadership Council Chair for the United Negro College Fund (UNCF) Seattle, and is also on the St. Jude Advisory Council for Seattle. In 2019, Chief Best was the recipient of the Vision from the Mountaintop Award from Urban Impact for her commitment to justice and community. In 2021, she published her memoir, *Black in Blue: Lessons on Leadership, Breaking Barriers, and Racial Reconciliation.*

**Jim Bueermann** has spent more than 40 years in policing. From 1978 to 2011, he was a member of the Redlands (CA) Police Department, where he served his last 13 years as the chief of police and director of Housing, Recreation, and Senior Services. After his retirement in 2011, he worked for a year for the US Department of Justice, National Institute of Justice, as an Executive Fellow. In 2012, he was appointed as the president of the National Police Foundation—America's oldest nonpartisan, nonprofit police research organization (and now the National Policing Institute). He retired from the Foundation in late 2018. In January 2019, he founded Future Policing Strategies, a California-based consultancy that helps practitioners, policy makers, and community members envision and advance policing for the future.

**David C. Couper** is a retired chief of police in Madison, Wisconsin. He was hired as chief in 1972 at 34 years old and continued in this position until 1993. Couper brought much change and reform to Madison—he developed a new way to address management conflict and public protest, he broke open the employment barriers that kept women and racial minorities from the police ranks, and he instituted a new and collaborative style of leadership. In 1993, he was chosen by his peers to receive the National Police Leadership Award. He has graduate degrees from the University of Minnesota and Edgewood College in Madison. He studied police in Europe, has authored three books on policing and the role of forgiveness in government, and maintains a blog at https://improvingpolice.wordpress.com/. Couper has served as priest in charge at St. Peter's Episcopal Church in North Lake, Wisconsin, since 2005.

**Charles Fitzgerald**, assistant chief, has been with the Detroit Police Department since March 1994. He currently holds the position of assistant chief over the Office of Enforcement Operations. The Office of Enforcement Operations is comprised of the Detective Bureau, Eastern and Western Operations, and Crime Control Strategies. He has a bachelor's degree from Capella University and master's degree from Wayne State University. He is a graduate of the FBI National Academy and the Eastern Michigan University School of Police Staff and Command. During his career, he has worked in many different capacities throughout his department, such as tactical services, narcotics, homicide, patrol, and investigative operations at various ranks. Assistant Chief Fitzgerald previously held the rank of deputy chief since November 2014 and was responsible for the Detective Bureau and Neighborhood Policing Bureau—West, until his promotion to assistant chief in January 2022.

**Dan B. Haley**, Major, is a 27-year veteran of the Kansas City Police Department (KCPD). He is currently assigned as the Research & Development Division Commander, which is responsible for producing the policies and procedures of the KCPD. He has command experience in employment, budget, diversity, logistical support (communications and fleet), staff inspection/night commander, and patrol as the South Patrol Division Commander. He holds a BS in Personal Financial Management Services (University of Missouri–Columbia), an MPA in Government/Business Relations with Honors (Park University), an MS in Criminal Justice (University of Missouri–Kansas City), and a JD (University of Missouri–Kansas City School of Law). He is a licensed attorney in Missouri and Kansas. A graduate of the FBI National Academy Session #263, Dan serves on multiple nonprofit boards: Tri-County Mental Health Services (Board President), KC Mothers in Charge (Immediate Past Board Co-Chair), Genesis Charter School-K-8th (Immediate Past Board President), Black Community Fund (Board Member), Rose Brooks Center for Domestic Violence (Board Member), and Commanders Lodge 102 (Past First Vice President/Past Board Member). He is also a member of 100 Black Men of Greater KC. He is a proud member of Kappa Alpha Psi Fraternity, Inc., where he is involved with the Kappa League and mentoring tomorrow's young leaders. His greatest accomplishment is being a husband of 24 years and father to his high school daughter.

**Michael S. Harrison** was sworn in as the Baltimore Police Department's 41st Commissioner on March 12, 2019. Before coming to Baltimore, Commissioner Harrison served the New Orleans Police Department (NOPD) for nearly three decades, joining in 1991 and ascending through the ranks. He was appointed to Superintendent in 2014 and led the NOPD for over four years. Commissioner Harrison was appointed to the Police Executive Research Forum Board of Directors in 2019, where he now serves as President. He is a member of the Major Cities Chiefs Association, International Association of Chiefs of Police, the National Organization of Black Law Enforcement Executives, and the Law Enforcement Immigration Task Force. He received a Bachelor's degree in Criminal Justice from the University of Phoenix and a Master's of Criminal Justice from Loyola University New Orleans. He is also a graduate of the Senior Management Institute for Police, Northwestern University's School of Police Staff and Command, and the FBI's National Executive Institute. He has considerable experience in navigating a policing agency operating under a federal consent decree, having led two large police departments under such oversight. He honorably served with the Louisiana Air National Guard. Commissioner Harrison has been married to his high school sweetheart since 1992, and they are the loving parents of two adult children.

**W. Craig Hartley Jr.,** joined the Commission on Accreditation for Law Enforcement Agencies in 2008 and was appointed executive director in 2014. He began his career with the Greensboro (NC) Police Department and served in a number of positions before becoming an assistant chief of police. During his tenure with Greensboro, he worked in the functional areas of patrol operations, tactical operations, accreditation, internal affairs, personnel, training, budget and planning, information, and technology and served as the chief of staff. Craig also worked for the Virginia Department of Criminal Justice Services, leading the department's Policy, Planning, and Research Division and coordinating legislative affairs and public information. A graduate of Appalachian State University and the University of North Carolina at Greensboro, he has also received specialized police management and leadership training from the Southern Police Institute, the Center for Creative Leadership, and the FBI National Academy.

**John P. Jarvis** serves as the academic dean of the FBI Academy and oversees the training activities of 37,000 employees as well as thousands of law enforcement and public safety personnel worldwide. He has been employed with the FBI since July 1991, where he also served in the Criminal Justice Services Division, the Training Division with the Behavioral Science Unit (BSU), and the Critical Incident Response Group as part of the National Center for the Analysis of Violent Crime. He has 31 years of experience in criminal justice research, analysis, and teaching, especially with the FBI National Academy. Prior to his Bureau career, Dr. Jarvis was employed by the Virginia Department of Corrections, the Virginia Department of Criminal Justice Services, and the University of Virginia. He holds a PhD in Sociology from the University of Virginia in Charlottesville and undergraduate degrees in sociology and mathematics from Old Dominion University in Norfolk, Virginia. Dr. Jarvis also conducts research and instructs both at the FBI Academy and with academic partners. As the academic dean, he is committed to providing ongoing leadership in the execution of law enforcement training as well as advancing research relating to law enforcement practices, futures, and investigative responses to violent crime.

**Joseph McHale** is a Senior Manager at the Institute for Intergovernmental Research, a nonprofit corporation that provides services and expertise in program development, management, data, training, and technology. Previously, he served as Chief of Police at the Marion (IA) Police Department (MPD), one of the most progressive law enforcement agencies in the state of Iowa. The MPD is a metro leader among area law enforcement agencies by growing with excellence through an emphasis on employee development and strategic, collaborative partnerships with their community, city departments, and other law enforcement agencies. Chief McHale retired from the Kansas City (MO) Police Department (KCPD) in 2016 at the rank of major. He is a graduate of the Southern Police Institute's 122nd Administrative Officer Course at the University of Louisville. Chief McHale has held supervisory/command-level positions in patrol, tactical response (SWAT), narcotics and vice, and the Midwest High-Intensity Drug Trafficking Area (HIDTA). He was the project manager for the Kansas City No Violence Alliance, which implemented focused deterrence in Kansas City and created the Violent Crime Enforcement Division, which was the largest reorganization of KCPD in three decades. Chief McHale also commanded the East Patrol Division, which had nearly 200 sworn staff and encompassed one of the busiest patrol districts in the Midwest United States.

**Renée J. Mitchell** served in the Sacramento Police Department for 22 years and is currently a Senior Police Researcher with RTI International. She holds a BS in Psychology, an MA in Counseling Psychology, an MBA, a JD, and a PhD in Criminology from the University of Cambridge. She was a 2009/2010 Fulbright Police Research Fellow. You can view her TEDx talks, "Research Not Riots" and "Policing Needs to Change: Trust Me I'm a Cop," where she advocates for evidence-based policing. She is the American Society of

Evidence-Based Policing co-founder and executive committee member. She has taught and lectured internationally on evidence-based policing. Her research areas include policing, evidence-based crime prevention, 911 calls for service, and implicit bias training. She has published her work in the *Journal of Experimental Criminology, Justice Quarterly,* and the *Cambridge Journal of Evidence-Based Policing.* Her books include *Evidence Based Policing: An introduction, Implementing Evidence-Based Research: A How to Guide for Police Organizations,* and *Twenty-One Mental Models That Can Change Policing: A Framework for Using Data and Research for Overcoming Cognitive Bias.*

**Richard Myers** served as the executive director of the Major Cities Chiefs Association from 2017 to 2019, representing the police chiefs of the 68 largest cities in the United States and the nine largest cities in Canada. Myers was appointed to that position after more than 40 years of police service, including chief of police positions in Newport News (VA), Colorado Springs (CO), Appleton (W(), Lisle (IL), Plymouth (MI), and Atlas Township (MI). He also served as the interim chief in Sanford (FL) following the Trayvon Martin homicide. Myers attended the FBI National Academy, the FBI Law Enforcement Executive Development Seminar, and the FBI National Executive Institute. A founding member of an international police futurist organization, Myers also served as president/chair of the Commission on Accreditation for Law Enforcement Agencies. Chief Myers continues to study emerging trends and practices and has contributed to many publications on a variety of current and future critical issues in policing, homeland security, and overall quality of life in communities. He holds both a BS and an MS from Michigan State University (MSU) and is on the MSU School of Criminal Justice Alumni Wall of Fame.

**Charles Ramsey**, commissioner (ret.), has held numerous leadership positions throughout his law enforcement career. He was deputy chief of the Patrol Division and deputy superintendent in the Chicago Police Department, chief of the Metropolitan Police Department of the District of Columbia, and commissioner of the Philadelphia Police Department. A graduate of the FBI's National Academy, he holds a graduate degree from Lewis University, has also served as president of the Major Cities Chiefs Association and the Police Executive Research Forum, and was co-chair of the President's Task Force on Twenty-First Century Policing.

**Darrel Stephens** consults on a wide range of police leadership and management issues. He is an accomplished police executive with over 50 years of experience in policing. His career began as a police officer in Kansas City (MO) in 1968. He has 26 years of experience in a police executive capacity, including nine years (September 1999 to June 2008) as the chief of police of the 2,100-member Charlotte–Mecklenburg Police Department and seven years as the executive director of the Major Cities Chiefs Association. In addition to his police experience, he served for two years as the City Administrator in St. Petersburg (FL). He also served as a member of the faculty of the Public Safety Leadership Program in the School of Education at Johns Hopkins University from 2008 to 2013. In addition, he was the executive director of the Police Executive Research Forum from 1986 until 1992. He served as one of two technical advisors to the President's Task Force on Twenty-First Century Policing, is one of the co-founders of the MCCA Police Executive Leadership Institute, and continues to serve on the faculty and as the program administrator. He holds a Bachelor's degree in Administration Of Justice from the University of Missouri–Kansas City and a Master's of Science degree in Public Services Administration from Central Missouri State University.

# GLOSSARY

**abuse of authority** Misuse of power by police that tends to injure a member of the police constituency. It can take the form of excessive physical force, psychological abuse, or violation of civil rights.

**accountability** Willing acceptance of responsibility for one's actions. In police departments, two kinds of accountability mechanisms are oversight (internal and external) and standards (professional and ethical).

**accreditation** A process by which police departments are assessed in terms of standards of competency and professionalism. Accreditation typically involves a rigorous process of self-study followed by external review by an accreditation team made up of an official body of organizations. See also *Commission on Accreditation for Law Enforcement Agencies*.

**active shooter response** Doctrine that directs the first officers on the scene to immediately confront the shooter in order to save as many lives as possible. Distinguished from a hostage situation, in which the practice is to slow things down and negotiate..

**actual danger** Strong likelihood of harm in a situation based on the actual numbers and rates of deaths and injuries that have resulted from similar situations.

**acute stress** A form of high-level distress caused by sudden emergencies, such as shootings or high-speed chases.

**affidavit** A written oath establishing probable cause to obtain a search warrant; an officer describes exactly what is to be seized and exactly what is to be searched.

**affirmative action plan** An attempt to remedy past discriminatory employment and promotional practices.

**andragogy** An instructional method promoting the involvement of students and instructors in the learning process, stressing analytical and conceptual skills. See also *pedagogy*.

***Arnold v. Ballard*** (1975) US Supreme Court ruling that upheld the notion educational requirements are legitimate and quantitatively verifiable conditions for employment as a police officer.

**arrest** The act of depriving a person of their liberty by legal authority; done for the purposes of interrogation or criminal prosecution.

**balance of power** The autonomy, authority, power, or status of groups or units compared with each other within an organization or a community.

**battery** Harmful or offensive bodily contact between two people, such as when an officer applies any force to an individual without justification.

**bias crime** A crime that is racially or sexually motivated; a hate crime.

**body-worn cameras** Cameras worn by police to record their interactions with citizens, ostensibly to increase police accountability. Despite a dearth of research on the topic, the use of body-worn cameras is increasing.

**bona fide occupational qualification** A permissible job-related standard (Title VII of the Civil Rights Act) if a particular characteristic can be shown to be necessary for successful job performance despite the fact that it may discriminate against minorities.

**bright-line rule** A clear, easily understood, and easily applied standard in a specific situation.

**broad function** Idea that the mission of the police is not confined to enforcing laws and apprehending lawbreakers but also encompasses conflict resolution, victim assistance, accident prevention, problem solving, reducing fear, and social work. Broad police function is one of the central ideas underlying community policing.

**broken windows theory** A theory proposed by James Q. Wilson and George L. Kelling that posits officers should pay more attention to minor infractions such as public drunkenness and vagrancy. Attention to these minor violations may ease citizen fears and deter more serious crime from occurring.

**career growth** Occurs after an individual is recruited, selected, trained, and has completed probation in a police department. Career growth can involve officers learning new skills and techniques in their current positions as well as training for specific positions within or outside a department, new assignments, and promotion.

**Carroll doctrine** Provides for warrantless searches of motor vehicles if the vehicle is in fact mobile and if there is probable cause.

**case law** Written rulings of state and federal appellate courts that define when and how a procedure is to be used.

**case screening** A screening strategy used to reduce attention to cases with a marginal probability of being solved so that detectives can give greater attention to solvable cases.

***Castro v. Beecher*** **(1972)** US Supreme Court ruling (1972) that affirmed the legitimacy of the Boston Police Department's requirement that police officers have at least a high school education.

**centralization** Retention of authority and decision making by the top levels of a police department.

**certification** A document (license or certificate) that states a department or individual has met professional standards; typically given by a state-level organization.

**chain of command** Levels in an organizational (departmental) hierarchy; the higher the level, the greater the power, authority, and influence.

**chronic stress** A form of low-level, cumulative distress that includes the day-to-day routine of the job.

**citizen input** Community-policing belief that citizens should have open access to police organizations and input to police policies and decisions. Individual neighborhoods and communities should have the opportunity to influence how they are policed, legitimate interest groups in the community should be able to discuss their views and concerns directly with police officials, and police departments should be responsive and accountable.

**civil laws** Laws concerned with relationships between individuals (e.g., contracts, business transactions, or family relations), as distinct from criminal laws.

**civil service system** A selection method for filling government jobs typically based on a written exam, oral interview, and physical, medical, and personal requirements; designed to be objectively fair and eliminate political influence, but often lacking in job relatedness and therefore may be discriminatory. Also known as the *merit system*.

**civilian review board** Group of citizens charged with investigating allegations of police misconduct.

**class-control theory** One of four theories to explain the development of police departments, which is to dominate the working class for the benefit of the industrial elite.

**classical principles** Rules governing a bureaucracy, including specialization of work, assigning of authority and responsibility, discipline, unity of command, scalar chain of authority, centralization of decision making, and small spans of control.

**code of silence** The secrecy that line-level officers maintain about their activities, both from the public and from police administrators.

**coercion** Occurs any time the police require citizens to act in a particular way.

**cognitive learning** Training that goes beyond learning a specific skill or task and instead focuses on the process that establishes logical and valid thinking patterns.

**color of law** The misuse of power possessed by an individual who is a state actor and derives power from the government.

**command voice** Firmly spoken order.

**Commission on Accreditation for Law Enforcement Agencies** National commission that accredits police agencies, public safety training academies, and public safety communication centers based on established standards and a process of self-study and on-site review.

**community-based approaches** Policing tactics that capitalize on the resources of communities to identify and control crime.

**community crime prevention** An approach based on the assumption that if a community can be changed, so too can the behavior of those who live there.

**community policing** A mode of policing that is highly responsive to the identities and needs of the communities a department serves. Among other things, community policing (also known as community-oriented policing) is characterized by philosophies and programs that promote ongoing police–community interaction, strong community partnerships, and a broad view of police responsibilities.

**Compstat** A process that utilized current crime data to analyze crime patterns on which to base appropriate responses; also known as an anti-crime program.

**computer-aided dispatching** A system that includes call taking, dispatching, and call disposition. The system also includes resource management, allowing departments to map crimes and alert officers of past problems in that jurisdiction.

**conducted energy devices** Weapons designed to disrupt a subject's central nervous system through the use of electrical energy (e.g., the Taser).

**consolidated agencies** A type of police agency created through the integration of two or more police departments. This may involve two or more departments becoming one, or it may include two or more departments sharing functions, such as communications or training.

**constable** In medieval England, an official appointed to assist the sheriff; later, a British police officer.

**constable–nightwatch system** A system of law enforcement that began in England and prevailed in northeastern US cities from the 1600s to the early 1800s. The constable provided limited daytime police services, whereas the nightwatch patrolled after dark.

**constitutional or federally protected rights** Title 42 USC § 1983 established that these rights must be violated for plaintiffs to seek redress in federal courts against police officers or departments; these rights are outlined in the

Bill of Rights or the equal protection clause of the Fourteenth Amendment.

**contingency theory** Management based on the recognition that many internal and external factors influence police behavior and that there is no one best way to run a department.

**continuum of force** A range of possible responses police officers use, from mere presence to deadly force, according to the intensity of resistance of suspects. The continuum provides officers with a standard for training in the use of force.

**contract law enforcement** A contractual arrangement between two units of government in which one agrees to provide law enforcement services for the other.

**controlling** The process by which managers determine how the quality or quantity of departmental systems and services can be improved if goals and objectives are to be accomplished.

**counterterrorism** Policing that aims to protect citizens from terrorist attacks. Counterterrorism activities must take into account the particular motivations and tools of terrorists and require new forms of cooperation between local police and federal agencies. Many current counterterrorism policies are controversial because of their effects on individual freedom.

**crime analysis** The analysis of crime data by police departments for the purpose of understanding the nature and extent of crime across geographic boundaries as well as the most effective and efficient means of responding to crime.

**crime-control theory** One of four theories to explain the development of police departments, which is to prevent or suppress criminal activity.

**crime-detection technology** Technology that is used to detect weapons and drugs, such as cameras that can record illegal behavior, listening devices that can intercept illicit conversations, and

biometric techniques that can identify wanted persons.

**Crime Gun Intelligence Centers** Interagency partnerships that utilize technologies such as National Integrated Ballistic Information Network (NIBIN) and eTrace to collect, manage, and analyze information on crime gun evidence.

**crime-solving technology** A host of technologies that focus on solving crimes that have already occurred but are associated with few privacy implications relative to crime-detection technologies. Examples include the collection and analysis of crime-scene fingerprints, DNA, and hairs.

**crime suppression** Control and prevention of crime through the actual or implied presence of police.

**criminal justice system** Includes the police, judicial system, and correctional institutions. The police function as the gatekeepers of the criminal justice system, because they make initial contact with lawbreakers and determine who will be cited or arrested.

**criminal laws** Laws concerned with the relationship between the individual and the government, especially in the areas of public safety and order (e.g., driving licenses, theft, rape, and murder), as distinct from civil laws.

**criminal procedure** The process by which a person accused of a crime is processed through the criminal justice system.

**crisis intervention team** Specially trained police officers given the responsibility to handle situations involving mental health crises. The team may work in partnership with other mental health agencies to bring understanding and compassion to the situation. A goal is to de-escalate the situation and perhaps resolve the situation without making an arrest.

**critical-incident debriefing** Counseling services provided to officers after an extremely stressful event.

**custody** Situation where a person is deprived of freedom in a significant way, such as during an arrest.

**cybercrime** Computer crime, involving the computer as a target, the computer as a tool for the commission of a crime, or the computer as incidental to the crime itself.

***Davis v. City of Dallas* (1985)** US Supreme Court ruling that upheld the Dallas Police Department's requirement of 45 hours of college credit, in spite of the fact that it discriminated against minorities, because of the professional and complex nature of police work.

**deadly force** Level of force capable of killing a person; used to incapacitate a suspect who presents an immediate and potentially deadly threat to an officer or other person.

**decentralization** Delegation of authority and decision making to lower organizational levels.

**de-escalation** Techniques that involve the use of communication and tactics designed to provide officers with time when dealing with combative suspects, the mentally ill, or distraught persons.

**de-feminization** The process whereby women who do not conform to sex-role stereotypes and are tough enough to gain respect as officers may be labeled "bitches" or "lesbians" in an attempt to neutralize their threat to male dominance.

**defense-of-life policy** Policies that restrict the use of deadly force to those situations in which the officer's life or that of another person is in jeopardy or to prevent the escape of a person who is extremely dangerous.

**de-institutionalization** Because the practice of committing people with serious psychiatric illness to mental hospitals was deemed unfair and inhumane, patients were released to underfunded community-based and outpatient services. Consequently, more people with serious mental health issues are "on the street" and have become a police problem.

**depolicing** Phenomenon where, in the wake of a lawsuit, officers may feel the need to engage in fewer interactions with the public, particularly officer-initiated encounters. Officers rationalize this as a normal response to what they feel is an unjust situation and rationalize that their own likelihood of being named as a defendant in a lawsuit decreases if they interact with fewer citizens.

**differential police response** Differential response programs classify incoming calls according to their degree of seriousness and base the type of action police taken on that classification. Such programs can decrease costs and increase efficiency.

**directed patrol** A proactive patrol method that uses uncommitted time for a specified activity and is based on crime and problem analysis. It utilizes computerized crime analysis and mapping to identify crime patterns and direct patrols to primary crime areas at primary crime times.

**discretion** The decision-making latitude of the police on whether to invoke legal sanctions. It may include the decision to investigate or not, to arrest or not, or to pursue or not.

**disorder-control theory** One of four theories to explain the development of police departments, which is to prevent or suppress mob violence.

**disparate impact** A selection method can be considered to have a legally disparate impact when the selection rate of a group is less than 80 percent of the most successful group; also known as the *four-fifths rule.*

**displacement** Shifting patterns of crime to another place, another target, or another time due to an intervention (e.g., spillover effect).

**distress** Negative stress.

**diversity** A wide variation in racial, ethnic, and gender makeup of a police department; also of a community within society.

**domestic terrorism** When a country's citizens/residents unlawfully use violence and intimidation in pursuit of political aims. As contrasted with international terrorism, which originates outside the country..

**double marginality** The situation in which minority police officers are not fully accepted by either the police or members of their own racial or ethnic group.

**early identification system** See *early warning system.*

**early warning system** A modern approach to police officer accountability that combines the bureaucratic and internal investigation methods; these systems track specific types of officer behaviors and then alert management when individual officers exceed the threshold for such behavior.

**economic corruption** The breaking of the law by officers to seek personal financial gain, such as keeping drug money confiscated from dealers.

**education** Instruction in a general body of knowledge on which decisions can be based as to *why* something should be done on the job; concerned with theories, concepts, issues, and alternatives. See also *training.*

**empirical evidence** Proof based on systematic study of data.

**ethical formalism** Idea of the absolute importance of doing one's duty. An officer who believes that police should "go by the book" is an ethical formalist.

**ethical relativism** Idea that what is considered good varies with the particular values of groups and individuals.

**ethical utilitarianism** Idea that it is the good results of one's actions that determine whether the action itself is good.

For example, telling a lie (generally an unethical act) might save a life (a good result).

**eustress** Positive stress.

**event analysis** Refers to the police being aware of important dates, celebrations, anniversaries of events, and how these important dates may relate to upcoming situations. For example, the police must be aware of the anniversary date of an act of terrorism and be alert to activity occurring on that date.

**evidence-based policing** A method of policing guided by evidence that shows certain practices to be the most effective and efficient.

**excessive force** More violence than is needed to carry out a legitimate police task.

**exclusionary rule** Refers to a legal remedy created by the Supreme Court as a response to evidence obtained in conflict with the Constitution of the United States where such evidence may not be introduced at criminal trial to determine guilt.

**exoneration** Clearing an officer of blame when an investigation finds a complaint is essentially true, but the officer's behavior is considered justified, legal, and within departmental policy.

**extralegal police aggression** Acts committed by a police officer that are intended to injure someone physically or psychologically with no legitimate police function.

**false complaints** Unfounded allegations of misconduct.

**federalism** A form of government in which some powers are exercised by the national government, while many others are delegated to state and local units of government.

**federalization** A strong trend throughout the second half of the twentieth century, the US Congress has passed more and more federal criminal laws, giving wider jurisdiction to federal prosecutors and police. Many crimes today, especially those involving guns or drugs, can be investigated and prosecuted federally as well as by state and local law enforcement.

**field operations** Consist primarily of patrol and investigations, but may also include units to handle traffic, crime prevention, victim assistance, and so on.

**field training officer** An experienced, well-qualified officer selected and taught to act as a mentor to a new recruit by providing on-the-job training.

**fleeing-felon rule** Common law doctrine authorizing the use of deadly force to capture an escaped felon or someone hastening from the scene of a suspected grave crime; overturned by the US Supreme Court in *Garner v. Tennessee* (1985).

**flexible operations** An operational style that provides officers with the freedom to engage in practices that achieve the traditional goals of policing while also promoting the ideals of community policing.

**focused deterrence** A multiagency approach to address a particular crime problem that couples supportive services and community engagement with enhanced certainty of punishment for high-risk offenders and groups.

**follow-up investigation** An official inquiry generally conducted by a detective to develop a case; includes identifying and locating a suspect, possibly obtaining a confession, and disposing of the case.

**formal social control** The regulation of behavior that is shaped by sanctions external to the community, such as the police or the criminal justice system.

**four-fifths rule** A selection method can be considered to have a legally disparate impact when the selection rate of a group is less than 80 percent of the most successful group; also known as the *disparate impact*.

**frankpledge system** A system for keeping order in medieval England based on tithings (10 families) and hundreds (10 tithings).

**fruit of the poisonous tree doctrine** An extension of the exclusionary rule, which indicates that not only evidence seized improperly but also any additional evidence seized after that police action must be excluded from criminal court.

**Garrity interview** Compelled testimony for internal (administrative) investigations; a routine practice not protected by the Fifth Amendment, such testimony cannot normally be used in a criminal proceeding.

**general deterrence** Patrol deterrence strategy focused on maximizing police interventions (e.g., attempting to reduce firearm violence by increasing motor vehicle stops for the purpose of seizing illegal weapons).

**generalists** Police officers who perform a variety of activities, some of which could be assigned to a specialist.

**geographic focus** A community-policing strategy emphasizing the geographic basis of assignment and responsibility by shifting the fundamental unit of patrol accountability from time of day to place. Seeks to establish 24-hour responsibility for smaller areas rather than responsibility for wide areas for 8- to 10-hour shifts; also seeks permanency of assignment for officers so that they will know their community better.

**Global Positioning System (GPS)** A system or device that uses satellites to pinpoint locations on earth, such as the longitude and latitude coordinates of a crime scene, traffic crash, or police vehicle.

**grass eaters** Police officers who accept graft when it comes their way but do not actively solicit opportunities for graft; distinct from *meat eaters*.

**gratuity** Something of value, such as free or reduced-cost beverages or meals, discount buying privileges, free admission to athletic events or movies, gifts, and small rewards. Most commonly, it is beverages or meals. Some officers accept such gratuities from the public.

**grievance arbitration** In unionized agencies, this is an option for officers appealing recommended disciplinary action they believe is inappropriate.

*Griggs v. Duke Power Co.* **(1971)** US Supreme Court ruling that held that even if an employment practice has discriminatory outcomes, it may be allowed if the practice is job related (a "business necessity").

**group norms** Expected behavior from group members, which can be a powerful factor in resistance to organizational change.

**informal social control** When an individual's behavior toward conformity is shaped by norms and values of groups (e.g., community, friends, family, and church).

**highway patrol** A state police force whose duties are generally limited to enforcing traffic laws and dealing with accidents on state roads and highways. See also *state police.*

**homeland security** The mission of protecting the nation as well as local communities from all kinds of serious threats, including terrorism and natural disasters.

**hot-pursuit exception** A common exception to warrant requirements. Police may follow a felon or otherwise dangerous criminal into a place typically protected by the Fourth Amendment, such as a home, or may cross jurisdictional boundaries. Hot pursuits must be based on probable cause, and the gravity of the offense must be taken into consideration. Once in a constitutionally protected area, the officer may search for the suspect and for weapons or evidence, but once the suspect is found, the search must cease.

**hot spots** Locations that have a greater amount of crime or disorder than other areas. Hot spot policing is a strategy that deploys police officers to locations that have a greater amount of crime and disorder than other areas, with instructions to be present for a specific amount of time and/or to carry out specific activities at the locations.

**inertia** A condition of doing things as they have always been done before; it is a strong influence in resisting change in police departments.

**in-group solidarity** A closeness and loyalty among officers brought about by the perceived danger of police work, the close-knit working relations among officers, concerns that outsiders cannot be trusted, and a common basis of patrol activity.

**innovation** The development and use of new ideas and methods.

**in-service training** A program to regularly update all department members on a wide variety of subjects.

**intelligence-led policing** Operational strategy to reduce crime in which crime analysis and criminal intelligence are used to guide police activities and priorities.

**intentional torts** Tort (wrongs) that an officer plans to cause some physical or mental harm.

**internal affairs** Section in a police department to respond to complaints.

**international terrorism** When unlawful violence and intimidation in pursuit of political aims is carried out in one country by individuals or groups who are not citizens/residents of that country. As contrasted with domestic terrorism, which originates within the country..

**interrogations** Circumstances when the police ask questions that tend to incriminate the citizen.

**job task analysis** Validating selection and testing methods by identifying the behaviors necessary for adequate job performance.

**jurisdiction** The geographic area or type of crime for which a police force is responsible.

**kin policing** In early or nonindustrial societies, enforcement of customary rules of conduct by family, clan, or tribe.

**lateral entry** The ability of a police officer, at the patrol or supervisory level, to transfer from one unit to another, usually without losing seniority.

**law enforcement** Activities in which police make arrests, issue citations, conduct investigations, and attempt to prevent or deter criminal activity. A primary function of patrol officers.

**Law Enforcement Assistance Administration** An agency through which the federal government spent billions of dollars on the criminal justice system, focusing on the police in an attempt to improve effectiveness and reduce crime.

**Law Enforcement Education Program** Established under the Law Enforcement Assistance Administration to provide financial assistance to police personnel, as well as to others who wished to enter police service, to pursue a college education; it significantly increased police programs in higher education in the mid-1970s.

**leading** Motivating others to perform various tasks that will contribute to the accomplishment of goals and objectives.

**learning organization** An organization that benefits from, and adapts to, its own and others' experiences.

**legalistic style** Policing that insists on enforcing the law in maintaining order.

**legitimacy** Public confidence in the police as fair and equitable; the legitimacy of the police may be associated with the community's willingness to accept and obey the law.

**less-lethal weapons** Weapons that are intended to knock down or incapacitate a dangerous suspect who has not responded to other techniques. They include conducted energy devices (e.g., Tasers), bean bags, and pepper sprays.

**management** Directing individuals to achieve departmental goals efficiently and effectively.

**marshals** Federal officials appointed to keep order in federal territories (US marshals); also, a federally appointed local police officer (deputy marshal) and a locally appointed official (town marshal).

**meat eaters** Police officers who actively solicit opportunities for financial gain and are involved in more widespread and serious corruption than *grass eaters*.

**mere presence** An officer's being in view in a situation; the mildest level of force.

**militarization** Involvement of the military with law enforcement. Traditionally kept separate, these two bodies now frequently work together in the so-called war on drugs and in anti-terrorism efforts.

**merit system** See *civil service system*.

**Miranda warnings** Based on the Fifth Amendment privilege from self-incrimination, police must take appropriate safeguards to ensure that a defendant's rights are not violated during arrest. Specifically, police must advise defendants that (1) they have the right to remain silent, (2) any statement made may be used against the defendant in court, (3) the defendant has the right to have an attorney present during questioning, and (4) if a defendant cannot afford an attorney, then the state will appoint one prior to questioning. The defendant must intelligently and voluntarily waive these rights prior to questioning.

**National Advisory Commission on Criminal Justice Standards and Goals** Commission that authored the highly influential 1973 *Report on Police*, a document that further advanced the higher-education recommendations made by previous commissions. The report included a graduated timetable for requiring additional higher education of all police officers at the time of initial employment.

**National Advisory Commission on Higher Education for Police Officers** Commission that studied the problems of college and graduate education for police in the 1970s and called for significant changes in virtually all phases of police higher education, including institution, curriculum, and faculty.

**negligent torts** Tort (wrongs) resulting from a breach of lawful duty to act reasonably toward an individual whom a police officer might harm.

**nightwatch** Developed after the fall of the Roman Empire, a group of citizens who patrolled at night looking for fires and other problems.

**noble-cause corruption** The abandonment of ethical and legal means to achieve good ends. Occurs when police use violence and subjugation of rights because they are more concerned about the noble cause (e.g., getting bad guys off the streets and protecting victims and children) than about the morality of technically legal behavior.

**occupational deviance** Illegal behavior by an officer in the course of work or under the cloak of police authority.

**office of professional standards** An internal investigatory unit most often found in larger police departments that responds to citizen complaints or officer concerns about police behavior.

**officer survival** Major risks faced by police officers, such as officer stress, suicide, and threats, are countered through officer survival training.

**Omnibus Crime Control and Safe Streets Act** A major piece of legislation in 1968 to deal with the national concern about crime; it created the Law Enforcement Assistance Administration.

**open-fields doctrine** A search doctrine indicating that items in open fields are not protected by the Fourth Amendment's guarantee against unreasonable searches and seizures, so they can properly be taken by an officer without a warrant or probable cause.

**order maintenance** Patrol goal that may or may not involve a violation of the law (usually minor), during which officers tend to use alternatives other than arrest.

**organizational change** A department's adoption of new ideas or behavior; a term often associated with community policing.

**organizational design** The formal patterns of arrangements and relationships developed by police management to accomplish departmental goals.

**organizing** The process of arranging personnel and physical resources to carry out plans and accomplish goals and objectives.

**paramilitary model** Formal pattern where the police are organized along military lines, with emphasis on a legalistic approach.

**particularistic perspectives** Views of the police that emphasize difference among police officers, as distinct from universalistic perspectives.

**partnerships** Programs, organizations, or police–community relationships that facilitate the community's participation in its own protection.

**patronage system** Unofficial practice in which public jobs are given as rewards for supporting the political party in power.

**Peace Officer Standards and Training** Organization that, in many states, sets standards for the evaluation of police personnel.

**pedagogy** An instructional method involving a one-way transfer of knowledge, usually facts and procedures, from the instructor to the student; distinct from *andragogy*.

**peer-counseling program** A program in which police officers who are specially trained to recognize problems associated with stress from critical incidents provide support to colleagues and make referrals as deemed necessary.

**perceived danger** Harm that an officer or the public believes to be potential in a situation.

**personal service** Stresses the personal, long-term relationship between a police official and the individuals they encounter. Police attention to personalized service can help create trust and confidence in the communities where they work.

**person-based approaches** Policing innovations that focus resources on the small proportion of the population responsible for a disproportionate amount of crime.

**person-initiated danger** An attack against a police officer by another person.

**physical force** Use of physical means to control or apprehend citizen suspects.

**physiological stress** A state resulting from physical, chemical, or emotional factors that can cause biological disease, such as high blood pressure and ulcers.

**place-based approaches** Policing approach that capitalizes on crime concentration among a small proportion of locations in the jurisdiction.

**plain-view doctrine** The principle that what police discover during the performance of their normal duties can be seized. For example, if a police officer stops a person who committed a traffic violation and the officer sees illegal items in the back seat of the car, that contraband is in plain view and can be legally seized.

**planning** The process of preparing for the future by setting goals and objectives and developing courses of action for accomplishing them.

**police auditor systems** Developed more recently than civilian review boards, these systems do not usually investigate or monitor individual citizen complaints; that is, these are left to internal affairs. Instead, the auditor model focuses on the police organization and its policies and practices, ensuring that legal requirements are being met and that the most efficient and effective practices are being followed.

**police brutality** Excessive force, including violence, that does not support a legitimate police function.

**police–community relations** Philosophy emphasizing the importance of communication and mutual understanding between a police agency and its community.

**police corruption** Any forbidden act that involves misuse of an officer's position for gain.

**police culture** The informal but important relationship among police officers and the values they share. Police work is characterized by its own occupational beliefs and values, which traditionally include a perception of the police as sexist and macho.

**police deviance** Activities of officers that are inconsistent with their legal authority, the department's authority, and standards of ethical conduct.

**Police Executive Research Forum** An association made up of college-educated police chief executives; established in the 1970s to encourage research, education, and debate.

**police misconduct** Actions that violate departmental guidelines (policies, procedures, rules, and regulations) that define both appropriate and inappropriate conduct for officers.

**police pursuit** An event in which a suspect attempts to flee from police, typically to avoid arrest.

**police stressors** Sources of stress for police, including departmental practices (e.g., authoritarian structure) and the inherent nature of police work (e.g., shift work, boredom, and exposure to human misery).

**police training officer** A new type of field training program developed for the purpose of initiating and training recruits in the two main components of community policing: community partnerships and problem solving. Differs significantly from traditional models and emphasizes adult learning (andragogical) principles and problem-based learning.

**police violence** Use of force to obtain confessions.

**police*women*** Female officers who attempt to maintain a feminine manner while performing police duties.

***police*women** Female officers who tend to emphasize the traditional police culture, especially its law enforcement aspects.

**political model** Model of policing in America from the middle of the eighteenth century to the 1920s, during which police derived their authority from powerful local politicians (who utilized the police to maintain the status quo and retain political power).

**positive interaction** Positive interaction occurs when police talk with, assist, or form relationships with community members in their day-to-day activities. Positive interaction can help offset the negative (yet inevitable) effects of the more punitive and confrontational aspects of policing.

**posse comitatus** Group in medieval England called out to pursue fleeing felons.

**posttraumatic stress disorder** A psychological state caused by frequent or prolonged exposure to crises or trauma.

**potential danger** Harm that could exist in a situation.

**predictive policing** A form of policing that uses data analysis to respond to crime more quickly and anticipate its "when and where" so that police can engage in preventative and preemptive practices.

**predispositional theory** The idea that the behavior of police officers is primarily explained by their characteristics, values, and attitudes of that person before they were employed.

**preliminary investigation** An initial inquiry conducted by patrol officers for the purposes of establishing that a crime has been committed and to protect the scene of the crime from those not involved in the inquiry.

**President's Commission on Law Enforcement and Administration of Justice** Commission that issued the 1967 report *Challenge of Crime in a Free Society*.

**pretextual stops** Officers stopping a suspect for a minor violation with the goal of eliciting another, more serious violation.

**prevention emphasis** Community-policing strategy that emphasizes a more proactive and preventive orientation, encouraging better use of police officers' time by devoting the substantial resource of free patrol time to directed enforcement activities, specific crime prevention efforts, problem solving, community engagement, citizen interaction, or similar kinds of activities. Officers are encouraged to look beyond individual-incident calls for service and reported crimes to discover underlying problems and conditions.

**private police** Police employed and paid by an individual or nongovernmental organization.

**privatization** Trend in which public police are increasingly replaced or augmented by privately employed security forces. Privatization raises questions about racial and economic inequality.

**proactive** Police work that emphasizes police-initiated activities by individual officers and departments.

**proactive arrests** Arrests that result from a police initiative to focus on a narrow set of high-risk targets.

**probable cause** According to the Supreme Court, probable cause exists where the facts and circumstances within the officers' knowledge, and of which they have reasonably trustworthy information, are sufficient in themselves to warrant a belief by a man of reasonable caution that a crime is being committed. Hence, the officer has reason to believe that a particular individual has more likely than not committed a certain crime. Probable cause is the minimum legal standard necessary to make a custodial arrest of a person, and it is a more rigorous standard than reasonable suspicion.

**problem-based approaches** Policing innovations that seek to identify problems and patterns as well as the causes of these problems.

**problem-based learning** Teaching method in which police trainees are presented with real-life problems that they must attempt to solve. Often part of police training officer–type field training programs.

**problem-oriented policing** An approach to police work that is concerned primarily with identifying and solving community problems, with or without input from the community.

**problem solving** Techniques to gain deeper insight into the issues that police are called on to address and to develop tailored solutions that have a longer-lasting impact on the problem.

**procedural justice** Refers to being treated fairly by police officers who are acting under the authority of criminal law; that is, being treated in an even-handed manner by police performing their law enforcement duties.

**procedural laws** Criminal laws that govern how the police enforce substantive laws.

**professionalism** Occupation where actors behave according to "professional" standards, often including specialized training and expertise in a specialized body of knowledge.

**professionalization** Movement to help the police be more objective and effective in their decisions by forming a code of ethics, developing a scientifically derived body of knowledge and skill, and providing extensive education and training. These are all means to turn police work from an occupation into a profession.

**protective sweep** A limited examination of a home to determine whether others are present who could pose a safety risk for officers.

**psychological force** The use of nonphysical methods of coercion, particularly to obtain an admission or confession from a suspect.

**psychological stress** Anxiety, which may challenge the individual's ability to handle or cope with the situation.

**public police** Police who are employed, trained, and paid by a government agency.

**public safety agencies** Represent the integration of police and firefighting services (or other services like disaster preparedness, hazardous waste disposal, and emergency medical services). This integration can be limited to administrative matters or the cross-training of personnel to handle both functions. If cross-trained, usually the police are trained in firefighting more often than the firefighters are trained in policing.

**quality-of-life policing** Police strategy that targets the reduction of physical and social disorder so that community members will work together to promote neighborhood safety and concomitantly reduce crime.

**quid pro quo harassment** A situation requiring the employee to choose between the job and meeting a supervisor's sexual demands.

**racial profiling** When race is used as the sole or primary factor influencing officers' decisions, particularly within the context of traffic stops. Race rather than behavior influences officers' behavior.

**rapid-response technology** Technology that helps police respond to crimes and incidents more quickly and effectively, such as gunshot detection systems and drones that provide an "eye in the sky" for situational awareness and tactical guidance.

**reactive** Police work that is characterized by police responses to incidents when assistance is specifically requested by citizens.

**reasonable suspicion** Suspicion based on objective facts and logical conclusions that a crime has been or is about to be committed, given the circumstances at hand; crime *may* be being committed.

**reform/professional model** Approach to policing and police administration designed to overcome problems encountered in the political era of American policing.

**regional police** Police organizations that are jointly operated by two or more local governments across their respective jurisdictions. Often overseen by a board or commission with representation from all participating jurisdictions and with funding provided by each on a proportional basis.

**reliability** The consistency of a measure in yielding results over time. If other observers conduct the same research in the same setting, they will probably come to similar conclusions.

**representative bureaucracy** A perspective suggesting that diversity within the public workforce, especially in terms of characteristics such as race and ethnicity, will help ensure that the interests of diverse groups are represented in policy formulation. The belief is that public agencies that are more representative of their population reveal a commitment to equal access to power, accurately reflect group preferences, enhance group willingness to cooperate, and use resources more efficiently.

**research and development** A unit to help police departments become learning organizations by going beyond mere statistical descriptions of departmental inputs and outputs and trying to develop new ideas.

**rotten-apple theory of corruption** The idea that corruption is limited to a small number of officers who were probably dishonest prior to their employment. The term stems from the metaphor that a few rotten apples will spoil the barrel; in other words, a few bad officers can spoil a department.

**rule of law** A principle of constitutional democracy whereby the exercise of power is based on laws, not on an individual or an organization.

**SARA model** A four-step, problem-solving or problem-oriented policing process that includes scanning, analysis, response, and assessment.

**screening in** Process of identifying police applicants who are the best-qualified candidates for the applicant pool.

**screening out** Process of identifying police applicants who are unqualified and removing them from consideration, while leaving all those who minimally qualify in the applicant pool.

**sensitization training** Instructing an officer to be aware of the problems of victims as well as their own victimization; it should be conducted early in their careers.

**search incident to arrest** Officers may search an arrestee without articulating probable cause that the person is in possession of criminal evidence or contraband.

**search warrant** a "written order, issued by a magistrate, directing a peace officer to search for property connected with a crime and bring it before the court" (del Carmen 2001, 181).

**separation of powers** Principle of government by which power is divided among separate branches of a government. In the United States, power is divided among the executive, judicial, and legislative branches.

**service style** Style of policing that emphasizes the service function over law enforcement or peacekeeping.

**sexual harassment** Unwelcome sexual advances that unreasonably interfere with a person's work or create a hostile working environment.

**sheriff** Originally, an English official appointed to levy fines and keep order in the shire; later in the United States, an official, usually elected, who enforces the law in rural areas. In addition to patrol and investigations, a sheriff's duties often include managing a jail and providing services for courts.

**situational danger** A particular problem on the job, such as a high-speed chase that threatens an officer's safety.

**social services** Police responsibilities that involve taking reports and providing information and assistance to the public; everything from helping a stranded motorist to checking Grandma's house to make sure she is all right.

**socialization theory** Theory that police behavior, both positive and negative, is determined more by work experiences and peers than by preemployment values and attitudes.

**social-supports model** An approach to police stress based on the premise that individuals are insulated against stressors when they have a support network of friends, family, and coworkers.

**solvability factors** The factors examined during case screening that help police identify the unsolved cases that are the most and least likely to be solved.

**specialists** Police officers who perform a particular kind of activity such as investigation; as distinguished from a *generalist.*

**specialized training** Instruction to prepare officers for particular categories of tasks or jobs.

**special jurisdiction police** Police agencies that have limited functional jurisdiction (e.g., fish and wildlife enforcement) or limited geographic jurisdiction (e.g., campus police or transit police).

**specific deterrence** Patrol deterrence strategy focused on targeted police interventions (e.g., attempting to reduce firearm violence by targeting and stopping suspicious-looking motorists for the purpose of seizing illegal weapons).

**state police** A state force that has broad law enforcement power, conducts criminal investigations, patrols roads and highways, and frequently has forensic science laboratories.

**stop and frisk** Practice where an officer may stop a person, temporarily depriving them of freedom of movement, if the officer has reasonable suspicion that the person is involved in a crime. Furthermore, the officer may frisk the person if there is reasonable suspicion to believe the citizen is armed and poses a threat to the officer for the duration of the stop.

**stressor-outcome model** An approach to police stress based on the premise that circumstances of strain or tension lead to psychological or physiological stress.

**structural characteristics** The features that police departments emphasize or do not emphasize, which may be discriminatory, especially against women.

**subjugation of a defendant's rights** Overriding a citizen's civil rights to obtain a confession or other evidence.

**substantive laws** Criminal laws that identify behavior and punishment; distinct from procedural laws.

**suicide prevention training** Instruction aimed at reducing police suicides by recognizing depression, developing communication skills, resolving conflicts, and maintaining close relationships.

**sustained complaints** Allegations of misdeeds by police that an investigation finds to be justified.

**symbolic assailant** Type of person the police officer thinks is potentially dangerous or troublesome, usually because of the way the person walks, talks, and dresses.

**systemic theory of corruption** Concept that suggests corruption stems from the nature of police work itself, and if anticorruption protocols are inadequate, corruption will spread throughout the department.

**systems theory** The idea that all parts of a system (organization) are interrelated and interdependent.

**target oriented** A concept used by police officers to assess likely targets in their districts. A target-oriented approach monitors not only obvious places and persons who might be of danger but also safe areas that may be vulnerable to disruption.

**task forces** A team of officers from two or more police agencies who work to solve a particular problem that transcends jurisdictional limits (e.g., a drug task force).

**team policing** An early version of community policing based on organizational decentralization and increased community participation.

**testimonial evidence** Proof based on the opinions of others.

**thief catcher** In seventeenth- and eighteenth-century England, a person hired to secure the return of stolen property.

**third degree** Historical term for coercive police methods used to obtain confessions.

**total quality management** A customer-oriented approach that emphasizes human resources and quantitative methods in an attempt at continuous improvement.

**training** Instruction of an individual in how to do a job; concerned with specific facts and procedures. See also *education*.

**transparency** Clear and honest representation of practices; a police department whose policies and procedures are open to the public can be said to have achieved transparency.

**trauma-informed policing** Practices that enhance officers' ability to understand and respond to victims in a manner that increases trust and engagement while also reducing victimization

**tribal police** Law enforcement bodies on Native American reservations.

**unfounded complaints** Allegations of police misdeeds that an investigation finds did not occur as stated.

**universalistic perspectives** Views of police behavior that look for the ways officers are similar; as distinct from *particularistic perspectives*.

**unmanned aerial vehicles** Drones used by select departments nationwide for purposes of search and rescue and disaster assessment.

**unsubstantiated complaints** Allegations that, in the opinion of those making the decision, cannot be sustained as either true or false.

**urban-dispersion theory** One of four theories to explain the development of the police department, which is to provide an important part of government.

**use corruption** Illegal use of drugs by officers.

**use of force** The legal authority to maintain order, demand compliance, detain individuals, use weapons, and if necessary, inflict violence. Police are granted this authority to shield victims from dangerous felons; to control unruly, hostile, or physically abusive citizens; and to protect against immediate threats to human life. Use of force is the most controversial aspect of the legal authority of the police.

**validity** Justifiability of a measure as an accurate assessment of the attribute it is designed to assess. Other people are likely to see the same thing the observers see.

**verbal force** Persuasive use of words to control a situation.

**vigilante** Member of a voluntary band (usually men) who organize to respond to real or imagined threats to their safety; to protect their lives, property, or power; or to seek revenge. Characteristic of the Old West, they are also active today.

**watchman style** Policing that allows great latitude in maintaining order.

**winning hearts and minds** A process to secure the cooperation of rank-and-file members of a department in implementing organizational change.

**wrongful death** Civil lawsuits that may arise when an unjustified police action results in the death of a citizen.

# PHOTO CREDITS

**Chapter 1:** page 2, Courtesy of the Kansas City (MO) Police Department.

**Chapter 2:** page 30, Courtesy, W. D. Smith Commercial Photography, Inc. Collection, Special Collections, The University of Texas at Arlington Libraries.

**Chapter 3:** page 60, Andrew Harrer/Bloomberg via Getty Images; page 71, Jackson County Prosecutor's Office.

**Chapter 4:** page 98, Courtesy of the Kansas City (MO) Police Department; page 101, Courtesy of Major Cities Chiefs Association.

**Chapter 5:** page 134, Baltimore PD.

**Chapter 6:** page 176, Courtesy of the Kansas City (MO) Police Department.

**Chapter 7:** page 214, Courtesy of the Kansas City (MO) Police Department; page 227, Courtesy of the Kansas City (MO) Police Department; page 232, Courtesy of the Detroit Police Department.

**Chapter 8:** page 240, Photo by Joshua Lott/Getty Images.

**Chapter 9:** page 270, Courtesy of the Kansas City (MO) Police Department.

**Chapter 10:** page 312, Courtesy of the Kansas City (MO) Police Department; page 326, Reprinted with permission of the National Policing Institute, Washington, DC, www.policefoundation.org.

**Chapter 11:** page 348, Courtesy of the Kansas City (MO) Police Department.

**Chapter 12:** page 386, Baltimore PD; page 412, Photo courtesy of Seattle Police Department.

**Chapter 13:** page 420, Courtesy of the Kansas City (MO) Police Department.

**Chapter 14:** page 456, Photo by Dale Stockton.

**Chapter 15:** page 482, Baltimore PD.

# NAME INDEX

# SUBJECT INDEX

Note: Page references followed by a "t" indicate table; "f" indicate figure.